Cay Horstmann
San Jose State University

Rance Necaise
Randolph-Macon College

Python for Everyone

3/e

WILEY

VICE PRESIDENT AND EXECUTIVE PUBLISHER	Laurie Rosatone
EXECUTIVE EDITOR	Joanna Dingle
PROJECT MANAGER/DEVELOPMENT EDITOR	Cindy Johnson
EDITORIAL ASSISTANT	Crystal Franks
LEAD PRODUCT DESIGNER	Tom Kulesa
MARKETING MANAGER	Michael MacDougald
PRODUCTION MANAGER	Nichole Urban
PRODUCTION MANAGER	Nicole Repasky
PRODUCTION MANAGEMENT SERVICES	Cindy Johnson, Publishing Services
PHOTO EDITOR	Anindita Adiyal
COVER DESIGNER	Joanna Vieira
COVER PHOTOS	(castle) © Tom Watson/EyeEm/Getty Images; (chalice) © Paul Fleet/Getty Images, Inc.; (balloon) © Mikhail Mishchenko/123RFLimited; (trumpets) © modella/123RF.com.

This book was set in 10.5/12 Stempel Garamond LT Std by Publishing Services, and printed and bound by Quad Graphics/Versailles. The cover was printed by Quad Graphics/Versailles.

Founded in 1807, John Wiley & Sons, Inc. has been a valued source of knowledge and understanding for more than 200 years, helping people around the world meet their needs and fulfill their aspirations. Our company is built on a foundation of principles that include responsibility to the communities we serve and where we live and work. In 2008, we launched a Corporate Citizenship Initiative, a global effort to address the environmental, social, economic, and ethical challenges we face in our business. Among the issues we are addressing are carbon impact, paper specifications and procurement, ethical conduct within our business and among our vendors, and community and charitable support. For more information, please visit our website: www.wiley.com/go/citizenship.

This book is printed on acid-free paper. ∞

Evaluation copies are provided to qualified academics and professionals for review purposes only, for use in their courses during the next academic year. These copies are licensed and may not be sold or transferred to a third party. Upon completion of the review period, please return the evaluation copy to Wiley. Return instructions and a free of charge return shipping label are available at: www.wiley.com/go/returnlabel. If you have chosen to adopt this textbook for use in your course, please accept this book as your complimentary desk copy. Outside of the United States, please contact your local representative.

ePUB ISBN 978-1-119-49853-7

Printed in the United States of America.

The inside back cover will contain printing identification and country of origin if omitted from this page. In addition, if the ISBN on the back cover differs from the ISBN on this page, the one on the back cover is correct.

PREFACE

This book is an introduction to computer programming using Python that focuses on the essentials—and on effective learning. Designed to serve a wide range of student interests and abilities, it is suitable for a first course in programming for computer scientists, engineers, and students in other disciplines. No prior programming experience is required, and only a modest amount of high school algebra is needed. For pedagogical reasons, the book uses Python 3, which is more regular than Python 2.

Here are the book's key features:

Present fundamentals first.

The book takes a traditional route, first stressing control structures, functions, procedural decomposition, and the built-in data structures. Objects are used when appropriate in the early chapters. Students start designing and implementing their own classes in Chapter 9.

Guidance and worked examples help students succeed.

Beginning programmers often ask "How do I start? Now what do I do?" Of course, an activity as complex as programming cannot be reduced to cookbook-style instructions. However, step-by-step guidance is immensely helpful for building confidence and providing an outline for the task at hand. "Problem Solving" sections stress the importance of design and planning. "How To" guides help students with common programming tasks. Numerous "Worked Examples" demonstrate how to apply chapter concepts to interesting problems.

Problem solving strategies are made explicit.

Practical, step-by-step illustrations of techniques help students devise and evaluate solutions to programming problems. Introduced where they are most relevant, these strategies address barriers to success for many students. Strategies included are:

- Algorithm Design (with pseudocode)
- First Do It By Hand (doing sample calculations by hand)
- Flowcharts
- Test Cases
- Hand-Tracing
- Storyboards
- Solve a Simpler Problem First
- Reusable Functions
- Stepwise Refinement
- Adapting Algorithms
- Discovering Algorithms by Manipulating Physical Objects
- Tracing Objects
- Patterns for Object Data
- Thinking Recursively
- Estimating the Running Time of an Algorithm

Practice makes perfect.

Of course, programming students need to be able to implement nontrivial programs, but they first need to have the confidence that they can succeed. Each section contains numerous exercises that ask students to carry out progressively more complex tasks: trace code and understand its effects, produce program snippets from prepared parts, and complete simple programs. Additional review and programming problems are provided at the end of each chapter.

A visual approach motivates the reader and eases navigation.

Photographs present visual analogies that explain the nature and behavior of computer concepts. Step-by-step figures illustrate complex program operations. Syntax boxes and example tables present a variety of typical and special cases in a compact format. It is easy to get the "lay of the land" by browsing the visuals, before focusing on the textual material.

Visual features help the reader with navigation.

Focus on the essentials while being technically accurate.

An encyclopedic coverage is not helpful for a beginning programmer, but neither is the opposite—reducing the material to a list of simplistic bullet points. In this book, the essentials are presented in digestible chunks, with separate notes that go deeper into good practices or language features when the reader is ready for the additional information.

New to This Edition

Interactive Learning

With this edition, interactive content is front and center. Immersive activities integrate with this text and engage students in activities designed to foster in-depth learning. Students don't just watch animations and code traces, they work on generating them. Live code samples invite the reader to experiment and to learn programming constructs first hand. The activities provide instant feedback to show students what they did right and where they need to study more.

A Focus on Data Science

The methods of data science are becoming so important that students in many disciplines, and not just computer scientists, are eager to learn the fundamentals of programming. Python is uniquely positioned as the "go to" language for budding data scientists, due to its logical structure, interactive programming libraries that invite exploration, and a wealth of libraries for data manipulation.

This book employs a proven pedagogy for teaching programming that is not limited to computer science majors. In this edition, we provide additional examples and exercises that focus on various aspects of data science.

Just the Right Amount of Python

When we wrote this book, our goal was to teach good programming and computer science, using Python as the means of instruction and not an end in itself.

Following suggestions of users of prior editions, we accelerated the coverage of convenience operations for working with strings and lists in this edition.

More Toolboxes

A popular enhancement of the previous edition was the introduction of optional "Toolbox" sections that introduce useful packages in the wonderful ecosystem of Python libraries. Students are empowered to perform useful work such as statistical computations, drawing graphs and charts, sending e-mail, processing spreadsheets, and analyzing web pages. The libraries are placed in the context of computer science principles, and students learn how those principles apply to solving real-world problems. Each Toolbox is accompanied by many new review and programming exercises.

New to this edition are additional Toolboxes on turtle graphics and game programming.

A Tour of the Book

Figure 1 shows the dependencies between the chapters and how topics are organized. The core material of the book is Chapters 1–8. Chapters 9 and 10 cover object-oriented programming, and Chapters 11 and 12 support a course that goes more deeply into algorithm design and analysis.

Appendices   Six appendices provide a handy reference for students on operator precedence, reserved words, Unicode, the Python standard library, and more.

Graphics and Image Processing

Writing programs that create drawings or process images can provide students with effective visualizations of complex topics. Chapter 2 introduces the EzGraphics open-source library and how to use it to create basic graphical drawings. The library,

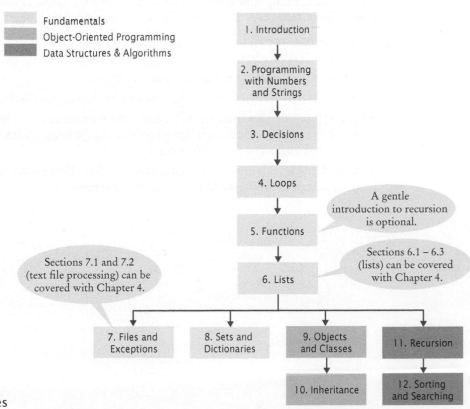

Figure 1
Chapter Dependencies

which students find easier to use than Python's standard Tkinter library, also supports simple image processing. Chapter 5 contains an optional Toolbox on turtle graphics. Graphics Worked Examples and exercises are provided throughout the text, all of which are optional.

Exercises

Review exercises contain a broad mix of review and programming questions, with optional questions from graphics, science, and business. Designed to engage students, the exercises illustrate the value of programming in applied fields.

Interactive eText Designed for Programming Students

Available online through wiley.com, vitalsource.com, or at your local bookstore, the interactive eText features integrated student coding activities that foster in-depth learning. Designed by Cay Horstmann, these activities provide instant feedback to show students what they did right and where they need to study more. Students do more than just watch animations and code traces; they work on generating them right in the eText environment.

Customized formats are also available in both print and digital formats and provide your students with curated content based on your unique syllabus.

Please contact your Wiley sales rep for more information about any of these options.

Web Resources

This book is complemented by a complete suite of online resources. Visit the online companion sites at www.Wiley.com. The online resources include

- Source code for all example programs, Toolboxes, and Worked Examples in the book.
- Lecture presentation slides (for instructors only).
- Solutions to all review and programming exercises (for instructors only).
- A test bank that focuses on skills, not just terminology (for instructors only). This extensive set of multiple-choice questions can be used with a word processor or imported into a course management system.
- CodeCheck®, an innovative online service that allows instructors to design their own automatically graded programming exercises.

A Walkthrough of the Learning Aids

The pedagogical elements in this book work together to focus on and reinforce key concepts and fundamental principles of programming, with additional tips and detail organized to support and deepen these fundamentals. In addition to traditional features, such as chapter objectives and a wealth of exercises, each chapter contains elements geared to today's visual learner.

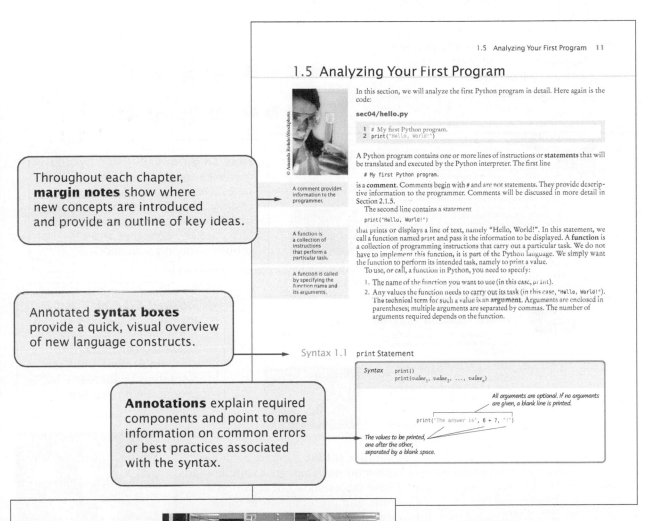

Throughout each chapter, **margin notes** show where new concepts are introduced and provide an outline of key ideas.

Annotated **syntax boxes** provide a quick, visual overview of new language constructs.

Annotations explain required components and point to more information on common errors or best practices associated with the syntax.

1.5   Analyzing Your First Program   11

1.5 Analyzing Your First Program

In this section, we will analyze the first Python program in detail. Here again is the code:

sec04/hello.py

```
1  # My first Python program.
2  print("Hello, World!")
```

A Python program contains one or more lines of instructions or **statements** that will be translated and executed by the Python interpreter. The first line

```
# My first Python program.
```

is a **comment**. Comments begin with # and are not statements. They provide descriptive information to the programmer. Comments will be discussed in more detail in Section 2.1.5.

The second line contains a statement

```
print("Hello, World!")
```

that prints or displays a line of text, namely "Hello, World!". In this statement, we call a function named print and pass it the information to be displayed. A **function** is a collection of programming instructions that carry out a particular task. We do not have to implement this function, it is part of the Python language. We simply want the function to perform its intended task, namely to print a value.

To use, or call, a function in Python, you need to specify:

1. The name of the function you want to use (in this case, print).
2. Any values the function needs to carry out its task (in this case, "Hello, World!"). The technical term for such a value is an **argument**. Arguments are enclosed in parentheses; multiple arguments are separated by commas. The number of arguments required depends on the function.

A comment provides information to the programmer.

A function is a collection of instructions that perform a particular task.

A function is called by specifying the function name and its arguments.

Syntax 1.1   **print Statement**

Syntax   print()
          print(*value₁*, *value₂*, ..., *valueₙ*)

All arguments are optional. If no arguments are given, a blank line is printed.

```
print("The answer is", 6 + 7, "!")
```

The values to be printed, one after the other, separated by a blank space.

Like a variable in a computer program, a parking space has an identifier and a contents.

Analogies to everyday objects are used to explain the nature and behavior of concepts such as variables, data types, loops, and more.

Memorable photos reinforce analogies and help students remember the concepts.

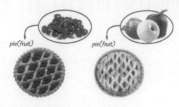

A recipe for a fruit pie may say to use any kind of fruit. Here, "fruit" is an example of a parameter variable. Apples and cherries are examples of arguments.

Problem Solving sections teach techniques for generating ideas and evaluating proposed solutions, often using pencil and paper or other artifacts. These sections emphasize that most of the planning and problem solving that makes students successful happens away from the computer.

6.6 Problem Solving: Discovering Algorithms by Manipulating Physical Objects   311

Now how does that help us with our problem, switching the first and the second half of the list?

Let's put the first coin into place, by swapping it with the fifth coin. However, as Python programmers, we will say that we swap the coins in positions 0 and 4:

HOW TO 1.1

Describing an Algorithm with Pseudocode

This is the first of many "How To" sections in this book that give you step-by-step procedures for carrying out important tasks in developing computer programs.

Before you are ready to write a program in Python, you need to develop an algorithm—a method for arriving at a solution for a particular problem. Describe the algorithm in pseudocode: a sequence of precise steps formulated in English.

Problem Statement You have the choice of buying two cars. One is more fuel efficient than the other, but also more expensive. You know the price and fuel efficiency (in miles per gallon, mpg) of both cars. You plan to keep the car for ten years. Assume a price of $4 per gallon of gas and usage of 15,000 miles per year. You will pay cash for the car and not worry about financing costs. Which car is the better deal?

© David H. Lewis/Getty Images.

How To guides give step-by-step guidance for common programming tasks, emphasizing planning and testing. They answer the beginner's question, "Now what do I do?" and integrate key concepts into a problem-solving sequence.

Step 1   Determine the inputs and outputs.

In our sample problem, we have these inputs:

WORKED EXAMPLE 1.1

Writing an Algorithm for Tiling a Floor

Problem Statement Make a plan for tiling a rectangular bathroom floor with alternating black and white tiles measuring 4 × 4 inches. The floor dimensions, measured in inches, are multiples of 4.

Step 1   Determine the inputs and outputs.

The inputs are the floor dimensions (length × width), measured in inches. The output is a tiled floor.

Step 2   Break down the problem into smaller tasks.

A natural subtask is to lay one row of tiles. If you can solve that, then you can solve the problem by laying one row next to the other, starting from a wall, until you reach the opposite wall.

How do you lay a row? Start with
If it is white, put a black one next to
you reach the opposite wall. The ro

© kilukilu/Shutterstock.

Worked Examples apply the steps in the How To to a different example, showing how they can be used to plan, implement, and test a solution to another programming problem.

Table 1 Number Literals in Python		
Number	Type	Comment
6	int	An integer has no fractional part.
–6	int	Integers can be negative.
0	int	Zero is an integer.
0.5	float	A number with a fractional part has type float.
1.0	float	An integer with a fractional part .0 has type float.
1E6	float	A number in exponential notation: 1×10^6 or 1000000. Numbers in exponential notation always have type float.
2.96E-2	float	Negative exponent: $2.96 \times 10^{-2} = 2.96 / 100 = 0.0296$
⊘ 100,000		**Error:** Do not use a comma as a decimal separator.
⊘ 3 1/2		**Error:** Do not use fractions; use decimal notation: 3.5.

Example tables support beginners with multiple, concrete examples. These tables point out common errors and present another quick reference to the section's topic.

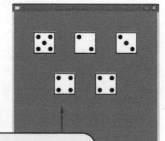

Optional **graphics programming examples** demonstrate constructs with engaging drawings, visually reinforcing programming concepts.

Progressive figures trace code segments to help students visualize the program flow. Color is used consistently to make variables and other elements easily recognizable.

Figure 3
Parameter Passing

1 Function call
```
result1 = cubeVolume(2)
```
result1 =

sideLength =

2 Initializing function parameter variable
```
result1 = cubeVolume(2)
```
result1 =

sideLength = 2

3 About to return to the caller
```
volume = sideLength ** 3
return volume
```
result1 =

sideLength = 2

volume = 8

4 After function call
```
result1 = cubeVolume(2)
```
result1 = 8

Consider the function call illustrated in Figure 3:
```
result1 = cubeVolume(2)
```
- The parameter variable sideLength of the cubeVolume function is created when the function is called. **1**
- The parameter variable is initialized with the value of the argument that was passed in the call. In our case, sideLength is set to 2. **2**
- The function computes the expression sideLength ** 3, which has the value 8. That value is stored in the variable volume. **3**
- The function returns. All of its variables are removed. The return value is trans-

sec01/elevatorsim.py
```
1  ##
2  #  This program simulates an elevator panel that skips the 13th floor.
3  #
4
5  # Obtain the floor number from the user as an integer.
6  floor = int(input("Floor: "))
7
8  # Adjust floor if necessary.
9  if floor > 13 :
10     actualFloor = floor - 1
11 else :
12     actualFloor = floor
13
14 # Print the result.
15 print("The elevator will travel to the actual floor", actualFloor)
```

Program listings are carefully designed for easy reading, going well beyond simple color coding. Students can run and change the same programs right in the eText.

The following program puts the if statement to work. This program asks for the desired floor and then prints out the actual floor.

elevatorsim.py
```
1  ##
2  #  This program simulates an elevator panel that skips the 13th floor.
3  #
4
5  # Obtain the floor number from the user as an integer.
6  floor = int(input("Floor: "))
7
8  # Adjust floor if necessary.
9  if floor > 13 :
10     actualFloor = floor - 1
11 else :
12     actualFloor = floor
13
14 # Print the result.
15 print("The elevator will travel to the actual floor", actualFloor)
```
Input
```
1  20
```
[Run] [Reset]

SELF CHECK

** 2. For each of the following, indicate whether it is appropriate to define a constant variable for the given value.

✓ [True] [False] Number of days per week

The number of days in a week is a constant.

[True] [False] The total purchase price based on a quantity of items purchased

[True] [False] Number of days per month

[True] [False] Hours per day

One correct, 0 errors

Self-check exercises in the eText are designed to engage students with the new material and check understanding before they continue to the next topic.

** Business P4.28 *Currency conversion.* Write a program that first asks the user to type today's price for one dollar in Japanese yen, then reads U.S. dollar values and converts each to yen. Use 0 as a sentinel.

Optional **science, graphics, and business exercises** engage students with realistic applications.

** Graphics P2.30 Write a program that displays the Olympic rings. Color the rings in the Olympic colors.

• Science P4.37 Radioactive decay of radioactive materials can be modeled by the equation $A = A_0 e^{-t(\log 2 / h)}$ where A is the amount of the material at time t, A_0 is the amount at time 0, and h is the half-life.

Technetium-99 is a radioisotope that is used in imaging of the brain. It has a half-life of 6 hours. Your program should display the relative amount A/A_0 in a patient body every hour for 24 hours after receiving a dose.

Toolbox sections teach students how to use Python libraries for solving real-world problems.

TOOLBOX 7.1
Working with CSV Files

You have seen how to read and write text files and to process data stored in various formats, but what if you need to process data stored in a spreadsheet? For example, suppose you need to print a list of all the movies released in the 1990s from a spreadsheet filled with movie data, such as the one shown below.

Common Errors describe the kinds of errors that students often make, with an explanation of why the errors occur, and what to do about them.

Common Error 3.2
Exact Comparison of Floating-Point Numbers

Floating-point numbers have only a limited precision, and calculations can introduce roundoff errors. You must take these inevitable roundoffs into account when comparing floating-point numbers. For example, the following code multiplies the square root of 2 by itself. Ideally, we expect to get the answer 2:

```
from math import sqrt

r = sqrt(2.0)
if r * r == 2.0 :
    print("sqrt(2.0) squared is 2.0")
else :
    print("sqrt(2.0) squared is not 2.0 but", r * r)
```

This program displays

```
sqrt(2.0) squared is not 2.0 but 2.0000000000000004
```

© caracterdesign/iStockphoto.

Take limited precision into account when comparing floating-point numbers.

Programming Tips explain good programming practices, and encourage students to be more productive with tips and techniques such as hand-tracing.

Programming Tip 3.2
Hand-Tracing

A very useful technique for understanding whether a program works correctly is called *hand-tracing*. You simulate the program's activity on a sheet of paper. You can use this method with pseudocode or Python code.

Get an index card, a cocktail napkin, or whatever sheet of paper is within reach. Make a column for each variable. Have the program code ready. Use a marker, such as a paper clip, to mark the current statement. In your mind, execute statements one at a time. Every time the value of a variable changes, cross out the old value and write the new value below the old one.

Let's trace the taxes.py program on page 88 with the inputs from the program run that follows it. In lines 12 and 13, income and maritalStatus are initialized by input statements.

```
 5  # Initialize constant variables for the tax rates and rate limits.
 6  RATE1 = 0.10
 7  RATE2 = 0.25
 8  RATE1_SINGLE_LIMIT = 32000.0
 9  RATE1_MARRIED_LIMIT = 64000.0
10
11  # Read income and marital status.
12  income = float(input("Please enter your income: "))
13  maritalStatus = input("Please enter s for single, m for married: ")
```

© thomasd007/iStockphoto.

Hand-tracing helps you understand whether a program works correctly.

tax1	tax2	income	marital status
		30000	m

Computing & Society presents social and historical information on computing—for interest and to fulfill the "historical and social context" requirements of the ACM/IEEE curriculum guidelines.

Computing & Society 1.1 Computers Are Everywhere

When computers were first invented in the 1940s, a computer filled an entire room. The photo below shows the ENIAC (electronic numerical integrator and computer), completed in 1946 at the University of Pennsylvania. The ENIAC was used by the military to compute the trajectories of projectiles. Nowadays, computing facilities of search engines, Internet shops, and social networks fill huge buildings called data centers. At the other end of the spectrum, computers are all around us. Your cell phone has a computer inside, as do many credit cards and fare cards for public transit. A modern car

The advent of ubiquitous computing changed many aspects of our lives. Factories used to employ people to do repetitive assembly tasks that are today carried out by computer-controlled robots, operated by a few people who know how to work with those computers. Books, music, and movies nowadays are often consumed on computers, and computers are almost always involved

This transit card contains a computer.

Special Topics present optional topics and provide additional explanation of others.

Special Topic 3.4
Short-Circuit Evaluation of Boolean Operators

The and and or operators are computed using **short-circuit evaluation**. In other words, logical expressions are evaluated from left to right, and evaluation stops as soon as the truth value is determined. When an and is evaluated and the first condition is false, the second condition is not evaluated, because it does not matter what the outcome of the second test is.

For example, consider the expression

```
quantity > 0 and price / quantity < 10
```

Suppose the value of quantity is zero. Then the test quantity > 0 fails, and the second test is not attempted. That is just as well, because it is illegal to divide by zero.

Similarly, when the first condition of an or expression is true, then the remainder is not evaluated because the result must be true.

The and and or operators are computed using short-circuit evaluation: As soon as the truth value is determined, no further conditions are evaluated.

In a short circuit, electricity travels along the path of least resistance. Similarly, short-circuit evaluation takes the fastest path for computing the result of a Boolean expression.

© YouraPechkin/iStockphoto.

Interactive activities in the eText
engage students in active reading as they...

Trace through a code segment

3. In this activity, trace through the tax calculation with four different sets of inputs. For each input set, click on the conditions of the if statement that are tested and then on the statement that is executed (which may be another if statement).

Select the next line to be executed.

```
income = float(input("Income: "))
maritalStatus = input("Marital status: ")
if maritalStatus == "s" :
    if income <= 32000 :
        tax = 0.10 * income
    else :
        tax = 3200 + 0.25 * (income - 32000)
else :
    if income <= 64000 :
        tax = 0.10 * income
    else :
        tax = 6400 + 0.25 * (income - 64000)
```

maritalStatus	income	tax
	30000	
s		3000
	40000	
s		

4 correct, 0 errors

Start over

4. Consider the following statement:

```
if hour < 21 :
    response = "Goodbye"
else :
    response = "Goodnight"
```

Determine the value of response when hour has the values given in the table below. (You do not need to put quotes around the response strings.)

Complete the second column. Press Enter to submit

Build an example table

hour	response	Explanation
20	Goodbye	20 < 21, and the first branch of the statement executes.
22	Goodnight	It is not true that 22 < 21, so the else clause executes.

Start over

3. Play with the following activity to learn how to find the largest value in a sequence of inputs. You examine each input in turn and when you find one that is larger than the largest one that you have seen so far, store it as the largest. When you see the sentinel value (the letter Q), you have found the largest value.

Select the next action.

Explore common algorithms

next: 30

largest: 90

Next input   Store as largest   Done

6 correct, 0 errors

4. The half life of Cesium 90, a dangerous radioactive isotope released in the Fukushima reactor accident, is 30 years. That is, half of its radioactive material will decay every 30 years. Rearrange the following lines to produce a program that computes when 99 percent of the material is gone.

Order the statements by moving them into the left window. Use the guide

Done

Arrange code to fulfill a task

```
percentage = 100
year = 0
while percentage > 1.0 :
    percentage = percentage * 0.5
```

```
year = year + 30
print(year)
```

0 correct, 0 errors

3. It is a common beginner's error to forget to include the self reference when accessing the instance variables, thereby creating and accessing local variables instead. Consider this example from a CashRegister class that has instance variables _totalPrice and _payment:

```
def giveChange(self) :
    change = self._payment - self._totalPrice;  ① ②
    _totalPrice = 0   ③ ④   # ERROR! This creates a local variable.
    _payment = 0   ⑤ ⑥   # ERROR! The instance variable is not updated.
    return change   ⑦
```

Trace through the method with the object shown and the self parameter variable already created and initialized. Observe that the local variables are set to zero and then removed when the method exits. The state of the CashRegister object is not changed.

Create a memory diagram

② Initialize the local variable change.
Enter the new value.

reg =

self =

change =

CashRegister	
_totalPrice =	15
_payment =	20

5. Complete the following program that computes and prints the sum of the first 100 po

intsum.py

```
1  number = 1
2  intSum = 0
3  while . . . :
4      intSum = intSum + number
5      number = number + 1
6
7  print(intSum)
```

CodeCheck   Reset

Complete a program and get immediate feedback

Start over

Acknowledgments

Many thanks to Joanna Dingle, Crystal Franks, Graig Donini, and Michael Mac-Dougald at John Wiley & Sons, and Vickie Piercey at Publishing Services for their help with this project. An especially deep acknowledgment and thanks goes to Cindy Johnson for her hard work, sound judgment, and amazing attention to detail.

We are grateful to Ben Stephenson, *University of Calgary,* for his excellent work preparing and reviewing the supplemental materials.

Many thanks to the individuals who worked through the many new activities for this edition, reviewed the manuscript, made valuable suggestions, and brought errors and omissions to our attention. They include:

William Bulko, *University of Texas, Austin*
John Conery, *University of Oregon*
Lee D. Cornell, *Minnesota State University, Mankato*
Mike Domaratzki, *University of Manitoba*
Rich Enbody, *Michigan State University*
Jackie Horton, *University of Vermont*
Winona Istre, *University of Louisiana, Lafayette*
Swami Iyer, *University of Massachusetts, Boston*
ToniAnn Marini, *North Carolina State University*
Melinda McDaniel, *Georgia Institute of Technology*
Shyamal Mitra, *University of Texas, Austin*
Ben Stephenson, *University of Calgary*
Mehmet Ulema, *Manhattan College*
David Wilkins, *University of Oregon*

Every new edition builds on the suggestions of prior reviewers, contributors, and users. We are grateful for the invaluable contributions these individuals have made:

Claude Anderson, *Rose Hulman Institute of Technology*
Jim Carrier, *Guilford Technical Community College*
Gokcen Cilingir, *Washington State University*
Lee Cornell, *Minnesota State University, Mankato*
Akshaye Dhawan, *Ursinus College*
Dirk Grunwald, *University of Colorado Boulder*
Andrew Harrington, *Loyola University Chicago*
Byron Hoy, *Stockton University*
Debbie Keen, *University of Kentucky*
Nicholas A. Kraft, *University of Alabama*

Aaron Langille, *Laurentian University*
Maria Laurent-Rice, *Orange Coast College*
John McManus, *Randolph-Macon College*
Shyamal Mitra, *University of Texas Austin*
Chandan R. Rupakheti, *Rose-Hulman Institute of Technology*
John Schneider, *Washington State University*
Amit Singhal, *University of Rochester*
Ben Stephenson, *University of Calgary*
Amanda Stouder, *Rose-Hulman Institute of Technology*

Dave Sullivan, *Boston University*
Jay Summet, *Georgia Institute of Technology*
James Tam, *University of Calgary*
Krishnaprasad Thirunarayan, *Wright State University*
Leon Tietz, *Minnesota State University, Mankato*
Peter Tucker, *Whitworth University*
Frances VanScoy, *West Virginia University*
Dean Zeller, *University of Northern Colorado*

CONTENTS

*In your eText or on the companion site at www.Wiley.com.

Programming Tips

Special Topics

Computing & Society

CHAPTER	Common Errors		Toolboxes and Worked Examples		How Tos and Worked Examples	
6	Out-of-Range Errors	250	Plotting Trigonometric Functions	265	Working with Lists	276
			Editing Sound Files	273	Rolling the Dice	278
					A World Population Table	290
					Graphics: Drawing Regular Polygons	293
7	Backslashes in File Names	303	Working with CSV Files	314	Processing Text Files	319
			Working with Files and Directories	325	Analyzing Baby Names	322
			Reading Web Pages	343	Graphics: Displaying a Scene File	334
			Statistical Analysis	348		
			Creating a Bubble Chart	352		
8			Harvesting JSON Data from the Web	388	Counting Unique Words	364
					Translating Text Messages	375
					Graphics: Pie Charts	384
9	Trying to Call a Constructor	404			Implementing a Class	410
					Implementing a Bank Account Class	414
					Graphics: A Die Class	436
10	Confusing Super- and Subclasses	451			Developing an Inheritance Hierarchy	463
	Forgetting to Use the super Function When Invoking a Superclass Method	458			Implementing an Employee Hierarchy for Payroll Processing	468
	Don't Use Type Tests	463				
11	Infinite Recursion	493	Analyzing Web Pages with Beautiful Soup	519	Finding Files	497
					Towers of Hanoi	512
12					Enhancing the Insertion Sort Algorithm	549

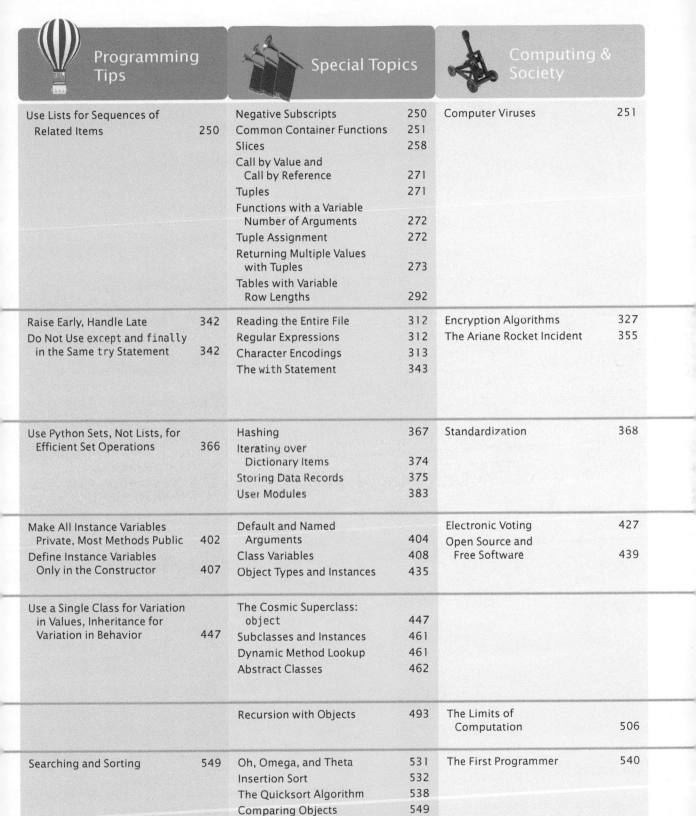

© JanPietruszka/iStockphoto.

To learn about computers and programming

To write and run your first Python program

To recognize compile-time and run-time errors

To describe an algorithm with pseudocode

Just as you gather tools, study a project, and make a plan for tackling it, in this chapter you will gather up the basics you need to start learning to program. After a brief introduction to computer hardware, software, and programming in general, you will learn how to write and run your first Python program. You will also learn how to diagnose and fix programming errors, and how to use pseudocode to describe an *algorithm*—a step-by-step description of how to solve a problem—as you plan your computer programs.

1.1 Computer Programs

Computers execute very basic instructions in rapid succession.

You have probably used a computer for work or fun. Many people use computers for everyday tasks such as electronic banking or writing a term paper. Computers are good for such tasks. They can handle repetitive chores, such as totaling up numbers or placing words on a page, without getting bored or exhausted.

The flexibility of a computer is quite an amazing phenomenon. The same machine can balance your checkbook, lay out your term paper, and play a game. In contrast, other machines carry out a much narrower range of tasks; a car drives and a toaster toasts. Computers can carry out a wide range of tasks because they execute different programs, each of which directs the computer to work on a specific task.

A computer program is a sequence of instructions and decisions.

The computer itself is a machine that stores data (numbers, words, pictures), interacts with devices (the monitor, the sound system, the printer), and executes programs. A **computer program** tells a computer, in minute detail, the sequence of steps that are needed to fulfill a task. The physical computer and peripheral devices are collectively called the **hardware**. The programs the computer executes are called the **software**.

Today's computer programs are so sophisticated that it is hard to believe that they are composed of extremely primitive instructions. A typical instruction may be one of the following:

- Put a red dot at a given screen position.
- Add up two numbers.
- If this value is negative, continue the program at a certain instruction.

The computer user has the illusion of smooth interaction because a program contains a huge number of such instructions, and because the computer can execute them at great speed.

Programming is the act of designing and implementing computer programs.

The act of designing and implementing computer programs is called **programming**. In this book, you will learn how to program a computer—that is, how to direct the computer to execute tasks.

To write a computer game with motion and sound effects or a word processor that supports fancy fonts and pictures is a complex task that requires a team of many highly-skilled programmers. Your first programming efforts will be more mundane. The concepts and skills you learn in this book form an important foundation, and you should not be disappointed if your first programs do not rival the sophisticated software that is familiar to you. Actually, you will find that there is an immense thrill even in simple programming tasks. It is an amazing experience to see the computer precisely and quickly carry out a task that would take you hours of drudgery, to make small changes in a program that lead to immediate improvements, and to see the computer become an extension of your mental powers.

1.2 The Anatomy of a Computer

To understand the programming process, you need to have a rudimentary understanding of the building blocks that make up a computer. We will look at a personal computer. Larger computers have faster, larger, or more powerful components, but they have fundamentally the same design.

At the heart of the computer lies the **central processing unit (CPU)** (see Figure 1). The inside wiring of the CPU is enormously complicated. The CPUs used for personal computers at the time of this writing are composed of several hundred million structural elements, called *transistors*.

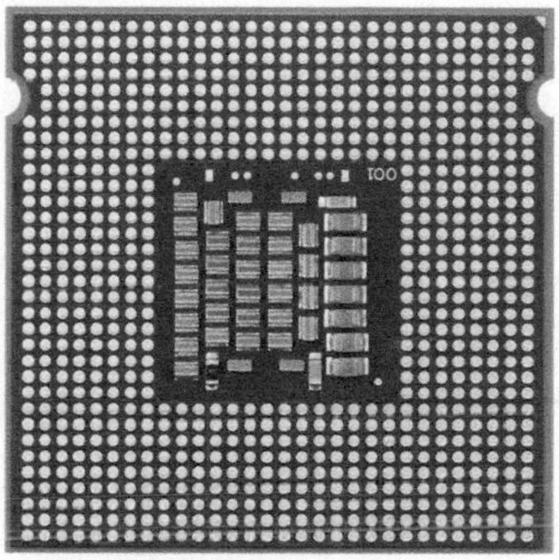

The central processing unit (CPU) performs program control and data processing.

The CPU performs program control and data processing. That is, the CPU locates and executes the program instructions; it carries out arithmetic operations such as addition, subtraction, multiplication, and division; it fetches data from external memory or devices and places processed data into storage.

Storage devices include memory and secondary storage.

There are two kinds of storage. **Primary storage** is made from memory chips: electronic circuits that can store data, provided they are supplied with electric power. **Secondary storage**, usually a **hard disk** (see Figure 2), provides slower and less expensive storage that persists without electricity. A hard disk consists of rotating platters, which are coated with a magnetic material, and read/write heads, which can detect and change the magnetic flux on the platters.

© Amorphis/iStockphoto.

Figure 1 Central Processing Unit

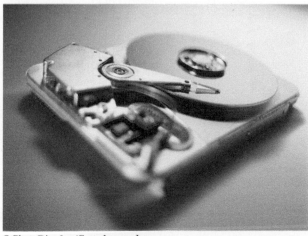

© PhotoDisc, Inc./Getty Images, Inc.

Figure 2 A Hard Disk

The computer stores both data and programs. They are located in secondary storage and loaded into memory when the program starts. The program then updates the data in memory and writes the modified data back to secondary storage.

To interact with a human user, a computer requires peripheral devices. The computer transmits information (called *output*) to the user through a display screen, speakers, and printers. The user can enter information (called *input*) for the computer by using a keyboard or a pointing device such as a mouse.

Some computers are self-contained units, whereas others are interconnected through **networks**. Through the network cabling, the computer can read data and programs from central storage locations or send data to other computers. To the user of a networked computer, it may not even be obvious which data reside on the computer itself and which are transmitted through the network.

Figure 3 gives a schematic overview of the architecture of a personal computer. Program instructions and data (such as text, numbers, audio, or video) are stored on the hard disk, on a compact disk (or DVD), or elsewhere on the network. When a program is started, it is brought into memory, where the CPU can read it. The CPU reads the program one instruction at a time. As directed by these instructions, the CPU reads data, modifies it, and writes it back to memory or the hard disk. Some program instructions will cause the CPU to place dots on the display screen or printer or to vibrate the speaker. As these actions happen many times over and at great speed, the human user will perceive images and sound. Some program instructions read user input from the keyboard or mouse. The program analyzes the nature of these inputs and then executes the next appropriate instruction.

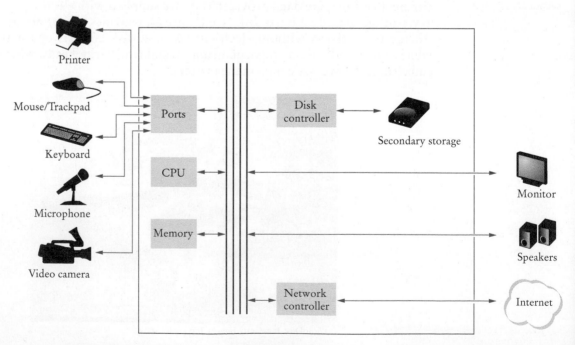

Figure 3 Schematic Design of a Personal Computer

Computing & Society 1.1   **Computers Are Everywhere**

When computers were first invented in the 1940s, a computer filled an entire room. The photo below shows the ENIAC (electronic *numerical integrator and computer*), completed in 1946 at the University of Pennsylvania. The ENIAC was used by the military to compute the trajectories of projectiles. Nowadays, computing facilities of search engines, Internet shops, and social networks fill huge buildings called data centers. At the other end of the spectrum, computers are all around us. Your cell phone has a computer inside, as do many credit cards and fare cards for public transit. A modern car has several computers—to control the engine, brakes, lights, and the radio.

The advent of ubiquitous computing changed many aspects of our lives. Factories used to employ people to do repetitive assembly tasks that are today carried out by computer-controlled robots, operated by a few people who know how to work with those computers. Books, music, and movies nowadays are often consumed on computers, and computers are almost always involved in their production. The book that you

© Maurice Savage/Alamy Limited.

This transit card contains a computer.

are reading right now could not have been written without computers.

Knowing about computers and how to program them has become an essential skill in many careers. Engineers design computer-controlled cars and medical equipment that preserve lives. Computer scientists develop programs that help people come together to support social causes. For example, activists used social networks to share videos showing abuse by repressive regimes, and this information was instrumental in changing public opinion.

As computers, large and small, become ever more embedded in our everyday lives, it is increasingly important for everyone to understand how they work, and how to work with them. As you use this book to learn how to program a computer, you will develop a good understanding of computing fundamentals that will make you a more informed citizen and, perhaps, a computing professional.

© UPPA/Photoshot.

The ENIAC

1.3 The Python Programming Language

In order to write a computer program, you need to provide a sequence of instructions that the CPU can execute. A computer program consists of a large number of simple CPU instructions, and it is tedious and error-prone to specify them one by one. For that reason, **high-level programming languages** have been created. These languages allow a programmer to specify the desired program actions at a high level. The high-level instructions are then automatically translated into the more detailed instructions required by the CPU.

In this book, we will use a high-level programming language called Python, which was developed in the early 1990s by Guido van Rossum. Van Rossum needed to carry out repetitive tasks for administering computer systems. He was dissatisfied with other available languages that were optimized for writing large and fast programs. He needed to write smaller programs that didn't have to run at optimum speed. It was important to him that he could author the programs quickly and update them quickly as his needs changed. Therefore, he designed a language that made it very easy to work with complex data. Python has evolved considerably since its beginnings. In this book, we use version 3 of the Python language. Van Rossum is still the principal author of the language, but the effort now includes many volunteers.

Guido van Rossum

Python is portable and easy to learn and use.

Python has become popular for business, scientific, and academic applications and is very suitable for the beginning programmer. There are many reasons for the success of Python. Python has a much simpler and cleaner syntax than other popular languages such as Java, C, and C++, which makes it easier to learn. Moreover, you can try out short Python programs in an interactive environment, which encourages experimentation and rapid turnaround. Python is also very portable between computer systems. The same Python program will run, without change, on Windows, UNIX, Linux, and Macintosh.

A package provides code for a particular problem domain.

Nowadays, many programmers choose Python because of the availability of packages—bundles of code that solve a particular problem. You can find an astounding number of packages for a wide variety of domains, such as computational biology, machine learning, statistics, data visualization, and many others. Expert developers produce these packages and distribute them, often free of charge. By using a package, you can leverage that expertise in your own projects. For example, you can use a machine learning package to find patterns in your data and a visualization package to display the results. In this book, we introduce you to some of these packages in the optional Toolbox sections.

1.4 Becoming Familiar with Your Programming Environment

Set aside some time to become familiar with the programming environment that you will use for your class work.

Many students find that the tools they need as programmers are very different from the software with which they are familiar. You should spend some time making yourself familiar with your programming environment. Because computer systems vary widely, this book can only give an outline of the steps you need to follow. It is a good idea to participate in a hands-on lab, or to ask a knowledgeable friend to give you a tour.

Step 1 Install the Python development environment.

Your instructor may have given you installation instructions for the environment that is used in your course. If not, follow the installation instructions that we provide at http://horstmann.com/python4everyone/install.html.

Step 2 Start the Python development environment.

Computer systems differ greatly in this regard. On many computers there is an **integrated development environment** in which you can write and test your programs. On other computers you first launch a **text editor**, a program that functions like a word processor, in which you can enter your Python instructions; you then open a **terminal window** and type commands to execute your program. Follow the instructions from your instructor or those at http://horstmann.com/python4everyone/install. html.

> A text editor is a program for entering and modifying text, such as a Python program.

Step 3 Write a simple program.

The traditional choice for the very first program in a new programming language is a program that displays a simple greeting: "Hello, World!". Let us follow that tradition. Here is the "Hello, World!" program in Python:

```
# My first Python program.
print("Hello, World!")
```

We will examine this program in the next section.

No matter which programming environment you use, you begin your activity by typing the program instructions into an editor window.

Create a new file and call it hello.py, using the steps that are appropriate for your environment. (If your environment requires that you supply a project name in addition to the file name, use the name hello for the project.) Enter the program instructions *exactly* as they are given above. Alternatively, locate the electronic copy in this book's companion code and paste it into your editor.

As you write this program, pay careful attention to the various symbols, and keep in mind that Python is **case sensitive**. You must enter upper- and lowercase letters exactly as they appear in the program listing. You cannot type Print or PRINT. If you are not careful, you will run into problems—see Common Error 1.1.

> Python is case sensitive. You must be careful about distinguishing between upper- and lowercase letters.

Step 4 Run the program.

The process for running a program depends greatly on your programming environment. You may have to click a button or enter some commands. When you run the test program, the message

```
Hello, World!
```

will appear somewhere on the screen (see Figure 4 and Figure 5).

Figure 4 Running the hello.py Program in a Terminal Window

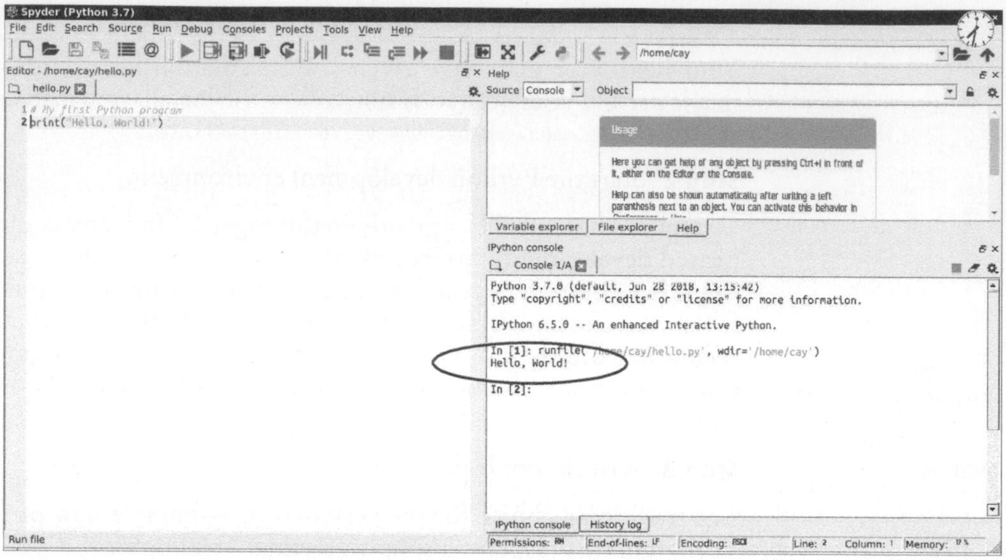

Figure 5   Running the hello.py Program in an Integrated Development Environment

The Python interpreter reads Python programs and executes the program instructions.

A Python program is executed using the **Python interpreter**. The interpreter reads your program and executes all of its steps. (Special Topic 1.1 explains in more detail what the Python interpreter does.) In some programming environments, the Python interpreter is automatically launched when you click on a "Run" button or select the "Run" option from a menu. In other environments, you have to launch the interpreter explicitly.

Step 5   Organize your work.

As a programmer, you write programs, try them out, and improve them. If you want to keep your programs, or turn them in for grading, you store them in **files**. A Python program can be stored in a file with any name, provided it ends with .py. For example, we can store our first program in a file named hello.py or welcome.py.

Files are stored in **folders** or **directories**. A folder can contain files as well as other folders, which themselves can contain more files and folders (see Figure 6). This hierarchy can be quite large, and you need not be concerned with all of its branches. However, you should create folders for organizing your work. It is a good idea to make a separate folder for your programming class. Inside that folder, make a separate folder for each program.

Some programming environments place your programs into a default location if you don't specify a folder. In that case, you need to find out where those files are located. Be sure that you understand where your files are located in the folder hierarchy. This information is essential when you submit files for grading, and for making backup copies (see Programming Tip 1.2).

Figure 6
A Folder Hierarchy

Programming Tip 1.1

Interactive Mode

When you write a complete program, you place the program instructions in a file and let the Python interpreter execute your program file. The interpreter, however, also provides an interactive mode in which Python instructions can be entered one at a time. To launch the Python interactive mode from a terminal window, enter the command

```
python
```

(On systems where multiple versions of Python are installed, use the command python3 to run version 3 of Python.) Interactive mode can also be started from within most Python integrated development environments.

The interface for working in interactive mode is known as the **Python shell**. First, you will see an informational message similar to the following:

```
Python 3.1.4 (default, Nov 3 2014, 14:38:10)
[GCC 4.9.1 20140930 (Red Hat 4.9.1-11)] on linux
Type "help", "copyright", "credits" or "license" for more information.
>>>
```

The >>> at the bottom of the output is the **prompt**. It indicates that you can enter Python instructions. (Your prompt may look different, such as In [1]:.) After you type an instruction and press the Enter key, the code is immediately executed by the Python interpreter. For example, if you enter

```
print("Hello, World!")
```

the interpreter will respond by executing the print function and displaying the output, followed by another prompt:

```
>>> print("Hello, World!")
Hello World!
>>>
```

Interactive mode is very useful when you are first learning to program. It allows you to experiment and test individual Python instructions to see what happens. You can also use interactive mode as a simple calculator. Just enter mathematical expressions using Python syntax:

```
>>> 7035 * 0.15
1055.25
>>>
```

Make it a habit to use interactive mode as you experiment with new language constructs.

Programming Tip 1.2
Backup Copies

You will spend many hours creating and improving Python programs. It is easy to delete a file by accident, and occasionally files are lost because of a computer malfunction. Retyping the contents of lost files is frustrating and time-consuming. It is therefore crucially important that you learn how to safeguard files and get in the habit of doing so *before* disaster strikes. Backing up files on a memory stick is an easy and convenient storage method for many people. Another increasingly popular form of backup is Internet file storage.

© Tatiana Popova/iStockphoto.

Here are a few pointers to keep in mind:

> Develop a strategy for keeping backup copies of your work before disaster strikes.

- *Back up often.* Backing up a file takes only a few seconds, and you will hate yourself if you have to spend many hours recreating work that you could have saved easily. We recommend that you back up your work once every thirty minutes.

- *Rotate backups.* Use more than one directory for backups, and rotate them. That is, first back up onto the first directory. Then back up onto the second directory. Then use the third, and then go back to the first. That way you always have three recent backups. If your recent changes made matters worse, you can then go back to the older version.

- *Pay attention to the backup direction.* Backing up involves copying files from one place to another. It is important that you do this right—that is, copy from your work location to the backup location. If you do it the wrong way, you will overwrite a newer file with an older version.
- *Check your backups once in a while.* Double-check that your backups are where you think they are. There is nothing more frustrating than to find out that the backups are not there when you need them.
- *Relax, then restore.* When you lose a file and need to restore it from a backup, you are likely to be in an unhappy, nervous state. Take a deep breath and think through the recovery process before you start. It is not uncommon for an agitated computer user to wipe out the last backup when trying to restore a damaged file.

Special Topic 1.1
The Python Interpreter

When you use the Python interpreter to execute a program, you can imagine it reading your program and executing it, one step at a time. However, that is not actually what is happening. Because one typically runs a program many times, the Python interpreter employs a division of labor. The time-consuming task of reading a program and comprehending its instructions is carried out once, by a component called a **compiler**. The compiler reads the file containing your **source code** (that is, the Python instructions that you wrote), and translates the instructions into **byte code**. Byte codes are very simple instructions understood by the **virtual machine**, a separate program that is similar to the CPU of a computer. After the compiler has translated your program into virtual machine instructions, they are executed by the virtual machine, as often as you like.

Your source code doesn't contain all the information that the virtual machine needs. For example, it does not contain the implementation of the print function. The virtual machine locates functions such as print in the standard Python library. You need not do anything special to access functionality in the standard library. However, when you want to do specialized tasks, such as graphics programming, you may need to install the required packages. The details depend on your Python environment.

You may find files containing virtual machine instructions in your file system. These files have the extension .pyc and are produced by the compiler. You don't have to pay much attention to these files, but don't turn them in for grading. They are only useful for the Python virtual machine, not a human grader.

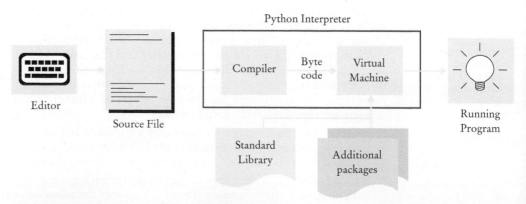

Figure 7   From Source Code to Running Program

1.5 Analyzing Your First Program

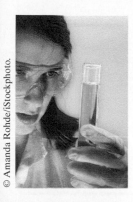

© Amanda Rohde/iStockphoto.

In this section, we will analyze the first Python program in detail. Here again is the code:

sec04/hello.py

```
1  # My first Python program.
2  print("Hello, World!")
```

A Python program contains one or more lines of instructions or **statements** that will be translated and executed by the Python interpreter. The first line

```
# My first Python program.
```

A comment provides information to the programmer.

is a **comment**. Comments begin with # and are not statements. They provide descriptive information to the programmer. Comments will be discussed in more detail in Section 2.1.5.

The second line contains a statement

```
print("Hello, World!")
```

A function is a collection of instructions that perform a particular task.

that prints or displays a line of text, namely "Hello, World!". In this statement, we call a function named print and pass it the information to be displayed. A **function** is a collection of programming instructions that carry out a particular task. We do not have to implement this function, it is part of the Python language. We simply want the function to perform its intended task, namely to print a value.

A function is called by specifying the function name and its arguments.

To use, or call, a function in Python, you need to specify:

1. The name of the function you want to use (in this case, print).
2. Any values the function needs to carry out its task (in this case, "Hello, World!"). The technical term for such a value is an **argument**. Arguments are enclosed in parentheses; multiple arguments are separated by commas. The number of arguments required depends on the function.

A string is a sequence of characters enclosed in a pair of single or double quotation marks.

A sequence of characters enclosed in quotation marks

```
"Hello, World!"
```

is called a **string**. You must enclose the contents of the string inside quotation marks to make it clear that you literally mean "Hello, World!". There is a reason for this requirement. Suppose you need to work with the word *print*. By enclosing it in quotation marks, it is clear that "print" means the sequence of characters p r i n t, not the function named print. The rule is simply that you must enclose all text strings in a pair of either single (') or double (") quotation marks.

You can also print numerical values. For example, the statement

```
print(3 + 4)
```

evaluates the expression 3 + 4 and displays the number 7. You can pass multiple values to the function. For example,

```
print("The answer is", 6 * 7)
```

displays The answer is 42. Each value passed to the print function will be displayed, one after the other in the order they are given and separated by a blank space. By default, the print function starts a new line after its arguments are printed.

Syntax 1.1 print Statement

Syntax
```
print()
print(value₁, value₂, ..., valueₙ)
```

All arguments are optional. If no arguments are given, a blank line is printed.

```
print("The answer is", 6 + 7, "!")
```

The values to be printed, one after the other, separated by a blank space.

For example,

```
print("Hello")
print("World!")
```

prints two lines of text:

```
Hello
World
```

If no arguments are given to the print function, it starts a new line. This is similar to pressing the Enter key in a text editor.

For example,

```
print("Hello")
print()
print("World!")
```

prints three lines of text including a blank line:

```
Hello

World
```

Statements in a Python program must begin in the same column. For example, the following program

```
print("Hello")
   print("World!")
```

is not valid because the indenting is inconsistent.

A sample program that demonstrates the use of the print function is below.

sec05/printtest.py

```
 1  ##
 2  #   Sample program that demonstrates the print function.
 3  #
 4
 5  # Prints 7.
 6  print(3 + 4)
 7
 8  # Prints "Hello World!" in two lines.
 9  print("Hello")
10  print("World!")
11
```

```
12  # Prints multiple values with a single print function call.
13  print("My favorite numbers are", 3 + 4, "and", 3 + 10)
14
15  # Prints three lines of text with a blank line.
16  print("Goodbye")
17  print()
18  print("Hope to see you again")
```

Program Run

```
7
Hello
World!
My favorite numbers are 7 and 13
Goodbye

Hope to see you again
```

1.6 Errors

Experiment a little with the hello.py program. What happens if you make a typing error such as

```
print("Hello, World!)
```

(Note the missing quotation marks at the end of the greeting.) When you attempt to run the program, the interpreter will stop and display the following message

```
File "hello.py", line 2
    print("Hello, World)
                        ^
SyntaxError: EOL while scanning string literal
```

© Martin Carlsson/iStockphoto.

Programmers spend a fair amount of time fixing compile-time and run-time errors.

> A compile-time error is a violation of the programming language rules that is detected when the code is translated into executable form.

This is a **compile-time error**. (The process of transforming Python instructions into an executable form is called *compilation*—see Special Topic 1.1). Something is wrong according to the rules of the language, and the error is detected before your program is actually run. For this reason, compile-time errors are sometimes called **syntax errors**. When such an error is found, no executable program is created. You must fix the error and attempt to run the program again. The interpreter is quite picky, and it is common to go through several rounds of fixing compile-time errors before the program runs for the first time. In this case, the fix is simple: add a quotation mark at the end of the string.

Unfortunately, the interpreter is not very smart and often provides no help in identifying the syntax error. For example, suppose you forget both quotation marks around a string

```
print(Hello, World!)
```

The error report looks like this:

```
File "hello.py", line 2
    print(Hello, World!)
                       ^
SyntaxError: invalid syntax
```

It is up to you to realize that you need to enclose strings in quotation marks.

Some errors can only be found when the program executes. For example, suppose your program includes the statement

```
print(1 / 0)
```

This statement does not violate the rules of the Python language, and the program will start running. However, when the division by zero occurs, the program will stop and display the following error message:

```
Traceback (most recent call last):
    File "hello.py", line 3, in <module>
ZeroDivisionError: int division or modulo by zero
```

An exception occurs when an instruction is syntactically correct, but impossible to perform.

This is called an **exception**. Unlike a compile-time error, which is reported as the program code is analyzed, an exception occurs when the program runs. An exception is a **run-time error**.

There is another kind of run-time error. Consider a program that contains the following statement:

```
print("Hello, Word!")
```

A run-time error is any error that occurs when the program compiles and runs, but produces unexpected results.

The program is syntactically correct and runs without exceptions, but it doesn't produce the results we expected. Instead of printing "Hello, World!", it prints "Word" in place of "World".

Some people use the term **logic error** instead of run-time error. After all, when the program misbehaves, something is wrong with the program logic. A well-written program would make sure that there are no divisions by zero and no faulty outputs.

During program development, errors are unavoidable. Once a program is longer than a few lines, it would require superhuman concentration to enter it correctly without slipping up once. You will find yourself misspelling words, omitting quotation marks, or trying to perform an invalid operation more often than you would like. Fortunately, these problems are reported at compile-time, and you can fix them.

Run-time errors are more troublesome. They are the harder to find and fix because the interpreter cannot flag them for us. It is the responsibility of the program author to test the program and prevent any run-time errors.

Common Error 1.1

Misspelling Words

If you accidentally misspell a word, then strange things may happen, and it may not always be completely obvious from the error message what went wrong. Here is a good example of how simple spelling errors can cause trouble:

```
Print("Hello, World!")
print("How are you?")
```

The first statement calls the Print function. This is not the same as the print function because Print starts with an uppercase letter and the Python language is case sensitive. Upper- and lowercase letters are considered to be completely different from each other; to the interpreter Print is no better match for print than pint. Of course, the message Name 'Print' is not defined should give you a clue where to look for the error.

If you get an error message that seems to indicate that the Python interpreter is on the wrong track, it is a good idea to check for spelling and capitalization.

1.7 Problem Solving: Algorithm Design

You will soon learn how to program calculations and decision making in Python. But before we look at the mechanics of implementing computations in the next chapter, let's consider how you can describe the steps that are necessary for finding a solution to a problem.

You may have run across advertisements that encourage you to pay for a computerized service that matches you up with a romantic partner. Think how this might work. You fill out a form and send it in. Others do the same. The data are processed by a computer program. Is it reasonable to assume that the computer can perform the task of finding the best match for you?

© mammamaart/iStockphoto.

Finding the perfect partner is not a problem that a computer can solve.

Suppose your younger brother, not the computer, had all the forms on his desk. What instructions could you give him? You can't say, "Find the best-looking person who likes inline skating and browsing the Internet". There is no objective standard for good looks, and your brother's opinion (or that of a computer program analyzing the digitized photo) will likely be different from yours. If you can't give written instructions for someone to solve the problem, there is no way the computer can magically find the right solution. The computer can only do what you tell it to do. It just does it faster, without getting bored or exhausted. For that reason, a computerized match-making service cannot guarantee to find the optimal match for you.

Contrast the problem of finding partners with the following problem:

> You put $10,000 into a bank account that earns 5 percent interest per year. How many years does it take for the account balance to be double the original?

Could you solve this problem by hand? Sure, you could. You figure out the balance as follows:

year	interest	balance
0		10000
1	10000.00 x 0.05 = 500.00	10000.00 + 500.00 = 10500.00
2	10500.00 x 0.05 = 525.00	10500.00 + 525.00 = 11025.00
3	11025.00 x 0.05 = 551.25	11025.00 + 551.25 = 11576.25
4	11576.25 x 0.05 = 578.81	11576.25 + 578.81 = 12155.06

You keep going until the balance is at least $20,000. Then the last number in the year column is the answer.

Of course, carrying out this computation is intensely boring to you (and your younger brother). But computers are very good at carrying out repetitive calculations quickly and flawlessly. What is important to the computer is a description of the steps for finding the solution. Each step must be clear and unambiguous, requiring no guesswork.

Here is such a description:

Set year to 0, balance to 10000.

year	interest	balance
0		10000

While the balance is less than $20,000
 Add 1 to the year.
 Set the interest to balance × 0.05 (i.e., 5 percent interest).
 Add the interest to the balance.

year	interest	balance
0		10000
1	500.00	10500.00
14	942.82	19799.32
(15)	989.96	20789.28

Report year as the answer.

Pseudocode is an informal description of a sequence of steps for solving a problem.

Of course, these steps are not yet in a language that a computer can understand, but you will soon learn how to formulate them in Python. This informal description is called **pseudocode**.

There are no strict requirements for pseudocode because it is read by human readers, not a computer program. Here are the kinds of pseudocode statements that we will use in this book:

- Use statements such as the following to describe how a value is set or changed:

  total cost = purchase price + operating cost
  Multiply the balance value by 1.05.
  Remove the first and last character from the word.

- You can describe decisions and repetitions as follows:

  If total cost 1 < total cost 2
  While the balance is less than $20,000
  For each picture in the sequence

  Use indentation to indicate which statements should be selected or repeated:

  For each car
   operating cost = 10 x annual fuel cost
   total cost = purchase price + operating cost

  Here, the indentation indicates that both statements should be executed for each car.

- Indicate results with statements such as:

  Choose car2.
  Report year as the answer.

The exact wording is not important. What is important is that pseudocode describes a sequence of steps that is

- Unambiguous
- Executable
- Terminating

The step sequence is *unambiguous* when there are precise instructions for what to do at each step and where to go next. There is no room for guesswork or personal opinion. A step is *executable* when it can be carried out in practice. Had we said to use the actual interest rate that will be charged in years to come, and not a fixed rate of 5 percent per year, that step would not have been executable, because there is no way for anyone to know what that interest rate will be. A sequence of steps is *terminating* if it will eventually come to an end. In our example, it requires a bit of thought to see that the sequence will not go on forever: With every step, the balance goes up by at least $500, so eventually it must reach $20,000.

A sequence of steps that is unambiguous, executable, and terminating is called an **algorithm**. We have found an algorithm to solve our investment problem, and thus we can find the solution by programming a computer. The existence of an algorithm is an essential prerequisite for programming a task. You need to first discover and describe an algorithm for the task that you want to solve before you start programming (see Figure 8).

© Claudiad/iStockphoto.

An algorithm is a recipe for finding a solution.

An algorithm for solving a problem is a sequence of steps that is unambiguous, executable, and terminating.

Understand the problem

Develop and describe an algorithm

Test the algorithm with simple inputs

Translate the algorithm into Python

Compile and test your program

Figure 8
The Software Development Process

Computing & Society 1.2 **Data Is Everywhere**

We humans are built to analyze data about our environment and answer questions such as: "Where will the ball land?" or "What will people buy on the market?" As our means of data collection improve, we look for new methods that help us make sense of the data.

In the 18th and 19th centuries, scientists and engineers learned how to understand the physical world through mathematical models. With the modest computing power available to them, their tool of choice was calculus. The 20th century brought statistical methods and, with the advent of digital computers, the ability to model systems that are not easily manageable with the rules of calculus.

Nowadays, the ease of data collection and the availability of computational power gives rise to innovative methods of analyzing data, which are often collectively called "data science".

One aspect of data science is "data mining", the ability to find patterns in vast amounts of data. Using tools from mathematics, one can find clusters of related data points. Statistical methods can provide "classification"—algorithms for grouping data into different categories. For example, a business can identify different groups of customers from their past shopping behavior and then make specific purchase recommendations for each group. Data mining is also useful for identifying abnormal behavior, which might be a sign of fraud or an imminent danger.

Another powerful part of data science is "machine learning"—building systems that loosely mimic the processing of our brains. Such systems can be trained by presenting them with certain patterns that have been pre-categorized. After the training phase, they are able to recognize similar patterns. For example, one can build a "neural net" and train it with thousands of photos of cats, then a similar number of dogs. Subsequently, the neural net can recognize with great reliability a given picture as a dog or cat. This may not sound so impressive at first. But think about how you might program such a task, given a grid of colored pixels. How would you formulate an algorithm that can tell dogs and cats apart, using only statements such as "If the color of the pixel at location ___ is ___, do ___"?

Data science has led to many advances such as self-driving cars and computer-assisted medical diagnoses. The ability to apply data science methods is helpful for practitioners in many disciplines. A certain amount of programming is required to apply such methods. Python is an excellent programming language for this purpose. A wealth of high-quality Python packages provides data science tools. You will see some simple examples in the "Toolbox" sections of this book. Moreover, Python supports an exploratory programming style. You can quickly try out ideas in an interactive environment until you find patterns in the data. In this book, you will learn all the Python fundamentals that you need to become a successful data scientist.

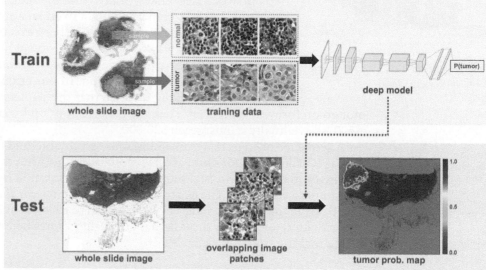

Courtesy of Andrew H. Beck, BIDMC, Harvard Medical School.

Machine learning can aid physicians with detecting malignant tumors.

HOW TO 1.1

Describing an Algorithm with Pseudocode

This is the first of many "How To" sections in this book that give you step-by-step procedures for carrying out important tasks in developing computer programs.

Before you are ready to write a program in Python, you need to develop an algorithm—a method for arriving at a solution for a particular problem. Describe the algorithm in pseudocode: a sequence of precise steps formulated in English.

Problem Statement   You have the choice of buying two cars. One is more fuel efficient than the other, but also more expensive. You know the price and fuel efficiency (in miles per gallon, mpg) of both cars. You plan to keep the car for ten years. Assume a price of $4 per gallon of gas and usage of 15,000 miles per year. You will pay cash for the car and not worry about financing costs. Which car is the better deal?

© David H. Lewis/Getty Images.

Step 1   Determine the inputs and outputs.

In our sample problem, we have these inputs:
- *purchase price1* and *fuel efficiency1*, the price and fuel efficiency (in mpg) of the first car
- *purchase price2* and *fuel efficiency2*, the price and fuel efficiency of the second car

We simply want to know which car is the better buy. That is the desired output.

Step 2   Break down the problem into smaller tasks.

For each car, we need to know the total cost of driving it. Let's do this computation separately for each car. Once we have the total cost for each car, we can decide which car is the better deal.

The total cost for each car is *purchase price + operating cost.*

We assume a constant usage and gas price for ten years, so the operating cost depends on the cost of driving the car for one year.

The operating cost is *10 x annual fuel cost.*

The annual fuel cost is *price per gallon x annual fuel consumed.*

The annual fuel consumed is *annual miles driven / fuel efficiency.* For example, if you drive the car for 15,000 miles and the fuel efficiency is 15 miles/gallon, the car consumes 1,000 gallons.

Step 3   Describe each subtask in pseudocode.

In your description, arrange the steps so that any intermediate values are computed before they are needed in other computations. For example, list the step

> *total cost = purchase price + operating cost*

after you have computed *operating cost.*
    Here is the algorithm for deciding which car to buy:

> *For each car, compute the total cost as follows:*
>   *annual fuel consumed = annual miles driven / fuel efficiency*
>   *annual fuel cost = price per gallon x annual fuel consumed*
>   *operating cost = 10 x annual fuel cost*
>   *total cost = purchase price + operating cost*
> *If total cost of car1 < total cost of car2*
>   *Choose car1.*
> *Else*
>   *Choose car2.*

Step 4   Test your pseudocode by working a problem.

We will use these sample values:

> Car 1: $25,000, 50 miles/gallon
> Car 2: $20,000, 30 miles/gallon

Here is the calculation for the cost of the first car:

> *annual fuel consumed = annual miles driven / fuel efficiency = 15000 / 50 = 300*
> *annual fuel cost = price per gallon x annual fuel consumed = 4 x 300 = 1200*
> *operating cost = 10 x annual fuel cost = 10 x 1200 = 12000*
> *total cost = purchase price + operating cost = 25000 + 12000 = 37000*

Similarly, the total cost for the second car is $40,000. Therefore, the output of the algorithm is to choose car 1.

WORKED EXAMPLE 1.1

Writing an Algorithm for Tiling a Floor

Problem Statement Make a plan for tiling a rectangular bathroom floor with alternating black and white tiles measuring 4 × 4 inches. The floor dimensions, measured in inches, are multiples of 4.

Step 1 Determine the inputs and outputs.

The inputs are the floor dimensions (length × width), measured in inches. The output is a tiled floor.

Step 2 Break down the problem into smaller tasks.

A natural subtask is to lay one row of tiles. If you can solve that, then you can solve the problem by laying one row next to the other, starting from a wall, until you reach the opposite wall.

© kilukilu/Shutterstock.

How do you lay a row? Start with a tile at one wall. If it is white, put a black one next to it. If it is black, put a white one next to it. Keep going until you reach the opposite wall. The row will contain *width / 4* tiles.

Step 3 Describe each subtask in pseudocode.

In the pseudocode, you want to be more precise about exactly where the tiles are placed.

> *Place a black tile in the northwest corner.*
> *While the floor is not yet filled, repeat the following steps:*
> * Repeat this step width / 4 – 1 times:*
> *   If the previously placed tile was white*
> *   Pick a black tile.*
> *   Else*
> *   Pick a white tile.*
> *   Place the picked tile east of the previously placed tile.*
> * Locate the tile at the beginning of the row that you just placed. If there is space to the south,*
> * place a tile of the opposite color below it.*

Step 4 Test your pseudocode by working a sample problem.

Suppose you want to tile an area measuring 20 × 12 inches. The first step is to place a black tile in the northwest corner.

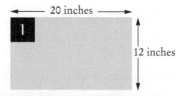

Next, alternate four tiles until reaching the east wall. (*width / 4 – 1 = 20 / 4 – 1 = 4*)

There is room to the south. Locate the tile at the beginning of the completed row. It is black. Place a white tile south of it.

Complete the row.

There is still room to the south. Locate the tile at the beginning of the completed row. It is white. Place a black tile south of it.

1	2	3	4	5
6	7	8	9	10
11				

Complete the row.

1	2	3	4	5
6	7	8	9	10
11	12	13	14	15

Now the entire floor is filled, and you are done.

CHAPTER SUMMARY

Define "computer program" and programming.

- Computers execute very basic instructions in rapid succession.
- A computer program is a sequence of instructions and decisions.
- Programming is the act of designing and implementing computer programs.

Describe the components of a computer.

- The central processing unit (CPU) performs program control and data processing.
- Storage devices include memory and secondary storage.

Describe the benefits of the Python language.

- Python is portable and easy to learn and use.
- A package provides code for a particular problem domain.

Become familiar with your Python programming environment.

- Set aside some time to become familiar with the programming environment that you will use for your class work.
- A text editor is a program for entering and modifying text, such as a Python program.
- Python is case sensitive. You must be careful about distinguishing between upper- and lowercase letters.
- The Python interpreter reads Python programs and executes the program instructions.
- Develop a strategy for keeping backup copies of your work before disaster strikes.

Describe the building blocks of a simple program.

- A comment provides information to the programmer.
- A function is a collection of instructions that perform a particular task.
- A function is called by specifying the function name and its arguments.
- A string is a sequence of characters enclosed in a pair of single or double quotation marks.

Classify program errors as compile-time and run-time errors.

- A compile-time error is a violation of the programming language rules that is detected when the code is translated into executable form.
- An exception occurs when an instruction is syntactically correct, but impossible to perform.
- A run-time error is any error that occurs when the program compiles and runs, but produces unexpected results.

Write pseudocode for simple algorithms.

- Pseudocode is an informal description of a sequence of steps for solving a problem.
- An algorithm for solving a problem is a sequence of steps that is unambiguous, executable, and terminating.

REVIEW EXERCISES

- **R1.1** Explain the difference between using a computer program and programming a computer.

- **R1.2** Which parts of a computer can store program code? Which can store user data?

- **R1.3** Which parts of a computer serve to give information to the user? Which parts take user input?

- **R1.4** A toaster is a single-function device, but a computer can be programmed to carry out different tasks. Is your cell phone a single-function device, or is it a programmable computer? (Your answer will depend on your cell phone model.)

- **R1.5** Which programming languages were mentioned in this chapter? When were they invented? By whom? (Look it up on the Internet.)

- **R1.6** On your own computer or on a lab computer, find the exact location (folder or directory name) of
    - **a.** The sample file `hello.py`, which you wrote with the editor.
    - **b.** The Python program launcher `python`, `python.exe`, or `python.app`.

- **R1.7** What does this program print?

    ```
    print("39 + 3")
    print(39 + 3)
    ```

- **R1.8** What does this program print? Pay close attention to spaces.

    ```
    print("Hello", "World", "!")
    ```

- **R1.9** What is the compile-time error in this program?

    ```
    print("Hello", "World!)
    ```

- **R1.10** Write three versions of the `hello.py` program that have different compile-time errors. Write a version that has a run-time error.

- **R1.11** How do you discover compile-time errors? How do you discover run-time errors?

- **R1.12** Write an algorithm to settle the following question: A bank account starts out with $10,000. Interest is compounded monthly at 0.5 percent per month. Every month, $500 is withdrawn to meet college expenses. After how many years is the account depleted?

- **R1.13** Consider the question in Exercise •• R1.12. Suppose the numbers ($10,000, 6 percent, $500) were user selectable. Are there values for which the algorithm you developed would not terminate? If so, change the algorithm to make sure it always terminates.

- **R1.14** In order to estimate the cost of painting a house, a painter needs to know the surface area of the exterior. Develop an algorithm for computing that value. Your inputs are the width, length, and height of the house, the number of windows and doors, and their dimensions. (Assume the windows and doors have a uniform size.)

- **R1.15** You want to decide whether you should drive your car to work or take the train. You know the one-way distance from your home to your place of work, and the fuel efficiency of your car (in miles per gallon). You also know the one-way price of a train ticket. You assume the cost of gas at \$4 per gallon, and car maintenance at 5 cents per mile. Write an algorithm to decide which commute is cheaper.

•• **R1.16** You want to find out which fraction of your car's use is for commuting to work, and which is for personal use. You know the one-way distance from your home to work. For a particular period, you recorded the beginning and ending mileage on the odometer and the number of work days. Write an algorithm to settle this question.

• **R1.17** In How To 1.1, you made assumptions about the price of gas and annual usage to compare cars. Ideally, you would like to know which car is the better deal without making these assumptions. Why can't a computer program solve that problem?

••• **R1.18** The value of π can be computed according to the following formula:

$$\frac{\pi}{4} = 1 - \frac{1}{3} + \frac{1}{5} - \frac{1}{7} + \frac{1}{9} - \cdots$$

Write an algorithm to compute π. Because the formula is an infinite series and an algorithm must stop after a finite number of steps, you should stop when you have the result determined to six significant digits.

•• **R1.19** Suppose you put your younger brother in charge of backing up your work. Write a set of detailed instructions for carrying out his task. Explain how often he should do it, and what files he needs to copy from which folder to which location. Explain how he should verify that the backup was carried out correctly.

• **Business R1.20** Imagine that you and a number of friends go to a luxury restaurant, and when you ask for the bill you want to split the amount and the tip (15 percent) between all. Write pseudocode for calculating the amount of money that everyone has to pay. Your program should print the amount of the bill, the tip, the total cost, and the amount each person has to pay. It should also print how much of what each person pays is for the bill and for the tip.

PROGRAMMING EXERCISES

• **P1.1** Write a program that prints a greeting of your choice, perhaps in a language other than English.

•• **P1.2** Write a program that prints the sum of the first ten positive integers, $1 + 2 + \cdots + 10$.

•• **P1.3** Write a program that prints the product of the first ten positive integers, $1 \times 2 \times \cdots \times 10$. (Use * to indicate multiplication in Python.)

•• **P1.4** Write a program that prints the balance of an account after the first, second, and third year. The account has an initial balance of \$1,000 and earns 5 percent interest per year.

• **P1.5** Write a program that displays your name inside a box on the screen, like this:

$$\boxed{\text{Dave}}$$

Do your best to approximate lines with characters such as | - +.

■■■ **P1.6** Write a program that prints your name in large letters, such as

```
*   *   **   ****   ****   *   *
*   *  *  *  *      *       *   *
*****  *    *  ****   ****    * *
*   *  ******  *      *        *
*   *  *    *  *      *        *
```

■■ **P1.7** Write a program that prints a face similar to (but different from) the following:

```
     /////
    +"""""+
   (| o o |)
    |  ^  |
    | '-' |
    +-----+
```

■■ **P1.8** Write a program that prints an imitation of a Piet Mondrian painting. (Search the Internet if you are not familiar with his paintings.) Use character sequences such as @@@ or ::: to indicate different colors, and use - and | to form lines.

■■ **P1.9** Write a program that prints a house that looks exactly like the following:

```
      +
     + +
    +   +
   +-----+
   | .-. |
   | | | |
   +-+-+-+
```

■■■ **P1.10** Write a program that prints an animal speaking a greeting, similar to (but different from) the following:

```
   /\_/\      -----
  ( ' ' )   / Hello \
  (  -  ) < Junior |
   | | |    \ Coder!/
  (_|_)      -----
```

■ **P1.11** Write a program that prints three items, such as the names of your three best friends or favorite movies, on three separate lines.

■ **P1.12** Write a program that prints a poem of your choice. If you don't have a favorite poem, search the Internet for "Emily Dickinson" or "e e cummings".

■■ **P1.13** Write a program that prints the United States flag, using * and = characters.

■ **Business P1.14** Write a program that prints a two-column list of your friends' birthdays. In the first column, print the names of your best friends; in the second column, print their birthdays.

■ **Business P1.15** In the United States there is no federal sales tax, so every state may impose its own sales taxes. Look on the Internet for the sales tax charged in five U.S. states, then write a program that prints the tax rate for five states of your choice.

```
Sales Tax Rates
-----------
Alaska: 0%
Hawaii: 4%
. . .
```

■ **Business P1.16** The ability to speak more than one language is a valuable skill in today's labor market. One of the basic skills is learning to greet people. Write a program that prints a two-column list with the greeting phrases shown in the following table; in the first column, print the phrase in English, in the second column, print the phrase in a language of your choice. If you don't speak any language other than English, use an online translator or ask a friend.

List of Phrases to Translate
Good morning.
It is a pleasure to meet you.
Please call me tomorrow.
Have a nice day!

© samxmeg/iStockphoto.

CHAPTER 2

PROGRAMMING WITH NUMBERS AND STRINGS

CHAPTER GOALS

To define and use variables and constants

To understand the properties and limitations of integers and floating-point numbers

To appreciate the importance of comments and good code layout

To write arithmetic expressions and assignment statements

To create programs that read and process inputs, and display the results

To learn how to use Python strings

To create simple graphics programs using basic shapes and text

CHAPTER CONTENTS

Numbers and character strings (such as the ones on this display board) are important data types in any Python program. In this chapter, you will learn how to work with numbers and text, and how to write simple programs that perform useful tasks with them.

2.1 Variables

When your program carries out computations, you will want to store values so that you can use them later. In a Python program, you use *variables* to store values. In this section, you will learn how to define and use variables.

To illustrate the use of variables, we will develop a program that solves the following problem. Soft drinks are sold in cans and bottles. A store offers a six-pack of 12-ounce cans for the same price as a two-liter bottle. Which should you buy? (Twelve fluid ounces equal approximately 0.355 liters.)

In our program, we will define variables for the number of cans per pack and for the volume of each can. Then we will compute the volume of a six-pack in liters and print out the answer.

cans: © blackred/iStockphoto. bottle: © travismanley/iStockphoto.

What contains more soda? A six-pack of 12-ounce cans or a two-liter bottle?

2.1.1 Defining Variables

A variable is a storage location with a name.

A **variable** is a storage location in a computer program. Each variable has a name and holds a value.

A variable is similar to a parking space in a parking garage. The parking space has an identifier (such as "J 053"), and it can hold a vehicle. A variable has a name (such as cansPerPack), and it can hold a value (such as 6).

Like a variable in a computer program, a parking space has an identifier and contents.

Javier Larrea/Age Fotostock.

Syntax 2.1   Assignment

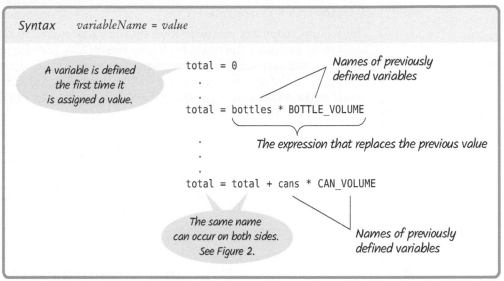

Syntax   *variableName = value*

A variable is defined the first time it is assigned a value.

total = 0

Names of previously defined variables

total = bottles * BOTTLE_VOLUME

The expression that replaces the previous value

total = total + cans * CAN_VOLUME

The same name can occur on both sides. See Figure 2.

Names of previously defined variables

An assignment statement stores a value in a variable.

You use the **assignment statement** to place a value into a variable. Here is an example

```
cansPerPack = 6  ❶ ❷
```

The left-hand side of an assignment statement consists of a variable. The right-hand side is an expression that has a value. That value is stored in the variable.

A variable is created the first time it is assigned a value.

The first time a variable is assigned a value, the variable is created and initialized with that value. After a variable has been defined, it can be used in other statements. For example,

```
print(cansPerPack)
```

will print the value stored in the variable cansPerPack.

Assigning a value to an existing variable replaces the previously stored value.

If an existing variable is assigned a new value, that value replaces the previous contents of the variable. For example,

```
cansPerPack = 8  ❸
```

changes the value contained in variable cansPerPack from 6 to 8. Figure 1 illustrates the two assignment statements used above.

The assignment operator = does *not* denote mathematical equality.

The = sign does not mean that the left-hand side is *equal* to the right-hand side. Instead, the value on the right-hand side is placed into the variable on the left.

Do not confuse this *assignment operator* with the = used in algebra to denote equality. Assignment is an instruction to do something—namely, place a value into a variable.

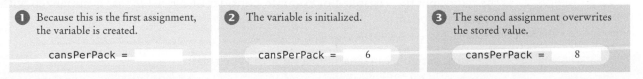

❶ Because this is the first assignment, the variable is created.

```
cansPerPack =
```

❷ The variable is initialized.

```
cansPerPack =   6
```

❸ The second assignment overwrites the stored value.

```
cansPerPack =   8
```

Figure 1   Executing Two Assignments

For example, in Python, it is perfectly legal to write

```
cansPerPack = cansPerPack + 2
```

The second statement means to look up the value stored in the variable cansPerPack, add 2 to it, and place the result back into cansPerPack. (See Figure 2.) The net effect of executing this statement is to increment cansPerPack by 2. If cansPerPack was 8 before execution of the statement, it is set to 10 afterwards. Of course, in mathematics it would make no sense to write that $x = x + 2$. No value can equal itself plus 2.

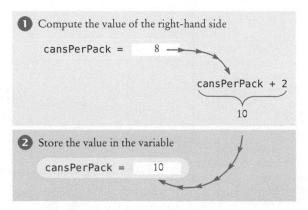

Figure 2
Executing the Assignment
cansPerPack = cansPerPack + 2

2.1.2 Number Types

The data type of a value specifies how the value is stored in the computer and what operations can be performed on the value.

Computers manipulate data values that represent information and these values can be of different types. In fact, each value in a Python program is of a specific type. The **data type** of a value determines how the data is represented in the computer and what operations can be performed on that data. A data type provided by the language itself is called a **primitive data type**. Python supports quite a few data types: numbers, text strings, files, containers, and many others. Programmers can also define their own **user-defined data types**, which we will cover in detail in Chapter 9.

Integers are whole numbers without a fractional part.

In Python, there are several different types of numbers. An **integer** value is a whole number without a fractional part. For example, there must be an integer number of cans in any pack of cans—you cannot have a fraction of a can. In Python, this type is called int. When a fractional part is required (such as in the number 0.355), we use **floating-point numbers**, which are called float in Python.

Floating-point numbers contain a fractional part.

When a value such as 6 or 0.355 occurs in a Python program, it is called a **number literal**. If a number literal has a decimal point, it is a floating-point number; otherwise, it is an integer. Table 1 shows how to write integer and floating-point literals in Python.

A variable in Python can store a value of any type. The data type is associated with the *value*, not the variable. For example, consider this variable that is initialized with a value of type int:

```
taxRate = 5
```

The same variable can later hold a value of type float:

```
taxRate = 5.5
```

Table 1 Number Literals in Python

Number	Type	Comment
6	int	An integer has no fractional part.
–6	int	Integers can be negative.
0	int	Zero is an integer.
0.5	float	A number with a fractional part has type float.
1.0	float	An integer with a fractional part .0 has type float.
1E6	float	A number in exponential notation: 1×10^6 or 1000000. Numbers in exponential notation always have type float.
2.96E-2	float	Negative exponent: $2.96 \times 10^{-2} = 2.96 / 100 = 0.0296$
🚫 100,000		**Error:** Do not use a comma as a decimal separator.
🚫 3 1/2		**Error:** Do not use fractions; use decimal notation: 3.5.

It could even hold a string:

```
taxRate = "Non-taxable"   # Not recommended
```

However, that is not a good idea. If you use the variable and it contains a value of an unexpected type, an error will occur in your program. Instead, once you have initialized a variable with a value of a particular type, you should take care that you keep storing values of the same type in that variable.

For example, because tax rates are not necessarily integers, it is a good idea to initialize the taxRate variable with a floating-point value, even if it happens to be a whole number:

```
taxRate = 5.0   # Tax rates can have fractional parts
```

This helps you remember that taxRate can contain a floating-point value, even though the initial value has no fractional part.

> Once a variable is initialized with a value of a particular type, it should always store values of that same type.

2.1.3 Variable Names

When you define a variable, you need to give it a name that explains its purpose. Whenever you name something in Python, you must follow a few simple rules:

1. Names must start with a letter or the underscore (_) character, and the remaining characters must be letters, numbers, or underscores.
2. You cannot use other symbols such as ? or %. Spaces are not permitted inside names either. You can use upper-case letters to denote word boundaries, as in cansPerPack. This naming convention is called *camel case* because the uppercase letters in the middle of the name look like the humps of a camel.

© GlobalP/iStockphoto.

3. Names are **case sensitive**, that is, `canVolume` and `canvolume` are different names.

4. You cannot use **reserved words** such as `if` or `class` as names; these words are reserved exclusively for their special Python meanings. (See Appendix B for a listing of all reserved words in Python.)

> By convention, variable names should start with a lowercase letter.

These are firm rules of the Python language. There are two "rules of good taste" that you should also respect.

1. It is better to use a descriptive name, such as `cansPerPack`, than a terse name, such as `cpp`.

2. Most Python programmers use names for variables that start with a lowercase letter (such as `cansPerPack`). In contrast, names that are all uppercase (such as `CAN_VOLUME`) indicate constants. Names that start with an uppercase letter are commonly used for user-defined data types (such as `GraphicsWindow`).

Table 2 shows examples of legal and illegal variable names in Python.

Table 2 Variable Names in Python

Variable Name	Comment
`canVolume1`	Variable names consist of letters, numbers, and the underscore character.
`x`	In mathematics, you use short variable names such as x or y. This is legal in Python, but not very common, because it can make programs harder to understand (see Programming Tip 2.1).
⚠ `CanVolume`	**Caution:** Variable names are case sensitive. This variable name is different from `canVolume`, and it violates the convention that variable names should start with a lowercase letter.
🚫 `6pack`	**Error:** Variable names cannot start with a number.
🚫 `can volume`	**Error:** Variable names cannot contain spaces.
🚫 `class`	**Error:** You cannot use a reserved word as a variable name.
🚫 `ltr/fl.oz`	**Error:** You cannot use symbols such as . or /.

2.1.4 Constants

> Use constants for values that should remain unchanged throughout your program.

A constant variable, or simply a **constant**, is a variable whose value should not be changed after it has been assigned an initial value. Some languages provide an explicit mechanism for marking a variable as a constant and will generate a syntax error if you attempt to assign a new value to the variable. Python leaves it to the programmer to make sure that constants are not changed. Thus, it is common practice to specify a constant variable by using all capital letters for its name.

```
BOTTLE_VOLUME = 2.0
MAX_SIZE = 100
```

By following this convention, you provide information to yourself and others that you intend for a variable in all capital letters to be constant throughout the program.

It is good programming style to use named constants in your program to explain numeric values. For example, compare the statements

```
totalVolume = bottles * 2
```

and

```
totalVolume = bottles * BOTTLE_VOLUME
```

A programmer reading the first statement may not understand the significance of the number 2. The second statement, with a named constant, makes the computation much clearer.

2.1.5 Comments

As your programs get more complex, you should add **comments**, explanations for human readers of your code. For example, here is a comment that explains the value used in a constant:

```
CAN_VOLUME = 0.355    # Liters in a 12-ounce can
```

This comment explains the significance of the value 0.355 to a human reader. The interpreter does not execute comments at all. It ignores everything from a # delimiter to the end of the line.

© jgroup/iStockphoto.

Just as a television commentator explains the news, you use comments in your program to explain its behavior.

It is a good practice to provide comments. This helps programmers who read your code understand your intent. In addition, you will find comments helpful when you review your own programs. Provide a comment at the top of your source file that explains the purpose of the program. In the textbook, we use the following style for these comments,

> Use comments to add explanations for humans who read your code. The interpreter ignores comments.

```
##
#   This program computes the volume (in liters) of a six-pack of soda cans.
#
```

Now that you have learned about variables, constants, the assignment statement, and comments, we are ready to write a program that solves the problem from the beginning of chapter. The program displays the volume of a six-pack of cans and the total volume of the six-pack and a two-liter bottle. We use constants for the can and bottle volumes. The totalVolume variable is initialized with the volume of the cans. Using an assignment statement, we add the bottle volume. As you can see from the program output, the six-pack of cans contains over two liters of soda.

sec01/volume1.py

```
 1  ##
 2  #   This program computes the volume (in liters) of a six-pack of soda
 3  #   cans and the total volume of a six-pack and a two-liter bottle.
 4  #
 5
 6  # Liters in a 12-ounce can and a two-liter bottle.
 7  CAN_VOLUME = 0.355
 8  BOTTLE_VOLUME = 2.0
 9
```

```
10  # Number of cans per pack.
11  cansPerPack = 6
12
13  # Calculate total volume in the cans.
14  totalVolume = cansPerPack * CAN_VOLUME
15  print("A six-pack of 12-ounce cans contains", totalVolume, "liters.")
16
17  # Calculate total volume in the cans and a two-liter bottle.
18  totalVolume = totalVolume + BOTTLE_VOLUME
19  print("A six-pack and a two-liter bottle contain", totalVolume, "liters.")
```

Program Run

```
A six-pack of 12-ounce cans contains 2.13 liters.
A six-pack and a two-liter bottle contain 4.13 liters.
```

Common Error 2.1

Using Undefined Variables

A variable must be created and initialized before it can be used for the first time. For example, a program starting with the following sequence of statements would not be legal:

```
canVolume = 12 * literPerOunce   # Error: literPerOunce has not yet been created.
literPerOunce = 0.0296
```

In your program, the statements are executed in order. When the first statement is executed by the virtual machine, it does not know that literPerOunce will be created in the next line, and it reports an "undefined name" error. The remedy is to reorder the statements so that each variable is created and initialized before it is used.

Programming Tip 2.1

Choose Descriptive Variable Names

We could have saved ourselves a lot of typing by using shorter variable names, as in

```
cv = 0.355
```

Compare this declaration with the one that we actually used, though. Which one is easier to read? There is no comparison. Just reading canVolume is a lot less trouble than reading cv and then *figuring out* it must mean "can volume".

This is particularly important when programs are written by more than one person. It may be obvious to *you* that cv stands for can volume and not current velocity, but will it be obvious to the person who needs to update your code years later? For that matter, will you remember yourself what cv means when you look at the code three months from now?

Programming Tip 2.2

Do Not Use Magic Numbers

A **magic number** is a numeric constant that appears in your code without explanation. For example,

```
totalVolume = bottles * 2
```

Why 2? Are bottles twice as voluminous as cans? No, the reason is that every bottle contains 2 liters. Use a named constant to make the code self-documenting:

```
BOTTLE_VOLUME = 2.0
totalVolume = bottles * BOTTLE_VOLUME
```

There is another reason for using named constants. Suppose circumstances change, and the bottle volume is now 1.5 liters. If you used a named constant, you make a single change, and you are done. Otherwise, you have to look at every value of 2 in your program and ponder whether it meant a bottle volume or something else. In a program that is more than a few pages long, that is incredibly tedious and error-prone.

© FinnBrandt/iStockphoto.

We prefer programs that are easy to understand over those that appear to work by magic.

Even the most reasonable cosmic constant is going to change one day. You think there are 365 days per year? Your customers on Mars are going to be pretty unhappy about your silly prejudice. Make a constant

```
DAYS_PER_YEAR = 365
```

2.2 Arithmetic

In the following sections, you will learn how to carry out arithmetic calculations in Python.

2.2.1 Basic Arithmetic Operations

© hocus-focus/iStockphoto.

Python supports the same four basic arithmetic operations as a calculator—addition, subtraction, multiplication, and division—but it uses different symbols for multiplication and division.

You must write a * b to denote multiplication. Unlike in mathematics, you cannot write a b, a · b, or a × b. Similarly, division is always indicated with a /, never a ÷ or a fraction bar.

For example, $\frac{a + b}{2}$ becomes (a + b) / 2.

The symbols + - * / for the arithmetic operations are called *operators*. The combination of variables, literals, operators, and parentheses is called an **expression**. For example, (a + b) / 2 is an expression.

Parentheses are used just as in algebra: to indicate in which order the parts of the expression should be computed. For example, in the expression (a + b) / 2, the sum a + b is computed first, and then the sum is divided by 2. In contrast, in the expression

```
a + b / 2
```

only b is divided by 2, and then the sum of a and b / 2 is formed. As in regular algebraic notation, multiplication and division have a *higher precedence* than addition and subtraction. For example, in the expression a + b / 2, the / is carried out first, even though the + operation occurs further to the left. Again, as in algebra, operators with the same precedence are executed left-to-right. For example, 10 - 2 - 3 is 8 - 3 or 5.

If you mix integer and floating-point values in an arithmetic expression, the result is a floating-point value. For example, 7 + 4.0 is the floating-point value 11.0.

Mixing integers and floating-point values in an arithmetic expression yields a floating-point value.

2.2.2 Powers

Python uses the exponential operator `**` to denote the power operation. For example, the Python equivalent of the mathematical expression a^2 is `a ** 2`. Note that there can be no space between the two asterisks. As in mathematics, the exponential operator has a higher order of precedence than the other arithmetic operators. For example, `10 * 2 ** 3` is $10 \cdot 2^3 = 80$. Unlike the other arithmetic operators, power operators are evaluated from right to left. Thus, the Python expression `10 ** 2 ** 3` is equivalent to $10^{(2^3)} = 10^8 = 100,000,000$.

In algebra, you use fractions and exponents to arrange expressions in a compact two-dimensional form. In Python, you have to write all expressions in a linear arrangement. For example, the mathematical expression

$$b \times \left(1 + \frac{r}{100}\right)^n$$

becomes

```
b * (1 + r / 100) ** n
```

Figure 3 shows how to analyze such an expression.

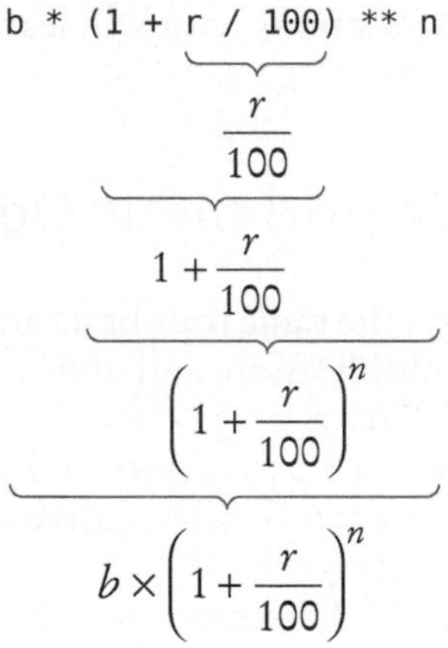

$$b \text{ * } (1 + \underbrace{r \text{ / } 100}) \text{ ** } n$$

$$\underbrace{\frac{r}{100}}$$

$$\underbrace{1 + \frac{r}{100}}$$

$$\underbrace{\left(1 + \frac{r}{100}\right)^n}$$

$$b \times \left(1 + \frac{r}{100}\right)^n$$

Figure 3 Analyzing an Expression

2.2.3 Floor Division and Remainder

The `//` operator computes floor division, in which the remainder is discarded.

When you divide two integers with the `/` operator, you get a floating-point value. For example,

```
7 / 4
```

yields 1.75. However, we can also perform **floor division** by using the `//` operator. For positive integers, floor division computes the quotient and discards the fractional part. The floor division

```
7 // 4
```

evaluates to 1 because 7 divided by 4 is 1.75 with a fractional part of 0.75 (which is discarded).

The % operator computes the remainder of a floor division.

If you are interested in the remainder of a floor division, use the % operator. The value of the expression

```
7 % 4
```

is 3, the remainder of the floor division of 7 by 4. The % symbol has no analog in algebra. It was chosen because it looks similar to /, and the remainder operation is related to division. The operator is called **modulus**. (Some people call it *modulo* or *mod*.) It has no relationship with the percent operation that you find on some calculators.

Here is a typical use for the // and % operations. Suppose you have an amount of pennies in a piggybank:

```
pennies = 1729
```

You want to determine the value in dollars and cents. You obtain the dollars through a floor division by 100:

```
dollars = pennies // 100    # Sets dollars to 17
```

The floor division discards the remainder. To obtain the remainder, use the % operator:

```
cents = pennies % 100    # Sets cents to 29
```

© Michael Flippo/iStockphoto.

See Table 3 for additional examples.

Floor division and modulus are also defined for negative integers and floating-point numbers. However, those definitions are rather technical, and we do not cover them in this book.

Floor division and the % operator yield the dollar and cent values of a piggybank full of pennies.

Table 3 Floor Division and Remainder

Expression (where n = 1729)	Value	Comment
n % 10	9	For any positive integer n, n % 10 is the last digit of n.
n // 10	172	This is n without the last digit.
n % 100	29	The last two digits of n.
n % 2	1	n % 2 is 0 if n is even, 1 if n is odd (provided n is not negative).
-n // 10	-173	−173 is the largest integer ≤ −172.9. We will not use floor division for negative numbers in this book.

2.2.4 Calling Functions

You learned in Chapter 1 that a function is a collection of programming instructions that carry out a particular task. We have been using the print function to display information, but there are many other functions available in Python. In this section, you will learn more about functions that work with numbers.

A function can return a value that can be used as if it were a literal value.

Most functions return a value. That is, when the function completes its task, it passes a value back to the point where the function was called. One example is the abs function that returns the absolute value—the value without a sign—of its numerical argument. For example, the call abs(-173) returns the value 173.

Syntax 2.2   Calling Functions

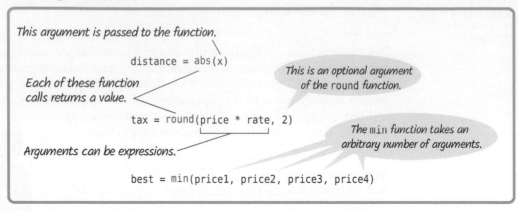

The value returned by a function can be stored in a variable:

```
distance = abs(x)
```

In fact, the returned value can be used anywhere that a value of the same type can be used:

```
print("The distance from the origin is", abs(x))
```

The abs function requires data to perform its task, namely the number from which to compute the absolute value. As you learned earlier, data that you provide to a function are the arguments of the call. For example, in the call

```
abs(-10)
```

the value −10 is the argument passed to the abs function.

When calling a function, you must provide the correct number of arguments. The abs function takes exactly one argument. If you call

```
abs(-10, 2)
```

or

```
abs()
```

your program will generate an error message.

Some functions have optional arguments that you only provide in certain situations. An example is the round function. When called with one argument, such as

```
round(7.625)
```

the function returns the nearest integer; in this case, 8. When called with two arguments, the second argument specifies the desired number of fractional digits.

For example,

```
round(7.627, 2)
```

is 7.63.

There are two common styles for illustrating optional arguments. One style, which we use in this book, shows different function calls with and without the optional arguments.

```
round(x)      # Returns x rounded to a whole number.
round(x, n)   # Returns x rounded to n decimal places.
```

The second style, which is used in Python's standard documentation, uses square brackets to denote the optional arguments.

```
round(x[, n])    # Returns x rounded to a whole number or to n decimal places.
```

Finally, some functions, such as the `max` and `min` functions, take an arbitrary number of arguments. For example, the call

```
cheapest = min(7.25, 10.95, 5.95, 6.05)
```

sets the variable `cheapest` to the minimum of the function's arguments; in this case, the number 5.95.

Table 4 shows the functions that we introduced in this section.

<table>
<tr><td colspan="2" align="center">Table 4 Built-in Mathematical Functions</td></tr>
<tr><th align="center">Function</th><th align="center">Returns</th></tr>
<tr><td>abs(x)</td><td>The absolute value of x.</td></tr>
<tr><td>round(x)
round(x, n)</td><td>The floating-point value x rounded to a whole number or to n decimal places.</td></tr>
<tr><td>max(x_1, x_2, ..., x_n)</td><td>The largest value from among the arguments.</td></tr>
<tr><td>min(x_1, x_2, ..., x_n)</td><td>The smallest value from among the arguments.</td></tr>
</table>

2.2.5 Mathematical Functions

Python has a standard library that provides functions and data types for your code.

The Python language itself is relatively simple, but Python contains a standard library that can be used to create powerful programs. A **library** is a collection of code that has been written and translated by someone else, ready for you to use in your program. A **standard library** is a library that is considered part of the language and must be included with any Python system.

Python's standard library is organized into *modules*. Related functions and data types are grouped into the same module. Functions defined in a module must be explicitly loaded into your program before they can be used. Python's `math` module includes a number of mathematical functions. To use any function from this module, you must first *import* the function. For example, to use the `sqrt` function, which computes the square root of its argument, first include the statement

A library function must be imported into your program before it can be used.

```
from math import sqrt
```

at the top of your program file. Then you can simply call the function as

```
y = sqrt(x)
```

Table 5 shows additional functions defined in the `math` module.

While most functions are defined in a module, a small number of functions (such as `print` and the functions introduced in the preceding section) can be used without importing any module. These functions are called **built-in functions** because they are defined as part of the language itself and can be used directly in your programs.

Table 5 Selected Functions in the math Module

Function	Returns
sqrt(x)	The square root of x ($x \geq 0$).
trunc(x)	Truncates floating-point value x to an integer.
cos(x)	The cosine of x in radians.
sin(x)	The sine of x in radians.
tan(x)	The tangent of x in radians.
exp(x)	e^x
degrees(x)	Convert x radians to degrees (i.e., returns $x \cdot 180/\pi$).
radians(x)	Convert x degrees to radians (i.e., returns $x \cdot \pi/180$).
log(x) log(x, *base*)	The natural logarithm of x (to base e) or the logarithm of x to the given *base*.

Table 6 Arithmetic Expression Examples

Mathematical Expression	Python Expression	Comments
$\dfrac{x + y}{2}$	(x + y) / 2	The parentheses are required; x + y / 2 computes $x + \dfrac{y}{2}$.
$\dfrac{xy}{2}$	x * y / 2	Parentheses are not required; operators with the same precedence are evaluated left to right.
$\left(1 + \dfrac{r}{100}\right)^n$	(1 + r / 100) ** n	The parentheses are required.
$\sqrt{a^2 + b^2}$	sqrt(a ** 2 + b ** 2)	You must import the sqrt function from the math module.
π	pi	pi is a constant declared in the math module.

Common Error 2.2
Roundoff Errors

Roundoff errors are a fact of life when calculating with floating-point numbers. You probably have encountered that phenomenon yourself with manual calculations. If you calculate 1/3 to two decimal places, you get 0.33. Multiplying again by 3, you obtain 0.99, not 1.00.

In the processor hardware, numbers are represented in the binary number system, using only digits 0 and 1. As with decimal numbers, you can get roundoff errors when binary digits are lost. They just may crop up at different places than you might expect.

Here is an example:

```
price = 4.35
quantity = 100
total = price * quantity   # Should be 100 * 4.35 = 435
print(total)   # Prints 434.99999999999994
```

In the binary system, there is no exact representation for 4.35, just as there is no exact representation for 1/3 in the decimal system. The representation used by the computer is just a little less than 4.35, so 100 times that value is just a little less than 435.

You can deal with roundoff errors by rounding to the nearest integer or by displaying a fixed number of digits after the decimal separator (see Section 2.5.3).

Common Error 2.3

Unbalanced Parentheses

Consider the expression

```
((a + b) * t / 2 * (1 - t)
```

What is wrong with it? Count the parentheses. There are three (and two). The parentheses are *unbalanced*. This kind of typing error is very common with complicated expressions. Now consider this expression.

```
(a + b) * t) / (2 * (1 - t)
```

This expression has three (and three), but it still is not correct. In the middle of the expression,

```
(a + b) * t) / (2 * (1 - t)
          ↑
```

there is only one (but two), which is an error. At any point in an expression, the count of (must be greater than or equal to the count of), and at the end of the expression the two counts must be the same.

Here is a simple trick to make the counting easier without using pencil and paper. It is difficult for the brain to keep two counts simultaneously. Keep only one count when scanning the expression. Start with 1 at the first opening parenthesis, add 1 whenever you see an opening parenthesis, and subtract one whenever you see a closing parenthesis. Say the numbers aloud as you scan the expression. If the count ever drops below zero, or is not zero at the end, the parentheses are unbalanced. For example, when scanning the previous expression, you would mutter

© Croko/iStockphoto.

```
(a + b) * t) / (2 * (1 - t)
1       0  -1
```

and you would find the error.

Programming Tip 2.3

Use Spaces in Expressions

It is easier to read

```
x1 = (-b + sqrt(b ** 2 - 4 * a * c)) / (2 * a)
```

than

```
x1=(-b+sqrt(b**2-4*a*c))/(2*a)
```

Simply put spaces around all operators (+ - * / % =, and so on). However, don't put a space after a *unary* minus: a – used to negate a single quantity, such as -b. That way, it can be easily distinguished from a *binary* minus, as in a - b.

It is customary *not* to put a space after a function name. That is, write sqrt(x) and not sqrt (x).

Special Topic 2.1
Other Ways to Import Modules

Python provides several different ways to import functions from a module into your program. You can import multiple functions from the same module like this:

```
from math import sqrt, sin, cos
```

You can also import the entire contents of a module into your program:

```
from math import *
```

Alternatively, you can import the module with the statement

```
import math
```

With this form of the import statement, you need to add the module name and a period before each function call, like this:

```
y = math.sqrt(x)
```

Some programmers prefer this style because it makes it very explicit to which module a particular function belongs.

Special Topic 2.2
Combining Assignment and Arithmetic

In Python, you can combine arithmetic and assignment. For example, the instruction

```
total += cans
```

is a shortcut for

```
total = total + cans
```

Similarly,

```
total *= 2
```

is another way of writing

```
total = total * 2
```

Many programmers find this a convenient shortcut especially when incrementing or decrementing by 1:

```
count += 1
```

If you like it, go ahead and use it in your own code. For simplicity, we won't use it in this book.

Special Topic 2.3
Line Joining

If you have an expression that is too long to fit on a single line, you can continue it on another line *provided the line break occurs inside parentheses*. For example,

```
x1 = ((-b + sqrt(b ** 2 - 4 * a * c))
    / (2 * a))   # Ok
```

However, if you omit the outermost parentheses, you get an error:

```
x1 = (-b + sqrt(b ** 2 - 4 * a * c))
    / (2 * a)   # Error
```

The first line is a complete statement, which the Python interpreter processes. The next line, `/ (2 * a)`, makes no sense by itself.

There is a second form of joining long lines. If the *last* character of a line is a backslash, the line is joined with the one following it:

```
x1 = (-b + sqrt(b ** 2 - 4 * a * c)) \
    / (2 * a)    # Ok
```

You must be very careful not to put any spaces or tabs after the backslash. In this book, we only use the first form of line joining.

2.3 Problem Solving: First Do It By Hand

In the preceding section, you learned how to express computations in Python. When you are asked to write a program for solving a problem, you may naturally think about the Python syntax for the computations. However, before you start programming, you should first take a very important step: carry out the computations *by hand*. If you can't compute a solution yourself, it's unlikely that you'll be able to write a program that automates the computation.

To illustrate the use of hand calculations, consider the following problem: A row of black and white tiles needs to be placed along a wall. For aesthetic reasons, the architect has specified that the first and last tile shall be black.

Your task is to compute the number of tiles needed and the gap at each end, given the space available and the width of each tile.

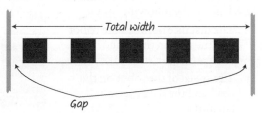

Pick concrete values for a typical situation to use in a hand calculation.

To make the problem more concrete, let's assume the following dimensions:

- Total width: 100 inches
- Tile width: 5 inches

The obvious solution would be to fill the space with 20 tiles, but that would not work—the last tile would be white.

Instead, look at the problem this way: The first tile must always be black, and then we add some number of white/black pairs:

The first tile takes up 5 inches, leaving 95 inches to be covered by pairs. Each pair is 10 inches wide. Therefore the number of pairs is 95/10 = 9.5. However, we need to discard the fractional part because we can't have fractions of tile pairs.

Therefore, we will use 9 tile pairs or 18 tiles, plus the initial black tile. Altogether, we require 19 tiles.

The tiles span 19 × 5 = 95 inches, leaving a total gap of 100 – 19 × 5 = 5 inches.

The gap should be evenly distributed at both ends. At each end, the gap is (100 – 19 × 5) / 2 = 2.5 inches.

This computation gives us enough information to devise an algorithm with arbitrary values for the total width and tile width.

> *number of pairs = integer part of (total width – tile width) / (2 x tile width)*
> *number of tiles = 1 + 2 x number of pairs*
> *gap at each end = (total width – number of tiles x tile width) / 2*

As you can see, doing a hand calculation gives enough insight into the problem that it becomes easy to develop an algorithm.

EXAMPLE CODE See sec03/tiles.py in your eText or companion code for the complete program.

WORKED EXAMPLE 2.1

Computing Travel Time

Problem Statement A robot needs to retrieve an item that is located in rocky terrain next to a road. The robot can travel at a faster speed on the road than on the rocky terrain, so it will want to do so for a certain distance before moving in a straight line to the item. Calculate by hand how much time it takes to reach the item.

Courtesy of NASA.

Your task is to compute the total time taken by the robot to reach its goal, given the following inputs:

- The distance between the robot and the item in the x- and y-direction (dx and dy)
- The speed of the robot on the road and the rocky terrain (s_1 and s_2)
- The length l_1 of the first segment (on the road)

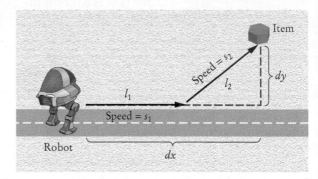

To make the problem more concrete, let's assume the following dimensions:

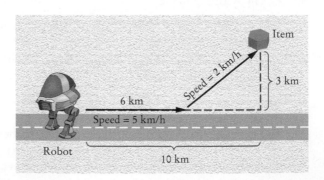

The total time is the time for traversing both segments. The time to traverse the first segment is simply the length of the segment divided by the speed: 6 km divided by 5 km/h, or 1.2 hours.

To compute the time for the second segment, we first need to know its length. It is the hypotenuse of a right triangle with side lengths 3 and 4.

Therefore, its length is $\sqrt{3^2 + 4^2} = 5$. At 2 km/h, it takes 2.5 hours to traverse it. That makes the total travel time 3.7 hours.

This computation gives us enough information to devise an algorithm for the total travel time with arbitrary arguments:

Time for segment 1 = l_1 / s_1
Length of segment 2 = square root of $[(dx - l_1)^2 + dy^2]$
Time for segment 2 = length of segment 2 / s_2
Total time = time for segment 1 + time for segment 2

Translated into Python, the computations are

```python
segment1Time = segment1Length / segment1Speed
segment2Length = sqrt((xDistance - segment1Length) ** 2 + yDistance ** 2)
segment2Time = segment2Length / segment2Speed
totalTime = segment1Time + segment2Time
```

Note that we use variable names that are longer and more descriptive than dx or s_1. When you do hand calculations, it is convenient to use the shorter names, but you should change them to descriptive names in your program. In real life, programs are commonly developed by multiple people. A variable with a short name like s1 may have meaning to you, but it may have no meaning for someone who works on the program at a later time.

EXAMPLE CODE   See worked_example_1/traveltime.py in your eText or companion code for the complete program.

2.4 Strings

Strings are sequences of characters.

Many programs process text, not numbers. Text consists of **characters**: letters, numbers, punctuation, spaces, and so on. A **string** is a sequence of characters. For example, the string "Hello" is a sequence of five characters.

© essxboy/iStockphoto.

2.4.1 The String Type

You have already seen strings in print statements such as

```python
print("Hello")
```

A string can be stored in a variable

```
greeting = "Hello"
```

and later accessed when needed just as numerical values can be:

```
print(greeting)
```

A **string literal** denotes a particular string (such as "Hello"), just as a number literal (such as 2) denotes a particular number. In Python, string literals are specified by enclosing a sequence of characters within a matching pair of either single or double quotes.

```
print("This is a string.", 'So is this.')
```

By allowing both types of delimiters, Python makes it easy to include an apostrophe or quotation mark within a string.

```
message = 'He said "Hello"'
```

In this book, we use double quotation marks around strings because this is a common convention in many other programming languages. However, the interactive Python interpreter always displays strings with single quotation marks.

The number of characters in a string is called the *length* of the string. For example, the length of "Harry" is 5. You can compute the length of a string using Python's len function:

```
length = len("World!")    # length is 6
```

A string of length 0 is called the *empty string*. It contains no characters and is written as "" or ''.

2.4.2 Concatenation and Repetition

Given two strings, such as "Harry" and "Morgan", you can **concatenate** them to one long string. The result consists of all characters in the first string, followed by all characters in the second string. In Python, you use the + operator to concatenate two strings. For example,

```
firstName = "Harry"
lastName = "Morgan"
name = firstName + lastName
```

results in the string

```
"HarryMorgan"
```

What if you'd like the first and last name separated by a space? No problem:

```
name = firstName + " " + lastName
```

This statement concatenates three strings: firstName, the string literal " ", and lastName. The result is

```
"Harry Morgan"
```

When the expression to the left or the right of a + operator is a string, the other one must also be a string or a syntax error will occur. You cannot concatenate a string with a numerical value.

You can also produce a string that is the result of repeating a string multiple times. For example, suppose you need to print a dashed line. Instead of specifying a literal string with 50 dashes, you can use the * operator to create a string that is comprised of the string "-" repeated 50 times. For example,

```
dashes = "-" * 50
```

results in the string

```
"--------------------------------------------------"
```

A string of any length can be repeated using the * operator. For example, the statements

```
message = "Echo..."
print(message * 5)
```

display

```
Echo...Echo...Echo...Echo...Echo...
```

The factor by which the string is replicated must be an integer value. The factor can appear on either side of the * operator, but it is common practice to place the string on the left side and the integer factor on the right.

2.4.3 Converting Between Numbers and Strings

Sometimes it is necessary to convert a numerical value to a string. For example, suppose you need to append a number to the end of a string. You cannot concatenate a string and a number:

```
name = "Agent " + 1729    # Error: Can only concatenate strings
```

Because string concatenation can only be performed between two strings, we must first convert the number to a string.

To produce the string representation of a numerical value, use the str function. The statement

```
str(1729)
```

converts the integer value 1729 to the string "1729". The str function solves our problem:

```
id = 1729
name = "Agent " + str(id)
```

The str function can also be used to convert a floating-point value to a string.

Conversely, to turn a string containing a number into a numerical value, use the int and float functions:

```
id = int("1729")
price = float("17.29")
```

This conversion is important when the strings come from user input (see Section 2.5.1).

The string passed to the int or float functions can only consist of those characters that comprise a literal value of the indicated type. For example, the statement

```
value = float("17x29")
```

will generate a run-time error because the letter "x" cannot be part of a floating-point literal.

Blank spaces at the front or back will be ignored: int(" 1729 ") is still 1729.

2.4.4 Strings and Characters

Strings are sequences of **Unicode** characters (see Computing & Society 2.1). You can access the individual characters of a string based on their position within the string. This position is called the *index* of the character.

© slpix/iStockphoto.

The first character has index 0, the second has index 1, and so on.

A string is a sequence of characters.

```
H  a  r  r  y
0  1  2  3  4
```

An individual character is accessed using a special subscript notation in which the position is enclosed within square brackets. For example, if the variable name is defined as

```
name = "Harry"
```

the statements

```
first = name[0]
last = name[4]
```

extract two different characters from the string. The first statement extracts the first character as the string "H" and stores it in variable first. The second statement extracts the character at position 4, which in this case is the last character, and stores it in variable last.

```
H  a  r  r  y
0  1  2  3  4

first = H          last = y
```

The index value must be within the valid range of character positions or an "index out of range" exception will be generated at run time. The len function can be used to determine the position of the last index, or the last character in a string.

```
pos = len(name) - 1   # Length of "Harry" is 5
last = name[pos]     # last is set to "y"
```

© Rich Legg/iStockphoto.

Initials are formed from the first letter of each name.

The following program puts these concepts to work. The program initializes two variables with strings, one with your name and the other with that of your significant other. It then prints out your initials.

The operation first[0] makes a string consisting of one character, taken from the start of first. The operation second[0] does the same for the second name. Finally, you concatenate the resulting one-character strings with the string literal "&" to get a string of length 3, the initials string. (See Figure 4.)

```
first =  R  o  d  o  l  f  o
         0  1  2  3  4  5  6

second = S  a  l  l  y
         0  1  2  3  4

initials = R  &  S
           0  1  2
```

Figure 4   Building the initials String

sec04/initials.py

```
1   ##
2   #   This program prints a pair of initials.
3   #
4
5   # Set the names of the couple.
6   first = "Rodolfo"
7   second = "Sally"
8
9   # Compute and display the initials.
10  initials = first[0] + "&" + second[0]
11  print(initials)
```

Program Run

```
R&S
```

Table 7 String Operations

Statement	Result	Comment
string = "Py" string = string + "thon"	string is set to "Python"	When applied to strings, + denotes concatenation.
print("Please" + " enter your name: ")	Prints Please enter your name:	Use concatenation to break up strings that don't fit into one line.
team = str(49) + "ers"	team is set to "49ers"	Because 49 is an integer, it must be converted to a string.
greeting = "H & S" n = len(greeting)	n is set to 5	Each space counts as one character.
string = "Sally" ch = string[1]	ch is set to "a"	Note that the initial position is 0.
last = string[len(string) - 1]	last is set to the string containing the last character in string	The last character has position len(string) - 1.

2.4.5 String Methods

In computer programming, an **object** is a software entity that represents a value with certain behavior. The value can be simple, such as a string, or complex, like a graphical window or data file. You will learn much more about objects in Chapter 9. For now, you need to master a small amount of notation for working with string objects.

The behavior of an object is given through its **methods**. A method, like a function, is a collection of programming instructions that carry out a particular task. But unlike a function, which is a standalone operation, a method can only be applied to an object of the type for which it was defined. For example, you can apply the upper method to any string, like this:

```
name = "John Smith"
uppercaseName = name.upper()    # Sets uppercaseName to "JOHN SMITH"
```

Note that the method name follows the object, and that a dot (.) separates the object and method name.

There is another string method called `lower` that yields the lowercase version of a string:

```
print(name.lower())   # Prints john smith
```

It is a bit arbitrary when you need to call a function (such as `len(name)`) and when you need to call a method (`name.lower()`). You will simply need to remember or look it up in a printed or online Python reference.

Just like function calls, method calls can have arguments. For example, the string method `replace` creates a new string in which every occurrence of a given substring is replaced with a second string. Here is a call to that method with two arguments:

```
name2 = name.replace("John", "Jane")   # Sets name2 to "Jane Smith"
```

Note that none of the method calls change the contents of the string on which they are invoked. After the call `name.upper()`, the `name` variable still holds `"John Smith"`. The method call returns the uppercase version. Similarly, the `replace` method returns a new string with the replacements, without modifying the original.

Table 8 lists the string methods introduced in this section.

Table 8 Useful String Methods	
Method	Returns
`s.lower()`	A lowercase version of string *s*.
`s.upper()`	An uppercase version of *s*.
`s.replace(old, new)`	A new version of string *s* in which every occurrence of the substring *old* is replaced by the string *new*.

Special Topic 2.4

Character Values

A character is stored internally as an integer value. The specific value used for a given character is based on a standard set of codes. You can find the values of the characters that are used in Western European languages in Appendix D. For example, if you look up the value for the character `"H"`, you can see that it is actually encoded as the number 72.

Python provides two functions related to character encodings. The `ord` function returns the number used to represent a given character. The `chr` function returns the character associated with a given code. For example,

```
print("The letter H has a code of", ord("H"))
print("Code 97 represents the character", chr(97))
```

produces the following output

```
The letter H has a code of 72
Code 97 represents the character a
```

Special Topic 2.5
Escape Sequences

Sometimes you may need to include both single and double quotes in a literal string. For example, to include double quotes around the word `Welcome` in the literal string "You're Welcome", precede the quotation marks with a backslash (\), like this:

```
"You're \"Welcome\""
```

The backslash is not included in the string. It indicates that the quotation mark that follows should be a part of the string and not mark the end of the string. The sequence \" is called an **escape sequence**.

To include a backslash in a string, use the escape sequence \\, like this:

```
"C:\\Temp\\Secret.txt"
```

Another common escape sequence is \n, which denotes a **newline** character. Printing a newline character causes the start of a new line on the display. For example, the statement

```
print("*\n**\n***")
```

prints the characters

```
*
**
***
```

on three separate lines.

Computing & Society 2.1   International Alphabets and Unicode

The English alphabet is pretty simple: upper- and lowercase *a* to *z*. Other European languages have accent marks and special characters. For example, German has three so-called *umlaut* characters, ä, ö, ü, and a *double-s* character ß. These are not optional frills; you couldn't write a page of German text without using these characters a few times. German keyboards have keys for these characters.

Many countries don't use the Roman script at all. Russian, Greek, Hebrew, Arabic, and Thai letters, to name just a few, have completely different shapes. To complicate matters, Hebrew and Arabic are typed from right to left. Each of these alphabets has about as many characters as the English alphabet.

© Joel Carillet/iStockphoto.

Hebrew, Arabic, and English

The Chinese languages as well as Japanese and Korean use Chinese characters. Each character represents an idea or

© pvachier/iStockphoto.

The German Keyboard Layout

thing. Words are made up of one or more of these ideographic characters. Over 70,000 ideographs are known.

Starting in 1988, a consortium of hardware and software manufacturers developed a uniform encoding scheme called **Unicode** that is capable of encoding text in essentially all written languages of the world.

Python 3 fully supports Unicode. You can form strings containing any Unicode characters. Consider for example

```
str = "🎺 £100"
```

Note the the trumpet emoticon 🎺 and the British pound sign £. Each index position in the string corresponds to a Unicode character:

```
trumpet = str[0]   # "🎺"
space = str[1]     # " "
britishPound = str[2]  # "£"
code = ord(trumpet)  # 127930
```

Today Unicode defines over 100,000 characters. There are even plans to add codes for extinct languages, such as Egyptian hieroglyphics.

© Saipg/iStockphoto.

The Chinese Script

2.5 Input and Output

Most interesting programs ask the program user to provide input values, then the programs produce outputs that depend on the user input. In the following sections, you will see how to read user input and how to control the appearance of the output that your programs produce.

2.5.1 User Input

You can make your programs more flexible if you ask the program user for inputs rather than using fixed values. Consider, for example, the initials.py program from Section 2.4.4 that prints a pair of initials. The two names from which the initials are derived are specified as literal values. If the program user entered the names as inputs, the program could be used for any pair of names.

When a program asks for user input, it should first print a message that tells the user which input is expected. Such a message is called a **prompt**. In Python, displaying a prompt and reading the keyboard input is combined in one operation.

```
first = input("Enter your first name: ")
```

Use the input function to read keyboard input.

The input function displays the string argument in the console window and places the cursor on the same line, immediately following the string.

```
Enter your first name: ▮
```

Note the space between the colon and the cursor. This is common practice in order to visually separate the prompt from the input. After the prompt is displayed, the program waits until the user types a name. After the user supplies the input,

```
Enter your first name: Rodolfo▮
```

the user presses the Enter key. Then the sequence of characters is returned from the input function as a string. In our example, we store the string in the variable first so it can be used later. The program then continues with the next statement.

The following version of the `initials.py` program is changed to obtain the two names from the user.

sec05_01/initials2.py

```
1  ##
2  #   This program obtains two names from the user and prints a pair of initials.
3  #
4
5  # Obtain the two names from the user.
6  first = input("Enter your first name: ")
7  second = input("Enter your significant other's first name: ")
8
9  # Compute and display the initials.
10 initials = first[0] + "&" + second[0]
11 print(initials)
```

Program Run

```
Enter your first name: Sally
Enter your significant other's first name: Harry
S&H
```

2.5.2 Numerical Input

The `input` function can only obtain a string of text from the user. But what if we need to obtain a numerical value? Consider, for example, a program that asks for the price and quantity of soda containers. To compute the total price, the number of soda containers needs to be an integer value, and the price per container needs to be a floating-point value.

To read an integer value, first use the `input` function to obtain the data as a string, then convert it to an integer using the `int` function.

> To read an integer or floating-point value, use the input function followed by the int or float function.

```
userInput = input("Please enter the number of bottles: ")
bottles = int(userInput)
```

In this example, `userInput` is a temporary variable that is used to store the string representation of the integer value (see Figure 5). After the input string is converted to an integer value and stored in `bottles`, it is no longer needed.

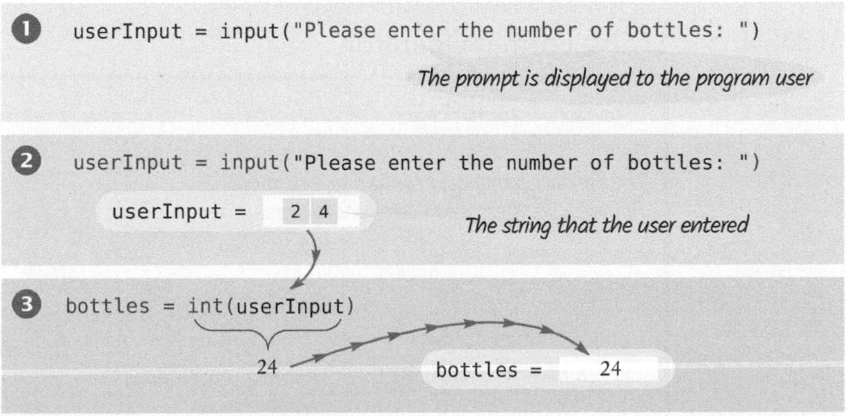

Figure 5   Extracting an Integer Value

To read a floating-point value from the user, the same approach is used, except the input string has to be converted to a float.

```
userInput = input("Enter price per bottle: ")
price = float(userInput)
```

2.5.3 Formatted Output

When you print the result of a computation, you often want to control its appearance. For example, when you print an amount in dollars and cents, you usually want it to be rounded to two significant digits. That is, you want the output to look like

```
Price per liter: 1.22
```

instead of

```
Price per liter: 1.215962441314554
```

The following command displays the price with two digits after the decimal point:

```
print("%.2f" % price)    # Prints 1.22
```

You can also specify a field width (the total number of characters, including spaces), like this:

```
print("%10.2f" % price)
```

The price is printed right-justified using ten characters: six spaces followed by the four characters 1.22.

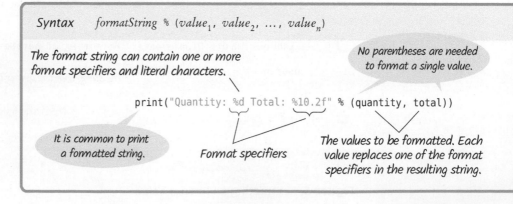

The argument passed to the print function

```
"%10.2f" % price
```

specifies how the string is to be formatted. The result is a string that can be printed or stored in a variable.

You learned earlier that the % symbol is used to compute the remainder of floor division, but that is only the case when the values left and right of the operator are both numbers. If the value on the left is a string, then the % symbol becomes the **string format operator**.

The construct %10.2f is called a *format specifier*: it describes how a value should be formatted. The letter f at the end of the format specifier indicates that we are

> Use the string format operator to specify how values should be formatted.

Syntax 2.3   **String Format Operator**

Syntax   *formatString* % (*value₁*, *value₂*, ..., *valueₙ*)

The format string can contain one or more format specifiers and literal characters.

No parentheses are needed to format a single value.

```
print("Quantity: %d Total: %10.2f" % (quantity, total))
```

It is common to print a formatted string.

Format specifiers

The values to be formatted. Each value replaces one of the format specifiers in the resulting string.

formatting a floating-point value. Use d for an integer value and s for a string; see Table 9 for examples.

Table 9 Format Specifier Examples

Format String	Sample Output	Comments
"%d"	2 4	Use d with an integer.
"%5d"	2 4	Spaces are added so that the field width is 5.
"%05d"	0 0 0 2 4	If you add 0 before the field width, zeroes are added instead of spaces.
"Quantity:%5d"	Q u a n t i t y : 2 4	Characters inside a format string but outside a format specifier appear in the output.
"%f"	1 . 2 1 9 9 7	Use f with a floating-point number.
"%.2f"	1 . 2 2	Prints two digits after the decimal point.
"%7.2f"	1 . 2 2	Spaces are added so that the field width is 7.
"%s"	H e l l o	Use s with a string.
"%d %.2f"	2 4 1 . 2 2	You can format multiple values at once.
"%9s"	H e l l o	Strings are right-justified by default.
"%-9s"	H e l l o	Use a negative field width to left-justify.
"%d%%"	2 4 %	To add a percent sign to the output, use %%.
"%+5d"	+ 2 4	Use a + to show a plus sign with positive numbers.

The *format string* (the string on the left side of the string format operator) can contain one or more format specifiers and literal characters. Any characters that are not format specifiers are included verbatim. For example, the command

```
"Price per liter:%10.2f" % price
```

produces the string

```
"Price per liter:      1.22"
```

You can format multiple values with a single string format operation, but you must enclose them in parentheses and separate them by commas. Here is a typical example:

```
print("Quantity: %d Total: %10.2f" % (quantity, total))
```

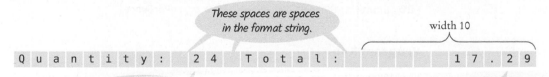

The values to be formatted (quantity and total in this case) are used in the order listed. That is, the first value is formatted based on the first format specifier (%d), the second value (stored in total) is based on the second format specifier (%10.2f), and so on.

When a field width is specified, the values are right-justified within the given number of columns. While this is the common layout used with numerical values printed in table format, it's not the style used with string data. For example, the statements

```
title1 = "Quantity:"
title2 = "Price:"
print("%10s %10d" % (title1, 24))
print("%10s %10.2f" % (title2, 17.29))
```

result in the following output:

```
 Quantity:         24
    Price:      17.29
```

The output would look nicer, however, if the titles were left-justified. To specify left justification, add a minus sign before the string field width:

```
print("%-10s %10d" % (title1, 24))
print("%-10s %10.2f" % (title2, 17.29))
```

The result is the far more pleasant

```
Quantity:          24
Price:          17.29
```

Our next example program will prompt for the price of a six-pack and the volume of each can, then print out the price per ounce. The program puts to work what you just learned about reading input and formatting output.

sec05_03/volume2.py

```
 1  ##
 2  #   This program prints the price per ounce for a six-pack of cans.
 3  #
 4
 5  # Define constant for pack size.
 6  CANS_PER_PACK = 6
 7
 8  # Obtain price per pack and can volume.
 9  userInput = input("Please enter the price for a six-pack: ")
10  packPrice = float(userInput)
11
12  userInput = input("Please enter the volume for each can (in ounces): ")
13  canVolume = float(userInput)
14
15  # Compute pack volume.
16  packVolume = canVolume * CANS_PER_PACK
17
18  # Compute and print price per ounce.
19  pricePerOunce = packPrice / packVolume
20  print("Price per ounce: %8.2f" % pricePerOunce)
```

Program Run

```
Please enter the price for a six-pack: 2.95
Please enter the volume for each can (in ounces): 12
Price per ounce:     0.04
```

Programming Tip 2.4
Don't Wait to Convert

When obtaining numerical values from input, you should convert the string representation to the corresponding numerical value immediately after the input operation.

Obtain the string and save it in a temporary variable that is then converted to a number by the next statement. Don't save the string representation and convert it to a numerical value every time it's needed in a computation:

```
unitPrice = input("Enter the unit price: ")
price1 = float(unitPrice)
price2 = 12 * float(unitPrice)    # Bad style
```

It is bad style to repeat the same computation multiple times. And if you wait, you could forget to perform the conversion.

Instead, convert the string input immediately to a number:

```
unitPriceInput = input("Enter the unit price: ")
unitPrice = float(unitPriceInput)    # Do this immediately after reading the input
price1 = unitPrice
price2 = 12 * unitPrice
```

Or, even better, combine the calls to input and float in a single statement:

```
unitPrice = float(input("Enter the unit price: "))
```

The string returned by the input function is passed directly to the float function, not saved in a variable.

HOW TO 2.1
Writing Simple Programs

This How To shows you how to turn a problem statement into pseudocode and, ultimately, a Python program.

Problem Statement Write a program that simulates a vending machine. A customer selects an item for purchase and inserts a bill into the vending machine. The vending machine dispenses the purchased item and gives change. Assume that all item prices are multiples of 25 cents, and the machine gives all change in dollar coins and quarters. Your task is to compute how many coins of each type to return.

Step 1 Understand the problem: What are the inputs? What are the desired outputs?

In this problem, there are two inputs:

- The denomination of the bill that the customer inserts
- The price of the purchased item

There are two desired outputs:

- The number of dollar coins that the machine returns
- The number of quarters that the machine returns

Jupiterimages/Getty Images, Inc.

A vending machine takes bills and gives change in coins.

Step 2 Work out examples by hand.

This is a very important step. If you can't compute a couple of solutions by hand, it's unlikely that you'll be able to write a program that automates the computation.

Let's assume that a customer purchased an item that cost $2.25 and inserted a $5 bill. The customer is due $2.75, or two dollar coins and three quarters, in change.

That is easy for you to see, but how can a Python program come to the same conclusion? The key is to work in pennies, not dollars. The change due the customer is 275 pennies. Dividing by 100 yields 2, the number of dollars. Dividing the remainder (75) by 25 yields 3, the number of quarters.

Step 3 Write pseudocode for computing the answers.

In the previous step, you worked out a specific instance of the problem. You now need to come up with a method that works in general.

Given an arbitrary item price and payment, how can you compute the coins due? First, compute the change due in pennies:

change due = 100 x bill value - item price in pennies

To get the dollars, divide by 100 and discard the fractional part:

num dollar coins = change due divided by 100 (without the fractional part)

If you prefer, you can use the Python symbol for floor division:

num dollar coins = change due // 100

But you don't have to. The purpose of pseudocode is to describe the computation in a humanly readable form, not to use the syntax of a particular programming language.

The remaining change due can be computed in two ways. If you are aware that one can compute the remainder of a floor division (in Python, with the modulus operator), you can simply compute

change due = remainder of dividing change due by 100

Alternatively, subtract the penny value of the dollar coins from the change due:

change due = change due - 100 x num dollar coins

To get the quarters due, divide by 25:

num quarters = change due // 25

Note that our use of floor division means that if prices are not multiples of 25, any excess pennies due the customer are ignored.

Step 4 Declare the variables and constants that you need, and decide what types of values they hold.

Here, we have five variables:

- billValue
- itemPrice
- changeDue
- dollarCoins
- quarters

Should we introduce constants to explain 100 and 25 as PENNIES_PER_DOLLAR and PENNIES_PER_QUARTER? Doing so will make it easier to convert the program to international markets, so we will take this step.

Because we use floor division and the modulus operator, we want all values to be integers.

Step 5 Turn the pseudocode into Python statements.

If you did a thorough job with the pseudocode, this step should be easy. Of course, you have to know how to express mathematical operations (such as floor division and modulus) in Python.

```
changeDue = PENNIES_PER_DOLLAR * billValue - itemPrice
dollarCoins = changeDue // PENNIES_PER_DOLLAR
changeDue = changeDue % PENNIES_PER_DOLLAR
quarters = changeDue // PENNIES_PER_QUARTER
```

Step 6 Provide input and output.

Before starting the computation, we prompt the user for the bill value and item price:

```
userInput = input("Enter bill value (1 = $1 bill, 5 = $5 bill, etc.): ")
billValue = int(userInput)
userInput = input("Enter item price in pennies: ")
itemPrice = int(userInput)
```

When the computation is finished, we display the result. For extra credit, we format the output strings to make sure that the output lines up neatly:

```
print("Dollar coins: %6d" % dollarCoins)
print("Quarters:     %6d" % quarters)
```

Step 7 Provide a Python program.

Your computation needs to be placed into a program. Find a name for the program that describes the purpose of the computation. In our example, we will choose the name vending.

In the program, you need to declare constants and variables (Step 4), carry out computations (Step 5), and provide input and output (Step 6). Clearly, you will want to first get the input, then do the computations, and finally show the output. Define the constants at the beginning of the program, and define each variable just before it is needed.

Here is the complete program.

how_to_1/vending.py

```
1  ##
2  #   This program simulates a vending machine that gives change.
3  #
4
5  # Define constants.
6  PENNIES_PER_DOLLAR = 100
7  PENNIES_PER_QUARTER = 25
8
9  # Obtain input from user.
10 userInput = input("Enter bill value (1 = $1 bill, 5 = $5 bill, etc.): ")
11 billValue = int(userInput)
12 userInput = input("Enter item price in pennies: ")
13 itemPrice = int(userInput)
14
15 # Compute change due.
16 changeDue = PENNIES_PER_DOLLAR * billValue - itemPrice
17 dollarCoins = changeDue // PENNIES_PER_DOLLAR
18 changeDue = changeDue % PENNIES_PER_DOLLAR
19 quarters = changeDue // PENNIES_PER_QUARTER
20
21 # Print change due.
22 print("Dollar coins: %6d" % dollarCoins)
23 print("Quarters:     %6d" % quarters)
```

Program Run

```
Enter bill value (1 = $1 bill, 5 = $5 bill, etc.): 5
Enter item price in pennies: 225
Dollar coins:      2
Quarters:          3
```

WORKED EXAMPLE 2.2

Computing the Cost of Stamps

Problem Statement   Simulate a postage stamp vending machine. A customer inserts dollar bills into the vending machine and then pushes a "purchase" button. The vending machine gives out as many first-class stamps as the customer paid for, and returns the change in penny (one-cent) stamps. A first-class stamp cost 49 cents at the time this book was written.

Step 1 Understand the problem: What are the inputs? What are the desired outputs?

In this problem, there is one input:

- The amount of money the customer inserts

There are two desired outputs:

- The number of first-class stamps the machine returns
- The number of penny stamps the machine returns

Step 2 Work out examples by hand.

Let's assume that a first-class stamp costs 49 cents and the customer inserts $1.00. That's enough for two stamps (98 cents) but not enough for three stamps ($1.47). Therefore, the machine returns two first-class stamps and two penny stamps.

Step 3 Write pseudocode for computing the answers.

Given an amount of money and the price of a first-class stamp, how can you compute how many first-class stamps can be purchased with the money? Clearly, the answer is related to the quotient

$$\frac{\text{amount of money}}{\text{price of first-class stamp}}$$

For example, suppose the customer paid $1.00. Use a pocket calculator to compute the quotient: $1.00/$0.49 = 2.04.

How do you get "2 stamps" out of 2.04? It's the quotient without the fractional part. In Python, this is easy to compute if both arguments are integers. Therefore, let's switch our computation to pennies. Then we have

number of first-class stamps = 100 / 49 (without remainder)

What if the user inputs two dollars? Then the numerator becomes 200. What if the price of a stamp goes up? A more general equation is

number of first-class stamps = 100 x dollars / price of first-class stamp in cents (without remainder)

How about the change? Here is one way of computing it. When the customer gets the stamps, the change is the customer payment, reduced by the value of the stamps purchased. In our example, the change is 2 cents—the difference between 100 and 2 · 49. Here is the general formula:

change = 100 x dollars – number of first-class stamps x price of first-class stamp

Step 4   Define the variables and constants that you need, and decide what types of values they hold.

Here, we have three variables:

- `dollars`
- `firstClassStamps`
- `change`

There is one constant, `FIRST_CLASS_STAMP_PRICE`. By using a constant, we can change the price in one place without having to search and replace every occurrence of 49 used as the stamp price in the program.

The variable `dollars` and constant `FIRST_CLASS_STAMP_PRICE` must be integers because the computation of `firstClassStamps` uses floor division. The remaining variables are also integers, counting the number of first-class and penny stamps.

Step 5   Turn the pseudocode into Python statements.

Our computation depends on the number of dollars that the user provides. Translating the math into Python yields the following statements:

```
firstClassStamps = 100 * dollars // FIRST_CLASS_STAMP_PRICE
change = 100 * dollars - firstClassStamps * FIRST_CLASS_STAMP_PRICE
```

Step 6   Provide input and output.

Before the computation, we prompt the user for the number of dollars and obtain the value:

```
dollarStr = input("Enter number of dollars: ")
dollars = int(dollarStr)
```

When the computation is finished, we display the result.

```
print("First class stamps: %6d" % firstClassStamps)
print("Penny stamps:       %6d" % change)
```

Step 7   Write a Python program.

Here is the complete program.

worked_example_2/stamps.py

```
 1  ##
 2  #   This program simulates a stamp machine that receives dollar bills and
 3  #   dispenses first class and penny stamps.
 4  #
 5
 6  # Define the price of a stamp in pennies.
 7  FIRST_CLASS_STAMP_PRICE = 49
 8
 9  # Obtain the number of dollars.
10  dollarStr = input("Enter number of dollars: ")
11  dollars = int(dollarStr)
12
13  # Compute and print the number of stamps to dispense.
14  firstClassStamps = 100 * dollars // FIRST_CLASS_STAMP_PRICE
15  change = 100 * dollars - firstClassStamps * FIRST_CLASS_STAMP_PRICE
16  print("First class stamps: %6d" % firstClassStamps)
17  print("Penny stamps:       %6d" % change)
```

Program Run

```
Enter number of dollars: 5
First class stamps:     10
Penny stamps:           10
```

Computing & Society 2.2   Bugs in Silicon

In the summer of 1994, Dr. Thomas Nicely of Lynchburg College in Virginia ran an extensive set of computations to analyze the sums of reciprocals of certain sequences of prime numbers, using a newly released Intel Pentium processor. The results were not always what his theory predicted, even after he took into account the inevitable roundoff errors. Then Dr. Nicely noted that the same program did produce the correct results when running on the slower 486 processor that preceded the Pentium in Intel's lineup. This should not have happened. The optimal roundoff behavior of floating-point calculations has been standardized by the Institute for Electrical and Electronics Engineers (IEEE) and Intel claimed to adhere to the IEEE standard in both the 486 and the Pentium processors. Upon further checking, Dr. Nicely discovered that indeed there was a very small set of numbers for which the product of two numbers was computed differently on the two processors. For example,

$$4,195,835 - ((4,195,835/3,145,727) \times 3,145,727)$$

is mathematically equal to 0, and it did compute as 0 on a 486 processor. On his Pentium processor the result was 256.

As it turned out, Intel had independently discovered the bug in its testing and had started to produce chips that fixed it. The bug was caused by an error in a table that was used to speed up the floating-point multiplication algorithm of the processor. Intel determined that the problem was exceedingly rare. They claimed that under normal use, a typical consumer would only notice the problem once every 27,000 years. Unfortunately for Intel, Dr. Nicely had not been a normal user.

Intel had to replace the defective chips, at a cost of about 475 million dollars.

In 2018, security researchers found flaws that are present in nearly every computer chip manufactured in the previous twenty years. These chips exploit an optimization called "speculative execution"—computing results ahead of time and discarding those that are not needed. Normally, a program cannot read data belonging to another program. But an adversary can make the processor read the data speculatively, and then use it in a way that has a measurable effect. The details are complex and require chip manufacturers to make fundamental changes in processor designs.

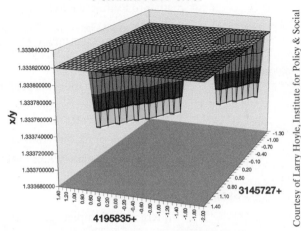

This graph shows a set of numbers for which the original Pentium processor obtained the wrong quotient.

2.6 Graphics: Simple Drawings

There are times when you may want to include simple drawings such as figures, graphs, or charts in your programs. Although the Python library provides a module for creating full graphical applications, it is beyond the scope of this book.

To help you create simple drawings, we have included an ezgraphics module with the book that is a simplified version of Python's more complex library module. The module code and usage instructions are included with this book's companion code.

In the following sections, you will learn all about this module, and how to use it to create simple drawings that consist of basic geometric shapes and text.

© Alexey Avdeev/iStockphoto.

You can make simple drawings out of lines, rectangles, and circles.

2.6.1 Creating a Window

A graphical application shows information inside a **window** on the desktop with a rectangular area and a title bar, as shown in Figure 6. In the `ezgraphics` module, this window is called a *graphics window*.

To create a graphical application using the `ezgraphics` module, carry out the following:

1. Import the `GraphicsWindow` class:

   ```
   from ezgraphics import GraphicsWindow
   ```

   As you will see in Chapter 9, a class defines the behavior of its objects. We will create a single object of the `GraphicsWindow` class and call methods on it.

2. Create a graphics window:

   ```
   win = GraphicsWindow()
   ```

   > A graphics window is used for creating graphical drawings.

   The new window will automatically be shown on the desktop and contain a canvas that is 400 pixels wide by 400 pixels tall. To create a graphics window with a canvas that is of a specific size, you can specify the width and height of the canvas as arguments:

   ```
   win = GraphicsWindow(500, 500)
   ```

   When a graphics window is created, the object representing the window is returned and must be stored in a variable, as it will be needed in the following steps. Several methods that can be used with a `GraphicsWindow` object are shown in Table 10.

3. Access the canvas contained in the graphics window:

   ```
   canvas = win.canvas()
   ```

   > Geometric shapes and text are drawn on a canvas that is contained in a graphics window.

   To create a drawing, you draw the geometric shapes on a canvas just as an artist would to create a painting. An object of the `GraphicsCanvas` class is automatically created when you create the `GraphicsWindow` object. The `canvas` method gives you access to the object representing that canvas. It will be used in the next step.

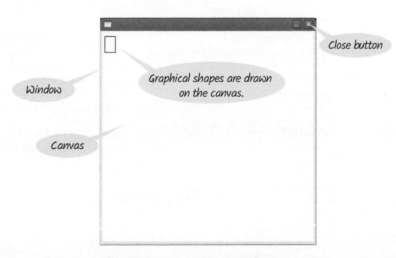

Figure 6   A Graphics Window

4. Create your drawing.

Geometric shapes and text are drawn on the canvas using methods defined in the GraphicsCanvas class. These methods will be described in the following sections. For now, we'll draw a rectangle:

```
canvas.drawRect(15, 10, 20, 30)
```

5. Wait for the user to close the graphics window:

```
win.wait()
```

After drawing the scene on the canvas, the program has to stop or pause and wait for the user to close the window (by clicking the close button). Without this statement, the program would terminate immediately and the graphics window would disappear, leaving no time for you to see your drawing.

The simple program below produces the graphics window shown in Figure 6.

sec06_01/window.py

```
1  ##
2  #  This program creates a graphics window with a rectangle. It provides the
3  #  template used with all of the graphical programs used in the book.
4  #
5
6  from ezgraphics import GraphicsWindow
7
8  # Create the window and access the canvas.
9  win = GraphicsWindow()
10 canvas = win.canvas()
11
12 # Draw on the canvas.
13 canvas.drawRect(5, 10, 20, 30)
14
15 # Wait for the user to close the window.
16 win.wait()
```

Table 10 GraphicsWindow Methods

Method	Description
w = GraphicsWindow() w = GraphicsWindow(*width*, *height*)	Creates a new graphics window with an empty canvas. The size of the canvas is 400 × 400 unless another size is specified.
w.canvas()	Returns the object representing the canvas contained in the graphics window.
w.wait()	Keeps the graphics window open and waits for the user to click the "close" button.

2.6.2 Lines and Polygons

To draw a shape on the canvas, you call one of the "draw" methods defined for a canvas. The call

```
canvas.drawLine(x1, y1, x2, y2)
```

draws a line on the canvas between the points (x_1, y_1) and (x_2, y_2). The call

```
canvas.drawRect(x, y, width, height)
```

draws a rectangle that has its upper-left corner positioned at (x, y) and the given width and height.

> The canvas has methods for drawing lines, rectangles, and other shapes.

Geometric shapes and text are drawn on a canvas by specifying points in the two-dimensional discrete Cartesian coordinate system. The coordinate system, however, is different from the one used in mathematics. The origin (0, 0) is at the upper-left corner of the canvas and the y-coordinate grows downward.

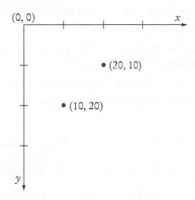

The points on the canvas correspond to pixels on the screen. Thus, the actual size of the canvas and the geometric shapes depends on the resolution of your screen.

Here is the code for a simple program that draws the bar chart shown in Figure 7.

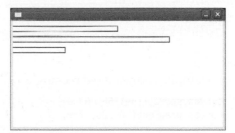

Figure 7 Drawing a Bar Chart

sec06_02/barchart1.py

```
1  ##
2  #   This program draws three rectangles on a canvas.
3  #
4
5  from ezgraphics import GraphicsWindow
6
7  # Create the window and access the canvas.
8  win = GraphicsWindow(400, 200)
9  canvas = win.canvas()
10
11 # Draw on the canvas.
12 canvas.drawRect(0, 10, 200, 10)
13 canvas.drawRect(0, 30, 300, 10)
14 canvas.drawRect(0, 50, 100, 10)
```

```
15
16  # Wait for the user to close the window.
17  win.wait()
```

2.6.3 Filled Shapes and Color

The canvas stores the current drawing parameters used to draw shapes and text.

The canvas stores the drawing parameters (the current color, font, line width, and so on) that are used for drawing shapes and text. When you first start drawing on a canvas, all shapes are drawn using a black pen.

To change the pen color, use one of the method calls,

```
canvas.setOutline(red, green, blue)
canvas.setOutline(colorName)
```

The method arguments can be integer values between 0 and 255 that specify a color value, or one of the strings describing a color in Table 11.

Colors can be specified by name or by their red, green, and blue components.

Table 11 Common Color Names			
Color Name	Color Name	Color Name	Color Name
"black"	"magenta"	"maroon"	"pink"
"blue"	"yellow"	"darkblue"	"orange"
"red"	"white"	"darkred"	"seagreen"
"green"	"gray"	"darkgreen"	"lightgray"
"cyan"	"gold"	"darkcyan"	"tan"

For example, to draw a red rectangle, call

```
canvas.setOutline(255, 0, 0)
canvas.drawRect(10, 20, 100, 50)
```

or

```
canvas.setOutline("red")
canvas.drawRect(10, 20, 100, 50)
```

The geometric shapes can be drawn in one of three styles—outlined, filled, or outlined and filled.

Outlined   Filled   Outlined and filled

The style used to draw a specific shape depends on the current *fill color* and *outline color* as set in the canvas. If you use the default setting (not changing the fill or outline), shapes are outlined in black and there is no fill color.

To set the fill color, use one of the method calls

```
canvas.setFill(red, green, blue)
canvas.setFill(colorName)
```

The following statements

```
canvas.setOutline("black")
canvas.setFill(0, 255, 0)
canvas.drawRect(10, 20, 100, 50)
```

draw a rectangle that is outlined in black and filled with green:

To fill without an outline, call the setOutline method with no arguments:

```
canvas.setOutline()    # Clears the outline color
```

You can also clear the fill color by calling the setFill method with no arguments. This is necessary if you set a fill color in order to draw a filled shape, but then would like to draw an unfilled shape.

Finally, you can set both fill and outline color to the same color with the setColor method. For example, the call

```
canvas.setColor("red")
```

sets both the fill and outline color to red.

Table 12 GraphicsCanvas Color Methods

Method	Description
c.setColor(*colorName*) c.setColor(*red, green, blue*)	Sets both the fill and outline color to the same color. Color can be set by the *colorName* or by values for its *red*, *green*, and *blue* components. (See Section 4.10 for more about RGB values.)
c.setFill() c.setFill(*colorName*) c.setFill(*red, green, blue*)	Sets the color used to fill a geometric shape. If no argument is given, the fill color is cleared.
c.setOutline() c.setOutline(*colorName*) c.setOutline(*red, green, blue*)	Sets the color used to draw lines and text. If no argument is given, the outline color is cleared.

The following program is a version of the barchart1.py program modified to create three filled rectangles, as shown in Figure 8.

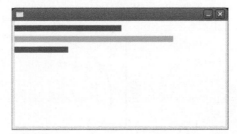

Figure 8   Drawing a Bar Chart with Color Bars

sec06_03/barchart2.py

```
1  ##
2  #   This programs draws three colored rectangles on a canvas.
3  #
```

```
4
5  from ezgraphics import GraphicsWindow
6
7  # Create the window and access the canvas.
8  win = GraphicsWindow(400, 200)
9  canvas = win.canvas()
10
11 # Draw on the canvas.
12 canvas.setColor("red")
13 canvas.drawRect(0, 10, 200, 10)
14
15 canvas.setColor("green")
16 canvas.drawRect(0, 30, 300, 10)
17
18 canvas.setColor("blue")
19 canvas.drawRect(0, 50, 100, 10)
20
21 # Wait for the user to close the window.
22 win.wait()
```

2.6.4 Ovals, Circles, and Text

Now that you've learned how to draw lines and rectangles, let's turn to additional graphical elements.

To draw an oval, you specify its *bounding box* (see Figure 9) in the same way that you would specify a rectangle, namely by the x- and y-coordinates of the top-left corner and the width and height of the box. To draw an oval, use the method call

```
canvas.drawOval(x, y, width, height)
```

As with a rectangle, the oval will be drawn filled, with an outline, or both depending on the current drawing context. To draw a circle, set the width and height to the same values:

```
canvas.drawOval(x, y, diameter, diameter)
```

Notice that (x, y) is the top-left corner of the bounding box, not the center of the circle.

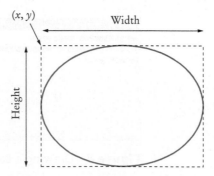

Figure 9 An Oval and its Bounding Box

You often want to put text inside a drawing, for example, to label some of the parts. Use the canvas method drawText to draw a string anywhere on a canvas. You must specify the string and the *x*- and *y*-coordinates of the top-left corner of the bounding box (the "anchor point"—see Figure 10). For example

```
canvas.drawText(50, 100, "Message")
```

Figure 10 Bounding Box and Anchor Point

Table 13 provides a list of drawing methods available for use with the canvas.

Table 13 GraphicsCanvas Drawing Methods

Method	Result	Notes
`c.drawLine(`x_1`, `y_1`, `x_2`, `y_2`)`	/	(x_1, y_1) and (x_2, y_2) are the endpoints.
`c.drawRect(x, y, width, height)`	▭	(x, y) is the top-left corner.
`c.drawOval(x, y, width, height)`	⬭	(x, y) is the top-left corner of the box that bounds the ellipse. To draw a circle, use the same value for *width* and *height*.
`c.drawText(x, y, text)`	Anchor point Message	(x, y) is the anchor point.

HOW TO 2.2

Graphics: Drawing Graphical Shapes

Suppose you want to write a program that displays graphical shapes such as cars, aliens, charts, or any other images that can be obtained from rectangles, lines, and ellipses. These instructions give you a step-by-step procedure for decomposing a drawing into parts and implementing a program that produces the drawing.

Problem Statement Create a program to draw a national flag.

Step 1 Determine the shapes that you need for the drawing.

You can use the following shapes:

- Squares and rectangles
- Circles and ovals
- Lines

The outlines of these shapes can be drawn in any color, and you can fill the insides of these shapes with any color. You can also use text to label parts of your drawing.

Some national flag designs consist of three equally wide sections of different colors, side by side, as in the Italian flag shown here.

You could draw such a flag using three rectangles. But if the middle rectangle is white, as it is,

© Punchstock.

for example, in the flag of Italy (green, white, red), it is easier and looks better to draw a line on the top and bottom of the middle portion:

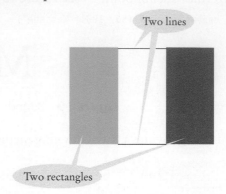

Step 2 Find the coordinates for the shapes.

You now need to find the exact positions for the geometric shapes.

- For rectangles, you need the x- and y-position of the top-left corner, the width, and the height.
- For ellipses, you need the top-left corner, width, and height of the bounding rectangle.
- For lines, you need the x- and y-positions of the starting point and the end point.
- For text, you need the x- and y-position of the anchor point.

A commonly-used size for a window is 300 by 300 pixels. You may not want the flag crammed all the way to the top, so perhaps the upper-left corner of the flag should be at point (100, 100).

Many flags, such as the flag of Italy, have a width : height ratio of 3 : 2. (You can often find exact proportions for a particular flag by doing a bit of Internet research on one of several Flags of the World sites.) For example, if you make the flag 90 pixels wide, then it should be 60 pixels tall. (Why not make it 100 pixels wide? Then the height would be $100 \cdot 2 / 3 \approx 67$, which seems more awkward.)

Now you can compute the coordinates of all the important points of the shape:

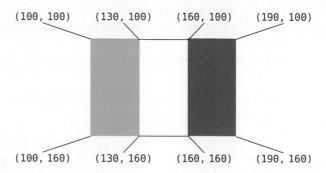

Step 3 Write Python statements to draw the shapes.

In our example, there are two rectangles and two lines:

```
canvas.setColor("green")
canvas.drawRect(100, 100, 30, 60)

canvas.setColor("red")
canvas.drawRect(160, 100, 30, 60)
```

```
canvas.setColor("black")
canvas.drawLine(130, 100, 160, 100)
canvas.drawLine(130, 160, 160, 160)
```

If you are more ambitious, then you can express the coordinates in terms of a few variables. In the case of the flag, we have arbitrarily chosen the top-left corner and the width. All other coordinates follow from those choices. If you decide to follow the ambitious approach, then the rectangles and lines are determined as follows:

```
canvas.drawRect(xLeft, yTop, width / 3, width * 2 / 3)
. . .
canvas.drawRect(xLeft + 2 * width / 3, yTop, width / 3, width * 2 / 3)
. . .
canvas.drawLine(xLeft + width / 3, yTop, xLeft + width * 2 / 3, yTop)
canvas.drawLine(xLeft + width / 3, yTop + width * 2 / 3,
                xLeft + width * 2 / 3, yTop + width * 2 / 3)
```

Step 4   Write the program that creates the graphics window and includes the drawing instructions at the proper spot in the template.

```
win = GraphicsWindow("The Italian Flag", 300, 300)
canvas = win.canvas()

Drawing instructions

win.wait()
```

The complete program for drawing the flag is provided below.

how_to_2/italianflag.py

```
 1  ##
 2  #   This program draws an Italian flag using the ezgraphics module.
 3  #
 4
 5  from ezgraphics import GraphicsWindow
 6
 7  win = GraphicsWindow(300, 300)
 8  canvas = win.canvas()
 9
10  # Define variables with the upper-left position and the size.
11  xLeft = 100
12  yTop = 100
13  width = 90
14
15  # Draw the flag.
16  canvas.setColor("green")
17  canvas.drawRect(xLeft, yTop, width / 3, width * 2 / 3)
18
19  canvas.setColor("red")
20  canvas.drawRect(xLeft + 2 * width / 3, yTop, width / 3, width * 2 / 3)
21
22  canvas.setColor("black")
23  canvas.drawLine(xLeft + width / 3, yTop, xLeft + width * 2 / 3, yTop)
24  canvas.drawLine(xLeft + width / 3, yTop + width * 2 / 3,
25                  xLeft + width * 2 / 3, yTop + width * 2 / 3)
26
27  # Wait for the user to close the window.
28  win.wait()
```

TOOLBOX 2.1
Symbolic Processing with SymPy

This is the first of many optional "Toolbox" sections in this book. Python is not only a very nice programming language, but it has a large ecosystem of useful packages. If you need to carry out complex computations in a particular problem domain, chances are that someone has put together a library of code that gets you started. There are packages for statistics, drawing graphs and charts, sending e-mail, analyzing web pages, and many other tasks. Many of them are developed by volunteers and are freely available on the Internet.

In this section, you will be introduced to the SymPy package for symbolic mathematics. In Section 2.2, you saw how to use Python to compute the value of mathematical expressions such as x ** 2 * sin(x) for a particular value of x. The SymPy package can do much more than that. It can give you a plot of the function and compute a wide variety of formulas. If you have taken a calculus course, you know that there is a formula for computing the derivative of a product. SymPy knows these rules and can carry out all the tedious routine manipulations, so that you don't have to. It is like having a calculus course in a box!

Of course, programs that can process math formulas have been around for over fifty years, but SymPy has two great advantages. It is not a separate program, it is one you use within Python. Second, other math programs come with their own programming languages that are different from Python. When you use SymPy, your investment in mastering Python pays off.

Getting Started

Before being able to use a package such as SymPy, it must be installed on your system. Your instructor may have given you specific installation instructions. If not, we recommend that you follow the instructions at http://horstmann.com/python4everyone/install.html.

The activities in this section work best when you run them in interactive mode (see Programming Tip 1.1). And if you use the IPython console, you can get a very attractive display of your results. If you follow our installation instructions, you can use the IPython console inside the Spyder IDE.

The functionality of a third-party code package such as SymPy is organized in one or more *modules*. You need to *import* the modules that you need, as described in Special Topic 2.1. Here, we import the entire contents of the sympy module:

```
from sympy import *
```

Now we have access to the functions in that module.

Working with Expressions

One useful function is sympify, which turns an expression contained in a string into SymPy form. For example,

```
f = sympify("x ** 2 * sin(x)")
```

When you print f, you will see

```
x**2*sin(x)
```

What you get is a symbolic expression, not Python code. The letters x that you see in the display are not Python variables but *symbols*, a special data type that is manipulated by SymPy. You can see that by displaying sympify(x * x ** 2). The result is

```
x ** 3
```

SymPy knows that $x^2 \cdot x = x^3$.

Alternatively, you can first define the symbolic expression x and store it in a variable. It is convenient to name that variable x as well.

Then use operators and functions to build up a SymPy expression:

```
x = sympify("x")
f = x ** 2 * sin(x)
```

The sympy module contains definitions of the mathematical operators and functions for symbolic expressions, so you can combine symbols in the same way as you would Python expressions.

If you use the IPython notebook, you can display results in mathematical notation with the command

```
init_printing()
```

See Figure 11. We will use mathematical notation for the remainder of this section. If you don't have the IPython notebook, everything will work, but you will see the formulas in the plain computer notation.

As you have seen, working with symbols is useful for simplifying algebraic expressions. Here are a few more examples:

```
expand((x - 1) * (x + 1)) # Yields x² − 1
expand((x - 1) ** 5) # Yields x⁵ − 5x⁴ + 10x³ − 10x² + 5x −1
```

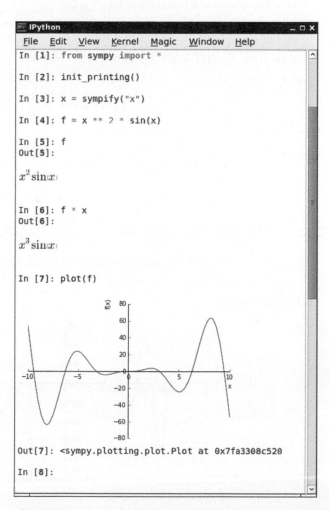

Figure 11   An IPython Notebook with SymPy Computations

Solving Equations

SymPy can solve quadratic equations and many others. When you pass an expression to the solve method, you get a list of values where the expression equals zero.

```
solve(x**2 + 2 * x - 8) # Yields [-4, 2]
solve(sin(x) - cos(x)) # Yields [-3π/4, π/4]
```

You still need to know something about mathematics to interpret the results that you get. There are infinitely many solutions to the second equation, because you can add π to any solution and get another. SymPy gives you two solutions from which you can derive the others.

SymPy can compute the derivative:

```
diff(f) # Yields x² cos(x) + 2x sin(x)
```

Computing integrals is just as easy:

```
g = integrate(f) # -x² cos(x) + 2x sin(x) + 2 cos(x)
```

In a typical calculus problem, you often obtain the derivative or integral of a function, and then compute the resulting expression for a given value of x. Substitute a value for the variable with the subs method, then turn the expression into a floating-point value with the evalf method:

```
result = g.subs(x, 0).evalf() # result is 2.0
```

Finally, you may want to plot a function. Calling plot gives you a plot with x ranging from −10 to 10. For example,

```
plot(-x**2 * cos(x) + 2 * x * sin(x) + 2 * cos(x))
```

yields

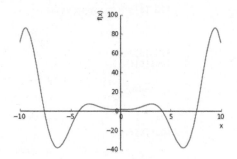

You can provide a different range for x, from −20 to 20, like this:

```
plot(-x**2 * cos(x) + 2 * x * sin(x) + 2 * cos(x), (x, -20, 20))
```

Here is the result:

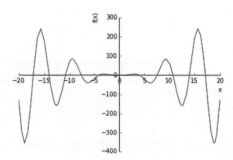

If you use the IPython notebook, you can integrate plots into the notebook. If plots are shown in a separate window, use the directive

```
%matplotlib inline
```

As you have seen, SymPy can make quick work of your calculus assignment. It is also a great reason for learning about Python libraries. The creators of SymPy have packaged a great amount of expertise—namely, how to manipulate mathematical symbols—into a form that you can use easily. Other Python packages that we will introduce throughout the book provide expertise from other domains that you can call upon in your programs.

CHAPTER SUMMARY

Declare variables with appropriate names and types.

- A variable is a storage location with a name.
- An assignment statement stores a value in a variable.
- A variable is created the first time it is assigned a value.
- Assigning a value to an existing variable replaces the previously stored value.
- The assignment operator = does *not* denote mathematical equality.
- The data type of a value specifies how the value is stored in the computer and what operations can be performed on the value.
- Integers are whole numbers without a fractional part.
- Floating-point numbers contain a fractional part.
- Once a variable is initialized with a value of a particular type, it should always store values of that same type.
- By convention, variable names should start with a lowercase letter.
- Use constants for values that should remain unchanged throughout your program.

- Use comments to add explanations for humans who read your code. The interpreter ignores comments.

Write arithmetic expressions in Python.

- Mixing integers and floating-point values in an arithmetic expression yields a floating-point value.
- The // operator computes floor division, in which the remainder is discarded.
- The % operator computes the remainder of a floor division.
- A function can return a value that can be used as if it were a literal value.
- Python has a standard library that provides functions and data types for your code.
- A library module must be imported into your program before it can be used.

Carry out hand calculations when developing an algorithm.

- Pick concrete values for a typical situation to use in a hand calculation.

Write programs that process strings.

- Strings are sequences of characters.
- A string literal denotes a particular string.
- The len function returns the number of characters in a string.
- Use the + operator to *concatenate* strings; that is, to put them together to yield a longer string.
- A string can be repeated using the * operator.
- The str function converts an integer or floating-point value to a string.

- The int and float functions convert a string containing a number to the numerical value.
- String positions are counted starting with 0.

Write programs that read user input and print formatted output.

- Use the input function to read keyboard input.
- To read an integer or floating-point value, use the input function followed by the int or float function.
- Use the string format operator to specify how values should be formatted.

Make simple graphical drawings.

- A graphics window is used for creating graphical drawings.
- Geometric shapes and text are drawn on a canvas that is contained in a graphics window.
- The canvas has methods for drawing lines, rectangles, and other shapes.
- The canvas stores the current drawing parameters used to draw shapes and text.
- Colors can be specified by name or by their red, green, and blue components.

REVIEW EXERCISES

■ **R2.1** What is the value of mystery after this sequence of statements?

```
mystery = 1
mystery = 1 - 2 * mystery
mystery = mystery + 1
```

■ **R2.2** What is the value of mystery after this sequence of statements?

```
mystery = 1
mystery = mystery + 1
mystery = 1 - 2 * mystery
```

■■ **R2.3** Write the following mathematical expressions in Python.

$$s = s_0 + v_0 t + \frac{1}{2} g t^2 \qquad\qquad FV = PV \cdot \left(1 + \frac{INT}{100}\right)^{YRS}$$

$$G = 4\pi^2 \frac{a^3}{p^2(m_1 + m_2)} \qquad\qquad c = \sqrt{a^2 + b^2 - 2ab \cos \gamma}$$

■■ **R2.4** Write the following Python expressions in mathematical notation.

a. `dm = m * (sqrt(1 + v / c) / sqrt(1 - v / c) - 1)`

b. `volume = pi * r * r * h`

c. `volume = 4 * pi * r ** 3 / 3`

d. `z = sqrt(x * x + y * y)`

■■ **R2.5** What are the values of the following expressions? In each line, assume that

```
x = 2.5
y = -1.5
m = 18
n = 4
```

a. `x + n * y - (x + n) * y`

b. `m // n + m % n`

c. `5 * x - n / 5`

d. `1 - (1 - (1 - (1 - (1 - n))))`

e. `sqrt(sqrt(n))`

■ **R2.6** What are the values of the following expressions, assuming that n is 17 and m is 18?

a. `n // 10 + n % 10`

b. `n % 2 + m % 2`

c. `(m + n) // 2`

d. `(m + n) / 2.0`

e. `int(0.5 * (m + n))`

f. `int(round(0.5 * (m + n)))`

■■ R2.7 What are the values of the following expressions? In each line, assume that

```
s = "Hello"
t = "World"
```

a. len(s) + len(t)

b. s[1] + s[2]

c. s[len(s) // 2]

d. s + t

e. t + s

f. s * 2

■ R2.8 Find at least three *compile-time* errors in the following program.

```
int x = 2
print(x, squared is, x * x)
xcubed = x *** 3
```

■■ R2.9 Find two *run-time* errors in the following program.

```
from math import sqrt
x = 2
y = 4
print("The product of ", x, "and", y, "is", x + y)
print("The root of their difference is ", sqrt(x - y))
```

■ R2.10 Consider the following code segment.

```
purchase = 19.93
payment = 20.00
change = payment - purchase
print(change)
```

The code segment prints the change as 0.07000000000000028. Explain why. Give a recommendation to improve the code so that users will not be confused.

■ R2.11 Explain the differences between 2, 2.0, '2', "2", and "2.0".

■ R2.12 Explain what each of the following program segments computes.

a. x = 2
   y = x + x

b. s = "2"
   t = s + s

■■ R2.13 Write pseudocode for a program that reads a word and then prints the first character, the last character, and the character in the middle. For example, if the input is Harry, the program prints H y r. If the word has even length, print the character right before the middle.

■■ R2.14 Write pseudocode for a program that prompts the user to enter a name (such as Harold James Morgan) and then prints a monogram consisting of the initial letters of the first, middle, and last name (such as HJM).

■■■ R2.15 Write pseudocode for a program that computes the first and last digit of a number. For example, if the input is 23456, the program should print 2 and 6. Use % and log(x, 10).

■ R2.16 Modify the pseudocode for the program in How To 2.1 so that the program gives change in quarters, dimes, and nickels. You can assume that the price is a multiple of 5 cents. To develop your pseudocode, first work with a couple of specific values.

•• **R2.17** A cocktail shaker is composed of three cone sections.

The volume of a cone section with height h and top and bottom radius r_1 and r_2 is

$$V = \pi \frac{\left(r_1^2 + r_1 r_2 + r_2^2\right)h}{3}$$

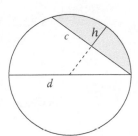

© Media Bakery.

Compute the total volume by hand for one set of realistic values for the radii and heights. Then develop an algorithm that works for arbitrary dimensions.

••• **R2.18** You are cutting off a piece of pie like this, where c is the length of the straight part (called the chord length) and h is the height of the piece.

There is an approximate formula for the area:

$$A \approx \frac{2}{3}ch + \frac{h^3}{2c}$$

However, h is not so easy to measure, whereas the diameter d of a pie is usually well-known. Calculate the area where the diameter of the pie is 12 inches and the chord length of the segment is 10 inches. Generalize to an algorithm that yields the area for any diameter and chord length.

•• **R2.19** The following pseudocode describes how to obtain the name of a day, given the day number (0 = Sunday, 1 = Monday, and so on.)

> *Define a string called names containing "SunMonTueWedThuFriSat".*
> *Compute the starting position as 3 x the day number.*
> *Get the characters at position, position + 1, position + 2.*
> *Concatenate them.*

Check this pseudocode, using the day number 4. Draw a diagram of the string that is being computed, similar to Figure 4.

•• **R2.20** The following pseudocode describes how to swap two letters in a word.

> *We are given a string myString and two letters l_1 and l_2.*
> *Change all occurrences of l_1 to the asterisk character. **
> *Change all occurrences of l_2 to l_1.*
> *Change all occurrences of * to l_2.*

Check this pseudocode, using the string `"marmalade"` and the letters a and e.

•• **R2.21** How do you get the first character of a string? The last character? The middle character (if the length is odd?) The middle two characters (if the length is even?)

• **R2.22** This chapter contains a number of recommendations regarding variables and constants that make programs easier to read and maintain. Briefly summarize these recommendations.

• **R2.23** Give instructions for drawing an outlined oval within its bounding box. Use green lines for the bounding box.

• **Toolbox R2.24** How do you compute the derivative and integral of $f(x) = x^2$ in SymPy?

• **Toolbox R2.25** What is `diff(integrate(f))` in SymPy?

- **Toolbox R2.26** How would you write a Python program that uses SymPy to display the solution for an arbitrary quadratic equation, $ax^2 + bx + c = 0$?
- **Toolbox R2.27** How would you use SymPy to plot the curve $y = \sin(1 / x)$, where x ranges from -0.5 to 0.5?
- **Toolbox R2.28** When you plot `sin(x) / x`, what do you guess the limit is as x approaches zero?

PROGRAMMING EXERCISES

- **P2.1** Write a program that displays the dimensions of a letter-size (8.5 × 11 inch) sheet of paper in millimeters. There are 25.4 millimeters per inch. Use constants and comments in your program.

- **P2.2** Write a program that computes and displays the perimeter of a letter-size (8.5 × 11 inch) sheet of paper and the length of its diagonal.

- **P2.3** Write a program that reads a number and displays the square, cube, and fourth power. Use the ** operator only for the fourth power.

- **P2.4** Write a program that prompts the user for two integers and then prints
  - The sum
  - The difference
  - The product
  - The average
  - The distance (absolute value of the difference)
  - The maximum (the larger of the two)
  - The minimum (the smaller of the two)

  Hint: Python defines max and min functions that accept a sequence of values, each separated with a comma.

- **P2.5** Enhance the output of Exercise •• P2.4 so that the numbers are properly aligned:
  ```
  Sum:             45
  Difference:      -5
  Product:         500
  Average:         22.50
  Distance:         5
  Maximum:          25
  Minimum:          20
  ```

- **P2.6** Write a program that prompts the user for a measurement in meters and then converts it to miles, feet, and inches.

- **P2.7** Write a program that prompts the user for a radius and then prints
  - The area and circumference of a circle with that radius
  - The volume and surface area of a sphere with that radius

- **P2.8** Write a program that asks the user for the lengths of the sides of a rectangle. Then print
  - The area and perimeter of the rectangle
  - The length of the diagonal

■ **P2.9** Improve the program discussed in How To 2.1 to allow input of quarters in addition to bills.

■■■ **P2.10** Write a program that helps a person decide whether to buy a hybrid car. Your program's inputs should be:

- The cost of a new car
- The estimated miles driven per year
- The estimated gas price
- The efficiency in miles per gallon
- The estimated resale value after five years

© asiseeit/iStockphoto.

Compute the total cost of owning the car for five years. (For simplicity, we will not take the cost of financing into account.) Obtain realistic prices for a new and used hybrid and a comparable car from the Web. Run your program twice, using today's gas price and 15,000 miles per year. Include pseudocode and the program runs with your assignment.

■■ **P2.11** Write a program that asks the user to input

- The number of gallons of gas in the tank
- The fuel efficiency in miles per gallon
- The price of gas per gallon

Then print the cost per 100 miles and how far the car can go with the gas in the tank.

■ **P2.12** *File names and extensions.* Write a program that prompts the user for the drive letter (C), the path (\Windows\System), the file name (Readme), and the extension (txt). Then print the complete file name C:\Windows\System\Readme.txt. (If you use UNIX or a Macintosh, skip the drive name and use / instead of \ to separate directories.)

■■■ **P2.13** Write a program that reads a number between 10,000 and 99,999 from the user, where the user enters a comma in the input. Then print the number without a comma. Here is a sample dialog; the user input is in color:

```
Please enter an integer between 10,000 and 99,999: 23,456
23456
```

Hint: Read the input as a string. Turn the strings consisting of the first two characters and the last three characters into numbers, and combine them.

■■ **P2.14** Write a program that reads a number between 1,000 and 999,999 from the user and prints it with a comma separating the thousands.

Here is a sample dialog; the user input is in color:

```
Please enter an integer between 1000 and 999999: 23456
23,456
```

■ **P2.15** *Printing a grid.* Write a program that prints the following grid to play tic-tac-toe.

```
+--+--+--+
|  |  |  |
+--+--+--+
|  |  |  |
+--+--+--+
|  |  |  |
+--+--+--+
```

Of course, you could simply write seven statements of the form

```
print("+--+--+--+")
```

You should do it the smart way, though. Declare string variables to hold two kinds of patterns: a comb-shaped pattern and the bottom line. Print the comb three times and the bottom line once.

■■ **P2.16**   Write a program that reads a five-digit positive integer and breaks it into a sequence of individual digits. For example, the input 16384 is displayed as

```
1 6 3 8 4
```

■■ **P2.17**   Write a program that reads two times in military format (0900, 1730) and prints the number of hours and minutes between the two times. Here is a sample run. User input is in color.

```
Please enter the first time: 0900
Please enter the second time: 1730
8 hours 30 minutes
```

Extra credit if you can deal with the case where the first time is later than the second:

```
Please enter the first time: 1730
Please enter the second time: 0900
15 hours 30 minutes
```

■■■ **P2.18**   *Writing large letters.* A large letter H can be produced like this:

```
*   *
*   *
*****
*   *
*   *
```

It can be declared as a string literal like this:

```
LETTER_H = "*   *\n*   *\n*****\n*   *\n*   *\n"
```

(The \n escape sequence denotes a "newline" character that causes subsequent characters to be printed on a new line.) Do the same for the letters E, L, and O. Then write the message

```
H
E
L
L
O
```

in large letters.

■■ **P2.19**   Write a program that transforms numbers 1, 2, 3, ..., 12 into the corresponding month names January, February, March, ..., December. *Hint:* Make a very long string "January February March ...", in which you add spaces such that each month name has *the same length*. Then concatenate the characters of the month that you want. If you are bothered by the trailing spaces, use the strip method to remove them (see Appendix C).

© José Luis Gutiérrez/iStockphoto.

■■ **P2.20** Write a program that prints a Christmas tree:

Remember to use escape sequences.

■■ **P2.21** Easter Sunday is the first Sunday after the first full moon of spring. To compute the date, you can use this algorithm, invented by the mathematician Carl Friedrich Gauss in 1800:

   1. Let y be the year (such as 1800 or 2001).
   2. Divide y by 19 and call the remainder a. Ignore the quotient.
   3. Divide y by 100 to get a quotient b and a remainder c.
   4. Divide b by 4 to get a quotient d and a remainder e.
   5. Divide 8 * b + 13 by 25 to get a quotient g. Ignore the remainder.
   6. Divide 19 * a + b - d - g + 15 by 30 to get a remainder h. Ignore the quotient.
   7. Divide c by 4 to get a quotient j and a remainder k.
   8. Divide a + 11 * h by 319 to get a quotient m. Ignore the remainder.
   9. Divide 2 * e + 2 * j - k - h + m + 32 by 7 to get a remainder r. Ignore the quotient.
   10. Divide h - m + r + 90 by 25 to get a quotient n. Ignore the remainder.
   11. Divide h - m + r + n + 19 by 32 to get a remainder p. Ignore the quotient.

Then Easter falls on day p of month n. For example, if y is 2001:

```
a = 6          g = 6        m = 0    n = 4
b = 20, c = 1  h = 18       r = 6    p = 15
d = 5, e = 0   j = 0, k = 1
```

Therefore, in 2001, Easter Sunday fell on April 15. Write a program that prompts the user for a year and prints out the month and day of Easter Sunday.

■■ **P2.22** Write a program that initializes a string variable and prints the first three characters, followed by three periods, and then the last three characters. For example, if the string is initialized to "Mississippi", then print Mis...ppi.

■■ **Graphics P2.23** Write a graphics program that draws your name in red, contained inside a blue rectangle.

■■ **Graphics P2.24** Write a graphics program that draws two solid squares: one in pink and one in purple. Use a standard color for one of them and a custom color for the other.

■■ **Graphics P2.25** Write a program to plot the following face.

▪▪ Graphics P2.26 Draw a "bull's eye"—a set of concentric rings in alternating black and white colors.

▪▪ Graphics P2.27 Write a program that draws a picture of a house. It could be as simple as the accompanying figure, or if you like, make it more elaborate (3-D, skyscraper, marble columns in the entryway, whatever). Use at least three different colors.

▪▪ Graphics P2.28 Draw the coordinate system figure shown in Section 2.6.2.

▪▪ Graphics P2.29 Modify the italianflag.py program in How To 2.2 to draw a flag with three horizontal colored stripes, such as the German flag.

▪▪ Graphics P2.30 Write a program that displays the Olympic rings. Color the rings in the Olympic colors.

▪▪ Graphics P2.31 Make a bar chart to plot the following data set. Label each bar.

Bridge Name	Longest Span (ft)
Golden Gate	4,200
Brooklyn	1,595
Delaware Memorial	2,150
Mackinac	3,800

▪▪ Business P2.32 The following pseudocode describes how a bookstore computes the price of an order from the total price and the number of the books that were ordered.

Read the total book price and the number of books.
Compute the tax (7.5 percent of the total book price).
Compute the shipping charge ($2 per book).
The price of the order is the sum of the total book price, the tax, and the shipping charge.
Print the price of the order.

Translate this pseudocode into a Python program.

■■ Business P2.33 The following pseudocode describes how to turn a string containing a ten-digit phone number (such as "4155551212") into a more readable string with parentheses and dashes, like this: "(415) 555-1212".

> *Take the string consisting of the first three characters and surround it with "(" and ")". This is the area code.*
>
> *Concatenate the area code, the string consisting of the next three characters, a hyphen, and the string consisting of the last four characters. This is the formatted number.*

Translate this pseudocode into a Python program that reads a telephone number into a string variable, computes the formatted number, and prints it.

■■ Business P2.34 The following pseudocode describes how to extract the dollars and cents from a price given as a floating-point value. For example, a price of 2.95 yields values 2 and 95 for the dollars and cents.

> *Convert the price to an integer and store it in a variable dollars.*
> *Multiply the difference price – dollars by 100 and add 0.5.*
> *Convert the result to an integer variable and store it in a variable cents.*

Translate this pseudocode into a Python program. Read a price and print the dollars and cents. Test your program with inputs 2.95 and 4.35.

■■ Business P2.35 *Giving change.* Implement a program that directs a cashier how to give change. The program has two inputs: the amount due and the amount received from the customer. Display the dollars, quarters, dimes, nickels, and pennies that the customer should receive in return. In order to avoid roundoff errors, the program user should supply both amounts in pennies, for example 274 instead of 2.74.

© Captainflash/iStockphoto.

■ Business P2.36 An online bank wants you to create a program that shows prospective customers how their deposits will grow. Your program should read the initial balance and the annual interest rate. Interest is compounded monthly. Print out the balances after the first three months. Here is a sample run:

```
Initial balance: 1000
Annual interest rate in percent: 6.0
After first month:     1005.00
After second month:    1010.03
After third month:     1015.08
```

■ Business P2.37 A video club wants to reward its best members with a discount based on the member's number of movie rentals and the number of new members referred by the member. The discount is in percent and is equal to the sum of the rentals and the referrals, but it cannot exceed 75 percent. Write a program to calculate the value of the discount.

Here is a sample run:

```
Enter the number of movie rentals: 56
Enter the number of members referred to the video club: 3
The discount is equal to:     59.00 percent.
```

• Science P2.38   Consider the following circuit.

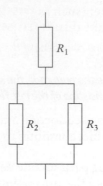

Write a program that reads the resistances of the three resistors and computes the total resistance, using Ohm's law.

•• Science P2.39   The dew point temperature T_d can be calculated (approximately) from the relative humidity RH and the actual temperature T by

$$T_d = \frac{b \cdot f(T, RH)}{a - f(T, RH)}$$

$$f(T, RH) = \frac{a \cdot T}{b + T} + \ln(RH)$$

where $a = 17.27$ and $b = 237.7°$ C.

Write a program that reads the relative humidity (between 0 and 1) and the temperature (in degrees C) and prints the dew point value. Use the Python function log to compute the natural logarithm.

••• Science P2.40   The pipe clip temperature sensors shown here are robust sensors that can be clipped directly onto copper pipes to measure the temperature of the liquids in the pipes.

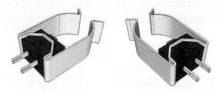

Each sensor contains a device called a *thermistor*. Thermistors are semiconductor devices that exhibit a temperature-dependent resistance described by:

$$R = R_0 \, e^{\beta \left(\frac{1}{T} - \frac{1}{T_0} \right)}$$

where R is the resistance (in Ω) at the temperature T (in °K), and R_0 is the resistance (in Ω) at the temperature T_0 (in °K). β is a constant that depends on the material used to make the thermistor. Thermistors are specified by providing values for R_0, T_0, and β.

The thermistors used to make the pipe clip temperature sensors have $R_0 = 1075$ Ω at $T_0 = 85$ °C, and $\beta = 3969$ °K. (Notice that β has units of °K. Recall that the temperature in °K is obtained by adding 273.15 to the temperature in °C.) The liquid temperature, in °C, is determined from the resistance R, in Ω, using

$$T = \frac{\beta T_0}{T_0 \ln\left(\dfrac{R}{R_0}\right) + \beta} - 273$$

Write a Python program that prompts the user for the thermistor resistance R and prints a message giving the liquid temperature in °C.

■■■ **Science P2.41** The circuit shown below illustrates some important aspects of the connection between a power company and one of its customers. The customer is represented by three parameters, V_t, P, and pf. V_t is the voltage accessed by plugging into a wall outlet. Customers depend on having a dependable value of V_t in order for their appliances to work properly. Accordingly, the power company regulates the value of V_t carefully. P describes the amount of power used by the customer and is the primary factor in determining the customer's

© TebNad/iStockphoto.

electric bill. The power factor, pf, is less familiar. (The power factor is calculated as the cosine of an angle so that its value will always be between zero and one.) In this problem you will be asked to write a Python program to investigate the significance of the power factor.

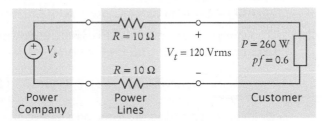

In the figure, the power lines are represented, somewhat simplistically, as resistances in Ohms. The power company is represented as an AC voltage source. The source voltage, V_s, required to provide the customer with power P at voltage V_t can be determined using the formula

$$V_s = \sqrt{\left(V_t + \frac{2RP}{V_t}\right)^2 + \left(\frac{2RP}{pf V_t}\right)^2 \left(1 - pf^2\right)}$$

(V_s has units of Vrms.) This formula indicates that the value of V_s depends on the value of pf. Write a Python program that prompts the user for a power factor value and then prints a message giving the corresponding value of V_s, using the values for P, R, and V_t shown in the figure above.

••• Science P2.42 Consider the following tuning circuit connected to an antenna, where C is a variable capacitor whose capacitance ranges from C_{min} to C_{max}.

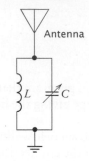

The tuning circuit selects the frequency $f = \dfrac{1}{2\pi\sqrt{LC}}$. To design this circuit for a given frequency, take $C = \sqrt{C_{min}C_{max}}$ and calculate the required inductance L from f and C. Now the circuit can be tuned to any frequency in the range

$$f_{min} = \frac{1}{2\pi\sqrt{LC_{max}}} \text{ to } f_{max} = \frac{1}{2\pi\sqrt{LC_{min}}}.$$

Write a Python program to design a tuning circuit for a given frequency, using a variable capacitor with given values for C_{min} and C_{max}. (A typical input is $f = 16.7$ MHz, $C_{min} = 14$ pF, and $C_{max} = 365$ pF.) The program should read in f (in Hz), C_{min} and C_{max} (in F), and print the required inductance value and the range of frequencies to which the circuit can be tuned by varying the capacitance.

• Science P2.43 According to the Coulomb force law, the electric force between two charged particles of charge Q_1 and Q_2 Coulombs, that are a distance r meters apart, is

$$F = \frac{Q_1 Q_2}{4\pi\varepsilon r^2} \text{ Newtons, where } \varepsilon = 8.854 \times 10^{-12} \text{ Farads/meter. Write a program that}$$

calculates and displays the force on a pair of charged particles, based on the user input of Q_1 Coulombs, Q_2 Coulombs, and r meters.

DECISIONS

© zennie/iStockphoto.

CHAPTER CONTENTS

One of the essential features of computer programs is their ability to make decisions. Like a train that changes tracks depending on how the switches are set, a program can take different actions depending on inputs and other circumstances.

In this chapter, you will learn how to program simple and complex decisions. You will apply what you learn to the task of checking user input.

3.1 The if Statement

The if statement allows a program to carry out different actions depending on the nature of the data to be processed.

The if statement is used to implement a decision (see Syntax 3.1). When a condition is fulfilled, one set of statements is executed. Otherwise, another set of statements is executed.

Here is an example using the if statement: In many countries, the number 13 is considered unlucky. Rather than offending superstitious tenants, building owners sometimes skip the thirteenth floor; floor 12 is immediately followed by floor 14. Of course, floor 13 is not usually left empty or, as some conspiracy theorists believe, filled with secret offices and research labs. It is simply called floor 14. The computer that controls the building elevators needs to compensate for this foible and adjust all floor numbers above 13.

Let's simulate this process in Python. We will ask the user to type in the desired floor number and then compute the actual floor. When the input is above 13, then we need to decrement the input to obtain the actual floor.

© DrGrounds/iStockphoto.

This elevator panel "skips" the thirteenth floor. The floor is not actually missing—the computer that controls the elevator adjusts the floor numbers above 13.

An if statement is like a fork in the road. Depending upon a decision, different parts of the program are executed.

© Media Bakery.

Figure 1
Flowchart for if Statement

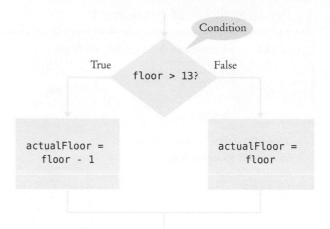

For example, if the user provides an input of 20, the program determines the actual floor as 19. Otherwise, we simply use the supplied floor number.

```
actualFloor = 0

if floor > 13 :
    actualFloor = floor - 1
else :
    actualFloor = floor
```

The flowchart in Figure 1 shows the branching behavior.

In our example, each branch of the if statement contains a single statement. You can include as many statements in each branch as you like. Sometimes, it happens that there is nothing to do in the else branch of the statement. In that case, you can omit it entirely, such as in this example:

```
actualFloor = floor

if floor > 13 :
    actualFloor = actualFloor − 1
```

See Figure 2 for the flowchart.

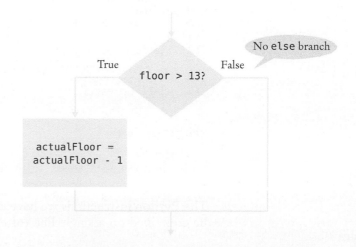

Figure 2
Flowchart for if Statement
with No else Branch

Syntax 3.1 if Statement

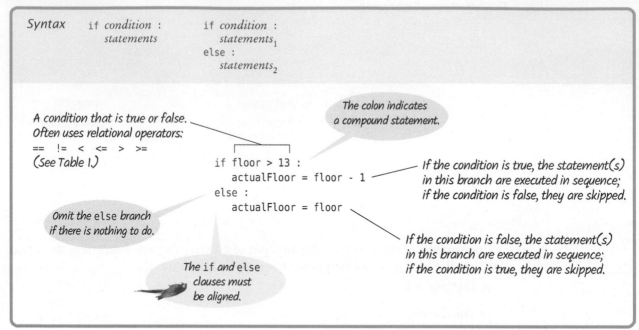

The following program puts the if statement to work. This program asks for the desired floor and then prints out the actual floor.

sec01/elevatorsim.py

```
1  ##
2  #   This program simulates an elevator panel that skips the 13th floor.
3  #
4
5  # Obtain the floor number from the user as an integer.
6  floor = int(input("Floor: "))
7
8  # Adjust floor if necessary.
9  if floor > 13 :
10    actualFloor = floor - 1
11 else :
12    actualFloor = floor
13
14 # Print the result.
15 print("The elevator will travel to the actual floor", actualFloor)
```

Program Run

```
Floor: 20
The elevator will travel to the actual floor 19
```

The Python instructions we have used so far have been simple statements that must be contained on a single line (or explicitly continued to the next line—see Special

Topic 2.3). Some constructs in Python are **compound statements,** which span multiple lines and consist of a *header* and a **statement block**. The if statement is an example of a compound statement.

> **Compound statements consist of a header and a statement block.**

```
if totalSales > 100.0 :    # The header ends in a colon.
    discount = totalSales * 0.05    # Lines in the block are indented to the same level
    totalSales = totalSales - discount
    print("You received a discount of", discount)
```

Compound statements require a colon (:) at the end of the header. The statement block is a group of one or more statements, all of which are indented to the same indentation level. A statement block begins on the line following the header and ends at the first statement indented less than the first statement in the block. You can use any number of spaces to indent statements within a block, but all statements within the block must have the same indentation level. Note that comments are not statements and thus can be indented to any level.

> **Statements in a statement block must be indented to the same level.**

Statement blocks, which can be nested inside other blocks, signal that one or more statements are part of the given compound statement. In the case of the if construct, the statement block specifies the instructions that will be executed if the condition is true or skipped if the condition is false.

Common Error 3.1

Tabs

Block-structured code has the property that nested statements are indented by one or more levels:

```
if totalSales > 100.0 :
↑   discount = totalSales * 0.05
|   totalSales = totalSales − discount
|   print("You received a discount of $%.2f" % discount)
else :
↑   diff = 100.0 − totalSales
|   if diff < 10.0 :
|   ↑   print("If you were to purchase our item of the day you can receive a 5% discount.")
|   else :
|   ↑   print("You need to spend $%.2f more to receive a 5% discount." % diff)
|   |   ↑
|   |   |
0   1   2   Indentation level
```

Python requires block-structured code as part of its syntax. The alignment of statements within a Python program specifies which statements are part of a given statement block.

How do you move the cursor from the leftmost column to the appropriate indentation level? A perfectly reasonable strategy is to hit the space bar a sufficient number of times. With most editors, you can use the Tab key instead. A tab moves the cursor to the next indentation level. Some editors even have an option to fill in the tabs automatically.

While the Tab *key* is nice, some editors use *tab characters* for alignment, which is not so nice. Python is very picky as to how you align the statements within a statement block. All of the statements must be aligned with either blank spaces or tab characters, but not a mixture of the two. In addition, tab characters can lead to problems when you send your file to another person or a printer. There is no universal agreement on the width of a tab character, and some software will ignore tab characters altogether. It is therefore best to save your files with spaces instead of tabs. Most editors have a setting to automatically convert all tabs to spaces.

Look at the documentation of your development environment to find out how to activate this useful setting.

Programming Tip 3.1

Avoid Duplication in Branches

Look to see whether you *duplicate code* in each branch. If so, move it out of the if statement. Here is an example of such duplication:

```python
if floor > 13 :
    actualFloor = floor - 1
    print("Actual floor:", actualFloor)
else :
    actualFloor = floor
    print("Actual floor:", actualFloor)
```

The output statement is exactly the same in both branches. This is not an error—the program will run correctly. However, you can simplify the program by moving the duplicated statement, like this:

```python
if floor > 13 :
    actualFloor = floor - 1
else :
    actualFloor = floor
print("Actual floor:", actualFloor)
```

Removing duplication is particularly important when programs are maintained for a long time. When there are two sets of statements with the same effect, it can easily happen that a programmer modifies one set but not the other.

Special Topic 3.1

Conditional Expressions

Python has a conditional operator of the form

> *value₁* if *condition* else *value₂*

The value of that expression is either *value₁* if the condition is true or *value₂* if it is false. For example, we can compute the actual floor number as

```python
actualFloor = floor - 1 if floor > 13 else floor
```

which is equivalent to

```python
if floor > 13 :
    actualFloor = floor - 1
else :
    actualFloor = floor
```

Note that a conditional expression is a single statement that must be contained on a single line or continued to the next line (see Special Topic 2.3). Also note that a colon is not needed because a conditional expression is not a compound statement.

You can use a conditional expression anywhere that a value is expected, for example:

```python
print("Actual floor:", floor - 1 if floor > 13 else floor)
```

We don't use the conditional expression in this book, but it is a convenient construct that you will find in some Python programs.

3.2 Relational Operators

In this section, you will learn how to compare numbers and strings in Python.

Every if statement contains a condition. In many cases, the condition involves comparing two values. For example, in the previous examples we tested floor > 13. The comparison > is called a **relational operator**. Python has six relational operators (see Table 1).

As you can see, only two Python relational operators (> and <) look as you would expect from the mathematical notation. Computer keyboards do not have keys for ≥, ≤, or ≠, but the >=, <=, and != operators are easy to remember because they look similar. The == operator is initially confusing to most newcomers to Python.

© arturbo/iStockphoto.

In Python, you use a relational operator to check whether one value is greater than another.

Table 1 **Relational Operators**		
Python	Math Notation	Description
>	>	Greater than
>=	≥	Greater than or equal
<	<	Less than
<=	≤	Less than or equal
==	=	Equal
!=	≠	Not equal

In Python, = already has a meaning, namely assignment. The == operator denotes equality testing:

```
floor = 13    # Assign 13 to floor
if floor == 13 :   # Test whether floor equals 13
```

You must remember to use == inside tests and to use = outside tests.

Strings can also be compared using Python's relational operators. For example, to test whether two strings are equal, use the == operator

```
if name1 == name2 :
    print("The strings are identical.")
```

or to test if they are not equal, use the != operator

```
if name1 != name2 :
    print("The strings are not identical.")
```

For two strings to be equal, they must be of the same length and contain the same sequence of characters:

If even one character is different, the two strings will not be equal:

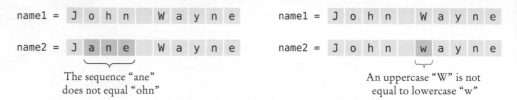

The relational operators in Table 1 have a lower precedence than the arithmetic operators. That means you can write arithmetic expressions on either side of the relational operator without using parentheses. For example, in the expression

```
floor - 1 < 13
```

both sides (floor - 1 and 13) of the < operator are evaluated, and the results are compared. Appendix A shows a table of the Python operators and their precedences.

Table 2 summarizes how to compare values in Python.

Table 2 Relational Operator Examples		
Expression	Value	Comment
3 <= 4	True	3 is less than 4; <= tests for "less than or equal".
⊘ 3 =< 4	**Error**	The "less than or equal" operator is <=, not =<. The "less than" symbol comes first.
3 > 4	False	> is the opposite of <=.
4 < 4	False	The left-hand side must be strictly smaller than the right-hand side.
4 <= 4	True	Both sides are equal; <= tests for "less than or equal".
3 == 5 - 2	True	== tests for equality.
3 != 5 - 1	True	!= tests for inequality. It is true that 3 is not 5 − 1.
⊘ 3 = 6 / 2	**Error**	Use == to test for equality.
1.0 / 3.0 == 0.333333333	False	Although the values are very close to one another, they are not exactly equal. See Common Error 3.2.
⊘ "10" > 5	**Error**	You cannot compare a string to a number.

The following program demonstrates comparisons using logical expressions.

sec02/compare.py

```python
1  ##
2  #    This program demonstrates comparisons of numbers and strings.
3  #
4
5  from math import sqrt
6
7  # Comparing integers
8  m = 2
9  n = 4
10
11 if m * m == n :
12    print("2 times 2 is four.")
13
14 # Comparing floating-point numbers
15 x = sqrt(2)
16 y = 2.0
17
18 if x * x == y :
19    print("sqrt(2) times sqrt(2) is 2")
20 else :
21    print("sqrt(2) times sqrt(2) is not two but %.18f" % (x * x))
22
23 EPSILON = 1E-14
24 if abs(x * x - y) < EPSILON :
25    print("sqrt(2) times sqrt(2) is approximately 2")
26
27 # Comparing strings
28 s = "120"
29 t = "20"
30
31 if s == t :
32    comparison = "is the same as"
33 else :
34    comparison = "is not the same as"
35
36 print("The string '%s' %s the string '%s'." % (s, comparison, t))
37
38 u = "1" + t
39 if s != u :
40    comparison = "not "
41 else :
42    comparison = ""
43
44 print("The strings '%s' and '%s' are %sidentical." % (s, u, comparison))
```

Program Run

```
2 times 2 is four.
sqrt(2) times sqrt(2) is not two but 2.000000000000000444
sqrt(2) times sqrt(2) is approximately 2
The string '120' is not the same as the string '20'.
The strings '120' and '120' are identical.
```

Common Error 3.2

Exact Comparison of Floating-Point Numbers

Floating-point numbers have only a limited precision, and calculations can introduce roundoff errors. You must take these inevitable roundoffs into account when comparing floating-point numbers. For example, the following code multiplies the square root of 2 by itself. Ideally, we expect to get the answer 2:

© caracterdesign/iStockphoto.

```
from math import sqrt

r = sqrt(2.0)
if r * r == 2.0 :
    print("sqrt(2.0) squared is 2.0")
else :
    print("sqrt(2.0) squared is not 2.0 but", r * r)
```

This program displays

Take limited precision into account when comparing floating-point numbers.

```
sqrt(2.0) squared is not 2.0 but 2.0000000000000004
```

It does not make sense in most circumstances to compare floating-point numbers exactly. Instead, we should test whether they are *close enough*. That is, the magnitude of their difference should be less than some threshold. Mathematically, we would write that x and y are close enough if

$$|x - y| < \varepsilon$$

for a very small number, ε. ε is the Greek letter epsilon, a letter used to denote a very small quantity. It is common to set ε to 10^{-14} when comparing floating-point numbers:

```
from math import sqrt

EPSILON = 1E-14
r = sqrt(2.0)
if abs(r * r - 2.0) < EPSILON :
    print("sqrt(2.0) squared is approximately 2.0")
```

Special Topic 3.2

Lexicographic Ordering of Strings

If two strings are not identical to each other, you still may want to know the relationship between them. Python's relational operators compare strings in "lexicographic" order. This ordering is very similar to the way in which words are sorted in a dictionary. If

```
string1 < string2
```

then the string `string1` comes before the string `string2` in the dictionary. For example, this is the case if `string1` is `"Harry"`, and `string2` is `"Hello"`. If

```
string1 > string2
```

then `string1` comes after `string2` in dictionary order.

As you have seen in the preceding section, if

```
string1 == string2
```

then `string1` and `string2` are equal.

Fuse/Getty Images.

To see which of two terms comes first in the dictionary, consider the first letter in which they differ.

There are a few technical differences between the ordering in a dictionary and the lexicographic ordering in Python.

In Python:

- All uppercase letters come before the lowercase letters. For example, "Z" comes before "a".
- The space character comes before all printable characters.
- Numbers come before letters.
- For the ordering of punctuation marks, see Appendix D.

The relational operators compare strings in lexicographic order.

When comparing two strings, you compare the first letters of each word, then the second letters, and so on, until one of the strings ends or you find the first letter pair that doesn't match.

If one of the strings ends, the longer string is considered the "larger" one. For example, compare "car" with "cart". The first three letters match, and we reach the end of the first string. Therefore "car" comes before "cart" in the lexicographic ordering.

When you reach a mismatch, the string containing the "larger" character is considered "larger". For example, let's compare "cat" with "cart". The first two letters match. Because t comes after r, the string "cat" comes after "cart" in the lexicographic ordering.

c	a	r

c	a	r	t

c	a	t

Letters match — r comes before t

Lexicographic Ordering

HOW TO 3.1

Implementing an if Statement

This How To walks you through the process of implementing an if statement.

Problem Statement The university bookstore has a Kilobyte Day sale every October 24, giving an 8 percent discount on all computer accessory purchases if the price is less than $128, and a 16 percent discount if the price is at least $128. Write a program that asks the cashier for the original price and then prints the discounted price.

Step 1 Decide upon the branching condition.

In our sample problem, the obvious choice for the condition is:

original price < 128?

That is just fine, and we will use that condition in our solution.

But you could equally well come up with a correct solution if you choose the opposite condition: Is the original price at least $128? You might choose this condition if you put yourself into the position of a shopper who wants to know when the bigger discount applies.

© MikePanic/iStockphoto.

Sales discounts are often higher for expensive products. Use the if statement to implement such a decision.

Step 2 Give pseudocode for the work that needs to be done when the condition is true.

In this step, you list the action or actions that are taken in the "positive" branch. The details depend on your problem. You may want to print a message, compute values, or even exit the program.

In our example, we need to apply an 8 percent discount:

discounted price = 0.92 x original price

Step 3   Give pseudocode for the work (if any) that needs to be done when the condition is *not* true.

What do you want to do in the case that the condition of Step 1 is not satisfied? Sometimes, you want to do nothing at all. In that case, use an if statement without an else branch.

In our example, the condition tested whether the price was less than $128. If that condition is *not* true, the price is at least $128, so the higher discount of 16 percent applies to the sale:

discounted price = 0.84 x original price

Step 4   Double-check relational operators.

First, be sure that the test goes in the right *direction*. It is a common error to confuse > and <. Next, consider whether you should use the < operator or its close cousin, the <= operator.

What should happen if the original price is exactly $128? Reading the problem carefully, we find that the lower discount applies if the original price is *less than* $128, and the higher discount applies when it is *at least* $128. A price of $128 should therefore *not* fulfill our condition, and we must use <, not <=.

Step 5   Remove duplication.

Check which actions are common to both branches, and move them outside.
In our example, we have two statements of the form

discounted price = ___ x original price

They only differ in the discount rate. It is best to just set the rate in the branches, and to do the computation afterwards:

If original price < 128
    discount rate = 0.92
Else
    discount rate = 0.84
discounted price = discount rate x original price

Step 6   Test both branches.

Formulate two test cases, one that fulfills the condition of the if statement, and one that does not. Ask yourself what should happen in each case. Then follow the pseudocode and act each of them out.

In our example, let us consider two scenarios for the original price: $100 and $200. We expect that the first price is discounted by $8, the second by $32.

When the original price is 100, then the condition 100 < 128 is true, and we get

discount rate = 0.92
discounted price = 0.92 x 100 = 92

When the original price is 200, then the condition 200 < 128 is false, and

discount rate = 0.84
discounted price = 0.84 x 200 = 168

In both cases, we get the expected answer.

Step 7   Assemble the if statement in Python.

Type the skeleton

```
if :
else :
```

and fill it in, as shown in Syntax 3.1. Omit the else branch if it is not needed.

In our example, the completed statement is

```
if originalPrice < 128 :
    discountRate = 0.92
else :
    discountRate = 0.84
discountedPrice = discountRate * originalPrice
```

how_to_1/sale.py

```
1  ##
2  #    Compute the discount for a given purchase.
3  #
4
5  # Obtain the original price.
6  originalPrice = float(input("Original price before discount: "))
7
8  # Determine the discount rate.
9  if originalPrice < 128 :
10     discountRate = 0.92
11 else :
12     discountRate = 0.84
13
14 # Compute and print the discount.
15 discountedPrice = discountRate * originalPrice
16 print("Discounted price: %.2f" % discountedPrice)
```

WORKED EXAMPLE 3.1

Extracting the Middle

Problem Statement Your task is to extract a string containing the middle character from a given string. For example, if the string is "crate", the result is the string "a". However, if the string has an even number of letters, extract the middle two characters. If the string is "crates", the result is "at".

Step 1 Decide on the branching condition.

We need to take different actions for strings of odd and even length. Therefore, the condition is

Is the length of the string odd?

In Python, you use the remainder of division by 2 to find out whether a value is even or odd. Then the test to determine whether the length of the string is odd becomes

```
if len(string) % 2 == 1
```

Step 2 Give pseudocode for the work that needs to be done when the condition is true.

We need to find the position of the middle character. If the length is 5, the position is 2.

```
 c   r   a   t   e
 0   1   2   3   4
```

In general,

position = len(string) / 2 (with the remainder discarded)
result = string[position]

Step 3   Give pseudocode for the work (if any) that needs to be done when the condition is *not* true.

Again, we need to find the position of the middle characters. If the length is 6, the starting position is 2, and the ending position is 3. That is, we would call

  result = string[2] + string[3]

In general,

  position = len(string) / 2 – 1 (with the remainder discarded)
  result = string[position] + string[position + 1]

Step 4   Double-check relational operators.

Do we really want `len(string) % 2 == 1`? For example, when the length is 5, 5 % 2 is the remainder of the division 5 / 2, which is 1. In general, dividing an odd number by 2 leaves a remainder of 1. Therefore, our condition is correct.

Step 5   Remove duplication.

Here is the statement that we have developed:

  If the length of string is odd
    position = len(string) / 2 (with remainder discarded)
    result = string[position]
  Else
    position = len(string) / 2 – 1 (with remainder discarded)
    result = string[position] + string[position + 1]

The first statement in each branch is almost identical. Could we make them the same? We can, if we adjust the position in the second branch:

  If the length of string is odd
    position = len(string) / 2 (with remainder discarded)
    result = string[position]
  Else
    position = len(string) / 2 (with remainder discarded)
    result = string[position – 1] + string[position]

Now we can move the duplicated computation outside the `if` statement:

  position = len(string) / 2 (with remainder discarded)
  If the length of string is odd
    result = string[position]
  Else
    result = string[position – 1] + string[position]

Step 6   Test both branches.

We will use a different set of strings for testing. For an odd-length string, consider `"monitor"`. We get

  position = len(string) / 2 = 7 / 2 = 3 (with remainder discarded)
  result = string[3] = "i"

For the even-length string `"monitors"`, we get

  position = len(string) / 2 = 4
  result = string[3] + string[4] = "it"

Step 7   Assemble the `if` statement in Python.

Here's the completed code segment.

```
position = len(string) // 2
if len(string) % 2 == 1 :
    result = string[position]
else :
    result = string[position - 1] + string[position]
```

EXAMPLE CODE   See worked_example_1/middle.py in your eText or companion code for the complete program.

3.3 Nested Branches

When a decision statement is contained inside the branch of another decision statement, the statements are *nested*.

It is often necessary to include an if statement inside another. Such an arrangement is called a *nested* set of statements.

Here is a typical example: In the United States, different tax rates are used depending on the taxpayer's marital status. There are different tax schedules for single and for married taxpayers. Married taxpayers add their income together and pay taxes on the total. Table 3 gives the tax rate computations, using a simplification of the schedules in effect for the 2008 tax year. A different tax rate applies to each "bracket". In this schedule, the income in the first bracket is taxed at 10 percent, and the income in the second bracket is taxed at 25 percent. The income limits for each bracket depend on the marital status.

Table 3 Federal Tax Rate Schedule		
If your status is Single and if the taxable income is	the tax is	of the amount over
at most $32,000	10%	$0
over $32,000	$3,200 + 25%	$32,000
If your status is Married and if the taxable income is	the tax is	of the amount over
at most $64,000	10%	$0
over $64,000	$6,400 + 25%	$64,000

Nested decisions are required for problems that have multiple levels of decision making.

Now compute the taxes due, given a marital status and an income figure. The key point is that there are two *levels* of decision making. First, you must branch on the marital status. Then, for each marital status, you must have another branch on income level.

Computing income taxes requires multiple levels of decisions.   © ericsphotography/iStockphoto.

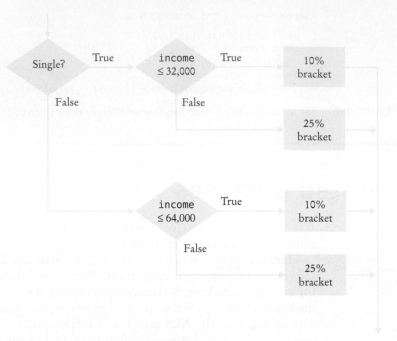

Figure 3   Income Tax Computation

The two-level decision process is reflected in two levels of if statements in the program below. (See Figure 3 for a flowchart.) In theory, nesting can go deeper than two levels. A three-level decision process (first by state, then by marital status, then by income level) requires three nesting levels.

sec03/taxes.py

```
1   ##
2   #  This program computes income taxes, using a simplified tax schedule.
3   #
4
5   # Initialize constant variables for the tax rates and rate limits.
6   RATE1 = 0.10
7   RATE2 = 0.25
8   RATE1_SINGLE_LIMIT = 32000.0
9   RATE1_MARRIED_LIMIT = 64000.0
10
11  # Read income and marital status.
12  income = float(input("Please enter your income: "))
13  maritalStatus = input("Please enter s for single, m for married: ")
14
15  # Compute taxes due.
16  tax1 = 0.0
17  tax2 = 0.0
18
19  if maritalStatus == "s" :
20      if income <= RATE1_SINGLE_LIMIT :
21          tax1 = RATE1 * income
22      else :
23          tax1 = RATE1 * RATE1_SINGLE_LIMIT
24          tax2 = RATE2 * (income - RATE1_SINGLE_LIMIT)
```

```
25  else :
26      if income <= RATE1_MARRIED_LIMIT :
27          tax1 = RATE1 * income
28      else :
29          tax1 = RATE1 * RATE1_MARRIED_LIMIT
30          tax2 = RATE2 * (income - RATE1_MARRIED_LIMIT)
31
32  totalTax = tax1 + tax2
33
34  # Print the results.
35  print("The tax is $%.2f" % totalTax)
```

Program Run

```
Please enter your income: 80000
Please enter s for single, m for married: m
The tax is $10400.00
```

Programming Tip 3.2

Hand-Tracing

A very useful technique for understanding whether a program works correctly is called *hand-tracing*. You simulate the program's activity on a sheet of paper. You can use this method with pseudocode or Python code.

Get an index card, a cocktail napkin, or whatever sheet of paper is within reach. Make a column for each variable. Have the program code ready. Use a marker, such as a paper clip, to mark the current statement. In your mind, execute statements one at a time. Every time the value of a variable changes, cross out the old value and write the new value below the old one.

Let's trace the taxes.py program on page 88 with the inputs from the program run that follows it. In lines 12 and 13, income and maritalStatus are initialized by input statements.

© thomasd007/iStockphoto.

Hand-tracing helps you understand whether a program works correctly.

```
5   # Initialize constant variables for the tax rates and rate limits.
6   RATE1 = 0.10
7   RATE2 = 0.25
8   RATE1_SINGLE_LIMIT = 32000.0
9   RATE1_MARRIED_LIMIT = 64000.0
10
11  # Read income and marital status.
12  income = float(input("Please enter your income: "))
13  maritalStatus = input("Please enter s for single, m for married: ")
```

tax1	tax2	income	marital status
		80000	m

In lines 16 and 17, tax1 and tax2 are initialized to 0.0.

```
16  tax1 = 0.0
17  tax2 = 0.0
```

tax1	tax2	income	marital status
0	0	80000	m

Because maritalStatus is not "s", we move to the else branch of the outer if statement (line 25).

```
19  if maritalStatus == "s" :
20      if income <= RATE1_SINGLE_LIMIT :
21          tax1 = RATE1 * income
22      else :
23          tax1 = RATE1 * RATE1_SINGLE_LIMIT
24          tax2 = RATE2 * (income - RATE1_SINGLE_LIMIT)
25  else :
```

Because income is not <= 64000, we move to the else branch of the inner if statement (line 28).

```
26    if income <= RATE1_MARRIED_LIMIT :
27        tax1 = RATE1 * income
28    else :
29        tax1 = RATE1 * RATE1_MARRIED_LIMIT
30        tax2 = RATE2 * (income - RATE1_MARRIED_LIMIT)
```

The values of tax1 and tax2 are updated.

```
28    else :
29        tax1 = RATE1 * RATE1_MARRIED_LIMIT
30        tax2 = RATE2 * (income - RATE1_MARRIED_LIMIT)
```

tax1	tax2	income	marital status
~~0~~	~~0~~	80000	m
6400	4000		

The sum totalTax is computed and printed. Then the program ends.

```
32 totalTax = tax1 + tax2
   . . .
35 print("The tax is $%.2f" % totalTax)
```

Because the program trace shows the expected output ($10,400), it successfully demonstrates that this test case works correctly.

tax1	tax2	income	marital status	total tax
~~0~~	~~0~~	80000	m	
6400	4000			10400

Computing & Society 3.1 Dysfunctional Computerized Systems

Making decisions is an essential part of any computer program. Nowhere is this more obvious than in a computer system that helps sort luggage at an airport. After scanning the luggage identification codes, the system sorts the items and routes them to different conveyor belts. Human operators then place the items onto trucks. When the city of Denver built a huge airport to replace an outdated and congested facility, the luggage system contractor went a step further. The new system was designed to replace the human operators with robotic carts. Unfortunately, the system plainly did not work. It was plagued by mechanical problems, such as luggage falling onto the tracks and jamming carts. Equally frustrating were the software glitches. Carts would uselessly accumulate at some locations when they were needed elsewhere.

The airport had been scheduled to open in 1993, but without a functioning luggage system, the opening was delayed for over a year while the contractor tried to fix the problems.

The contractor never succeeded, and ultimately a manual system was installed. The delay cost the city and airlines close to a billion dollars, and the contractor, once the leading luggage systems vendor in the United States, went bankrupt.

Clearly, it is very risky to build a large system based on a technology that has never been tried on a smaller scale. In 2013, the rollout of universal healthcare in the United States was put in jeopardy by a dysfunctional web site for selecting insurance plans. The system promised an insurance shopping experience similar to booking airline flights. But, the HealthCare.gov site didn't simply present the available insurance plans. It also had to check the income level of each applicant and use that information to determine the subsidy level. That task turned out to be quite a bit harder than checking whether a credit card had sufficient credit to pay for an airline ticket. The Obama administration would have been well advised to design a signup process that did not rely on an untested computer program.

Lyn Alweis/Contributor/Getty Images.

The Denver airport originally had a fully automatic system for moving luggage, replacing human operators with robotic carts. Unfortunately, the system never worked and was dismantled before the airport was opened.

Multiple Alternatives

Multiple if statements can be combined to evaluate complex decisions.

In Section 3.1, you saw how to program a two-way branch with an if statement. In many situations, there are more than two cases. In this section, you will see how to implement a decision with multiple alternatives.

For example, consider a program that displays the effect of an earthquake, as measured by the Richter scale (see Table 4).

© kevinruss/iStockphoto.

The 1989 Loma Prieta earthquake that damaged the Bay Bridge in San Francisco and destroyed many buildings measured 7.1 on the Richter scale.

Table 4 Richter Scale	
Value	Effect
8	Most structures fall
7	Many buildings destroyed
6	Many buildings considerably damaged, some collapse
4.5	Damage to poorly constructed buildings
<4.5	No destruction of buildings

The Richter scale is a measurement of the strength of an earthquake. Every step in the scale, for example from 6.0 to 7.0, signifies a tenfold increase in the strength of the quake.

In this case, there are five branches: one each for the four descriptions of damage, and one for no destruction. Figure 4 shows the flowchart for this multiple-branch statement.

You could use multiple if statements to implement multiple alternatives, like this:

```python
if richter >= 8.0 :
   print("Most structures fall")
else :
   if richter >= 7.0 :
      print("Many buildings destroyed")
   else :
      if richter >= 6.0 :
         print("Many buildings considerably damaged, some collapse")
      else :
         if richter >= 4.5 :
            print("Damage to poorly constructed buildings")
         else :
            print("No destruction of buildings")
```

but this becomes difficult to read and, as the number of branches increases, the code begins to shift further and further to the right due to the required indentation. Python provides the special construct elif for creating if statements containing multiple branches. Using the elif statement, the above code segment can be rewritten as

```python
if richter >= 8.0 :
   print("Most structures fall")
elif richter >= 7.0 :
   print("Many buildings destroyed")
elif richter >= 6.0 :
   print("Many buildings considerably damaged, some collapse")
```

```
    elif richter >= 4.5 :
        print("Damage to poorly constructed buildings")
    else :
        print("No destruction of buildings")
```

As soon as one of the four tests succeeds, the effect is displayed, and no further tests are attempted. If none of the four cases applies, the final else clause applies, and a default message is printed.

Here you must sort the conditions and test against the largest cutoff first. Suppose we reverse the order of tests:

```
    if richter >= 4.5 :    # Tests in wrong order
        print("Damage to poorly constructed buildings")
    elif richter >= 6.0 :
        print("Many buildings considerably damaged, some collapse")
    elif richter >= 7.0 :
        print("Many buildings destroyed")
    elif richter >= 8.0 :
        print("Most structures fall")
```

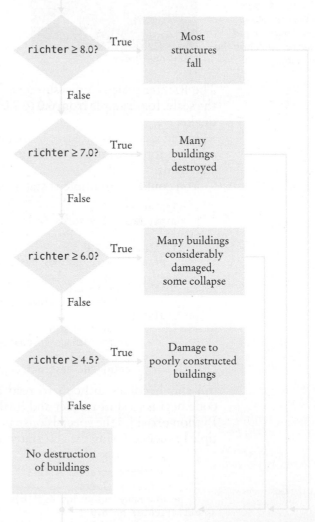

Figure 4
Multiple Alternatives

When using multiple if statements, test general conditions after more specific conditions.

This does not work. Suppose the value of richter is 7.1. That value is at least 4.5, matching the first case. The other tests will never be attempted.

The remedy is to test the more specific conditions first. Here, the condition richter >= 8.0 is more specific than the condition richter >= 7.0, and the condition richter >= 4.5 is more general (that is, fulfilled by more values) than either of the first two.

In this example, it is also important that we use an if/elif sequence, not just multiple independent if statements. Consider this sequence of independent tests.

```python
if (richter >= 8.0) :    # Didn't use else
    print("Most structures fall")
if richter >= 7.0 :
    print("Many buildings destroyed")
if richter >= 6.0 :
    print("Many buildings considerably damaged, some collapse")
if richter >= 4.5 :
    print("Damage to poorly constructed buildings")
```

Now the alternatives are no longer exclusive. If richter is 7.1, then the last *three* tests all match, and three messages are printed.

The complete program for printing the description of an earthquake given the Richter scale magnitude is provided below.

sec04/earthquake.py

```python
1  ##
2  #   This program prints a description of an earthquake, given the Richter scale
3  #   magnitude.
4  #
5
6  # Obtain the user input.
7  richter = float(input("Enter a magnitude on the Richter scale: "))
8
9  # Print the description.
10 if richter >= 8.0 :
11     print("Most structures fall")
12 elif richter >= 7.0 :
13     print("Many buildings destroyed")
14 elif richter >= 6.0 :
15     print("Many buildings considerably damaged, some collapse")
16 elif richter >= 4.5 :
17     print("Damage to poorly constructed buildings")
18 else :
19     print("No destruction of buildings")
```

TOOLBOX 3.1

Sending E-mail

Suppose you work as a teaching assistant and have to notify many students of their test scores. It would be a lot of work to type out each message in your e-mail program. Fortunately, you can automate this process using Python's email module.

Assembling an E-mail Message

First, you need to assemble the message. In general, messages can be combinations of text and attachments, such as images and files. A specification with the abbreviation MIME (Multi-Purpose Internet Mail Extensions) describes how e-mail messages need to be formatted.

Fortunately, you don't have to know the details of the formatting. Simply use the MIME classes that Python provides. Import them with the following statements:

```
from email.mime.multipart import MIMEMultipart
from email.mime.text import MIMEText
from email.mime.image import MIMEImage
from email.mime.application import MIMEApplication
```

You start by making a message that can consist of multiple parts:

```
msg = MIMEMultipart()
```

Specify the e-mail addresses of the sender and one or more recipients:

```
msg.add_header("From", sender)
msg.add_header("To", recipient1)
msg.add_header("To", recipient2)
```

For copying and "blind copying" additional recipients, use the following statements:

```
msg.add_header("Cc", recipient3)
msg.add_header("Bcc", recipient4)
```

Set the subject line with this command:

```
msg.add_header("Subject", subjectLine)
```

Now you are ready to include your message body. If it is a plain text string, call

```
msg.attach(MIMEText(body, "plain"))
```

You can also attach an HTML version by calling

```
msg.attach(MIMEText(htmlBody, "html"))
```

If you provide both, then the recipient's mail program will display one or the other, depending on the preferences of the user and the capabilities of the receiving device.

If you want to include an image, you need to first read it from a file. We discuss file input in detail in Chapter 7, but it is easy to do in this case. You open the file for "reading binary data", read the data, and make a MIMEImage object. Then close the file and attach the image to the message:

```
file = open("myimage.jpg", "rb")
img = MIMEImage(file.read())
file.close()
msg.attach(img)
```

For other attachments, such as PDF files or spreadsheets, you create a MIMEApplication object from the file. Add a header to tell the recipient that this file is an attachment that can be saved.

```
fp = open("/somedir/myfile.pdf", "rb")
attachment = MIMEApplication(fp.read())
fp.close()
attachment.add_header("Content-Disposition",
    "attachment; filename=myfile.pdf")  # The file name without directory
msg.attach(attachment)
```

The recipient can then save the file by clicking on some icon. By default, the file will have the given name, but with most e-mail readers, the recipient can change it. (You should not include the directory name in the attachment header because the recipient may not have the same directories as the sender.)

Of course, not every e-mail has image and file attachments. Just skip those parts to send a text message.

Sending a Message

Once you have assembled the message, you need to send it, using the smtplib module. SMTP is an abbreviation for the "Simple Mail Transport Protocol", the specification for communicating with mail servers. Import the module:

```
import smtplib
```

Then connect to the mail server. You specify the host name and "port number". Here we use Google's Gmail service as an example. With Gmail (and with most other mail servers), you use port 587 for "transport level security". That means, the communication between your computer and the mail server is encrypted. If you use a different e-mail service, you will need to find out the host name and port number.

```
host = "smtp.gmail.com"
port = 587
server = smtplib.SMTP(host, port)
```

The `SMTP` function returns an object that you use to communicate with the server. First, turn on secure communications:

```
server.starttls()
```

Then log in with your e-mail username and password (for the e-mail service specified above).

```
server.login(username, password)
```

Now send your e-mail with the `send_message` method, and quit the session.

```
server.send_message(msg)
server.quit()
```

A Sample E-mail Program

As you can see, it is easy to send e-mail with a Python program. You assemble a message and send it to the server. Let's return to the teaching assistant who wants to notify students of their exam grade. If the student did well, you want to send a cheerful message, and if the student seems in need of tutoring, you want to include directions to the tutoring center.

When you write such a program, you should include your information (e-mail address, account name, server name, and so on) in the program so that you don't have to type it in each time. However, it seems wise not to store your password in your program. Instead, read it in whenever the program is run.

Here is how to start out:

```
from email.mime.multipart import MIMEMultipart
from email.mime.text import MIMEText
import smtplib

sender = "sally.smith@mycollege.edu"
username = "sallysmith"
password = input("Password: ")
host = "smtp.myserver.com"
port = 587
```

Then prompt for the recipient's e-mail address and test score. Create a message body depending on the score.

```
recipient = input("Student email: ")
score = int(input("Score: "))
body = "Your score on the last exam is " + str(score) + "\n"
if score <= 50 :
   body = body + "To do better next time, why not visit the tutoring center?"
elif score >= 90 :
   body = body + "Fantastic job! Keep it up."
```

Now assemble the message. Here, we will simply send a plain text message. Exercises • Toolbox P3.53–•• Toolbox P3.56 at the end of this chapter give some suggestions for enhancement.

```
msg = MIMEMultipart()
msg.add_header("From", sender)
msg.add_header("To", recipient)
msg.add_header("Subject", "Exam score")
msg.attach(MIMEText(body, "plain"))
```

Finally, send off the message:

```
server = smtplib.SMTP(host, port)
server.starttls()
server.login(username, password)
server.send_message(msg)
server.quit()
```

That's it. A customized message is on its way to the recipient.

This program sends a single e-mail message. In Chapter 4, you will learn how to program loops that can send multiple messages. Chapter 7 shows you how a program can read data from a spreadsheet. Then you can enhance this program to automatically send messages to all students whose e-mail addresses and test scores are in a spreadsheet.

EXAMPLE CODE See `toolbox_1/mail.py` in your eText or companion code for the complete program.

3.5 Problem Solving: Flowcharts

Flowcharts are made up of elements for tasks, input/output, and decisions.

You have seen examples of flowcharts earlier in this chapter. A flowchart shows the structure of decisions and tasks that are required to solve a problem. When you have to solve a complex problem, it is a good idea to draw a flowchart to visualize the flow of control. The basic flowchart elements are shown in Figure 5.

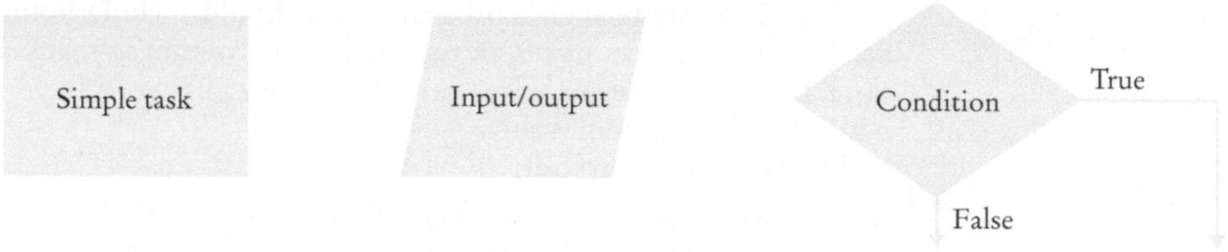

Simple task
Input/output
Condition
True
False

Figure 5
Flowchart Elements

Each branch of a decision can contain tasks and further decisions.

The basic idea is simple enough. Link tasks and input/output boxes in the sequence in which they should be executed. Whenever you need to make a decision, draw a diamond with two outcomes (see Figure 6).

Each branch can contain a sequence of tasks and even additional decisions. If there are multiple choices for a value, lay them out as in Figure 7.

Condition
True
False
False branch
True branch

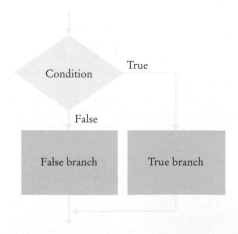

Figure 6
Flowchart with Two Outcomes

Figure 7
Flowchart with Multiple Choices

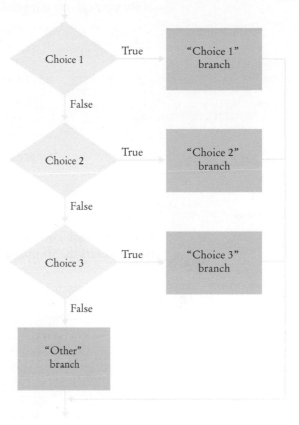

There is one issue that you need to be aware of when drawing flowcharts. Unconstrained branching and merging can lead to "spaghetti code", a messy network of possible pathways through a program.

There is a simple rule for avoiding spaghetti code: Never point an arrow *inside another branch*.

To understand the rule, consider this example: Shipping costs are $5 inside the United States, except that to Hawaii and Alaska they are $10. International shipping costs are also $10.

You might start out with a flowchart like the following:

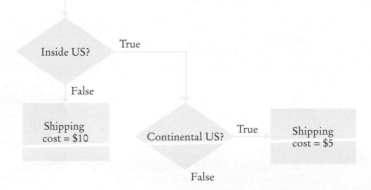

Now you may be tempted to reuse the "shipping cost = $10" task:

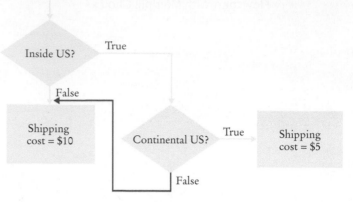

Don't do that! The red arrow points inside a different branch. Instead, add another task that sets the shipping cost to $10, like this:

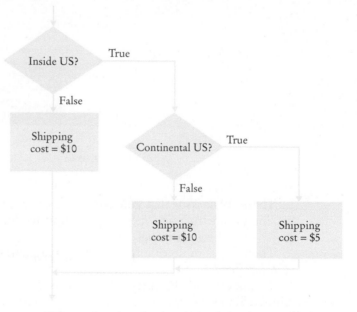

Not only do you avoid spaghetti code, but it is also a better design. In the future it may well happen that the cost for international shipments is different from that to Alaska and Hawaii.

Spaghetti code has so many pathways that it becomes impossible to understand.

© Ekspansio/iStockphoto.

Flowcharts can be very useful for getting an intuitive understanding of the flow of an algorithm. However, they get large rather quickly when you add more details. At that point, it makes sense to switch from flowcharts to pseudocode.

The complete program computing the shipping costs is provided below.

sec05/shipping.py

```
1  ##
2  #   A program to compute shipping costs.
3  #
4
5  # Obtain the user input.
6  country = input("Enter the country: ")
7  state = input("Enter the state or province: ")
8
9  # Compute the shipping cost.
10 shippingCost = 0.0
11
12 if country == "USA" :
13    if state == "AK" or state == "HI" :    # See Section 3.7 for the or operator
14       shippingCost = 10.0
15    else :
16       shippingCost = 5.0
17 else :
18    shippingCost = 10.0
19
20 # Print the results.
21 print("Shipping cost to %s, %s: $%.2f" % (state, country, shippingCost))
```

Program Run

```
Enter the country: USA
Enter the state or province: VA
Shipping cost to VA, USA: $5.00
```

3.6 Problem Solving: Test Cases

Consider how to test the tax computation program from Section 3.3. Of course, you cannot try out all possible inputs of marital status and income level. Even if you could, there would be no point in trying them all. If the program correctly computes one or two tax amounts in a given bracket, then we have good reason to believe that all amounts will be correct.

You want to aim for complete *coverage* of all decision points. Here is a plan for obtaining a comprehensive set of test cases:

Each branch of your program should be covered by a test case.

- There are two possibilities for the marital status and two tax brackets for each status, yielding four test cases.
- Test a handful of *boundary* conditions, such as an income that is at the boundary between two brackets, and a zero income.
- If you are responsible for error checking (which is discussed in Section 3.9), also test an invalid input, such as a negative income.

Make a list of the test cases and the expected outputs:

Test Case		Expected Output	Comment
30,000	s	3,000	10% bracket
72,000	s	13,200	3,200 + 25% of 40,000
50,000	m	5,000	10% bracket
104,000	m	16,400	6,400 + 25% of 40,000
32,000	s	3,200	boundary case
0	m	0	boundary case

When you develop a set of test cases, it is helpful to have a flowchart of your program (see Section 3.5). Check off each branch that has a test case. Include test cases for the boundary cases of each decision. For example, if a decision checks whether an input is less than 100, test with an input of 100.

It is a good idea to design test cases before implementing a program.

It is always a good idea to design test cases *before* starting to code. Working through the test cases gives you a better understanding of the algorithm that you are about to implement.

Programming Tip 3.3

Make a Schedule and Make Time for Unexpected Problems

Commercial software is notorious for being delivered later than promised. For example, Microsoft originally promised that its Windows Vista operating system would be available late in 2003, then in 2005, then in March 2006; it finally was released in January 2007. Some of the early promises might not have been realistic. It was in Microsoft's interest to let prospective customers expect the imminent availability of the product. Had customers known the actual delivery date, they might have switched to a different product in the meantime. Undeniably, though, Microsoft had not anticipated the full complexity of the tasks it had set itself to solve.

Microsoft can delay the delivery of its product, but it is likely that you cannot. As a student or a programmer, you are expected to manage your time wisely and to finish your assignments on time. You can probably do simple programming exercises the night before the due date, but an assignment that looks twice as hard may well take four times as long, because more things can go wrong. You should therefore make a schedule whenever you start a programming project.

First, estimate realistically how much time it will take you to:

- Design the program logic.
- Develop test cases.
- Type the program in and fix syntax errors.
- Test and debug the program.

For example, for the income tax program I might estimate an hour for the design, 30 minutes for developing test cases, an hour for data entry and fixing syntax errors, and an hour for testing and debugging. That is a total of 3.5 hours. If I work two hours a day on this project, it will take me almost two days.

Then think of things that can go wrong. Your computer might break down. You

Bananastock/Media Bakery.

Make a schedule for your programming work and build in time for problems.

might be stumped by a problem with the computer system. (That is a particularly important concern for beginners. It is *very* common to lose a day over a trivial problem just because it takes time to track down a person who knows the magic command to overcome it.) As a rule of thumb, *double* the time of your estimate. That is, you should start four days, not two days, before the due date. If nothing went wrong, great; you have the program done two days early. When the inevitable problem occurs, you have a cushion of time that protects you from embarrassment and failure.

3.7 Boolean Variables and Operators

The Boolean type bool has two values, False and True.

Jon Patton/E+/iStockphoto.

A Boolean variable is also called a flag because it can be either up (true) or down (false).

Sometimes, you need to evaluate a logical condition in one part of a program and use it elsewhere. To store a condition that can be true or false, you use a *Boolean variable*. Boolean variables are named after the mathematician George Boole (1815–1864), a pioneer in the study of logic.

In Python, the bool data type has exactly two values, denoted False and True. These values are not strings or integers; they are special values, just for Boolean variables. Here is the initialization of a variable set to True:

```
failed = True
```

You can use the value later in your program to make a decision:

```
if failed :    # Only executed if failed has been set to true
    . . .
```

When you make complex decisions, you often need to combine Boolean values. An operator that combines Boolean conditions is called a **Boolean operator**. In Python, the and operator yields True only when both conditions are true. The or operator yields True if at least one of the conditions is true.

Suppose you write a program that processes temperature values, and you want to test whether a given temperature corresponds to liquid water. (At sea level, water freezes at 0 degrees Celsius and boils at 100 degrees.) Water is liquid if the temperature is greater than zero and less than 100:

```
if temp > 0 and temp < 100 :
    print("Liquid")
```

© toos/iStockphoto.

At this geyser in Iceland, you can see ice, liquid water, and steam.

Python has two Boolean operators that combine conditions: and and or.

The condition of the test has two parts, joined by the and operator. Each part is a Boolean value that can be true or false. The combined expression is true if both individual expressions are true. If either one of the expressions is false, then the result is also false (see Figure 8).

A	B	A and B
true	true	true
true	false	false
false	true	false
false	false	false

A	B	A or B
true	true	true
true	false	true
false	true	true
false	false	false

A	not A
true	false
false	true

Figure 8 Boolean Truth Tables

The Boolean operators and and or have a lower precedence than the relational operators. For that reason, you can write relational expressions on either side of the Boolean operators without using parentheses. For example, in the expression

```
temp > 0 and temp < 100
```

the expressions temp > 0 and temp < 100 are evaluated first. Then the and operator combines the results. Appendix A shows a table of the Python operators and their precedence. (For complex expressions, however, parentheses make the code more readable.)

Conversely, let's test whether water is not liquid at a given temperature. That is the case when the temperature is at most 0 or at least 100. Use the or operator to combine the expressions:

```
if temp <= 0 or temp >= 100 :
    print("Not liquid")
```

Figure 9 shows flowcharts for these examples.

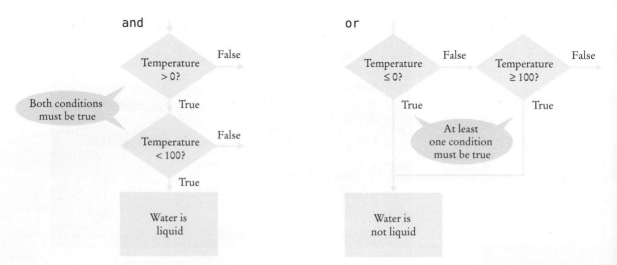

Figure 9 Flowcharts for *and* and *or* Combinations

To invert a condition, use the not operator.

Sometimes you need to *invert* a condition with the not Boolean operator. The not operator takes a single condition and evaluates to True if that condition is false and to False if the condition is true. In this example, output occurs if the value of the Boolean variable frozen is False:

```
if not frozen :
    print("Not frozen")
```

Table 5 illustrates additional examples of evaluating Boolean operators.

Table 5 Boolean Operator Examples

Expression	Value	Comment
0 < 200 and 200 < 100	False	Only the first condition is true.
0 < 200 or 200 < 100	True	The first condition is true.
0 < 200 or 100 < 200	True	The or is not a test for "either-or". If both conditions are true, the result is true.
0 < x and x < 100 or x == -1	(0 < x and x < 100) or x == -1	The and operator has a higher precedence than the or operator (see Appendix A).
not (0 < 200)	False	0 < 200 is true, therefore its negation is false.
frozen == True	frozen	There is no need to compare a Boolean variable with True.
frozen == False	not frozen	It is clearer to use not than to compare with False.

The following program demonstrates the use of Boolean expressions.

sec07/compare2.py

```
1  ##
2  #   This program demonstrates comparisons of numbers, using Boolean expressions.
3  #
4
5  x = float(input("Enter a number (such as 3.5 or 4.5): "))
6  y = float(input("Enter a second number: "))
7
8  if x == y :
9      print("They are the same.")
10 else :
11     if x > y :
12         print("The first number is larger")
13     else :
14         print("The first number is smaller")
15
16     if -0.01 < x - y and x - y < 0.01 :
17         print("The numbers are close together")
18
19     if x > 0 and y > 0 or x < 0 and y < 0 :
20         print("The numbers have the same sign")
```

```
21    else :
22        print("The numbers have different signs")
```

Program Run

```
Enter a number (such as 3.5 or 4.5): 3.25
Enter a second number: -1.02
The first number is larger
The numbers have different signs
```

Common Error 3.3

Confusing and **and** or **Conditions**

It is a surprisingly common error to confuse and and or conditions. A value lies between 0 and 100 if it is at least 0 *and* at most 100. It lies outside that range if it is less than 0 *or* greater than 100. There is no golden rule; you just have to think carefully.

Often the and or or is clearly stated, and then it isn't too hard to implement it. But sometimes the wording isn't as explicit. It is quite common that the individual conditions are nicely set apart in a bulleted list, but with little indication of how they should be combined. Consider these instructions for filing a tax return. You can claim single filing status if any one of the following is true:

- You were never married.
- You were legally separated or divorced on the last day of the tax year.
- You were widowed, and did not remarry.

Because the test passes if *any one* of the conditions is true, you must combine the conditions with or. Elsewhere, the same instructions state that you may use the more advantageous status of "married filing jointly" if all five of the following conditions are true:

- Your spouse died less than two years ago and you did not remarry.
- You have a child whom you can claim as dependent.
- That child lived in your home for all of the tax year.
- You paid over half the cost of keeping up your home for this child.
- You filed a joint return with your spouse the year he or she died.

Because *all* of the conditions must be true for the test to pass, you must combine them with an and operator.

Programming Tip 3.4

Readability

Programs are more than just instructions to be executed by a computer. A program implements an algorithm and is commonly read by other people. Thus, it is important for your programs not only to be correct but also to be easily read by others. While many programmers focus only on a readable layout for their code, the choice of syntax can also have an impact on readability.

To help provide readable code, you should never compare against a literal Boolean value (True or False) in a logical expression. For example, consider the expression in this if statement:

```
if frozen == False :
    print("Not frozen")
```

A reader of this code may be confused as to the condition that will cause the if statement to be executed. Instead, you should use the more acceptable form

```
if not frozen :
    print("Not frozen")
```

which is easier to read and explicitly states the condition.

It is also important to have appropriate names for variables that contain Boolean values. Choose names such as done or valid, so that it is clear what action should be taken when the variable is set to True or False.

Special Topic 3.3

Chaining Relational Operators

In mathematics, it is very common to combine multiple relational operators to compare a variable against multiple values. For example, consider the expression

```
0 <= value <= 100
```

Python also allows you to chain relational operators in this fashion. When the expression is evaluated, the Python interpreter automatically inserts the Boolean operator and to form two separate relational expressions

```
value >= 0 and value <= 100
```

Relational operators can be chained arbitrarily. For example, the expression a < x > b is perfectly legal. It means the same as a < x and x > b. In other words, x must exceed both a and b.

Most programming languages do not allow multiple relational operators to be combined in this fashion; they require explicit Boolean operators. Thus, when first learning to program, it is good practice to explicitly insert the Boolean operators. That way, if you must later change to a different programming language, you will avoid syntax errors generated by chaining relational operators in a logical expression.

Special Topic 3.4

Short-Circuit Evaluation of Boolean Operators

The and and or operators are computed using **short-circuit evaluation**. In other words, logical expressions are evaluated from left to right, and evaluation stops as soon as the truth value is determined. When an and is evaluated and the first condition is false, the second condition is not evaluated, because it does not matter what the outcome of the second test is.

For example, consider the expression

```
quantity > 0 and price / quantity < 10
```

> The and and or operators are computed using *short-circuit evaluation:* As soon as the truth value is determined, no further conditions are evaluated.

Suppose the value of quantity is zero. Then the test quantity > 0 fails, and the second test is not attempted. That is just as well, because it is illegal to divide by zero.

Similarly, when the first condition of an or expression is true, then the remainder is not evaluated because the result must be true.

In a short circuit, electricity travels along the path of least resistance. Similarly, short-circuit evaluation takes the fastest path for computing the result of a Boolean expression.

© YouraPechkin/iStockphoto.

Special Topic 3.5

De Morgan's Law

Humans generally have a hard time comprehending logical conditions with *not* operators applied to *and/or* expressions. De Morgan's Law, named after the logician Augustus De Morgan (1806–1871), can be used to simplify these Boolean expressions.

Suppose we want to charge a higher shipping rate if we don't ship within the continental United States.

```
if not (country == "USA" and state != "AK" and state != "HI") :
    shippingCharge = 20.00
```

This test is a little bit complicated, and you have to think carefully through the logic. When it is *not* true that the country is USA *and* the state is not Alaska *and* the state is not Hawaii, then charge $20.00. Huh? It is not true that some people won't be confused by this code.

The computer doesn't care, but it takes human programmers to write and maintain the code. Therefore, it is useful to know how to simplify such a condition.

De Morgan's Law has two forms: one for the negation of an and expression and one for the negation of an or expression:

> De Morgan's law tells you how to negate and and or conditions.

not (A and B)	is the same as	not A or not B
not (A or B)	is the same as	not A and not B

Pay particular attention to the fact that the and and or operators are *reversed* by moving the not inward. For example, the negation of "the state is Alaska *or* it is Hawaii",

```
not (state == "AK" or state == "HI")
```

is "the state is not Alaska *and* it is not Hawaii":

```
state != "AK" and state != "HI"
```

Now apply the law to our shipping charge computation:

```
not (country == "USA" and state != "AK" and state != "HI")
```

is equivalent to

```
not (country == "USA") or not (state != "AK") or not (state != "HI")
```

Because two negatives cancel each other out, the result is the simpler test

```
country != "USA" or state == "AK" or state == "HI"
```

In other words, higher shipping charges apply when the destination is outside the United States or to Alaska or Hawaii.

To simplify conditions with negations of *and* or *or* expressions, it is usually a good idea to apply De Morgan's Law to move the negations to the innermost level.

3.8 Analyzing Strings

> Use the in operator to test whether a string occurs in another.

Sometimes it is necessary to determine whether a string contains a given substring. That is, one string contains an exact match of another string. Given this code segment,

```
name = "John Wayne"
```

the expression

```
"Way" in name
```

yields True because the substring "Way" occurs within the string stored in variable name.

Python also provides the inverse of the `in` operator, `not in`:

```
if "-" not in name :
    print("The name does not contain a hyphen.")
```

Sometimes we need to determine not only whether a string contains a given substring, but also whether the string begins or ends with that substring. For example, suppose you are given the name of a file and need to ensure that it has the correct extension.

```
if filename.endswith(".html") :
    print("This is an HTML file.")
```

The `endswith` string method is applied to the string stored in `filename` and returns `True` if the string ends with the substring `".html"` and `False` otherwise. Table 6 describes additional string methods available for testing substrings.

Table 6 Operations for Testing Substrings

Operation	Description
substring `in` *s*	Returns `True` if the string *s* contains *substring* and `False` otherwise.
s.`count`(*substring*)	Returns the number of non-overlapping occurrences of *substring* in the string *s*.
s.`endswith`(*substring*)	Returns `True` if the string *s* ends with the `substring` and `False` otherwise.
s.`find`(*substring*)	Returns the lowest index in the string *s* where *substring* begins, or −1 if *substring* is not found.
s.`startswith`(*substring*)	Returns `True` if the string *s* begins with *substring* and `False` otherwise.

We can also examine a string to test for specific characteristics. For example, the `islower` string method examines the string and determines whether all letters in the string are lowercase. The code segment

```
line = "Four score and seven years ago"
if line.islower() :
    print("The string contains only lowercase letters.")
else :
    print("The string contains uppercase letters.")
```

prints

```
The string also contains uppercase letters.
```

because the string in `line` begins with an uppercase letter. If the string contains non-letters, they are ignored and do not affect the Boolean result. But what if we need to determine whether a string contains only letters of the alphabet? There is a string method for that as well.

```
if line.isalpha() :
    print("The string is valid.")
else :
    print("The string must contain only upper and lowercase letters.")
```

Python provides several string methods that test for specific characteristics as described in Table 7.

Table 7 Methods for Testing String Characteristics

Method	Description
s.isalnum()	Returns True if string *s* consists of only alphanumeric characters (letters or digits) and contains at least one character. Otherwise it returns False.
s.isalpha()	Returns True if string *s* consists of only letters and contains at least one character. Otherwise it returns False.
s.isdigit()	Returns True if string *s* consists of only digits and contains at least one character. Otherwise, it returns False.
s.islower()	Returns True if string *s* contains at least one letter and all letters in the string are lowercase. Otherwise, it returns False.
s.isspace()	Returns True if string *s* consists of only white space characters (blank, newline, tab) and it contains at least one character. Otherwise, it returns False.
s.isupper()	Returns True if string *s* contains at least one letter and all letters in the string are uppercase. Otherwise, it returns False.

Table 8 summarizes how to compare and examine strings in Python.

Table 8 Comparing and Analyzing Strings

Expression	Value	Comment
"John" == "John"	True	== is also used to test the equality of two strings.
"John" == "john"	False	For two strings to be equal, they must be identical. An uppercase "J" does not equal a lowercase "j".
"john" < "John"	False	Based on lexicographical ordering of strings an uppercase "J" comes before a lowercase "j" so the string "john" follows the string "John". See Special Topic 3.2.
"john" in "John Johnson"	False	The substring "john" must match exactly.
name = "John Johnson" "ho" not in name	True	The string does not contain the substring "ho".
name.count("oh")	2	All non-overlapping substrings are included in the count.
name.find("oh")	1	Finds the position or string index where the first substring occurs.
name.find("ho")	–1	The string does not contain the substring ho.
name.startswith("john")	False	The string starts with "John" but an uppercase "J" does not match a lowercase "j".
name.isspace()	False	The string contains non-white space characters.
name.isalnum()	False	The string also contains a blank space.

Table 8 Comparing and Analyzing Strings

Expression	Value	Comment
`"1729".isdigit()`	True	The string contains only characters that are digits.
`"-1729".isdigit()`	False	A negative sign is not a digit.

The following program demonstrates the use of operators and methods for examining substrings.

sec08/substrings.py

```
1  ##
2  #  This program demonstrates the various string methods that test substrings.
3  #
4
5  # Obtain a string and substring from the user.
6  theString = input("Enter a string: ")
7  theSubString = input("Enter a substring: ")
8
9  if theSubString in theString :
10     print("The string does contain the substring.")
11
12     howMany = theString.count(theSubString)
13     print("   It contains", howMany, "instance(s)")
14
15     where = theString.find(theSubString)
16     print("   The first occurrence starts at position", where)
17
18     if theString.startswith(theSubString) :
19        print("   The string starts with the substring.")
20     else :
21        print("   The string does not start with the substring.")
22
23     if theString.endswith(theSubString) :
24        print("   The string ends with the substring.")
25     else :
26        print("   The string does not end with the substring.")
27
28  else :
29     print("The string does not contain the substring.")
```

Program Run

```
Enter a string: The itsy bitsy spider went up the water spout
Enter a substring: itsy
The string does contain the substring.
   It contains 2 instance(s)
   The first occurrence starts at position 4
   The string does not start with the substring.
   The string does not end with the substring.
```

3.9 Application: Input Validation

An important application for the `if` statement is *input validation*. Whenever your program accepts user input, you need to make sure that the user-supplied values are valid before you use them in your computations.

Consider our `elevatorsim.py` program on page 76. Assume that the elevator panel has buttons labeled 1 through 20 (but not 13). The following are illegal inputs:

- The number 13
- Zero or a negative number
- A number larger than 20
- An input that is not a sequence of digits, such as `five`

Tetra Images/Media Bakery.

Like a quality control worker, you want to make sure that user input is correct before processing it.

In each of these cases, we will want to give an error message and exit the program.

> If the user provides an input that is not in the expected range, print an error message and don't process the input.

It is simple to guard against an input of 13:

```
if floor == 13 :
    print("Error: There is no thirteenth floor.")
```

Here is how you ensure that the user doesn't enter a number outside the valid range:

```
if floor <= 0 or floor > 20 :
    print("Error: The floor must be between 1 and 20.")
```

However, dealing with an input that is not a valid integer is a more serious problem. When the statement

```
floor = int(input("Floor: "))
```

is executed, and the user types in an input that is not an integer (such as `five`), then the variable `floor` is not set. Instead, a run-time exception occurs and the program is terminated. Python's exception mechanism is needed to help verify integer and floating-point values. We will cover more advanced input verifications in Chapter 7, when exceptions are covered in detail.

Here is a revised elevator simulation program with input validation.

sec09/elevatorsim2.py

```
 1  ##
 2  #   This program simulates an elevator panel that skips the 13th floor,
 3  #   checking for input errors.
 4  #
 5
 6  # Obtain the floor number from the user as an integer.
 7  floor = int(input("Floor: "))
 8
 9  # Make sure the user input is valid.
10  if floor == 13 :
11      print("Error: There is no thirteenth floor.")
12  elif floor <= 0 or floor > 20 :
13      print("Error: The floor must be between 1 and 20.")
14  else :
```

```
15    # Now we know that the input is valid.
16    actualFloor = floor
17    if floor > 13 :
18       actualFloor = floor - 1
19
20    print("The elevator will travel to the actual floor", actualFloor)
```

Program Run

```
Floor: 13
Error: There is no thirteenth floor.
```

Programs that prompt the user to enter a character in order to perform some action or to specify a certain condition are also very common. Consider the income tax computation program from Section 3.3. The user is prompted for marital status and asked to enter a single letter

```
maritalStatus = input("Please enter s for single, m for married: ")
```

Note the specification of lowercase letters for the status. It is common, however, for a user to enter an uppercase letter accidentally or because the caps lock key is on. Instead of flagging this as an error, we can allow the user to enter either an upper- or lowercase letter. When validating the user input, we must compare against both cases:

```
if maritalStatus == "s" or maritalStatus == "S" :
    Process the data for single status.
elif maritalStatus == "m" or maritalStatus == "M" :
    Process the data for married status.
else :
    print("Error: the marital status must be either s or m.")
```

One-letter inputs are easy to validate by simply comparing against both the upper- and lowercase letters. But what if the user is asked to enter a multi-letter code? For example, in the shipping cost program, the user is asked to enter codes for the country and state or province. In the original version of the program, we only checked the user input against uppercase versions of the codes:

```
if country == "USA" :
    if state == "AK" or state == "HI" :
```

It's not uncommon for a user to enter a multi-letter code using lowercase letters or a mix of upper- and lowercase. It would be tedious to compare the input against all possible combinations of upper- and lowercase letters. Instead, we can first convert the user input to either all upper- or lowercase letters and then compare against a single version. This can be done using the lower or upper string method.

```
state = input("Enter the state or province: ")
state = state.upper()

country = input("Enter the country: ")
country = country.upper()

if country == "USA" :
    if state == "AK" or state == "HI" :
        Compute the shipping cost.
```

Special Topic 3.6

Terminating a Program

In text-based programs (those without a graphical user interface) it is common to abort the program if the user enters invalid input. As we saw in the main text, we check the user input and process the data only if valid input was provided. This requires the use of an if/elif/else statement to process the data only if the input is valid. This works fine with small programs where the input value is examined only once. But in larger programs, we may need to examine the input value in multiple locations. Instead of having to validate and display an error message each time the input value is used, we can validate the input once and immediately abort the program when invalid data is entered.

The exit function defined in the sys standard library module immediately aborts the program when executed. An optional message can be displayed to the terminal before the program aborts.

```
from sys import exit

if not (userResponse == "n" or userResponse == "y") :
    exit("Error: you must enter either n or y.")
```

This function, when used as part of the input validation process, can be used to abort the program when an error occurs and to construct cleaner and more readable code.

Special Topic 3.7

Interactive Graphical Programs

In a program that uses the ezgraphics module, you can read and validate user input in the same way as in any other Python program. Simply put calls to the input function before the call to the wait method. For example,

```
from ezgraphics import GraphicsWindow
from sys import exit

win = GraphicsWindow()
canvas = win.canvas()
x = int(input("Please enter the x-coordinate: "))
y = int(input("Please enter the y-coordinate: "))
if x < 0 or y < 0 :
    exit("Error: x and y must be >= 0".)
canvas.drawOval(x - 5, y - 5, 10, 10)
win.wait()
```

The ezgraphics module also allows you to get simple graphical information from the user. The GraphicsWindow method getMouse pauses execution until the user clicks a mouse button somewhere in the graphics window.

The x- and y-coordinates of the point where the mouse button was clicked are returned as a list of two elements. If we insert the following code before the win.wait() statement in the example above,

```
point = win.getMouse()
x = point[0]
y = point[1]
canvas.drawRectangle(x, y, 40, 50)
```

a rectangle will be drawn with its upper-left corner positioned at the point where the user clicked the mouse button.

Worked Example 3.2 shows a more complex graphical application with input validation.

Computing & Society 3.2   Artificial Intelligence

When one uses a sophisticated computer program such as a tax preparation package, one is bound to attribute some intelligence to the computer. The computer asks sensible questions and makes computations that we find a mental challenge. After all, if doing one's taxes were easy, we wouldn't need a computer to do it for us.

As programmers, however, we know that all this apparent intelligence is an illusion. Human programmers have carefully "coached" the software in all possible scenarios, and it simply replays the actions and decisions that were programmed into it.

Would it be possible to write computer programs that are genuinely intelligent in some sense? From the earliest days of computing, there was a sense that the human brain might be nothing but an immense computer, and that it might well be feasible to program computers to imitate some processes of human thought. Serious research into *artificial intelligence* began in the mid-1950s, and the first twenty years brought some impressive successes. Programs that play chess—surely an activity that appears to require remarkable intellectual powers—have become so good that they now routinely beat all but the best human players. As far back as 1975, an *expert-system* program called Mycin gained fame for being better at diagnosing meningitis in patients than the average physician.

From the very outset, one of the stated goals of the AI community was to produce software that could translate text from one language to another, for example from English to Russian. That undertaking proved to be enormously complicated. Human language appears to be much more subtle and interwoven with the human experience than had originally been thought. Systems such as Apple's Siri can answer common questions about the weather, appointments, and traffic. However, beyond a narrow range, they are more entertaining than useful.

In some areas, artificial intelligence technology has seen substantial advances. One of the most astounding examples is the advent of self-driving cars. In 2004, the Defense Advanced Research Projects Agency (DARPA) invited competitors to submit a computer-controlled vehicle that had to complete an obstacle course without a human driver or remote control. The event was a disappointment, with none of the entrants finishing the route. However, by 2007, a competition in an "urban" environment—an abandoned air force base—had vehicles successfully interact with each other and follow California traffic laws. Within the next decade, technologies for partially or fully autonomous driving became commercially viable. We can now envision a future where self-driving vehicles become ubiquitous.

When a system with artificial intelligence replaces a human in an activity such as giving medical advice or driving a vehicle, an important question arises. Who is responsible for mistakes? We accept that human doctors and drivers occasionally make mistakes with lethal consequences. Will we do the same for medical expert systems and self-driving cars?

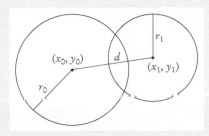

Vaughn Youtz/Zuma Press.

Winner of the 2007 DARPA Urban Challenge

WORKED EXAMPLE 3.2

Graphics: Intersecting Circles

Problem Statement Develop a graphics program that draws two circles, each defined by its center and radius, and determines whether the two circles intersect.

Given two circles, each defined by a center point and radius, we can determine whether they intersect.

Two circles may intersect at a single point, at two points, or at an unlimited number of points (when the

two circles are coincident). If the circles do not intersect, one circle may be contained entirely within the other, or the two circles may be completely separate.

Your task is to write a graphics program that obtains the parameters for two circles from the user and draws each circle in the graphics window with a message that reports whether the circles intersect. Each circle should be drawn immediately after its parameters have been input by the user and validated by the program. The result message should appear at the bottom of the window and should be one of the following:

The circles are completely separate.
One circle is contained within the other.
The circles intersect at a single point.
The circles are coincident.
The circles intersect at two points.

The center of each circle should be inside the graphics window and the radius should be at least five pixels.

Step 1   Determine the data to be extracted from the user and the appropriate input validation tests.

In order to define and draw a circle, the user must enter the *x*- and *y*-coordinates of the center point and the radius. Because the circle will be drawn in a graphics window using the ezgraphics module, these parameters must be integers.

The data extracted from the user must be validated to ensure that the circles will be visible in the window and large enough to see. The size of the graphics window can be specified at the time it is created.

```
WIN_WIDTH = 500
WIN_HEIGHT = 500
win = GraphicsWindow(WIN_WIDTH, WIN_HEIGHT)
```

The constant variables used to create the window can also be used to validate the center coordinates. The validation tests required for each set of inputs include

If x < 0 or x >= WIN_WIDTH or y < 0 or y >= WIN_HEIGHT
    Exit the program indicating a bad center coordinate.
If radius < MIN_RADIUS
    Exit the program indicating a bad radius size.

Step 2   Draw a circle.

The ezgraphics module does not define a method for drawing a circle. But it does define the drawOval method:

```
canvas.drawOval(x, y, width, height)
```

This method requires the coordinates of the upper-left corner and the dimensions (width and height) of the bounding box that encloses the oval.

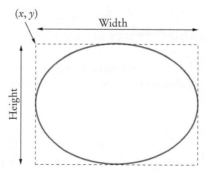

To draw a circle, we use the same value for the width and height parameters. This will be the diameter of the circle. As a reminder, the diameter of a circle is twice its radius:

diameter = 2 x radius

Because the user enters the *x*- and *y*-coordinates for the *center* of the circle, we need to compute the coordinates for the upper-left corner of the bounding box.

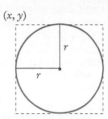

This is simple because the distance between the center of the circle and the top, or the center and the left side, of the bounding box is equal to the radius of the circle.

left side = centerX – radius
top side = centerY – radius

Step 3   Determine whether the two circles intersect.

To determine whether the two circles intersect, we must compute the Euclidean distance between the two center points

$$d = \sqrt{(x_1 - x_0)^2 + (y_1 - y_0)^2}$$

and compare it with the radiuses of the two circles as follows:

- If $d > r_0 + r_1$, the two circles do not intersect and are completely separate.
- If $d < |r_0 - r_1|$, the two circles do not intersect and one is contained within the other.
- If $d = r_0 + r_1$, the two circles intersect at a single point.
- If $d = 0$ and $r_0 = r_1$, the two circles are coincident.
- Otherwise, the two circles intersect at two points.

With this explanation, the mathematical conditions can be converted to an algorithm for selecting the appropriate message:

Set dist to the Euclidean distance between the two center points.
If dist > r_0 + r_1
    Set message to "The circles are completely separate."
Else if dist < abs(r_0 – r_1)
    Set message to "One circle is contained within the other."
Else if dist == r_0 + r_1
    Set message to "The circles intersect at a single point."
Else if dist == 0 and r_0 == r_1
    Set message to "The circles are coincident."
Else
    Set message to "The circles intersect at two points."

Step 4   Determine where to draw the message in the graphics window.

The message can be drawn anywhere in the graphics window, but for simplicity, we will draw it along the bottom of the window. The drawText method left-aligns text to the right of and below a given anchor point. A good position for the *x*- and *y*-coordinates is 15 pixels from the bottom and 15 pixels from the left edge of the window. Having defined constant variables earlier for the size of the window, we can specify the position of the text like this:

```
canvas.drawText(15, WIN_HEIGHT - 15, message)
```

Step 5   Implement your solution in Python.

The complete program is provided below.

worked_example_1/circles.py

```
1  ##
2  #   Draws and determines if two circles intersect. The parameters of both
3  #   circles are obtained from the user.
4  #
5
6  from ezgraphics import GraphicsWindow
7  from math import sqrt
8  from sys import exit
9
10 # Define constant variables.
11 MIN_RADIUS = 5
12 WIN_WIDTH = 500
13 WIN_HEIGHT = 500
14
15 # Create the graphics window and get the canvas.
16 win = GraphicsWindow(WIN_WIDTH, WIN_HEIGHT)
17 canvas = win.canvas()
18
19 # Obtain the parameters of the first circle.
20 print("Enter parameters for the first circle:")
21 x0 = int(input("  x-coord: "))
22 y0 = int(input("  y-coord: "))
23 if x0 < 0 or x0 >= WIN_WIDTH or y0 < 0 or y0 >= WIN_HEIGHT :
24    exit("Error: the center of the circle must be within the area of the window.")
25
26 r0 = int(input("  radius: "))
27 if r0 <= MIN_RADIUS :
28    exit("Error: the radius must be >", MIN_RADIUS)
29
30 # Draw the first circle.
31 canvas.setOutline("blue")
32 canvas.drawOval(x0 - r0, y0 - r0, 2 * r0, 2 * r0)
33
34 # Obtain the parameters of the second circle.
35 print("Enter parameters for the second circle:")
36 x1 = int(input("  x-coord: "))
37 y1 = int(input("  y-coord: "))
38 if x1 < 0 or x1 >= WIN_WIDTH or y1 < 0 or y1 >= WIN_HEIGHT :
39    exit("Error: the center of the circle must be within the area of the window.")
40
41 r1 = int(input("  radius: "))
42 if r1 <= MIN_RADIUS :
43    exit("Error: the radius must be >", MIN_RADIUS)
44
45 # Draw the second circle.
46 canvas.setOutline("red")
47 canvas.drawOval(x1 - r1, y1 - r1, 2 * r1, 2 * r1)
48
49 # Determine if the two circles intersect and select appropriate message.
50 dist = sqrt((x1 - x0) ** 2 + (y1 - y0) ** 2)
51
52 if dist > r0 + r1 :
53    message = "The circles are completely separate."
54 elif dist < abs(r0 - r1) :
```

```
55     message = "One circle is contained within the other."
56 elif dist == r0 + r1 :
57     message = "The circles intersect at a single point."
58 elif dist == 0 and r0 == r1 :
59     message = "The circles are coincident."
60 else :
61     message = "The circles intersect at two points."
62
63 # Display the result at the bottom of the graphics window.
64 canvas.setOutline("black")
65 canvas.drawText(15, WIN_HEIGHT - 15, message)
66
67 # Wait until the user closes the window.
68 win.wait()
```

TOOLBOX 3.2

Plotting Simple Graphs

A graph provides a visual representation of data by showing the relationship between sets of numbers. The matplotlib module provides a collection of easy to use tools for creating many types of graphs. We will explore several of them in this book.

For example, suppose you have been offered a job in beautiful Fairbanks, Alaska, and you are considering whether to accept. Perhaps you are concerned about the climate. This is how warm it gets on average each month:

Jan	Feb	Mar	Apr	May	Jun	Jul	Aug	Sep	Oct	Nov	Dec
1.1	10.0	25.4	44.5	61.0	71.6	72.7	65.9	54.6	31.9	10.9	4.8

You can scan through the numbers and try to make sense of them, or you can create a graph to help you see patterns that may not be so obvious from the raw numbers. From a visual inspection, you can quickly determine that it stays below freezing for six months out of the year, but also that the summer temperatures seem quite pleasant (see Figure 10).

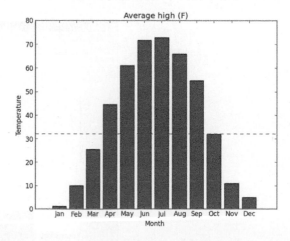

Figure 10 Average High Temperatures in Fairbanks

Creating a Graph

To create and display a graph using the `matplotlib` module, carry out the following steps:

1. Import the `pyplot` submodule.

```
from matplotlib import pyplot
```

The `pyplot` module has functions for adding elements to and displaying a graph.

2. Plot data on the graph.

To display data on the graph, you invoke functions in the `pyplot` module. Here, we use the `bar` function to plot several values as bars on a bar graph:

```
pyplot.bar(1, 1.1)
pyplot.bar(2, 10.0)
pyplot.bar(3, 25.4)
pyplot.bar(4, 44.5)
pyplot.bar(5, 61.0)
```

As a shortcut, you can also place the *x*- and *y*-values into *lists*—sequences of values enclosed in square brackets (Lists will be covered in Chapter 6.):

```
pyplot.bar([1, 2, 3, 4, 5], [1.1, 10.0, 25.4, 44.5, 61.0])
```

By default, each bar has width 0.8. Exercises • Toolbox P3.32 and ••• Toolbox P3.35 show you how you can change bar colors and widths.

3. Improve the appearance of the graph.

For example, you can change the labels of the axes:

```
pyplot.xlabel("Month")
pyplot.ylabel("Temperature")
```

You will see additional ways of changing the appearance of a graph later in this section.

4. Display the graph.

After you have configured the graph, call the `show` function:

```
pyplot.show()
```

The program pauses at this point and waits for the user to close the window. This allows you to view the graph during the execution of your Python program—see Figure 11. (If you use the IPython notebook, you can display graphs inside the notebook. See Toolbox 2.1 for instructions.) The buttons at the bottom of the window are tools that can be used with the graph. The one most commonly used is the Save button, which allows you to save the graph to a file in a variety of formats.

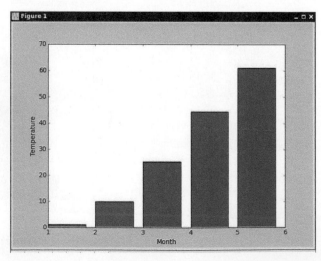

Figure 11
A Simple Bar Graph

The following program created the simple graph in this worked example.

toolbox_2/samplegraph.py

```
 1  ##
 2  #   This program illustrates the steps required to create a bar graph
 3  #   using the matplotlib module.
 4  #
 5
 6  from matplotlib import pyplot
 7
 8  # Plot data on the graph.
 9  pyplot.bar(1, 1.1)
10  pyplot.bar(2, 10.0)
11  pyplot.bar(3, 25.4)
12  pyplot.bar(4, 44.5)
13  pyplot.bar(5, 61.0)
14
15  # Add descriptive information.
16  pyplot.xlabel("Month")
17  pyplot.ylabel("Temperature")
18
19  # Display the graph.
20  pyplot.show()
```

EXAMPLE CODE See `toolbox_2/fairbanks.py` in your eText or companion code for the program that created the graph in Figure 10.

Creating a Line Graph

A line graph connects data points with line segments. You pass lists of the x- and y-coordinates to the plot function:

```
pyplot.plot([1, 2, 3, 4, 5], [1.1, 10.0, 25.4, 44.5, 61.0])
```

This call plots a line with five data points.

You can plot multiple lines on the same graph. For example, you can also plot the low temperatures in each month:

```
pyplot.plot([1, 2, 3, 4, 5], [1.1, 10.0, 25.4, 44.5, 61.0])   # Highs
pyplot.plot([1, 2, 3, 4, 5], [-16.9, -12.7, -2.5, 20.6, 37.8]) # Lows
```

To distinguish the different lines, matplotlib uses a different color for each line. Here, the first line is drawn in blue and the second in green.

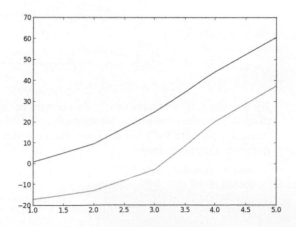

You can change the color as well as the style of the lines and points by supplying a format string to the plot function. Table 9 shows some of the more common style elements. For example, the call

```
pyplot.plot([1, 2, 3, 4, 5], [1.1, 10.0, 25.4, 44.5, 61.0], "r--o")
```

plots a red dashed line, and marks each point as a circle.

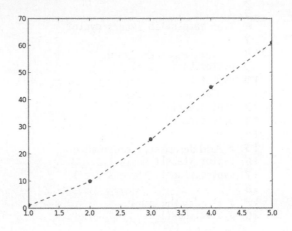

Changing the Appearance of a Graph

Adding a grid to a graph can help the viewer identify the data points. To show a grid, call

```
pyplot.grid("on")
```

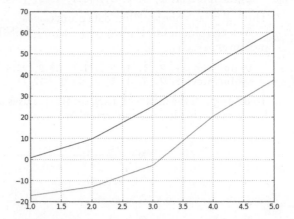

By default, matplotlib automatically chooses limits for the x- and y-axes that include all data points. To change the limits, for example, to increase the padding, or to choose a range that is more appropriate for your data, use the xlim and ylim functions and pass the minimum and maximum of the desired range:

```
pyplot.xlim(0.5, 5.5)
pyplot.ylim(-40, 100)
```

Table 9 Color Codes, Line Styles, and Marker Types

Character	Color Code	Character	Line Style	Character	Marker Type
b	Blue	-	Solid	.	Point marker
g	Green	--	Dashed	o	Circle marker
r	Red	:	Dotted	v	Triangle down marker
c	Cyan	-.	Alternating dashes and dots	^	Triangle up marker
m	Magenta			s	Square marker
y	Yellow			*	Star marker
k	Black			D	Diamond marker
w	White				

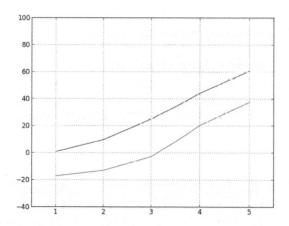

Graphs typically contain descriptive information that helps viewers understand what they are seeing. At a minimum, this information should include a title and labels for both axes.

```
pyplot.title("Average Temperatures in Fairbanks")
pyplot.xlabel("Month")
pyplot.ylabel("Temperature")
```

For graphs that contain more than one line, add a legend that describes the lines. After plotting the lines, call the legend function and provide a list of descriptions:

```
pyplot.legend(["High", "Low"])
```

The first string in the list will be associated with the first line, the second string with the second line, and so on.

You can also change the labels of the "tick marks" along the axes. For example, in our graph, it is helpful to label the months. Call the xticks or yticks function and supply two lists, the first with the tick locations and the second with the labels. Figure 12 shows the result of the following command for a line graph of temperature data for twelve months in Fairbanks.

```
pyplot.xticks(
  [1, 2, 3, 4, 5, 6, 7, 8, 9, 10, 11, 12],
  ["Jan", "Feb", "Mar", "Apr", "May", "Jun",
    "Jul", "Aug", "Sep", "Oct", "Nov", "Dec"])
```

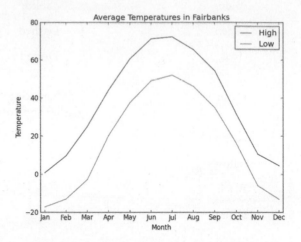

Figure 12   A Line Graph of Temperature Data

Here is the program that constructs the graph in Figure 12.

toolbox_2/linegraph.py

```
 1  ##
 2  #  This program creates a simple line graph that illustrates many
 3  #  of the features of the matplotlib module.
 4  #
 5
 6  from matplotlib import pyplot
 7
 8  # Plot data on the graph.
 9  pyplot.plot([1, 2, 3, 4, 5, 6, 7, 8, 9, 10, 11, 12],
10     [1.1, 10.0, 25.4, 44.5, 61.0, 71.6, 72.7, 65.9, 54.6, 31.9, 10.9, 4.8])
11  pyplot.plot([1, 2, 3, 4, 5, 6, 7, 8, 9, 10, 11, 12],
12     [-16.9, -12.7, -2.5, 20.6, 37.8, 49.3, 52.3, 46.4, 35.1, 16.5, -5.7, -12.9])
13
14  # Change the x limits to give some padding
15  pyplot.xlim(0.8, 12.2)
16
17  # Add descriptive information.
18  pyplot.title("Average Temperatures in Fairbanks")
19  pyplot.xlabel("Month")
20  pyplot.ylabel("Temperature")
21  pyplot.legend(["High", "Low"])
22
23  pyplot.xticks(
24     [1, 2, 3, 4, 5, 6, 7, 8, 9, 10, 11, 12],
25     ["Jan", "Feb", "Mar", "Apr", "May", "Jun",
26        "Jul", "Aug", "Sep", "Oct", "Nov", "Dec"])
27
28  # Display the graph.
29  pyplot.show()
```

Table 10 Plotting Functions

Function	Description
`pyplot.bar(`*x-value*`, `*y-value*`)` `pyplot.bar([`*x-values*`], [`*y-values*`])`	Plots a single bar on the graph or multiple bars when the *x*- and *y*-values are provided as lists.
`pyplot.plot([`*x-coords*`], [`*y-coords*`])` `pyplot.plot([`*x-coords*`], [`*y-coords*`], `*format*`)`	Plots a line graph. The color and style of the line can be specified with a format string.
`pyplot.grid("on")`	Adds a grid to the graph.
`pyplot.xlim(`*min*`, `*max*`)` `pyplot.ylim(`*min*`, `*max*`)`	Sets the range of *x*- or *y*-values shown on the graph.
`pyplot.title(`*text*`)`	Adds a title to the graph.
`pyplot.xlabel(`*text*`)` `pyplot.ylabel(`*text*`)`	Adds a label below the *x*-axis or to the left of the *y*-axis.
`pyplot.legend([`$label_1$`, `$label_2$`, ...])`	Adds a legend for multiple lines.
`pyplot.xticks([`$x\text{-}coord_1$`, `$x\text{-}coord_2$`, ...],` `            [`$label_1$`, `$label_2$`, ...])`	Adds labels below the tick marks along the *x*-axis.
`pyplot.yticks([`$y\text{-}coord_1$`, `$y\text{-}coord_2$`, ...],` `            [`$label_1$`, `$label_2$`, ...])`	Adds labels to the left of the tick marks along the *y*-axis.
`pyplot.show()`	Displays the plot.

CHAPTER SUMMARY

Use the `if` statement to implement a decision.

- The `if` statement allows a program to carry out different actions depending on the nature of the data to be processed.
- Compound statements consist of a header and a statement block.
- Statements in a statement block must be indented to the same level.

Implement comparisons of numbers and strings.

- Use relational operators (< <= > >= == !=) to compare numbers and strings.
- The relational operators compare strings in lexicographic order.

Implement decisions whose branches require further decisions.

- When a decision statement is contained inside the branch of another decision statement, the statements are *nested.*
- Nested decisions are required for problems that have multiple levels of decision making.

Implement complex decisions that require multiple `if` statements.

- Multiple `if` statements can be combined to evaluate complex decisions.
- When using multiple `if` statements, test general conditions after more specific conditions.

Draw flowcharts for visualizing the control flow of a program.

- Flowcharts are made up of elements for tasks, input/output, and decisions.
- Each branch of a decision can contain tasks and further decisions.
- Never point an arrow inside another branch.

Condition   True

False

Design test cases for your programs.

- Each branch of your program should be covered by a test case.
- It is a good idea to design test cases before implementing a program.

Use the Boolean data type to store and combine conditions that can be true or false.

- The Boolean type `bool` has two values, `False` and `True`.
- Python has two Boolean operators that combine conditions: `and` and `or`.
- To invert a condition, use the `not` operator.
- The `and` and `or` operators are computed using *short-circuit evaluation:* As soon as the truth value is determined, no further conditions are evaluated.
- De Morgan's law tells you how to negate `and` and `or` conditions.

Examine strings for specific characteristics.

- Use the `in` operator to test whether a string occurs in another.

Apply `if` statements to detect whether user input is valid.

- If the user provides an input that is not in the expected range, print an error message and don't process the input.

REVIEW EXERCISES

■ **R3.1** What is the value of each variable after the if statement?

a.
```
n = 1
k = 2
r = n
if k < n :
    r = k
```

b.
```
n = 1
k = 2
if n < k :
    r = k
else :
    r = k + n
```

c.
```
n = 1
k = 2
r = k
if r < k :
    n = r
else :
    k = n
```

d.
```
n = 1
k = 2
r = 3
if r < n + k :
    r = 2 * n
else :
    k = 2 * r
```

■■ **R3.2** Explain the difference between

```
s = 0
if x > 0 :
    s = s + 1
if y > 0 :
    s = s + 1
```

and

```
s = 0
if x > 0 :
    s = s + 1
elif y > 0 :
    s = s + 1
```

■■ **R3.3** Find the errors in the following if statements.

a.
```
if x > 0 then
    print(x)
```

b.
```
if 1 + x > x ** sqrt(2) :
    y = y + x
```

c.
```
if x = 1 :
    y += 1
```

d.
```
xStr = input("Enter an integer value")
x = int(xStr)
if xStr.isdigit() :
    sum = sum + x
else :
    print("Bad input for x")
```

```
     e. letterGrade = "F"
        if grade >= 90 :
            letterGrade = "A"
        if grade >= 80 :
            letterGrade = "B"
        if grade >= 70 :
            letterGrade = "C"
        if grade >= 60 :
            letterGrade = "D"
```

■ **R3.4** What do these code fragments print?

```
   a. n = 1
      m = -1
      if n < -m :
          print(n)
      else :
          print(m)
```

```
   b. n = 1
      m = -1
      if -n >= m :
          print(n)
      else :
          print(m)
```

```
   c. x = 0.0
      y = 1.0
      if abs(x - y) < 1 :
          print(x)
      else :
          print(y)
```

```
   d. x = sqrt(2.0)
      y = 2.0
      if x * x == y :
          print(x)
      else :
          print(y)
```

■■ **R3.5** Suppose x and y are variables, each of which contains a number. Write a code fragment that sets y to x if x is positive and to 0 otherwise.

■■ **R3.6** Suppose x and y are variables, each of which contains a number. Write a code fragment that sets y to the absolute value of x without calling the abs function. Use an if statement.

■■ **R3.7** Explain why it is more difficult to compare floating-point numbers than integers. Write Python code to test whether an integer n equals 10 and whether a floating-point number x is approximately equal to 10.

■ **R3.8** It is easy to confuse the = and == operators. Write a test program containing the statement

```
   if floor = 13
```

What error message do you get? Write another test program containing the statement

```
   count == 0
```

What happens when you run the program?

■■ R3.9 Each square on a chess board can be described by a letter and number, such as g5 in this example:

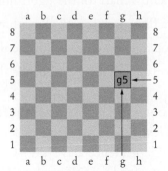

The following pseudocode describes an algorithm that determines whether a square with a given letter and number is dark (black) or light (white).

> *If the letter is an a, c, e, or g*
>   *If the number is odd*
>   *color = "black"*
>   *Else*
>   *color = "white"*
> *Else*
>   *If the number is even*
>   *color = "black"*
>   *Else*
>   *color = "white"*

Using the procedure in Programming Tip 3.2, trace this pseudocode with input g5.

■■ R3.10 Give a set of four test cases for the algorithm of Exercise ●● R3.9 that covers all branches.

■■ R3.11 In a scheduling program, we want to check whether two appointments overlap. For simplicity, appointments start at a full hour, and we use military time (with hours 0–23). The following pseudocode describes an algorithm that determines whether the appointment with start time *start1* and end time *end1* overlaps with the appointment with start time *start2* and end time *end2*.

> *If start1 > start2*
>   *s = start1*
> *Else*
>   *s = start2*
> *If end1 < end2*
>   *e = end1*
> *Else*
>   *e = end2*
> *If s < e*
>   *The appointments overlap.*
> *Else*
>   *The appointments don't overlap.*

Trace this algorithm with an appointment from 10–12 and one from 11–13, then with an appointment from 10–11 and one from 12–13.

- **R3.12** Draw a flowchart for the algorithm in Exercise •• R3.11.

- **R3.13** Draw a flowchart for the algorithm in Exercise •• P3.18.

- **R3.14** Draw a flowchart for the algorithm in Exercise •• P3.20.

- ■ **R3.15** Develop a set of test cases for the algorithm in Exercise •• R3.11.

- ■ **R3.16** Develop a set of test cases for the algorithm in Exercise •• P3.20.

- ■ **R3.17** Write pseudocode for a program that prompts the user for a month and day and prints out whether it is one of the following four holidays:
  - New Year's Day (January 1)
  - Independence Day (July 4)
  - Veterans Day (November 11)
  - Christmas Day (December 25)

- ■ **R3.18** Write pseudocode for a program that assigns letter grades for a quiz, according to the following table:

  ```
  Score    Grade
  90-100     A
  80-89      B
  70-79      C
  60-69      D
  < 60       F
  ```

- ■ **R3.19** Explain how the lexicographic ordering of strings in Python differs from the ordering of words in a dictionary or telephone book. *Hint:* Consider strings such as IBM, wiley.com, Century 21, and While-U-Wait.

- ■ **R3.20** Of the following pairs of strings, which comes first in lexicographic order?
  - **a.** `"Tom"`, `"Jerry"`
  - **b.** `"Tom"`, `"Tomato"`
  - **c.** `"church"`, `"Churchill"`
  - **d.** `"car manufacturer"`, `"carburetor"`
  - **e.** `"Harry"`, `"hairy"`
  - **f.** `"Python"`, `" Car"`
  - **g.** `"Tom"`, `"Tom"`
  - **h.** `"Car"`, `"Carl"`
  - **i.** `"car"`, `"bar"`

- ■ **R3.21** Explain the difference between an `if`/`elif`/`else` sequence and nested `if` statements. Give an example of each.

- ■ **R3.22** Give an example of an `if`/`elif`/`else` sequence where the order of the tests does not matter. Give an example where the order of the tests matters.

- ■ **R3.23** Rewrite the condition in Section 3.4 to use `<` operators instead of `>=` operators. What is the impact on the order of the comparisons?

- ■ **R3.24** Give a set of test cases for the tax program in Exercise ••• P3.25. Manually compute the expected results.

- ■ ■ **R3.25** Complete the following truth table by finding the truth values of the Boolean expressions for all combinations of the Boolean inputs p, q, and r.

p	q	r	(p and q) or not r	not (p and (q or not r))
False	False	False		
False	False	True		
False	True	False		
. . .				
5 more combinations				
. . .				

■■■ R3.26 True or false? *A* and *B* is the same as *B* and *A* for any Boolean conditions *A* and *B*.

■ R3.27 The "advanced search" feature of many search engines allows you to use Boolean operators for complex queries, such as "(cats OR dogs) AND NOT pets". Contrast these search operators with the Boolean operators in Python.

■■ R3.28 Suppose the value of b is False and the value of x is 0. What is the value of each of the following expressions?

a. b and x == 0   **e.** b and x != 0
b. b or x == 0   **f.** b or x != 0
c. not b and x == 0   **g.** not b and x != 0
d. not b or x == 0   **h.** not b or x != 0

■■ R3.29 Simplify the following expressions. Here, b is a variable of type bool.

a. b == True
b. b == False
c. b != True
d. b != False

■■■ R3.30 Simplify the following statements. Here, b is a variable that contains a Boolean value and n is a variable that contains an integer value.

a.
```
if n == 0 :
    b = True
else :
    b = False
```

b.
```
if n == 0 :
    b = False
else :
    b = True
```

c.
```
b = False
if n > 1 :
    if n < 2 :
        b = True
```

d.
```
if n < 1 :
    b = True
else :
    b = n > 2
```

■ **R3.31** What is wrong with the following program?

```
inputStr = input("Enter the number of quarters: ")
quarters = int(inputStr)
if inputStr.isdigit() :
    total = quarters * 0.25
    print("Total: ", total)
else :
    print("Input error.")
```

■ **Toolbox R3.32** How do you show a bar graph that displays the values of the first four square numbers (1, 4, 9, 16)?

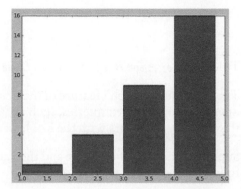

■ **Toolbox R3.33** The graph in Exercise • Toolbox R3.32 has tick marks on the *x*-axis at 1.0, 1.5, 2.0, 2.5, …. What can you do to get tick marks at 1, 2, 3, and 4?

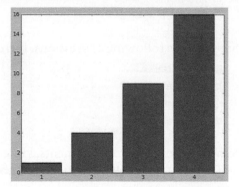

■ **Toolbox R3.34** In the graph of Exercise • Toolbox R3.32, the axes are scaled to contain the data points, so it looks like the values grow more slowly than they do. How can you accurately display the growth?

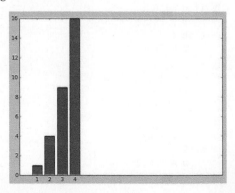

- **Toolbox R3.35** What does the following call produce?

    ```
    pyplot.plot([1, 2, 3, 4, 5], [1.1, 10.0, 25.4, 44.5, 61.0], "ro")
    ```

- **Toolbox R3.36** How can you draw the red markers of Exercise • Toolbox R3.35 on top of a green line?

PROGRAMMING EXERCISES

- **P3.1** Write a program that reads an integer and prints whether it is negative, zero, or positive.

- **P3.2** Write a program that reads a floating-point number and prints "zero" if the number is zero. Otherwise, print "positive" or "negative". Add "small" if the absolute value of the number is less than 1, or "large" if it exceeds 1,000,000.

- **P3.3** Write a program that reads an integer and prints how many digits the number has, by checking whether the number is ≥ 10, ≥ 100, and so on. (Assume that all integers are less than ten billion.) If the number is negative, first multiply it by –1.

- **P3.4** Write a program that reads three numbers and prints "all the same" if they are all the same, "all different" if they are all different, and "neither" otherwise.

- **P3.5** Write a program that reads three numbers and prints "increasing" if they are in increasing order, "decreasing" if they are in decreasing order, and "neither" otherwise. Here, "increasing" means "strictly increasing", with each value larger than its predecessor. The sequence 3 4 4 would not be considered increasing.

- **P3.6** Repeat Exercise •• P3.5, but before reading the numbers, ask the user whether increasing/decreasing should be "strict" or "lenient". In lenient mode, the sequence 3 4 4 is increasing and the sequence 4 4 4 is both increasing and decreasing.

- **P3.7** Write a program that reads in three integers and prints "in order" if they are sorted in ascending *or* descending order, or "not in order" otherwise. For example,

    ```
    1 2 5   in order
    1 5 2   not in order
    5 2 1   in order
    1 2 2   in order
    ```

- **P3.8** Write a program that reads four integers and prints "two pairs" if the input consists of two matching pairs (in some order) and "not two pairs" otherwise. For example,

    ```
    1 2 2 1   two pairs
    1 2 2 3   not two pairs
    2 2 2 2   two pairs
    ```

- **P3.9** Write a program that reads a temperature value and the letter C for Celsius or F for Fahrenheit. Print whether water is liquid, solid, or gaseous at the given temperature at sea level.

- **P3.10** The boiling point of water drops by about one degree Celsius for every 300 meters (or 1,000 feet) of altitude. Improve the program of Exercise • P3.9 to allow the user to supply the altitude in meters or feet.

- **P3.11** Add error handling to Exercise • P3.10. If the user provides an invalid unit for the altitude, print an error message and end the program.

■■ **P3.12** Write a program that translates a letter grade into a number grade. Letter grades are A, B, C, D, and F, possibly followed by + or –. Their numeric values are 4, 3, 2, 1, and 0. There is no F+ or F–. A + increases the numeric value by 0.3, a – decreases it by 0.3. However, an A+ has value 4.0.

```
Enter a letter grade: B-
The numeric value is 2.7.
```

■■ **P3.13** Write a program that translates a number between 0 and 4 into the closest letter grade. For example, the number 2.8 (which might have been the average of several grades) would be converted to B–. Break ties in favor of the better grade; for example 2.85 should be a B.

■■ **P3.14** Write a program that takes user input describing a playing card in the following shorthand notation:

```
A          Ace
2 ... 10   Card values
J          Jack
Q          Queen
K          King
D          Diamonds
H          Hearts
S          Spades
C          Clubs
```

Your program should print the full description of the card. For example,

```
Enter the card notation: QS
Queen of Spades
```

■■ **P3.15** Write a program that reads in three floating-point numbers and prints the largest of the three inputs without using the max function. For example:

```
Enter a number: 4
Enter a number: 9
Enter a number: 2.5
The largest number is 9.0
```

■■ **P3.16** Write a program that reads in three strings and sorts them lexicographically.

```
Enter a string: Charlie
Enter a string: Able
Enter a string: Baker
Able
Baker
Charlie
```

■■ **P3.17** Write a program that reads in a string and prints whether it

- contains only letters.
- contains only uppercase letters.
- contains only lowercase letters.
- contains only digits.
- contains only letters and digits.
- starts with an uppercase letter.
- ends with a period.

•• P3.18 When two points in time are compared, each given as hours (in military time, ranging from 0 to 23) and minutes, the following pseudocode determines which comes first.

> *If hour1 < hour2*
>   *time1 comes first.*
> *Else if hour1 and hour2 are the same*
>   *If minute1 < minute2*
>   *time1 comes first.*
>   *Else if minute1 and minute2 are the same*
>   *time1 and time2 are the same.*
>   *Else*
>   *time2 comes first.*
> *Else*
>   *time2 comes first.*

Write a program that prompts the user for two points in time and prints the time that comes first, then the other time.

• P3.19 Write a program that prompts the user to provide a single character from the alphabet. Print Vowel or Consonant, depending on the user input. If the user input is not a letter (between a and z or A and Z), or is a string of length > 1, print an error message.

•• P3.20 The following algorithm yields the season (Spring, Summer, Fall, or Winter) for a given month and day.

> *If month is 1, 2, or 3, season = "Winter"*
> *Else if month is 4, 5, or 6, season = "Spring"*
> *Else if month is 7, 8, or 9, season = "Summer"*
> *Else if month is 10, 11, or 12, season = "Fall"*
> *If month is divisible by 3 and day >= 21*
>   *If season is "Winter", season = "Spring"*
>   *Else if season is "Spring", season = "Summer"*
>   *Else if season is "Summer", season = "Fall"*
>   *Else season = "Winter"*

© rotofrank/iStockphoto.

Write a program that prompts the user for a month and day and then prints the season, as determined by this algorithm.

•• P3.21 Write a program that reads in two floating-point numbers and tests whether they are the same up to two decimal places. Here are two sample runs.

```
Enter a floating-point number: 2.0
Enter a floating-point number: 1.99998
They are the same up to two decimal places.
Enter a floating-point number: 2.0
Enter a floating-point number: 1.98999
They are different.
```

•• P3.22 Write a program that prompts for the day and month of the user's birthday and then prints a horoscope. Make up fortunes for programmers, like this:

```
Please enter your birthday.
  month: 6
  day: 16
Gemini are experts at figuring out the behavior
of complicated programs. You feel where bugs are
coming from and then stay one step ahead. Tonight,
your style wins approval from a tough critic.
```

Each fortune should contain the name of the astrological sign. (You will find the sign names and date ranges at a distressingly large number of sites on the Internet.)

© lillisphotography/iStockphoto.

•• P3.23 The original U.S. income tax of 1913 was quite simple. The tax was

- 1 percent on the first $50,000.
- 2 percent on the amount over $50,000 up to $75,000.
- 3 percent on the amount over $75,000 up to $100,000.
- 4 percent on the amount over $100,000 up to $250,000.
- 5 percent on the amount over $250,000 up to $500,000.
- 6 percent on the amount over $500,000.

There was no separate schedule for single or married taxpayers. Write a program that computes the income tax according to this schedule.

••• P3.24 The taxes.py program uses a simplified version of the 2008 U.S. income tax schedule. Look up the tax brackets and rates for the current year, for both single and married filers, and implement a program that computes the actual income tax.

••• P3.25 Write a program that computes taxes for the following schedule.

If your status is Single and if the taxable income is over	but not over	the tax is	of the amount over
$0	$8,000	10%	$0
$8,000	$32,000	$800 + 15%	$8,000
$32,000		$4,400 + 25%	$32,000
If your status is Married and if the taxable income is over	but not over	the tax is	of the amount over
$0	$16,000	10%	$0
$16,000	$64,000	$1,600 + 15%	$16,000
$64,000		$8,800 + 25%	$64,000

••• P3.26 *Unit conversion.* Write a unit conversion program that asks the users from which unit they want to convert (fl. oz, gal, oz, lb, in, ft, mi) and to which unit they want to convert (ml, l, g, kg, mm, cm, m, km). Reject incompatible conversions (such as gal km). Ask for the value to be converted, then display the result:

```
Convert from? gal
Convert to? ml
Value? 2.5
2.5 gal = 9463.5 ml
```

■■■ P3.27 A year with 366 days is called a leap year. Leap years are necessary to keep the calendar synchronized with the sun because the earth revolves around the sun once every 365.25 days. Actually, that figure is not entirely precise, and for all dates after 1582 the *Gregorian correction* applies. Usually years that are divisible by 4 are leap years (for example, 1996). However, years that are divisible by 100 (for example, 1900) are not leap years, but years that are divisible by 400 are leap years (for example, 2000). Write a program that asks the user for a year and computes whether that year is a leap year. Use a single if statement and Boolean operators.

■■■ P3.28 *Roman numbers.* Write a program that converts a positive integer into the Roman number system. The Roman number system has digits

I	1
V	5
X	10
L	50
C	100
D	500
M	1,000

© Charles Schultz/iStockphoto.

Numbers are formed according to the following rules.

a. Only numbers up to 3,999 are represented.

b. As in the decimal system, the thousands, hundreds, tens, and ones are expressed separately.

c. The numbers 1 to 9 are expressed as

I	1
II	2
III	3
IV	4
V	5
VI	6
VII	7
VIII	8
IX	9

As you can see, an I preceding a V or X is subtracted from the value, and you can never have more than three I's in a row.

d. Tens and hundreds are done the same way, except that the letters X, L, C and C, D, M are used instead of I, V, X, respectively.

Your program should take an input, such as 1978, and convert it to Roman numerals, MCMLXXVIII.

••• **P3.29**   Write a program that asks the user to enter a month (1 for January, 2 for February, and so on) and then prints the number of days in the month. For February, print "28 or 29 days".

```
Enter a month: 5
30 days
```

Do not use a separate if/else branch for each month. Use Boolean operators.

••• **P3.30**   French country names are feminine when they end with the letter e, masculine otherwise, except for the following which are masculine even though they end with e:

- le Belize
- le Cambodge
- le Mexique
- le Mozambique
- le Zaïre
- le Zimbabwe

Write a program that reads the French name of a country and adds the article: le for masculine or la for feminine, such as le Canada or la Belgique.

However, if the country name starts with a vowel, use l'; for example, l'Afghanistan.

For the following plural country names, use les:

- les Etats-Unis
- les Pays-Bas

•• **Toolbox P3.31**   Add curves for the average high and low temperatures in your hometown to the line graph program in Toolbox 3.2.

• **Toolbox P3.32**   You can change the color of a bar in a bar chart by calling

```
pyplot.bar(x, y, color="...")
```

Valid color strings are listed in Table 9. Use pyplot with this option to create a vertical version of the bar chart in Section 2.6.3.

••• **Toolbox P3.33**   Repeat Exercise P2.31 using pyplot to create the bar chart.

•• **Toolbox P3.34**   Change the color of the bar chart in Toolbox 3.2. Draw bars that stay below 32 degrees in blue, the others in yellow.

••• **Toolbox P3.35**   You can change the width of a bar in a bar chart by calling

```
pyplot.bar(x, y, width="...")
```

Use this option to produce a graph with two sets of bars (with a different color for the low and high temperatures) using the Fairbanks data from Toolbox 3.2, as shown here.

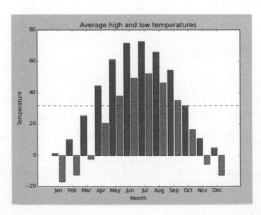

■■ **Toolbox P3.36** The pie command in the pyplot module draws a pie chart. You supply a list of the values. Draw a pie chart of the areas of all continents. Provide a legend for the chart as described in Toolbox 3.2.

■■■ **Business P3.37** Write a program to simulate a bank transaction. There are two bank accounts: checking and savings. First, ask for the initial balances of the bank accounts; reject negative balances. Then ask for the transaction; options are deposit, withdrawal, and transfer. Then ask for the account; options are checking and savings. Then ask for the amount; reject transactions that overdraw an account. At the end, print the balances of both accounts.

■■ **Business P3.38** Write a program that reads in the name and salary of an employee. Here the salary will denote an *hourly* wage, such as $9.25. Then ask how many hours the employee worked in the past week. Be sure to accept fractional hours. Compute the pay. Any overtime work (over 40 hours per week) is paid at 150 percent of the regular wage. Print a paycheck for the employee.

■■ **Business P3.39** When you use an automated teller machine (ATM) with your bank card, you need to use a personal identification number (PIN) to access your account. If a user fails more than three times when entering the PIN, the machine will block the card. Assume that the user's PIN is "1234" and write a program that asks the user for the PIN no more than three times, and does the following:

© Mark Evans/iStockphoto.

- If the user enters the right number, print a message saying, "Your PIN is correct", and end the program.
- If the user enters a wrong number, print a message saying, "Your PIN is incorrect" and, if you have asked for the PIN less than three times, ask for it again.
- If the user enters a wrong number three times, print a message saying "Your bank card is blocked" and end the program.

■ **Business P3.40** A supermarket awards coupons depending on how much a customer spends on groceries. For example, if you spend $50, you will get a coupon worth eight percent of that amount. The following table shows the percent used to calculate the coupon awarded for different amounts spent. Write a program that calculates and prints the value of the coupon a person can receive based on groceries purchased.

Here is a sample run:

```
Please enter the cost of your groceries: 14
You win a discount coupon of $ 1.12. (8% of your purchase)
```

Money Spent	Coupon Percentage
Less than $10	No coupon
From $10 to $60	8%
More than $60 to $150	10%
More than $150 to $210	12%
More than $210	14%

■ **Business P3.41** Calculating the tip when you go to a restaurant is not difficult, but your restaurant wants to suggest a tip according to the service diners receive. Write a program that calculates a tip according to the diner's satisfaction as follows:

- Ask for the diners' satisfaction level using these ratings: 1 = Totally satisfied, 2 = Satisfied, 3 = Dissatisfied.
- If the diner is totally satisfied, calculate a 20 percent tip.
- If the diner is satisfied, calculate a 15 percent tip.
- If the diner is dissatisfied, calculate a 10 percent tip.
- Report the satisfaction level and tip in dollars and cents.

■ **Graphics P3.42** Modify the program in Worked Example 3.2 to use the getMouse method to obtain the center coordinates of the two circles.

■ **Science P3.43** Write a program that prompts the user for a wavelength value and prints a description of the corresponding part of the electromagnetic spectrum, as given in Table 11.

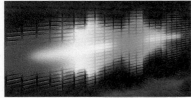

© drxy/iStockphoto.

Table 11 Electromagnetic Spectrum		
Type	Wavelength (m)	Frequency (Hz)
Radio Waves	$> 10^{-1}$	$< 3 \times 10^{9}$
Microwaves	10^{-3} to 10^{-1}	3×10^{9} to 3×10^{11}
Infrared	7×10^{-7} to 10^{-3}	3×10^{11} to 4×10^{14}
Visible light	4×10^{-7} to 7×10^{-7}	4×10^{14} to 7.5×10^{14}
Ultraviolet	10^{-8} to 4×10^{-7}	7.5×10^{14} to 3×10^{16}
X-rays	10^{-11} to 10^{-8}	3×10^{16} to 3×10^{19}
Gamma rays	$< 10^{-11}$	$> 3 \times 10^{19}$

■ **Science P3.44** Repeat Exercise • Science P3.43, modifying the program so that it prompts for the frequency instead.

■■ **Science P3.45** Repeat Exercise • Science P3.43, modifying the program so that it first asks the user whether the input will be a wavelength or a frequency.

■■■ **Science P3.46** A minivan has two sliding doors. Each door can be opened by either a dashboard switch, its inside handle, or its outside handle. However, the inside handles do not work if a child lock switch is activated. In order for the sliding doors to open, the gear shift must be in park, *and* the master unlock switch must be activated. (This book's author is the long-suffering owner of just such a vehicle.)

© nano/iStockphoto.

Your task is to simulate a portion of the control software for the vehicle. The input is a sequence of values for the switches and the gear shift, in the following order:

- Dashboard switches for left and right sliding door, child lock, and master unlock (0 for off or 1 for activated)
- Inside and outside handles on the left and right sliding doors (0 or 1)
- The gear shift setting (one of P N D 1 2 3 R).

A typical input would be 0 0 0 1 0 1 0 0 P.

Print "left door opens" and/or "right door opens" as appropriate. If neither door opens, print "both doors stay closed".

■ **Science P3.47** Sound level L in units of decibel (dB) is determined by

$$L = 20 \log_{10}(p/p_0)$$

where p is the sound pressure of the sound (in Pascals, abbreviated Pa), and p_0 is a reference sound pressure equal to 20×10^{-6} Pa (where L is 0 dB).

The following table gives descriptions for certain sound levels.

© Photobuff/iStockphoto.

Threshold of pain	130 dB
Possible hearing damage	120 dB
Jack hammer at 1 m	100 dB
Traffic on a busy roadway at 10 m	90 dB
Normal conversation	60 dB
Calm library	30 dB
Light leaf rustling	0 dB

Write a program that reads a value and a unit, either dB or Pa, and then prints the closest description from the list above.

■■ **Science P3.48** The electric circuit shown below is designed to measure the temperature of the gas in a chamber.

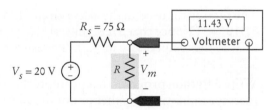

The resistor R represents a temperature sensor enclosed in the chamber. The resistance R, in Ω, is related to the temperature T, in °C, by the equation

$$R = R_0 + kT$$

In this device, assume $R_0 = 100 \ \Omega$ and $k = 0.5$. The voltmeter displays the value of the voltage, V_m, across the sensor. This voltage V_m indicates the temperature, T, of the gas according to the equation

$$T = \frac{R}{k} - \frac{R_0}{k} = \frac{R_s}{k} \frac{V_m}{V_s - V_m} - \frac{R_0}{k}$$

Suppose the voltmeter voltage is constrained to the range $V_{\min} = 12$ volts $\leq V_m \leq V_{\max} = 18$ volts. Write a program that accepts a value of V_m and checks that it's between 12 and 18. The program should return the gas temperature in degrees Celsius when V_m is between 12 and 18 and an error message when it isn't.

■■■ **Science P3.49**

© rotofrank/iStockphoto.

Crop damage due to frost is one of the many risks confronting farmers. The figure below shows a simple alarm circuit designed to warn of frost. The alarm circuit uses a device called a thermistor to sound a buzzer when the temperature drops below freezing. Thermistors are semiconductor devices that exhibit a temperature dependent resistance described by the equation

$$R = R_0 e^{\beta\left(\frac{1}{T} - \frac{1}{T_0}\right)}$$

where R is the resistance, in Ω, at the temperature T, in °K, and R_0 is the resistance, in Ω, at the temperature T_0, in °K. β is a constant that depends on the material used to make the thermistor.

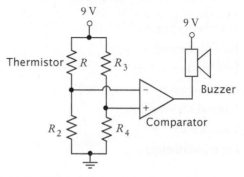

The circuit is designed so that the alarm will sound when

$$\frac{R_2}{R + R_2} < \frac{R_4}{R_3 + R_4}$$

The thermistor used in the alarm circuit has $R_0 = 33{,}192\ \Omega$ at $T_0 = 40\ °C$, and $\beta = 3{,}310\ °K$. (Notice that β has units of °K. The temperature in °K is obtained by adding 273° to the temperature in °C.) The resistors R_2, R_3, and R_4 have a resistance of 156.3 k$\Omega = 156{,}300\ \Omega$.

Write a Python program that prompts the user for a temperature in °F and prints a message indicating whether or not the alarm will sound at that temperature.

■ **Science P3.50** A mass $m = 2$ kilograms is attached to the end of a rope of length $r = 3$ meters. The mass is whirled around at high speed. The rope can withstand a maximum tension of $T = 60$ Newtons. Write a program that accepts a rotation speed v and determines whether such a speed will cause the rope to break. *Hint:* $T = mv^2/r$.

■ **Science P3.51** A mass m is attached to the end of a rope of length $r = 3$ meters. The rope can only be whirled around at speeds of 1, 10, 20, or 40 meters per second. The rope can withstand a maximum tension of $T = 60$ Newtons. Write a program where the user enters the value of the mass m, and the program determines the greatest speed at which it can be whirled without breaking the rope. *Hint:* $T = mv^2/r$.

■■ Science P3.52 The average person can jump off the ground with a velocity of 7 mph without fear of leaving the planet. However, if an astronaut jumps with this velocity while standing on Halley's Comet, will the astronaut ever come back down? Create a program that allows the user to input a launch velocity (in mph) from the surface of Halley's Comet and determine whether a jumper will return to the surface. If not, the program should calculate how much more massive the comet must be in order to return the jumper to the surface.

NASA/JPL-Caltech.

Hint: Escape velocity is $v_{escape} = \sqrt{2\dfrac{GM}{R}}$, where $G = 6.67 \times 10^{-11} N\,m^2/kg^2$ is the gravitational constant, M is the mass of the heavenly body, and R is its radius. Halley's comet has a mass of 2.2×10^{14} kg and a diameter of 9.4 km.

■ Toolbox P3.53 Modify the program in Toolbox 3.1 so that it copies the professor on all messages.

■ Toolbox P3.54 Modify the program in Toolbox 3.1 so that it "blind copies" the tutoring lab for students in need of tutoring. Provide the address of the lab (such as cs-tutoring-lab@ mycollege.edu) as a constant string in your program.

■■ Toolbox P3.55 Modify the program in Toolbox 3.1 so that it adds an image (goldstar.jpg) for students with a score of at least 90 or a map to the tutoring center (tutoring.jpg) for those with a score of at most 50.

■■ Toolbox P3.56 Modify the program in Toolbox 3.1 to prompt whether to attach a file to the message. If so, prompt for the file location and attach it.

LOOPS

© photo75/iStockphoto.

In a loop, a part of a program is repeated over and over, until a specific goal is reached. Loops are important for calculations that require repeated steps and for processing input consisting of many data items. In this chapter, you will learn about loop statements in Python, as well as techniques for writing programs that process input and simulate activities in the real world.

4.1 The while Loop

In this section, you will learn about *loop statements* that repeatedly execute instructions until a goal has been reached.

Recall the investment problem from Chapter 1. You put $10,000 into a bank account that earns 5 percent interest per year. How many years does it take for the account balance to be double the original investment?

In Chapter 1 we developed the following algorithm for this problem:

© AlterYourReality/iStockphoto.

Because the interest earned also earns interest, a bank balance grows exponentially.

Start with a year value of 0, a column for the interest, and a balance of $10,000.

year	interest	balance
0		$10,000

Repeat the following steps while the balance is less than $20,000.
  Add 1 to the year value.
  Compute the interest as balance x 0.05 (i.e., 5 percent interest).
  Add the interest to the balance.
Report the final year value as the answer.

You now know how to create and update the variables in Python. What you don't yet know is how to carry out "Repeat steps while the balance is less than $20,000".

In a particle accelerator, subatomic particles traverse a loop-shaped tunnel multiple times, gaining the speed required for physical experiments. Similarly, in computer science, statements in a loop are executed while a condition is true.

© mmac72/iStockphoto.

Figure 1 Flowchart of a while Loop

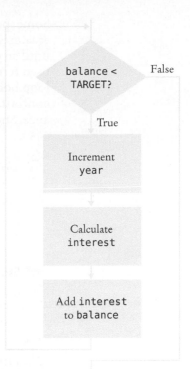

A while loop executes instructions repeatedly while a condition is true.

In Python, the while statement implements such a repetition (see Syntax 4.1). It has the form

```
while condition :
    statements
```

As long as the condition remains true, the statements inside the while statement are executed. This statement block is called the **body** of the while statement.

In our case, we want to increment the year counter and add interest while the balance is less than the target balance of $20,000:

```
while balance < TARGET :
    year = year + 1
    interest = balance * RATE / 100
    balance = balance + interest
```

A while statement is an example of a **loop**. If you draw a flowchart, the flow of execution loops again to the point where the condition is tested (see Figure 1).

It often happens that you want to execute a sequence of statements a given number of times. You can use a while loop that is controlled by a counter, as in the following:

```
counter = 1    # Initialize the counter.
while counter <= 10 :    # Check the counter.
    print(counter)
    counter = counter + 1    # Update the loop variable.
```

Syntax 4.1 while Statement

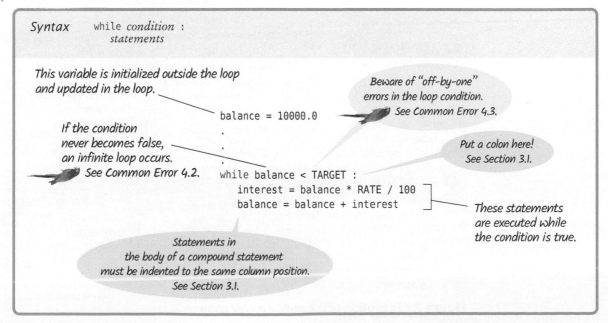

```
Syntax      while condition :
                statements
```

This variable is initialized outside the loop and updated in the loop.

Beware of "off-by-one" errors in the loop condition. See Common Error 4.3.

If the condition never becomes false, an infinite loop occurs. See Common Error 4.2.

```
balance = 10000.0
.
.
.
while balance < TARGET :
    interest = balance * RATE / 100
    balance = balance + interest
```

Put a colon here! See Section 3.1.

These statements are executed while the condition is true.

Statements in the body of a compound statement must be indented to the same column position. See Section 3.1.

Some people call this loop *count-controlled*. In contrast, the `while` loop in the `doubleinv.py` program below can be called an *event-controlled* loop because it executes until an event occurs; namely that the balance reaches the target. Another commonly used term for a count-controlled loop is *definite*. You know from the outset that the loop body will be executed a definite number of times; in our example, ten times. In contrast, you do not know how many iterations it takes to accumulate a target balance. Such a loop is called *indefinite*.

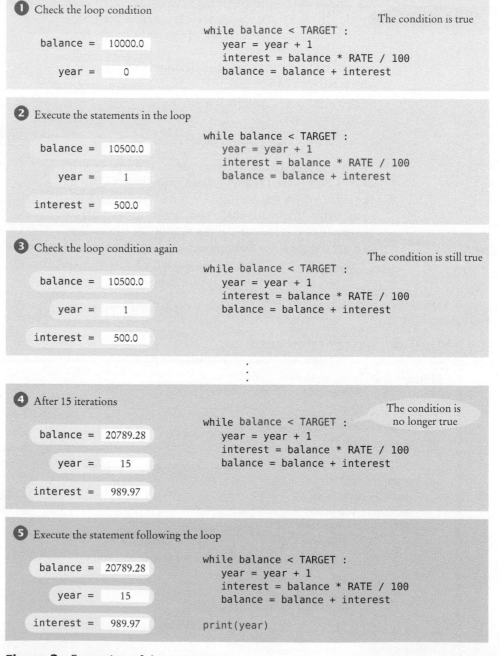

Figure 2   Execution of the `doubleinv.py` Loop

Here is the program that solves the investment problem. Figure 2 illustrates the program's execution.

sec01/doubleinv.py

```
1  ##
2  #   This program computes the time required to double an investment.
3  #
4
5  # Create constant variables.
6  RATE = 5.0
7  INITIAL_BALANCE = 10000.0
8  TARGET = 2 * INITIAL_BALANCE
9
10 # Initialize variables used with the loop.
11 balance = INITIAL_BALANCE
12 year = 0
13
14 # Count the years required for the investment to double.
15 while balance < TARGET :
16     year = year + 1
17     interest = balance * RATE / 100
18     balance = balance + interest
19
20 # Print the results.
21 print("The investment doubled after", year, "years.")
```

Program Run

```
The investment doubled after 15 years.
```

Table 1 shows examples of simple loops.

Table 1 while Loop Examples

Loop	Output	Explanation

`i = 0`
`total = 0`
`while total < 10 :`
`    i = i + 1`
`    total = total + i`
`    print(i, total)`
	1 1
	2 3
	3 6
	4 10
		When total is 10, the loop condition is false, and the loop ends.

`i = 0`
`total = 0`
`while total < 10 :`
`    i = i + 1`
`    total = total - 1`
`    print(i, total)`
	1 -1
	2 -3
	3 -6
	4 -10
	. . .
		Because total never reaches 10, this is an "infinite loop" (see Common Error 4.2).

`i = 0`
`total = 0`
`while total < 0 :`
`    i = i + 1`
`    total = total - i`
`    print(i, total)`
	(No output)	The statement total < 0 is false when the condition is first checked, and the loop is never executed.

Table 1 while Loop Examples

Loop	Output	Explanation

``
i = 0
total = 0
while total >= 10 :
    i = i + 1
    total = total + i
    print(i, total)
``
	(No output)	The programmer probably thought, "Stop when the sum is at least 10." However, the loop condition controls when the loop is executed, not when it ends (see Common Error 4.1).

``
i = 0
total = 0
while total >= 0 :
    i = i + 1
    total = total + i
print(i, total)
``
	(No output, program does not terminate)	Because total will always be greater than or equal to 0, the loop runs forever. It produces no output because the print function is outside the body of the loop, as indicated by the indentation.

Common Error 4.1

Don't Think "Are We There Yet?"

When doing something repetitive, most of us want to know when we are done. For example, you may think, "I want to get at least $20,000," and set the loop condition to

```
balance >= TARGET
```

But the while loop thinks the opposite: How long am I allowed to keep going? The correct loop condition is

```
while balance < TARGET :
```

In other words: "Keep at it while the balance is less than the target."

When writing a loop condition, don't ask, "Are we there yet?" The condition determines how long the loop will keep going.

© MsSponge/iStockphoto.

Common Error 4.2

Infinite Loops

A very annoying loop error is an *infinite loop:* a loop that runs forever and can be stopped only by killing the program or restarting the computer. If there are output statements in the loop, then many lines of output flash by on the screen. Otherwise, the program just sits there and *hangs*, seeming to do nothing. On some systems, you can stop a hanging program by hitting Ctrl + C. On others, you can close the window in which the program runs.

A common reason for infinite loops is forgetting to update the variable that controls the loop:

```
year = 1
while year <= 20 :
    interest = balance * RATE / 100
    balance = balance + interest
```

Here the programmer forgot to add a year = year + 1 command in the loop. As a result, the year always stays at 1, and the loop never comes to an end.

Another common reason for an infinite loop is accidentally incrementing a counter that should be decremented (or vice versa). Consider this example:

```
year = 20
while year > 0 :
    interest = balance * RATE / 100
    balance = balance + interest
    year = year + 1
```

© ohiophoto/iStockphoto.

Like this hamster who can't stop running in the treadmill, an infinite loop never ends.

The year variable really should have been decremented, not incremented. This is a common error because incrementing counters is so much more common than decrementing that your fingers may type the + on autopilot. As a consequence, year is always larger than 0, and the loop never ends.

Common Error 4.3

Off-by-One Errors

Consider our computation of the number of years that are required to double an investment:

```
year = 0
while balance < TARGET :
    year = year + 1
    interest = balance * RATE / 100
    balance = balance + interest
print("The investment doubled after", year, "years.")
```

Should year start at 0 or at 1? Should you test for balance < TARGET or for balance <= TARGET? It is easy to be *off by one* in these expressions.

Some people try to solve **off-by-one errors** by randomly inserting +1 or -1 until the program seems to work, which is a terrible strategy. It can take a long time to test all the various possibilities. Expending a small amount of mental effort is a real time saver.

Fortunately, off-by-one errors are easy to avoid, simply by thinking through a couple of test cases and using the information from the test cases to come up with a rationale for your decisions.

Should year start at 0 or at 1? Look at a scenario with simple values: an initial balance of $100 and an interest rate of 50 percent. After year 1, the balance is $150, and after year 2 it is $225, or over $200. So the investment doubled after 2 years. The loop executed two times, incrementing year each time. Hence year must start at 0, not at 1.

year	balance
0	$100
1	$150
2	$225

In other words, the balance variable denotes the balance after the end of the year. At the outset, the balance variable contains the balance after year 0 and not after year 1.

Next, should you use a < or <= comparison in the test? This is harder to figure out, because it is rare for the balance to be exactly twice the initial balance. There is one case when this happens, namely when the interest rate is 100 percent. The loop executes once. Now year is 1, and balance is exactly equal to 2 * INITIAL_BALANCE. Has the investment doubled after one year? It has. Therefore, the loop should not execute again. If the test condition is balance < TARGET, the loop stops, as it should. If the test condition had been balance <= TARGET, the loop would have executed once more.

In other words, you keep adding interest while the balance *has not yet doubled*.

Special Topic 4.1

Special Form of the print Function

Python provides a special form of the print function that prevents it from starting a new line after its arguments are displayed.

```
print(value₁, value₂, . . ., valueₙ, end="")
```

For example, the output of the two statements

```
print("00", end="")
print(3 + 4)
```

is the single line

```
007
```

By including end="" as the last argument to the first print function, we indicate that an empty string is to be printed after the first argument is displayed instead of starting a new line. The output of the next print function starts on the same line where the previous one left off.

The end="" argument is called a *named argument*. Named arguments allow you to specify the contents of a specific optional argument defined for a function or method. Although named arguments can be used with many of Python's built-in functions and methods, we limit their use in this book to the print function.

Computing & Society 4.1   The First Bug

According to legend, the first bug was found in the Mark II, a huge electromechanical computer at Harvard University. It really was caused by a bug—a moth was trapped in a relay switch.

Actually, from the note that the operator left in the log book next to the moth (see the photo), it appears as if the term "bug" had already been in active use at the time.

The pioneering computer scientist Maurice Wilkes wrote, "Somehow, at the Moore School and afterwards, one had always assumed there would be no particular difficulty in get-ting programs right. I can remember the exact instant in time at which it dawned on me that a great part of my future life would be spent finding mistakes in my own programs."

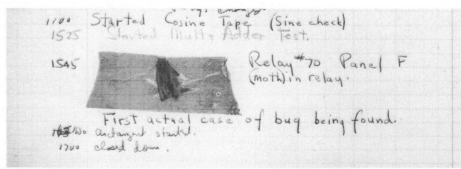

The First Bug   Courtesy of the Naval Surface Warfare Center, Dahlgren, VA, 1988. NHHC Collection.

4.2 Problem Solving: Hand-Tracing

Hand-tracing is a simulation of code execution in which you step through instructions and track the values of the variables.

In Programming Tip 3.2, you learned about the method of hand-tracing. When you hand-trace code or pseudocode, you write the names of the variables on a sheet of paper, mentally execute each step of the code, and update the variables.

It is best to have the code written or printed on a sheet of paper. Use a marker, such as a paper clip, to mark the current line. Whenever a variable changes, cross out the old value and write the new value below. When a program produces output, also write down the output in another column.

Consider this example. What value is displayed?

```python
n = 1729
total = 0
while n > 0 :
    digit = n % 10
    total = total + digit
    n = n // 10

print(total)
```

There are three variables: n, total, and digit.

The first two variables are initialized with 1729 and 0 before the loop is entered.

Because n is greater than zero, enter the loop. The variable digit is set to 9 (the remainder of dividing 1729 by 10). The variable total is set to 0 + 9 = 9.

Finally, n becomes 172. (Recall that the remainder in the division 1729 // 10 is discarded because the // operator performs floor division.)

Cross out the old values and write the new ones under the old ones.

```
n = 1729
total = 0
while n > 0 :
    digit = n % 10
    total = total + digit
    n = n // 10

print(total)
```

n	total	digit
~~1729~~	~~0~~	
172	9	9

Now check the loop condition again.

```
n = 1729
total = 0
while n > 0 :
    digit = n % 10
    total = total + digit
    n = n // 10

print(total)
```

Because n is still greater than zero, repeat the loop. Now digit becomes 2, total is set to 9 + 2 = 11, and n is set to 17.

n	total	digit
~~1729~~	~~0~~	
~~172~~	~~9~~	~~9~~
17	11	2

Repeat the loop once again, setting digit to 7, total to 11 + 7 = 18, and n to 1.

n	total	digit
~~1729~~	~~0~~	
~~172~~	~~9~~	~~9~~
~~17~~	~~11~~	~~2~~
1	18	7

Enter the loop for one last time. Now digit is set to 1, total to 19, and n becomes zero.

n	total	digit
~~1729~~	~~0~~	
~~172~~	~~9~~	~~9~~
~~17~~	~~11~~	~~2~~
~~1~~	~~18~~	~~7~~
0	19	1

```
    n = 1729
    total = 0
⌦  while n > 0 :
        digit = n % 10
        total = total + digit
        n = n // 10

    print(total)
```

*Because n equals zero,
this condition is not true.*

The condition n > 0 is now false. Continue with the statement after the loop.

```
    n = 1729
    total = 0
    while n > 0 :
        digit = n % 10
        total = total + digit
        n = n // 10

⌦  print(total)
```

n	total	digit	output
1729	0		
172	9	9	
17	11	2	
1	18	7	
0	19	1	19

This statement is an output statement. The value that is output is the value of total, which is 19.

Of course, you can get the same answer by just running the code. However, hand-tracing can give you *insight* that you would not get if you simply ran the code. Consider again what happens in each iteration:

- We extract the last digit of n.
- We add that digit to total.
- We strip the digit off of n.

Hand-tracing can help you understand how an unfamiliar algorithm works.

In other words, the loop computes the sum of the digits in n. You now know what the loop does for any value of n, not just the one in the example. (Why would anyone want to compute the sum of the digits? Operations of this kind are useful for checking the validity of credit card numbers and other forms of ID numbers—see Exercise ••• Business P4.35.)

Hand-tracing does not just help you understand code that works correctly. It is a powerful technique for finding errors in your code. When a program behaves in a way that you don't expect, get out a sheet of paper and track the values of the variables as you mentally step through the code.

Hand-tracing can show errors in code or pseudocode.

You don't need a working program to do hand-tracing. You can hand-trace pseudocode. In fact, it is an excellent idea to hand-trace your pseudocode before you go to the trouble of translating it into actual code, to confirm that it works correctly.

4.3 Application: Processing Sentinel Values

In this section, you will learn how to write loops that read and process a sequence of input values.

Whenever you read a sequence of inputs, you need to have some method of indicating the end of the sequence. Sometimes you are lucky and no input value can be zero. Then you can prompt the user to keep entering numbers, or 0 to finish the sequence. If zero is allowed but negative numbers are not, you can use –1 to indicate termination.

In the military, a sentinel guards a border or passage. In computer science, a sentinel value denotes the end of an input sequence or the border between input sequences

© Rhoberazzi/iStockphoto.

> A sentinel value denotes the end of a data set, but it is not part of the data.

Such a value, which is not an actual input, but serves as a signal for termination, is called a **sentinel**.

Let's put this technique to work in a program that computes the average of a set of salary values. In our sample program, we will use any negative value as the sentinel. An employee would surely not work for a negative salary, but there may be volunteers who work for free.

Inside the loop, we read an input. If the input is non-negative, we process it. In order to compute the average, we need the total sum of all salaries, and the number of inputs.

```
while . . . :
    salary = float(input("Enter a salary or -1 to finish: "))
    if salary >= 0.0 :
        total = total + salary
        count = count + 1
```

Any negative number can end the loop, but we prompt for a sentinel of –1 so that the user need not ponder which negative number to enter. Note that we stay in the loop as long as the sentinel value is not detected.

```
while salary >= 0.0 :
    . . .
```

There is just one problem: When the loop is entered for the first time, no data value has been read. We must make sure to initialize salary with a value that will satisfy the while loop condition so that the loop will be executed at least once.

```
salary = 0.0    # Any non-negative value will do.
```

After the loop has finished, we compute and print the average.

Here is the complete program.

sec03/sentinel.py

```
 1  ##
 2  #   This program prints the average of salary values that are terminated with
 3  #   a sentinel.
 4  #
 5
 6  # Initialize variables to maintain the running total and count.
 7  total = 0.0
 8  count = 0
 9
10  # Initialize salary to any non-sentinel value.
11  salary = 0.0
12
13  # Process data until the sentinel is entered.
14  while salary >= 0.0 :
15      salary = float(input("Enter a salary or -1 to finish: "))
16      if salary >= 0.0 :
17          total = total + salary
18          count = count + 1
19
```

```
20  # Compute and print the average salary.
21  if count > 0 :
22      average = total / count
23      print("Average salary is", average)
24  else :
25      print("No data was entered.")
```

Program Run

```
Enter a salary or -1 to finish: 10000
Enter a salary or -1 to finish: 10000
Enter a salary or -1 to finish: 40000
Enter a salary or -1 to finish: -1
Average salary is 20000.0
```

A pair of input operations, known as the priming and modification reads, can be used to read a sentinel-terminated sequence of values.

Some programmers don't like the "trick" of initializing the input variable with a value other than a sentinel. Although it solves the problem, it requires the use of an if statement in the body of the loop to test for the sentinel value. Another approach is to use two input statements, one before the loop to obtain the first value and another at the bottom of the loop to read additional values:

```
salary = float(input("Enter a salary or -1 to finish: "))
while salary >= 0.0 :
    total = total + salary
    count = count + 1
    salary = float(input("Enter a salary or -1 to finish: "))
```

If the first value entered by the user is the sentinel, then the body of the loop is never executed. Otherwise, the value is processed just as it was in the earlier version of the loop. The input operation before the loop is known as the *priming read*, because it prepares or initializes the loop variable.

The input operation at the bottom of the loop is used to obtain the next input. It is known as the *modification read*, because it modifies the loop variable inside the loop. Note that this is the last statement to be executed before the next iteration of the loop. If the user enters the sentinel value, then the loop terminates. Otherwise, the loop continues, processing the input.

Special Topic 4.2 shows a third approach for processing sentinel values that uses a Boolean variable.

Now consider the case in which any number (positive, negative, or zero) can be an acceptable input. In such a situation, you must use a sentinel that is not a number (such as the letter Q).

Because the input function obtains data from the user and returns it as a string, you can examine the string to see if the user entered the letter Q before converting the string to a numeric value for use in the calculations:

```
inputStr = input("Enter a value or Q to quit: ")
while inputStr != "Q" :
    value = float(inputStr)
    Process value.
    inputStr = input("Enter a value or Q to quit: ")
```

Note that the conversion to a floating-point value is performed as the first statement within the loop. By including it as the first statement, it handles the input string for both the priming read and the modification read.

Finally, consider the case where you prompt for multiple strings, for example, a sequence of names. We still need a sentinel to flag the end of the data extraction. Using a string such as Q is not such a good idea because that might be a valid input. You can use the empty string instead. When a user presses the Enter key without pressing any other keys, the input function returns the empty string:

```python
name = input("Enter a name or press the Enter key to quit: ")
while name != "" :
    Process name.
    name = input("Enter a name or press the Enter key to quit: ")
```

Special Topic 4.2

Processing Sentinel Values with a Boolean Variable

Sentinel values can also be processed using a Boolean variable for the loop termination:

```python
done = False
while not done :
    value = float(input("Enter a salary or -1 to finish: "))
    if value < 0.0 :
        done = True
    else :
        Process value.
```

The actual test for loop termination is in the middle of the loop, not at the top. This is called a **loop and a half** because one must go halfway into the loop before knowing whether one needs to terminate. As an alternative, you can use the break statement:

```python
while True :
    value = float(input("Enter a salary or -1 to finish: "))
    if value < 0.0 :
        break
    Process value.
```

The break statement breaks out of the enclosing loop, independent of the loop condition. When the break statement is encountered, the loop is terminated, and the statement following the loop is executed.

In the loop-and-a-half case, break statements can be beneficial. But it is difficult to lay down clear rules as to when they are safe and when they should be avoided. We do not use the break statement in this book.

Special Topic 4.3

Redirection of Input and Output

Consider the sentinel.py program that computes the average value of an input sequence. If you use such a program, then it is quite likely that you already have the values in a file, and it seems a shame that you have to type them all in again. The command line interface of your operating system provides a way to link a file to the input of a program, as if all the characters in the file had actually been typed by a user. If you type

```
python sentinel.py < numbers.txt
```

the program is executed, but it no longer expects input from the keyboard. All input commands get their input from the file numbers.txt. This process is called *input redirection*.

Input redirection is an excellent tool for testing programs. When you develop a program and fix its bugs, it is boring to keep entering the same input every time you run the program. Spend a few minutes putting the inputs into a file, and use redirection.

You can also redirect output. In this program, that is not terribly useful. If you run

```
python sentinel.py < numbers.txt > output.txt
```

Use input redirection to read input from a file. Use output redirection to capture program output in a file.

the file output.txt contains the input prompts and the output, such as

```
Enter a salary or -1 to finish:
Enter a salary or -1 to finish:
Enter a salary or -1 to finish:
Enter a salary or -1 to finish:
Average salary is 15000.0
```

However, redirecting output is obviously useful for programs that produce lots of output. You can format or print the file containing the output.

4.4 Problem Solving: Storyboards

When you design a program that interacts with a user, you need to make a plan for that interaction. What information does the user provide, and in which order? What information will your program display, and in which format? What should happen when there is an error? When does the program quit?

> A storyboard consists of annotated sketches for each step in an action sequence.

This planning is similar to the development of a movie or a computer game, where *storyboards* are used to plan action sequences. A storyboard is made up of panels that show a sketch of each step. Annotations explain what is happening and note any special situations. Storyboards are also used to develop software—see Figure 3.

Making a storyboard is very helpful when you begin designing a program. You need to ask yourself which information you need in order to compute the answers that the program user wants. You need to decide how to present those answers. These are important considerations that you want to settle before you design an algorithm for computing the answers.

Let's look at a simple example. We want to write a program that helps users with questions such as "How many tablespoons are in a pint?" or "How many inches are in 30 centimeters?"

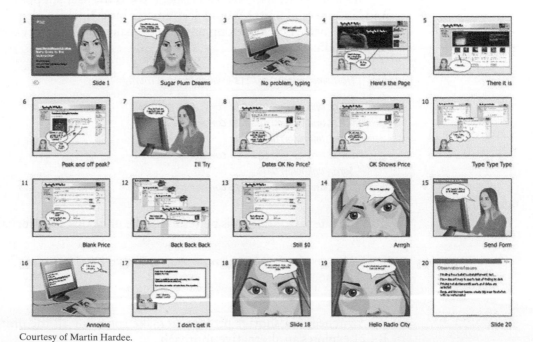

Figure 3
Storyboard for the Design of a Web Application

Courtesy of Martin Hardee.

Developing a storyboard helps you understand the inputs and outputs that are required for a program.

What information does the user provide?

- The quantity and unit to convert from
- The unit to convert to

What if there is more than one quantity? A user may have a whole table of centimeter values that should be converted into inches.

What if the user enters units that our program doesn't know how to handle, such as ångström?

What if the user asks for impossible conversions, such as inches to gallons?

Let's get started with a storyboard panel. It is a good idea to write the user inputs in a different color. (Underline them if you don't have a color pen handy.)

Converting a Sequence of Values

What unit do you want to convert from? *cm*
What unit do you want to convert to? *in*
Enter values, terminated by zero ————— Allows conversion of multiple values
30
30 cm = 11.81 in ——
100   ———— Format makes clear what got converted
100 cm = 39.37 in
0
What unit do you want to convert from?

The storyboard shows how we deal with a potential confusion. A user who wants to know how many inches are 30 centimeters may not read the first prompt carefully and specify inches. But then the output is "30 in = 76.2 cm", alerting the user to the problem.

The storyboard also raises an issue. How is the user supposed to know that "cm" and "in" are valid units? Would "centimeter" and "inches" also work? What happens when the user enters a wrong unit? Let's make another storyboard to demonstrate error handling.

Handling Unknown Units (needs improvement)

What unit do you want to convert from? *cm*
What unit do you want to convert to? *inches*
Sorry, unknown unit.
What unit do you want to convert to? *inch*
Sorry, unknown unit.
What unit do you want to convert to? *gmr*

To eliminate frustration, it is better to list the units that the user can supply.

From unit (in, ft, mi, mm, cm, m, km, oz, lb, g, kg, tsp, tbsp, pint, gal): *cm*
To unit: *in* ——
———— No need to list the units again

We switched to a shorter prompt to make room for all the unit names. Exercise •
R4.21 explores an alternative approach.

There is another issue that we haven't addressed yet. How does the user quit the program? The first storyboard suggests that the program will go on forever. We can ask the user after seeing the sentinel that terminates an input sequence.

Exiting the Program

From unit (in, ft, mi, mm, cm, m, km, oz, lb, g, kg, tsp, tbsp, pint, gal): cm
To unit: in
Enter values, terminated by zero
30
30 cm = 11.81 in
0   —— Sentinel triggers the prompt to exit
More conversions (y, n)? n
(Program exits)

As you can see from this case study, a storyboard is essential for developing a working program. You need to know the flow of the user interaction in order to structure your program.

4.5 Common Loop Algorithms

In the following sections, we discuss some of the most common algorithms that are implemented as loops. You can use them as starting points for your loop designs.

4.5.1 Sum and Average Value

To compute an average, keep a total and a count of all values.

Computing the sum of a number of inputs is a very common task. Keep a *running total*, a variable to which you add each input value. Of course, the total should be initialized with 0.

```
total = 0.0
inputStr = input("Enter value: ")
while inputStr != "" :
    value = float(inputStr)
    total = total + value
    inputStr = input("Enter value: ")
```

Note that the total variable is created and initialized outside the loop. We want the loop to add each value entered by the user to the variable.

To compute an average, count how many values you have, and divide by the count. Be sure to check that the count is not zero.

```
total = 0.0
count = 0
inputStr = input("Enter value: ")
while inputStr != "" :
    value = float(inputStr)
    total = total + value
    count = count + 1
    inputStr = input("Enter value: ")

if count > 0 :
    average = total / count
else :
    average = 0.0
```

4.5.2 Counting Matches

To count values that fulfill a condition, check all values and increment a counter for each match.

You often want to know how many values fulfill a particular condition. For example, you may want to count how many negative values are included in a sequence of integers. Keep a *counter*, a variable that is initialized with 0 and incremented whenever there is a match.

© Hiob/iStockphoto.

In a loop that counts matches, a counter is incremented whenever a match is found.

```
negatives = 0
inputStr = input("Enter value: ")
while inputStr != "" :
    value = int(inputStr)
    if value < 0 :
        negatives = negatives + 1
    inputStr = input("Enter value: ")

print("There were", negatives, "negative values.")
```

Note that the negatives variable is created and initialized outside the loop. We want the loop to increment negatives by 1 for each negative value entered by the user.

4.5.3 Prompting Until a Match is Found

In Chapter 3, we checked to be sure the user-supplied values were valid before they were used in a computation. If invalid data was entered, we printed an error message and ended the program. Instead of ending the program, however, you should keep asking the user to enter the data until a correct value is provided. For example, suppose you are asking the user to enter a positive integer value < 100:

```
valid = False
while not valid :
    value = int(input("Please enter a positive integer value < 100: "))
    if value > 0 and value < 100 :
        valid = True
    else :
        print("Invalid input.")
```

4.5.4 Maximum and Minimum

To find the largest value, update the largest value seen so far whenever you see a larger one.

To compute the largest value in a sequence, keep a variable that stores the largest element that you have encountered and update the variable when you find a larger one:

```
largest = float(input("Enter a value: "))
inputStr = input("Enter a value: ")
while inputStr != "" :
    value = float(inputStr)
    if value > largest :
        largest = value
    inputStr = input("Enter a value: ")
```

This algorithm requires that there is at least one input, which is used to initialize the largest variable. The second input operation acts as the priming read for the loop.

To compute the smallest value, simply reverse the comparison:

```python
smallest = float(input("Enter a value: "))
inputStr = input("Enter a value: ")
while inputStr != "" :
    value = float(inputStr)
    if value < smallest :
        smallest = value
    inputStr = input("Enter a value: ")
```

To find the height of the tallest bus rider, remember the largest value so far, and update it whenever you see a taller one.

© CEFutcher/iStockphoto.

4.5.5 Comparing Adjacent Values

To compare adjacent inputs, store the preceding input in a variable.

When processing a sequence of values in a loop, you sometimes need to compare a value with the value that just preceded it. For example, suppose you want to check whether a sequence of inputs such as 1 7 2 9 9 4 9 contains adjacent duplicates.

Now you face a challenge. Consider the typical loop for reading an integer:

```python
inputStr = input("Enter an integer value: ")
while inputStr != "" :
    value = int(inputStr)
    . . .
    inputStr = input("Enter an integer value: ")
```

How can you compare the current input with the preceding one? At any time, `value` contains the current input, overwriting the previous one.

The answer is to store the previous input, like this:

```python
inputStr = input("Enter an integer value: ")
while inputStr != "" :
    previous = value
    value = int(inputStr)
    if value == previous :
        print("Duplicate input")
    inputStr = input("Enter an integer value: ")
```

© tingberg/iStockphoto.

When comparing adjacent values, store the previous value in a variable.

One problem remains. When the loop is entered for the first time, `value` has not yet been assigned a value. You can solve this problem with an initial input operation outside the loop:

```python
value = int(input("Enter an integer value: "))
inputStr = input("Enter an integer value: ")
while inputStr != "" :
    previous = value
    value = int(inputStr)
    if value == previous :
        print("Duplicate input")
    inputStr = input("Enter an integer value: ")
```

Here is a sample program that illustrates some of the common loop algorithms.

sec05/grades.py

```
1    ##
2    #   This program computes information related to a sequence of grades obtained
3    #   from the user. It computes the number of passing and failing grades,
4    #   computes the average grade and finds the highest and lowest grade.
5    #
6
7    # Initialize the counter variables.
8    numPassing = 0
9    numFailing = 0
10
11   # Initialize the variables used to compute the average.
12   total = 0
13   count = 0
14
15   # Initialize the min and max variables.
16   minGrade = 100.0    # Assuming 100 is the highest grade possible.
17   maxGrade = 0.0
18
19   # Use a while loop with a priming read to obtain the grades.
20   grade = float(input("Enter a grade or -1 to finish: "))
21   while grade >= 0.0 :
22       # Increment the passing or failing counter.
23       if grade >= 60.0 :
24           numPassing = numPassing + 1
25       else :
26           numFailing = numFailing + 1
27
28       # Determine if the grade is the min or max grade.
29       if grade < minGrade :
30           minGrade = grade
31       if grade > maxGrade :
32           maxGrade = grade
33
34       # Add the grade to the running total.
35       total = total + grade
36       count = count + 1
37
38       # Read the next grade.
39       grade = float(input("Enter a grade or -1 to finish: "))
40
41   # Print the results.
42   if count > 0 :
43       average = total / count
44       print("The average grade is %.2f" % average)
45       print("Number of passing grades is", numPassing)
46       print("Number of failing grades is", numFailing)
47       print("The maximum grade is %.2f" % maxGrade)
48       print("The minimum grade is %.2f" % minGrade)
```

4.6 The for Loop

Often, you will need to visit each character in a string. The for loop (see Syntax 4.2) makes this process particularly easy to program. For example, suppose we want to print a string, with one character per line. We cannot simply print the string using the print function. Instead, we need to iterate over the characters in the string and print each character individually. Here is how you use the for loop to accomplish this task:

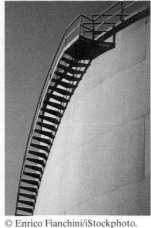

```
stateName = "Virginia"
for letter in stateName :
    print(letter)
```

which results in the output

```
V
i
r
g
i
n
i
a
```

© Enrico Fianchini/iStockphoto.

You can visualize the for *loop as an orderly sequence of steps.*

The loop body is executed for each character in the string stateName, starting with the first character. At the beginning of each loop iteration, the next character is assigned to the variable letter. Then the loop body is executed. You should read this loop as "for each letter in stateName". This loop is equivalent to the following while loop that uses an explicit index variable:

```
i = 0
while i < len(stateName) :
    letter = stateName[i]
    print(letter)
    i = i + 1
```

Note an important difference between the for loop and the while loop. In the for loop, the *element variable* letter is assigned stateName[0], stateName[1], and so on. In the while loop, the *index variable* i is assigned 0, 1, and so on.

Syntax 4.2   for Statement

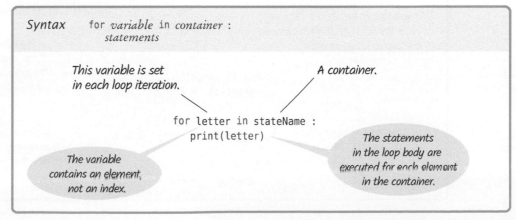

Syntax   for *variable* in *container* :
          statements

This variable is set in each loop iteration.

A container.

```
for letter in stateName :
    print(letter)
```

The variable contains an element, not an index.

The statements in the loop body are executed for each element in the container.

Use a for loop when you need to access the characters of a string one at a time.

The for loop can be used with the range function to iterate over a range of integer values.

The for loop can be used to iterate over the contents of any **container**, which is an object that contains or stores a collection of elements. Thus, a string is a container that stores the collection of characters in the string. In later chapters, we will explore other types of containers available in Python.

As you have seen in prior sections, loops that iterate over a range of integer values are very common. To simplify the creation of such loops, Python provides the range function for generating a sequence of integers that can be used with the for loop. The loop

```
for i in range(1, 10) :    # i = 1, 2, 3, ..., 9
    print(i)
```

prints the sequential values from 1 to 9. The range function generates a sequence of values based on its arguments. The first argument of the range function is the first value in the sequence. Values are included in the sequence while they are less than the second argument. This loop is equivalent to the following while loop:

```
i = 1
while i < 10 :
    print(i)
    i = i + 1
```

Note that the ending value (the second argument to the range function) is not included in the sequence, so the equivalent while loop stops before reaching that value, too.

By default, the range function creates the sequence in steps of 1. This can be changed by including a step value as the third argument to the function:

```
for i in range(1, 10, 2) :    # i = 1, 3, 5, ..., 9
    print(i)
```

Now, only the odd values from 1 to 9 are printed. We can also have the for loop count down instead of up:

```
for i in range(10, 0, -1) :    # i = 10, 9, 8, ..., 1
    print(i)
```

Syntax 4.3 for Statement with range Function

Syntax   for *variable* in range(...) :
              statements

This variable is set, at the beginning of each iteration, to the next integer in the sequence generated by the range function.

The range *function generates a sequence of integers over which the loop iterates.*

With one argument, the sequence starts at 0. The argument is the first value NOT included in the sequence.

```
for i in range(5) :
    print(i)   # Prints 0, 1, 2, 3, 4
```

With three arguments, the third argument is the step value.

```
for i in range(1, 5) :
    print(i)   # Prints 1, 2, 3, 4
```

With two arguments, the sequence starts with the first argument.

```
for i in range(1, 11, 2) :
    print(i)   # Prints 1, 3, 5, 7, 9
```

Finally, you can use the range function with a single argument. When you do, the range of values starts at zero.

```
for i in range(10) :   # i = 0, 1, 2, ..., 9
    print("Hello")    # Prints Hello ten times
```

With a single argument, the sequence is the values from 0 to one less than the argument, in steps of 1. This form is very useful when we need to simply execute the body of a loop a given number of times, as in the preceding example. See Table 2 for additional examples.

Table 2 for Loop Examples		
Loop	Values of i	Comment
`for i in range(6) :`	0, 1, 2, 3, 4, 5	Note that the loop executes 6 times.
`for i in range(10, 16) :`	10, 11, 12, 13, 14, 15	The ending value is never included in the sequence.
`for i in range(0, 9, 2) :`	0, 2, 4, 6, 8	The third argument is the step value.
`for i in range(5, 0, -1) :`	5, 4, 3, 2, 1	Use a negative step value to count down.

Here is a typical use of the for loop. We want to print the balance of our savings account over a period of years, as shown in this table:

Year	Balance
1	10500.00
2	11025.00
3	11576.25
4	12155.06
5	12762.82

The for loop pattern applies because the variable year starts at 1 and then moves in constant increments until it reaches the target:

```
for year in range(1, numYears + 1) :
    Update balance.
    Print year and balance.
```

Following is the complete program. Figure 4 shows the corresponding flowchart.

Figure 4   Flowchart of a for Loop

sec06/investment.py

```
1  ##
2  #   This program prints a table showing the growth of an investment.
3  #
4
5  # Define constant variables.
6  RATE = 5.0
7  INITIAL_BALANCE = 10000.0
8
9  # Obtain the number of years for the computation.
10  numYears = int(input("Enter number of years: "))
11
12  # Print the table of balances for each year.
13  balance = INITIAL_BALANCE
14  for year in range(1, numYears + 1) :
15      interest = balance * RATE / 100
16      balance = balance + interest
17      print("%4d %10.2f" % (year, balance))
```

Program Run

```
Enter number of years: 10
   1   10500.00
   2   11025.00
   3   11576.25
   4   12155.06
   5   12762.82
   6   13400.96
   7   14071.00
   8   14774.55
   9   15513.28
  10   16288.95
```

Programming Tip 4.1

Count Iterations

Finding the correct lower and upper bounds for a loop can be confusing. Should you start at 0 or at 1? Should you use <= b or < b as a termination condition?

Counting the number of iterations is a very useful device for better understanding a loop. Counting is easier for loops with asymmetric bounds. The loop

```
i = a
while i < b :
    . . .
    i = i + 1
```

is executed b - a times. The same is true for the equivalent for loop

```
for i in range(a, b) :
```

These asymmetric bounds are particularly useful for traversing the characters in a string. The loop

```
for i in range(0, len(string)) :
    Do something with i and string[i]
```

runs len(string) times, and i traverses all valid string positions from 0 to len(string) - 1. (Because these loops are so common, you can omit the 0 in the call to the range function.)

The loop with symmetric bounds,

```
i = a
while i <= b :
    . . .
    i = i + 1
```

is executed b - a + 1 times. That "+1" is the source of many programming errors. For example, when a is 10 and b is 20, then i assumes the values 10, 11, 12, 13, 14, 15, 16, 17, 18, 19, and 20. Those are eleven values: $20 - 10 + 1$.

One way to visualize this "+1" error is by looking at a fence. Each section has one fence post to the left, and there is a final post on the right of the last section. Forgetting to count the last value is often called a "fence post error".

In a Python for loop, the "+1" can be quite noticeable:

```
for year in range(1, numYears + 1) :
```

You must specify an upper bound that is one more than the last value to be included in the range.

How many posts do you need for a fence with four sections? It is easy to be "off by one" with problems such as this one.

© akaplummer/iStockphoto.

HOW TO 4.1
Writing a Loop

This How To walks you through the process of implementing a loop statement.

Problem Statement Read twelve temperature values (one for each month), and display the number of the month with the highest temperature. For example, according to http://worldclimate.com, the average maximum temperatures for Death Valley are (in order by month, in degrees Celsius):

18.2 22.6 26.4 31.1 36.6 42.2
45.7 44.5 40.2 33.1 24.2 17.6

In this case, the month with the highest temperature (45.7 degrees Celsius) is July, and the program should display 7.

© Stevegeer/iStockphoto.

Step 1   Decide what work must be done *inside* the loop.

Every loop needs to do some kind of repetitive work, such as

- Reading another item.
- Updating a value (such as a bank balance or total).
- Incrementing a counter.

If you can't figure out what needs to go inside the loop, start by writing down the steps that you would take if you solved the problem by hand. For example, with the maximum temperature problem, you might write

> *Read the first value.*
> *Read the second value.*
> *If the second value is higher than the first value*
>   *Set highest temperature to the second value.*
>   *Set highest month to 2.*
> *Read the next value.*
> *If the value is higher than the first and second values*
>   *Set highest temperature to the value.*
>   *Set highest month to 3.*
> *Read the next value.*
> *If the value is higher than the highest temperature seen so far*
>   *Set highest temperature to the value.*
>   *Set highest month to 4.*
>   . . .

Now look at these steps and reduce them to a set of *uniform* actions that can be placed into the loop body. The first action is easy:

> *Read the next value.*

The next action is trickier. In our description, we used tests "higher than the first", "higher than the first and second", "higher than the highest temperature seen so far". We need to settle on one test that works for all iterations. The last formulation is the most general.

Similarly, we must find a general way of setting the highest month. We need a variable that stores the current month, running from 1 to 12. Then we can formulate the second loop action:

> *If the value is higher than the highest temperature*
>   *Set highest temperature to the value.*
>   *Set highest month to current month.*

Altogether our loop is

> *Repeat*
>   *Read the next value.*
>   *If the value is higher than the highest temperature*
>   *Set the highest temperature to the value.*
>   *Set highest month to current month.*
>   *Increment current month.*

Step 2   Specify the loop condition.

What goal do you want to reach in your loop? Typical examples are

- Has a counter reached its final value?
- Have you read the last input value?
- Has a value reached a given threshold?

In our example, we simply want the current month to reach 12.

Step 3 Determine the loop type.

We distinguish between two major loop types. A *count-controlled* loop is executed a definite number of times. In an *event-controlled* loop, the number of iterations is not known in advance—the loop is executed until some event happens.

Count-controlled loops can be implemented as for statements. The for statement can either iterate over the individual elements of a container, such as a string, or be used with the range function to iterate over a sequence of integers.

Event-controlled loops are implemented as while statements in which the loop condition determines when the loop terminates. Sometimes, the condition for terminating a loop changes in the middle of the loop body. In that case, you can use a Boolean variable that specifies when you are ready to leave the loop; such a variable is called a **flag**. Follow this pattern:

```
done = False
while not done :
    Do some work.
    If all work has been completed :
        done = True
    else :
        Do more work.
```

In summary,

- If you need to iterate over all the elements of a container, without regard to their positions, use a plain for loop.
- If you need to iterate over a range of integers, use a for loop with the range function.
- Otherwise, use a while loop.

In our example, we read 12 temperature values. Therefore, we choose a for loop that uses the range function to iterate over a sequence of integers.

Step 4 Set up variables for entering the loop for the first time.

List all variables that are used and updated in the loop, and determine how to initialize them. Commonly, counters are initialized with 0 or 1, totals with 0.

In our example, the variables are

current month
highest value
highest month

We need to be careful how we set up the highest temperature value. We can't simply set it to 0. After all, our program needs to work with temperature values from Antarctica, all of which may be negative.

A good option is to set the highest temperature value to the first input value. Of course, then we need to remember to read in only 11 more values, with the current month starting at 2.

We also need to initialize the highest month with 1. After all, in an Australian city, we may never find a month that is warmer than January.

Step 5 Process the result after the loop has finished.

In many cases, the desired result is simply a variable that was updated in the loop body. For example, in our temperature program, the result is the highest month. Sometimes, the loop computes values that contribute to the final result. For example, suppose you are asked to average the temperatures. Then the loop should compute the sum, not the average. After the loop has completed, you are ready to compute the average: divide the sum by the number of inputs.

Here is our complete loop:

Read value.
highest temperature = value
highest month = 1

> *For current month from 2 to 12*
>   *Read next value.*
>   *If the value is higher than the highest temperature*
>   *Set highest temperature to the value.*
>   *Set highest month to current month.*

Step 6   Trace the loop with typical examples.

Hand trace your loop code, as described in Section 4.2. Choose example values that are not too complex—executing the loop 3–5 times is enough to check for the most common errors. Pay special attention when entering the loop for the first and last time.

Sometimes, you want to make a slight modification to make tracing feasible. For example, when hand-tracing the investment doubling problem, use an interest rate of 20 percent rather than 5 percent. When hand-tracing the temperature loop, use 4 data values, not 12.

Let's say the data are 22.6 36.6 44.5 24.2. Here is the trace:

current month	current value	highest month	highest value
		1̸	22.6
2̸	36.6	2	36.6
3̸	44.5	3	44.5
4	24.2		

The trace demonstrates that *highest month* and *highest value* are properly set.

Step 7   Implement the loop in Python.

Here's the loop for our example. Exercise •• P4.4 asks you to complete the program.

```python
highestValue = float(input("Enter a value: "))
highestMonth = 1
for currentMonth in range(2, 13) :
    nextValue = float(input("Enter a value: "))
    if nextValue > highestValue :
        highestValue = nextValue
        highestMonth = currentMonth

print(highestMonth)
```

4.7 Nested Loops

When the body of a loop contains another loop, the loops are nested. A typical use of nested loops is printing a table with rows and columns.

In Section 3.3, you saw how to nest two if statements. Similarly, complex iterations sometimes require a **nested loop**: a loop inside another loop statement. When processing tables, nested loops occur naturally. An outer loop iterates over all rows of the table. An inner loop deals with the columns in the current row.

The hour and minute displays in a digital clock are an example of nested loops. The hours loop 12 times, and for each hour, the minutes loop 60 times. © davejkahn/iStockphoto.

In this section you will see how to print a table. For simplicity, we will print the powers of x, x^n, as in the table at right.

Here is the pseudocode for printing the table:

Print table header.
For x from 1 to 10
    Print table row.
    Print new line.

How do you print a table row? You need to print a value for each exponent. This requires a second loop.

For n from 1 to 4
    Print x^n.

x^1	x^2	x^3	x^4
1	1	1	1
2	4	8	16
3	9	27	81
...	...	...	...
10	100	1000	10000

This loop must be placed inside the preceding loop. We say that the inner loop is *nested* inside the outer loop.

There are 10 rows in the outer loop. For each x, the program prints four columns in the inner loop (see Figure 5). Thus, a total of $10 \times 4 = 40$ values are printed.

In this program, we want to show the results of multiple print statements on the same line. This is achieved by adding the argument end="" to the print function (see Special Topic 4.1).

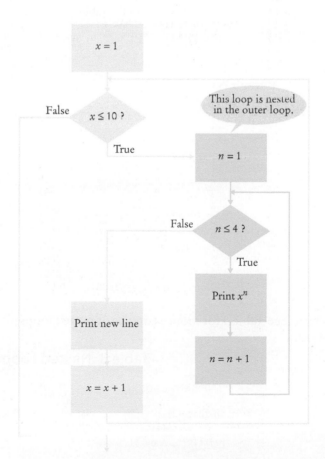

Figure 5 Flowchart of a Nested Loop

Following is the complete program. Note that we also use loops to print the table header. However, those loops are not nested.

sec07/powertable.py

```
1   ##
2   #  This program prints a table of powers of x.
3   #
4
5   # Initialize constant variables for the max ranges.
6   NMAX = 4
7   XMAX = 10
8
9   # Print table header.
10  for n in range(1, NMAX + 1) :
11      print("%10d" % n, end="")
12
13  print()
14  for n in range(1, NMAX + 1) :
15      print("%10s" % "x ", end="")
16
17  print("\n", "      ", "-" * 35)
18
19  # Print table body.
20  for x in range(1, XMAX + 1) :
21      # Print the x row in the table.
22      for n in range(1, NMAX + 1) :
23          print("%10.0f" % x ** n, end="")
24
25      print()
```

Program Run

```
         1         2         3         4
         x         x         x         x
-----------------------------------
         1         1         1         1
         2         4         8        16
         3         9        27        81
         4        16        64       256
         5        25       125       625
         6        36       216      1296
         7        49       343      2401
         8        64       512      4096
         9        81       729      6561
        10       100      1000     10000
```

See Table 3 for more examples of nested loops.

Table 3 Nested Loop Examples		
Nested Loops	Output	Explanation

`for i in range(3) :`
`    for j in range(4) :`
`        print("*", end="")`
`    print()`
	****
	****
	****
		Prints 3 rows of 4 asterisks each.

Table 3 Nested Loop Examples

Nested Loops	Output	Explanation
| ```
for i in range(4) :
    for j in range(3) :
        print("*", end="")
    print()
``` | ***<br>***<br>***<br>*** | Prints 4 rows of 3 asterisks each. |
| ```
for i in range(4) :
    for j in range(i + 1) :
        print("*", end="")
    print()
``` | *<br>**<br>***<br>**** | Prints 4 rows of lengths 1, 2, 3, and 4. |
| ```
for i in range(3) :
    for j in range(5) :
        if j % 2 == 1 :
            print("*", end="")
        else :
            print("-", end="")
    print()
``` | -*-*-<br>-*-*-<br>-*-*- | Prints alternating dashes and asterisks. |
| ```
for i in range(3) :
    for j in range(5) :
        if i % 2 == j % 2 :
            print("*", end="")
        else :
            print(" ", end="")
    print()
``` | * * *<br> * *<br>* * * | Prints a checkerboard pattern. |

WORKED EXAMPLE 4.1

Average Exam Grades

Problem Statement It is common to repeatedly read and process multiple groups of values. Write a program that can be used to compute the average exam grade for multiple students. Each student has the same number of exam grades.

Fuse/Getty Images, Inc.

Step 1 Understand the problem.

To compute the average exam grade for one student, we must enter and tally all of the grades for that student. This can be done with a loop. But we need to compute the average grade for multiple students. Thus, computing an individual student's average grade must be repeated for each student in the course. This requires a nested loop. The inner loop will process the grades for one student and the outer loop will repeat the process for each student.

> *Prompt user for the number of exams.*
> *Repeat for each student*
> *   Process the student's exam grades.*
> *   Print the student's exam average.*

Step 2   Compute the average grade for one student.

The algorithm from Section 4.5.1 can be used to extract the grades and compute the average. The difference in this problem, however, is that we can read a fixed number of grades for each student instead of reading until a sentinel value is entered. Because we know how many grades need to be read, we can use a for loop with the range function:

```
total score = 0
for i in range(1, numExams + 1) :
    Read the next exam score.
    Add the exam score to the total score.
Compute the exam average.
Print the exam average.
```

Step 3   Repeat the process for each student.

Because we are computing the average exam grade for multiple students, we must repeat the task in Step 2 for each student. Because we do not know how many students there are, we will use a while loop with a sentinel value. But what should the sentinel be? For simplicity, it can be based on a simple yes or no question. After the user enters the grades for a student, we can prompt the user whether they wish to enter grades for another student:

```
moreGrades = input("Enter exam grades for another student (Y/N)? ")
moreGrades = moreGrades.upper()
```

A no response serves as the terminating condition. Thus, each time the user enters "Y" at the prompt, the loop will be executed again.

We will use a loop condition set to moreGrades == "Y", and initialize the loop variable to contain the string "Y". This allows the loop to be executed at least once so the user can enter the grades for the first student before being prompted for a yes or no response.

```
moreGrades = "Y"
while moreGrades == "Y" :
    Enter grades for one student.
    Compute average grade for one student.
    moreGrades = input("Enter exam grades for another student (Y/N)? ")
    moreGrades = moreGrades.upper()
```

Step 4   Implement your solution in Python.

Here is the complete program.

worked_example_1/examaverages.py

```
1   ##
2   #   This program computes the average exam grade for multiple students.
3   #
4
5   # Obtain the number of exam grades per student.
6   numExams = int(input("How many exam grades does each student have? "))
7
8   # Initialize moreGrades to a non-sentinel value.
9   moreGrades = "Y"
10
11  # Compute average exam grades until the user wants to stop.
12  while moreGrades == "Y" :
13
14      # Compute the average grade for one student.
15      print("Enter the exam grades.")
16      total = 0
```

```
17    for i in range(1, numExams + 1) :
18        score = int(input("Exam %d: " % i))   # Prompt for each exam grade.
19        total = total + score
20
21    average = total / numExams
22    print("The average is %.2f" % average)
23
24    # Prompt as to whether the user wants to enter grades for another student.
25    moreGrades = input("Enter exam grades for another student (Y/N)? ")
26    moreGrades = moreGrades.upper()
```

WORKED EXAMPLE 4.2

A Grade Distribution Histogram

Problem Statement   Histograms are used to show the distribution of data across a fixed number of categories. They are essentially bar charts in which the height of a bar indicates the number of items in a category. Your task is to construct a histogram to visualize the distribution of letter grades for a single class, using the plotting package described in Toolbox 3.2. The grades are entered as numerical values that must be converted to the appropriate letter grade.

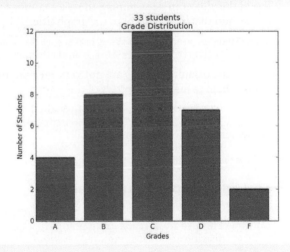

Step 1   Initialize grade counters.

To build the histogram, we must first tally the number of students with each letter grade. This will require 5 counters, one for each letter grade:

```
numAs = 0
numBs = 0
numCs = 0
numDs = 0
numFs = 0
```

Step 2   Read and process the grades.

The grades are numerical values between 0 and 100. These must be read, one at a time, using a while loop with a sentinel value as described in Section 4.3. After reading each numerical grade, we must determine the corresponding letter grade and update the appropriate grade counter.

To determine the letter grade, we will assume the traditional grading scale: A: $grade \geq 90$, B: $80 \leq grade < 90$, C: $70 \leq grade < 80$, D: $60 \leq grade < 70$, and F: $grade < 60$.

> *Prompt the user for the first numerical grade.*
> *Repeat for each grade*
> > *Determine the letter grade.*
> > *Update the grade count.*

Step 3   Construct the bar chart.

After reading and processing the grades, we can construct the bar chart. The height of each bar represents the count for the given letter grade.

```
pyplot.bar(1, numAs)
pyplot.bar(2, numBs)
pyplot.bar(3, numCs)
pyplot.bar(4, numDs)
pyplot.bar(5, numFs)
```

Step 4   Format the chart.

After the bars are added to the chart, we need to label both axes appropriately.

```
pyplot.xlabel("Grades")
pyplot.ylabel("Number of Students")
```

To aid the viewer in determining the total number of students for which grades were entered, we can add that information to the graph title:

```
numStudents = numAs + numBs + numCs + numDs + numFs
pyplot.title("%d students\nGrade Distribution" % numStudents)
```

Finally, the default *x*-values are not very meaningful for describing the individual bars, so we change them to match the letters of the grades.

```
pyplot.xticks([1.4, 2.4, 3.4, 4.4, 5.4], ["A", "B", "C", "D", "F"])
```

Step 5   Implement your solution in Python.

Here is the complete program.

worked_example_2/histogram.py

```
 1  ##
 2  #   This program reads exam grades from the user and produces a grade
 3  #   distribution histogram.
 4  #
 5
 6  from matplotlib import pyplot
 7
 8  # Initialize the variables used to maintain the grade counts.
 9  numAs = 0
10  numBs = 0
11  numCs = 0
12  numDs = 0
13  numFs = 0
14
15  # Use a while loop with a priming read to obtain the exam grades.
16  grade = int(input("Enter exam grade or -1 to finish: "))
17  while grade >= 0 :
18     if grade >= 90.0 :
19        numAs = numAs + 1
```

```
20      elif grade >= 80.0 :
21          numBs = numBs + 1
22      elif grade >= 70.0 :
23          numCs = numCs + 1
24      elif grade >= 60.0 :
25          numDs = numDs + 1
26      else :
27          numFs = numFs + 1
28
29      grade = int(input("Enter exam grade or -1 to finish: "))
30
31  # Plot the grade distribution.
32  pyplot.bar(1, numAs)
33  pyplot.bar(2, numBs)
34  pyplot.bar(3, numCs)
35  pyplot.bar(4, numDs)
36  pyplot.bar(5, numFs)
37
38  # Add axis labels.
39  pyplot.xlabel("Grades")
40  pyplot.ylabel("Number of Students")
41
42  # Add a title that indicates the total number of students.
43  numStudents = numAs + numBs + numCs + numDs + numFs
44  pyplot.title("%d students\nGrade Distribution" % numStudents)
45
46  # Add the letter grades as labels under the bars.
47  pyplot.xticks([1.4, 2.4, 3.4, 4.4, 5.4], ["A", "B", "C", "D", "F"])
48
49  # Display the graph.
50  pyplot.show()
```

4.8 Processing Strings

A common use of loops is to process or evaluate strings. For example, you may need to count the number of occurrences of one or more characters in a string or verify that the contents of a string meet certain criteria. In this section, we explore several basic string processing algorithms.

4.8.1 Counting Matches

In Section 4.5.2, we saw how to count the number of values that fulfill a particular condition. We can also apply this task to strings. For example, suppose you need to count the number of uppercase letters contained in a string.

```
uppercase = 0
for char in string :
    if char.isupper() :
        uppercase = uppercase + 1
```

This loop iterates through the characters in the string and checks each one to see if it is an uppercase letter. When an uppercase letter is found, the uppercase counter is incremented. For example, if string contains "My Fair Lady", uppercase is incremented three times (when char is M, F, and L).

Sometimes, you need to count the number of occurrences of multiple characters within a string. For example, suppose we would like to know how many vowels are contained in a word. Instead of individually comparing each letter in the word against the five vowels, you can use the in operator and a literal string that contains the five letters:

Use the in operator to compare a character against multiple options.

```
vowels = 0
for char in word :
   if char.lower() in "aeiou" :
      vowels = vowels + 1
```

Note the use of the lower method in the logical expression. This method is used to convert each uppercase letter to its corresponding lowercase letter before checking to see if it is a vowel. That way, we limit the number of characters that must be specified in the literal string.

4.8.2 Finding All Matches

When you need to examine every character within a string, independent of its position, you can use the for statement to iterate over the individual characters. This is the approach we used to count the number of uppercase letters in a string. Sometimes, however, you may need to find the position of each match within a string. For example, suppose you are asked to print the position of each uppercase letter in a sentence. You cannot use the for statement that iterates over all characters because you need to know the positions of the matches. Instead, iterate over the positions (using for with range) and look up the character at each position:

```
sentence = input("Enter a sentence: ")
for i in range(len(sentence)) :
   if sentence[i].isupper() :
      print(i)
```

4.8.3 Finding the First or Last Match

If your goal is to find a match, exit the loop when the match is found.

When you count the values that fulfill a condition, you need to look at all values. However, if your task is to find a match, then you can stop as soon as the condition is fulfilled.

Here is a loop that finds the position of the first digit in a string.

```
found = False
position = 0
while not found and position < len(string) :
   if string[position].isdigit() :
      found = True
   else :
      position = position + 1

if found :
   print("First digit occurs at position", position)
else :
   print("The string does not contain a digit.")
```

If a match was found, then `found` will be `True` and `position` will contain the index of the first match. If the loop did not find a match, then `found` remains `False` after the loop terminates. We can use the value of `found` to determine which of the two messages to print.

What if we need to find the position of the last digit in the string? Traverse the string from back to front:

```
found = False
position = len(string) - 1
while not found and position >= 0 :
    if string[position].isdigit() :
        found = True
    else :
        position = position - 1
```

When searching, you look at items until a match is found.   © drflet/iStockphoto.

4.8.4 Validating a String

In Chapter 3, you learned the importance of validating user input before it is used in computations. But data validation is not limited to verifying that user input is a specific value or falls within a valid range. It is also common to require user input to be entered in a specific format. For example, consider the task of verifying whether a string contains a correctly formatted telephone number.

> Validating a string can ensure that it contains correctly formatted data.

In the United States, telephone numbers consist of three parts—area code, exchange, and line number—which are commonly specified in the form (###)###-####. We can examine a string to ensure that it contains a correctly formatted phone number with 13 characters. To do this, we must not only verify that it contains digits and the appropriate symbols, but that each are in the appropriate spots in the string. This requires an event-controlled loop that can exit early if an invalid character or an out of place symbol is encountered while processing the string:

```
valid = len(string) == 13
position = 0
while valid and position < len(string) :
    if position == 0 :
        valid = string[position] == "("
    elif position == 4 :
        valid = string[position] == ")"
    elif position == 8 :
        valid = string[position] == "-"
    else :
        valid = string[position].isdigit()
    position = position + 1

if valid :
    print("The string contains a valid phone number.")
else :
    print("The string does not contain a valid phone number.")
```

As an alternative, we can combine the four logical conditions into a single expression to produce a more compact loop:

```
valid = len(string) == 13
position = 0
while valid and position < len(string) :
    valid = ((position == 0 and string[position] == "(")
        or (position == 4 and string[position] == ")")
        or (position == 8 and string[position] == "-")
        or (position != 0 and position != 4 and position != 8
            and string[position].isdigit()))
    position = position + 1
```

4.8.5 Building a New String

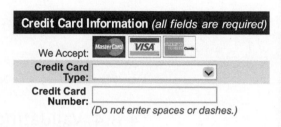

One of the minor annoyances of online shopping is that many web sites require you to enter a credit card without spaces or dashes, which makes double-checking the number rather tedious. How hard can it be to remove dashes or spaces from a string?

You build a string by concatenating individual characters.

As you learned in Chapter 2, the contents of a string cannot be changed. But nothing prevents us from building a new string. For example, if the user enters a string that contains a credit card number in the format `"4123-5678-9012-3450"`, we can remove the dashes by building a new string that contains only the digits: start with an empty string and append to it each character in the original string that is not a space or dash. In Python, characters can be appended to a string using the string concatenation operator (+):

```
newString = newString + "x"
```

Here is a loop that builds a new string containing a credit card number with spaces and dashes removed:

```
userInput = input("Enter a credit card number: ")
creditCardNumber = ""
for char in userInput :
    if char != " " and char != "-" :
        creditCardNumber = creditCardNumber + char
```

If the user enters `"4123-5678-9012-3450"`, `creditCardNumber` will contain the string `"4123567890123450"` after the loop executes.

As another example, suppose we need to build a new string in which all uppercase letters in the original are converted to lowercase and all lowercase letters are converted to uppercase. Using the same technique of string concatenation used in the previous example, this is rather easy:

```
newString = ""
for char in original :
    if char.isupper() :
        newChar = char.lower()
    elif char.islower() :
        newChar = char.upper()
```

```
else :
    newChar = char
newString = newString + newChar
```

The following program demonstrates several of the string processing algorithms presented in this section. This program reads a string that contains a test taker's answers to a multiple choice exam and grades the test.

sec08/multiplechoice.py

```python
1  ##
2  #   This program grades a multiple choice exam in which each question has four
3  #   possible choices: a, b, c, or d.
4  #
5
6  # Define a string containing the correct answers.
7  CORRECT_ANSWERS = "adbdcacbdac"
8
9  # Obtain the user's answers, and make sure enough answers are provided.
10 done = False
11 while not done :
12     userAnswers = input("Enter your exam answers: ")
13     if len(userAnswers) == len(CORRECT_ANSWERS) :
14         done = True
15     else :
16         print("Error: an incorrect number of answers given.")
17
18 # Check the exam.
19 numQuestions = len(CORRECT_ANSWERS)
20 numCorrect = 0
21 results = ""
22
23 for i in range(numQuestions) :
24     if userAnswers[i] == CORRECT_ANSWERS[i] :
25         numCorrect = numCorrect + 1
26         results = results + userAnswers[i]
27     else :
28         results = results + "X"
29
30 # Grade the exam.
31 score = round(numCorrect / numQuestions * 100)
32
33 if score == 100 :
34     print("Very Good!")
35 else :
36     print("You missed %d questions: %s" % (numQuestions - numCorrect, results))
37
38 print("Your score is: %d percent" % score)
```

Program Run

```
Enter your exam answers: acddcbcbcac
You missed 4 questions: aXXdcXcbXac
Your score is: 64 percent
```

4.9 Application: Random Numbers and Simulations

In a simulation, you use the computer to simulate an activity.

A *simulation program* uses the computer to simulate an activity in the real world (or an imaginary one). Simulations are commonly used for predicting climate change, analyzing traffic, picking stocks, and many other applications in science and business. In many simulations, one or more loops are used to modify the state of a system and observe the changes. You will see examples in the following sections.

4.9.1 Generating Random Numbers

Many events in the real world are difficult to predict with absolute precision, yet we can sometimes know the average behavior quite well. For example, a store may know from experience that a customer arrives every five minutes. Of course, that is an average—customers don't arrive in five minute intervals. To accurately model customer traffic, you want to take that random fluctuation into account. Now, how can you run such a simulation in the computer?

You can introduce randomness by calling the random number generator.

The Python library has a *random number generator* that produces numbers that appear to be completely random. Calling `random()` yields a random floating-point number that is ≥ 0 and < 1. Call `random()` again, and you get a different number. The `random` function is defined in the `random` module.

The following program calls `random()` ten times.

sec09_01/randomtest.py

```
1  ##
2  #   This program prints ten random numbers between 0 and 1.
3  #
4
5  from random import random
6
7  for i in range(10) :
8      value = random()
9      print(value)
```

Program Run

```
0.580742512361
0.907222103296
0.102851584902
0.196652864583
0.957267274444
0.439101769744
0.299604096229
0.679313379668
0.0903726139666
0.801120553331
```

Actually, the numbers are not completely random. They are drawn from sequences of numbers that don't repeat for a long time. These sequences are actually computed from fairly simple formulas; they just behave like random numbers (see Exercise • P4.27). For that reason, they are often called **pseudorandom** numbers.

4.9.2 Simulating Die Tosses

In actual applications, you need to transform the output from the random number generator into a specific range. For example, to simulate the throw of a die, you need random integers between 1 and 6.

Python provides a separate function for generating a random integer within a given range. The function

```
randint(a, b)
```

which is defined in the random module, returns a random integer that is between a and b, including the bounds themselves.

Here is a program that simulates the throw of a pair of dice.

© ktsimage/iStockphoto.

sec09_02/dice.py

```
1   ##
2   #   This program simulates tosses of a pair of dice.
3   #
4
5   from random import randint
6
7   for i in range(10) :
8       # Generate two random numbers between 1 and 6, inclusive.
9       d1 = randint(1, 6)
10      d2 = randint(1, 6)
11
12      # Print the two values.
13      print(d1, d2)
```

Program Run

```
1 5
6 4
1 1
4 5
6 4
3 2
4 2
3 5
5 2
4 5
```

4.9.3 The Monte Carlo Method

The Monte Carlo method is an ingenious method for finding approximate solutions to problems that cannot be precisely solved. (The method is named after the famous casino in Monte Carlo.)

Here is a typical example. It is difficult to compute the number π, but you can approximate it quite well with the following simulation.

© timstarkey/iStockphoto.

Simulate shooting a dart into a square surrounding a circle of radius 1. That is easy: generate random x- and y-coordinates between –1 and 1.

If the generated point lies inside the circle, we count it as a *hit*. That is the case when $x^2 + y^2 \leq 1$. Because our shots are entirely random, we expect that the ratio of *hits/tries* is approximately equal to the ratio of the areas of the circle and the square, that is, $\pi/4$. Therefore, our estimate for π is $4 \times$ *hits/tries*. This method yields an estimate for π, using nothing but simple arithmetic.

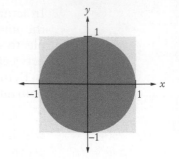

To generate a random floating-point value between two bounds a and b, you compute:

```
r = random()    # 0 ≤ r < 1
x = a + (b - a) * r    # a ≤ x < b
```

As r ranges from 0 (inclusive) to 1 (exclusive), x ranges from a (inclusive) to b (exclusive). In our application, it does not matter that x never reaches the upper bound (b = 1). The points that fulfill the equation $x = 1$ lie on a line with area 0.

Here is the program that carries out the simulation.

sec09_03/montecarlo.py

```
 1  ##
 2  #   This program computes an estimate of pi by simulating
 3  #   dart throws onto a square.
 4  #
 5
 6  from random import random
 7
 8  TRIES = 10000
 9
10  hits = 0
11  for i in range(TRIES) :
12
13      # Generate two random numbers between -1 and 1
14      r = random()
15      x = -1 + 2 * r
16      r = random()
17      y = -1 + 2 * r
18
19      # Check whether the point lies in the unit circle
20      if x * x + y * y <= 1 :
21          hits = hits + 1
22
23  # The ratio hits / tries is approximately the same as the ratio
24  # circle area / square area = pi / 4.
25
26  piEstimate = 4.0 * hits / TRIES
27  print("Estimate for pi:", piEstimate)
```

Program Run

```
Estimate for pi: 3.1464
```

WORKED EXAMPLE 4.3

Graphics: Bull's Eye

Problem Statement   Develop a graphics program that draws a target with alternating black and white rings on a light gray background and a red bull's eye in the center.

The number of rings in the target should be obtained from the user but it must be between two and ten. Each ring should be 25 pixels wide and the bull's eye should have a diameter that is twice the width of a ring. The outermost ring must be colored black with each subsequent ring alternating between white and black. Finally, the size of the graphics window should be based on the size of the target with the outer ring offset ten pixels from all four sides of the window.

Step 1   Define constant variables.

You should define constant variables for the constraints and sizes specified in the problem statement. This also makes it easy to change these constraints, if necessary.

The problem description specifies several magic numbers:

```
MIN_NUM_RINGS = 2
MAX_NUM_RINGS = 10
RING_WIDTH = 25
TARGET_OFFSET = 10
```

Step 2   Obtain the number of rings from the user.

Because there is a limitation on the number of rings contained in the target, we need to validate the user input:

```
numRings = int(input("Enter # of rings in the target: "))
While number of rings is outside the valid range
    Print an error message.
    numRings = int(input("Re-enter # of rings in the target: "))
```

Step 3   Determine how the rings will be drawn.

Each ring can be drawn as a filled circle, with the individual circles drawn on top of each other, starting with the outside circle. The inner circles will fill the center part of the larger circles, thus creating the ring effect.

Step 4   Determine the size of the graphics window.

The size of the window is based on the size of the target, which is the size of the outer ring. To determine the radius of the outer ring we can sum the widths of all the rings and the radius of the bull's eye (which is equal to the width of a ring). We know the number of rings and the width of each ring, so the computation is

outer ring radius = (number of rings + 1) x RING_WIDTH

The size of the target is simply the diameter of the outer ring, or 2 times its radius:

target size = 2 x outer ring radius

Finally, the target is offset from the window border by TARGET_OFFSET pixels. Accounting for the offset and the size of the target, we can compute the size of the window as

window size = target size + 2 x TARGET_OFFSET

Step 5   Draw the rings of the target.

To draw the rings of the target, we start with the outermost circle and work our way inward. We can use a basic for loop that iterates once for each ring and includes several steps:

```
Initialize circle parameters.
for i in range(numRings) :
    Select circle color.
    Draw the circle.
    Adjust circle parameters.
```

The parameters of the outer circle, which is drawn first, must be initialized before the first iteration of the loop. The diameter of the outer circle is equal to the size of the target. Its bounding box is offset from the window border by TARGET_OFFSET pixels in both the horizontal and vertical directions.

```
diameter = target size
x = TARGET_OFFSET
y = TARGET_OFFSET
```

To select the color used to draw the circle, we can base our decision on the value of the loop variable i. Because the loop variable starts at 0, a black circle will be drawn each time the loop variable is even and a white circle will be drawn each time it's odd.

```
If i is even
    canvas.setColor("black")
Else
    canvas.setColor("white")
```

To draw the circle, use the drawOval canvas method with both the width and height of the bounding box set to the diameter of the circle. The drawOval method also requires the position of the upper-left corner of the bounding box:

```
canvas.drawOval(x, y, diameter, diameter)
```

The diameter of each inner circle will decrease by 2 times the ring width and the position of the bounding box will move inward by a ring width in both directions.

```
diameter = diameter - 2 * RING_WIDTH
x = x + RING_WIDTH
y = y + RING_WIDTH
```

Step 6   Draw the bull's eye in the center.

After drawing the black and white rings, we still have to draw the bull's eye in the center as a red filled circle. When the loop terminates, the circle parameters (position and diameter) will be set to the values needed to draw that circle.

Step 7   Implement your solution in Python.

The complete program is provided below. Note that we use the setBackground canvas method to set the background color of the canvas to a light gray instead of the default white. (See http://ezgraphics.org for a complete description of the ezgraphics module.)

worked_example_3/bullseye.py

```
1  ##
2  #   Draws a target with a bull's eye using the number of rings
3  #   specified by the user.
4  #
5
6  from ezgraphics import GraphicsWindow
```

```
 7
 8  # Define constant variables.
 9  MIN_NUM_RINGS = 2
10  MAX_NUM_RINGS = 10
11  RING_WIDTH = 25
12  TARGET_OFFSET = 10
13
14  # Obtain number of rings in the target.
15  numRings = int(input("Enter # of rings in the target: "))
16  while numRings < MIN_NUM_RINGS or numRings > MAX_NUM_RINGS :
17      print("Error: the number of rings must be between",
18            MIN_NUM_RINGS, "and", MAX_NUM_RINGS)
19      numRings = int(input("Re-enter # of rings in the target: "))
20
21  # Determine the diameter of the outermost circle. It has to be drawn first.
22  diameter = (numRings + 1) * RING_WIDTH * 2
23
24  # Determine the size of the window based on the size of the outer circle.
25  winSize = diameter + 2 * TARGET_OFFSET
26
27  # Create the graphics window and get the canvas.
28  win = GraphicsWindow(winSize, winSize)
29  canvas = win.canvas()
30
31  # Use a light gray background for the canvas.
32  canvas.setBackground("light gray")
33
34  # Draw the rings, alternating between black and white.
35  x = TARGET_OFFSET
36  y = TARGET_OFFSET
37  for ring in range(numRings) :
38      if ring % 2 == 0 :
39          canvas.setColor("black")
40      else :
41          canvas.setColor("white")
42      canvas.drawOval(x, y, diameter, diameter)
43
44      diameter = diameter - 2 * RING_WIDTH
45      x = x + RING_WIDTH
46      y = y + RING_WIDTH
47
48  # Draw the bull's eye in red.
49  canvas.setColor("red")
50  canvas.drawOval(x, y, diameter, diameter)
51
52  win.wait()
```

4.10 Graphics: Digital Image Processing

Digital image processing is the use of computer algorithms to manipulate digital images. This technique has a wide range of uses, from digital photography to applications in data compression, computer graphics, computer vision, and robotics. In this section, you will learn how to manipulate images with the ezgraphics package.

4.10.1 Filtering Images

A digital image is made of distinct pixels organized into a grid.

A digital image is made of "pixels" arranged in a grid of rows and columns. You don't typically see the individual pixels, but they are there. An image on a computer screen appears smooth or continuous because very small points on the screen are used to reproduce the individual pixels.

The pixels store data representing a color from the visible spectrum. There are different ways to specify a color, but the most common is to use the discrete RGB color model, where the individual colors are specified by the amount of red, green, and blue light needed to produce the given color. The values are given as integers between 0 (no light present) and 255 (maximum amount present).

Image colors are specified using RGB values.

Filtering an image results in the color component values of each pixel being modified in some way. For example, you can darken a bright image, create the negative of an image, or convert an image to grayscale. Table 4 approximates the results of applying several common filters to a variety of RGB values.

Table 4 Sample RGB Values			
RGB Values	15% Darker	Negative	Grayscale
255, 255, 255	217, 217, 217	0, 0, 0	254, 254, 254
0, 0, 255	0, 0, 217	255, 255, 0	18, 18, 18
128, 128, 128	109, 109, 109	127, 127, 127	128, 128, 128
0, 255, 0	0, 217, 0	255, 0, 255	182, 182, 182
255, 0, 0	217, 0, 0	0, 255, 255	54, 54, 54
35, 178, 200	30, 151, 170	220, 77, 55	149, 149, 149
255, 255, 0	217, 217, 0	0, 0, 255	236, 236, 236
0, 255, 255	0, 217, 217	255, 0, 0	200, 200, 200

To process an image, you must first load it into your program. In the `ezgraphics` module, an image is stored in an instance of the `GraphicsImage` class. Table 5 on page 174 shows the methods of the class. You can load an image from a file like this:

```
filename = "queen-mary.gif"
image = GraphicsImage(filename)
```

Use drawImage to display an image in a GraphicsWindow.

To display the image, you draw it on the canvas of a `GraphicsWindow`:

```
win = GraphicsWindow()
canvas = win.canvas()
canvas.drawImage(image)
win.wait()
```

EXAMPLE CODE See sec10_01/viewimage.py in your eText or companion code for an image file viewer program.

However, before showing the image, we will want to filter, or transform, it. Let us start with something simple—replacing an image with its negative, the kind of image that old-fashioned film cameras used to produce (see Figure 6).

Courtesy of Cay Horstmann.

Figure 6 An Image and Its Negative

Filtering an image modifies the pixel colors.

To filter an image, you must get the red, green, and blue component values for each pixel. The pixels are organized into a two-dimensional grid of size *width* × *height*.

The rows and columns are numbered sequentially starting at 0, with pixel (0, 0) in the upper-left corner. The row numbers range from 0 to *height* – 1; the column numbers from 0 to *width* – 1.

Pixels are identified by row and column.

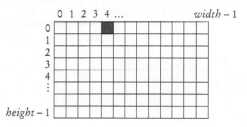

To get the three component values of an individual pixel, you use the getRed, getGreen, and getBlue methods. The following gets the color of the pixel in row 0, column 4:

```
red = image.getRed(0, 4)
green = image.getGreen(0, 4)
blue = image.getBlue(0, 4)
```

To create the negative of an image, adjust the RGB component values using the equations:

```
newRed = 255 - red
newGreen = 255 - green
newBlue = 255 - blue
```

After the values have been adjusted, update the pixel with the new color:

```
image.setPixel(0, 4, newRed, newGreen, newBlue)
```

To process the entire image, use nested loops to iterate over the individual pixels:

```
width = image.width()
height = image.height()
for row in range(height) :
    for col in range(width) :
        Get the current pixel color.
        Filter the pixel.
        Set the pixel to the new color.
```

After creating the negative of the original image, you can save the result by calling

```
image.save("negative" + filename)
```

Following is the complete source code for a program that processes an image file, producing a negative of the original.

sec10_01/filterimage.py

```
 1  ##
 2  #   This program processes a digital image by creating a negative of
 3  #   the original.
 4  #
 5
 6  from ezgraphics import GraphicsImage, GraphicsWindow
 7
 8  filename = input("Enter the name of the image file: ")
 9
10  # Load the image from the file.
11  image = GraphicsImage(filename)
12
13  # Process the image.
14  width = image.width()
15  height = image.height()
16  for row in range(height) :
17      for col in range(width) :
18          # Get the current pixel color.
19          red = image.getRed(row, col)
20          green = image.getGreen(row, col)
21          blue = image.getBlue(row, col)
22
23          # Filter the pixel.
24          newRed = 255 - red
25          newGreen = 255 - green
26          newBlue = 255 - blue
27
28          # Set the pixel to the new color.
29          image.setPixel(row, col, newRed, newGreen, newBlue)
30
31  # Display the image on screen.
32  win = GraphicsWindow()
33  canvas = win.canvas()
34  canvas.drawImage(image)
35  win.wait()
36
37  # Save the new image with a new name.
38  image.save("negative-" + filename)
```

4.10.2 Reconfiguring Images

Other manipulations can change the grid structure of the image without modifying the pixel values. For example, you may want to flip or rotate an image, or enlarge the image and add a border.

Reconfiguring an image requires the use of a second image into which the original pixels can be copied. The size of the new image depends on the type of reconfiguration to be performed. To vertically flip an image, for example, the new image must be the same size as the original.

> An image can be reconfigured without modifying the pixel colors.

```
origImage = GraphicsImage("queen-mary.gif")
width = origImage.width()
height = origImage.height()
newImage = GraphicsImage(width, height)
```

The colors of the individual pixels will not be modified; they simply have to be copied to the new image. You can copy the red, green, and blue components separately, as you saw in the preceding section, or you can move a pixel in its entirety. The getPixel method returns all three colors in a "tuple"—a data structure that holds three values at once (see Special Topic 6.5 for more on tuples). Then call the setPixel method to set the pixel in the new image.

For example, to create a duplicate image, copy the pixels to the same location in the new image:

```
for row in range(height) :
    for col in range(width) :
        pixel = origImage.getPixel(row, col)
        newImage.setPixel(row, col, pixel)
```

To flip an image vertically (see Figure 7), entire rows of pixels have to be copied to different rows in the new image. The first row will become the last row in the new image, the second row will be the next to last row in the new image, and so on.

Courtesy of Cay Horstmann.

Figure 7 A Flipped Version of an Image

To do so, you iterate over the pixels in the original image, computing their location in the new image and keeping track of them with a second set of row and column variables. Here, we use newRow and newCol:

```
newRow = height - 1
for row in range(height) :
    for col in range(width) :
        newCol = col
        pixel = origImage.getPixel(row, col)
        newImage.setPixel(newRow, newCol, pixel)

    newRow = newRow - 1
```

The following program creates and saves the image that results from vertically flipping a GIF image.

sec10_02/flipimage.py

```
1  ##
2  #  This program creates a new flipped version of a GIF image.
3  #
4
5  from ezgraphics import GraphicsImage
6
7  filename = input("Enter the name of the image file: ")
8
9  # Load the original image.
10 origImage = GraphicsImage(filename)
11
```

```
12  # Create an empty image that will contain the new flipped image.
13  width = origImage.width()
14  height = origImage.height()
15  newImage = GraphicsImage(width, height)
16
17  # Iterate over the image and copy the pixels to the new image to
18  # produce the flipped image.
19  newRow = height - 1
20  for row in range(height) :
21     for col in range(width) :
22        newCol = col
23        pixel = origImage.getPixel(row, col)
24        newImage.setPixel(newRow, newCol, pixel)
25     newRow = newRow - 1
26
27  # Save the new image with a new name.
28  newImage.save("flipped-" + filename)
```

A list of the methods that can be used with a graphics image are shown in Table 5.

Table 5 GraphicsImage Methods

Method	Description
GraphicsImage(*filename*)	Reads the file into a GraphicsImage object.
GraphicsImage(*width*, *height*)	Constructs a blank image of the given size.
img.setPixel(*row, col, red, green, blue*) *img*.setPixel(*row, col, pixel*)	Sets the color of the pixel at position (row, col) to the given RGB values, or to a tuple containing the RGB values.
img.getRed(*row, col*) *img*.getGreen(*row, col*) *img*.getBlue(*row, col*) *img*.getPixel(*row, col*)	Returns the red, green, or blue value of the pixel at position (row, col), or a tuple of all three values.
img.save(*filename*)	Saves the image to a GIF file.
img.copy()	Creates and returns a new image that is a duplicate copy of this image.
img.width() *img*.height()	Returns the width or height of the image.

4.11 Problem Solving: Solve a Simpler Problem First

When developing a solution to a complex problem, first solve a simpler task.

As you learn more about programming, the complexity of the tasks that you are asked to solve will increase. When you face a complex task, you should apply an important skill: simplifying the problem and solving the simpler problem first.

This is a good strategy for several reasons. Usually, you learn something useful from solving the simpler task. Moreover, the complex problem can seem insurmountable, and you may find it difficult to know where to get started. When you are successful with a simpler problem first, you will be much more motivated to try the harder one.

It takes practice and a certain amount of courage to break down a problem into a sequence of simpler ones. The best way to learn this strategy is to practice it. When you work on your next assignment, ask yourself what is the absolutely simplest part of the task that is helpful for the end result, and start from there. With some experience, you will be able to design a plan that builds up a complete solution as a manageable sequence of intermediate steps.

Let us look at an example. You are asked to arrange pictures, lining them up along the top edges, separating them with small gaps, and starting a new row whenever you run out of room in the current row.

National Gallery of Art (see Credits page for details.)

Instead of tackling the entire assignment at once, here is a plan that solves a series of simpler problems.

> Make a plan consisting of a series of tasks, each a simple extension of the previous one, and ending with the original problem.

1. Draw one picture.

2. Draw two pictures next to each other.

3. Draw two pictures with a gap between them.

4. Draw three pictures with a gap between them.

5. Draw all pictures in a long row.

...

6. Draw a row of pictures until you run out of room, then put one more picture in the next row.

Let's get started with this plan.

1. The `GraphicsImage` class that is part of the `ezgraphics` module and that was introduced in Section 4.10 can be used to load the pictures for this problem. As it turns out, the pictures are in files named `picture1.gif`, `picture2.gif`, ... `picture20.gif`. Let's load the first one:

```
pic = GraphicsImage("picture1.gif")
```

To show the picture, first get a canvas in a `GraphicsWindow` to draw on:

```
win = GraphicsWindow(750, 350)
canvas = win.canvas()
```

To draw the image, specify the canvas coordinates where the upper-left corner of the image is to be positioned. Here, we want to draw the first picture in the upper-left corner of the canvas and wait for the user to close the window.

```
canvas.drawImage(0, 0, pic)
win.wait()
```

That's enough to show the picture.

2. Now let's put the next picture after the first. It needs to be drawn so that its left-most edge is positioned at the right-most *x*-coordinate of the preceding picture. This can be determined by obtaining the width of the first picture and using that value as the *x*-coordinate for the second picture.

pic.width()

```
win = GraphicsWindow(750, 350)
canvas = win.canvas()
pic = GraphicsImage("picture1.gif")
canvas.drawImage(0, 0, pic)
pic2 = GraphicsImage("picture2.gif")
x = pic.width()
canvas.drawImage(x, 0, pic2)
win.wait()
```

3. The next step is to separate the two by a small gap:

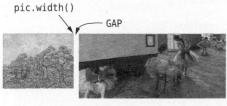

```
GAP = 10
win = GraphicsWindow(750, 350)
canvas = win.canvas()
pic = GraphicsImage("picture1.gif")
canvas.drawImage(0, 0, pic)
pic2 = GraphicsImage("picture2.gif")
x = pic.width() + GAP
canvas.drawImage(x, 0, pic2)
win.wait()
```

4. To draw the third picture, it's not sufficient to know the width of the preceding picture. We also need to know the *x*-coordinate where it was drawn so we can add that value to the width of the preceding image, plus the gap between the images.

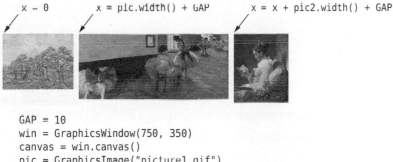

```
GAP = 10
win = GraphicsWindow(750, 350)
canvas = win.canvas()
pic = GraphicsImage("picture1.gif")
canvas.drawImage(0, 0, pic)
pic2 = GraphicsImage("picture2.gif")
x = pic.width() + GAP
canvas.drawImage(x, 0, pic2)
pic3 = GraphicsImage("picture3.gif")
x = x + pic2.width() + GAP
canvas.drawImage(x, 0, pic3)
win.wait()
```

5. Now let's put all of the pictures in a row. Load the pictures in a loop, and then put each picture to the right of the one that preceded it. In each iteration, you need to track two pictures: the one that is being loaded, and the one that preceded it (see Section 4.5.5).

```
GAP = 10
NUM_PICTURES = 20

win = GraphicsWindow(750, 350)
canvas = win.canvas()
pic = GraphicsImage("picture1.gif")
canvas.drawImage(0, 0, pic)

x = 0
for i in range(2, NUM_PICTURES + 1) :
   previous = pic
   filename = "picture%d.gif" % i
   pic = GraphicsImage(filename)
   x = x + previous.width() + GAP
   canvas.drawImage(x, 0, pic)
win.wait()
```

6. Of course, we don't want to have all pictures in a row. The right margin of a picture should not extend past MAX_WIDTH.

```
x = previous.width() + GAP
if x + pic.width() < MAX_WIDTH :
   Place pic on current row.
else :
   Place pic on next row.
```

If the image doesn't fit any more, then we need to put it on the next row, below all the pictures in the current row. We'll set a variable maxY to the maximum *y*-coordinate of all placed pictures, updating it whenever a new picture is placed:

```
maxY = max(maxY, pic.height())
```

The following statement places a picture on the next row:

```
canvas.drawImage(0, maxY + GAP, pic)
```

Using this, we can complete the last preliminary stage for constructing the gallery program:

```
GAP = 10
NUM_PICTURES = 5   # Temporarily set to 5 for testing Step 6
MAX_WIDTH = 720

win = GraphicsWindow(750, 350)
canvas = win.canvas()
pic = GraphicsImage("picture1.gif")
canvas.drawImage(0, 0, pic)
```

```
          x = 0
          maxY = 0
          for i in range(2, NUM_PICTURES + 1) :
             maxY = max(maxY, pic.height())
             previous = pic
             filename = "picture%d.gif" % i
             pic = GraphicsImage(filename)
             x = x + previous.width() + GAP
             if x + pic.width() < MAX_WIDTH :
                canvas.drawImage(x, 0, pic)
             else :
                canvas.drawImage(0, maxY + GAP, pic)

          win.wait()
```

Now we have written complete programs for all preliminary stages. We know how to line up the pictures, how to separate them with gaps, how to find out when to start a new row, and where to start it.

EXAMPLE CODE   With this knowledge, producing the final version is straightforward. Here is the program listing.

sec11/gallery.py

```
 1  ##
 2  #   This program arranges a collection of pictures into rows by lining
 3  #   them up along the top edges and separating them with small gaps.
 4  #
 5
 6  from ezgraphics import GraphicsImage, GraphicsWindow
 7
 8  GAP = 10
 9  NUM_PICTURES = 20
10  MAX_WIDTH = 720
11
12  win = GraphicsWindow(750, 750)   # Taller window to show all pictures
13  canvas = win.canvas()
14
15  pic = GraphicsImage("picture1.gif")
16  canvas.drawImage(0, 0, pic)
17
18  x = 0
19  y = 0
20  maxY = 0
21  for i in range(2, NUM_PICTURES + 1) :
22     maxY = max(maxY, pic.height())
23     previous = pic
24     filename = "picture%d.gif" % i
25     pic = GraphicsImage(filename)
26     x = x + previous.width() + GAP
27     if x + pic.width() < MAX_WIDTH :
28        canvas.drawImage(x, y, pic)
29     else :
30        x = 0
31        y = y + maxY + GAP
32        canvas.drawImage(x, y, pic)
33
34  win.wait()
```

Computing & Society 4.2 Digital Piracy

As you read this, you will have written a few computer programs and experienced firsthand how much effort it takes to write even the humblest of programs. Writing a real software product, such as a financial application or a computer game, takes a lot of time and money. Few people, and fewer companies, are going to spend that kind of time and money if they don't have a reasonable chance to make more money from their effort. Revenue comes from licensing fees or advertising.

When a mass market for personal computer software first appeared, it was an easy matter for an unscrupulous person to make copies of computer programs without paying for them. In most countries that is illegal. Most governments provide legal protection, such as copyright laws and patents, to encourage the development of new products. Countries that tolerate widespread piracy have found that they have an ample cheap supply of foreign software, but no local manufacturers willing to design good software for their own citizens, such

as word processors in the local script or financial programs adapted to the local tax laws.

Because it is so easy and inexpensive to pirate software, and the chance of being found out is minimal, you have to make a moral choice for yourself. If a package that you would really like to have is too expensive for your budget, do you steal it, or do you stay honest and get by with a more affordable product?

Of course, piracy is not limited to software. The same issues arise for other digital products as well. You may have had the opportunity to obtain copies of songs or movies without payment. Or you may have been frustrated by a copy protection device on your music player that made it difficult for you to listen to songs that you paid for. Admittedly, it can be difficult to have a lot of sympathy for a musical ensemble whose publisher charges a lot of money for what seems to have been very little effort on their part, at least when compared to the effort that goes into designing and implementing a software package. Nevertheless,

it seems only fair that artists and authors receive some compensation for their efforts.

How to pay artists, authors, and programmers fairly, without burdening honest customers, is an unsolved problem at the time of this writing, and many computer scientists are engaged in research in this area.

© RapidEye/iStockphoto.

CHAPTER SUMMARY

Explain the flow of execution in a loop.

- A while loop executes instructions repeatedly while a condition is true.
- An off-by-one error is a common error when programming loops. Think through simple test cases to avoid this type of error.

Use the technique of hand-tracing to analyze the behavior of a program.

- Hand-tracing is a simulation of code execution in which you step through instructions and track the values of the variables.
- Hand-tracing can help you understand how an unfamiliar algorithm works.
- Hand-tracing can show errors in code or pseudocode.

Implement loops that read sequences of input data.

- A sentinel value denotes the end of a data set, but it is not part of the data.
- A pair of input operations, known as the priming and modification reads, can be used to read a sentinel-terminated sequence of values.
- Use input redirection to read input from a file. Use output redirection to capture program output in a file.

Use the technique of storyboarding for planning user interactions.

- A storyboard consists of annotated sketches for each step in an action sequence.
- Developing a storyboard helps you understand the inputs and outputs that are required for a program.

Know the most common loop algorithms.

- To compute an average, keep a total and a count of all values.
- To count values that fulfill a condition, check all values and increment a counter for each match.
- To find the largest value, update the largest value seen so far whenever you see a larger one.
- To compare adjacent inputs, store the preceding input in a variable.

Use for loops to iterate over the elements of a container.

- Use the for loop when you need to access the characters of a string one at a time.
- The for loop can be used with the range function to iterate over a range of integer values.

Use nested loops to implement multiple levels of iteration.

- When the body of a loop contains another loop, the loops are nested. A typical use of nested loops is printing a table with rows and columns.

Use loops to process strings.

- Use the in operator to compare a character against multiple options.
- If your goal is to find a match, exit the loop when the match is found.
- Validating a string can ensure that it contains correctly formatted data.
- You build a string by concatenating individual characters.

Apply loops to the implementation of simulations.

- In a simulation, you use the computer to simulate an activity.
- You can introduce randomness by calling the random number generator.

Design computer algorithms to manipulate digital images.

- A digital image is made of distinct pixels organized into a grid.
- Image colors are specified using RGB values.
- Use drawImage to display an image in a GraphicsWindow.
- Filtering an image modifies the pixel colors.
- Pixels are identified by row and column.
- An image can be reconfigured without modifying the pixel colors.

Design programs that carry out complex tasks.

- When developing a solution to a complex problem, first solve a simpler task.
- Make a plan consisting of a series of tasks, each a simple extension of the previous one, and ending with the original problem.

- **R4.1** Write a while loop that prints
  - **a.** All squares less than n. For example, if n is 100, print 0 1 4 9 16 25 36 49 64 81.
  - **b.** All positive numbers that are divisible by 10 and less than n. For example, if n is 100, print 10 20 30 40 50 60 70 80 90
  - **c.** All powers of two less than n. For example, if n is 100, print 1 2 4 8 16 32 64.

- **R4.2** Write a loop that computes
  - **a.** The sum of all even numbers between 2 and 100 (inclusive).
  - **b.** The sum of all squares between 1 and 100 (inclusive).
  - **c.** The sum of all odd numbers between a and b (inclusive).
  - **d.** The sum of all odd digits of n. (For example, if n is 32677, the sum would be $3 + 7 + 7 = 17$.)

- **R4.3** Provide trace tables for these loops.

  a.
  ```
  i = 0
  j = 10
  n = 0
  while i < j :
      i = i + 1
      j = j - 1
      n = n + 1
  ```

  b.
  ```
  i = 0
  j = 0
  n = 0
  while i < 10 :
      i = i + 1
      n = n + i + j
      j = j + 1
  ```

  c.
  ```
  i = 10
  j = 0
  n = 0
  while i > 0 :
      i = i - 1
      j = j + 1
      n = n + i - j
  ```

  d.
  ```
  i = 0
  j = 10
  n = 0
  while i != j :
      i = i + 2
      j = j - 2
      n = n + 1
  ```

- **R4.4** What do these loops print?
  - **a.**
    ```
    for i in range(1, 10) :
        print(i)
    ```
  - **b.**
    ```
    for i in range(1, 10, 2) :
        print(i)
    ```
  - **c.**
    ```
    for i in range(10, 1, -1) :
        print(i)
    ```
  - **d.**
    ```
    for i in range(10) :
        print(i)
    ```
  - **e.**
    ```
    for i in range(1, 10) :
        if i % 2 == 0 :
            print(i)
    ```

- **R4.5** What is an infinite loop? On your computer, how can you terminate a program that executes an infinite loop?

- **R4.6** Write a program trace for the pseudocode in Exercise • P4.6, assuming the input values are 4 7 –2 –5 0.

- **R4.7** What is an "off-by-one" error? Give an example from your own programming experience.

■ **R4.8** What is a sentinel value? Give a simple rule when it is appropriate to use a numeric sentinel value.

■ **R4.9** Which loop statements does Python support? Give simple rules for when to use each loop type.

■ **R4.10** How many iterations do the following loops carry out?

    a. `for i in range(1, 11) . . .`
    b. `for i in range(10) . . .`
    c. `for i in range(10, 0, -1) . . .`
    d. `for i in range(-10, 11) . . .`
    e. `for i in range(10, 0) . . .`
    f. `for i in range(-10, 11, 2) . . .`
    g. `for i in range(-10, 11, 3) . . .`

■■ **R4.11** Give an example of a `for` loop where symmetric bounds are more natural. Give an example of a `for` loop where asymmetric bounds are more natural.

■■ **R4.12** Write pseudocode for a program that prints a calendar such as the following:

```
Su  M  T  W Th  F Sa
          1  2  3  4
 5  6  7  8  9 10 11
12 13 14 15 16 17 18
19 20 21 22 23 24 25
26 27 28 29 30 31
```

■ **R4.13** Write pseudocode for a program that prints a Celsius/Fahrenheit conversion table such as the following:

```
Celsius | Fahrenheit
--------+-----------
      0 |         32
     10 |         50
     20 |         68
   . . .         . . .
    100 |        212
```

■ **R4.14** Write pseudocode for a program that reads a student record, consisting of the student's first and last name, followed by a sequence of test scores and a sentinel of –1. The program should print the student's average score. Then provide a trace table for this sample input:

```
Harry
Morgan
94
71
86
95
-1
```

■■ **R4.15** Write pseudocode for a program that reads a sequence of student records and prints the total score for each student. Each record has the student's first and last name, followed by a sequence of test scores and a sentinel of –1. The sequence of records is terminated by the word END. Here is a sample sequence:

```
Harry
Morgan
94
71
```

```
86
95
-1
Sally
Lin
99
98
100
95
90
-1
END
```

Provide a trace table for this sample input.

- **R4.16** Rewrite the following for loop as a while loop.

```
s = 0
for i in range(1, 10) :
    s = s + i
```

- **R4.17** Provide trace tables of the following loops.

a.
```
s = 1
n = 1
while s < 10 :
    s = s + n
```
b.
```
s = 1
for n in range(1, 5) :
    s = s + n
```

- **R4.18** What do the following loops print? Work out the answer by tracing the code, not by using the computer.

a.
```
s = 1
for n in range(1, 6) :
    s = s + n
    print(s)
```
b.
```
s = 1
for n in range(1, 11) :
    n = n + 2
    s = s + n
    print(s)
```
c.
```
s = 1
for n in range(1, 6) :
    s = s + n
    n = n + 1
print(s, n)
```

- **R4.19** What do the following program segments print? Find the answers by tracing the code, not by using the computer.

a.
```
n = 1
for i in range(2, 5) :
    n = n + i
print(n)
```
b.
```
n = 1 / 2
i = 2
while i < 6 :
    n = n + 1 / i
    i = i + 1
print(i)
```

c.
```
x = 1.0
y = 1.0
i = 0
while y >= 1.5 :
    x = x / 2
    y = x + y
    i = i + 1
print(i)
```

- **R4.20** Add a storyboard panel for the conversion program in Section 4.4 that shows a scenario where a user enters incompatible units.

- **R4.21** In Section 4.4, we decided to show users a list of all valid units in the prompt. If the conversion program supports many more units, this approach is unworkable. Give a storyboard panel that illustrates an alternate approach: If the user enters an unknown unit, a list of all known units is shown.

- **R4.22** Change the storyboards in Section 4.4 to support a menu that asks users whether they want to convert units, see program help, or quit the program. The menu should be displayed at the beginning of the program, when a sequence of values has been converted, and when an error is displayed.

- **R4.23** Draw a flowchart for a program that carries out unit conversions as described in Section 4.4.

- ■ **R4.24** In Section 4.5.4, the code for finding the largest and smallest input initializes the largest and smallest variables with an input value. Why can't you initialize them with zero?

- **R4.25** What are nested loops? Give an example where a nested loop is typically used.

- ■ **R4.26** The nested loops

```
for i in range(height) :
    for j in range(width) :
        print("*", end="")
    print()
```

display a rectangle of a given width and height, such as

```
****
****
****
```

Write a *single* for loop that displays the same rectangle.

- ■ **R4.27** Suppose you design an educational game to teach children how to read a clock. How do you generate random values for the hours and minutes?

- ■■ **R4.28** In a travel simulation, Harry will visit one of his 15 friends who are located in three states. He has ten friends in California, three in Nevada, and two in Utah. How do you produce a random number between 1 and 3, denoting the destination state, with a probability that is proportional to the number of friends in each state?

- **Graphics R4.29** How would you modify the filterimage.py program in Section 4.10.1 to produce a new image that only shows the green color of each pixel?

- **Graphics R4.30** What changes would be needed in the flipimage.py program in Section 4.10.2 to flip the image horizontally instead of vertically?

■ **Graphics R4.31** What would be the size of the new image if you wanted to rotate an image 90 degrees counter-clockwise?

■ **Graphics R4.32** Improve the picture gallery program in Section 4.11 to adjust the size of the canvas so that it fits tightly around the gallery of images.

■ **Graphics R4.33** Design a new version of the picture gallery program in Section 4.11 that arranges the pictures by lining them up along the left edges instead of the top edges. A small gap should still be used to separate the pictures and a new column started whenever you run out of room in the current column.

PROGRAMMING EXERCISES

■ **P4.1** Write programs with loops that compute

 a. The sum of all even numbers between 2 and 100 (inclusive).

 b. The sum of all squares between 1 and 100 (inclusive).

 c. All powers of 2 from 2^0 up to 2^{20}.

 d. The sum of all odd numbers between a and b (inclusive), where a and b are inputs.

 e. The sum of all odd digits of an input. (For example, if the input is 32677, the sum would be $3 + 7 + 7 = 17$.)

■■ **P4.2** Write programs that read a sequence of integer inputs and print

 a. The smallest and largest of the inputs.

 b. The number of even and odd inputs.

 c. Cumulative totals. For example, if the input is 1 7 2 9, the program should print 1 8 10 19.

 d. All adjacent duplicates. For example, if the input is 1 3 3 4 5 5 6 6 6 2, the program should print 3 5 6.

■■ **P4.3** Write programs that read a line of input as a string and print

 a. Only the uppercase letters in the string.

 b. Every second letter of the string.

 c. The string, with all vowels replaced by an underscore.

 d. The number of digits in the string.

 e. The positions of all vowels in the string.

■■ **P4.4** Complete the program in How To 4.1. Your program should read twelve temperature values and print the month with the highest temperature.

■■ **P4.5** Write a program that reads a set of floating-point values. Ask the user to enter the values, then print

 • the average of the values.

 • the smallest of the values.

 • the largest of the values.

 • the range, that is the difference between the smallest and largest.

■ **P4.6** Translate the following pseudocode for finding the minimum value from a set of inputs into a Python program.

> *Set a Boolean variable "first" to true.*
> *While another value has been read successfully*
>> *If first is true*
>>> *Set the minimum to the value.*
>>> *Set first to false.*
>> *Else if the value is less than the minimum*
>>> *Set the minimum to the value.*
> *Print the minimum.*

■■■ **P4.7** Translate the following pseudocode for randomly permuting the characters in a string into a Python program.

> *Read a word.*
> *Repeat len(word) times*
>> *Pick a random position i in the word, but not the last position.*
>> *Pick a random position j > i in the word.*
>> *Swap the letters at positions j and i.*
> *Print the word.*

© Anthony Rosenberg/iStockphoto.

To swap the letters, construct substrings as follows:

```
first     i     middle     j     last
```

Then replace the string with

```
first + word[j] + middle + word[i] + last
```

■ **P4.8** Write a program that reads a word and prints each character of the word on a separate line. For example, if the user provides the input "Harry", the program prints

```
H
a
r
r
y
```

■■ **P4.9** Write a program that reads a word and prints the word in reverse. For example, if the user provides the input "Harry", the program prints

```
yrraH
```

■ **P4.10** Write a program that reads a word and prints the number of vowels in the word. For this exercise, assume that a e i o u y are vowels. For example, if the user provides the input "Harry", the program prints 2 vowels.

■■■ **P4.11** Write a program that reads a word and prints the number of syllables in the word. For this exercise, assume that syllables are determined as follows: Each sequence of adjacent vowels a e i o u y, except for the last e in a word, is a syllable. However, if that algorithm yields a count of 0, change it to 1. For example,

Word	Syllables
Harry	2
hairy	2
hare	1
the	1

■■■ **P4.12** Write a program that reads a word and prints all substrings, sorted by length. For example, if the user provides the input "rum", the program prints

```
r
u
m
ru
um
rum
```

■■ **P4.13** Write a program that reads an integer value and prints all of its *binary digits* in reverse order: Print the remainder number % 2, then replace the number with number // 2. Keep going until the number is 0. For example, if the user provides the input 13, the output should be

```
1
0
1
1
```

■■ **P4.14** *Mean and standard deviation*. Write a program that reads a set of floating-point data values. Choose an appropriate mechanism for prompting for the end of the data set.

When all values have been read, print out the count of the values, the average, and the standard deviation. The average of a data set $\{x_1, \ldots, x_n\}$ is $\bar{x} = \sum x_i / n$, where $\sum x_i = x_1 + \cdots + x_n$ is the sum of the input values. The standard deviation is

$$s = \sqrt{\frac{\sum (x_i - \bar{x})^2}{n - 1}}$$

However, this formula is not suitable for the task. By the time the program has computed $\bar{x}$, the individual x_i are long gone. Until you know how to save these values, use the numerically less stable formula

$$s = \sqrt{\frac{\sum x_i^2 - \frac{1}{n}\left(\sum x_i\right)^2}{n - 1}}$$

You can compute this quantity by keeping track of the count, the sum, and the sum of squares as you process the input values.

■■ **P4.15** The *Fibonacci numbers* are defined by the sequence

$$f_1 = 1$$
$$f_2 = 1$$
$$f_n = f_{n-1} + f_{n-2}$$

Reformulate that as

© GlobalP/iStockphoto.

```
fold1 = 1
fold2 = 1
fnew = fold1 + fold2
```

Fibonacci numbers describe the growth of a rabbit population.

After that, discard fold2, which is no longer needed, and set fold2 to fold1 and fold1 to fnew. Repeat an appropriate number of times.

Implement a program that prompts the user for an integer *n* and prints the *n*th Fibonacci number, using the above algorithm.

■■■ **P4.16** *Factoring of integers.* Write a program that asks the user for an integer and then prints out all its factors. For example, when the user enters 150, the program should print

```
2
3
5
5
```

■■■ **P4.17** *Prime numbers.* Write a program that prompts the user for an integer and then prints out all prime numbers up to that integer. For example, when the user enters 20, the program should print

```
2
3
5
7
11
13
17
19
```

Recall that a number is a prime number if it is not divisible by any number except 1 and itself.

■ **P4.18** Write a program that prints a multiplication table, like this:

```
 1   2   3   4   5   6   7   8   9  10
 2   4   6   8  10  12  14  16  18  20
 3   6   9  12  15  18  21  24  27  30
   . . .
10  20  30  40  50  60  70  80  90 100
```

■■ **P4.19** Modify the examaverages.py program from Worked Example 4.1 so it will also compute the overall average exam grade.

■■ **P4.20** Modify the examaverages.py program from Worked Example 4.1 to have it validate the input when the user is prompted as to whether they want to enter grades for another student.

■■ **P4.21** Write a program that reads an integer and displays, using asterisks, a filled and hollow square, placed next to each other. For example if the side length is 5, the program should display

```
***** *****
***** *   *
***** *   *
***** *   *
***** *****
```

■■ **P4.22** Write a program that reads an integer and displays, using asterisks, a filled diamond of the given side length. For example, if the side length is 4, the program should display

```
   *
  ***
 *****
*******
 *****
  ***
   *
```

■■■ **P4.23** *The game of Nim.* This is a well-known game with a number of variants. The following variant has an interesting winning strategy. Two players alternately take marbles from a pile. In each move, a player chooses how many marbles to take. The player must take at least one but at most half of the marbles. Then the other player takes a turn. The player who takes the last marble loses.

Write a program in which the computer plays against a human opponent. Generate a random integer between 10 and 100 to denote the initial size of the pile. Generate a random integer between 0 and 1 to decide whether the computer or the human takes the first turn. Generate a random integer between 0 and 1 to decide whether the computer plays *smart* or *stupid*. In stupid mode the computer simply takes a random legal value (between 1 and $n/2$) from the pile whenever it has a turn. In smart mode the computer takes off enough marbles to make the size of the pile a power of two minus one—that is, 3, 7, 15, 31, or 63. That is always a legal move, except when the size of the pile is currently one less than a power of two. In that case, the computer makes a random legal move.

You will note that the computer cannot be beaten in smart mode when it has the first move, unless the pile size happens to be 15, 31, or 63. Of course, a human player who has the first turn and knows the winning strategy can win against the computer.

■■ **P4.24** *The Drunkard's Walk.* A drunkard in a grid of streets randomly picks one of four directions and stumbles to the next intersection, then again randomly picks one of four directions, and so on. You might think that on average the drunkard doesn't move far because the choices cancel each other out, but that is actually not the case.

Represent locations as integer pairs (x, y). Implement the drunkard's walk over 100 intersections, starting at $(0, 0)$, and print the ending location.

■■ **P4.25** *The Monty Hall Paradox.* Marilyn vos Savant described the following problem (loosely based on a game show hosted by Monty Hall) in a popular magazine: "Suppose you're on a game show, and you're given the choice of three doors: Behind one door is a car; behind the others, goats. You pick a door, say No. 1, and the host, who knows what's behind the doors, opens another door, say No. 3, which has a goat. He then says to you, 'Do you want to pick door No. 2?' Is it to your advantage to switch?"

Ms. vos Savant proved that it is to your advantage, but many of her readers, including some mathematics professors, disagreed, arguing that the probability would not change because another door was opened.

Your task is to simulate this game show. In each iteration, randomly pick a door number between 1 and 3 for placing the car. Randomly have the player pick a door. Randomly have the game show host pick a door having a goat (but not the door that the player picked). Increment a counter for strategy 1 if the player wins by switching to the third door, and increment a counter for strategy 2 if the player wins by sticking with the original choice. Run 1,000 iterations and print both counters.

■■ **P4.26** *The Buffon Needle Experiment.* The following experiment was devised by Comte Georges-Louis Leclerc de Buffon (1707–1788), a French naturalist. A needle of length 1 inch is dropped onto paper that is ruled with lines 2 inches apart. If the needle drops onto a line, we count it as a *hit*. (See Figure 8.) Buffon discovered that the quotient *tries/hits* approximates π.

For the Buffon needle experiment, you must generate two random numbers: one to describe the starting position and one to describe the angle of the needle with the x-axis. Then you need to test whether the needle touches a grid line.

Generate the *lower* point of the needle. Its x-coordinate is irrelevant, and you may assume its y-coordinate y_{low} to be any random number between 0 and 2. The angle α between the needle and the x-axis can be any value between 0 degrees and 180 degrees (π radians). The upper end of the needle has y-coordinate

$$y_{high} = y_{low} + \sin \alpha$$

The needle is a hit if y_{high} is at least 2, as shown in Figure 9. Stop after 10,000 tries and print the quotient *tries/hits*. (This program is not suitable for computing the value of π. You need π in the computation of the angle.)

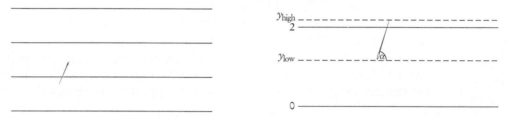

Figure 8 The Buffon Needle Experiment **Figure 9** A Hit in the Buffon Needle Experiment

■ **P4.27** A simple random generator is obtained by the formula

$$r_{new} = (a \cdot r_{old} + b)\%m$$

and then setting r_{old} to r_{new}.

Write a program that asks the user to enter an initial value for r_{old}. (Such a value is often called a *seed*). Then print the first 100 random integers generated by this formula, using $a = 32310901$, $b = 1729$, and $m = 2^{24}$.

■■ **Toolbox P4.28** Generate 1,000 random die tosses and show a histogram with the number of times that the result is 1, 2, 3, 4, 5, or 6. Use the technique of Worked Example 4.2.

■■ **Toolbox P4.29** Generate 1,000 random integers between 1 and 999,999. Show a histogram with the number of times that the *first* digit of the result is 1, 2, 3, 4, 5, 6, 7, 8, or 9. Use the technique of Worked Example 4.2.

■■ **Business P4.30** *Currency conversion*. Write a program that first asks the user to type today's price for one dollar in Japanese yen, then reads U.S. dollar values and converts each to yen. Use 0 as a sentinel.

© hatman12/iStockphoto.

■■ **Business P4.31** Write a program that first asks the user to type in today's price of one dollar in Japanese yen, then reads U.S. dollar values and converts each to Japanese yen. Use 0 as the sentinel value to denote the end of dollar inputs. Then the program reads a sequence of yen amounts and converts them to dollars. The second sequence is terminated by another zero value.

■■ Business P4.32 Your company has shares of stock it would like to sell when their value exceeds a certain target price. Write a program that reads the target price and then reads the current stock price until it is at least the target price. Your program should read a sequence of floating-point values from standard input. Once the minimum is reached, the program should report that the stock price exceeds the target price.

■■ Business P4.33 Write an application to pre-sell a limited number of cinema tickets. Each buyer can buy as many as 4 tickets. No more than 100 tickets can be sold. Implement a program that prompts the user for the desired number of tickets and then displays the number of remaining tickets. Repeat until all tickets have been sold, and then display the total number of buyers.

■■ Business P4.34 You need to control the number of people who can be in an oyster bar at the same time. Groups of people can always leave the bar, but a group cannot enter the bar if they would make the number of people in the bar exceed the maximum of 100 occupants. Write a program that reads the sizes of the groups that arrive or depart. Use negative numbers for departures. After each input, display the current number of occupants. As soon as the bar holds the maximum number of people, report that the bar is full and exit the program.

■■■ Business P4.35 *Credit Card Number Check*. The last digit of a credit card number is the *check digit*, which protects against transcription errors such as an error in a single digit or switching two digits. The following method is used to verify actual credit card numbers but, for simplicity, we will describe it for numbers with 8 digits instead of 16:

- Starting from the rightmost digit, form the sum of every other digit. For example, if the credit card number is 4358 9795, then you form the sum 5 + 7 + 8 + 3 = 23.
- Double each of the digits that were not included in the preceding step. Add all digits of the resulting numbers. For example, with the number given above, doubling the digits, starting with the next-to-last one, yields 18 18 10 8. Adding all digits in these values yields 1 + 8 + 1 + 8 + 1 + 0 + 8 = 27.
- Add the sums of the two preceding steps. If the last digit of the result is 0, the number is valid. In our case, 23 + 27 = 50, so the number is valid.

Write a program that implements this algorithm. The user should supply an 8-digit number, and you should print out whether the number is valid or not. If it is not valid, you should print the value of the check digit that would make it valid.

■■ Science P4.36 In a predator-prey simulation, you compute the populations of predators and prey, using the following equations:

$$prey_{n+1} = prey_n \times (1 + A - B \times pred_n)$$
$$pred_{n+1} = pred_n \times (1 - C + D \times prey_n)$$

Here, A is the rate at which prey birth exceeds natural death, B is the rate of predation, C is the rate at which predator deaths exceed births without food, and D represents predator increase in the presence of food.

© Charles Gibson/iStockphoto.

Write a program that prompts users for these rates, the initial population sizes, and the number of periods. Then print the populations for the given number of periods. As inputs, try $A = 0.1$, $B = C = 0.01$, and $D = 0.00002$ with initial prey and predator populations of 1,000 and 20.

•• Science P4.37 *Projectile flight.* Suppose a cannonball is propelled straight into the air with a starting velocity v_0. Any calculus book will state that the position of the ball after t seconds is $s(t) = -1/2gt^2 + v_0t$, where $g = 9.81$ m/s^2 is the gravitational force of the earth. No calculus textbook ever mentions why someone would want to carry out such an obviously dangerous experiment, so we will do it in the safety of the computer.

© MOF/iStockphoto.

In fact, we will confirm the theorem from calculus by a simulation. In our simulation, we will consider how the ball moves in very short time intervals Δt. In a short time interval the velocity v is nearly constant, and we can compute the distance the ball moves as $\Delta s = v\Delta t$. In our program, we will simply set

```
DELTA_T = 0.01
```

and update the position by

```
s = s + v * DELTA_T
```

The velocity changes constantly—in fact, it is reduced by the gravitational force of the earth. In a short time interval, $\Delta v = -g\Delta t$, so we must keep the velocity updated as

```
v = v - g * DELTA_T
```

In the next iteration the new velocity is used to update the distance.

Now run the simulation until the cannonball falls back to the earth. Get the initial velocity as an input (100 m/s is a good value). Update the position and velocity 100 times per second, but print out the position only every full second. Also printout the values from the exact formula $s(t) = -1/2gt^2 + v_0t$ for comparison.

Note: You may wonder whether there is a benefit to this simulation when an exact formula is available. Well, the formula from the calculus book is *not* exact. Actually, the gravitational force diminishes the farther the cannonball is away from the surface of the earth. This complicates the algebra sufficiently that it is not possible to give an exact formula for the actual motion, but the computer simulation can simply be extended to apply a variable gravitational force. For cannonballs, the calculus-book formula is actually good enough, but computers are necessary to compute accurate trajectories for higher-flying objects such as ballistic missiles.

••• Science P4.38 A simple model for the hull of a ship is given by

$$|y| = \frac{B}{2}\left[1 - \left(\frac{2x}{L}\right)^2\right]\left[1 - \left(\frac{z}{T}\right)^2\right]$$

where B is the beam, L is the length, and T is the draft.

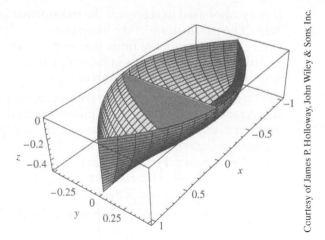

(*Note:* There are two values of y for each x and z because the hull is symmetric from starboard to port.)

The cross-sectional area at a point x is called the "section" in nautical parlance. To compute it, let z go from 0 to $-T$ in n increments, each of size T/n. For each value of z, compute the value for y. Then sum the areas of trapezoidal strips. At right are the strips where $n = 4$.

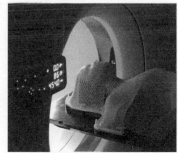

Write a program that reads in values for B, L, T, x, and n and then prints out the cross-sectional area at x.

■ **Science P4.39** Radioactive decay of radioactive materials can be modeled by the equation $A = A_0 e^{-t(\log 2/h)}$, where A is the amount of the material at time t, A_0 is the amount at time 0, and h is the half-life.

Technetium-99 is a radioisotope that is used in imaging of the brain. It has a half-life of 6 hours. Your program should display the relative amount A/A_0 in a patient body every hour for 24 hours after receiving a dose.

■■■ **Science P4.40** The photo on the left shows an electric device called a "transformer". Transformers are often constructed by wrapping coils of wire around a ferrite core. The figure below illustrates a situation that occurs in various audio devices such as cell phones and music players. In this circuit, a transformer is used to connect a speaker to the output of an audio amplifier.

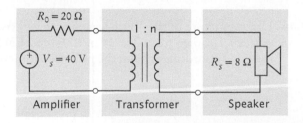

The symbol used to represent the transformer is intended to suggest two coils of wire. The parameter n of the transformer is called the "turns ratio" of the transformer. (The number of times that a wire is wrapped around the core to form a coil is called the number of turns in the coil. The turns ratio is literally the ratio of the number of turns in the two coils of wire.)

When designing the circuit, we are concerned primarily with the value of the power delivered to the speakers—that power causes the speakers to produce the sounds we want to hear. Suppose we were to connect the speakers directly to the amplifier without using the transformer. Some fraction of the power available from the amplifier would get to the speakers. The rest of the available power would be lost in the amplifier itself. The transformer is added to the circuit to increase the fraction of the amplifier power that is delivered to the speakers.

The power, P_s, delivered to the speakers is calculated using the formula

$$P_s = R_s \left(\frac{n V_s}{n^2 R_0 + R_s} \right)^2$$

Write a program that models the circuit shown and varies the turns ratio from 0.01 to 2 in 0.01 increments, then determines the value of the turns ratio that maximizes the power delivered to the speakers.

■■ **Graphics P4.41** Write a graphical application that displays a checkerboard with 64 squares, alternating white and black.

■ **Graphics P4.42** Using the technique of Section 2.6, generate the image of a sine wave. Draw a line of pixels for every five degrees.

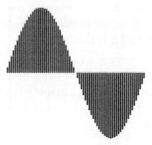

■■ **Graphics P4.43** It is easy and fun to draw graphs of curves with the ezgraphics module provided with the book. Simply draw 100 line segments joining the points $(x, f(x))$ and $(x + d, f(x + d))$, where x ranges from x_{min} to x_{max} and $d = (x_{max} - x_{min}) / 100$.

Draw the curve $f(x) = 0.00005x^3 - 0.03x^2 + 4x + 200$, where x ranges from 0 to 400 in this fashion.

■■■ **Graphics P4.44** Draw a picture of the "four-leaved rose" whose equation in polar coordinates is $r = \cos(2\theta)$. Let θ go from 0 to 2π in 100 steps. Each time, compute r and then compute the (x, y) coordinates from the polar coordinates by using the formula

$$x = r \cdot \cos(\theta), \ y = r \cdot \sin(\theta)$$

Transform the x- and y-coordinates so that the curve fits inside the window. Choose suitable values for a and b:

$$x' = a \cdot x + b$$
$$y' = a \cdot y + b$$

■■■ **Graphics P4.45** Write a graphical application that draws a spiral, such as the following:

■■ **Graphics P4.46** Implement a "sunset" effect by increasing the red level of each pixel of an image by 30 percent (up to a value of 255).

Courtesy of Cay Horstmann.

■■ **Graphics P4.47** Add black vertical stripes to an image, each spaced five pixels from the next. The partial image below is enlarged to show the lines.

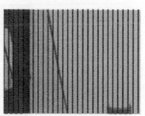

Courtesy of Cay Horstmann.

■■ **Graphics P4.48** Add black diagonal stripes to an image, each spaced five pixels apart. The partial image below is enlarged to show the lines.

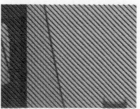

Courtesy of Cay Horstmann.

■■ Graphics P4.49   Rotate an image 90 degrees clockwise.

Courtesy of Cay Horstmann.

■■ Graphics P4.50   Replicate an image four times.

Python for Everyone/John Wiley & Sons, Inc.

■■ Graphics P4.51   Replicate each pixel of an image four times, so that the image is twice as large and wide as the original, with "blocky" pixels. The partial image below is enlarged to show the pixels.

Python for Everyone/John Wiley & Sons, Inc.

■■ Graphics P4.52   Convert an image to grayscale by changing each pixel to a gray one. Because the color receptors in the human eye have different sensitivities, you cannot simply average the original red, green, and blue values. Instead, compute the gray level as

$$gray = 0.2126 \times red + 0.7152 \times green + 0.0722 \times blue$$

Courtesy of Cay Horstmann.

■■ Graphics P4.53 Detect edges in an image, coloring each pixel black or white depending on whether it is significantly different from the neighboring pixels to the east, south, and southeast. Average the red, green, and blue components of the three neighbors. Then compute

$$distance = |red - red_{neighbors}| + |green - green_{neighbors}| + |blue - blue_{neighbors}|$$

If that distance is > 30, color the pixel black. Otherwise, color it white.

Note that you can update the pixels without constructing a new image because you are only looking at neighbors that haven't yet been changed.

Courtesy of Cay Horstmann.

■■ Graphics P4.54 Repeat Exercise ●● Graphics P4.53, but now use the neighbors of each pixel in all eight compass directions. You will need to construct a new image.

■■ Graphics P4.55 Add a "telescope" effect to an image, coloring all pixels black that are more than half the distance between the center and the closest edge.

Courtesy of Cay Horstmann.

■■ Graphics P4.56 Write a program that creates and saves a 200 × 200 pixel image of four triangles, like this:

■■■ Graphics P4.57 Repeat Exercise ●● Graphics P4.56, drawing a black border, ten pixels wide, around the square formed by the triangles.

## CHAPTER 5

FUNCTIONS

© attator/iStockphoto.

To be able to implement functions

To become familiar with the concept of parameter passing

To develop strategies for decomposing complex tasks into simpler ones

To be able to determine the scope of a variable

To learn how to think recursively (optional)

A function packages a computation consisting of multiple steps into a form that can be easily understood and reused. (The person in the image to the left is in the middle of executing the function "make two cups of espresso".) In this chapter, you will learn how to design and implement your own functions. Using the process of stepwise refinement, you will be able to break up complex tasks into sets of cooperating functions.

5.1 Functions as Black Boxes

A function is a named sequence of instructions.

A **function** is a sequence of instructions with a name. You have already encountered several functions. For example, the round function, which was introduced in Chapter 2, contains instructions to round a floating-point value to a specified number of decimal places.

You *call* a function in order to execute its instructions. For example, consider the following program statement:

    price = round(6.8275, 2)   # Sets result to 6.83

By using the expression round(6.8275, 2), your program *calls* the round function, asking it to round 6.8275 to two decimal digits. The instructions of the round function execute and compute the result. The round function *returns* its result back to where the function was called and your program resumes execution (see Figure 1).

Arguments are supplied when a function is called.

When a program calls the round function, it provides "inputs", such as the values 6.8275 and 2 in the call round(6.8275, 2). These values are called the **arguments** of the function call. Note that they are not necessarily inputs provided by a human user. They are simply the values for which we want the function to compute a result. The "output" that the round function computes is called the **return value**.

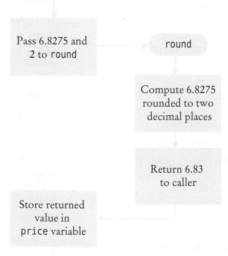

Figure 1   Execution Flow of a Function Call

Figure 2
The round Function as a Black Box

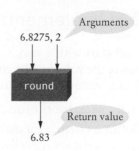

Functions can receive multiple arguments, but they return only one value. It is also possible to have functions with no arguments. An example is the random function that requires no argument to produce a random number.

> The return value is the result that the function computes.

The return value of a function is returned to the point in your program where the function was called. It is then processed according to the statement containing the function call. For example, suppose your program contains a statement

```
price = round(6.8275, 2)
```

When the round function returns its result, the return value is stored in the variable price.

> Returning a value from a function is not the same as producing program output.

Do not confuse returning a value with producing program output. If you want the return value to be printed, you need to add a statement such as print(price).

At this point, you may wonder how the round function performs its job. For example, how does round compute that 6.8275 rounded to two decimal digits is 6.83? Fortunately, as a user of the function, you *don't need to know* how the function is implemented. You just need to know the *specification* of the function: If you provide arguments x and n, the function returns x rounded to n decimal digits. Engineers use the term *black box* for a device with a given specification but unknown implementation. You can think of round as a black box, as shown in Figure 2.

When you design your own functions, you will want to make them appear as black boxes to other programmers. Those programmers want to use your functions without knowing what goes on inside. Even if you are the only person working on a program, making each function into a black box pays off: there are fewer details that you need to keep in mind.

Although a thermostat is usually white, you can think of it as a black box. The input is the desired temperature, and the output is a signal to the heater or air conditioner.

© yenwen/iStockphoto.

5.2 Implementing and Testing Functions

In this section, you will learn how to implement a function from a given specification, and how to call it with test inputs.

5.2.1 Implementing a Function

We will start with a very simple example: a function to compute the volume of a cube with a given side length.

When writing this function, you need to

© studioaraminta/iStockphoto.

- Pick a name for the function (cubeVolume).
- Define a variable for each argument (sideLength). These variables are called the **parameter variables**.

Put all this information together along with the def reserved word to form the first line of the function's definition:

```
def cubeVolume(sideLength) :
```

The cubeVolume function uses a given side length to compute the volume of a cube.

This line is called the **header** of the function. Next, specify the **body** of the function. The body contains the statements that are executed when the function is called.

The volume of a cube of side length s is $s \times s \times s = s^3$. However, for greater clarity, our parameter variable has been called sideLength, not s, so we need to compute sideLength ** 3.

We will store this value in a variable called volume:

```
volume = sideLength ** 3
```

In order to return the result of the function, use the return statement:

```
return volume
```

A function is a compound statement, which requires the statements in the body to be indented to the same level. Here is the complete function:

```
def cubeVolume(sideLength) :
    volume = sideLength ** 3
    return volume
```

The return statement gives the function's result to the caller.

© princessdlaf/iStockphoto.

> When defining a function, you provide a name for the function and a variable for each argument.

5.2.2 Testing a Function

In the preceding section, you saw how to write a function. If you run a program containing just the function definition, then nothing happens. After all, nobody is calling the function.

Syntax 5.1   **Function Definition**

Syntax   def *functionName*(*parameterName₁*, *parameterName₂*, . . .) :
                   statements

Name of function

Name of parameter variable

Function header

```
def cubeVolume(sideLength) :
    volume = sideLength ** 3
    return volume
```

Function body, executed when function is called.

return *statement exits function and returns result.*

In order to test the function, your program should contain

- The definition of the function.
- Statements that call the function and print the result.

Here is such a program:

```
def cubeVolume(sideLength) :
    volume = sideLength ** 3
    return volume

result1 = cubeVolume(2)
result2 = cubeVolume(10)

print("A cube with side length 2 has volume", result1)
print("A cube with side length 10 has volume", result2)
```

Note that the function returns different results when it is called with different arguments. Consider the call cubeVolume(2). The argument 2 corresponds to the sideLength parameter variable. Therefore, in this call, sideLength is 2. The function computes side-Length ** 3, or 2 ** 3. When the function is called with a different argument, say 10, then the function computes 10 ** 3.

5.2.3 Programs that Contain Functions

When you write a program that contains one or more functions, you need to pay attention to the order of the function definitions and statements in the program.

Have another look at the program of the preceding section. Note that it contains

- The definition of the cubeVolume function.
- Several statements, two of which call that function.

As the Python interpreter reads the source code, it reads each function definition and each statement. The statements in a function definition are not executed until the function is called. Any statement not in a function definition, on the other hand, is executed as it is encountered. Therefore, it is important that you define each function before you call it. For example, the following will produce a compile-time error:

```
print(cubeVolume(10))

def cubeVolume(sideLength) :
    volume = sideLength ** 3
    return volume
```

The compiler does not know that the cubeVolume function will be defined later in the program.

However, a function can be called from within another function before the former has been defined. For example, the following is perfectly legal:

```
def main() :
    result = cubeVolume(2)
    print("A cube with side length 2 has volume", result)

def cubeVolume(sideLength) :
    volume = sideLength ** 3
    return volume

main()
```

Note that the cubeVolume function is called from within the main function even though cubeVolume is defined after main. To see why this is not a problem, consider the flow of execution. The definitions of the main and cubeVolume functions are processed. The statement in the last line is not contained in any function. Therefore, it is executed directly. It calls the main function. The body of the main function executes, and it calls cubeVolume, which is now known.

When defining and using functions in Python, it is good programming practice to place all statements into functions, and to specify one function as the starting point. In the previous example, the main function is the point at which execution begins. Any legal name can be used for the starting point, but we chose main because it is the required function name used by other common languages.

Of course, we must have one statement in the program that calls the main function. That statement is the last line of the program, main().

The complete program including comments is provided below. Note that both functions are in the same file. Also note the comment that describes the behavior of the cubeVolume function. (Programming Tip 5.1 describes the format of the comment.)

Syntax 5.2 Program with Functions

By convention, main is the starting point of the program.

The cubeVolume function is defined below.

```
def main() :
    result = cubeVolume(2)
    print("A cube with side length 2 has volume", result)

def cubeVolume(sideLength) :
    volume = sideLength ** 3
    return volume

main()
```

This statement is outside any function definitions.

sec02/cubes.py

```
1  ##
2  #   This program computes the volumes of two cubes.
3  #
4
5  def main() :
6      result1 = cubeVolume(2)
7      result2 = cubeVolume(10)
8      print("A cube with side length 2 has volume", result1)
9      print("A cube with side length 10 has volume", result2)
10
11  ## Computes the volume of a cube.
12  #   @param sideLength the length of a side of the cube
13  #   @return  the volume of the cube
14  #
15  def cubeVolume(sideLength) :
16      volume = sideLength ** 3
17      return volume
18
19  # Start the program.
20  main()
```

Program Run

```
A cube with side length 2 has volume 8
A cube with side length 10 has volume 1000
```

Programming Tip 5.1

Function Comments

Whenever you write a function, you should *comment* its behavior. Comments are for human readers, not compilers. Various individuals prefer different layouts for function comments. In this book, we will use the following layout:

```
## Computes the volume of a cube.
#   @param sideLength the length of a side of the cube
#   @return the volume of the cube
#
def cubeVolume(sideLength) :
    volume = sideLength ** 3
    return volume
```

This particular documentation style is borrowed from the Java programming language. It is supported by a wide variety of documentation tools such as Doxygen (http://www.doxygen.org), which extracts the documentation in HTML format from the Python source.

Each line of the function comment begins with a hash symbol (#) in the first column. The first line, which is indicated by two hash symbols, describes the purpose of the function. Each @param clause describes a parameter variable and the @return clause describes the return value.

There is an alternative (but, in our opinion, somewhat less descriptive) way of documenting the purpose of a Python function. Add a string, called a "docstring", as the first statement of the function body, like this:

```
def cubeVolume(sideLength) :
    "Computes the volume of a cube."
    volume = sideLength ** 3
    return volume
```

We don't use this style, but many Python programmers do.

Function comments explain the purpose of the function, the meaning of the parameter variables and return value, as well as any special requirements.

Note that the function comment does not document the implementation (*how* the function does what it does) but rather the design (*what* the function does, its inputs, and its results). The comment allows other programmers to use the function as a "black box".

Programming Tip 5.2
Naming Functions

The name of a function can be any legal identifier, including the name of a previously defined variable. You should never use the same name for a function and a variable.

Python does not distinguish between identifiers used to name variables and those used to name functions. If you name your function the same as a previously-defined variable, or vice versa, the previous definition is overwritten. For example, suppose we initialize a variable named cubeVolume and then attempt to call the cubeVolume function:

```
def cubeVolume(sideLength) :
    volume = sideLength ** 3
    return volume

cubeVolume = 0
cubeVolume = cubeVolume(2)
```

This would result in a TypeError exception indicating that an integer is not callable.

The reason for the error is that, after the cubeVolume function was defined, the identifier cubeVolume was redefined to refer to a variable containing an integer. Then when the program made the function call cubeVolume(2), Python assumed it was trying to call a function, but cubeVolume referred to an integer variable at that point.

5.3 Parameter Passing

Parameter variables hold the arguments supplied in the function call.

In this section, we examine the mechanism of parameter passing more closely. When a function is called, variables are created for receiving the function's arguments. These variables are called **parameter variables**. (Another commonly used term is **formal parameters**.) The values that are supplied to the function when it is called are the **arguments** of the call. (These values are also commonly called the **actual parameters**.) Each parameter variable is initialized with the corresponding argument.

A recipe for a fruit pie may say to use any kind of fruit. Here, "fruit" is an example of a parameter variable. Apples and cherries are examples of arguments.

© DNY59/iStockphoto (cherry pie);
© inhausecreative/iStockphoto (apple pie);
© RedHelga/iStockphoto (cherries);
© ZoneCreative/iStockphoto (apples).

Figure 3
Parameter Passing

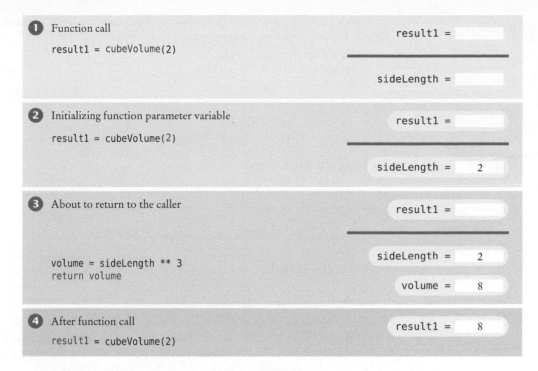

Consider the function call illustrated in Figure 3:

```
result1 = cubeVolume(2)
```

- The parameter variable `sideLength` of the `cubeVolume` function is created when the function is called. ❶
- The parameter variable is initialized with the value of the argument that was passed in the call. In our case, `sideLength` is set to 2. ❷
- The function computes the expression `sideLength ** 3`, which has the value 8. That value is stored in the variable `volume`. ❸
- The function returns. All of its variables are removed. The return value is transferred to the *caller*, that is, the statement calling the `cubeVolume` function. The caller puts the return value in the `result1` variable. ❹

Now consider what happens in a subsequent call, `cubeVolume(10)`. A new parameter variable is created. (Recall that the previous parameter variable was removed when the first call to `cubeVolume` returned.) It is initialized with 10, and the process repeats. After the second function call is complete, its variables are again removed.

Programming Tip 5.3
Do Not Modify Parameter Variables

In Python, a parameter variable is just like any other variable. You can modify the values of the parameter variables in the body of a function. For example,

```
def totalCents(dollars, cents) :
    cents = dollars * 100 + cents   # Modifies parameter variable.
    return cents
```

However, many programmers find this practice confusing (see Common Error 5.1). To avoid the confusion, simply introduce a separate variable:

```
def totalCents(dollars, cents) :
    result = dollars * 100 + cents
    return result
```

Common Error 5.1

Trying to Modify Arguments

The following function contains a common error: trying to modify an argument.

```
def addTax(price, rate) :
    tax = price * rate / 100
    price = price + tax    # Has no effect outside the function.
    return tax
```

Now consider this call:

```
total = 10
addTax(total, 7.5)    # Does not modify total.
```

When the addTax function is called, price is set to the value of total, that is, 10. Then price is changed to 10.75. When the function returns, all of its variables, including the price parameter variable, are removed. Any values that have been assigned to them are simply forgotten. Note that total is *not* changed.

In Python, a function can never change the contents of a variable that was passed as an argument. When you call a function with a variable as argument, you don't actually pass the variable, just the value that it contains.

5.4 Return Values

> The return statement terminates a function call and yields the function result.

You use the return statement to specify the result of a function. In the preceding examples, each return statement returned a variable. However, the return statement can return the value of any expression. Instead of saving the return value in a variable and returning the variable, it is often possible to eliminate the variable and return the value of a more complex expression:

```
def cubeVolume(sideLength) :
    return sideLength ** 3
```

When the return statement is processed, the function exits *immediately*. Some programmers find this behavior convenient for handling exceptional cases at the beginning of the function:

```
def cubeVolume(sideLength) :
    if sideLength < 0 :
        return 0
    # Handle the regular case.
    . . .
```

If the function is called with a negative value for sideLength, then the function returns 0 and the remainder of the function is not executed. (See Figure 4.)

Figure 4
A return Statement
Exits a Function
Immediately

© Tashka/iStockphoto.

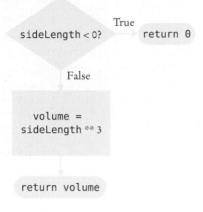

Every branch of a function should return a value. Consider the following incorrect function:

```python
def cubeVolume(sideLength) :
    if sideLength >= 0 :
        return sideLength ** 3
    # Error—no return value if sideLength < 0
```

The compiler will not report this as an error. Instead, the special value None will be returned from the function. A correct implementation is:

```python
def cubeVolume(sideLength) :
    if sideLength >= 0 :
        return sideLength ** 3
    else :
        return 0
```

Some programmers dislike the use of multiple return statements in a function. You can avoid multiple returns by storing the function result in a variable that you return in the last statement of the function. For example:

```python
def cubeVolume(sideLength) :
    if sideLength >= 0 :
        volume = sideLength ** 3
    else :
        volume = 0
    return volume
```

EXAMPLE CODE   See sec04/earthquake.py in your eText or companion code for a complete program demonstrating a function that returns a value.

Special Topic 5.1

Using Single-Line Compound Statements

Compound statements in Python are generally written across several lines. The header is on one line and the body on the following lines, with each body statement indented to the same level. When the body contains a single statement, however, compound statements may be written on a single line. For example, instead of constructing the following if statement:

```python
if digit == 1 :
    return "one"
```

you can use the special single-line form because the body contains a single statement

```
if digit == 1 : return "one"
```

This form can be very useful in functions that select a single value from among a collection and return it. For example, the single-line form used here produces condensed code that is easy to read.

```
if digit == 1 : return "one"
if digit == 2 : return "two"
if digit == 3 : return "three"
if digit == 4 : return "four"
if digit == 5 : return "five"
if digit == 6 : return "six"
if digit == 7 : return "seven"
if digit == 8 : return "eight"
if digit == 9 : return "nine"
```

Sometimes, the use of single-line compound statements can be distracting or cause the reader to accidentally skip over important details. Thus, in this book, we limit its use to `if` statements that contain a `return` clause.

HOW TO 5.1

Implementing a Function

A function is a computation that can be used multiple times with different arguments, either in the same program or in different programs. Whenever a computation may be needed more than once, turn it into a function.

Problem Statement Suppose that you are helping archae-ologists who research Egyptian pyramids. You have taken on the task of writing a function that determines the volume of a pyramid, given its height and base length.

© Holger Mette/iStockphoto.

Step 1 Describe what the function should do.

Provide a simple English description, such as "Compute the volume of a pyramid whose base is a square."

Step 2 Determine the function's "inputs".

Turn computations that can be reused into functions.

Make a list of *all* the parameters that can vary. It is common for beginners to implement functions that are overly specific. For example, you may know that the great pyramid of Giza, the largest of the Egyptian pyramids, has a height of 146 meters and a base length of 230 meters. You should *not* use these numbers in your calculation, even if the original problem only asked about the great pyramid. It is just as easy—and far more useful—to write a function that computes the volume of *any* pyramid. In our case, the parameters are the pyramid's height and base length.

Step 3 Determine the types of the parameter variables and the return value.

The height and base length can both be floating-point numbers. The computed volume is also a floating-point number, yielding a return type of `float`. Therefore, the documentation for the function will be

```
## Computes the volume of a pyramid whose base is a square.
#  @param height a float indicating the height of the pyramid
#  @param baseLength a float indicating the length of one side of the pyramid's base
#  @return the volume of the pyramid as a float
```

and the function will be defined as

```
def pyramidVolume(height, baseLength) :
```

Step 4 Write pseudocode for obtaining the desired result.

In most cases, a function needs to carry out several steps to find the desired answer. You may need to use mathematical formulas, branches, or loops. Express your function in pseudocode.
An Internet search yields the fact that the volume of a pyramid is computed as

volume = 1/3 x height x base area

Because the base is a square, we have

base area = base length x base length

Using these two equations, we can compute the volume from the arguments.

Step 5 Implement the function body.

In our example, the function body is quite simple. Note the use of the return statement to return the result.

```
def pyramidVolume(height, baseLength) :
    baseArea = baseLength * baseLength
    return height * baseArea / 3
```

Step 6 Test your function.

After implementing a function, you should test it in isolation. Such a test is called a **unit test**. Work out test cases by hand, and make sure that the function produces the correct results.
For example, for a pyramid with height 9 and base length 10, we expect the area to be 1/3 × 9 × 100 = 300. If the height is 0, we expect an area of 0.

```
def main() :
    print("Volume:" + pyramidVolume(9, 10))
    print("Expected: 300")
    print("Volume:" + pyramidVolume(0, 10))
    print("Expected: 0")
```

The output confirms that the function worked as expected:

```
Volume: 300.0
Expected: 300
Volume: 0.0
Expected: 0
```

EXAMPLE CODE The complete program for calculating a pyramid's volume is provided below.

how_to_1/pyramids.py

```
 1  ##
 2  #   This program defines a function for calculating a pyramid's volume and
 3  #   provides a unit test for the function.
 4  #
 5
 6  def main() :
 7      print("Volume:", pyramidVolume(9, 10))
 8      print("Expected: 300")
 9      print("Volume:", pyramidVolume(0, 10))
10      print("Expected: 0")
11
12  ## Computes the volume of a pyramid whose base is a square.
13  #   @param height a float indicating the height of the pyramid
14  #   @param baseLength a float indicating the length of one side of
15  #       the pyramid's base
```

```
16  #    @return the volume of the pyramid as a float
17  #
18  def pyramidVolume(height, baseLength) :
19     baseArea = baseLength * baseLength
20     return height * baseArea / 3
21
22  # Start the program.
23  main()
```

WORKED EXAMPLE 5.1

Generating Random Passwords

Problem Statement   Many web sites and software packages require you to create passwords that contain at least one digit and one special character. Your task is to write a program
that generates such a password of a given length. The characters should be chosen randomly.

> **Change Password**
>
> To protect the security of your account, please change your password frequently.
>
> ⓘ Learn more about Security Features and Protecting Your Account.
>
> **Choosing a Password**
>
> When selecting your password, please keep the following in mind:
>
> - **Length.** Use at least eight (8) characters without spaces.
> - **Characters.** Use at least one letter, one number, and one special character, excluding < \ >.
> - **Content.** Avoid numbers, names, or dates that are significant to you. For example, your phone number, first name, or date of birth. Try to base your password on a memory aid.
>
> Enter your current password: [_____]
>
> Enter your new password: [_____]
>
> Retype your new password: [_____]
>
> [Submit] [Cancel]

Step 1   Describe what the function should do.

The problem description asks you to write a program, not a function. We will write a
password-generating function and call it from the program's main function.

Let us be more precise about the function. It will generate a password with a given number
of characters. We could include multiple digits and special characters, but for simplicity, we
decide to include just one of each. We need to decide which special characters are valid. For
our solution, we will use the following set:

    + - * / ? ! @ # $ % &

The remaining characters of the password are letters. For simplicity, we will use only lowercase letters in the English alphabet.

Step 2   Determine the function's "inputs".

There is just one parameter: the length of the password.

Step 3   Determine the types of the parameter variables and the return value.

At this point, we have enough information to document and specify the function header:

```
## Generates a random password.
# @param length an integer that specifies the length of the password
# @return a string containing the password of the given length with one digit
#   and one special character
#
def makePassword(length) :
```

Step 4 Write pseudocode for obtaining the desired result.

Here is one approach for making a password:

Make an empty string called password.
Randomly generate length − 2 letters and append them to password.
Randomly generate a digit and insert it at a random location in password.
Randomly generate a symbol and insert it at a random location in password.

How do we generate a random letter, digit, or symbol? How do we insert a digit or symbol in a random location? We will delegate those tasks to helper functions. Each of those functions starts a new sequence of steps, which, for greater clarity, we will place after the steps for this function.

Step 5 Implement the function body.

We need to know the "black box" descriptions of the two helper functions described in Step 4 (which we will complete after this function). Here they are:

```
## Returns a string containing one character randomly chosen from a given string.
# @param characters the string from which to randomly choose a character
# @return a substring of length 1, taken at a random index
#
def randomCharacter(characters) :
```

```
## Inserts one string into another at a random position.
# @param string the string into which another string is inserted
# @param toInsert the string to be inserted
# @return the string that results from inserting toInsert into string
#
def insertAtRandom(string, toInsert) :
```

Now we can translate the pseudocode in Step 4 into Python:

```
def makePassword(length) :
   password = ""
   for i in range(length - 2) :
      password = password + randomCharacter("abcdefghijklmnopqrstuvwxyz")

   randomDigit = randomCharacter("0123456789")
   password = insertAtRandom(password, randomDigit)

   randomSymbol = randomCharacter("+-*/?!@#$%&")
   password = insertAtRandom(password, randomSymbol)

   return password
```

Step 6 Test your function.

Because our function depends on several helper functions, we must implement the helper functions first, as described in the following sections. (If you are impatient, you can use the technique of stubs that is described in Programming Tip 5.6.)

Here is a simple main function that calls the makePassword function:

```
def main() :
   result = makePassword(8)
   print(result)
```

Place all functions into a file named password.py. Add a call to main. Run the program a few times. Typical outputs are

```
u@taqr8f
i?fs1dgh
ot$3rvdv
```

Each output has length 8 and contains a digit and special symbol.

Repeat for the First Helper Function

Now it is time to turn to the helper function for generating a random letter, digit, or special symbol.

Step 1 Describe what the function should do.

How do we deal with the choice between letter, digit, or special symbol? Of course, we could write three separate functions, but it is better if we can solve all three tasks with a single function. We could require a parameter, such as 1 for letter, 2 for digit, and 3 for special symbol. But stepping back a bit, we can supply a more general function that simply selects a random character from *any* set. Passing the string "abcdefghijklmnopqrstuvwxyz" generates a random lowercase letter. To get a random digit, pass the string "0123456789" instead.

Now we know what our function should do. Given any string, it should return a random character in it.

Step 2 Determine the function's "inputs".

The input is any string.

Step 3 Determine the types of the parameter variables and the return value.

The input type is clearly a string, as is the return value.
The function header will be:

```
def randomCharacter(characters) :
```

Step 4 Write pseudocode for obtaining the desired result.

randomCharacter(characters)
n = len(characters)
r = a random integer between 0 and n − 1
Return the substring of characters of length 1 that starts at r.

Step 5 Implement the function body.

Simply translate the pseudocode into Python:

```
def randomCharacter(characters) :
    n = len(characters)
    r = randint(0, n - 1)
    return characters[r]
```

Step 6 Test your function.

Supply a program file for testing this function only:

```
from random import randint

def main() :
    for i in range(10) :
        print(randomCharacter("abcdef"), end="")
    print()

def randomCharacter(characters) :
    n = len(characters)
```

```
        r = randint(0, n - 1)
        return characters[r]

    main()
```

When you run this program, you might get an output such as

```
afcdfeefac
```

This confirms that the function works correctly.

Repeat for the Second Helper Function

Finally, we implement the second helper function, which inserts a string containing a single character at a random location in a string.

Step 1   Describe what the function should do.

Suppose we have a string "arxcsw" and a string "8". Then the second string should be inserted at a random location, returning a string such as "ar8xcsw" or "arxcsw8". Actually, it doesn't matter that the second string has length 1, so we will simply specify that our function should insert an arbitrary string into a given string.

Step 2   Determine the function's "inputs".

The first input is the string into which another string should be inserted. The second input is the string to be inserted.

Step 3   Determine the types of the parameter variables and the return value.

The inputs are both strings, and the result is also a string. We can now fully describe our function:

```
## Inserts one string into another at a random position.
#  @param string the string into which another string is inserted
#  @param toInsert the string to be inserted
#  @return a string that results from inserting toInsert into string
#
def insertAtRandom(string, toInsert) :
```

Step 4   Write pseudocode for obtaining the desired result.

There is no predefined function for inserting a string into another. Instead, we need to find the insertion position and then "break up" the first string by taking two substrings: the characters up to the insertion position, and the characters following it.

How many choices are there for the insertion position? If string has length 6, there are seven choices:

1. |arxcsw
2. a|rxcsw
3. ar|xcsw
4. arx|csw
5. arxc|sw
6. arxcs|w
7. arxcsw|

In general, if the string has length n, there are $n + 1$ choices, ranging from 0 (before the start of the string) to n (after the end of the string).

Here is the pseudocode:

insertAtRandom(string, toInsert)
n = len(string)
r = a random integer between 0 and n
Return the characters in string from 0 to r − 1 + toInsert + the remainder of string.

Step 5   Implement the function body.

Translate the pseudocode into Python:

```python
def insertAtRandom(string, toInsert) :
    n = len(string)
    r = randint(0, n)
    result = ""

    for i in range(r) :
        result = result + string[i]
    result = result + toInsert
    for i in range(r, n) :
        result = result + string[i]

    return result
```

Step 6   Test your function.

Supply a program file for testing this function only:

```python
from random import randint

def main() :
    for i in range(10) :
        print(insertAtRandom("arxcsw", "8")

def insertAtRandom(string, toInsert) :
    n = len(string) :
    r = randint(0, n)
    result = ""

    for i in range(r) :
        result = result + string[i]
    result = result + toInsert
    for i in range(r, n) :
        result = result + string[i]

    return result

main()
```

When you run this program, you might get an output such as

```
arxcsw8
ar8xcsw
arxc8sw
a8rxcsw
arxcsw8
ar8xcsw
arxcsw8
a8rxcsw
8arxcsw
8arxcsw
```

The output shows that the second string is being inserted at an arbitrary position, including the beginning and end of the first string.

EXAMPLE CODE   See worked_example_1/password.py in your eText or companion code for the complete program.

5.5 Functions Without Return Values

Some functions may not return a value, but they can produce output.

Sometimes, you need to carry out a sequence of instructions that does not yield a value. If that instruction sequence occurs multiple times, you will want to package it into a function.

Here is a typical example: Your task is to print a string in a box, like this:

```
-------
!Hello!
-------
```

However, different strings can be substituted for `Hello`. A function for this task can be defined as follows:

© jgroup/iStockphoto.

Some functions are called because they produce output, even though they don't return a value.

```
def boxString(contents) :
```

Now you develop the body of the function in the usual way, by formulating a general algorithm for solving the task.

n = the length of the string
Print a line that contains the - character n + 2 times.
Print a line containing the contents, surrounded with a ! to the left and right.
Print another line containing the - character n + 2 times.

Here is the function implementation:

```
## Prints a string in a box.
#   @param contents the string to enclose in a box
#
def boxString(contents) :
    n = len(contents) :
    print("-" * (n + 2))
    print("!" + contents + "!")
    print("-" * (n + 2))
```

Note that this function doesn't compute any value. It performs some actions and then returns to the caller. Actually, the function returns a special value, called `None`, but there is nothing that you can do with that value.

Because there is no useful return value, don't use `boxString` in an expression. You can call

```
boxString("Hello")
```

but don't call

```
result = boxString("Hello")   # No—boxString doesn't return a useful result.
```

If you want to return from a function that does not compute a value before reaching the end, you use a `return` statement without a value. For example,

```
def boxString(contents) :
    n = len(contents)
    if n == 0 :
        return   # Return immediately
    print("-" * (n + 2))
    print("!" + contents + "!")
    print("-" * (n + 2))
```

Computing & Society 5.1   Personal Computing

In 1971, Marcian E. "Ted" Hoff, an engineer at Intel Corporation, was working on a chip for a manufacturer of electronic calculators. He realized that it would be a better idea to develop a *general-purpose* chip that could be *programmed* to interface with the keys and display of a calculator, rather than to do yet another custom design. Thus, the *microprocessor* was born. At the time, its primary application was as a controller for calculators, washing machines, and the like. It took years for the computer industry to notice that a genuine central processing unit was now available as a single chip.

Hobbyists were the first to catch on. In 1974 the first computer *kit,* the Altair 8800, was available from MITS Electronics for about $350. The kit consisted of the microprocessor, a circuit board, a very small amount of memory, toggle switches, and a row of display lights. Purchasers had to solder and assemble it, then program it in machine language through the toggle switches. It was not a big hit. The first big hit was the Apple II. It was a real computer with a keyboard, a monitor, and a floppy disk drive. When it was first released, users had a $3,000 machine that could play Space Invaders, run a primitive bookkeeping program, or let users program it in BASIC. The original Apple II did not even support lowercase letters, making it worthless for word processing. The breakthrough came in 1979 with a new spreadsheet program, VisiCalc. In a spreadsheet, you enter financial data and their relationships into a grid of rows and columns (see the figure). Then you modify some of the data and watch in real time how the others change. For example, you can see how changing the mix of widgets in a manufacturing plant might affect estimated costs and profits. Corporate managers snapped up VisiCalc and the computer that was needed to run it. For them, the computer was a spreadsheet machine. More importantly, it was a personal device. The managers were free to do the calculations that they wanted to do, not just the ones

that the "high priests" in the data center provided.

Personal computers have been with us ever since, and countless users have tinkered with their hardware and software. This "freedom to tinker" is an important part of personal computing. On a personal device, you should be able to install the software that you want to install to make you more productive or creative, even if that's not the same software that most people use. For the first thirty years of personal computing, this freedom was largely taken for granted.

We are now entering an era where smartphones, tablets, and smart TV sets are replacing functions that were traditionally fulfilled by personal computers. While it is amazing to carry more computing power in your cell phone than in the best personal com-

puters of the 1990s, it is disturbing that we lose a degree of personal control. With some phone or tablet brands, you can only install those applications that the manufacturer publishes on the "app store". For example, Apple rejected MIT's iPad app for the educational language Scratch because it contained a virtual machine. You'd think it would be in Apple's interest to encourage the next generation to be enthusiastic about programming, but they have a general policy of denying programmability on "their" devices.

When you select a device for making phone calls or watching movies, it is worth asking who is in control. Are you purchasing a personal device that you can use in any way you choose, or are you being tethered to a flow of data that is controlled by somebody else?

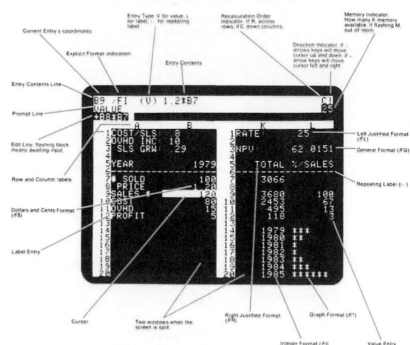

Courtesy of International Business Machines Corporation, © International Business Machines Corporation.

The VisiCalc Spreadsheet Running on an Apple II

Problem Solving: Reusable Functions

Eliminate replicated code or pseudocode by defining a function.

You have used many Python functions, both built-in and from the standard library. These functions have been provided as a part of the Python platform so that programmers need not recreate them. Of course, the Python library doesn't cover every conceivable need. You will often be able to save yourself time by designing your own functions that can be used for multiple problems.

When you write nearly identical code or pseudocode multiple times, either in the same program or in separate programs, consider introducing a function. Here is a typical example of code replication:

```python
hours = int(input("Enter a value between 0 and 23: "))
while hours < 0 or hours > 23 :
    print("Error: value out of range.")
    hours = int(input("Enter a value between 0 and 23: "))

minutes = int(input("Enter a value between 0 and 59: "))
while minutes < 0 or minutes > 59 :
    print("Error: value out of range.")
    minutes = int(input("Enter a value between 0 and 59: "))
```

This program segment reads two variables, making sure that each of them is within a certain range. It is easy to extract the common behavior into a function:

```python
## Prompts a user to enter a value up to a given maximum until the user provides
#  a valid input.
#  @param high an integer indicating the largest allowable input
#  @return the integer value provided by the user (between 0 and high, inclusive)
#
def readIntUpTo(high) :
    value = int(input("Enter a value between 0 and " + str(high) + ": "))
    while value < 0 or value > high :
        print("Error: value out of range.")
        value = int(input("Enter a value between 0 and " + str(high) + ": "))

    return value
```

Then use this function twice:

```python
hours = readIntUpTo(23)
minutes = readIntUpTo(59)
```

We have now removed the replication of the loop—it only occurs once, inside the function.

These homes weren't built by separate builders. Similarly, programmers use a function, not replicated code, to do the same task multiple times.

© LawrenceSawyer/iStockphoto.

Design your functions to be reusable. Supply parameter variables for the values that can vary when the function is reused.

Note that the function can be reused in other programs that need to read integer values. However, we should consider the possibility that the smallest value need not always be zero.

Here is a better alternative:

```
## Prompts a user to enter a value within a given range until the user provides
#    a valid input.
#    @param low an integer indicating the smallest allowable input
#    @param high an integer indicating the largest allowable input
#    @return the integer value provided by the user (between low and high, inclusive)
#
def readIntBetween(low, high) :
   value = int(input("Enter a value between " + str(low) + " and " +
                     str(high) + ": "))
   while value < low or value > high :
      print("Error: value out of range.")
      value = int(input("Enter a value between " + str(low) + " and " +
                        str(high) + ": "))
   return value
```

In our program, we call

```
hours = readIntBetween(0, 23)
```

Another program can call

```
month = readIntBetween(1, 12)
```

In general, you will want to provide parameter variables for the values that vary when a function is reused. A complete program demonstrating the readIntBetween function is provided below.

sec06/readtime.py

```
1   ##
2   #   This program demonstrates a reusable function.
3   #
4
5   def main() :
6      print("Please enter a time: hours, then minutes.")
7      hours = readIntBetween(0, 23)
8      minutes = readIntBetween(0, 59)
9      print("You entered %d hours and %d minutes." % (hours, minutes))
10
11  ## Prompts a user to enter a value within a given range until the user provides
12  #    a valid input.
13  #    @param low an integer indicating the smallest allowable input
14  #    @param high an integer indicating the largest allowable input
15  #    @return the integer value provided by the user (between low and high,
16  #    inclusive)
17  #
18  def readIntBetween(low, high) :
19     value = int(input("Enter a value between " + str(low) + " and " +
20                       str(high) + ": "))
21     while value < low or value > high :
22        print("Error: value out of range.")
23        value = int(input("Enter a value between " + str(low) + " and " +
24                          str(high) + ": "))
25
26     return value
27
```

```
28  # Start the program.
29  main()
```

Program Run

```
Please enter a time: hours, then minutes.
Enter a value between 0 and 23: 25
Error: value out of range.
Enter a value between 0 and 23: 20
Enter a value between 0 and 59: -1
Error: value out of range.
Enter a value between 0 and 59: 30
You entered 20 hours and 30 minutes.
```

5.7 Problem Solving: Stepwise Refinement

Use the process of stepwise refinement to decompose complex tasks into simpler ones.

One of the most powerful strategies for problem solving is the process of **stepwise refinement**. To solve a difficult task, break it down into simpler tasks. Then keep breaking down the simpler tasks into even simpler ones, until you are left with tasks that you know how to solve.

Now apply this process to a problem of everyday life. You get up in the morning and simply must *get coffee*. How do you get coffee? You see whether you can get someone else, such as your mother or mate, to bring you some. If that fails, you must *make coffee*. How do you make coffee? If there is instant coffee available, you can *make instant coffee*. How do you make instant coffee? Simply *boil water* and mix the boiling water with the instant coffee. How do you boil water? If there is a microwave, then you fill a cup with water, place it in the microwave and heat it for three minutes. Otherwise, you fill a kettle with water and heat it on the stove until the water comes to a boil.

On the other hand, if you don't have instant coffee, you must *brew coffee*. How do you brew coffee? You add water to the coffee maker, put in a filter, *grind coffee*, put the coffee in the filter, and turn the coffee maker on. How do you grind coffee? You add coffee beans to the coffee grinder and push the button for 60 seconds.

Figure 5 shows a flowchart view of the coffee-making solution. Refinements are shown as expanding boxes. In Python, you implement a refinement as a function. For example, a function brewCoffee would call grindCoffee, and brewCoffee would be called from a function makeCoffee.

A production process is broken down into sequences of assembly steps.

© AdShooter/iStockphoto.

Figure 5
Flowchart
of Coffee-
Making
Solution

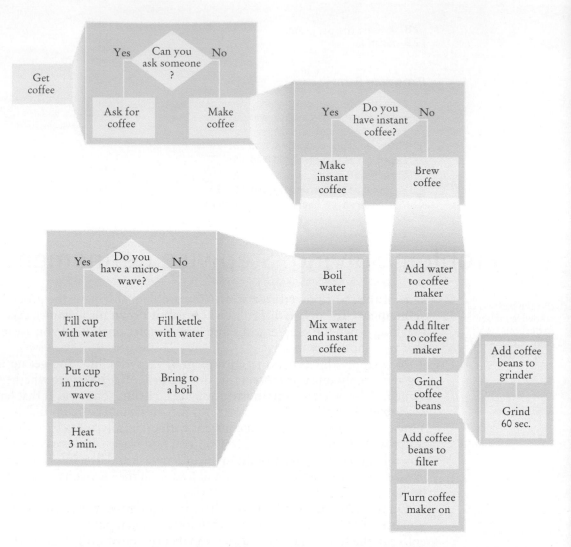

Let us apply the process of stepwise refinement to a programming problem.

When printing a check, it is customary to write the check amount both as a number ("$274.15") and as a text string ("two hundred seventy four dollars and 15 cents"). Doing so reduces the recipient's temptation to add a few digits in front of the amount.

For a human, this isn't particularly difficult, but how can a computer do this? There is no built-in function that turns 274 into `"two hundred seventy four"`. We need to program this function. Here is the description of the function we want to write:

© YinYang/iStockphoto.

```
## Turns a number into its English name.
#  @param number a positive integer < 1,000
#  @return the name of the number (e.g., "two hundred seventy four")
#
def intName(number) :
```

How can this function do its job? Consider a simple case first. If the number is between 1 and 9, we need to compute `"one"` ... `"nine"`. In fact, we need the same computation *again* for the hundreds (`two hundred`). Any time you need something more than once, it is a good idea to turn that into a function. Rather than writing the entire function, write only the comment:

When you discover that you need a function, write a description of the parameter variables and return values.

```
## Turns a digit into its English name.
#  @param digit an integer between 1 and 9
#  @return the name of digit ("one" ... "nine")
#
def digitName(digit) :
```

Numbers between 10 and 19 are special cases. Let's have a separate function `teenName` that converts them into strings `"eleven"`, `"twelve"`, `"thirteen"`, and so on:

A function may require simpler functions to carry out its work.

```
## Turns a number between 10 and 19 into its English name.
#  @param number an integer between 10 and 19
#  @return the name of the given number ("ten" ... "nineteen")
#
def teenName(number) :
```

Next, suppose that the number is between 20 and 99. The name of such a number has two parts, such as `"seventy four"`. We need a way of producing the first part, `"twenty"`, `"thirty"`, and so on. Again, we will put that computation into a separate function:

```
## Gives the name of the tens part of a number between 20 and 99.
#  @param number an integer between 20 and 99
#  @return the name of the tens part of the number ("twenty" ... "ninety")
#
def tensName(number) :
```

Now let us write the pseudocode for the `intName` function. If the number is between 100 and 999, then we show a digit and the word `"hundred"` (such as `"two hundred"`). We then remove the hundreds, for example reducing 274 to 74. Next, suppose the remaining part is at least 20 and at most 99. If the number is evenly divisible by 10, we use `tensName`, and we are done. Otherwise, we print the tens with `tensName` (such as `"seventy"`) and remove the tens, reducing 74 to 4. In a separate branch, we deal with numbers that are at between 10 and 19. Finally, we print any remaining single digit (such as `"four"`).

> *intName(number)*
> *part = number # The part that still needs to be converted*
> *name = ""*
>
> *If part >= 100*
>   *name = name of hundreds in part + " hundred"*
>   *Remove hundreds from part.*
>
> *If part >= 20*
>   *Append tensName(part) to name.*
>   *Remove tens from part.*
> *Else if part >= 10*
>   *Append teenName(part) to name.*
>   *part = 0*
>
> *If part > 0*
>   *Append digitName(part) to name.*

Translating the pseudocode into Python is straightforward. The result is shown in the source listing below.

Note how we rely on helper functions to do much of the detail work. Using the process of stepwise refinement, we now need to consider these helper functions.

Let's start with the `digitName` function. This function is so simple to implement that pseudocode is not really required. Simply use an `if` statement with nine branches:

```python
def digitName(digit) :
    if (digit == 1) : return "one"
    if (digit == 2) : return "two"
    . . .
```

The `teenName` and `tensName` functions are similar.

This concludes the process of stepwise refinement. Here is the complete program.

sec07/intname.py

```python
1   ##
2   #   This program turns an integer into its English name.
3   #
4
5   def main() :
6       value = int(input("Please enter a positive integer < 1000: "))
7       print(intName(value))
8
9   ## Turns a number into its English name.
10  #   @param number a positive integer < 1,000
11  #   @return the name of the number (e.g., "two hundred seventy four")
12  #
13  def intName(number) :
14      part = number    # The part that still needs to be converted.
15      name = ""     # The name of the number.
16
17      if part >= 100 :
18          name = digitName(part // 100) + " hundred"
19          part = part % 100
20
21      if part >= 20 :
22          name = name + " " + tensName(part)
23          part = part % 10
24      elif part >= 10 :
25          name = name + " " + teenName(part)
26          part = 0
27
28      if part > 0 :
29          name = name + " " + digitName(part)
30
31      return name
32
33  ## Turns a digit into its English name.
34  #   @param digit an integer between 1 and 9
35  #   @return the name of digit ("one" ... "nine")
36  #
37  def digitName(digit) :
38      if digit == 1 : return "one"
39      if digit == 2 : return "two"
40      if digit == 3 : return "three"
41      if digit == 4 : return "four"
42      if digit == 5 : return "five"
43      if digit == 6 : return "six"
```

```
44    if digit == 7 : return "seven"
45    if digit == 8 : return "eight"
46    if digit == 9 : return "nine"
47    return ""
48
49 ## Turns a number between 10 and 19 into its English name.
50 #  @param number an integer between 10 and 19
51 #  @return the name of the given number ("ten" ... "nineteen")
52 #
53 def teenName(number) :
54    if number == 10 : return "ten"
55    if number == 11 : return "eleven"
56    if number == 12 : return "twelve"
57    if number == 13 : return "thirteen"
58    if number == 14 : return "fourteen"
59    if number == 15 : return "fifteen"
60    if number == 16 : return "sixteen"
61    if number == 17 : return "seventeen"
62    if number == 18 : return "eighteen"
63    if number == 19 : return "nineteen"
64    return ""
65
66 ## Gives the name of the tens part of a number between 20 and 99.
67 #  @param number an integer between 20 and 99
68 #  @return the name of the tens part of the number ("twenty" ... "ninety")
69 #
70 def tensName(number) :
71    if number >= 90 : return "ninety"
72    if number >= 80 : return "eighty"
73    if number >= 70 : return "seventy"
74    if number >= 60 : return "sixty"
75    if number >= 50 : return "fifty"
76    if number >= 40 : return "forty"
77    if number >= 30 : return "thirty"
78    if number >= 20 : return "twenty"
79    return ""
80
81 # Start the program.
82 main()
```

Program Run

```
Please enter a positive integer < 1000: 729
seven hundred twenty nine
```

Programming Tip 5.4

Keep Functions Short

There is a certain cost for writing a function. You need to design, code, and test the function. The function needs to be documented. You need to spend some effort to make the function reusable rather than tied to a specific context. To avoid this cost, it is always tempting just to stuff more and more code into one place rather than going through the trouble of breaking up the code into separate functions. It is quite common to see inexperienced programmers produce functions that are several hundred lines long.

As a rule of thumb, a function that is so long that its code will not fit on a single screen in your development environment should probably be broken up.

Programming Tip 5.5

Tracing Functions

When you design a complex function, it is a good idea to carry out a manual walkthrough before entrusting your program to the computer.

Take an index card, or some other piece of paper, and write down the function call that you want to study. Write the name of the function and the names and values of the parameter variables, like this:

intName(number = 416)

Then write the names and initial values of the function variables. Write them in a table, because you will update them as you walk through the code.

intName(number = 416)	
part	*name*
416	*""*

We enter the test part >= 100. part // 100 is 4 and part % 100 is 16. digitName(4) is easily seen to be "four". (Had digitName been complicated, you would have started another sheet of paper to figure out that function call. It is quite common to accumulate several sheets in this way.)

Now name has changed to digitName(part // 100) + " hundred", that is "four hundred", and part has changed to part % 100, or 16.

intName(number = 416)	
part	*name*
~~*416*~~	~~*""*~~
16	*"four hundred"*

Now you enter the branch part >= 10. teenName(16) is sixteen, so the variables now have the values

intName(number = 416)	
part	*name*
~~*416*~~	~~*""*~~
~~*16*~~	~~*"four hundred"*~~
0	*"four hundred sixteen"*

Now it becomes clear why you need to set part to 0 in line 26. Otherwise, you would enter the next branch and the result would be "four hundred sixteen six". Tracing the code is an effective way to understand the subtle aspects of a function.

Programming Tip 5.6
Stubs

When writing a larger program, it is not always feasible to implement and test all functions at once. You often need to test a function that calls another, but the other function hasn't yet been implemented. Then you can temporarily replace the missing function with a **stub**. A stub is a function that returns a simple value that is sufficient for testing another function. Here are examples of stub functions:

© lillisphotography/iStockphoto.

```
## Turns a digit into its English name.
#  @param digit an integer between 1 and 9
#  @return the name of digit ("one" ... "nine")
#
def digitName(digit) :
    return "mumble"
```

Stubs are incomplete functions that can be used for testing.

```
## Gives the name of the tens part of a number
#  between 20 and 99.
#  @param number an integer between 20 and 99
#  @return the tens name of the number ("twenty" ... "ninety")
#
def tensName(number) :
    return "mumblety"
```

If you combine these stubs with the intName function and test it with an argument of 274, you will get a result of "mumble hundred mumblety mumble", which indicates that the basic logic of the intName function is working correctly.

WORKED EXAMPLE 5.2
Calculating a Course Grade

Problem Statement   Students in this course take four exams and earn a letter grade (A+, A, A–, B+, B, B–, C+, C, C–, D+, D, D–, or F) for each of them. The course grade is determined by dropping the lowest grade and averaging the three remaining grades. To average grades, first convert them to number grades, using the usual scheme A+ = 4.3, A = 4.0, A– = 3.7, B+ = 3.3, ..., D– = 0.7, F = 0. Then compute their average and convert it

© paul kline/iStockphoto.

back to the closest letter grade. For example, an average of 3.51 would be an A–.

Your task is to read four letter grades, one per line.

letterGrade1
letterGrade2
letterGrade3
letterGrade4

For example,

A–
B+
C
A

For each sequence of four input lines, your output should be the letter grade earned in the course, as just described. For example, A–.

The end of inputs will be indicated by a *letterGrade1* input of Q.

Step 1   Carry out stepwise refinement.

We will use the process of stepwise refinement. To process the inputs, we need to process all four grades of a student's grade set. Therefore, we define a task *Process grade set.*

To process one set of grades, we read the first grade and bail out if it is a Q. Otherwise, we read the four grades. Because we need them in their numeric form, we identify a task *Convert letter grade to number.*

We then have four numbers and need to find the smallest one. That is another task, *Find smallest of four numbers.* To average the remaining ones, we compute the sum of all values, subtract the smallest, and divide by three. Let's say that is not worth making into a subtask.

Next, we need to convert the result back into a letter grade. That is yet another subtask *Convert number grade to letter.* Finally, we print the letter grade. That is again so simple that it requires no subtask.

Step 2   Convert letter grade to number.

How do we convert a letter grade to a number? Follow this algorithm:

gradeToNumber(grade)
first = first character of grade
If first is A, B, C, D, or F
    Set result to 4, 3, 2, 1, or 0 respectively.
If the second character of grade is +
    Add 0.3 to result.
If the second character of grade is –
    Subtract 0.3 from result.
Return result.

Here is a function for that task:

```python
## Converts a letter grade to a number.
#   @param grade a letter grade (A+, A, A–, . . ., D–, F)
#   @return the equivalent number grade
#
def gradeToNumber(grade) :
   result = 0
   first = grade[0]
   first = first.upper()
   if first == "A" :
      result = 4
   elif first == "B" :
      result = 3
   elif first == "C" :
      result = 2
   elif first == "D" :
      result = 1

   if len(grade) > 1 :
      second = grade[1]
      if second == "+" :
```

```
            result = result + 0.3
      elif second == "-" :
            result = result - 0.3

    return result
```

Step 3 Convert number grade to letter.

How do we do the opposite conversion? Here, the challenge is that we need to convert to the *nearest* letter grade. For example, if x is the number grade, then we have:

$2.5 \leq x < 2.85$: B–
$2.85 \leq x < 3.15$: B
$3.15 \leq x < 3.5$: B+

We can make a function with 13 branches, one for each valid letter grade.

```
## Converts a number to the nearest letter grade.
#   @param x a number between 0 and 4.3
#   @return the nearest letter grade
#
def numberToGrade(x) :
    if x >= 4.15 : return "A+"
    if x >= 3.85 : return "A"
    if x >= 3.5 : return "A-"
    if x >= 3.15 : return "B+"
    if x >= 2.85 : return "B"
    if x >= 2.5 : return "B-"
    if x >= 2.15 : return "C+"
    if x >= 1.85 : return "C"
    if x >= 1.5 : return "C-"
    if x >= 1.15 : return "D+"
    if x >= 0.85 : return "D"
    if x >= 0.5 : return "D-"
    return "F"
```

Step 4 Find the minimum of four numbers.

Finally, how do we find the smallest of four numbers? Python provides the min function that accepts multiple values as its arguments and returns the minimum from among those values. For example:

```
result = min(5, 8, 2, 23)
```

will assign 2 to variable result.

Step 5 Process a grade set.

As previously described, to process a student's grade set, we follow these steps:

Read in the four input strings.
Convert grades to numbers.
Compute the average after dropping the lowest grade.
Print the grade corresponding to that average.

However, if we read the first input string and find a Q, we need to signal to the caller that we have reached the end of the input set and that no further calls should be made.

Our function will return a Boolean value, False if it was successful, True if it encountered the sentinel.

```
## Processes one student's set of grades.
#   @return True if the sentinel was encountered or False otherwise
#
def processGradeSet() :
```

```
# Read the first grade.
grade1 = input("Enter the first grade or Q to quit: ")
if grade1.upper() == "Q" :
    return True

# Read the next three grades.
grade2 = input("Enter the second grade: ")
grade3 = input("Enter the third grade: ")
grade4 = input("Enter the fourth grade: ")

# Compute and print their average.
x1 = gradeToNumber(grade1)
x2 = gradeToNumber(grade2)
x3 = gradeToNumber(grade3)
x4 = gradeToNumber(grade4)
xlow = min(x1, x2, x3, x4)
avg = (x1 + x2 + x3 + x4 - xlow) / 3
print(numberToGrade(avg))

return False
```

Step 6   Write the main function.

The main function is now utterly trivial. We keep calling processGradeSet while it returns False.

```
def main() :
    done = False
    while not done :
        done = processGradeSet()
```

We place all functions into a single Python file.

EXAMPLE CODE   See worked_example_2/grades.py in your eText or companion code for the complete program.

WORKED EXAMPLE 5.3

Using a Debugger

As you have undoubtedly realized by now, computer programs rarely run perfectly the first time. At times, it can be quite frustrating to find the errors, or bugs, as they are called by programmers. Of course, you can insert print statements into your code that show the program flow and values of key variables. You then run the program and try to analyze the printout. But if the printout does not clearly point to the problem, you need to add and remove print statements and run the program again. That can be a time-consuming process.

Modern development environments contain a *debugger*, a program that helps you locate bugs by letting you follow the execution of a program. You can stop and restart the program and see the contents of variables whenever the program is temporarily stopped. At each stop, you can decide how many program steps to run until the next stop.

Python Debuggers

Just like compilers, debuggers vary widely from one system to another. Most debuggers in integrated environments have a similar layout—see the examples below. You will have to find out how to prepare a program for debugging, and how to start the debugger on your system. With many development environments, you can simply pick a menu command to build your program for debugging and start the debugger.

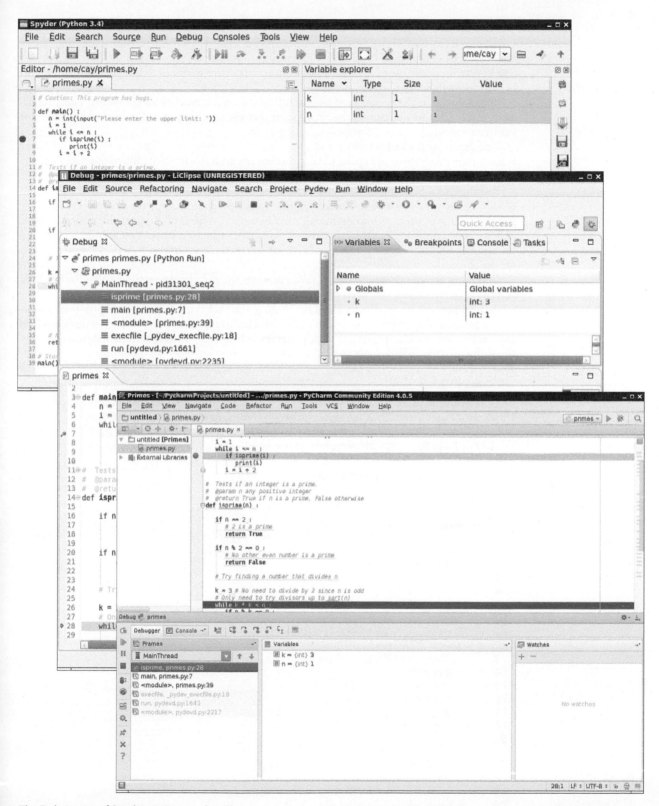

The Debuggers of Spyder, PyDev, and PyCharm

Debugger Essentials

Once you have started the debugger, you can go a long way with just four debugging commands: "set breakpoint", "run until breakpoint", "step over", and "step inside". The names and keystrokes or mouse clicks for these commands differ between debuggers, but all debuggers support these basic commands.

When you start the debugger, it runs at full speed until it reaches a *breakpoint*. Then execution stops. The line containing the breakpoint that causes the stop is displayed, but it has not yet been executed.

You can now inspect variables and step through the program a line at a time, or continue running the program at full speed until it reaches the next breakpoint. When the program terminates, the debugger stops as well.

Running to a breakpoint gets you there speedily, but you don't know what the program did along the way. For a better understanding of the program flow, you can step through the program a line at a time. One command, usually called "step into", steps inside function calls, and another command, called "step over" skips over function calls. You should step into a function to check whether it carries out its job correctly. Step over a function if you know it works correctly.

Finally, when the program has finished running, the debugging session is also finished. To run the program again, you need to start another debugging session.

A debugger can be an effective tool for finding and removing bugs in your program. However, it is no substitute for good design and careful programming. If the debugger does not find any errors, it does not mean that your program is bug-free. Testing and debugging can only show the presence of bugs, not their absence.

Debugging Practice

Here is a simple program for practicing the use of a debugger. The program is supposed to compute all prime numbers up to a number n. (An integer is defined to be prime if it is not evenly divisible by any number except by 1 and itself. Also, mathematicians find it convenient not to call 1 a prime. Thus, the first few prime numbers are 2, 3, 5, 7, 11, 13, 17, 19.)

worked_example_3/primes.py

```
1   # Caution: This program has bugs.
2
3   def main() :
4      n = int(input("Please enter the upper limit: "))
5      i = 1
6      while i <= n :
7         if isprime(i) :
8            print(i)
9         i = i + 2
10
11  #   Tests whether an integer is a prime.
12  #   @param n  any positive integer
13  #   @return True if n is a prime, False otherwise
14  def isprime(n) :
15
16     if n == 2 :
17        # 2 is a prime
18        return True
19
20     if n % 2 == 0 :
21        # No other even number is a prime
22        return False
23
24     # Try finding a number that divides n
25
```

```
26    k = 3 # No need to divide by 2 because n is odd
27    # Only need to try divisors up to sqrt(n)
28    while k * k < n :
29        if n % k == 0 :
30            # n is not a prime because it is divisible by k
31            return False
32        # Try next odd number
33        k = k + 2
34
35    # No divisor found. Therefore, n is a prime
36    return True
37
38 # Start the program
39 main()
```

When you run this program with an input of 10, then the output is

```
1
3
5
7
9
```

That is not very promising. It looks as if the program just prints all odd numbers. Let us find out what it does wrong by using the debugger.

First, set a breakpoint in line 7. With most debuggers, you right-click or double-click on the line to do so. Then pick the menu option to start debugging. On the way, the program will stop to input a value into n. Type 10 at the input prompt. The program will then stop at the breakpoint.

```
3 def main() :
4     n = int(input("Please enter the upper limit: "))
5     i = 1
6     while i <= n :
7         if isprime(i) :
8             print(i)
9         i = i + 2
10
```

Now we wonder why the program treats 1 as a prime. Locate the buttons for the "step over" and "step into" commands. With the Spyder debugger, they look like this:

Step into the isprime function. Execute the "step over" command a few times, until you reach the while loop. You will notice that the program skips the two if statements. Have a look at the variables.

Variable explorer			
Name ▾	Type	Size	Value
k	int	1	3
n	int	1	1

As you can see, n is 1 because we are currently testing whether 1 is a prime. The if statements were skipped because they handle even numbers. Then k is set to 3.

Continue stepping, and you will notice that the while loop is skipped because k * k is not less than n. Then the isprime function returns True, which is a bug. It looks like the function needs to be rewritten to treat 1 as a special case.

Next, we would like to know why the program doesn't print 2 as a prime even though the isprime function recognizes that 2 is a prime. Continue the debugger. It will stop at the breakpoint in line 7. Note that i is 3. Now it becomes clear. The loop in the main function only tests odd numbers. Either main should test both odd and even numbers, or better, it should just handle 2 as a special case.

Finally, we would like to find out why the program believes 9 is a prime. Continue debugging until the breakpoint is hit with i = 9. Step into the isprime function. Now use "step over" repeatedly. The two if statements are skipped, which is correct because 9 is an odd number. The program again skips past the while loop. Inspect k to find out why. Note that k is 3. Look at the condition in the while loop. It tests whether k * k < n. Now k * k is 9 and n is also 9, so the test fails.

When checking whether an integer n is prime, it makes sense to only test divisors up to $\sqrt{n}$. If n can be factored as $p \times q$, then the factors can't both be greater than $\sqrt{n}$. But actually that isn't quite true. If n is a perfect square of a prime, then its sole nontrivial divisor is equal to $\sqrt{n}$. That is exactly the case for $9 = 3 \times 3$. We should have tested for k * k ≤ n.

By running the debugger, we discovered three bugs in the program:

1. isprime falsely claims 1 to be a prime.
2. main doesn't test 2.
3. There is an off-by-one error in isprime. The condition of the while statement should be k * k ≤ n.

Here is the improved program.

```python
def main() :
    n = int(input("Please enter the upper limit: "))
    if n >= 2 :
        print(2)
    i = 3
    while i <= n :
        if isprime(i) :
            print(i)
        i = i + 2

#   Tests whether an integer is a prime.
#   @param n  any positive integer
#   @return  True if n is a prime, False otherwise
def isprime(n) :
    if n == 1 :
        return False

    if n == 2 :
        # 2 is a prime
        return True

    if n % 2 == 0 :
        # No other even number is a prime
        return False

    # Try finding a number that divides n
    k = 3 # No need to divide by 2 because n is odd
    # Only need to try divisors up to sqrt(n)
    while k * k <= n :
        if n % k == 0 :
            # n is not a prime because it is divisible by k
            return False
        # Try next odd number
        k = k + 2

    # No divisor found. Therefore, n is a prime
    return True
```

```
# Start the program.
main()
```

Is our program now free from bugs? That is not a question the debugger can answer. Remember, testing can only show the presence of bugs, not their absence.

5.8 Variable Scope

As your programs get larger and contain more variables, you may encounter problems where you cannot access a variable that is defined in a different part of your program, or where two variable definitions conflict with each other. In order to resolve these problems, you need to be familiar with the concept of *variable scope*.

The **scope** of a variable is the part of the program in which you can access it. For example, the scope of a function's parameter variable is the entire function. In the following code segment, the scope of the parameter variable sideLength is the entire cubeVolume function but *not* the main function.

> The scope of a variable is the part of the program in which it is visible.

```
def main() :
    print(cubeVolume(10))

def cubeVolume(sideLength) :
    return sideLength ** 3
```

A variable that is defined within a function is called a **local variable**. When a local variable is defined in a block, it becomes available from that point until the end of the function in which it is defined. For example, in the code segment below, the scope of the square variable is highlighted.

> A local variable is one defined within a function or code block.

```
def main() :
    sum = 0
    for i in range(11) :
        square = i * i
        sum = sum + square

    print(square, sum)
```

A loop variable in a for statement is a local variable. As with any local variable, its scope extends to the end of the function in which it was defined:

```
def main() :
    sum = 0
    for i in range(11) :
        square = i * i
        sum = sum + square

    print(i, sum)
```

Here is an example of a scope problem:

```
def main() :
    sideLength = 10
    result = cubeVolume()
    print(result)
```

```python
def cubeVolume() :
    return sideLength ** 3   # Error

main()
```

Note the scope of the variable `sideLength`. The `cubeVolume` function attempts to read the variable, but it cannot—the scope of `sideLength` does not extend outside the `main` function. The remedy is to pass it as an argument, as we did in Section 5.2.

It is possible to use the same variable name more than once in a program. Consider the `result` variables in the following example:

```python
def main() :
    result = square(3) + square(4)
    print(result)

def square(n) :
    result = n * n
    return result

main()
```

Each `result` variable is defined in a separate function, and their scopes do not overlap.

A global variable is defined outside of a function.

Python also supports **global variables**: variables that are defined outside functions. A global variable is visible to all functions defined after it. However, any function that wishes to update a global variable must include a `global` declaration, like this:

```python
balance = 10000   # A global variable

def withdraw(amount) :
    global balance    # This function intends to update the global balance variable
    if balance >= amount :
        balance = balance - amount
```

If you omit the `global` declaration, then the `balance` variable inside the `withdraw` function is considered a local variable.

Generally, global variables are not a good idea. When multiple functions update global variables, the result can be difficult to predict. Particularly in larger programs developed by multiple programmers, it is important that the effect of each function be clear and easy to understand. You should avoid global variables in your programs.

© jchamp/iStockphoto (Railway and Main); © StevenCarrieJohnson/iStockphoto (Main and N. Putnam); © jsmith/iStockphoto (Main and South St.).

In the same way that there can be a street named "Main Street" in different cities, a Python program can have multiple variables with the same name.

Programming Tip 5.7
Avoid Global Variables

Programs with global variables are difficult to maintain and extend because you can no longer view each function as a "black box" that simply receives arguments and returns a result. When functions modify global variables, it becomes more difficult to understand the effect of function calls. As programs get larger, this difficulty mounts quickly. Instead of using global variables, use function parameter variables and return values to transfer information from one part of a program to another.

Global constants, however, are fine. You can place them at the top of a Python source file and access (but not modify) them in any of the functions in the file. Do not use a `global` declaration to access constants.

WORKED EXAMPLE 5.4

Graphics: Rolling Dice

Problem Statement   Computer programs are often used to simulate the rolling of one or more dice (see Section 4.9.2). Your task is to write a graphics program that simulates the rolling of five dice and draws the resulting face of each die in a graphics window. Users should be able to repeatedly roll the five dice until they choose to quit the program.

Step 1   Carry out stepwise refinement.

Viewing the problem from a high-level, there are only a few steps involved. First, create and configure a graphics window. Next, roll and draw the five dice. Users should be able to repeatedly roll the dice until they quit the program, so we will ask the user whether to roll again. Now we have a simple algorithm for this problem:

> *Create and configure a graphics window.*
> *Repeat until user quits*
>   *Roll and draw the dice.*
>   *Query user about rolling again.*

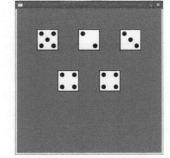

As part of the refinement process, we will implement the individual tasks in the following steps.

Here is the `main` function for implementing this algorithm:

```
DIE_SIZE = 60

def main() :
   canvas = configureWindow(DIE_SIZE * 7)
   rollDice(canvas, DIE_SIZE)
   while rollAgain() :
      rollDice(canvas, DIE_SIZE)
```

The size of the window that is passed to the `configureWindow` function is calculated based on `DIE_SIZE`. To evenly space the five dice across the window in two rows, we compute the width needed for seven dice, which leaves room between the border and the dice.

Step 2   Create and configure a graphics window.

To create a graphics program, we first create a graphics window and access its canvas. This can be done in a separate function, `configureWindow`. To allow for a more flexible program, we specify a parameter variable for the size of the window.

```
def configureWindow(winSize) :
```

In prior graphics programs, we had to use the wait method to prevent the window from closing. For this task, that method is not needed because we will be getting input from the user each time the dice are drawn on the canvas, thus stopping the window from closing.

The following function creates and configures the graphics window and returns the canvas. Note the use of the setBackground method to set a green background for the window.

```
## Create and configure the graphics window.
#  @param winSize the vertical and horizontal size of the window
#  @return the canvas used for drawing
#
def configureWindow(winSize) :
   win = GraphicsWindow(winSize, winSize)
   canvas = win.canvas()
   canvas.setBackground(0, 128, 0)
   return canvas
```

Step 3   Prompt the user to roll again or quit.

Each time the dice are rolled, we will ask the user whether to roll again or quit the program. This simple function implements that task, returning True if the dice should be rolled again.

```
## Prompt the user whether to roll again or quit.
#  @return True if the user wants to roll again
#
def rollAgain() :
   userInput = input("Press the Enter key to roll again or enter Q to quit: ")
   if userInput.upper() == "Q" :
      return False
   else :
      return True
```

Step 4   Roll and draw the dice.

How do we roll five dice? In Section 4.9.2, you learned how to simulate that using the random number generator. To roll five dice, call randint(1, 6) five times.

Drawing the result of the simulated roll requires a bit more thought. We need to determine how to position each die on the canvas. A quick way to do this is to lay out each die based on the size of the dice, similar to laying tiles on a floor.

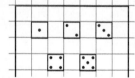

The rollDice function is shown below. We need to clear the canvas before each roll to remove the five dice from the previous roll, so the function calls the canvas method clear. The drawing of a single die is handled by the drawDie function, which we design in the next step.

```
## Simulates the rolling of 5 dice and draws the face of each die on a graphical
#  canvas in two rows with 3 dice in the first row and 2 in the second row.
#  @param canvas the graphical canvas on which to draw the dice
#  @param size an integer indicating the dimensions of a single die
#
def rollDice(canvas, size) :
   # Clear the canvas of all objects.
   canvas.clear()

   # Set the initial die offset from the upper-left corner of the canvas.
   xOffset = size
   yOffset = size

   # Roll and draw each of five dice.
   for die in range(5) :
      dieValue = randint(1, 6)
      drawDie(canvas, xOffset, yOffset, size, dieValue)
```

```
    if die == 2 :
        xOffset = size * 2
        yOffset = size * 3
    else :
        xOffset = xOffset + size * 2
```

Step 5 Draw a single die.

How do we layout the dots on the face of a die? Think of the die face as a grid consisting of five rows of five columns, and locate the seven possible dot positions on the grid as shown at right.

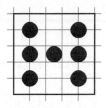

To draw the face for a specific die value, we need to draw the dots representing the given value in the correct positions. This task can be divided into several steps:

> *If dieValue is 1, 3, or 5*
>   *Draw the center dot.*
> *Else if dieValue is 6*
>   *Draw the middle dots in the left and right columns.*
> *If dieValue is >= 2*
>   *Draw the upper-left and lower-right dots.*
> *If dieValue is >= 4*
>   *Draw the lower-left and upper-right dots.*

The drawDie function implements the algorithm:

```
## Draws a single die on the canvas.
#  @param canvas  the canvas on which to draw the die
#  @param x  the x-coordinate for the upper-left corner of the die
#  @param y  the y-coordinate for the upper-left corner of the die
#  @param size  an integer indicating the dimensions of the die
#  @param dieValue  an integer indicating the number of dots on the die
#
def drawDie(canvas, x, y, size, dieValue) :
    # The size of the dot and positioning will be based on the size of the die.
    dotSize = size // 5
    offset1 = dotSize // 2
    offset2 = dotSize // 2 * 4
    offset3 = dotSize // 2 * 7

    # Draw the rectangle for the die.
    canvas.setFill("white")
    canvas.setOutline("black")
    canvas.setLineWidth(2)
    canvas.drawRect(x, y, size, size)

    # Set the color used for the dots.
    canvas.setColor("black")
    canvas.setLineWidth(1)
```

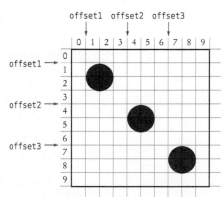

```
    # Draw the center dot or middle row of dots, if needed.
    if dieValue == 1 or dieValue == 3 or dieValue == 5 :
        canvas.drawOval(x + offset2, y + offset2, dotSize, dotSize)
    elif dieValue == 6 :
        canvas.drawOval(x + offset1, y + offset2, dotSize, dotSize)
        canvas.drawOval(x + offset3, y + offset2, dotSize, dotSize)

    # Draw the upper-left and lower-right dots, if needed.
    if dieValue >= 2 :
        canvas.drawOval(x + offset1, y + offset1, dotSize, dotSize)
        canvas.drawOval(x + offset3, y + offset3, dotSize, dotSize)
```

```
# Draw the lower-left and upper-right dots, if needed.
if dieValue >= 4 :
    canvas.drawOval(x + offset1, y + offset3, dotSize, dotSize)
    canvas.drawOval(x + offset3, y + offset1, dotSize, dotSize)
```

Put all of the functions together in a single Python source file.

EXAMPLE CODE   See worked_example_4/rolldice.py in your eText or companion code for the complete program.

5.9 Graphics: Building an Image Processing Toolkit

As you learned in Chapter 2, Python's standard library contains a large collection of functions and classes organized into modules. To help solve a given problem, you can import these "tools" instead of writing them yourself.

When the standard library doesn't have what you need, you can create your own collection of tools and organize them into one or more user-defined modules. This is known as a *software toolkit*. In this section, we walk through the development of a simple toolkit for processing digital images. Creating a toolkit makes it easy to reuse the same functions in multiple programs as needed.

5.9.1 Getting Started

A toolkit provides a collection of related functions or classes for solving a specific task.

The tools, or functions, in a toolkit should be related and easy to remember. An image processing toolkit would contain functions that are used to adjust or rearrange the individual pixels of an image, possibly changing its shape. To maintain a consistent interface, all of the functions in our toolkit will take a source image as an argument and return the new image that results from adjusting or rearranging the original.

In Python, you can place the functions of a toolkit into a separate file and then import them into any program of your choice. We'll place the image processing functions into a file called imgproctools.py.

In Section 4.10, we implemented an algorithm for creating the negative of an image and for flipping an image vertically. We can use the code from Chapter 4 to create the first two functions in our toolkit.

Here is the implementation of the createNegative function:

```
## Creates and returns a new image that is the negative of the original.
#  @param image the source image
#  @return the new negative image
#
def createNegative(image) :
    width = image.width()
    height = image.height()

    # Create a new image that is the same size as the original.
    newImage = GraphicsImage(width, height)
    for row in range(height) :
        for col in range(width) :

            # Get the color of the pixel in the original image.
            red = image.getRed(row, col)
```

```
        green = image.getGreen(row, col)
        blue = image.getBlue(row, col)

        # Filter the pixel.
        newRed = 255 - red
        newGreen = 255 - green
        newBlue = 255 - blue

        # Set the pixel in the new image to the new color.
        newImage.setPixel(row, col, newRed, newGreen, newBlue)

    return newImage
```

Here is the implementation of the `flipVertically` function:

```
## Creates and returns a new image that results from flipping an original
#  image vertically.
#  @param image the source image
#  @return the new vertically flipped image
#
def flipVertically(image) :
    # Create a new image that is the same size as the original.
    width = image.width()
    height = image.height()
    newImage = GraphicsImage(width, height)

    # Flip the image vertically.
    newRow = height - 1
    for row in range(height) :
        for col in range(width) :
            newCol = col
            pixel = image.getPixel(row, col)
            newImage.setPixel(newRow, newCol, pixel)
        newRow = newRow - 1

    return newImage
```

5.9.2 Comparing Images

Sometimes, you need to see whether two images are identical. For two images to be identical, they must be the exact same size, and corresponding pixels in the images must be the same color. The `sameImage` function is a useful one to include in the toolkit.

```
## Compares two images to determine if they are identical.
#  @param image1, image2 the two images to be compared
#  @return True if the images are identical, False otherwise
#
def sameImage(image1, image2) :
    # Make sure the images are the same size.
    width = image1.width()
    height = image1.height()
    if width != image2.width() or height != image2.height() :
        return False

    # Compare the two images, pixel by pixel.
    for row in range(height) :
        for col in range(width) :
            pixel1 = image1.getPixel(row, col)
            pixel2 = image2.getPixel(row, col)
```

```
# Compare the color components of corresponding pixels.
for i in range(3) :
    if pixel1[i] != pixel2[i] :
        return False

# Indicate the images are identical.
return True
```

5.9.3 Adjusting Image Brightness

The intensity levels, or brightness, of an image's pixels may cause it to appear too dark or too light. To darken a light image, you need to decrease the color component values of each pixel, and to brighten a dark image, you need to increase the values. A simple way to do this is to specify the amount by which the color components of each pixel should change. This amount should be between −100 and 100 percent. For example, to increase the brightness by 25 percent (see Figure 6), you would specify a positive percentage as 0.25 and increase each color component by that amount:

```
red = image.getRed(row, col)
green = image.getGreen(row, col)
blue = image.getBlue(row, col)

newRed = int(red + red * 0.25)
newGreen = int(green + green * 0.25)
newBlue = int(blue + blue * 0.25)
```

To darken a light image, you would specify a negative percentage:

```
newRed = int(red + red * -0.3)
newGreen = int(green + green * -0.3)
newBlue = int(blue + green * -0.3)
```

When adjusting the color component values in this fashion, it is possible for the new value to be outside the valid range of RGB values. Thus, if the adjusted component value is less than 0, it must be capped at 0, or if it is greater than 255, it must be capped at 255. Here is the adjustment for red pixels:

```
newRed = int(red + red * amount)
if newRed > 255 :
    newRed = 255
elif newRed < 0 :
    newRed = 0
```

Courtesy of Cay Horstmann.

Figure 6   An Image and a 25 Percent Brighter Version

The complete `adjustBrightness` function is shown below.

```
## Creates and returns a new image in which the brightness levels of
#  all three color components are adjusted by a given percentage.
#  @param image the source image
#  @param amount the percentage by which to adjust the brightness
#  @return the new image
#
def adjustBrightness(image, amount) :
    width = image.width()
    height = image.height()

    # Create a new image that is the same size as the original.
    newImage = GraphicsImage(width, height)
    for row in range(height) :
        for col in range(width) :

            # Get the color of the pixel in the original image.
            red = image.getRed(row, col)
            green = image.getGreen(row, col)
            blue = image.getBlue(row, col)

            # Adjust the brightness and cap the colors.
            newRed = int(red + red * amount)
            if newRed > 255 :
                newRed = 255
            elif newRed < 0 :
                newRed = 0
            newGreen = int(green + green * amount)
            if newGreen > 255 :
                newGreen = 255
            elif newGreen < 0 :
                newgreen = 0
            newBlue = int(blue + blue * amount)
            if newBlue > 255 :
                newBlue = 255
            elif newBlue < 0 :
                newBlue = 0

            # Set the pixel in the new image to the new color.
            newImage.setPixel(row, col, newRed, newGreen, newBlue)

    return newImage
```

5.9.4 Rotating an Image

Most cameras have a sensor that checks whether a photo is taken in portrait or landscape mode. But sometimes the sensor can be confused; then you need to rotate an image 90 degrees to the left or right (see Figure 7). When rotating an image, the width and height of the new image are the height and width of the original.

```
width = image.width()
height = image.height()
newImage = GraphicsImage(height, width)
```

To rotate the image to the left, the entire first row of pixels becomes the first column of the new image, the second row becomes the second column, and so on.

Figure 7
An Image Rotated Left

Courtesy of Cay Horstmann.

```
for row in range(height) :
   newCol = row
   for col in range(width) :
      newRow = col
      pixel = image.getPixel(row, col)
      newImage.setPixel(newRow, newCol, pixel)
```

The complete `rotateLeft` function is shown below.

```
## Rotates the image 90 degrees to the left.
#  @param image the image to be rotated
#  @return the new rotated image
#
def rotateLeft(image) :
   # Create a new image whose dimensions are the opposite of the original.
   width = image.width()
   height = image.height()
   newImage = GraphicsImage(height, width)

   # Rotate the image.
   for row in range(height) :
      newCol = row
      for col in range(width) :
         newRow = col
         pixel = image.getPixel(row, col)
         newImage.setPixel(newRow, newCol, pixel)

   return newImage
```

There are many other useful functions that could be added to the toolkit. You will find several of them in the exercises.

EXAMPLE CODE   See sec09/imgproctools.py in your eText or companion code for the complete toolkit program.

5.9.5 Using the Toolkit

After you create the functions and store them in the toolkit file, you can use them in the same way that you use the functions defined in the standard modules: You import

Functions defined
in a toolkit must
be imported before
they can be used in
your program.

the functions that you want to use. In the `processimg.py` example program below, we use the form of the `import` statement that imports all of the functions in the module (see Special Topic 2.1). The program prompts the user for the name of an image file, displays a menu of available operations, and processes the image based on the user's selection.

sec09/processimg.py

```python
1   ## This program illustrates the use of the tools
2   #  in the image processing toolkit.
3   #
4
5   from ezgraphics import GraphicsImage, GraphicsWindow
6   from imgproctools import *
7
8   # Read the name of the file to be processed
9   filename = input("Enter the name of the image file to be processed: ")
10
11  # Load the image from the file and display it in a window.
12  image = GraphicsImage(filename)
13
14  win = GraphicsWindow()
15  canvas = win.canvas()
16  canvas.drawImage(image)
17  done = False
18
19  while not done :
20      # Prompt the user for the type of processing.
21      print("How should the image be processed?")
22      print("1 - create image negative")
23      print("2 - adjust brightness")
24      print("3 - flip vertically")
25      print("4 - rotate to the left")
26      print("5 - save and quit")
27
28  response = int(input("Enter your choice: "))
29
30  # Process the image and display the new image in the window.
31      if response == 1 :
32          newImage = createNegative(image)
33      elif response == 2 :
34          amount = float(input("Adjust between -1.0 and 1.0: "))
35          newImage = adjustBrightness(image, amount)
36      elif response == 3 :
37          newImage = flipVertically(image)
38      elif response == 4 :
39          newImage = rotateLeft(image)
40
41      if response == 5 :
42          newImage.save("output.gif")
43          done = True
44      else :
45          canvas.drawImage(newImage)
46          image = newImage
```

WORKED EXAMPLE 5.5

Plotting Growth or Decay

When you put money into a savings account, the interest you earn is compounded. That is, you earn interest, not only on the money you put into the account, but also on the previous interest earned. With enough time, the balance can grow enormously, a phenomenon called "exponential growth".

The converse phenomenon occurs when a quantity keeps getting reduced by a given proportion. One example is radioactive decay. For example, the Carbon 14 isotope used in carbon dating decays at a rate of about 0.0121 percent per year. After 5,730 years, half of it is gone.

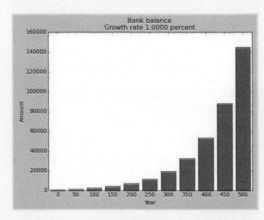 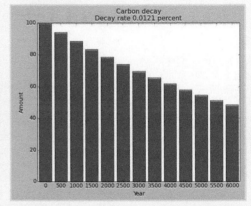

Figure 8 Examples of Growth and Decay

Problem Statement   Using the plotting package described in Toolbox 3.2, develop a function that produces a bar chart that tracks growth or decay over a long period of time. Limit the number of bars by drawing bars at specified points in time.

Step 1   Describe what the function should do.

The purpose of the bar chart is to illustrate the change in a quantity that increases or decreases by a given percentage every year. Every so many years, a bar with the current amount should be drawn, until the requested span of years has elapsed.

The function should build a nicely formatted bar chart similar to the example shown above. This will require adding a chart title and labels and tick marks for both axes.

Step 2   Determine the function's "inputs".

The function will need five inputs:

1. The initial amount
2. The annual percentage rate of change (which is negative for decay)
3. The number of years to track
4. The number of years between successive bars
5. A title for the chart

Step 3   Determine the type of the parameter variables and the return value.

The initial amount and the annual interest rate are clearly floating-point values. The number of years to show, and the years between bars are integers. The title is a string. The function does not return a value; it constructs a chart in a pyplot window.

We now have enough information to document and specify the function header:

```
## Constructs a bar chart that shows the cumulative increase or
#  decrease in a quantity over many years.
#  @param initial (float) the initial value of the quantity
#  @param rate (float) the percentage rate of change per year
#  @param years (int) the number of years to show in the chart
#  @param bardistance (int) the number of years between successive bars
#  @param title (string) the title of the graph
#
```

Step 4   Write pseudocode for obtaining the desired result.

Here is one approach for building the chart:

> *Plot the bar for the initial amount.*
> *Repeat for each year*
>   *Compute the change for the current year.*
>   *Update the amount.*
>   *If a bar should be drawn for the current year*
>   *Draw a bar for the amount at the next position.*
> *Add descriptive information.*
> *Configure the chart frame.*

Step 5   Implement the function body.

First, we'll draw the initial bar. You will notice that the *x*-axis values are centered under the bars. By default, bars are left aligned. To center the *x*-axis values, we add a named argument align = "center" to the pyplot.bar function:

```
def showGrowthChart(initial, rate, years, bardistance, title) :

    amount = initial
    bar = 0

    # Add the bar for the initial amount.
    pyplot.bar(bar, amount, align = "center")
    bar = bar + 1
```

The bar variable is a counter for the bars that we increment every time a bar is shown.

Next, we loop over the years and update the amount. For each year, we need to decide whether to draw a bar. The parameter bardistance provides the number of years between bars. If year is an exact multiple of bardistance, we draw a bar. For example, if bardistance is 500, a bar is drawn at year 500, 1000, 1500, and so on.

```
year = 1
while year <= years :
    # Update the amount
    change = amount * rate / 100
    amount = amount + change
    # If a bar should be drawn for this year, draw it
    if year % bardistance == 0 :
        pyplot.bar(bar, amount, align = "center")
        bar = bar + 1
    year = year + 1
```

The chart title is given, but we will add a subtitle that describes the growth or decay rate:

```
if rate >= 0 :
    subtitle = "Growth rate %.4f percent" % rate
else :
    subtitle = "Decay rate %.4f percent" % -rate

pyplot.title(title + "\n" + subtitle)
```

Here is how to configure the axes. We want a tick for each bar, and each tick should be labeled with the year at which it occurs. Note the use of the range function for producing the two lists for the ticks. For example, in the first graph of Figure 8, bar is 11 when the chart is plotted; year is 501 and bardistance is 50. So the range functions generate [0, 1, 2, 3, ..., 9, 10] and [0, 50, 100, 150, ..., 500].

```python
# Configure the axes
pyplot.xlabel("Year")
pyplot.ylabel("Amount")
pyplot.xticks(range(0, bar), range(0, year, bardistance))
```

Finally, we adjust the plot area. Because the bars are centered, we need to shift the area slightly to the left. Then we can show the chart, and we are done.

```python
# Fit the plot area tightly around the bar chart.
pyplot.xlim(-0.5, bar - 0.5)

pyplot.show()
```

Step 6 Test your function.

Here is a simple main function that calls the drawGrowthChart function with two typical scenarios:

```python
def main() :
    showGrowthChart(1000.0, 1.0, 500, 50, "Bank balance")
    showGrowthChart(100.0, -0.0121, 6000, 500, "Carbon decay")
```

The first graph shows that even at a puny interest rate of 1 percent per year, an investment of $1,000 can grow tremendously if you have a sufficiently long investment horizon. The second graph shows radioactive decay. You can see that after 6,000 years, about half of the original amount of Carbon 14 is left.

EXAMPLE CODE   See worked_example_5/growth.py in your eText or companion code for the complete program.

5.10 Recursive Functions (Optional)

A recursive function is a function that calls itself. This is not as unusual as it sounds at first. Suppose you face the arduous task of cleaning up an entire house. You may well say to yourself, "I'll pick a room and clean it, and then I'll clean the other rooms." In other words, the cleanup task calls itself, but with a simpler input. Eventually, all the rooms will be cleaned.

In Python, a recursive function uses the same principle. Here is a typical example. We want to print triangle patterns like this:

```
[]
[][]
[][][]
[][][][]
```

Specifically, our task is to provide a function

```python
def printTriangle(sideLength) :
```

© Janice Richard/iStockphoto.

Cleaning up a house can be solved recursively: Clean one room, then clean up the rest.

The triangle given above is printed by calling `printTriangle(4)`. To see how recursion helps, consider how a triangle with side length 4 can be obtained from a triangle with side length 3.

```
[]
[][]
[][][]
[][][][]
```

Print the triangle with side length 3.
Print a line with four [].

More generally, here are the Python instructions for an arbitrary side length:

```python
def printTriangle(sideLength) :
    printTriangle(sideLength - 1)
    print("[]" * sideLength)
```

There is just one problem with this idea. When the side length is 1, we don't want to call `printTriangle(0)`, `printTriangle(-1)`, and so on. The solution is simply to treat this as a special case, and not to print anything when `sideLength` is less than 1.

```python
def printTriangle(sideLength) :
    if sideLength < 1 : return
    printTriangle(sideLength - 1)
    print("[]" * sideLength)
```

A recursive computation solves a problem by using the solution to the same problem with simpler inputs.

Look at the `printTriangle` function one more time and notice how utterly reasonable it is. If the side length is 0, nothing needs to be printed. The next part is just as reasonable. Print the smaller triangle *and don't think about why that works*. Then print a row of []. Clearly, the result is a triangle of the desired size.

There are two key requirements to make sure that the recursion is successful:

This set of Russian dolls looks similar to the call pattern of a recursive function.

- Every recursive call must simplify the task in some way.
- There must be special cases to handle the simplest tasks directly.

For a recursion to terminate, there must be special cases for the simplest inputs.

The `printTriangle` function calls itself again with smaller and smaller side lengths. Eventually the side length must reach 0, and the function stops calling itself.

Here is what happens when we print a triangle with side length 4.

- The call `printTriangle(4)` calls `printTriangle(3)`.
  - The call `printTriangle(3)` calls `printTriangle(2)`.
    - The call `printTriangle(2)` calls `printTriangle(1)`.
      - The call `printTriangle(1)` calls `printTriangle(0)`.
        - The call `printTriangle(0)` returns, doing nothing.
      - The call `printTriangle(1)` prints [].
    - The call `printTriangle(2)` prints [][].
  - The call `printTriangle(3)` prints [][][].
- The call `printTriangle(4)` prints [][][][].

The call pattern of a recursive function looks complicated, and the key to the successful design of a recursive function is *not to think about it*.

Recursion is not really necessary to print triangle shapes. You can use nested loops, like this:

```python
def printTriangle(sideLength) :
    for i in range(1, sideLength + 1) :
        print("[]" * i)
```

However, this loop is a bit tricky. Many people find the recursive solution simpler to understand. The complete triangle.py program is provided below.

sec10/triangle.py

```python
1  ##
2  #   This program demonstrates how to print a triangle using recursion.
3  #
4
5  def main() :
6      printTriangle(4)
7
8  ## Prints a triangle with a given side length.
9  #  @param sideLength an integer indicating the length of the bottom row
10 #
11 def printTriangle(sideLength) :
12     if sideLength < 1 : return
13     printTriangle(sideLength - 1)
14
15     # Print the row at the bottom.
16     print("[]" * sideLength)
17
18 # Start the program.
19 main()
```

HOW TO 5.2
Thinking Recursively

Problem Statement   Solving a problem recursively requires a different mindset than solving it by programming loops. In fact, it helps if you are, or pretend to be, a bit lazy and let others do most of the work for you. If you need to solve a complex problem, pretend that "someone else" will do most of the heavy lifting and solve the problem for all simpler inputs. Then you only need to figure out how you can turn the solutions for simpler inputs into a solution for the whole problem. In this How To, we illustrate the recursive thinking process.

Problem Statement   Consider the problem of Section 4.2, computing the sum of the digits of a number. We want to design a function digitSum that computes the sum of the digits of an integer n. For example, digitSum(1729) = 1 + 7 + 2 + 9 = 19.

Step 1   Break the input into parts that can themselves be inputs to the problem.

The key to finding a recursive solution is reducing the input to a simpler input for the same problem.

In your mind, focus on a particular input or set of inputs for the task that you want to solve, and think how you can simplify the inputs. Look for simplifications that can be solved by the same task, and whose solutions are related to the original task.

In the digit sum problem, start by considering how to simplify an input such as n = 1729. Would it help to subtract 1? After all, digitSum(1729) = digitSum(1728) + 1. But consider n = 1000. There seems to be no obvious relationship between digitSum(1000) and digitSum(999).

A much more promising idea is to remove the last digit, that is, to compute n // 10 = 172. The digit sum of 172 is directly related to the digit sum of 1729.

Step 2   Combine solutions with simpler inputs into a solution of the original problem.

When designing a recursive solution, do not worry about multiple nested calls. Simply focus on reducing a problem to a slightly simpler one.

In your mind, consider the solutions for the simpler inputs that you have discovered in Step 1. Don't worry *how* those solutions are obtained. Simply have faith that the solutions are readily available. Just say to yourself: These are simpler inputs, so someone else will solve the problem for me.

In the case of the digit sum task, ask yourself how you can obtain digitSum(1729) if you know digitSum(172). You simply add the last digit (9) and you are done. How do you get the last digit? As the remainder n % 10. The value digitSum(n) can therefore be obtained as

```
digitSum(n // 10) + n % 10
```

Don't worry how digitSum(n // 10) is computed. The input is smaller, and therefore it works.

Step 3   Find solutions to the simplest inputs.

A recursive computation keeps simplifying its inputs. To make sure that the recursion comes to a stop, you must deal with the simplest inputs separately. Come up with special solutions for them. That is usually very easy.

Look at the simplest inputs for the digitSum problem:

- A number with a single digit
- 0

A number with a single digit is its own digit sum, so you can stop the recursion when n < 10, and return n in that case. Or, you can be even lazier. If n has a single digit, then digitSum(n // 10) + n % 10 equals digitSum(0) + n. You can simply terminate the recursion when n is zero.

Step 4   Implement the solution by combining the simple cases and the reduction step.

Now you are ready to implement the solution. Make separate cases for the simple inputs that you considered in Step 3. If the input isn't one of the simplest cases, then implement the logic you discovered in Step 2.

The complete digitSum function is provided below as part of a test program.

how_to_2/digits.py

```python
1  ##
2  #   This program illustrates the recursive digitSum function.
3  #
4
5  def main() :
6     print("Digit sum:", digitSum(1729))
7     print("Expected: 19")
8     print("Digit sum:", digitSum(1000))
9     print("Expected: 1")
10    print("Digit sum:", digitSum(9))
11    print("Expected: 9")
12    print("Digit sum:", digitSum(0))
13    print("Expected: 0")
14
15  ## Computes the sum of the digits of a number.
16  #  @param n an integer >= 0
17  #  @return the sum of the digits of n
18  #
19  def digitSum(n) :
20     if n == 0 : return 0    # Special case for terminating the recursion
21     return digitSum(n // 10) + n % 10    # General case
22
23  # Start the program.
24  main()
```

TOOLBOX 5.1

Turtle Graphics

In Section 2.6 you were introduced to the ezgraphics module, a simplified version of Python's more complex graphics library module. Python also includes a basic graphics package that can be used to create simple drawings. The Turtle Graphics package, which dates back to 1966, was originally designed to help teach programming to children. The package creates a turtle, which is a mechanical object or cursor, that you control by issuing basic commands. As the turtle moves, it draws on the screen using a pen that it carries. In this Toolbox, you will learn some of the basic commands for controlling the turtle to create simple figures.

Basic Turtle Commands

To create a drawing, first import the turtle graphics package into your program:

```
import turtle
```

The turtle carries a pen that can be either up or down. When the pen is down, the turtle draws on the screen as it moves. Initially, the pen is in the up position. To begin drawing, we need to put the pen down:

```
turtle.pendown()
```

The turtle starts in the center of a graphics window and faces towards the east. The turtle can be moved forward or backward relative to its current position. Here, we move the turtle forward 100 screen pixels:

```
turtle.forward(100)
```

which results in a horizontal line 100 pixels long (shown at left).

The turtle moves in the direction it currently faces. To change its direction, you turn the turtle either left or right and specify the angle by which it should turn. The angle is given in degrees. We can turn the turtle to the right 90° and draw a vertical line starting at its current position:

```
turtle.right(90)
turtle.forward(100)
```

This results in two sides of a square.

If we issue these commands two additional times, the result is a complete square:

```
turtle.right(90)
turtle.forward(100)
turtle.right(90)
turtle.forward(100)
```

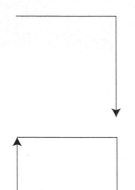

After drawing the scene, the program has to pause and wait for the user to terminate or end the program. This can be achieved using the input function and simply discarding the user input:

```
response = input("Press ENTER to quit.")
```

If you fail to wait for user input, the program terminates and you will not see the graphics window or the image drawn by the turtle. Note, this step performs the same function as the win.wait() method call used by ezgraphics.

Pen Attributes

The color and size of the pen can also be changed. To change the pen color, use one of the function calls,

```
turtle.color(colorName)
```

```
turtle.color(red,green,blue)
```

The strings for the color names are the same as those used in the ezgraphics module (see Table 11 on page 62). The red, green, and blue color values can be integer values between 0 and 255.

Suppose we want to draw a thick vertical line to the right of the square, as shown in Figure 9. To add the vertical line to the drawing, carry out the following steps:

1. Change the color and size of the pen.

   ```
   turtle.pensize(3)
   turtle.color("red")
   ```

2. Pick up the pen.

   Remember, the turtle draws as it moves when the pen is down. The turtle has to be moved to the top position of the vertical line without drawing on the screen. Pick up the pen using the command:

   ```
   turtle.penup()
   ```

3. Turn the turtle to face east.

   The turtle is currently at the upper-left corner of the square and facing north. The turtle has to be turned to face east before it can be moved.

   ```
   turtle.right(90)
   ```

4. Move the turtle 100 spaces to the right of the square.

   Because the turtle is at the upper-left corner of the square and the square is 100 pixels wide, the turtle has to be moved forward 200 pixels.

   ```
   turtle.forward(200)
   ```

5. Turn the turtle, put the pen down, and draw the line.

   ```
   turtle.right(90)
   turtle.pendown()
   turtle.forward(100)
   ```

Figure 9   The Turtle Draws a Line

Here is the complete program that constructs the image in Figure 9.

toolbox_1/turtlebox.py

```
 1  ##
 2  #   This program draws a rectangle and vertical line using Python's
 3  #   turtle graphics package.
 4  #
 5  import turtle
 6
 7  # Draw a square in the default color and pen size.
 8  turtle.pendown()
 9  turtle.forward(100)
10  turtle.right(90)
11  turtle.forward(100)
12  turtle.right(90)
13  turtle.forward(100)
14  turtle.right(90)
15  turtle.forward(100)
```

```
16
17  # Draw a larger red vertical line to the right of the box.
18  turtle.pensize(3)
19  turtle.pencolor("red")
20  turtle.penup()
21  turtle.right(90)
22  turtle.forward(200)
23  turtle.right(90)
24  turtle.pendown()
25  turtle.forward(100)
26
27  # Wait for user input to quit the program.
28  response = input("Press ENTER to quit.")
```

Advanced Commands

The turtle moves within a two-dimensional discrete Cartesian coordinate system similar to that used in mathematics. The origin is in the center of the graphics window and the positive y-axis extends upwards. (Note that this is not the same coordinate system used by ezgraphics.)

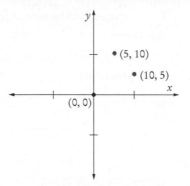

Commands are provided that work directly with the coordinate system. For example, to move the turtle to a given position, independent of the current direction in which the turtle faces, use the command

```
turtle.goto(x, y)
```

The turtle can be returned to the origin or its home position using the command

```
turtle.home()
```

If the pen is down, the turtle draws as it moves back to the origin. To clear the graphics window, use one of the commands

```
turtle.clear()
turtle.reset()
```

The clear function clears the window without moving the turtle. The reset function clears the screen, moves the turtle to the origin, and resets the turtle to its initial state.

There are a large number of commands available with the Turtle Graphics package. Some of the more commonly used commands are provided in Table 1.

Using Functions

If you want to produce a drawing with multiple related shapes, it is a good idea to provide a function for each kind of shape. For example, this function draws a rectangle and then ends up in the original position and orientation.

```
def square(width) :
    turtle.pendown()
```

```
turtle.forward(width)
turtle.right(90)
turtle.forward(width)
turtle.right(90)
turtle.forward(width)
turtle.right(90)
turtle.forward(width)
turtle.right(90)
turtle.penup()
```

You can now draw any number of rectangles:

```
for i in range(0, 10) :
    square(20)
    turtle.forward(30)
```

Table 1 Turtle Functions

Function	Description
turtle.backward(*distance*)	Moves backward *distance* in the opposite direction.
turtle.clear()	Clears the turtle's drawing from the window, but does not move the turtle.
turtle.forward(*distance*)	Moves forward *distance* in the current direction.
turtle.goto(x, y)	Moves to absolute position (x, y).
turtle.heading()	Returns the turtle's current heading in degrees.
turtle.hideturtle()	Hides the turtle.
turtle.home()	Moves to the origin (0,0) and sets the heading to the east.
turtle.left(*angle*)	Turns left by *angle* degrees.
turtle.pencolor(*colorname*) turtle.pencolor(*red*, *green*, *blue*)	Sets the pen color. The color can be specified by name or by *red*, *green*, and *blue* color values in the range [0 … 255].
turtle.pendown()	Puts the pen down to draw when moving.
turtle.pensize(*width*)	Sets the line thickness to *width*.
turtle.penup()	Picks the pen up to stop drawing when moving.
turtle.reset()	Clears the turtle's drawing from the window, moves the turtle to the origin (0, 0), and sets the heading to the east.
turtle.right(*angle*)	Turns right by *angle* degrees.
turtle.showturtle()	Shows the turtle.

A simpler way of implementing the square function is to repeat the drawing and turning four times:

```
def square(width) :
    turtle.pendown()
    for in in range(0, 4) :
        turtle.forward(width)
        turtle.right(90)
    turtle.penup()
```

We can generalize this function to draw pentagons, hexagons, and so on:

```
def regularPolygon(n, width) :
    turtle.pendown()
    for in in range(0, n) :
        turtle.forward(width)
        turtle.right(360 / n)
    turtle.penup()
```

Here are a number of polygons:

```
for n in range(3, 10) :
    regularPolygon(n, 20)
    turtle.forward(60)
```

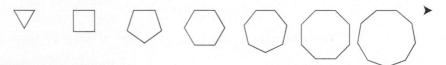

Of course, you can draw any shapes that can be made from lines. Exercise •• Toolbox P5.42 asks you to write a function that draws a house, and to call the function repeatedly to draw an urban scene.

Drawing Fractal Curves

A "fractal curve" is a curve whose small details resemble its broader shapes. For example, when you look at the undulating coast line of an island, and then focus on a small part, it too has a shape with nooks and crannies that is comparable to the larger part.

We will have our turtle draw a particular curve with "self similarity" — the Hilbert curve, which has the remarkable property that it wiggles around to visit all points with integer coordinates in a square. Figure 10 shows the Hilbert curves for $n = 1$, 2, and 3.

The figure below is a screen shot of our demo program plotting the Hilbert curve for $n = 6$. (The curves are named after the renowned mathematician David Hilbert who invented them

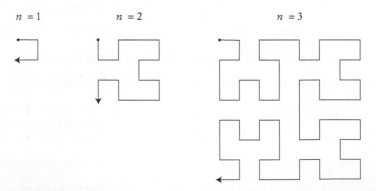

Figure 10 Hilbert Curves

for a different purpose. He scaled down all curves to fill a 1 × 1 square. As *n* goes towards infinity, the curve is "space filling", traversing all points in the square.)

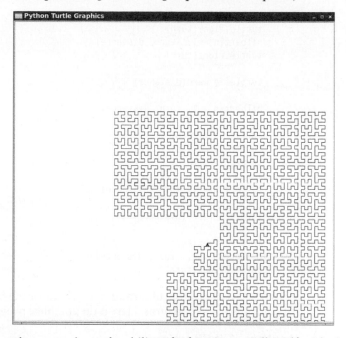

This section requires recursion—the ability of a function to call itself with simpler versions. If you skipped Section 5.10, feel free to skip this section as well. Or forge ahead and run the sample program. It is seductive to watch the turtle as it meticulously fills out a large square.

We will implement a function hilbert that makes a turtle traverse this curve. It is easy enough for *n* = 1.

```
def hilbert(n, turn, distance) :
   if n == 1 :
      turtle.forward(distance)
      turtle.right(turn)
      turtle.forward(distance)
      turtle.right(turn)
      turtle.forward(distance)
   else :
      . . .
```

We will call this function with turn = 90 or, if we want to draw a mirror image of the curve, with turn = –90.

Figure 11 shows how to draw the *n*th generation of the curve, provided that we know how to draw the previous generation. Note that the *n*th generation contains four curves of the previous generation, two of which are mirror images.

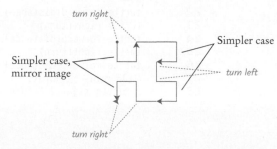

Figure 11
Drawing the *n*th
Generation Curve

The turtle also has to do certain turns before and after the recursive steps, as indicated in Figure 11. Here is the completion of the hilbert function:

```
else :
   turtle.right(turn)
   hilbert(n - 1, -turn, distance)
   turtle.right(turn)

   turtle.forward(distance)

   hilbert(n - 1, turn, distance)

   turtle.left(turn)
   turtle.forward(distance)
   turtle.left(turn)

   hilbert(n - 1, turn, distance)

   turtle.forward(distance)

   turtle.right(turn)
   hilbert(n - 1, -turn, distance)
   turtle.right(turn)
```

This is a nice application of turtle graphics because the Hilbert curve is produced as a sequence of pen movements and turns. Here is the complete program.

toolbox_1/hilbert.py

```
1   ##
2   #   This program draws a Hilbert curve using Python's turtle graphics package.
3   #
4   import turtle
5
6   def main() :
7      turtle.reset()
8      turtle.penup()
9      n = 6
10     turtle.goto(-n ** 2 * 10 / 2, n ** 2 * 10 / 2)
11     turtle.pendown()
12     hilbert(n, 90, 10)
13     response = input("Press ENTER to quit.")
14
15   ## Draws one generation of the Hilbert curve using Turtle graphics.
16   #   @param n an integer indicating the generation of the curve
17   #   @param turn the angle by which to turn the turtle
18   #   @param distance the number of pixels to move the turtle forward
19   #
20   def hilbert(n, turn, distance) :
21      if n == 1 :
22         turtle.forward(distance)
23         turtle.right(turn)
24         turtle.forward(distance)
25         turtle.right(turn)
26         turtle.forward(distance)
27         # Or, more elegantly,
28         # turtle.right(2 * turn)
```

```
29      else :
30          turtle.right(turn)
31          hilbert(n - 1, -turn, distance)
32          turtle.right(turn)
33          turtle.forward(distance)
34          hilbert(n - 1, turn, distance)
35          turtle.left(turn)
36          turtle.forward(distance)
37          turtle.left(turn)
38          hilbert(n - 1, turn, distance)
39          turtle.forward(distance)
40          turtle.right(turn)
41          hilbert(n - 1, -turn, distance)
42          turtle.right(turn)
43
44  main()
```

CHAPTER SUMMARY

Understand the concepts of functions, arguments, and return values.

- A function is a named sequence of instructions.
- Arguments are supplied when a function is called.
- The return value is the result that the function computes.
- Returning a value from a function is not the same as producing program output.

Be able to implement functions.

- When defining a function, you provide a name for the function and a variable for each argument.
- Function comments explain the purpose of the function, the meaning of the parameter variables and return value, as well as any special requirements.

Describe the process of parameter passing.

- Parameter variables hold the arguments supplied in the function call.

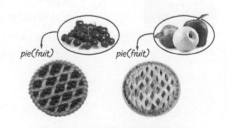

Describe the process of returning a value from a function.

- The return statement terminates a function call and yields the function result.
- Turn computations that can be reused into functions.

Design and implement functions without return values.

- Some functions may not return a value, but they can produce output.

Develop functions that can be reused for multiple problems.

- Eliminate replicated code or pseudocode by defining a function.
- Design your functions to be reusable. Supply parameter variables for the values that can vary when the function is reused.

Apply the design principle of stepwise refinement.

- Use the process of stepwise refinement to decompose complex tasks into simpler ones.
- When you discover that you need a function, write a description of the parameter variables and return values.
- A function may require simpler functions to carry out its work.

Determine the scope of variables in a program.

- The scope of a variable is the part of the program in which it is visible.
- A local variable is one defined within a function or code block.
- A global variable is defined outside of a function.

Design and build a software toolkit of related functions.

- A toolkit provides a collection of related functions or classes for solving a specific task.
- Functions defined in a toolkit must be imported before they can be used in your program.

Understand recursive function calls and implement simple recursive functions.

- A recursive computation solves a problem by using the solution to the same problem with simpler inputs.
- For a recursion to terminate, there must be special cases for the simplest inputs.
- The key to finding a recursive solution is reducing the input to a simpler input for the same problem.
- When designing a recursive solution, do not worry about multiple nested calls. Simply focus on reducing a problem to a slightly simpler one.

REVIEW EXERCISES

- **R5.1** Consider the function call len("black boxes"). How many arguments are passed to the function? What is the return value?

- **R5.2** In which sequence are the lines of the cubes.py program in Section 5.2 executed, starting with the first line of main?

- **R5.3** Write function headers with comments for the tasks described below.
  - **a.** Computing the larger of two integers
  - **b.** Computing the smallest of three floating-point numbers
  - **c.** Checking whether an integer is a prime number, returning True if it is and False otherwise
  - **d.** Checking whether a string is contained inside another string
  - **e.** Computing the balance of an account with a given initial balance, an annual interest rate, and a number of years of earning interest
  - **f.** Printing the balance of an account with a given initial balance and an annual interest rate over a given number of years
  - **g.** Printing the calendar for a given month and year
  - **h.** Computing the day of the week for a given day, month, and year (as a string such as "Monday")
  - **i.** Generating a random integer between 1 and n

- **R5.4** True or false?
  - **a.** A function has exactly one return statement.
  - **b.** A function has at least one return statement.
  - **c.** A function has at most one return value.
  - **d.** A function that does not return a value never has a return statement.
  - **e.** When executing a return statement, the function exits immediately.
  - **f.** A function that does not return a value must print a result.
  - **g.** A function without parameter variables always returns the same value.

- **R5.5** Consider these functions:

```
def f(x) :
    return g(x) + math.sqrt(h(x))

def g(x) :
    return 4 * h(x)

def h(x) :
    return x * x + k(x) - 1

def k(x) :
    return 2 * (x + 1)
```

  Without actually compiling and running a program, determine the results of the following function calls.
  - **a.** x1 = f(2)
  - **b.** x2 = g(h(2))

c. `x3 = k(g(2) + h(2))`

d. `x4 = f(0) + f(1) + f(2)`

e. `x5 = f(-1) + g(-1) + h(-1) + k(-1)`

■ **R5.6** What is the difference between an argument and a return value? How many arguments can a function call have? How many return values?

■■ **R5.7** Design a function that prints a floating-point number as a currency value (with a $ sign and two decimal digits).

　a. Indicate how the programs `ch02/sec05/volume2.py` and `ch04/sec06/investment.py` should change to use your function.

　b. What change is required if the programs should show a different currency, such as euros?

■■ **Business R5.8** Write pseudocode for a function that translates a telephone number with letters in it (such as 1-800-FLOWERS) into the actual phone number. Use the standard letters on a phone pad.

■■ **R5.9** For each of the variables in the following program, indicate the scope. Then determine what the program prints, without actually running the program.

© stacey_newman/iStockphoto.

■■ **R5.10** We have seen three kinds of variables in Python: global variables, parameter variables, and local variables. Classify the variables of Exercise •• R5.9 according to these categories.

■■ **R5.11** Use the process of stepwise refinement to describe the process of making scrambled eggs. Discuss what you do if you do not find eggs in the refrigerator.

■ **R5.12** Perform a walkthrough of the `intName` function with the following arguments:

　a. 5

　b. 12

　c. 21

　d. 301

　e. 324

　f. 0

　g. -2

■■ **R5.13** Consider the following function:

```python
def f(a) :
   if a < 0 : return -1
   n = a
   while n > 0 :
      if n % 2 == 0 :    # n is even
         n = n // 2
      elif n == 1 :
         return 1
      else :
         n = 3 * n + 1
   return 0
```

Perform traces of the computations `f(-1)`, `f(0)`, `f(1)`, `f(2)`, `f(10)`, and `f(100)`.

■■■ **R5.14** Consider the falseSwap function that is intended to swap the values of two integers:

```
def main() :
    x = 3
    y = 4
    falseSwap(x, y)
    print(x, y)

def falseSwap(a, b) :
    temp = a
    a = b
    b = temp

main()
```

Why doesn't the falseSwap function swap the contents of x and y?

■■■ **R5.15** Give pseudocode for a recursive function for printing all substrings of a given string. For example, the substrings of the string "rum" are "rum" itself, "ru", "um", "r", "u", "m", and the empty string. You may assume that all letters of the string are different.

■■■ **R5.16** Give pseudocode for a recursive function that sorts all letters in a string. For example, the string "goodbye" would be sorted into "bdegooy".

PROGRAMMING EXERCISES

■ **P5.1** Write the following functions and provide a program to test them.

  a. def smallest(x, y, z)   (returning the smallest of the arguments)

  b. def average(x, y, z)   (returning the average of the arguments)

■■ **P5.2** Write the following functions and provide a program to test them.

  a. def allTheSame(x, y, z)   (returning true if the arguments are all the same)

  b. def allDifferent(x, y, z)   (returning true if the arguments are all different)

  c. def sorted(x, y, z)   (returning true if the arguments are sorted, with the smallest one coming first)

■■ **P5.3** Write the following functions and provide a program to test them.

  a. def firstDigit(n)   (returning the first digit of the argument)

  b. def lastDigit(n)   (returning the last digit of the argument)

  c. def digits(n)   (returning the number of digits in the argument)

  For example, firstDigit(1729) is 1, lastDigit(1729) is 9, and digits(1729) is 4.

■ **P5.4** Write a function

```
def middle(string)
```

that returns a string containing the middle character in string if the length of string is odd, or the two middle characters if the length is even. For example, middle("middle") returns "dd".

■ **P5.5** Write a function

```
def repeat(string, n, delim)
```

that returns the string string repeated n times, separated by the string delim. For example, repeat("ho", 3, ", ") returns "ho, ho, ho".

■■ **P5.6** Write a function

```
def countVowels(string)
```

that returns a count of all vowels in the string `string`. Vowels are the letters a, e, i, o, and u, and their uppercase variants.

■■ **P5.7** Write a function

```
def countWords(string)
```

that returns a count of all words in the string `string`. Words are separated by spaces. For example, `countWords("Mary had a little lamb")` should return 5.

■■ **P5.8** It is a well-known phenomenon that most people are easily able to read a text whose words have two characters flipped, provided the first and last letter of each word are not changed. For example,

I dn'ot gvie a dman for a man taht can olny sepll a wrod one way. (Mrak Taiwn)

Write a function `scramble(word)` that constructs a scrambled version of a given word, randomly flipping two characters other than the first and last one. Then write a program that reads words and prints the scrambled words.

■ **P5.9** Write functions

```
def sphereVolume(r)
def sphereSurface(r)
def cylinderVolume(r, h)
def cylinderSurface(r, h)
def coneVolume(r, h)
def coneSurface(r, h)
```

that compute the volume and surface area of a sphere with radius r, a cylinder with a circular base with radius r and height h, and a cone with a circular base with radius r and height h. Then write a program that prompts the user for the values of r and h, calls the six functions, and prints the results.

■■ **P5.10** Write a function

```
def readFloat(prompt)
```

that displays the prompt string, followed by a space, reads a floating-point number in, and returns it. Here is a typical usage:

```
salary = readFloat("Please enter your salary:")
percentageRaise = readFloat("What percentage raise would you like?")
```

■■ **P5.11** Enhance the `intName` function so that it works correctly for values < 1,000,000,000.

■■ **P5.12** Enhance the `intName` function so that it works correctly for negative values and zero. *Caution:* Make sure the improved function doesn't print 20 as `"twenty zero"`.

■■■ **P5.13** For some values (for example, 20), the `intName` function returns a string with a leading space (`" twenty"`). Repair that blemish and ensure that spaces are inserted only when necessary. *Hint:* There are two ways of accomplishing this. Either ensure that leading spaces are never inserted, or remove leading spaces from the result before returning it.

■■■ **P5.14** Write a function `getTimeName(hours, minutes)` that returns the English name for a point in time, such as `"ten minutes past two"`, `"half past three"`, `"a quarter to four"`, or `"five o'clock"`. Assume that hours is between 1 and 12.

•• P5.15 Write a recursive function

```
def reverse(string)
```

that computes the reverse of a string. For example, reverse("flow") should return "wolf". *Hint:* Reverse the substring starting at the second character, then add the first character at the end. For example, to reverse "flow", first reverse "low" to "wol", then add the "f" at the end.

•• P5.16 Write a recursive function

```
def isPalindrome(string)
```

that returns True if string is a palindrome, that is, a word that is the same when reversed. Examples of palindromes are "deed", "rotor", or "aibohphobia". *Hint:* A word is a palindrome if the first and last letters match and the remainder is also a palindrome.

•• P5.17 Use recursion to implement a function find(string, match) that tests whether match is contained in string:

```
b = find("Mississippi", "sip") # Sets b to true
```

Hint: If string starts with match, you are done. If not, consider the string that you obtain by removing the first character.

• P5.18 Use recursion to determine the number of digits in an integer n. *Hint:* If n is < 10, it has one digit. Otherwise, it has one more digit than n // 10.

• P5.19 Use recursion to compute a^n, where n is a positive integer. *Hint:* If n is 1, then $a^n = a$. If n is even, then $a^n = (a^{n/2})^2$. Otherwise, $a^n = a \times a^{n-1}$.

•• P5.20 *Leap years.* Write a function

```
def isLeapYear(year)
```

that tests whether a year is a leap year: that is, a year with 366 days. Exercise P3.27 describes how to test whether a year is a leap year. In this exercise, use multiple if statements and return statements to return the result as soon as you know it.

© mbbirdy/Getty Images, Inc.

•• P5.21 In Exercise P3.28 you were asked to write a program to convert a number to its representation in Roman numerals. At the time, you did not know how to eliminate duplicate code, and as a consequence the resulting program was rather long. Rewrite that program by implementing and using the following function:

```
def romanDigit(n, one, five, ten)
```

That function translates one digit, using the strings specified for the one, five, and ten values. You would call the function as follows:

```
romanOnes = romanDigit(n % 10, "I", "V", "X")
n = n // 10
romanTens = romanDigit(n % 10, "X", "L", "C")
. . .
```

© Charles Schultz/iStockphoto.

•• Business P5.22 Write a function that computes the balance of a bank account with a given initial balance and interest rate, after a given number of years. Assume interest is compounded yearly.

■■ **Business P5.23** Write a program that prints a paycheck. Ask the program user for the name of the employee, the hourly rate, and the number of hours worked. If the number of hours exceeds 40, the employee is paid "time and a half", that is, 150 percent of the hourly rate on the hours exceeding 40. Your check should look similar to that in the figure below. Use fictitious names for the payer and the bank. Be sure to use stepwise refinement and break your solution into several functions. Use the intName function to print the dollar amount of the check.

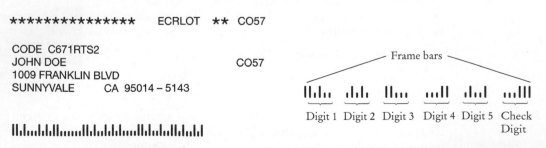

■■ **Business P5.24** Write a program that prints instructions to get coffee, asking the user for input whenever a decision needs to be made. Decompose each task into a function, for example:

```
def brewCoffee() :
    print("Add water to the coffee maker.")
    print("Put a filter in the coffee maker.")
    grindCoffee()
    print("Put the coffee in the filter.")
    . . .
```

■■ **Business P5.25** *Postal bar codes*. For faster sorting of letters, the United States Postal Service encourages companies that send large volumes of mail to use a bar code denoting the zip code (see Figure 12).

The encoding scheme for a five-digit zip code is shown in Figure 13. There are full-height frame bars on each side. The five encoded digits are followed by a check digit, which is computed as follows: Add up all digits, and choose the check digit to make the sum a multiple of 10. For example, the zip code 95014 has a sum of 19, so the check digit is 1 to make the sum equal to 20.

```
**************    ECRLOT  **  CO57

CODE  C671RTS2
JOHN DOE                          CO57
1009 FRANKLIN BLVD
SUNNYVALE      CA  95014 – 5143
```

Illhuludllhullhululhulullhululhulul

Figure 12 A Postal Bar Code

Frame bars

Illulu ulilu Illuu uulll ulul uulll

Digit 1 Digit 2 Digit 3 Digit 4 Digit 5 Check Digit

Figure 13 Encoding for Five-Digit Bar Codes

Each digit of the zip code, and the check digit, is encoded according to the table below, where 0 denotes a half bar and 1 a full bar:

Digit	Bar 1 (weight 7)	Bar 2 (weight 4)	Bar 3 (weight 2)	Bar 4 (weight 1)	Bar 5 (weight 0)
1	0	0	0	1	1
2	0	0	1	0	1
3	0	0	1	1	0
4	0	1	0	0	1
5	0	1	0	1	0
6	0	1	1	0	0
7	1	0	0	0	1
8	1	0	0	1	0
9	1	0	1	0	0
0	1	1	0	0	0

The digit can be computed easily from the bar code using the column weights 7, 4, 2, 1, 0. For example, 01100 is $0 \times 7 + 1 \times 4 + 1 \times 2 + 0 \times 1 + 0 \times 0 = 6$. The only exception is 0, which would yield 11 according to the weight formula.

Write a program that asks the user for a zip code and prints the bar code. Use : for half bars, | for full bars. For example, 95014 becomes

||:|:::|:|:||:::::::||:|::|:::|||

Provide these functions:

```
def printDigit(d)
def printBarCode(zipCode)
```

∎∎∎ **Business P5.26** Write a program that reads in a bar code (with : denoting half bars and | denoting full bars) and prints out the zip code it represents. Print an error message if the bar code is not correct.

∎∎ **Business P5.27** Write a program that converts a Roman number such as MCMLXXVIII to its decimal number representation. *Hint:* First write a function that yields the numeric value of each of the letters. Then use the following algorithm:

total = 0
string = roman number string
While string is not empty
  If string has length 1, or value(first character of string) is at least value(second character of string)
    Add value(first character of string) to total.
    Remove first character from string.
  Else
    difference = value(second character of string) - value(first character of string)
    Add difference to total.
    Remove first character and second character from string.

■■ **Business P5.28** A non-governmental organization needs a program to calculate the amount of financial assistance for needy families. The formula is as follows:

- If the annual household income is between $30,000 and $40,000 and the household has at least three children, the amount is $1,000 per child.
- If the annual household income is between $20,000 and $30,000 and the household has at least two children, the amount is $1,500 per child.
- If the annual household income is less than $20,000, the amount is $2,000 per child.

Implement a function for this computation. Write a program that asks for the household income and number of children for each applicant, printing the amount returned by your function. Use –1 as a sentinel value for the input.

■■■ **Business P5.29** In a social networking service, a user has friends, the friends have other friends, and so on. We are interested in knowing how many people can be reached from a person by following a given number of friendship relations. This number is called the "degree of separation": one for friends, two for friends of friends, and so on. Because we do not have the data from an actual social network, we will simply use an average of the number of friends per user.

© MichaelJay/iStockphoto.

Write a recursive function

```
def reachablePeople(degree, averageFriendsPerUser)
```

Use that function in a program that prompts the user for the desired degree and average, and then prints the number of reachable people. This number should include the original user.

■■ **Business P5.30** Having a secure password is a very important practice, when much of our information is stored online. Write a program that validates a new password, following these rules:

- The password must be at least 8 characters long.
- The password must have at least one uppercase and one lowercase letter.
- The password must have at least one digit.

Write a program that asks for a password, then asks again to confirm it. If the passwords don't match or the rules are not fulfilled, prompt again. Your program should include a function that checks whether a password is valid.

■■■ **Science P5.31** You are designing an element for a control panel that displays a temperature value between 0 and 100. The element's color should vary continuously from blue (when the temperature is 0) to red (when the temperature is 100). Write a function colorForValue(temperature) that returns a color value for the given temperature. Colors are encoded as red/green/blue values, each between 0 and 255. The three colors are combined into a single integer, using the formula

```
color = 65536 × red + 256 × green + blue
```

Each of the intermediate colors should be fully saturated; that is, it should be on the outside of the color cube, along the path that goes from blue through cyan, green, and yellow to red.

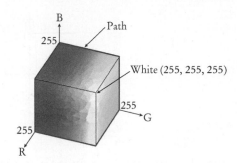

You need to know how to *interpolate* between values. In general, if an output y should vary from c to d as an input x varies from a to b, then y is computed as follows:

$$z = (x - a) / (b - a)$$

$$y = c(1 - z) + dz$$

If the temperature is between 0 and 25 degrees, interpolate between blue and cyan, whose (red, green, blue) components are (0, 0, 255) and (0, 255, 255). For temperature values between 25 and 50, interpolate between (0, 255, 255) and (0, 255, 0), which represents the color green. Do the same for the remaining two path segments.

You need to interpolate each color separately and then combine the interpolated colors to a single integer.

Be sure to use appropriate helper functions to solve your task.

■■ Science P5.32 In a movie theater, the angle θ at which a viewer sees the picture on the screen depends on the distance x of the viewer from the screen. For a movie theater with the dimensions shown in the picture below, write a function that computes the angle for a given distance.

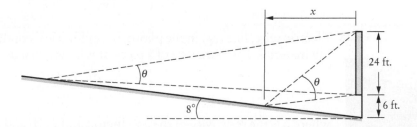

Next, provide a more general function that works for theaters with arbitrary dimensions.

■■ Science P5.33 The effective focal length f of a lens of thickness d that has surfaces with radii of curvature R_1 and R_2 is given by

$$\frac{1}{f} = (n - 1)\left[\frac{1}{R_1} - \frac{1}{R_2} + \frac{(n - 1)d}{nR_1R_2}\right]$$

where n is the refractive index of the lens medium.

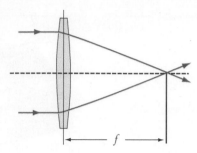

Write a function that computes f in terms of the other parameters.

■■ Science P5.34 A laboratory container is shaped like the frustum of a cone:

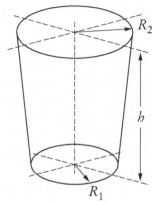

Write functions to compute the volume and surface area, using these equations:

$$V = \tfrac{1}{3}\pi h \left(R_1^2 + R_2^2 + R_1 R_2 \right)$$

$$S = \pi \left(R_1 + R_2 \right) \sqrt{\left(R_2 - R_1 \right)^2 + h^2} + \pi R_1^2$$

■■ Science P5.35 Electric wire, like that in the photo, is a cylindrical conductor covered by an insulating material. The resistance of a piece of wire is given by the formula

$$R = \frac{\rho L}{A} = \frac{4\rho L}{\pi d^2}$$

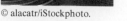
© alacatr/iStockphoto.

where ρ is the resistivity of the conductor, and L, A, and d are the length, cross-sectional area, and diameter of the wire. The resistivity of copper is $1.678 \times 10^{-8}\ \Omega$ m. The wire diameter, d, is commonly specified by the American wire gauge (AWG), which is an integer, n. The diameter of an AWG n wire is given by the formula

$$d = 0.127 \times 92^{\frac{36-n}{39}}\ \text{mm}$$

Write a function

```
def diameter(wireGauge)
```

that accepts the wire gauge and returns the corresponding wire diameter. Write another function

```
def copperWireResistance(length, wireGauge)
```

that accepts the length and gauge of a piece of copper wire and returns the resistance of that wire. The resistivity of aluminum is 2.82×10^{-8} Ω m. Write a third function

```
def aluminumWireResistance(length, wireGauge)
```

that accepts the length and gauge of a piece of aluminum wire and returns the resistance of that wire.

Write a program to test these functions.

•• **Science P5.36** The drag force on a car is given by

$$F_D = \frac{1}{2}\rho v^2 A C_D$$

where ρ is the density of air (1.23 kg/m^3), v is the velocity in units of m/s, A is the projected area of the car (2.5 m^2), and C_D is the drag coefficient (0.2).

The amount of power in watts required to overcome such drag force is $P = F_D v$, and the equivalent horsepower required is Hp = $P / 746$. Write a program that accepts a car's velocity and computes the power in watts and in horsepower needed to overcome the resulting drag force. *Note:* 1 mph = 0.447 m/s.

••• **Graphics P5.37** Add a function to the image processing toolkit that puts a border of a given color around an image. Update the processimg.py program to test your function.

••• **Graphics P5.38** Add a function to the image processing toolkit that reduces an image by half, discarding every second pixel. Update the processimg.py program to test your function.

••• **Graphics P5.39** Add a function to the image processing toolkit that doubles an image in size, replicating each pixel horizontally and vertically. Update the processimg.py program to test your function.

••• **Graphics P5.40** Add a function to the image processing toolkit that places two copies of an image next to each other, and another function that places two copies of an image below each other. Update the processimg.py program to test your functions.

••• **Graphics P5.41** Add a function to the image processing toolkit in Section 5.9.5 that changes an image to grayscale, following the approach of Exercise P4.52.

•• **Toolbox P5.42** Provide a function that uses turtle graphics to provide a house with a given number of stories and a given number of windows per story. Draw the house with a roof, an entrance, and the given windows. Then draw an urban scene by calling your function repeatedly.

••• **Toolbox P5.43** *The Koch Snowflake.* A snowflake-like shape is recursively defined as follows. Start with an equilateral triangle:

◁

Next, increase the size by a factor of three and replace each straight line with four line segments:

Repeat the process:

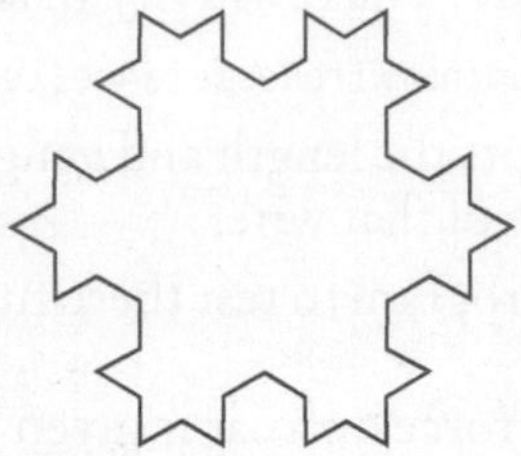

Write a turtle graphics program that draws the iterations of the snowflake shape. Supply a button that, when clicked, produces the next iteration.

CHAPTER 6

LISTS

© traveler1116/iStockphoto.

CHAPTER GOALS

To collect elements using lists

To use the for loop for traversing lists

To learn common algorithms for processing lists

To use lists with functions

To work with tables of data

CHAPTER CONTENTS

In many programs, you need to collect large numbers of values. In Python, you use the list structure for this purpose. A list is a container that stores a collection of elements that are arranged in a linear or sequential order. Lists can automatically grow to any desired size as new items are added and shrink as items are removed. In this chapter, you will learn about lists and several common algorithms for processing them.

6.1 Basic Properties of Lists

We start this chapter by introducing the list data type. Lists are the fundamental mechanism in Python for collecting multiple values. In the following sections, you will learn how to create lists and how to access list elements.

6.1.1 Creating Lists

Suppose you write a program that reads a sequence of values and prints out the sequence, marking the largest value, like this:

```
32
54
67.5
29
35
80
115 <= largest value
44.5
100
65
```

You do not know which value to mark as the largest one until you have seen them all. After all, the last value might be the largest one. Therefore, the program must first store all values before it can print them.

Could you simply store each value in a separate variable? If you know that there are ten values, then you could store the values in ten variables value1, value2, value3, ..., value10. However, such a sequence of variables is not very practical to use. You would have to write quite a bit of code ten times, once for each of the variables. In Python, a **list** is a much better choice for storing a sequence of values.

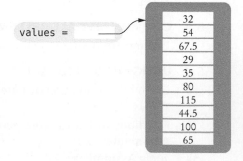

Figure 1 A List of Size 10

A list is a container that stores a sequence of values.

Here we create a list and specify the initial values that are to be stored in it (see Figure 1):

```
values = [32, 54, 67.5, 29, 35, 80, 115, 44.5, 100, 65] # A list with ten elements
```

The square brackets indicate that we are creating a list. The items are stored in the order they are provided. You will want to store the list in a variable so that you can access it later.

Syntax 6.1 Lists

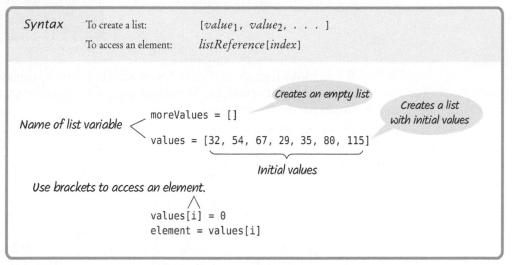

Syntax   To create a list: [*value*₁, *value*₂, . . .]

          To access an element: *listReference*[*index*]

Creates an empty list

Creates a list with initial values

Name of list variable

```
moreValues = []
values = [32, 54, 67, 29, 35, 80, 115]
```

Initial values

Use brackets to access an element.

```
values[i] = 0
element = values[i]
```

6.1.2 Accessing List Elements

Each individual element in a list is accessed by an integer i, using the notation *list*[i].

A list is a sequence of elements, each of which has an integer position or index. To access a list element, you specify which index you want to use. That is done with the subscript operator ([]) in the same way that you access individual characters in a string. For example,

```
print(values[5])    # Prints 80, the element at index 5   ①
```

This is not an accident. Both lists and strings are **sequences,** and the [] operator can be used to access an element in any sequence.

There are two differences between lists and strings. Lists can hold values of any type, whereas strings are sequences of characters. Moreover, strings are immutable—you cannot change the characters in the sequence. But lists are mutable. You can replace one list element with another, like this:

```
values[5] = 87   ②
```

Now the element at index 5 is filled with 87 (see Figure 2).

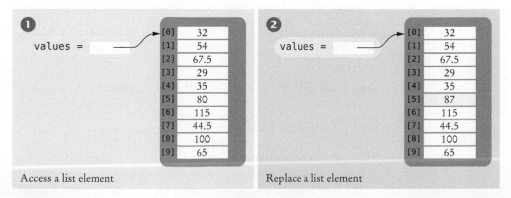

Access a list element   Replace a list element

Figure 2   Accessing a List Element

Like a mailbox that is identified by a box number, a list element is identified by an index.

© Luckie8/iStockphoto.

If you look carefully at Figure 2, you will find that the sixth element was modified when we changed `values[5]`. As with strings, list indexes start at 0. That is, the legal elements for the `values` list are

```
values[0],  the first element
values[1],  the second element
values[2],  the third element
values[3],  the fourth element
values[4],  the fifth element
    . . .
values[9],  the tenth element
```

In this list, an index can be any integer ranging from 0 to 9 (see Special Topic 6.1).

You have to be careful that the index stays within the valid range. Trying to access an element that does not exist in the list is a serious error. For example, if `values` has ten elements, you are not allowed to access `values[20]`. Attempting to access an element whose index is not within the valid index range is called an **out-of-range error** or a **bounds error**. When an out-of-range error occurs at run time, it causes a run-time exception.

Here is a very common out-of-range error:

```
values[10] = number
```

There is no `values[10]` in a list with ten elements – the index can range from 0 to 9. To avoid out-of-range errors, you will want to know how many elements are in a list. You can use the `len` function to obtain the length of the list; that is, the number of elements:

```
numElements = len(values)
```

The following code ensures that you only access the list when the index variable `i` is within the legal bounds:

```
if 0 <= i and i < len(values) :
    values[i] = number
```

Note that there are two distinct uses of the square brackets. When the square brackets immediately follow a variable name, they are treated as the subscript operator, as in

```
values[4]
```

When the square brackets *do not* a follow a variable name, they create a list. For example,

```
values = [4]
```

sets `values` to the list `[4]`; that is, the list containing the single element 4.

> A list index must be less than the number of elements in the list.

> An out-of-range error, which occurs if you supply an invalid list index, can cause your program to terminate.

6.1.3 Traversing Lists

There are two fundamental ways of visiting all elements of a list. You can loop over the index values and look up each element, or you can loop over the elements themselves.

We first look at a loop that traverses all index values. Given the `values` list that contains 10 elements, we will want to set a variable, say `i`, to 0, 1, 2, and so on, up to 9.

Then the expression values[i] yields each element in turn. This loop displays all index values and their corresponding elements in the values list.

```
for i in range(10) :
    print(i, values[i])
```

The variable i iterates through the integer values 0 through 9, which is appropriate because there is no element corresponding to values[10].

Instead of using the literal value 10 for the number of elements in the list, it is a good idea to use the len function to create a more reusable loop:

```
for i in range(len(values)) :
    print(i, values[i])
```

If you don't need the index values, you can iterate over the individual elements using a for loop in the form:

```
for element in values :
    print(element)
```

You can iterate over the index values or the elements of a list.

Note again the similarity between strings and lists. As was the case with looping over the characters in a string, the loop body is executed once for each element in the list values. At the beginning of each loop iteration, the next element is assigned to the loop variable element and the loop body is then executed.

6.1.4 List References

If you look closely at Figure 1, you will note that the variable values does not store any numbers. Instead, the list is stored elsewhere and the values variable holds a **reference** to the list. (The reference denotes the location of the list in memory.) When you access the elements in a list, you need not be concerned about the fact that Python uses list references. This only becomes important when copying list references.

A list reference specifies the location of a list. Copying the reference yields a second reference to the same list.

When you copy a list variable into another, both variables refer to the same list (see Figure 3). The second variable is an *alias* for the first because both variables reference the same list.

```
scores = [10, 9, 7, 4, 5]
values = scores    # Copying list reference  ❶
```

You can modify the list through either of the variables:

```
scores[3] = 10
print(values[3])    # Prints 10  ❷
```

Section 6.2.8 shows how you can make a copy of the *contents* of the list.

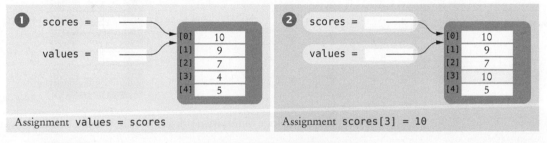

Figure 3   Two List Variables Referencing the Same List

Common Error 6.1

Out-of-Range Errors

Perhaps the most common error in using lists is accessing a nonexistent element.

```
values = [2.3, 4.5, 7.2, 1.0, 12.2, 9.0, 15.2, 0.5]
values[8] = 5.4
   # Error—values has 8 elements, and the index can range from 0 to 7
```

If your program accesses a list through an out-of-range index, the program will generate an exception at run time.

Programming Tip 6.1

Use Lists for Sequences of Related Items

Lists are intended for storing sequences of values with the same meaning. For example, a list of test scores makes perfect sense:

```
scores = [98, 85, 100, 89, 73, 92, 83, 65, 79, 80]
```

But a list

```
personalData = ["John Q. Public", 25, 485.25, "10 wide"]
```

that holds a person's name, age, bank balance, and shoe size in positions 0, 1, 2, and 3 is bad design. It would be tedious for the programmer to remember which of these data values is stored in which list location. In this situation, it is far better to use three separate variables.

Special Topic 6.1

Negative Subscripts

Python, unlike many other languages, also allows you to use negative subscripts when accessing an element of a list. The negative subscripts provide access to the list elements in reverse order. For example, a subscript of –1 provides access to the last element in the list:

```
last = values[-1]
print("The last element in the list is", last)
```

Similarly, values[-2] is the second-to-last element. Note that values[-10] is the first element.

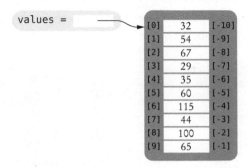

In general, the valid range of negative subscripts is between -1 and -len(values).

Special Topic 6.2

Common Container Functions

Python strives for simplicity and consistency when working with containers such as lists, strings (which are containers of characters), and the containers you will see in Chapter 8. For example, the `len` function is used to determine the number of characters in a string and the number of elements in a list. Likewise, the `in` operator can be used to determine whether a target is contained in a container:

```
sentence = ". . ."
if "?" in sentence :
    type = "question"

values = [ . . . ]
noneAreZero = not (0 in values)
```

The `min` and `max` functions can be used to locate the minimum or maximum element in a container. A common use of these functions is removing outlier values before processing the data. While the functions can be used with strings, there really is no good reason to do so.

For sequence type containers (such as strings, lists, and tuples), the subscript operator `[]` is used for accessing a specific element:

```
print(string[3])
print(values[2])
initialValue = values[0]
lastChar = sentence[len(sentence) - 1]
```

Python's `for` loop iterator can be used to iterate over the elements of any container:

```
numSpaces = 0
for ch in string :
    if ch == " " :
        numSpaces = numSpaces + 1

numZeroes = 0
for num in values :
    if num == 0 :
        numZeroes = numZeroes + 1
```

Not all functions, however, can be used with all containers. For example, the `sum` function can only be used with lists and tuples that contain numerical values. A run-time error would be raised if you attempted to use this function with a string. See Appendix C for built-in functions that can take a container as argument.

Computing & Society 6.1 Computer Viruses

In November 1988, Robert Morris, a student at Cornell University, launched a so-called virus program that infected a significant fraction of computers connected to the Internet (which was much smaller then than it is now).

In order to attack a computer, a virus has to find a way to get its instructions executed. This particular program carried out a "buffer overrun" attack, providing an unexpectedly large input to a program on another machine. That program allocated an array of 512 characters (an array is a sequence structure similar to a list), under the assumption that nobody would ever provide such a long input. Unfortunately, that program was written in the C programming language. C does not check that an array index is less than the length of the array. If you write into an array using an index that is too large, you simply overwrite memory locations that belong to some other objects. C programmers are supposed to provide safety checks, but that had not happened in the program under attack. The virus program purposefully filled the 512-character array with 536 bytes. The excess 24 bytes overwrote a return address, which the attacker knew was stored just after the array. When the function that read the input was finished, it didn't return to its caller but to code supplied by the virus (see the figure). The virus was thus able to execute its code on a remote machine and infect it.

In Python, as in C, all programmers must be very careful not to overrun the boundaries of a sequence. However, in Python, this error causes a runtime exception, and it never corrupts memory outside the list.

One may well speculate what would possess the virus author to spend weeks designing a program that disabled thousands of computers. It appears that the break-in was fully intended by the author, but the disabling of the computers was a bug caused by continuous reinfection. Morris was sentenced to three years probation, 400 hours of community service, and a $10,000 fine.

In recent years, computer attacks have intensified and the motives have become more sinister. Instead of disabling computers, viruses often take permanent residence in the attacked computers. Criminal enterprises rent out the processing power of millions of hijacked computers for sending spam e-mail or mining cryptocurrencies. Other viruses monitor every keystroke and send those that look like credit card numbers or banking passwords to their master.

Typically, a machine gets infected because a user executes code downloaded from the Internet, clicking on an icon or link that purports to be a game or video clip. Antivirus programs check all downloaded programs against an ever-growing list of known viruses.

When you use a computer for managing your finances, you need to be aware of the risk of infection. If a virus reads your banking password and empties your account, you will have a hard time convincing your financial institution that it wasn't your act, and you will most likely lose your money. Keep your operating system and antivirus program up to date, and don't click on suspicious links on a web page or in your e-mail inbox. Use banks that require "two-factor authentication" for major transactions, such as a callback on your cell phone.

Viruses are even used for military purposes. In 2010, a virus dubbed Stuxnet spread through Microsoft Windows and infected USB sticks. The virus looked for Siemens industrial computers and reprogrammed them in subtle ways. It appears that the virus was designed to damage the centrifuges of the Iranian nuclear enrichment operation. The computers controlling the centrifuges were not connected to the Internet, but they were configured with USB sticks, some of which were infected. Security researchers believe that the virus was developed by U.S. and Israeli intelligence agencies, and that it was successful in slowing down the Iranian nuclear program. Neither country has officially acknowledged or denied their role in the attacks.

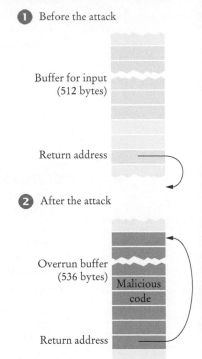

A "Buffer Overrun" Attack

6.2 List Operations

Many programming languages provide list constructs that are rather basic, with just the operations described in the preceding sections. In contrast, Python has a rich set of operations that make list processing quite convenient. We discuss these operations in the following sections.

6.2.1 Appending Elements

Earlier in the chapter, we created a list by specifying a sequence of initial values. Sometimes, however, we may not know the values that will be contained in the list when it's created. In this case, we can create an empty list and add elements as needed (see Figure 4). Here we start out with an empty list:

```
friends = []    ❶
```

A new element can be appended to the end of the list with the append method:

```
friends.append("Harry")    ❷
```

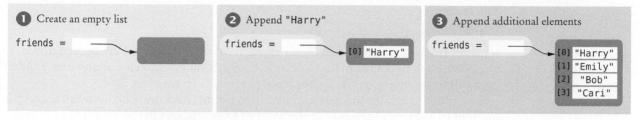

Figure 4 Appending Elements to a List

The size, or length, of the list increases after each call to the append method. Any number of elements can be added to a list:

```
friends.append("Emily")
friends.append("Bob")
friends.append("Cari")   ❸
```

6.2.2 Inserting an Element

You have just seen how to add a new element to the end of a list using the list method append. If the order of the elements does not matter, appending new elements is sufficient. Sometimes, however, the order is important and a new element has to be inserted at a specific position in the list. For example, given this list,

```
friends = ["Harry", "Emily", "Bob", "Cari"]   ❶
```

suppose we want to insert the string "Cindy" into the list following the first element, which contains the string "Harry" (see Figure 5).

Use the insert method to insert a new element at any position in a list.

❶ The newly created list

```
friends =
              [0] "Harry"
              [1] "Emily"
              [2]  "Bob"
              [3]  "Cari"
```

❷ After friends.insert(1, "Cindy")

```
friends =
              [0] "Harry"          New element added at index 1
              [1] "Cindy"
              [2] "Emily"          Elements at indexes 1-3
              [3]  "Bob"           moved to create slot
              [4] "Cari"           at index 1
```

❸ After friends.insert(5, "Bill")

```
friends =
              [0] "Harry"
              [1] "Cindy"
              [2] "Emily"
              [3]  "Bob"
              [4] "Cari"           New element appended
              [5] "Bill"           to the list
```

Figure 5
Inserting
Elements into
a List

The statement

```
friends.insert(1, "Cindy")   ②
```

achieves this task. All of the elements at and following position 1 are moved down by one position to make room for the new element, which is inserted at position 1. After each call to the insert method, the size of the list is increased by 1.

The index at which the new element is to be inserted must be between 0 and the number of elements currently in the list. For example, in a list of length 5, valid index values for the insertion are 0, 1, 2, 3, 4, and 5. The element is inserted before the element at the given index, except when the index is equal to the number of elements in the list. Then it is appended after the last element:

```
friends.insert(5, "Bill")   ③
```

This is the same as if we had used the append method.

6.2.3 Finding an Element

If you simply want to know whether an element is present in a list, use the in operator:

```
if "Cindy" in friends :
    print("She's a friend")
```

The in operator tests whether an element is contained in a list.

Often, you want to know the position at which an element occurs. The index method yields the index of the first match. For example,

```
friends = ["Harry", "Emily", "Bob", "Cari", "Emily"]
n = friends.index("Emily")    # Sets n to 1
```

If a value occurs more than once, you may want to find the position of all occurrences. You can call the index method and specify a starting position for the search. Here, we start the search after the index of the previous match:

```
n2 = friends.index("Emily", n + 1)    # Sets n2 to 4
```

When you call the index method, the element to be found must be in the list or a runtime exception occurs. It is usually a good idea to test with the in operator before calling the index method:

```
if "Cindy" in friends :
    n = friends.index("Cindy")
else :
    n = -1
```

6.2.4 Removing an Element

Use the pop method to remove an element from any position in a list.

The pop method removes the element at a given position. For example, suppose we start with the list

```
friends = ["Harry", "Cindy", "Emily", "Bob", "Cari", "Bill"]
```

To remove the element at index position 1 ("Cindy") in the friends list, you use the command

```
friends.pop(1)
```

All of the elements following the removed element are moved up one position to close the gap. The size of the list is reduced by 1 (see Figure 6). The index passed to the pop method must be within the valid range.

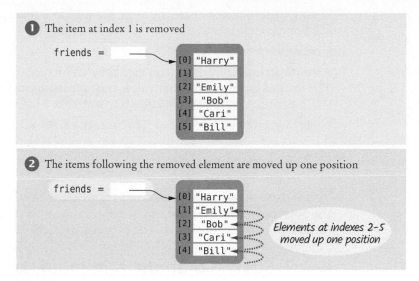

Figure 6 Removing an Element from a List

The element removed from the list is returned by the pop method. This allows you to combine two operations in one—accessing the element and removing it:

```
print("The removed item is", friends.pop(1))
```

If you call the pop method without an argument, it removes and returns the last element of the list. For example, friends.pop() removes "Bill".

The remove method removes an element by *value* instead of by *position*. For example, suppose we want to remove the string "Cari" from the friends list but we do not know where it's located in the list. Instead of having to find the position, we can use the remove method:

> Use the remove method to remove an element from a list by value.

```
friends.remove("Cari")
```

Note that the value being removed must be in the list or an exception is raised. To avoid a run-time error, you should first verify that the element is in the list before attempting to remove it:

```
element = "Cari"
if element in friends :
    friends.remove(element)
```

6.2.5 Concatenation and Replication

The concatenation of two lists is a new list that contains the elements of the first list, followed by the elements of the second. For example, suppose we have two lists

```
myFriends = ["Fritz", "Cindy"]
yourFriends = ["Lee", "Pat", "Phuong"]
```

> Two lists can be concatenated using the plus (+) operator.

and we want to create a new list that combines the two. Two lists can be concatenated by using the plus (+) operator:

```
ourFriends = myFriends + yourFriends
# Sets ourFriends to ["Fritz", "Cindy", "Lee", "Pat", "Phuong"]
```

If you want to concatenate the same list multiple times, use the replication operator (*). For example,

```
monthInQuarter = [1, 2, 3] * 4    # The list is [1, 2, 3, 1, 2, 3, 1, 2, 3, 1, 2, 3]
```

As with string replication, you can have an integer on either side of the * operator. The integer specifies how many copies of the list should be concatenated.

One common use of replication is to initialize a list with a fixed value. For example,

```
monthlyScores = [0] * 12   # The list is [0, 0, 0, 0, 0, 0, 0, 0, 0, 0, 0, 0]
```

6.2.6 Equality Testing

You can use the == operator to compare whether two lists have the same elements, in the same order. For example, [1, 4, 9] == [1, 4, 9] is True, but [1, 4, 9] == [4, 1, 9] is False. The opposite of == is !=. The expression [1, 4, 9] != [4, 9] is True.

6.2.7 Sum, Maximum, Minimum, and Sorting

If you have a list of numbers, the sum function yields the sum of all values in the list. For example:

```
sum([1, 4, 9, 16])    # Yields 30
```

For a list of numbers or strings, the max and min functions return the largest and smallest value:

```
max([1, 16, 9, 4])    # Yields 16
min(["Fred", "Ann", "Sue"])    # Yields "Ann"
```

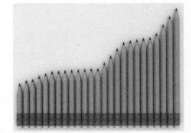

© ProstoVova/iStockphoto.

The sort method sorts a list of numbers or strings. For example,

```
values = [1, 16, 9, 4]
values.sort()    # Now values is [1, 4, 9, 16]
```

When sorting a list of strings, the strings are rearranged in lexicographic ordering (see Special Topic 3.2) in which lowercase letters follow the uppercase letters. For example, this code segment

```
names = ["Fred", "Ann", "Sue", "betsy"]
names.sort()
for name in names :
    print(name)
```

will produce the following output

```
Ann
Fred
Sue
betsy
```

6.2.8 Copying Lists

As discussed in Section 6.1.4, list variables do not themselves hold list elements. They hold a reference to the actual list. If you copy the reference, you get another reference to the same list (see Figure 7):

```
prices = values    ❶
```

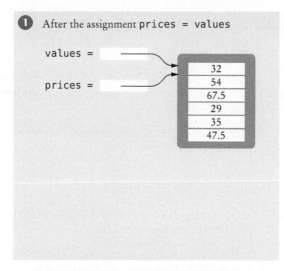

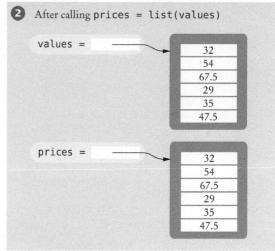

Figure 7   Copying a List Reference versus Copying a List

You can modify the list through either of the two references.

Sometimes, you want to make a copy of a list; that is, a new list that has the same elements in the same order as a given list. Use the list function:

> Use the `list` function to copy the elements of one list into a new list.

```
prices = list(values)  ②
```

Now, `values` and `prices` refer to different lists. Right after the copy, both lists have the same contents. But you can modify either without affecting the other.

The `list` function can be used to make a list out of any sequence. For example, when the argument is a string, you get a list of all characters in the string:

```
characters = list("Hello")   # The list is ["H", "e", "l", "l", "o"]
```

Table 1   Common Functions and Operators Used with Lists

Operation	Description
`[]` `[elem₁, elem₂, ..., elemₙ]`	Creates a new empty list or a list that contains the initial elements provided.
`len(l)`	Returns the number of elements in list l.
`list(sequence)`	Creates a new list containing all elements of the sequence.
`values * num`	Creates a new list by replicating the elements in the `values` list num times.
`values + moreValues`	Creates a new list by concatenating elements in both lists.
`l[from : to]`	Creates a sublist from a subsequence of elements in list l starting at position from and going through but not including the element at position to. Both from and to are optional. (See Special Topic 6.3.)
`sum(l)`	Computes the sum of the values in list l.
`min(l)` `max(l)`	Returns the minimum or maximum value in list l.
`l₁ == l₂`	Tests whether two lists have the same elements, in the same order.

Table 2 Common List Methods

Method	Description
l.pop() *l*.pop(*position*)	Removes the last element from the list or from the given position. All elements following the given position are moved up one place.
l.insert(*position*, *element*)	Inserts the element at the given position in the list. All elements at and following the given position are moved down.
l.append(*element*)	Appends the element to the end of the list.
l.index(*element*)	Returns the position of the given element in the list. The element must be in the list.
l.remove(*element*)	Removes the given element from the list and moves all elements following it up one position. The element must be in the list.
l.sort()	Sorts the elements in the list from smallest to largest.

Special Topic 6.3
Slices

Sometimes you want to look at a part of a list. For example, suppose you are given a list of temperatures, one per month:

```
temperatures = [18, 21, 24, 28, 33, 39, 40, 39, 36, 30, 22, 18]
```

You are interested in the temperatures only for the third quarter, with index values 6, 7, and 8. You can use Python's slice operator (:) to obtain them.

```
thirdQuarter = temperatures[6 : 9]
```

The arguments for the slice operator are the first index to include in the slice, followed by the first index to exclude.

This may seem a curious arrangement, but it has a useful property. The length of the slice temperatures[a : b] is the difference b - a. In our case, the difference 9 – 6 = 3 is the number of months in a quarter.

Both index values used with the slice operator (6 and 9 here) are optional. If the first index is omitted, all elements from the first element on are included. The slice

```
temperatures[ : 6]
```

contains all elements up to (but not including) position 6. That's the first half of the year. The slice

```
temperatures[6 : ]
```

includes all elements from index 6 to the end of the list; that is, the second half of the year. If you omit both index values, temperatures[:], you get a copy of the list. You can even assign values to a slice. For example, the assignment

```
temperatures[6 : 9] = [45, 44, 40]
```

replaces the values for the third quarter.

The size of the slice and the replacement don't have to match:

```
friends[ : 2] = ["Peter", "Paul", "Mary"]
```

replaces the first two elements of friends with three new elements, increasing the length of the list.

Slices work with all sequences, not just lists. They are particularly useful with strings. A slice of a string is a substring:

> Use the slice operator (:) to extract a sublist or substring.

```
greeting = "Hello, World!"
greeted = greeting[7 : 12]   # The substring "World"
```

6.3 Common List Algorithms

In the preceding sections, you saw how to use library functions and methods to work with lists in Python. In this section, you will see how to achieve common tasks that cannot be solved with the Python library. And even if there is a library function or method that carries out a particular task, it is worth knowing what goes on "under the hood". This helps you understand how efficient an operation is. Moreover, you won't be stranded if you use a programming language that doesn't have a library as rich as Python's.

6.3.1 Filling

This loop creates and fills a list with squares $(0, 1, 4, 9, 16, ..., (n-1)^2)$. Note that the element with index 0 contains 0^2, the element with index 1 contains 1^2, and so on.

```
values = []
for i in range(n) :
    values.append(i * i)
```

6.3.2 Combining List Elements

If you want to compute the sum of a list of numbers, you can simply call the sum function. But suppose you have a list of strings and want to concatenate them. Then the sum method doesn't work. Fortunately, you have already seen in Section 4.5.1 how to compute the sum of a sequence of values, and that algorithm can be easily modified. Here is how to compute a sum of numbers stored in a list values:

```
result = 0.0
for element in values :
    result = result + element
```

To concatenate strings stored in a list friends, you only need to change the initial value:

```
result = ""
for element in friends :
    result = result + element
```

This simply concatenates the elements to one long string, such as "HarryEmilyBob". The next section shows you how to separate the elements.

6.3.3 Element Separators

When you display the elements of a list, you usually want to separate them, often with commas or vertical lines, like this:

```
Harry, Emily, Bob
```

Note that there is one fewer separator than there are numbers. Add the separator before each element in the sequence *except the initial one* (with index 0), like this:

```
result = ""
for i in range(len(friends)) :
    if i > 0 :
        result = result + ", "
    result = result + friends[i]
```

If you want to print values without adding them to a string, you need to adapt the algorithm slightly. Suppose we want to print a list of numbers like this:

```
32 | 54 | 67.5 | 29 | 35
```

The following loop achieves that:

```
for i in range(len(values)) :
    if i > 0 :
        print(" | ", end="")
    print(values[i], end="")
print()
```

© trutenka/iStockphoto.

To print five elements, you need four separators.

Again, we skip the first separator.

The str function uses this algorithm to convert a list to a string. The expression

```
str(values)
```

returns a string describing the contents of the list in the form

```
[32, 54, 67.5, 29, 35]
```

The elements are surrounded by a pair of brackets and separated by commas. You can also print a list, without having to first convert it to a string, which can be convenient for debugging:

```
print("values = ", values)    # Prints values = [32, 54, 67.5, 29, 35]
```

6.3.4 Maximum and Minimum

Use the algorithm from Section 4.5.4 that keeps a variable for the largest element already encountered. Here is the implementation of that algorithm for a list:

```
largest = values[0]
for i in range(1, len(values)) :
    if values[i] > largest :
        largest = values[i]
```

© CEFutcher/iStockphoto.

Note that the loop starts at 1 because we initialize largest with values[0].

To compute the smallest element, reverse the comparison.

These algorithms require that the list contain at least one element.

Of course, in this case, you could have just called the max function. But now consider a slightly different situation. You have a list of strings and want to find the longest one.

```
names = ["Ann", "Charlotte", "Zachary", "Bill"]
```

If you call `max(names)`, you get the string that is highest in the dictionary order; in our example, `"Zachary"`. To get the longest string, you need to modify the algorithm, and compare the length of each element with the longest one already encountered:

```
longest = names[0]
for i in range(1, len(names)) :
    if len(names[i]) > len(longest) :
        longest = names[i]
```

6.3.5 Linear Search

© yekorzh/Getty Images.

To search for a specific element, visit the elements and stop when you encounter the match.

You often need to search for the position of a specific element in a list so that you can replace or remove it. If you simply want to find the position of a value, you can use the `index` method:

```
searchedValue = 100

if searchedValue in values :
    pos = values.index(searchedValue)
    print("Found at position:", pos)
else :
    print("Not found")
```

However, if you want to find the position of a value that has a given property, you have to know how the `index` method works. Consider the task of finding the first value that is > 100. You need to visit all elements until you have found a match or you have come to the end of the list:

```
limit = 100
pos = 0
found = False
while pos < len(values) and not found :
    if values[pos] > limit :
        found = True
    else :
        pos = pos + 1

if found :
    print("Found at position:", pos)
else :
    print("Not found")
```

A linear search inspects elements in sequence until a match is found.

This algorithm is called **linear search** or *sequential search* because you inspect the elements in sequence.

6.3.6 Collecting and Counting Matches

In the preceding section, you saw how to find the position of the first element that fulfills a particular condition. Suppose we want to find all matches. You can simply append them to an initially empty list.

Here, we collect all values that are > 100:

```
limit = 100
result = []
for element in values :
    if (element > limit) :
        result.append(element)
```

Sometimes you just want to know how many matches there are without collecting them. Then you increment a counter instead of collecting the matches:

```
limit = 100
counter = 0
for element in values :
   if (element > limit) :
      counter = counter + 1
```

6.3.7 Removing Matches

A common processing task is to remove all elements that match a particular condition. Suppose, for example, that we want to remove all strings of length < 4 from a list. Of course, you traverse the list and look for matching elements:

```
for i in range(len(words)) :
   word = words[i]
   if len(word) < 4 :
      Remove the element at index i.
```

But there is a subtle problem. After you remove the element, the for loop increments i, skipping past the *next* element.

Consider this concrete example, where words contains the strings "Welcome", "to", "the", "island!". When i is 1, we remove the word "to" at index 1. Then i is incremented to 2, and the word "the", which is now at position 1, is never examined.

i	words
0̸	~~"Welcome", "to",~~ "the", "island"
+̸	"Welcome", "the", "island"
2	

We should not increment the index when removing a word. The appropriate pseudocode is

> If the element at index i matches the condition
>   Remove the element at index i.
> Else
>   Increment i.

Because we don't always increment the index, a for loop is not appropriate for this algorithm. Instead, use a while loop:

```
i = 0
while i < len(words) :
   word = words[i]
   if len(word) < 4 :
      words.pop(i)
   else :
      i = i + 1
```

6.3.8 Swapping Elements

You often need to swap elements of a list. For example, you can sort a list by repeatedly swapping elements that are not in order.

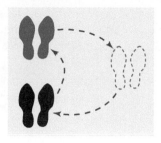

Consider the task of swapping the elements at positions i and j of a list values. We'd like to set values[i] to values[j]. But that overwrites the value that is currently stored in values[i], so we want to save that first:

Use a temporary variable when swapping two elements.

```
temp = values[i]      ❷
values[i] = values[j] ❸
```

Now we can set values[j] to the saved value.

```
values[j] = temp      ❹
```

To swap two elements, you need a temporary variable.

Figure 8 shows the process.

See Special Topic 6.7 for another way of swapping two elements.

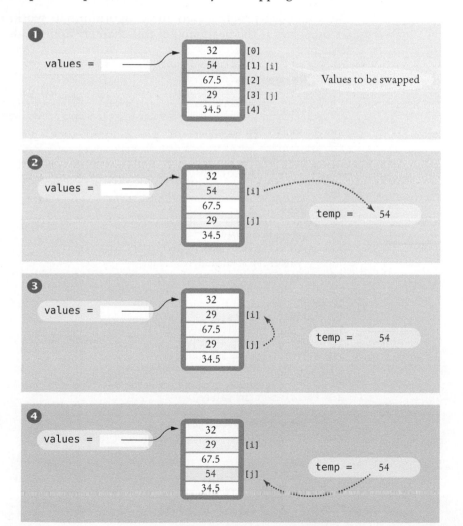

Figure 8 Swapping List Elements

6.3.9 Reading Input

It is very common to read input from a user and store it in a list for later processing. Start with an empty list and, as each value is read, append the value to the end of the list:

```
values = []
print("Please enter values, Q to quit:")
userInput = input("")    # Get user input without a prompt.
while userInput.upper() != "Q" :
   values.append(float(userInput))
   userInput = input("")
```

In this loop, the user enters one number on each line, like this:

```
Please enter values, Q to quit:
32
29
67.5
Q
```

The following program puts these algorithms to work, solving the task that we set ourselves at the beginning of this chapter: to mark the largest value in an input sequence.

sec03/largest.py

```
1   ##
2   #   This program reads a sequence of values and prints them, marking the
3   #   largest value.
4   #
5
6   # Create an empty list.
7   values = []
8
9   # Read the input values.
10  print("Please enter values, Q to quit:")
11  userInput = input("")
12  while userInput.upper() != "Q" :
13     values.append(float(userInput))
14     userInput = input("")
15
16  # Find the largest value.
17  largest = values[0]
18  for i in range(1, len(values)) :
19     if values[i] > largest :
20        largest = values[i]
21
22  # Print all values, marking the largest.
23  for element in values :
24     print(element, end="")
25     if element == largest :
26        print(" <== largest value", end="")
27     print()
```

Program Run

```
Please enter values, Q to quit:
32
54
```

```
67.5
29
35
80
115
44.5
100
65
Q
32.0
54.0
67.5
29.0
35.0
80.0
115.0 <== largest value
44.5
100.0
65.0
```

WORKED EXAMPLE 6.1

Plotting Trigonometric Functions

Problem Statement   Using the plotting package from Toolbox 3.2, your task is to plot a graph that contains the curves of the sine and cosine trigonometric functions for the angles between −180 degrees and 180 degrees.

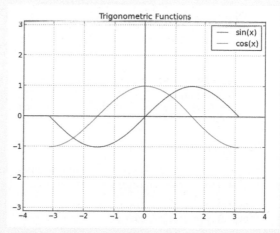

Step 1   Understand the problem.

The trigonometric functions are used for computing properties of triangles, especially right triangles. The most common of these include the sine, cosine, and tangent of an angle. Each of these functions takes an angle and returns the ratio between the lengths of two different sides of the triangle.

Plots of the trigonometric functions show the values of each function for a range of angles. You can use Python functions for computing the sine, cosine, and tangent with a sequence of data points to generate the values needed to plot the curve of the function. Because these

Python functions take an argument in radians, you first need to convert the angle to its equivalent value in radians using the formula

$$\text{radians} = \left(\frac{\pi}{180}\right) \times \text{degrees}$$

Step 2   Carry out stepwise refinement.

There are only three basic steps involved in solving this problem:

Compute the data points for the curves.
Plot the curves.
Improve the appearance of the graph.

Step 3   Build the list of data points.

In Toolbox 3.2, you learned how to plot a line graph of a curve using the plot function from the pyplot module. To do so, you must provide two lists, one with the *x*-coordinates and one with the *y*-coordinates of the data points to be plotted. In Chapter 3, we defined the lists using literal values, but it's more common to compute the data points and add them to the lists.

We start with three empty lists into which the coordinates can be added. Because both functions will be plotted for the same angles, you need to store the angle values (the *x*-coordinates) only once.

```
sinY = []
cosY = []
trigX = []
```

The data points can then be computed by iterating over the range of angles and computing the sine and cosine for each angle. The following loop increments the angle values, converts each to radians, and uses them to calculate the *y*-coordinates for the two functions. The results of the sine and cosine functions are appended to their respective lists.

```
angle = -180
while angle <= 180 :
    x = pi / 180 * angle   # Convert to radians
    trigX.append(x)   # Add the x-coordinate for both curves
    y = sin(x)
    sinY.append(y)   # Add the y-coordinate for the sine curve
    y = cos(x)
    cosY.append(y)   # Add the y-coordinate for the cosine curve
    angle = angle + 1
```

Step 4   Plot the curves.

Having computed and stored the data points in lists, pass the lists to the plot function to plot the curves for both trigonometric functions:

```
pyplot.plot(trigX, sinY)
pyplot.plot(trigX, cosY)
```

Step 5   Improve the appearance of the graph.

Add descriptive information, such as a title and legend, to help the viewer understand what they are seeing:

```
pyplot.title("Trigonometric Functions")
pyplot.legend(["sin(x)", "cos(x)"])
```

You can also include a grid to help the viewer identify the data points:

```
pyplot.grid("on")
```

For graphs that extend across the *x*- and *y*-axes, as is the case with the trigonometric functions, you may want to highlight those axes. This can be done using the axhline and axvline functions. Both accept an optional named argument for specifing the color of the line (see Table 9 in Chapter 3 for color codes). Here, "k" indicates black.

```
pyplot.axhline(color="k")
pyplot.axvline(color="k")
```

Finally, graphs should provide an accurate view of the data. One way that graphs can be misleading is when they use different scales for the values along the two axes. Consider the following graph of the trigonometric functions and compare it to the graph in the problem statement.

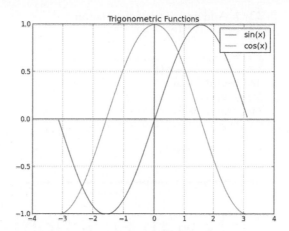

The distances between adjacent coordinates along the y-axis are much greater than along the x-axis. This results in a distorted view of the curves.

To rectify this problem, you can specify that both axes use the same distance between values by calling

```
pyplot.axis("equal")
```

EXAMPLE CODE   Here is the complete program.

worked_example_1/trigcurves.py

```
 1  ##
 2  #   This program creates a line graph containing the curves for the sine and
 3  #   cosine trigonometric functions for x-values between –180 and 180 degrees.
 4  #
 5
 6  from matplotlib import pyplot
 7  from math import pi, sin, cos
 8
 9  # Create empty lists to store the y-values for the sine and cosine curves.
10  sinY = []
11  cosY = []
12
13  # The x-values will be the same for both curves.
14  trigX = []
15
16  # Compute the y-values for the sine and cosine curves.
17  angle = -180
18  while angle <= 180 :
19      x = pi / 180 * angle
20      trigX.append(x)
21
22      y = sin(x)
23      sinY.append(y)
```

```
24
25      y = cos(x)
26      cosY.append(y)
27      angle = angle + 1
28
29  # Plot the two curves.
30  pyplot.plot(trigX, sinY)
31  pyplot.plot(trigX, cosY)
32
33  # Add descriptive information.
34  pyplot.title("Trigonometric Functions")
35
36  # Improve the appearance of the graph.
37  pyplot.legend(["sin(x)", "cos(x)"])
38  pyplot.grid("on")
39  pyplot.axis("equal")
40  pyplot.axhline(color="k")
41  pyplot.axvline(color="k")
42
43  pyplot.show()
```

6.4 Using Lists with Functions

Lists can occur as function arguments and return values.

A function can accept a list as an argument. For example, the following function computes the sum of values, a list of floating-point values:

```
def sum(values) :
    total = 0.0
    for element in values :
        total = total + element

    return total
```

When calling a function with a list argument, the function receives a list reference, not a copy of the list.

This function visits the list elements, but it does not modify them. It is also possible to modify the elements of a list. The following function multiplies all elements of a list by a given factor:

```
def multiply(values, factor) :
    for i in range(len(values)) :
        values[i] = values[i] * factor
```

Figure 9 traces the function call

```
multiply(scores, 10)
```

Note these steps:

- The parameter variables values and factor are created. ❶
- The parameter variables are initialized with the arguments that are passed in the call. In our case, values is set to scores and factor is set to 10. Note that values and scores are references to the *same* list. ❷
- The function multiplies all list elements by 10. ❸
- The function returns. Its parameter variables are removed. However, scores still refers to the list with the modified elements. ❹

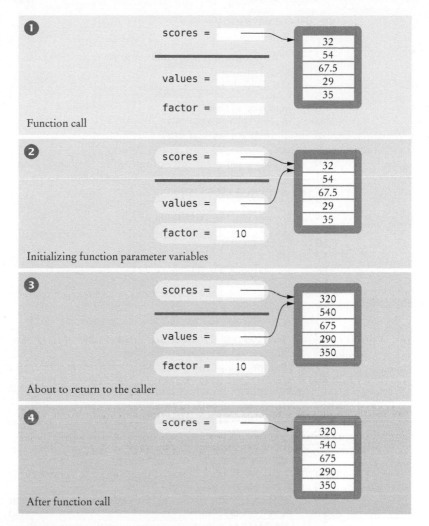

Figure 9   Trace of Call to the `multiply` Function

A function can return a list. Simply build up the result in the function and return it. In this example, the `squares` function returns a list of squares from 0^2 up to $(n-1)^2$:

```
def squares(n) :
   result = []
   for i in range(n) :
      result.append(i * i)

   return result
```

The following example program reads values from standard input, multiplies them by 10, and prints the result in reverse order. The program uses three functions:

- The `readFloats` function returns a list, using the algorithm of Section 6.3.1.
- The `multiply` function has a list argument. It modifies the list elements.
- The `printReversed` function also has a list argument, but it does not modify the list elements.

sec04/reverse.py

```python
1   ##
2   #  This program reads, scales, and reverses a sequence of numbers.
3   #
4
5   def main() :
6      numbers = readFloats(5)
7      multiply(numbers, 10)
8      printReversed(numbers)
9
10  ## Reads a sequence of floating-point numbers.
11  #  @param numberOfInputs  the number of inputs to read
12  #  @return  a list containing the input values
13  #
14  def readFloats(numberOfInputs) :
15     print("Enter", numberOfInputs, "numbers:")
16     inputs = []
17     for i in range(numberOfInputs) :
18        value = float(input(""))
19        inputs.append(value)
20
21     return inputs
22
23  ## Multiplies all elements of a list by a factor.
24  #  @param values  a list of numbers
25  #  @param factor  the value with which element is multiplied
26  #
27  def multiply(values, factor) :
28     for i in range(len(values)) :
29        values[i] = values[i] * factor
30
31  ## Prints a list in reverse order.
32  #  @param values  a list of numbers
33  #
34  def printReversed(values) :
35     # Traverse the list in reverse order, starting with the last element
36     i = len(values) - 1
37     while i >= 0 :
38        print(values[i], end=" ")
39        i = i - 1
40     print()
41
42  # Start the program.
43  main()
```

Program Run

```
Enter 5 numbers:
12
25
20
0
10
100.0 0.0 200.0 250.0 120.0
```

Special Topic 6.4

Call by Value and Call by Reference

We have told you that a Python function can never change the contents of a variable that was passed to it. If you call fun(var), then the contents of var is the same after the function as it was before. The reason is simple. When the function is called, the contents of var is copied into the corresponding parameter variable. When the function exits, the parameter variable is removed. At no point is the contents of var changed. Computer scientists refer to this call mechanism as "call by value".

Other programming languages, such as C++, support a mechanism, called "call by reference", that can change the arguments of a function call. You may sometimes hear that in Python "numbers are passed by value, lists are passed by reference". That is technically not quite correct. In Python, lists themselves are never passed as arguments; only their references are. Both numbers and *list references* are passed by value.

The confusion arises because a Python function can mutate the contents of a list when it receives a reference to it (see Figure 9). In Python, when you call fun(lst), the function can modify the contents of the list whose reference is stored in lst, but it cannot replace lst with a reference to a different list.

Special Topic 6.5

Tuples

Python provides a data type for immutable sequences of arbitrary data. A **tuple** is very similar to a list, but once created, its contents cannot be modified. A tuple is created by specifying its contents as a comma-separated sequence. You can enclose the sequence in parentheses:

```
triple = (5, 10, 15)
```

If you prefer, you can omit the parentheses:

```
triple = 5, 10, 15
```

> A tuple is created as a comma-separated sequence enclosed in parentheses.

However, we prefer to use them for greater clarity.

You have already seen the use of a tuple with string formatting:

```
print("Enter a value between %d and %d:" % (low, high))
```

Here the tuple (low, high) is used to pass the collection of values that are to replace the format specifiers in the format string.

Many of the operations defined for a list can also be used with a tuple:

- Access an individual element of a tuple by position (element = triple[1]).
- Obtain the number of elements in the tuple with the len function.
- Iterate over the elements of a tuple using for loops.
- Test for elements using the in and not in operators.

In fact, any list operation that does not modify the contents of the list can be used with a tuple. A tuple is simply an immutable version of a list.

In this book, we don't use tuples—we simply use lists, even if we never mutate them. But, as you can see in the Special Topics that follow, tuples can be very useful in Python functions.

Special Topic 6.6

Functions with a Variable Number of Arguments

In Python, it is possible to define functions that receive a variable number of arguments. For example, we can write a sum function that can compute the sum of any number of arguments:

```
a = sum(1, 3)        # Sets a to 4
b = sum(1, 7, 2, 9)  # Sets b to 19
```

The modified sum function must be declared as

```
def sum(*values) :
```

The asterisk before the parameter variable indicates that the function can receive any number of arguments. The values parameter variable is actually a tuple that contains all arguments that were passed to the function. The function implementation traverses the values tuple and processes the elements:

```
def sum(*values) :
   total = 0
   for element in values :
      total = total + element

   return total
```

Because the parameter variable is a tuple, any number of, including zero, arguments can be passed to the function:

```
c = sum()   # Sets c to 0
```

A function can also be defined to receive a fixed number of arguments followed by a variable number of arguments:

```
def studentGrades(idNum, name, *grades) :
```

In this example, the first two arguments are required and will be assigned to parameter variables idNum and name. Any remaining arguments will be stored in the grades tuple. When combined with fixed parameter variables, the tuple parameter variable must be the last one.

Special Topic 6.7

Tuple Assignment

In Python (but not in most other programming languages), you can assign to multiple variables in a single assignment statement:

```
(price, quantity) = (19.95, 12)
```

The left-hand side is a tuple of variables. Each variable in the tuple is assigned the corresponding element from the tuple on the right-hand side.

It is legal to omit the parentheses:

```
price, quantity = 19.95, 12
```

Most of the time, this isn't any more useful than the separate assignments

```
price = 19.95
quantity = 12
```

However, simultaneous assignment is a convenient shortcut for swapping two values:

```
(values[i], values[j]) = (values[j], values[i])
```

Of course, the assignment can't really be simultaneous. Behind the scenes, the values in the right-hand side are first stored in a temporary tuple, and then the tuple values are assigned.

Special Topic 6.8
Returning Multiple Values with Tuples

In Chapter 5, you learned that a function can only return a single value. It is common practice in Python, however, to return a tuple, which can contain multiple values. For example, suppose we define a function that obtains the date from the user as the integer values for the month, day, and year and returns the three values in a tuple:

```python
def readDate() :
    print("Enter a date:")
    month = int(input(" month: "))
    day = int(input(" day: "))
    year = int(input(" year: "))
    return (month, day, year)   # Returns a tuple
```

When the function is called, you can assign the entire tuple to a variable:

```python
date = readDate()
```

or you can use tuple assignment:

```python
(month, day, year) = readDate()
```

Some people prefer to omit the parentheses, making it look as if the function really returned multiple values:

```python
return month, day, year
```

Nevertheless, that's still a tuple.

If you like, you can also omit the parentheses in the tuple assignment:

```python
month, day, year = readDate()
```

For simplicity, we don't return tuples from functions in this book. Of course, we often implement and use functions that return lists. In our example, readDate can simply return a list [month, day, year].

TOOLBOX 6.1
Editing Sound Files

Sound vibrations originate from an object such as a violin string or a loudspeaker membrane. They are transmitted through a medium—usually air—until they reach a microphone or an eardrum. The changes in pressure give the sensation of sound. To measure sound, one determines the amount of pressure, over and over again. The rate of measurement is called the "sample rate". For example, audio CDs use a rate of 44,100 samples per second. You should simply think of a sound wave as a sequence of measurements, taken at regular intervals.

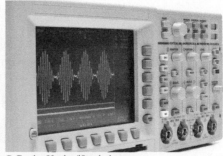

© GordonHeeley/iStockphoto.

There are many interesting ways in which you can manipulate sound data. In this Toolbox, we will use the SciPy library installed with other modules in Toolbox 2.1 to edit sound files.

About Sound Files

Many sound files, including audio CDs, represent sound values as 16-bit integers that vary between –32,768 and 32,767. When you process sounds, you are in effect working with a long list of integer values. Figure 10 shows a sound wave of a cat's meow.

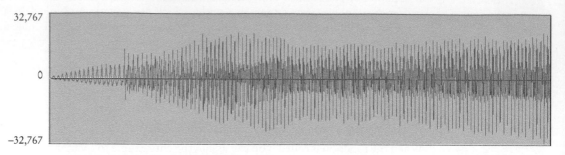

Figure 10 Sound Wave of a Cat's Meow

Some sound files contain stereo sound. Then you have two values for each sample: one each for the left and right speaker.

Sound files can be quite large. CD quality sound requires about 10MB per minute. CDs contain the raw sound data, but when you buy music over the Internet, the data are compressed, making for much smaller files. Currently, the most common compressed formats are encumbered by patents. For that reason, we will concentrate on processing uncompressed sound files. If you want to use the techniques of this section with compressed files, you should first uncompress them to the WAV format. We recommend the Audacity program (available at http://audacity.sourceforge.net), which is also useful for analyzing sound files that you make.

Reading and Writing Sound Files

We will use the scipy.io.wavfile module of the SciPy library to read and write sound files. You read a sound file with the read function. The function returns a tuple (see Special Topic 6.5) with two elements: the sample rate, and the sound data. The sound data are in a special format (a "NumPy array"), which we will convert to a Python list (using the NumPy array method tolist):

```
contents = scipy.io.wavfile.read("meow.wav")
samplerate = contents[0]
data = contents[1].tolist()
```

If the file contains mono sound, the sound data is a list of numbers. (See Exercise •• Toolbox P6.47 for processing stereo files.) You can process the list in some way and use the scipy.io.wavfile.write function to save the result to another file. Before passing the sound data to that function, you need to convert it back to a NumPy array with the numpy.asarray function:

```
scipy.io.wavfile.write("output.wav", samplerate,
    numpy.asarray(outputdata, dtype="int16"))
```

After running your Python program, listen to the output file with the audio player on your computer, or with the Audacity program.

Manipulating Sound Data

Here is a simple example of manipulating sound data that is quite surprising. Let's replace all positive values with 30,000 and all negative values with –30,000.

```
outputdata = []
for i in range(len(data)) :
    if (data[i] > 0) :
        outputdata.append(30000)
```

```
else :
    outputdata.append(-30000)
```

It seems as if this operation would completely mutilate the sound, but it doesn't. You have to experience this yourself! Go ahead and run the program with the input files provided with your source code (a cat's meow and a classical music clip). The results are quite scratchy, but you can clearly hear the original sounds.

EXAMPLE CODE   See toolbox_1/audio.py in your eText or companion code for the program and the sample audio files.

Exercises • Toolbox P6.39 to •• Toolbox P6.49 invite you to carry out several useful sound manipulations. You can add "fade in" and "fade out" effects by lowering the volume at the beginning or end of the list. You can mix two tracks by producing the average of the list values. You can produce an echo by shifting the sound wave, attenuating it, and mixing it back with the original. All these effects are easily achieved by manipulating lists of numbers.

6.5 Problem Solving: Adapting Algorithms

By combining fundamental operations and algorithms, you can solve complex programming tasks.

In Sections 6.2 and 6.3, you were introduced to a number of fundamental list operations and algorithms. These operations and algorithms form the building blocks for many programs that process lists. In general, it is a good problem-solving strategy to have a repertoire of fundamental algorithms that you can combine and adapt.

Consider this example problem: You are given the quiz scores of a student and are asked to drop the lowest score.

We do not have a ready-made algorithm for this situation, but it is easy to combine two standard operations:

Find the minimum.
Remove the minimum from the list.

For example, suppose we are given the list

[0]	[1]	[2]	[3]	[4]	[5]	[6]
8	7	8.5	9.5	7	4	10

The minimum is 4. After removing the minimum, we obtain:

[0]	[1]	[2]	[3]	[4]	[5]
8	7	8.5	9.5	7	10

This demonstrates that our strategy works. If we aren't concerned about efficiency, we can stop now. However, as computer scientists deal with ever larger data sets, it is worth going beyond solutions that work and asking whether we can get the correct result more efficiently.

You should be familiar with the implementation of fundamental algorithms so that you can adapt them.

This is where it is helpful to know how the library operations work. To remove a value, one must first find it, with a linear search (Section 6.3.5). That's exactly what the remove method does.

It is inefficient to determine the minimum and then make another pass through the list to find it again. If we remembered at which position the minimum occurred, we could simply call pop, and the inefficiency would be avoided.

We can adapt the algorithm for finding the minimum to yield the position. Here is the original algorithm:

```
smallest = values[0]
for i in range(1, len(values)) :
   if values[i] < smallest :
      smallest = values[i]
```

When we find the smallest value, we also want to update the position:

```
if values[i] < smallest :
   smallest = values[i]
   smallestPosition = i
```

In fact, then there is no reason to keep track of the smallest value any longer. It is simply values[smallestPosition]. With this insight, we can adapt the algorithm as follows:

```
smallestPosition = 0
for i in range(1, len(values)) :
   if values[i] < values[smallestPosition] :
      smallestPosition = i
```

HOW TO 6.1

Working with Lists

In many data processing situations, you need to process a sequence of values. This How To walks you through the steps for storing input values in a list and carrying out computations with the list elements.

Problem Statement A final quiz score is computed by adding all the scores, except for the lowest two. For example, if the scores are

8 4 7 8.5 9.5 7 5 10

then the final score is 50. Write a program to compute a final score in this way.

Thierry Dosogne/The Image Bank/Getty Images, Inc.

Step 1 Decompose your task into steps.

You will usually want to break down your task into multiple steps, such as

• Reading the data into a list.
• Processing the data in one or more steps.
• Displaying the results.

When deciding how to process the data, you should be familiar with the list operations and algorithms in Sections 6.2 and 6.3. Most processing tasks can be solved by using one or more of these algorithms.

In our sample problem, we will read the data. Then we will remove the minimum, repeat that to remove the second-lowest score, and compute the total. For example, if the input is 8 4 7 8.5 9.5 7 5 10, we will remove the two lowest scores (4 and 5), yielding 8 7 8.5 9.5 7 10. The sum of those values is the final score of 50.

Thus, we have identified these steps:

Read inputs into the list scores.
Remove the minimum from scores.
Remove the minimum from scores again.
total = sum of the elements in scores

Step 2   Determine which algorithm(s) you need.

Sometimes, a step corresponds to exactly one of the basic list operations and algorithms. That is the case with calculating the sum (Section 6.2.7) and reading the inputs (Section 6.3.9). At other times, you need to combine several algorithms. To remove the minimum value, you can find the minimum value and remove it. As discussed in Section 6.5, it is a bit more efficient to find the position of the minimum value and pop that.

Step 3   Use functions to structure the program.

Even though it may be possible to put all steps into the main function, this is rarely a good idea. It is better to make each processing step into a separate function. We don't need to write a function for computing the sum because we can simply call the sum function. However, we will implement two functions:

- readFloats
- removeMinimum

The main function simply calls these functions:

```
scores = readFloats()
removeMinimum(scores)
removeMinimum(scores)
total = sum(scores)
print("Final score:", total)
```

Step 4   Assemble and test the program.

Review your code and check that you handle both normal and exceptional situations. What happens with an empty list? One that contains a single element? When no match is found? When there are multiple matches? Consider these boundary conditions and make sure that your program works correctly.

In our example, it is impossible to compute the minimum if the list is empty or has length 1. In that case, we should terminate the program with an error message *before* attempting to call the removeMinimum function.

What if the minimum value occurs multiple times? That means that a student had more than one test with the same low score. We remove only two of the occurrences of that low score, and that is the desired behavior.

The following table shows test cases and their expected output:

Test Case	Expected Output	Comment
8 4 7 8.5 9.5 7 5 10	50	See Step 1.
8 7 7 7 9	24	Only two instances of the low score should be removed.
8 7	0	After removing the low scores, no score remains.
(no inputs)	**Error**	That is not a legal input.

EXAMPLE CODE   Here's the complete program.

how_to_1/scores.py

```
1  ##
2  #   This program computes a final score for a series of quiz scores: the sum after
3  #   dropping the two lowest scores. The program uses a list.
4  #
5
6  def main() :
7      scores = readFloats()
```

```
 8      if len(scores) > 1 :
 9         removeMinimum(scores)
10         removeMinimum(scores)
11         total = sum(scores)
12         print("Final score:", total)
13      else :
14         print("At least two scores are required.")
15
16  ## Reads a sequence of floating-point numbers.
17  #   @return a list containing the numbers
18  #
19  def readFloats() :
20      # Create an empty list.
21      values = []
22
23      # Read the input values into a list.
24      print("Please enter values, Q to quit:")
25      userInput = input("")
26      while userInput.upper() != "Q" :
27         values.append(float(userInput))
28         userInput = input("")
29
30      return values
31
32  ## Removes the minimum value from a list.
33  #   @param values a list of size >= 1
34  #
35  def removeMinimum(values) :
36      smallestPosition = 0
37      for i in range(1, len(values)) :
38         if values[i] < values[smallestPosition] :
39            smallestPosition = i
40
41      values.pop(smallestPosition)
42
43  # Start the program.
44  main()
```

WORKED EXAMPLE 6.2

Rolling the Dice

Problem Statement   Your task is to analyze whether a die
is fair by counting how often the values 1, 2, ..., 6 appear. Your
input is a sequence of die toss values. You should print a table
with the frequencies of each die value.

© ktsimage/iStockphoto.

Step 1   Decompose your task into steps.

Our first try at decomposition simply echoes the problem
statement:

Read the die values into a list.
Count how often the values 1, 2, ..., 6 appear in the list.
Print the counts.

But let's think about the task a little more. This decomposition suggests that we first read and store all die values. Do we really need to store them? After all, we only want to know how often each face value appears. If we keep a list of counters, we can discard each input after incrementing the counter.

This refinement yields the following outline:

> *For each input value i*
> *Increment the counter corresponding to i.*
> *Print the counters.*

Step 2 Determine which algorithm(s) you need.

We don't have a ready-made algorithm for reading inputs and incrementing a counter, but it is straightforward to develop one. Suppose we read an input into `value`. This is an integer between 1 and 6. If we have a list `counters` of length 6, then we simply call

```
counters[value - 1] = counters[value - 1] + 1
```

Alternatively, we can use a list of seven integers, "wasting" the element `counters[0]`. That trick makes it easier to update the counters. When reading an input value, we simply execute

```
counters[value] = counters[value] + 1
```

That is, we define the list as

```
counters = [0] * (sides + 1)
```

Why introduce a `sides` variable? Suppose you later changed your mind and wanted to investigate 12-sided dice:

© Ryan Ruffatti/iStockphoto.

Then the program can simply be changed by setting `sides` to 12.

The only remaining task is to print the counts. A typical output might look like this:

```
1:    3
2:    3
3:    2
4:    2
5:    2
6:    0
```

We haven't seen an algorithm for this exact output format. It is similar to the basic loop for printing all elements:

```
for element in counters :
    print(element)
```

However, that loop is not appropriate for two reasons. First, it displays the unused 0 entry. We cannot simply iterate over the elements of the list if we want to skip that entry. We need a traditional count-controlled loop instead:

```
for i in range(1, len(counters)) :
    print(counters[i])
```

This loop prints the counter values, but it doesn't quite match the sample output. We also want the corresponding face values:

```
for i in range(1, len(counters)) :
    print("%2d: %4d" % (i, counters[i]))
```

Step 3 Use functions to structure your program.

We will provide a function for each step:

- `countInputs(sides)`
- `printCounters(counters)`

The `main` function calls these functions:

```
counters = countInputs(6)
printCounters(counters)
```

The `countInputs` function reads all inputs, increments the matching counters, and returns the list of counters. The `printCounters` function prints the values of the faces and counters, as already described.

Step 4 Assemble and test the program.

The listing at the end of this section shows the complete program. There is one notable feature that we have not previously discussed. When updating a counter

```
counters[value] = counters[value] + 1
```

we want to be sure that the user did not provide a wrong input which would cause a list out-of-range error. Therefore, we reject inputs that are < 1 or > `sides`.

The following table shows test cases and their expected output. To save space, we only show the counters in the output.

Test Case	Expected Output	Comment
1 2 3 4 5 6	1 1 1 1 1 1	Each number occurs once.
1 2 3	1 1 1 0 0 0	Numbers that don't appear should have counts of zero.
1 2 3 1 2 3 4	2 2 2 1 0 0	The counters should reflect how often each input occurs.
(No input)	0 0 0 0 0 0	This is a legal input; all counters are zero.
0 1 2 3 4 5 6 7	**Error**	Each input should be between 1 and 6.

EXAMPLE CODE Here's the complete program.

worked_example_2/dice.py

```
1  ##
2  #   This program reads a sequence of die toss values and prints how many times
3  #   each value occurred.
4  #
5
6  def main() :
7      counters = countInputs(6)
8      printCounters(counters)
9
```

```
10   ## Reads a sequence of die toss values between 1 and sides (inclusive)
11   #  and counts how frequently each of them occurs.
12   #  @param sides the die's number of sides
13   #  @return a list whose ith element contains the number of times the value i
14   #  occurred in the input. The 0 element is unused.
15   #
16   def countInputs(sides) :
17      counters = [0] * (sides + 1)    # counters[0] is not used.
18
19      print("Please enter values, Q to quit:")
20      userInput = input("")
21      while userInput.upper() != "Q" :
22         value = int(userInput)
23
24         # Increment the counter for the input value.
25         if value >= 1 and value <= sides :
26            counters[value] = counters[value] + 1
27         else :
28            print(value, "is not a valid input.")
29
30         # Read the next value.
31         userInput = input("")
32
33      return counters
34
35   ## Prints a table of die value counters.
36   #  @param counters a list of counters. counters[0] is not printed.
37   #
38   def printCounters(counters) :
39      for i in range(1, len(counters)) :
40         print("%2d: %4d" % (i, counters[i]))
41
42   # Start the program.
43   main()
```

Program Run

```
Please enter values, Q to quit: 1
2
3
1
2
3
4
Q
 1:    2
 2:    2
 3:    2
 4:    1
 5:    0
 6:    0
```

Exercise •• P6.14 invites you to modify this solution to use randomly generated values to more accurately analyze whether a die is fair.

6.6 Problem Solving: Discovering Algorithms by Manipulating Physical Objects

In Section 6.5, you saw how to solve a problem by combining and adapting known operations and algorithms. But what do you do when none of the standard algorithms is sufficient for your task? In this section, you will learn a technique for discovering algorithms by manipulating physical objects.

Consider the following task: You are given a list whose size is an even number, and you are to switch the first and the second half. For example, if the list contains the eight numbers

9 13 21 4 11 7 1 3

then you should change it to

11 7 1 3 9 13 21 4

Many students find it quite challenging to come up with an algorithm. They may know that a loop is required, and they may realize that elements should be inserted (Section 6.2.2) or swapped (Section 6.3.8), but they may not have sufficient intuition to draw diagrams, describe an algorithm, or write down pseudocode.

One useful technique for discovering an algorithm is to manipulate physical objects. Start by lining up some objects to denote a list. Coins, playing cards, or small toys are good choices.

Use a sequence of coins, playing cards, or toys to visualize a list of values.

Manipulating physical objects can give you ideas for discovering algorithms.

© JenCon/iStockphoto.

Here we arrange eight coins:

(coins) © jamesbenet/iStockphoto; (dollar coins) © JordiDelgado/iStockphoto.

Now let's step back and see what we can do to change the order of the coins. We can remove a coin (Section 6.2.4):

Visualizing the removal of a list element

We can insert a coin (Section 6.2.2):

Visualizing the insertion of a list element

Or we can swap two coins (Section 6.3.8).

Visualizing the swapping of two list elements

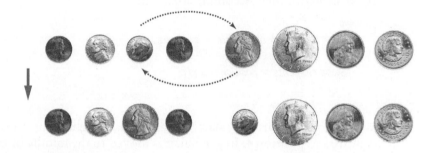

Go ahead—line up some coins and try out these three operations right now so that you get a feel for them.

Now how does that help us with our problem, switching the first and the second half of the list?

Let's put the first coin into place, by swapping it with the fifth coin. However, as Python programmers, we will say that we swap the coins in positions 0 and 4:

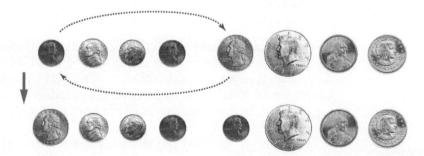

Next, we swap the coins in positions 1 and 5:

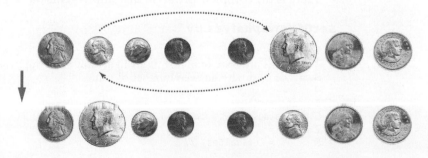

Two more swaps, and we are done:

Now an algorithm is becoming apparent:

```
i = 0
j = ... # We'll think about that in a minute
While ... # Don't know yet
    Swap elements at positions i and j.
    i = i + 1
    j = j + 1
```

Where does the variable *j* start? When we have eight coins, the coin at position zero is moved to position 4. In general, it is moved to the middle of the list, or to position *length // 2*.

And how many iterations do we make? We need to swap all coins in the first half. That is, we need to swap *length // 2* coins. The pseudocode is

```
i = 0
j = length // 2
While i < length // 2
    Swap elements at positions i and j.
    i = i + 1
    j = j + 1
```

It is a good idea to make a walkthrough of the pseudocode (see Section 4.2). You can use paper clips to denote the positions of the variables *i* and *j*. If the walkthrough is successful, then we know that there was no "off-by-one" error in the pseudocode. Exercise • P6.10 asks you to translate the pseudocode to Python. Exercise •• R6.24 suggests a different algorithm for switching the two halves of a list, by repeatedly removing and inserting coins.

Many people find that the manipulation of physical objects is less intimidating than drawing diagrams or mentally envisioning algorithms. Give it a try when you need to design a new algorithm!

Here is the complete program that implements our algorithm.

> You can use paper clips as position markers or counters.

sec06/swaphalves.py

```
1  ##
2  #   This program implements an algorithm that swaps the first and second halves
3  #   of a list with an even number of values.
4
5  def main() :
6      values = [9, 13, 21, 4, 11, 7, 1, 3]
7      i = 0
8      j = len(values) // 2
```

```
 9    while i < len(values) // 2 :
10        swap(values, i, j)
11        i = i + 1
12        j = j + 1
13
14    print(values)
15
16 ## Swaps the elements of a list at given positions.
17 #  @param a the list
18 #  @param i the first position
19 #  @param j the second position
20 #
21 def swap(a, i, j) :
22    temp = a[i]
23    a[i] = a[j]
24    a[j] = temp
25
26 # Start the program.
27 main()
```

6.7 Tables

It often happens that you want to store collections of values that have a two-dimensional tabular layout. Such data sets commonly occur in financial and scientific applications. An arrangement consisting of rows and columns of values is called a *table*, or a *matrix*.

Let's explore how to store the example data shown in Figure 11: the medal counts of the figure skating competitions at the 2014 Winter Olympics.

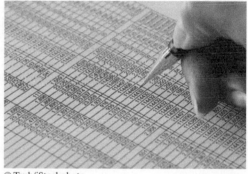

© Trub/iStockphoto.

© technotr/iStockphoto.

	Gold	Silver	Bronze
Canada	0	3	0
Italy	0	0	1
Germany	0	0	1
Japan	1	0	0
Kazakhstan	0	0	1
Russia	3	1	1
South Korea	0	1	0
United States	1	0	1

Figure 11 Figure Skating Medal Counts

6.7.1 Creating Tables

Python does not have a data type for creating tables. But a two-dimensional tabular structure can be created using Python lists. Here is the code for creating a table that contains 8 rows and 3 columns, which is suitable for holding our medal count data:

```
COUNTRIES = 8
MEDALS = 3

counts = [
     [ 0, 3, 0 ],
     [ 0, 0, 1 ],
     [ 0, 0, 1 ],
     [ 1, 0, 0 ],
     [ 0, 0, 1 ],
     [ 3, 1, 1 ],
     [ 0, 1, 0 ]
     [ 1, 0, 1 ]
   ]
```

This creates a list in which each element is itself another list (see Figure 12).

Sometimes, you may need to create a table with a size that is too large to initialize with literal values. To create such a table, you must work harder. First, create a list that will be used to store the individual rows.

```
table = []
```

Then create a new list using replication (with the number of columns as the size) for each row in the table and append it to the list of rows:

```
ROWS = 5
COLUMNS = 20

for i in range(ROWS) :
   row = [0] * COLUMNS
   table.append(row)
```

The result is a table that consists of 5 rows and 20 columns.

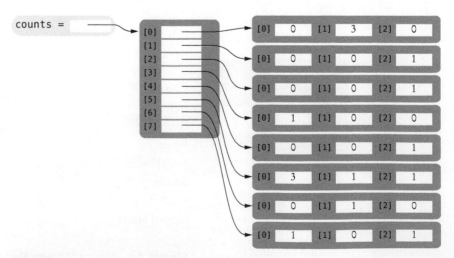

Figure 12 A Table Created Using a List of Lists

6.7.2 Accessing Elements

Individual elements in a table are accessed by using two index values, *table*[i][j].

To access a particular element in the table, you need to specify two index values in separate brackets to select the row and column, respectively (see Figure 13):

```
medalCount = counts[3][1]
```

To access all elements in a table, you use two nested loops. For example, the following loop prints all elements of counts:

```
for i in range(COUNTRIES) :
    # Process the ith row.
    for j in range(MEDALS) :
        # Process the jth column in the ith row.
        print("%8d" % counts[i][j], end="")

    print()    # Start a new line at the end of the row.
```

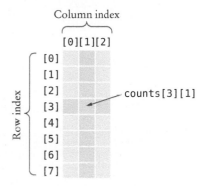

Figure 13
Accessing an Element in a Table

6.7.3 Locating Neighboring Elements

Some programs that work with tables need to locate the elements that are adjacent to an element. This task is particularly common in games. Figure 14 shows how to compute the index values of the neighbors of an element.

For example, the neighbors of counts[3][1] to the left and right are counts[3][0] and counts[3][2]. The neighbors to the top and bottom are counts[2][1] and counts[4][1].

You need to be careful about computing neighbors at the boundary of the list. For example, counts[0][1] has no neighbor to the top. Consider the task of computing the

[i - 1][j - 1]	[i - 1][j]	[i - 1][j + 1]
[i][j - 1]	[i][j]	[i][j + 1]
[i + 1][j - 1]	[i + 1][j]	[i + 1][j + 1]

Figure 14
Neighboring Locations in a Table

sum of the neighbors to the top and bottom of the element count[i][j]. You need to check whether the element is located at the top or bottom of the table:

```
total = 0
if i > 0 :
    total = total + counts[i - 1][j]
if i < ROWS - 1 :
    total = total + counts[i + 1][j]
```

6.7.4 Computing Row and Column Totals

A common task is to compute row or column totals. In our example, the row totals give us the total number of medals won by a particular country.

Finding the correct index values is a bit tricky, and it is a good idea to make a quick sketch. To compute the total of row i, we need to visit the following elements:

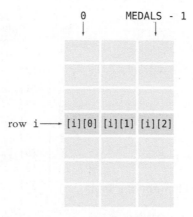

As you can see, we need to compute the sum of counts[i][j], where j ranges from 0 to MEDALS - 1. The following loop computes the total:

```
total = 0
for j in range(MEDALS) :
    total = total + counts[i][j]
```

Computing column totals is similar. Form the sum of counts[i][j], where i ranges from 0 to COUNTRIES - 1.

```
total = 0
for i in range(COUNTRIES) :
    total = total + counts[i][j]
```

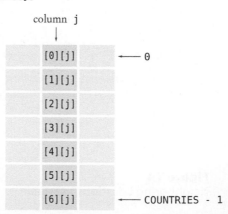

6.7.5 Using Tables with Functions

When you pass a table to a function, you will want to recover the dimensions of the table. If `values` is a table, then

- `len(values)` is the number of rows.
- `len(values[0])` is the number of columns.

(Note that `len(values[0])` is the length of first element in `values`, but because all of the elements (rows) are the same length, it is also the number of columns in the table.)
For example, the following function computes the sum of all elements in a table:

```python
def sum(values) :
    total = 0
    for i in range(len(values)) :
        for j in range(len(values[0])) :
            total = total + values[i][j]

    return total
```

Working with tables is illustrated in the following program. The program prints out the medal counts and the row totals.

sec07/medals.py

```python
 1  ##
 2  #   This program prints a table of medal winner counts with row totals.
 3  #
 4
 5  MEDALS = 3
 6  COUNTRIES = 8
 7
 8  # Create a list of country names.
 9  countries = [ "Canada",
10                "Italy",
11                "Germany",
12                "Japan",
13                "Kazakhstan",
14                "Russia",
15                "South Korea",
16                "United States" ]
17
18  # Create a table of medal counts.
19  counts = [
20              [ 0, 3, 0 ],
21              [ 0, 0, 1 ],
22              [ 0, 0, 1 ],
23              [ 1, 0, 0 ],
24              [ 0, 0, 1 ],
25              [ 3, 1, 1 ],
26              [ 0, 1, 0 ],
27              [ 1, 0, 1 ]
28          ]
29
30  # Print the table header.
31  print("         Country   Gold Silver Bronze   Total")
32
33  # Print countries, counts, and row totals.
34  for i in range(COUNTRIES) :
35     print("%15s" % countries[i], end="")
```

```
36
37    # Print each row element and update the row total.
38    total = 0
39    for j in range(MEDALS) :
40       print("%8d" % counts[i][j], end="")
41       total = total + counts[i][j]
42
43    # Display the row total and print a new line.
44    print("%8d" % total)
```

Program Run

```
      Country  Gold  Silver  Bronze  Total
       Canada     0       3       0      3
        Italy     0       0       1      1
      Germany     0       0       1      1
        Japan     1       0       0      1
   Kazakhstan     0       0       1      1
       Russia     3       1       1      5
  South Korea     0       1       0      1
United States     1       0       1      2
```

WORKED EXAMPLE 6.3

A World Population Table

Problem Statement Consider the following population data.

Population Per Continent (in millions)							
Year	1750	1800	1850	1900	1950	2000	2050
Africa	106	107	111	133	221	767	1766
Asia	502	635	809	947	1402	3634	5268
Australia	2	2	2	6	13	30	46
Europe	163	203	276	408	547	729	628
North America	2	7	26	82	172	307	392
South America	16	24	38	74	167	511	809

You are to print the data in tabular format and add column totals that show the total world population in the given years.

Step 1 First, we break down the task into steps:

Initialize the table data.
Print the table.
Compute and print the column totals.

Step 2   Initialize the table as a sequence of rows:

```
populations = [
      [ 106, 107, 111, 133, 221, 767, 1766 ],
      [ 502, 635, 809, 947, 1402, 3634, 5268 ],
      [ 2, 2, 2, 6, 13, 30, 46 ],
      [ 163, 203, 276, 408, 547, 729, 628 ],
      [ 2, 7, 26, 82, 172, 307, 392 ],
      [ 16, 24, 38, 74, 167, 511, 809 ]
      ]
```

Step 3   To print the row headers, we also need a list of the continent names. Note that it has the same number of rows as our table.

```
continents = [
      "Africa",
      "Asia",
      "Australia",
      "Europe",
      "North America",
      "South America"
      ]
```

To print a row, we first print the continent name, then all columns. This is achieved with two nested loops. The outer loop prints each row:

```
# Print population data.
for i in range(ROWS) :
   # Print the ith row.
   . . .
   print()    # Start a new line at the end of the row.
```

To print a row, we first print the row header, then all columns:

```
print("%20s" % continents[i], end="")
for j in range(COLUMNS) :
   print("%5d" % populations[i][j], end="")
```

Step 4   To print the column sums, we use the algorithm that was described in Section 6.7.4. We carry out that computation once for each column.

```
for j in range(COLUMNS) :
   total = 0
   for i in range(ROWS) :
      total = total + populations[i][j]

   print("%5d" % total, end="")
```

EXAMPLE CODE   Here is the complete program.

worked_example_3/population.py

```
 1  ##
 2  #   This program prints a table showing the world population growth over 300 years.
 3  #
 4
 5  ROWS = 6
 6  COLUMNS = 7
 7
 8  # Initialize the populations table.
 9  populations = [
10        [ 100, 107, 111, 133, 221, 767, 1766 ],
11        [ 502, 635, 809, 947, 1402, 3634, 5268 ],
12        [ 2, 2, 2, 6, 13, 30 46 ],
```

```
13          [ 163, 203, 276, 408, 547, 729, 628 ],
14          [ 2, 7, 26, 82, 172, 307, 392 ],
15          [ 16, 24, 38, 74, 167, 511, 809 ]
16      ]
17
18  # Define a list of continent names.
19  continents = [
20      "Africa",
21      "Asia",
22      "Australia",
23      "Europe",
24      "North America",
25      "South America"
26      ]
27
28  # Print the table header.
29  print("                      Year 1750 1800 1850 1900 1950 2000 2050")
30
31  # Print population data.
32  for i in range(ROWS) :
33      # Print the ith row.
34      print("%20s" % continents[i], end="")
35      for j in range(COLUMNS) :
36          print("%5d" % populations[i][j], end="")
37
38      print()    # Start a new line at the end of the row.
39
40  # Print column totals.
41  print("                   World", end="")
42  for j in range(COLUMNS) :
43      total = 0
44      for i in range(ROWS) :
45          total = total + populations[i][j]
46
47      print("%5d" % total, end="")
48
49  print()
```

Program Run

```
              Year 1750 1800 1850 1900 1950 2000 2050
            Africa  106  107  111  133  221  767 1766
              Asia  502  635  809  947 1402 3634 5268
         Australia    2    2    2    6   13   30   46
            Europe  163  203  276  408  547  729  628
     North America    2    7   26   82  172  307  392
     South America   16   24   38   74  167  511  809
             World  791  978 1262 1650 2522 5978 8909
```

Special Topic 6.9

Tables with Variable Row Lengths

The tables used in this section contain rows that all have the same length. It is possible, however, to create a table in which the row length varies.

For example, you can create a table that has a triangular shape, such as:

```
b[0][0]
b[1][0] b[1][1]
b[2][0] b[2][1] b[2][2]
```

To create such a table, you must use list replication within a loop (see Figure 15).

```
b = []
for i in range(3) :
    b.append([0] * (i + 1))
```

You can access each list element as b[i][j]. The expression b[i] selects the ith row, and the [j] operator selects the jth element in that row.

Note that the number of rows is len(b), and the length of the ith row is len(b[i]). For example, the following pair of loops prints a ragged table:

```
for i in range(len(b)) :
    for j in range(len(b[i])) :
        print(b[i][j], end=" ")
    print()
```

If you don't need the row and column index values, you can traverse the rows and elements directly:

```
for row in b :
    for element in row :
        print(element, end=" ")
    print()
```

Naturally, such "ragged" tables are not very common.

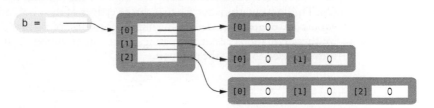

Figure 15   A Triangular Table

WORKED EXAMPLE 6.4

Graphics: Drawing Regular Polygons

A regular polygon is a polygon in which all sides have the same length and all interior angles are equal and less than 180 degrees. You may know regular polygons of specific sizes by their common names: equilateral triangle, square, pentagon, hexagon, heptagon, octagon.

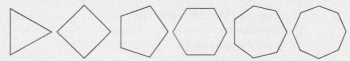

Problem Statement   Develop a graphics program that draws a regular polygon in the center of the window with the given number of sides as specified by the user.

Step 1   Understand the drawing task.

The problem decomposes into two separate tasks. First, it is useful to be able to draw an arbitrary polygon, given its list of vertices. Draw lines from each vertex to the next, and then close up the polygon by drawing a line from the last vertex to the first.

In order to draw a regular polygon with a given number of sides on the canvas, you must determine how to compute the vertices for the polygon. A regular polygon can be inscribed within a circle such that every vertex lies on the circle.

If the center of the polygon, which is the same as the center of the circle, is at the origin, the x- and y-coordinates of the vertices can be computed using polar coordinates.

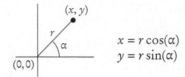

$$x = r\cos(\alpha)$$
$$y = r\sin(\alpha)$$

We can start by defining the first vertex on the x-axis (where $\alpha = 0$) and then compute each successive vertex by incrementing the angle by the amount that separates consecutive vertices (Δ). The computations for the first three vertices of the polygon are illustrated below, where Δ equals 360 degrees divided by the number of sides. Note that the coordinate values computed by these equations result in floating-point values which must be rounded to integers before they are used to draw the polygon.

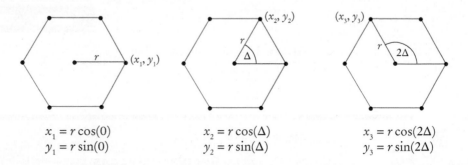

$$x_1 = r\cos(0)$$
$$y_1 = r\sin(0)$$

$$x_2 = r\cos(\Delta)$$
$$y_2 = r\sin(\Delta)$$

$$x_3 = r\cos(2\Delta)$$
$$y_3 = r\sin(2\Delta)$$

Step 2   Carry out stepwise refinement.

We will use the process of stepwise refinement in solving this problem. Viewing the problem from a high-level, there are only a few steps involved.

Create and configure a graphics window.
Obtain number of sides for the polygon.
Build the regular polygon.
Draw the polygon.

We can split up the tasks of obtaining the number of sides, building the polygon, and drawing the polygon into functions `getNumberSides`, `buildRegularPolygon`, and `drawPolygon`. The main function for solving this problem is then:

```
WIN_SIZE = 400
POLY_RADIUS = 150
POLY_OFFSET = WIN_SIZE // 2 - POLY_RADIUS

def main() :
    win = GraphicsWindow(WIN_SIZE, WIN_SIZE)
    canvas = win.canvas()
    canvas.setOutline("blue")
    numSides = getNumberSides()
    polygon = buildRegularPolygon(POLY_OFFSET, POLY_OFFSET, numSides, POLY_RADIUS)
    drawPolygon(polygon, canvas)
    win.wait()
```

Step 3   Query the user for the number of sides.

A polygon must have at least three sides. We can validate the user input by repeatedly prompting for a value until a valid value is entered. The code for this function is shown below.

```
## Obtain from the user the number of sides for the polygon.
#  @return the number of sides >= 3
#
def getNumberSides() :
    numSides = int(input("Enter number of polygon sides (>= 3): "))
    while numSides < 3 :
        print("Error!! the number of sides must be 3 or greater.")
        numSides = int(input("Enter number of polygon sides (>= 3): "))

    return numSides
```

Step 4   Build and draw the regular polygon.

First consider the task of drawing an arbitrary polygon, shown below.

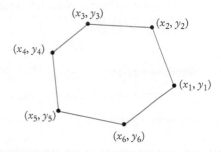

A polygon is specified by a list of points. Each point has an x- and y-coordinate, and we represent it as a list of length 2.

To draw a polygon, the caller must build up a vertex list of this form and pass it to the drawPolygon function:

```
vertexList = [[x1, y1], [x2, y2], [x3, y3], [x4, y4], [x5, y5], [x6, y6]]
drawPolygon(vertexList, canvas)
```

The code for that function draws $n - 1$ line segments, joining each point with its successor. Then it draws another line, joining the last point with the initial one.

```
def drawPolygon(vertexList, canvas) :
    last = len(vertexList) - 1
    for i in range(last) :
        start = vertexList[i]
        end = vertexList[i + 1]
        canvas.drawLine(start[0], start[1], end[0], end[1])
```

```
start = vertexList[last]
end = vertexList[0]
canvas.drawLine(start[0], start[1], end[0], end[1])
```

Now let us move on to the function for building a *regular* polygon. We let the user specify the position of the upper-left corner of a bounding square, and the desired radius.

The vertices computed using the equations from Step 1 assume the polygon is centered at the origin. To draw a polygon within the bounding square positioned with its upper-left corner at (x, y), the vertices will have to be offset by

```
xOffset = x + radius
yOffset = y + radius
```

Now, the vertices can be computed and saved in a list.

The function for this task is shown below. Note that as each coordinate is computed, it must be converted to an integer using the round function. In addition, the trigonometric functions require the angle be specified in radians. We use the radians function to convert from degrees to radians. This function, as well as sin and cos, are defined in the math module.

```
## Computes and builds a list of vertices for a regular convex polygon as
#  defined within a bounding square.
#  @param x  the x-coordinate of the upper-left corner of the bounding square
#  @param y  the y-coordinate of the upper-left corner of the bounding square
#  @param sides  the number of sides for the polygon
#  @param radius  the radius of regular polygon
#  @return  the list of vertices stored in the format [[x1, y1], ... [xn, yn]]
#
def buildRegularPolygon(x, y, sides, radius) :
   xOffset = x + radius
   yOffset = y + radius
   angle = 0.0
   angleInc = radians(360 / sides)
   vertexList = []
   for i in range(sides) :
      xVertex = xOffset + radius * cos(angle)
      yVertex = yOffset + radius * sin(angle)
      vertexList.append([round(xVertex), round(yVertex)])
      angle = angle + angleInc

   return vertexList
```

Step 5   Put all of the functions together in a single Python source file.

EXAMPLE CODE   See worked_example_4/drawpoly.py in your eText or companion code for the complete program.

CHAPTER SUMMARY

Use lists for collecting values.

- A list is a container that stores a sequence of values.
- Each individual element in a list is accessed by an integer index i, using the notation *list*[i].
- A list index must be less than the number of elements in the list.
- An out-of-range error, which occurs if you supply an invalid list index, can cause your program to terminate.

- You can iterate over the index values or the elements of a list.
- A list reference specifies the location of a list. Copying the reference yields a second reference to the same list.

Know and use the built-in operations for lists.

- Use the `insert` method to insert a new element at any position in a list.
- The `in` operator tests whether an element is contained in a list.
- Use the `pop` method to remove an element from any position in a list.
- Use the `remove` method to remove an element from a list by value.
- Two lists can be concatenated using the plus (+) operator.
- Use the `list` function to copy the elements of one list into a new list.
- Use the slice operator (:) to extract a sublist or substring.

Know and use common list algorithms.

- When separating elements, don't place a separator before the first element.
- A linear search inspects elements in sequence until a match is found.
- Use a temporary variable when swapping two elements.

Implement functions that process lists.

- Lists can occur as function arguments and return values.
- When calling a function with a list argument, the function receives a list reference, not a copy of the list.
- A tuple is created as a comma-separated sequence enclosed in parentheses.

Combine and adapt algorithms for solving a programming problem.

- By combining fundamental operations and algorithms, you can solve complex programming tasks.
- You should be familiar with the implementation of fundamental algorithms so that you can adapt them.

Discover algorithms by manipulating physical objects.

- Use a sequence of coins, playing cards, or toys to visualize a list of values.
- You can use paper clips as position markers or counters.

Use tables for data that is arranged in rows and columns.

- Individual elements in a table are accessed by using two index values, *table*[i][j].

REVIEW EXERCISES

■■ R6.1 Given the list values = [], write code that fills the list with each set of numbers below.

a. 1 2 3 4 5 6 7 8 9 10
b. 0 2 4 6 8 10 12 14 16 18 20
c. 1 4 9 16 25 36 49 64 81 100
d. 0 0 0 0 0 0 0 0 0 0
e. 1 4 9 16 9 7 4 9 11
f. 0 1 0 1 0 1 0 1 0 1
g. 0 1 2 3 4 0 1 2 3 4

■■ R6.2 Consider the following list:

```
a = [1, 2, 3, 4, 5, 4, 3, 2, 1, 0]
```

What is the value of total after each of the following loops complete?

a.
```
total = 0
for i in range(10) :
    total = total + a[i]
```
b.
```
total = 0
for i in range(0, 10, 2) :
    total = total + a[i]
```
c.
```
total = 0
for i in range(1, 10, 2) :
    total = total + a[i]
```
d.
```
total = 0
for i in range(2, 11) :
    total = total + a[i]
```
e.
```
total = 0
i = 1
while i < 10 :
    total = total + a[i]
    i = 2 * i
```
f.
```
total = 0
for i in range(9, -1, -1) :
    total = total + a[i]
```
g.
```
total = 0
for i in range(9, -1, -2) :
    total = total + a[i]
```
h.
```
total = 0
for i in range(0, 10) :
    total = a[i] - total
```

■ R6.3 Describe three different ways of making a copy of a list that don't involve the list function.

■■ R6.4 Consider the following list:

```
a = [1, 2, 3, 4, 5, 4, 3, 2, 1, 0]
```

What are the contents of the list a after each of the following loops complete? (For each part, assume the list a contains the original list of values.)

a.
```
for i in range(1, 10) :
    a[i] = a[i - 1]
```

b. `for i in range(9, 0, -1) :`
   `a[i] = a[i - 1]`

c. `for i in range(9) :`
   `a[i] = a[i + 1]`

d. `for i in range(8, -8, -1) :`
   `a[i] = a[i + 1]`

e. `for i in range(1, 10) :`
   `a[i] = a[i] + a[i - 1]`

f. `for i in range(1, 10, 2) :`
   `a[i] = 0`

g. `for i in range(5) :`
   `a[i + 5] = a[i]`

h. `for i in range(1, 5) :`
   `a[i] = a[9 - i]`

••• **R6.5** Write a loop that fills a list `values` with ten random numbers between 1 and 100. Write code for two nested loops that fill `values` with ten *different* random numbers between 1 and 100.

•• **R6.6** Write Python code for a loop that simultaneously computes both the maximum and minimum of a list.

• **R6.7** What is wrong with each of the following code segments?

   a. `values = [1, 2, 3, 4, 5, 6, 7, 8, 9, 10]`
      `for i in range(1, 11) :`
         `values[i] = i * i`

   b. `values = []`
      `for i in range(len(values)) :`
         `values[i] = i * i`

•• **R6.8** Write `for` loops that iterate over the elements of a list without the use of the `range` function for the following tasks.

   a. Printing all elements of a list in a single row, separated by spaces.

   b. Computing the product of all elements in a list.

   c. Counting how many elements in a list are negative.

• **R6.9** What is an index of a list? What are the legal index values? What is an out-of-range (or bounds) error?

• **R6.10** Write a program that contains an out-of-range error. Run the program. What happens on your computer?

• **R6.11** Write a loop that reads ten numbers and a second loop that displays them in the opposite order from which they were entered.

• **R6.12** For the operations on lists below, provide the header and function comment for a function. Do not implement the functions.

   a. Sort the elements in decreasing order.

   b. Print all elements, separated by a given string.

   c. Count how many elements are less than a given value.

   d. Remove all elements that are less than a given value.

   e. Place all elements that are less than a given value in another list.

R6.13 Trace the flow of the second loop in Section 6.3.3 with the given example. Show two columns, one with the value of i and one with the output.

R6.14 Trace the flow of the loop in Section 6.3.5, where values contains the elements 80 90 100 120 110. Show two columns, for pos and found. Repeat the trace when values contains the elements 80 90 120 70.

R6.15 Consider the following loop for collecting all elements that match a condition; in this case, that the element is larger than 100.

```
matches = []
for element in values :
    if element > 100 :
        matches.append(element)
```

Trace the flow of the loop, where values contains the elements 110 90 100 120 80. Show two columns, for element and matches.

R6.16 Trace the algorithm for removing an element described in Section 6.3.7. Use a list values with elements 110 90 100 120 80, and remove the element at index 2.

R6.17 Give pseudocode for an algorithm that rotates the elements of a list by one position, moving the initial element to the end of the list, like this:

R6.18 Give pseudocode for an algorithm that removes all negative values from a list, preserving the order of the remaining elements.

R6.19 Suppose values is a *sorted* list of integers. Give pseudocode that describes how a new value can be inserted in its proper position so that the resulting list stays sorted.

R6.20 A *run* is a sequence of adjacent repeated values. Give pseudocode for computing the length of the longest run in a list. For example, the longest run in the list with elements

```
1 2 5 5 3 1 2 4 3 2 2 2 2 3 6 5 5 6 3 1
```

has length 4.

R6.21 What is wrong with the following function that aims to fill a list with random numbers?

```
def fillWithRandomNumbers(values) :
    numbers = []
    for i in range(len(values)) :
        numbers[i] = random.random()
    values = numbers
```

R6.22 You are given two lists denoting x- and y-coordinates of a set of points in the plane. For plotting the point set, we need to know the x- and y-coordinates of the smallest rectangle containing the points. How can you obtain these values from the fundamental algorithms in Section 6.3?

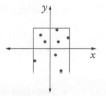

R6.23 Solve the problem described in How To 6.1 by sorting the list first. How do you need to modify the algorithm for computing the total?

■■ **R6.24** Solve the task described in Section 6.6 using an algorithm that removes and inserts elements instead of switching them. Write the pseudocode for the algorithm, assuming that functions for removal and insertion exist. Act out the algorithm with a sequence of coins and explain why it is less efficient than the swapping algorithm developed in Section 6.6.

■■ **R6.25** Develop an algorithm for finding the most frequently occurring value in a list of numbers. Use a sequence of coins. Place paper clips below each coin that count how many other coins of the same value are in the sequence. Give the pseudocode for an algorithm that yields the correct answer, and describe how using the coins and paper clips helped you find the algorithm.

■■ **R6.26** How do you perform the following tasks with lists in Python?

  a. Test that two lists contain the same elements in the same order.

  b. Copy one list to another.

  c. Fill a list with zeroes, overwriting all elements in it.

  d. Remove all elements from a list.

■ **R6.27** True or false?

  a. List index values must be integers.

  b. Lists can change their size, getting larger or smaller.

  c. A function cannot return a list.

  d. All elements of a list are of the same type.

  e. Lists cannot contain strings as elements.

  f. A function cannot change the length of a list argument.

■■ **R6.28** Write Python statements for performing the following tasks with a table of m rows and n columns.

  • Initialize the table with zeroes.

  • Fill all entries with ones.

  • Fill elements alternately with zeroes and ones in a checkerboard pattern.

  • Fill only the elements in the top and bottom row with zeroes.

  • Fill only the elements in the left and right column with ones.

  • Compute the sum of all elements.

  • Print the table.

■ **Toolbox R6.29** Why does stereo CD sound take up about 10 MB per minute?

■ **Toolbox R6.30** What happens when you read a sound file, divide all data values by two, and save the result?

■ **Toolbox R6.31** What happens when you read a sound file, keep the data values the same, divide the sampling rate by two, and save the result?

■ **Toolbox R6.32** What happens when you write a sound file that contains the same value (such as 30,000) repeated 44,100 times? Try it out if you aren't sure.

■ **Toolbox R6.33** What happens when you multiply all data of a sound file with –1 and save the result? Try it out if you are not sure.

PROGRAMMING EXERCISES

•• P6.1 Write a program that initializes a list with ten random integers and then prints four lines of output, containing

- Every element at an even index.
- Every even element.
- All elements in reverse order.
- Only the first and last element.

• P6.2 Write a program that reads numbers and adds them to a list if they aren't already contained in the list. When the list contains ten numbers, the program displays the contents and quits.

•• P6.3 Write a program that adds all numbers from 2 to 10,000 to a list. Then remove the multiples of 2 (but not 2), multiples of 3 (but not 3), and so on, up to the multiples of 100. Print the remaining values.

•• P6.4 Write list functions that carry out the following tasks for a list of integers. For each function, provide a test program.

- **a.** Swap the first and last elements in the list.
- **b.** Shift all elements by one to the right and move the last element into the first position. For example, 1 4 9 16 25 would be transformed into 25 1 4 9 16.
- **c.** Replace all even elements with 0.
- **d.** Replace each element except the first and last by the larger of its two neighbors.
- **e.** Remove the middle element if the list length is odd, or the middle two elements if the length is even.
- **f.** Move all even elements to the front, otherwise preserving the order of the elements.
- **g.** Return the second-largest element in the list.
- **h.** Return true if the list is currently sorted in increasing order.
- **i.** Return true if the list contains two adjacent duplicate elements.
- **j.** Return true if the list contains duplicate elements (which need not be adjacent).

• P6.5 Modify the largest.py program in Section 6.3 to mark both the smallest and the largest elements.

•• P6.6 Write a function sumWithoutSmallest that computes the sum of a list of values, except for the smallest one, in a single loop. In the loop, update the sum and the smallest value. After the loop, subtract the smallest value from the sum and return the difference.

• P6.7 Write a function removeMin that removes the minimum value from a list without using the min function or remove method.

•• P6.8 Compute the *alternating sum* of all elements in a list. For example, if your program reads the input

$$1 \quad 4 \quad 9 \quad 16 \quad 9 \quad 7 \quad 4 \quad 9 \quad 11$$

then it computes

$$1 - 4 + 9 - 16 + 9 - 7 + 4 - 9 + 11 = -2$$

■ **P6.9** Write a function that reverses the sequence of elements in a list. For example, if you call the function with the list

1 4 9 16 9 7 4 9 11

then the list is changed to

11 9 4 7 9 16 9 4 1

■ **P6.10** Write a function that implements the algorithm developed in Section 6.6.

■■ **P6.11** Write a function def equals(a, b) that checks whether two lists have the same elements in the same order.

■■ **P6.12** Write a function def sameSet(a, b) that checks whether two lists have the same elements in some order, ignoring duplicates. For example, the two lists

1 4 9 16 9 7 4 9 11

and

11 11 7 9 16 4 1

would be considered identical. You will probably need one or more helper functions.

■■■ **P6.13** Write a function def sameElements(a, b) that checks whether two lists have the same elements in some order, with the same multiplicities. For example,

1 4 9 16 9 7 4 9 11

and

11 1 4 9 16 9 7 4 9

would be considered identical, but

1 4 9 16 9 7 4 9 11

and

11 11 7 9 16 4 1 4 9

would not. You will probably need one or more helper functions.

■■ **P6.14** Modify the program in Worked Example 6.2 to use randomly-generated numbers for the die values instead of reading them from the user.

■■ **P6.15** A *run* is a sequence of adjacent repeated values. Write a program that generates a sequence of 20 random die tosses, stores them in a list, and prints the die values, marking the runs by including them in parentheses, like this:

1 2 (5 5) 3 1 2 4 3 (2 2 2 2) 3 6 (5 5) 6 3 1

Use the following pseudocode:

inRun = False
For each valid index i in the list
    If inRun
        If values[i] is different from the preceding value
            Print).
            inRun = False
    If not inRun

> *If values[i] is the same as the following value*
> > *Print (.*
> > *inRun = True*
> *Print values[i].*
> *If inRun, print).*

■■ **P6.16** Write a program that generates a sequence of 20 random die tosses, stores them in a list, and prints the die values, marking only the longest run, like this:

> 1 2 5 5 3 1 2 4 3 (2 2 2 2) 3 6 5 5 6 3 1

If there is more than one run of maximum length, mark the first one.

■■ **P6.17** Write a program that generates a sequence of 20 random values between 0 and 99, stores them in a list, prints the sequence, sorts it, and prints the sorted sequence. Use the list sort method.

■■■ **P6.18** Write a program that produces ten random permutations of the numbers 1 to 10. To generate a random permutation, you need to fill a list with the numbers 1 to 10 so that no two entries of the list have the same contents. You could do it by brute force, by generating random values until you have a value that is not yet in the list. But that is inefficient. Instead, follow this algorithm.

> *Make a second list and fill it with the numbers 1 to 10.*
> *Repeat 10 times*
> > *Pick a random position in the second list.*
> > *Remove the element at the position from the second list.*
> > *Append the removed element to the permutation list.*

■■ **P6.19** It is a well-researched fact that men in a rest room generally prefer to maximize their distance from already occupied stalls, by occupying the middle of the longest sequence of unoccupied places.

For example, consider the situation where ten stalls are empty.

_ _ _ _ _ _ _ _ _ _

The first visitor will occupy a middle position:

_ _ _ _ _ X _ _ _ _

The next visitor will be in the middle of the empty area at the left.

_ _ X _ _ X _ _ _ _

Write a program that reads the number of stalls and then prints out diagrams in the format given above when the stalls become filled, one at a time. *Hint:* Use a list of Boolean values to indicate whether a stall is occupied.

■■■ **P6.20** In this assignment, you will model the game of *Bulgarian Solitaire*. The game starts with 45 cards. (They need not be playing cards. Unmarked index cards work just as well.) Randomly divide them into some number of piles of random size. For example, you might start with piles of size 20, 5, 1, 9, and 10. In each round, you take one card from each pile, forming a new pile with these cards. For example, the sample starting configuration would be transformed into piles of size 19, 4, 8, 9, and 5. The solitaire is over when the piles have size 1, 2, 3, 4, 5, 6, 7, 8, and 9, in some order. (It can be shown that you always end up with such a configuration.)

In your program, produce a random starting configuration and print it. Then keep applying the solitaire step and print the result. Stop when the solitaire final configuration is reached.

■■■ **P6.21**   *Magic squares.* An $n \times n$ matrix that is filled with the numbers 1, 2, 3, ..., n^2 is a magic square if the sum of the elements in each row, in each column, and in the two diagonals is the same value.

Write a program that reads in 16 values from the keyboard and tests whether they form a magic square when put into a 4×4 table. You need to test two features:

16	3	2	13
5	10	11	8
9	6	7	12
4	15	14	1

1. Does each of the numbers 1, 2, ..., 16 occur in the user input?

2. When the numbers are put into a square, are the sums of the rows, columns, and diagonals equal to each other?

■■■ **P6.22**   Implement the following algorithm to construct magic $n \times n$ squares; it works only if n is odd. Here is the 5×5 square that you get if you follow this algorithm:

Set row = n − 1, column = n // 2.
For k = 1 ... n * n
    Place k at [row][column].
    Increment row and column.
    If the row or column is n, replace it with 0.
    If the element at [row][column] has already been filled
        Set row and column to their previous values.
        Decrement row.

11	18	25	2	9
10	12	19	21	3
4	6	13	20	22
23	5	7	14	16
17	24	1	8	15

Write a program whose input is the number n and whose output is the magic square of order n if n is odd.

■■ **P6.23**   Write a function def neighborAverage(values, row, column) that computes the average of the neighbors of a table element in the eight directions shown in Figure 14. However, if the element is located at the boundary of the table, only include the neighbors that are in the table. For example, if row and column are both 0, there are only three neighbors.

■■ **P6.24**   Write a program that reads a sequence of input values and displays a bar chart of the values, using asterisks, like this:

```
**********************
******************************************
****************************
***************************
*************
```

You may assume that all values are positive. First figure out the maximum value. That value's bar should be drawn with 40 asterisks. Shorter bars should use proportionally fewer asterisks.

■■■ **P6.25**   Improve the program of Exercise •• P6.24 to work correctly when the data set contains negative values.

■■ **P6.26**   Improve the program of Exercise •• P6.24 by adding captions for each bar. Prompt the user for the captions and data values. The output should look like this:

```
      Egypt **********************
     France ****************************************
      Japan ***************************
    Uruguay **************************
Switzerland *************
```

•• P6.27 A theater seating chart is implemented as a table of ticket prices, like this:

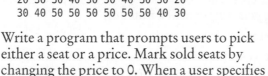

```
10 10 10 10 10 10 10 10 10 10
10 10 10 10 10 10 10 10 10 10
10 10 10 10 10 10 10 10 10 10
10 10 20 20 20 20 20 20 10 10
10 10 20 20 20 20 20 20 10 10
10 10 20 20 20 20 20 20 10 10
20 20 30 30 40 40 30 30 20 20
20 30 30 40 50 50 40 30 30 20
30 40 50 50 50 50 50 50 40 30
```

© lepas2004/iStockphoto.

Write a program that prompts users to pick either a seat or a price. Mark sold seats by changing the price to 0. When a user specifies a seat, make sure it is available. When a user specifies a price, find any seat with that price.

••• P6.28 Write a program that plays tic-tac-toe. The tic-tac-toe game is played on a 3 × 3 grid as in the photo at right.

The game is played by two players, who take turns. The first player marks moves with a circle, the second with a cross. The player who has formed a horizontal, vertical, or diagonal sequence of three marks wins. Your program should draw the game board, ask the user for the coordinates of the next mark, change the players after every successful move, and pronounce the winner.

© Kathy Muller/iStockphoto.

• P6.29 Write a function def appendList(a, b) that appends one list after another. For example, if a is

$$1 \quad 4 \quad 9 \quad 16$$

and b is

$$9 \quad 7 \quad 4 \quad 9 \quad 11$$

then appendList returns a new list containing the values

$$1 \quad 4 \quad 9 \quad 16 \quad 9 \quad 7 \quad 4 \quad 9 \quad 11$$

•• P6.30 Write a function def merge(a, b) that merges two lists, alternating elements from both lists. If one list is shorter than the other, then alternate as long as you can and then append the remaining elements from the longer list. For example, if a is

$$1 \quad 4 \quad 9 \quad 16$$

and b is

$$9 \quad 7 \quad 4 \quad 9 \quad 11$$

then merge returns a new list containing the values

$$1 \quad 9 \quad 4 \quad 7 \quad 9 \quad 4 \quad 16 \quad 9 \quad 11$$

•• P6.31 Write a function def mergeSorted(a, b) that merges two *sorted* lists, producing a new sorted list. Keep an index into each list, indicating how much of it has been processed already. Each time, append the smallest unprocessed element from either list, then advance the index. For example, if a is

$$1 \quad 4 \quad 9 \quad 16$$

and b is

4 7 9 9 11

then mergeSorted returns a new list containing the values

1 4 4 7 9 9 9 11 16

•• Business P6.32 A pet shop wants to give a discount to its clients if they buy one or more pets and at least five other items. The discount is equal to 20 percent of the cost of the other items, but not the pets. Implement a function

```
def discount(prices, isPet, nItems)
```

The function receives information about a particular sale. For the ith item, prices[i] is the price before any discount, and isPet[i] is true if the item is a pet.

Write a program that prompts a cashier to enter each price and then a Y for a pet or N for another item. Use a price of –1 as a sentinel. Save the inputs in a list. Call the function that you implemented, and display the discount.

© joshblake/iStockphoto.

•• Business P6.33 A supermarket wants to reward its best customer of each day, showing the customer's name on a screen in the supermarket. For that purpose, the customer's purchase amount is stored in a list and the customer's name is stored in a corresponding list. Implement a function

```
def nameOfBestCustomer(sales, customers)
```

that returns the name of the customer with the largest sale.

Write a program that prompts the cashier to enter all prices and names, adds them to two lists, calls the function that you implemented, and displays the result. Use a price of 0 as a sentinel.

••• Business P6.34 Improve the program of Exercise •• Business P6.33 so that it displays the top customers, that is, the topN customers with the largest sales, where topN is a value that the user of the program supplies. Implement a function

```
def nameOfBestCustomers(sales, customers, topN)
```

If there were fewer than topN customers, include all of them.

••• Science P6.35 You are given a table of values that give the height of a terrain at different points in a square. Write a function

```
def floodMap(heights, waterLevel)
```

that prints out a flood map, showing which of the points in the terrain would be flooded if the water level was the given value. In the flood map, print a * for each flooded point and a space for each point that is not flooded.

Here is a sample map:

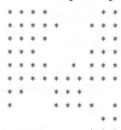

```
* * * *           * *
* * * * *         * * *
* * * *             * *
* * *               * *
* * * *         *   * * *
* * * * * * * * * * * *
* *         * * *
*           * * * *       *
                    * *
                  * * *
```

© nicolamargaret/iStockphoto.

Then write a program that reads one hundred terrain height values and shows how the terrain gets flooded when the water level increases in ten steps from the lowest point in the terrain to the highest.

•• **Science P6.36**   Sample values from an experiment often need to be smoothed out. One simple approach is to replace each value in a list with the average of the value and its two neighboring values (or one neighboring value if it is at either end of the list). Implement a function

```
def smooth(values, int size)
```

that carries out this operation. You should not create another list in your solution.

•• **Science P6.37**   Modify the ch06/exercises/animation.py program to show an animated sine wave. In the ith frame, shift the sine wave by $5 \times i$ degrees.

••• **Science P6.38**   Write a program that models the movement of an object with mass m that is attached to an oscillating spring. When a spring is displaced from its equilibrium position by an amount x, Hooke's law states that the restoring force is

$$F = -kx$$

where k is a constant that depends on the spring. (Use 10 N/m for this simulation.)

Start with a given displacement x (say, 0.5 meter). Set the initial velocity v to 0. Compute the acceleration a from Newton's law ($F = ma$) and Hooke's law, using a mass of 1 kg. Use a small time interval $\Delta t = 0.01$ second. Update the velocity—it changes by $a\Delta t$. Update the displacement—it changes by $v\Delta t$.

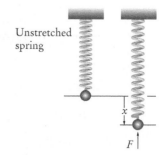

Every ten iterations, plot the spring displacement as a bar, where 1 pixel represents 1 cm. Use the technique in Section 2.6 for creating an image.

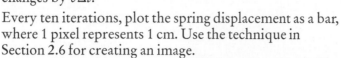

• **Toolbox P6.39**   Write a sound file that switches between the values 30,000 and –30,000, with each value repeated ten times before switching. Provide 44,100 values and set the sampling to 44,100. What sound do you get? Repeat with 15,000 and –15,000. What is the difference? What happens when you double the sampling rate? Cut it in half?

•• **Toolbox P6.40**   Write a program that reads a sound file and "fades in" the sound. Multiply the values of the first second with a factor that increases from 0 to 1.

■■ **Toolbox P6.41**   Repeat Exercise ●● Toolbox P6.40, but also fade out the sound at the end.

■ **Toolbox P6.42**   Write a program that reads two sound files and mixes them. Average the sound values. Your program should work even if the inputs have different lengths. You can assume that the inputs have the same sampling rate.

■■ **Toolbox P6.43**   Make the program of Exercise ● Toolbox P6.42 work if the inputs have different sampling rates. Use the higher of the two rates for the output.

■■ **Toolbox P6.44**   Write a program that reads a sound file and introduces an echo. For each data value, add 80 percent of the value from 0.2 seconds ago. When you are done, rescale the result so that no value is larger than 32,787.

■ **Toolbox P6.45**   Write a program that reads a sound file, reverses all values, and saves the result. Try it out with the recording of speech or a song.

■■■ **Toolbox P6.46**   Using the Audacity program described in Toolbox 6.1, produce recordings of yourself saying one, two, three, …, nine, ten, eleven, twelve, teen, twenty, thirty, …, fifty. Then write a program that asks the user to supply a time such as 9:53, and that produces a file announcing that time. In this example, you would put together the sounds for nine, fifty, and three.

■■ **Toolbox P6.47**   Write a program that reads in a stereo sound file and turns it to mono by averaging the left and right channel. When you read in the data and convert to a list, you will get a list of lists, each of which contains a data value for the left and right channel. *Hint:* To understand the format, use interactive mode (see Programming Tip 1.1) to load a stereo file, as described in Toolbox 6.1. Display the data list and observe that its elements are lists of length 2.

■■ **Toolbox P6.48**   Write a program that reads in a stereo sound file and flips the left and right channels. Test it with a file that has a noisy object moving from the left to the right.

■■ **Toolbox P6.49**   Write a program that reads in a stereo sound file and produces a mono file that contains (left - right) / 2 for each sample. Test it with sound files of songs. If the file records the singer's voice equally in both channels, the result will contain the instrumental music and remove the vocals!

James King-Holmes/Bletchley Park Trust/Photo Researchers, Inc.

CHAPTER 7

FILES AND EXCEPTIONS

In this chapter, you will learn how to read and write files—a very useful skill for processing real world data. As an application, you will learn how to encrypt data. (The Enigma machine shown at left is an encryption device used by Germany in World War II. Pioneering British computer scientists broke the code and were able to intercept encoded messages, which was a significant help in winning the war.) The remainder of this chapter tells you how your programs can report and recover from problems, such as missing files or malformed content, using the exception-handling mechanism of the Python language.

7.1 Reading and Writing Text Files

We begin this chapter by discussing the common task of reading and writing files that contain text. Examples of text files include not only files created with a simple text editor, such as Windows Notepad, but also Python source code and HTML files.

In the following sections, you will learn how to process data from files. File processing is a very useful skill in many disciplines because it is so common that large data sets to be analyzed or manipulated are stored in files.

7.1.1 Opening a File

To open a file, supply the name of the file stored on disk and the mode in which the file is to be opened.

To access a file, you must first *open* it. When you open a file, you give the name of the file, or, if the file is stored in a different directory, the file name preceded by the directory path. You also specify whether the file is to be opened for reading or writing. Suppose you want to read data from a file named input.txt, located in the same directory as the program. Then you use the following function call to open the file:

```
infile = open("input.txt", "r")
```

This statement opens the file for reading (indicated by the string argument "r") and returns a *file object* that is associated with the file named input.txt. When opening a file for reading, the file must exist or an exception occurs. Later in the chapter we will explore how to detect and handle exceptions.

The file object returned by the open function must be saved in a variable. All operations for accessing a file are made via the file object.

To open a file for writing, you provide the name of the file as the first argument to the open function and the string "w" as the second argument:

```
outfile = open("output.txt", "w")
```

If the output file already exists, it is emptied before the new data is written into it. If the file does not exist, an empty file is created. When you are done processing a file, be sure to *close* the file using the close method:

```
infile.close()
outfile.close()
```

If your program exits without closing a file that was opened for writing, some of the output may not be written to the disk file.

Syntax 7.1 Opening and Closing Files

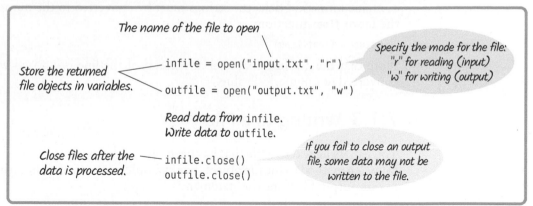

The name of the file to open

Store the returned
file objects in variables.

```
infile = open("input.txt", "r")

outfile = open("output.txt", "w")
```

Specify the mode for the file:
"r" for reading (input)
"w" for writing (output)

Read data from `infile`.
Write data to `outfile`.

Close files after the
data is processed.

```
infile.close()
outfile.close()
```

If you fail to close an output
file, some data may not be
written to the file.

**Close all files
when you are done
processing them.**

After a file has been closed, it cannot be used again until it has been reopened.
Attempting to do so will result in an exception.

7.1.2 Reading from a File

**Use the readline
method to obtain
lines of text from
a file.**

To read a line of text from a file, call the `readline` method on the file object that was
returned when you opened the file:

```
line = infile.readline()
```

When a file is opened, an input marker is positioned at the beginning of the file. The
`readline` method reads the text, starting at the current position and continuing until
the end of the line is encountered. The input marker is then moved to the next line.
The `readline` method returns the text that it read, including the newline character that
denotes the end of the line. For example, suppose `input.txt` contains the lines

```
flying
circus
```

The first call to `readline` returns the string `"flying\n"`. Recall that `\n` denotes the newline character that indicates the end of the line. If you call `readline` a second time, it
returns the string `"circus\n"`. Calling `readline` again yields the empty string `""` because
you have reached the end of the file.

If the file contains a blank line, then `readline` returns a string containing only the
newline character `"\n"`.

Reading multiple lines of text from a file is very similar to reading a sequence of
values with the `input` function. You repeatedly read a line of text and process it until
the sentinel value is reached:

```
line = infile.readline()
while line != "" :
    Process the line.
    line = infile.readline()
```

The sentinel value is an empty string, which is returned by the `readline` method after
the end of file has been reached.

As with the `input` function, the `readline` method can return only strings. If the file contains numerical data, the strings must be converted to the numerical value using the `int` or `float` function:

```
value = float(line)
```

Note that the newline character at the end of the line is ignored when the string is converted to a numerical value.

7.1.3 Writing to a File

You can write text to a file that has been opened for writing. This is done by applying the `write` method to the file object. For example, we can write the string `"Hello, World!"` to our output file using the statement:

```
outfile.write("Hello, World!\n")
```

As you learned in Chapter 1, the `print` function adds a newline character at the end of its output to start a new line. When writing text to an output file, however, you must explicitly write the newline character to start a new line.

The `write` method takes a single string as an argument and writes the string immediately. That string is appended to the end of the file, following any text previously written to the file.

You can also write formatted strings to a file with the `write` method:

```
outfile.write("Number of entries: %d\nTotal: %8.2f\n" % (count, total))
```

Alternatively, you can write text to a file with the `print` function. Supply the file object as an argument with name `file`, as follows:

```
print("Hello, World!", file=outfile)
```

If you don't want a newline, use the `end` argument:

```
print("Total: ", end="", file=outfile)
```

7.1.4 A File Processing Example

Here is a typical example of processing data from a file. Suppose you are given a text file that contains a sequence of floating-point values, stored one value per line. You need to read the values and write them to a new output file, aligned in a column and followed by their total and average value. If the input file has the contents

```
32.0
54.0
67.5
29.0
35.0
80.25
115.0
```

then the output file should contain

```
  32.00
  54.00
  67.50
  29.00
  35.00
  80.25
```

```
                115.00
               --------
   Total:      412.75
   Average:     58.96
```

The following program accomplishes this task.

sec01/total.py

```python
1  ##
2  #   This program reads a file containing numbers and writes the numbers to
3  #   another file, lined up in a column and followed by their total and average.
4  #
5
6  # Prompt the user for the name of the input and output files.
7  inputFileName = input("Input file name: ")
8  outputFileName = input("Output file name: ")
9
10 # Open the input and output files.
11 infile = open(inputFileName, "r")
12 outfile = open(outputFileName, "w")
13
14 # Read the input and write the output.
15 total = 0.0
16 count = 0
17
18 line = infile.readline()
19 while line != "" :
20    value = float(line)
21    outfile.write("%15.2f\n" % value)
22    total = total + value
23    count = count + 1
24    line = infile.readline()
25
26 # Output the total and average.
27 outfile.write("%15s\n" % "--------")
28 outfile.write("Total: %8.2f\n" % total)
29
30 avg = total / count
31 outfile.write("Average: %6.2f\n" % avg)
32
33 # Close the files.
34 infile.close()
35 outfile.close()
```

Common Error 7.1

Backslashes in File Names

When you specify a file name as a string literal, and the name contains backslash characters (as in a Windows file name), you must supply each backslash twice:

```python
infile = open("c:\\homework\\input.txt", "r")
```

A single backslash inside a quoted string is an **escape character** that is combined with the following character to form a special meaning, such as \n for a newline character. The \\ combination denotes a single backslash.

When a program user supplies a file name to a program, however, the user should not type the backslash twice.

7.2 Text Input and Output

In the following sections, you will learn how to process files with complex contents, and you will learn how to cope with challenges that often occur with real data.

7.2.1 Iterating over the Lines of a File

You can iterate over a file object to read the lines of text in the file.

You have seen how to read a file one line at a time. However, there is a simpler way. Python can treat an input file as though it were a container of strings in which each line is an individual string. To read the lines of text from the file, you can iterate over the file object using a for loop.

For example, the following loop reads all lines from a file and prints them:

```
for line in infile :
    print(line)
```

At the beginning of each iteration, the loop variable line is assigned a string that contains the next line of text in the file. Within the body of the loop, you simply process the line of text. In the loop above, we printed the line to the terminal.

There is one key difference between a file and a container, however. Once the file has been read, you cannot iterate over the file again without first closing and reopening the file.

As you saw in Section 7.1.2, each input line ends with a newline (\n) character. That is a bit unfortunate. For example, suppose we have an input file that contains a collection of words, stored one per line

```
spam
and
eggs
```

When the lines of input are printed to the terminal, they will be displayed with a blank line between each word:

```
spam

and

eggs
```

Remember, the print function prints its argument to the terminal and then starts a new line by printing a newline character. Because each line ends with a newline character, the second newline creates a blank line in the output.

Use the rstrip method to remove the newline character from a line of text.

Generally, the newline character must be removed before the input string is used. When the first line of the text file is read, the string line contains

$$\boxed{s}\ \boxed{p}\ \boxed{a}\ \boxed{m}\ \boxed{\backslash n}$$

To remove the newline character, apply the rstrip method to the string

```
line = line.rstrip()
```

which results in the new string

$$\boxed{s}\ \boxed{p}\ \boxed{a}\ \boxed{m}$$

By default, the `rstrip` method creates a new string in which all white space (blanks, tabs, and newlines) at the end of the string has been removed. For example, if there are two blank spaces following the word eggs in the third line of text

```
e  g  g  s        \n
```

the `rstrip` method will remove not only the newline character but also the blank spaces:

```
e  g  g  s
```

To remove specific characters from the end of a string, you can pass a string argument containing those characters to the `rstrip` method. For example, if we need to remove a period or a question mark from the end of string, we can use the command

```
line = line.rstrip(".?")
```

See Table 1 for additional string methods that can be used to strip characters from a string and Table 2 for examples of their use.

Table 1 Character Stripping Methods

Method	Returns
s.lstrip() s.lstrip(*chars*)	A new version of *s* in which white space (blanks, tabs, and newlines) is removed from the left (the front) of *s*. If provided, characters in the string *chars* are removed instead of white space.
s.rstrip() s.rstrip(*chars*)	Same as lstrip except characters are removed from the right (the end) of *s*.
s.strip() s.strip(*chars*)	Similar to lstrip and rstrip, except characters are removed from the front and end of *s*.

Table 2 Character Stripping Examples

Statement	Result	Comment
string = "James\n" result = string.rstrip()	James	The newline character is stripped from the end of the string.
string = "James \n" result = string.rstrip()	James	Blank spaces are also stripped from the end of the string.
string = "James \n" result = string.rstrip("\n")	James	Only the newline character is stripped.
name = " Mary " result = name.strip()	Mary	The blank spaces are stripped from the front and end of the string.
name = " Mary " result = name.lstrip()	Mary	The blank spaces are stripped only from the front of the string.

7.2.2 Reading Words

Sometimes you may need to read the individual words from a text file. For example, suppose our input file contains two lines of text

```
Mary had a little lamb,
whose fleece was white as snow.
```

that we would like to print to the terminal, one word per line

```
Mary
had
a
little
. . .
```

Because there is no method for reading a word from a file, you must first read a line and then split it into individual words. This can be done using the split method:

```
wordList = line.split()
```

The split method returns the list of substrings that results from splitting the string at each blank space. For example, if line contains the string

```
line =  M a r y    h a d    a    l i t t l e    l a m b ,
```

it will be split into 5 substrings that are stored in a list in the same order in which they occur in the string:

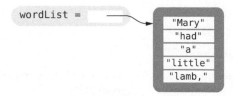

```
wordList =
                              "Mary"
                              "had"
                              "a"
                              "little"
                              "lamb,"
```

The blank spaces are not part of the substrings. They only act as the delimiters for where the string will be split. After splitting the string, you can iterate over the list of substrings to print the individual words

```
for word in wordList :
    print(word)
```

Notice that the last word in the line contains a comma. If we only want to print the words contained in the file without punctuation marks, then we can strip those from the substrings using the rstrip method introduced in the previous section:

```
word = word.rstrip(".,?!")
```

The complete solution for our original task is:

```
inputFile = open("lyrics.txt", "r")
for line in inputFile :
   line = line.rstrip()
   wordList = line.split()
   for word in wordList :
      word = word.rstrip(".,?!")
      print(word)

inputFile.close()
```

Use the split method to split a string into individual words.

The `split` method treats consecutive blank spaces as a single delimiter. Thus, if the string contains multiple spaces between some or all of the words,

line = `M a r y     h a d   a     l i t t l e   l a m b ,`

`line.split()` would still result in the same five substrings:

   `"Mary" "had" "a" "little" "lamb,"`

By default, the `split` method uses white space characters as the delimiter. You can also split a string using a different delimiter. For example, if the words were separated by a colon instead of blank spaces,

line = `a p p l e s : p e a r s : o r a n g e s : g r a p e s`

we can specify the colon as the delimiter to be used by the `split` method. The statement

   `substrings = line.split(":")`

splits the string into the four substrings

   `"apples" "pears" "oranges" "grapes"`

Note that when a delimiter is passed as an argument, consecutive delimiters are not treated as a single one, as was the case when no argument was supplied. Thus, the string

line = `a p p l e s : p e a r s : : g r a p e s`

would result in four substrings, with an empty string corresponding to the "word" between the two consecutive colons:

   `"apples" "pears" "" "grapes"`

Table 3 provides additional methods for splitting strings.

Table 3 String Splitting Methods

Method	Returns

`s.split()`
`s.split(sep)`
`s.split(sep, maxsplit)`
	Returns a list of words from string *s*. If the string *sep* is provided, it is used as the delimiter; otherwise, any white space character is used. If *sep* contains more than one character, then each character is treated as a separator. If *maxsplit* is provided, then only that number of splits will be made, resulting in at most *maxsplit* + 1 words.

`s.rsplit(sep, maxsplit)`	Same as `split` except the splits are made starting from the end of the string instead of from the front.
`s.splitlines()`	Returns a list containing the individual lines of a string split using the newline character `\n` as the delimiter.

Table 4 String Splitting Examples

Statement	Result	Comment
`string = "a,bc,d"` `string.split(",")`	`"a" "bc" "d"`	The string is split at each comma.

Table 4 String Splitting Examples

Statement	Result	Comment
```string = "a b c"``` ```string.split()```	```"a" "b" "c"```	The string is split using the blank space as the delimiter. Consecutive blank spaces are treated as one space.
```string = "a b c"``` ```string.split(" ")```	```"a" "b" "" "c"```	The string is split using the blank space as the delimiter. With an explicit argument, the consecutive blank spaces are treated as separate delimiters.
```string = "a:bc:d"``` ```string.split(":", 1)```	```"a" "bc:d"```	The string is split into 2 parts starting from the front. The split is made at the first colon.
```string = "a:bc:d"``` ```string.rsplit(":", 1)```	```"a:bc" "d"```	The string is split into 2 parts starting from the end. The split is made at the last colon.

7.2.3 Reading Characters

Read one or more characters with the read method.

Instead of reading an entire line, you can read individual characters with the read method. The read method takes a single argument that specifies the number of characters to read. The method returns a string containing the characters. When supplied with an argument of 1,

```
char = inputFile.read(1)
```

the read method returns a string consisting of the next character in the file. Or, if the end of the file is reached, it returns an empty string "". The following loop processes the contents of a file, one character at a time:

```
char = inputFile.read(1)
   while char != "" :
      Process character.
      char = inputFile.read(1)
```

Note that the read method will read and return the newline characters that terminate the individual lines as they are encountered.

Let us write a simple program that counts the number of times each letter of the English alphabet occurs in the lyrics.txt file from the previous section. Because there are 26 letters of the alphabet for which we must maintain a count, we can use a list of 26 counters represented by integer values.

```
letterCounts = [0] * 26    # Create a list with 26 elements initialized to 0.
```

The number of occurrences for letter "A" will be maintained in counts[0], the count for letter "B" in counts[1] and so on all the way through counts[25] for letter "Z".

Instead of using a large if/elif/else statement, we can use the ord function (see Special Topic 2.4) to return the Unicode value for each letter. The uppercase letters have codes in sequential order, from 65 for the letter A through 90 for the letter Z. By subtracting the code for the letter A, one obtains a value between 0 and 25 that can be used as an index to the letterCounts list:

```
code = ord(char) - ord("A")
letterCounts[code] = letterCounts[code] + 1
```

Note that all lowercase letters must be converted to uppercase before they are counted. The program that solves this task is provided below.

```
letterCounts = [0] * 26
inputFile = open("lyrics.txt", "r")
char = inputFile.read(1)
while char != "" :
    char = char.upper()    # Convert the character to uppercase.
    if char >= "A" and char <= "Z" :    # Make sure the character is a letter.
        code = ord(char) - ord("A")
        letterCounts[code] = letterCounts[code] + 1
        char = inputFile.read(1)
inputFile.close()
```

7.2.4 Reading Records

A text file can contain a collection of **data records** in which each record consists of multiple fields. For example, a file containing student data may consist of records composed of fields for an identification number, full name, address, and class year. A file containing bank account transactions may contain records composed of the transaction date, description, and amount fields.

When working with text files that contain data records, you generally have to read the entire record before you can process it:

For each record in the file
    Read the entire record.
    Process the record.

The organization or format of the records can vary, however, making some formats easier to read than others. Consider a simple example of a file with population data from the CIA Fact Book site (https://www.cia.gov/library/publications/the-world-factbook/index.html). Each record consists of two fields: the name of a country and its population. A typical format for such data is to store each field on a separate line of the file with all fields of a single record on consecutive lines:

```
China
1330044605
India
1147995898
United States
303824646
. . .
```

Reading the data in this format is rather easy. Because each record consists of two fields, we read two lines from the file for each record. This requires the use of the readline method and a while loop that checks for the end of file (the sentinel value):

```
line = infile.readline()       # Read the first field of the first record.
while line != "" :             # Check for end of file.
    countryName = line.rstrip() # Remove the \n character.
    line = infile.readline()    # Read the second field.
    population = int(line)      # Convert to an integer. The \n character is ignored.
    Process data record.
    line = infile.readline()    # Read the first field of the next record.
```

The first field of the first record has to be obtained as the "priming read" in case the file contains no records. Once inside the loop, the remaining fields of the record are read from the file. The newline character is stripped from the end of string fields, and strings containing numerical fields are converted to their appropriate type (here, int). At the end of the loop body, the first field of the next record is obtained as the "modification read".

Another common format stores each data record on a single line. If the record's fields are separated by a specific delimiter,

```
China:1330044605
India:1147995898
United States:303824646
. . .
```

you can extract the fields by splitting the line with the split method as described in Section 7.2.2.

```
for line in infile :
    fields = line.split(":")
    countryName = fields[0]
    population = int(fields[1])
    Process the record.
```

But what if the fields are not separated by a delimiter?

```
China 1330044605
India 1147995898
United States 303824646
. . .
```

Because some country names have more than one word, we cannot simply use a blank space as the delimiter because multi-word names would be split incorrectly. One approach for reading records in this format is to read the line, then search for the first digit in the string returned by readline:

```
i = 0
char = line[0]
while not line[0].isdigit() :
    i = i + 1
```

You can then extract the country name and population as substrings using the slice operator (see Special Topic 6.3):

```
countryName = line[0 : i - 1]
population = int(line[i : ])
```

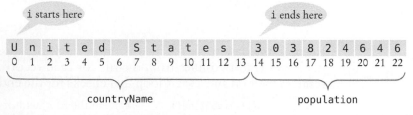

Alternatively, you can use the rsplit string method that splits a string starting from its right end. For example, if line contains the string

```
"United States 303824646"
```

the statement

```
fields = line.rsplit(" ", 1)
```

splits the string into two parts at the first blank space encountered starting from the end of the string.

Note that the substrings resulting from the `rsplit` method are stored in the list in the order in which they occur in the string.

Table 5 File Operations

Operation	Explanation
f = open(*filename*, *mode*)	Opens the file specified by the string *filename*. The *mode* parameter indicates whether the file is opened for reading ("r") or writing ("w"). A file object is returned.
f.close()	Closes a previously opened file. Once closed, the file cannot be used until it has been reopened.
string = f.readline()	Reads the next line of text from an input file and returns it as a string. An empty string "" is returned when the end of file is reached.
string = f.read(*num*) string = f.read()	Reads the next *num* characters from the input file and returns them as a string. An empty string is returned when all characters have been read from the file. If no argument is supplied, the entire contents of the file is read and returned in a single string.
f.write(*string*)	Writes the *string* to a file opened for writing.

Here is a program that reads and processes data records that contain text and numbers.

sec02/items.py

```
1  ##
2  #   This program reads a file whose lines contain items and prices, like this:
3  #   item name 1: price1
4  #   item name 2: price2
5  #   ...
6  #   Each item name is terminated with a colon.
7  #   The program writes a file in which the items are left-aligned and the
8  #   prices are right-aligned. The last line has the total of the prices.
9  #
10
11 # Prompt for the input and output file names.
12 inputFileName = input("Input file: ")
13 outputFileName = input("Output file: ")
14
15 # Open the input and output files.
16 inputFile = open(inputFileName, "r")
17 outputFile = open(outputFileName, "w")
18
19 # Read the input and write the output.
20 total = 0.0
```

```
21
22  for line in inputFile :
23      # Make sure there is a colon in the input line, otherwise skip the line.
24      if ":" in line :
25          # Split the record at the colon.
26          parts = line.split(":")
27
28          # Extract the two data fields.
29          item = parts[0]
30          price = float(parts[1])
31
32          # Increment the total.
33          total = total + price
34
35          # Write the output.
36          outputFile.write("%-20s%10.2f\n" % (item, price))
37
38  # Write the total price.
39  outputFile.write("%-20s%10.2f\n" % ("Total:", total))
40
41  # Close the files.
42  inputFile.close()
43  outputFile.close()
```

Special Topic 7.1

Reading the Entire File

There are two methods for reading an entire file. The call inputFile.read() returns a string with all characters in the file. The readlines method reads the entire contents of a text file into a list:

```
inputFile = open("sample.txt", "r")
listOfLines = inputFile.readlines()
inputFile.close()
```

Each element in the list returned by the readlines method is a string containing a single line from the file (including the newline character). Once the contents of the file are in the list, you can access lines in the list by position, as in listOfLines[2]. You can also iterate over the entire list:

```
for line in listOfLines :
    text = line.rstrip()
    print(text)
```

These methods are very useful when you need to load the contents of a small file. However, you should avoid using them for large files because they can require a large amount of memory to store all of the strings.

Special Topic 7.2

Regular Expressions

Regular expressions describe character patterns. For example, numbers have a simple form. They contain one or more digits. The regular expression describing numbers is [0-9]+. The set [0-9] denotes any digit between 0 and 9, and the + means "one or more".

The search commands of professional programming editors understand regular expressions. Moreover, several utility programs use regular expressions to locate matching text. A commonly used program that uses regular expressions is *grep* (which stands for "global regular expression print"). You can run grep from a command line environment. Grep is part of the UNIX operating system, and versions are available for Windows. It needs a regular expression and one or more files to search. When grep runs, it displays a set of lines that match the regular expression.

Suppose you want to find all magic numbers (see Programming Tip 2.2) in a file.

```
grep '[0-9]+' homework.py
```

lists all lines in the file homework.py that contain sequences of digits. That isn't terribly useful; lines with variable names x1 will be listed.

OK, you want sequences of digits that do *not* immediately follow letters:

```
grep '[^A-Za-z][0-9]+' homework.py
```

The set [^A-Za-z] denotes any characters that are *not* in the ranges A to Z and a to z. This works much better, and it shows only lines that contain actual numbers.

The re standard module contains a special version of the split function that accepts a regular expression to describe delimiters (the blocks of text that separate words). It takes the line to split as its second argument:

```
from re import split
line = "http://python.org"
regex = "[^A-Za-z]+"
tokens = split(regex, line)    # ["http", "python", "org"]
```

In this example, the string is split at all sequences of characters that are not letters.

For more information on regular expressions, consult one of the many tutorials on the Internet by pointing your search engine to "regular expression tutorial".

Special Topic 7.3

Character Encodings

A **character** (such as the letter A, the digit 0, the accented character é, the Greek letter π, the symbol $\int$, or the Chinese character 中) is encoded as a sequence of bytes. Each byte is a value between 0 and 255.

Unfortunately, the encoding is not uniform. In 1963, ASCII (the American Standard Code for Information Interchange) defined an encoding for 128 characters, which you can find in Appendix D. ASCII encodes all upper-and lowercase Latin letters and digits, as well as symbols such as + * %, as values between 0 and 127. For example, the code for the letter A is 65.

As different populations felt the need to encode their own alphabets, they designed their own codes. Many of them built upon ASCII, using the values in the range from 128 to 255 for their own language. For example, in Spain, the letter é was encoded as 233. But in Greece, the code 233 denoted the letter ι (a lowercase iota). As you can imagine, if a Spanish tourist named José sent an e-mail to a Greek hotel, this created a problem.

To resolve this issue, the design of Unicode was begun in 1987. As described in Computing & Society 2.1, each character in the world is given a unique integer value. However, there are still multiple encodings of those integers in binary. The most popular encoding is called UTF-8. It encodes each character as a sequence of one to four bytes. For example, an A is still 65, as in ASCII, but an é is 195 169.

The details of the encoding don't matter, as long as you specify that you want UTF-8 when you read and write a file.

As this book goes to print, the Windows and Macintosh operating systems have not yet made the switch to UTF-8. Python picks up the character encoding from the operating system (which in turn depends on the region in which the user lives). Unless you specifically request otherwise, the open function yields file objects that read and write files in that encoding. That's fine if your files contain only ASCII characters, or if the creator and the recipient use the same encoding. But if you need to process files with accented characters, Chinese characters, or special symbols, you should specifically request the UTF-8 encoding. Open a file with

```
infile = open("input.txt", "r", encoding="utf-8")
outfile = open("output.txt", "w", encoding="utf-8")
```

You may wonder why Python can't just figure out the character encoding. However, consider the string José. In UTF-8, that's 74 111 115 195 169. The first three bytes, for Jos, are in the ASCII range and pose no problem. But the next two bytes, 195 169, could be é in UTF-8 or Ã¡ in the traditional Spanish encoding. The interpreter doesn't understand Spanish, and it can't decide which encoding to choose. Therefore, you should always specify the UTF-8 encoding when you exchange files with users from other parts of the world.

TOOLBOX 7.1

Working with CSV Files

You have seen how to read and write text files and to process data stored in various formats, but what if you need to process data stored in a spreadsheet? For example, suppose you need to print a list of all the movies released in the 1990s from a spreadsheet filled with movie data, such as the one shown below.

	A	B	C	D
1	Detective Story	1951	William Wyler	
2	Airport 1975	1974	Jack Smight	
3	Hamlet	1996	Kenneth Branagh	
4	American Beauty	1999	Sam Mendes	
5	Bitter Moon	1992	Roman Polanski	
6	Million Dollar Baby	2004	Clint Eastwood	
7	Round Midnight	1986	Bertrand Tavernier	
8	Kiss of the Spider Woman	1985	Héctor Babenco	
9	Twin Falls Idaho	1999	Michael Polish	
10	Traffic	2000	Steven Soderbergh	
11				

Most spreadsheet applications store their data in proprietary file formats that cannot be accessed directly by other programs. Fortunately, most can save a copy of the data in a portable format known as *CSV* (Comma-Separated Values). A CSV file is simply a text file in which each row of the spreadsheet is stored as a line of text. The data values in each row are separated by commas. For example, the CSV file created from the spreadsheet shown above contains:

```
"Detective Story","1951","William Wyler"
"Airport 1975","1974","Jack Smight"
"Hamlet","1996","Kenneth Branagh"
"American Beauty","1999","Sam Mendes"
"Bitter Moon","1992","Roman Polanski"
"Million Dollar Baby","2004","Clint Eastwood"
"Round Midnight","1986","Bertrand Tavernier"
"Kiss of the Spider Woman","1985","Héctor Babenco"
"Twin Falls Idaho","1999","Michael Polish"
"Traffic","2000","Steven Soderbergh"
```

CSV files are so common that the Python standard library provides tools for working with them. In this section, we explore the csv module and how to work with CSV files in Python.

Reading a CSV File

To read the contents of a CSV file, you must first open the file as a regular text file,

```
infile = open("movies1.csv")
```

then create a CSV reader object using the reader function:

```
from csv import reader
csvReader = reader(infile)
```

You can use a for loop to iterate through the data in the CSV reader object. For example,

```
for row in csvReader :
    print(row)
```

reads and prints each row of data from the CSV file in this format:

```
['Detective Story', '1951', 'William Wyler']
['Airport 1975', '1974', 'Jack Smight']
. . .
['Kiss of the Spider Woman', '1985', 'Héctor Babenco']
['Twin Falls Idaho', '1999', 'Michael Polish']
['Traffic', '2000', 'Steven Soderbergh']
```

During each iteration of the loop, the data for one complete row is read from the file and stored in the loop variable row as a list of strings. For each row, the list can be processed like any other list. Here, we complete the original task of printing the titles of all movies that were released in the 1990s:

```
from csv import reader

# Open the text file and create a CSV reader.
infile = open("movies1.csv")
csvReader = reader(infile)

# Read the rows of data.
for row in csvReader :
    year = int(row[1])
    if year >= 1990 and year <= 1999 :
        print(row[0])
```

Because the data is read and stored as a list of strings, you have to convert numerical data to the appropriate numerical format before using those values. In our loop, we convert the year value to an integer before testing it.

You can skip a row by using Python's next function with the CSV reader. For example, if a spreadsheet contains descriptive information, such as a title or column headings, you can skip the row(s) containing that information:

```
next(csvReader)
```

Creating a CSV File

To create a CSV file from a Python program, first create a new text file using the open function:

```
outfile = open("newdata.csv", "w")
```

Then create a CSV writer using the writer function from the csv module:

```
from csv import writer
csvWriter = writer(outfile)
```

To add a row of data to the CSV file, use the writerow method. You pass a list of the row's data to this method. For example, to add a row of column headers, you would pass a list of strings, one for each column in the spreadsheet.

```
csvWriter.writerow(["Name", "Id", "Class", "Average"])
```

You can add numbers or a mixture of text and numbers:

```
csvWriter.writerow(["John Smith", 1607, "Senior", 3.28])
```

To skip a row in the CSV file, you pass an empty list to the writerow method.

```
csvWriter.writerow([])
```

After writing the data to the CSV file, you must remember to close the file:

```
outfile.close()
```

Processing a CSV File

Here is an example that illustrates both reading from and writing to a CSV file. Suppose you are given the task of creating a new CSV file that contains a limited amount of information from a much larger collection of movie data. Specifically, the new file should contain only the title, year of release, and list of the actors for those movies released in the 1990s. If the input CSV file contains the 5 columns

```
"Name","Year","Directors","Producers","Actors"
```

then the new file should contain only the first two and the last column of data and only those rows that contain movies from the 1990s, with the appropriate column headings.
The following program accomplishes this task.

toolbox_1/filter.py

```
 1  ##
 2  #   This program reads data from a csv file that contains movie information,
 3  #   filters out unwanted data, and produces a new csv file.
 4  #
 5
 6  from csv import reader, writer
 7
 8  # Open the two csv files.
 9  infile = open("movies.csv")
10  csvReader = reader(infile)
11
12  outfile = open("filtered.csv", "w")
13  csvWriter = writer(outfile)
14
15  # Add the list of column headers to the csv file.
16  headers = ["Name","Year","Actors"]
17  csvWriter.writerow(headers)
18
19  # Skip the row of column headers in the reader.
20  next(csvReader)
21
22  # Filter the rows of data.
23  for row in csvReader :
24    year = int(row[1])
25    if year >= 1990 and year <= 1999 :
26      newRow = [row[0], row[1], row[4]]
27      csvWriter.writerow(newRow)
28
29  infile.close()
30  outfile.close()
```

7.3 Command Line Arguments

Depending on the operating system and Python development environment used, there are different methods of starting a program—for example, by selecting "Run" in the development environment, by clicking on an icon, or by typing the name of the program at the prompt in a terminal window. The latter method is called "invoking the program from the command line". When you use this method, you must of course type the name of the program, but you can also type in additional information that the program can use. These additional strings are called **command line arguments**. For example, if you start a program with the command line

```
python program.py -v input.dat
```

then the program receives two command line arguments: the strings "-v" and "input. dat". It is entirely up to the program what to do with these strings. It is customary to interpret strings starting with a hyphen (-) as program options.

Should you support command line arguments for your programs, or should you prompt users, perhaps with a graphical user interface? For a casual and infrequent user, an interactive user interface is much better. The user interface guides the user along and makes it possible to navigate the application without much knowledge. But for a frequent user, a command line interface has a major advantage: it is easy to automate. If you need to process hundreds of files every day, you could spend all your time typing file names into file chooser dialog boxes. However, by using batch files or shell scripts (a feature of your computer's operating system), you can automatically call a program many times with different command line arguments.

Your program receives its command line arguments in the argv list defined in the sys module. In our example, the argv list has a length of 3 and contains the strings

```
argv[0]:    "program.py"
argv[1]:    "-v"
argv[2]:    "input.dat"
```

The first element (argv[0]) contains the name of the program, while the remaining elements contain the command-line arguments in the order they were specified.

Let us write a program that *encrypts* a file—that is, scrambles it so that it is unreadable except to those who know the decryption method. Ignoring 2,000 years of progress in the field of encryption, we will use a method familiar to Julius Caesar, replacing A with a D, B with an E, and so on (see Figure 1). Note that a Caesar cipher only modifies the upper- and lowercase letters. Spacing and punctuation marks are left unchanged.

> Programs that start from the command line receive the command line arguments in the argv list defined in the sys module.

The emperor Julius Caesar used a simple scheme to encrypt messages.

Plain text	M	e	e	t		m	e		a	t		t	h	e
	↓	↓	↓	↓		↓	↓		↓	↓		↓	↓	↓
Encrypted text	P	h	h	w		p	h		d	w		w	k	h

Figure 1
Caesar Cipher

The program takes the following command line arguments:

- An optional -d flag to indicate decryption instead of encryption
- The input file name
- The output file name

For example,

```
python cipher.py input.txt encrypt.txt
```

encrypts the file input.txt and places the result into encrypt.txt.

```
python cipher.py -d encrypt.txt output.txt
```

decrypts the file encrypt.txt and places the result into output.txt.

sec03/cipher.py

```
1   ##
2   #   This program encrypts a file using the Caesar cipher.
3   #
4
5   from sys import argv
6
7   DEFAULT_KEY = 3
8
9   def main() :
10     key = DEFAULT_KEY
11     infile = ""
12     outfile = ""
13
14     files = 0    # Number of command line arguments that are files.
15     for i in range(1, len(argv)) :
16        arg = argv[i]
17        if arg[0] == "-" :
18           # It is a command line option.
19           option = arg[1]
20           if option == "d" :
21              key = -key
22           else :
23              usage()
24              return
25
26        else :
27           # It is a file name.
28           files = files + 1
29           if files == 1 :
30              infile = arg
31           elif files == 2 :
32              outfile = arg
33
34     # There must be two files.
35     if files != 2 :
36        usage()
37        return
38
39     # Open the files.
40     inputFile = open(infile, "r")
41     outputFile = open(outfile, "w")
42
43     # Read the characters from the file.
44     for line in inputFile :
45        for char in line :
46           newChar = encrypt(char, key)
47           outputFile.write(newChar)
48
49     # Close the files.
50     inputFile.close()
51     outputFile.close()
52
53   ## Encrypts upper- and lowercase characters by shifting them according to a key.
54   #    @param ch  the letter to be encrypted
55   #    @param key  the encryption key
56   #    @return the encrypted letter
57   #
58   def encrypt(ch, key) :
59      LETTERS = 26    # Number of letters in the Roman alphabet.
```

```
60
61    if ch >= "A" and ch <= "Z" :
62        base = ord("A")
63    elif ch >= "a" and ch <= "z" :
64        base = ord("a")
65    else :
66        return ch      # Not a letter.
67
68    offset = ord(ch) - base + key
69    if offset > LETTERS :
70        offset = offset - LETTERS
71    elif offset < 0 :
72        offset = offset + LETTERS
73
74    return chr(base + offset)
75
76 ## Prints a message describing proper usage.
77 #
78 def usage() :
79    print("Usage: python cipher.py [-d] infile outfile")
80
81 # Start the program.
82 main()
```

HOW TO 7.1

Processing Text Files

Processing text files that contain real data can be surprisingly challenging. This How To gives you step-by-step guidance.

Problem Statement Read two country data files, `worldpop.txt` and `worldarea.txt` (in `how_to_1` in your companion code). Both files contain the same countries in the same order.

Write a file `world_pop_density.txt` that contains country names and population densities (people per square km), with the country names aligned left and the numbers aligned right:

```
Afghanistan           50.56
Akrotiri             127.64
Albania              125.91
Algeria               14.18
American Samoa       288.92
. . .
```

© Oksana Perkins/iStockphoto.

Singapore is one of the most densely populated countries in the world.

Step 1 Understand the processing task.

As always, you need to have a clear understanding of the task before designing a solution. Can you carry out the task by hand (perhaps with smaller input files)? If not, get more information about the problem.

One important aspect that you need to consider is whether you can process the data as it becomes available, or whether you need to store it first. For example, if you are asked to write out sorted data, you first need to collect all input, perhaps by placing it in a list. However, it is often possible to process the data "on the go", without storing it.

In our example, we can read each file a line at a time and compute the density for each line because our input files store the population and area data in the same order.

The following pseudocode describes our processing task.

> *While there are more lines to be read*
> *   Read a line from each file.*
> *   Extract the country name.*
> *   population = number following the country name in the line from the first file*
> *   area = number following the country name in the line from the second file*
> *   If area != 0*
> *   density = population / area*
> *   Print country name and density.*

Step 2   Determine which files you need to read and write.

This should be clear from the problem. In our example, there are two input files, the population data and the area data, and one output file.

Step 3   Choose a mechanism for obtaining the file names.

There are three options:

- Hard-coding the file names (such as `"worldpop.txt"`).
  ```
  filename = "worldpop.txt"
  ```
- Asking the user:
  ```
  filename = input("Enter filename: ")
  ```
- Using command-line arguments for the file names.

In our example, we use hard-coded file names for simplicity.

Step 4   Choose between iterating over the file or reading individual lines.

As a rule of thumb, iterate over the input data if the records are grouped by line. When gathering records in which the data is distributed over several lines, then you will need to read the individual lines and explicitly check for the end of file.

In our example, we have to read the individual lines because we are reading data from two input files. If we were only reading from one file, we could iterate over the file using a `for` loop.

Step 5   With line-oriented input, extract the required data.

It is simple to read the lines of input using a `for` loop. Then you need to extract the data for the individual fields. This can be done as described in Section 7.2.2. Typically, you can do this using either the `split` or `rsplit` methods.

Step 6   Use functions to factor out common tasks.

Processing input files usually has repetitive tasks, such as splitting strings and converting strings to numbers. It really pays off to develop functions to handle these tedious operations.

In our example, we have a common task that calls for a helper function: extracting the country name and the value that follows. Because both files have the same format, the name of the country followed by a value, we can use a single function to extract a data record. We will implement the function as described in Section 7.2.4:

```
extractDataRecord(infile)
```

Here is the complete source code.

how_to_1/population.py

```
1  ##
2  #   This program reads data files of country populations and areas and prints the
3  #   population density for each country.
4  #
```

```
5
6   POPULATION_FILE = "worldpop.txt"
7   AREA_FILE = "worldarea.txt"
8   REPORT_FILE = "world_pop_density.txt"
9
10  def main() :
11      # Open the files.
12      popFile = open(POPULATION_FILE, "r")
13      areaFile = open(AREA_FILE, "r")
14      reportFile = open(REPORT_FILE, "w")
15
16      # Read the first population data record.
17      popData = extractDataRecord(popFile)
18      while len(popData) == 2 :
19          # Read the next area data record.
20          areaData = extractDataRecord(areaFile)
21
22          # Extract the data components from the two lists.
23          country = popData[0]
24          population = popData[1]
25          area = areaData[1]
26
27          # Compute and print the population density.
28          density = 0.0
29          if area > 0 :    # Protect against division by zero.
30              density = population / area
31          reportFile.write("%-40s%15.2f\n" % (country, density))
32
33          # Read the next population data record.
34          popData = extractDataRecord(popFile)
35
36      # Close the files.
37      popFile.close()
38      areaFile.close()
39      reportFile.close()
40
41  ## Extracts and returns a record from an input file in which the data is
42  #  organized by line. Each line contains the name of a country (possibly
43  #  containing multiple words) followed by an integer (either population
44  #  or area for the given country).
45  #  @param infile the input text file containing the line oriented data
46  #  @return a list containing the country (string) in the first element
47  #  and the population (int) or area (int) in the second element. If the end of
48  #  file was reached, an empty list is returned
49  #
50  def extractDataRecord(infile) :
51      line = infile.readline()
52      if line == "" :
53          return []
54      else :
55          parts = line.rsplit(" ", 1)
56          parts[1] = int(parts[1])
57          return parts
58
59  # Start the program.
60  main()
```

WORKED EXAMPLE 7.1

Analyzing Baby Names

The Social Security Administration publishes lists of the most popular baby names on their web site at http://www.ssa.gov/OACT/babynames/. When you query the 1,000 most popular names for a given year, the browser displays the result on the screen (see the *Querying Baby Names* figure below).

To save the data as text, one simply selects it and pastes the result into a file. The companion code contains a file babynames.txt with the data for 2011.

Each line in the file contains five entries:

- The rank (from 1 to 1,000)
- The name and percentage of the male name of that rank

© Nancy Ross/iStockphoto.

- The name and percentage of the female name of that rank

For example, the line

```
6  Michael  0.8247%  Emily  0.7375%
```

shows that the 6th most common boy's name was Michael, with 0.8247 percent of the births in 2011. The 6th most common girl's name was Emily.

Problem Statement Why is Michael more common than Emily? Parents seem to use a wider set of girl's names, making each one of them less frequent. Your task is to test that conjecture, by determining the names given to the top 50 percent of boys and girls in the list. Simply print boy and girl names, together with their ranks, until you reach the 50 percent limit.

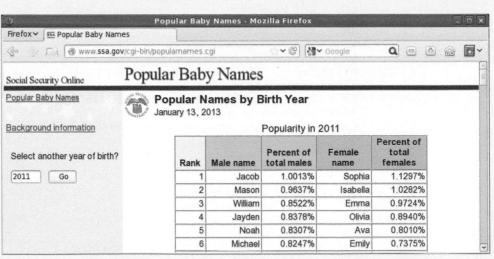

Querying Baby Names

Step 1 Understand the processing task.

To process each line, we read the entire line and split it at the blank spaces. We then extract the five values needed for the task at hand (rank, boy name, boy percentage, girl name, girl percentage), converting the rank to an integer and the percentages to floating-point values. To stop processing after reaching 50 percent, we can add up the percentages and stop when they reach 50 percent.

We need separate totals for boys and girls. When a total reaches 50 percent, we stop printing. When both totals reach 50 percent, we stop reading.

The following pseudocode describes our processing task:

boyTotal = 0
girlTotal = 0
While boyTotal < 50 or girlTotal < 50
    Read a line of values and split it.
    Extract the individual values.
    If boyTotal < 50
        Print boy name.
    Add percentage to boyTotal.
    Repeat for girl part.

Step 2   Determine which files you need to read and write.

We only need to read a single file, `babynames.txt`. We were not asked to save the output to a file, so we will just send it to the terminal.

Step 3   Choose a mechanism for obtaining the file names.

We do not need to prompt the user for the file name.

Step 4   Choose between iterating over the file or reading individual lines.

Since we will not be reading the entire file, but stopping when we reach 50 percent for either the boy names or the girl names, we need to read the individual lines. A `for` loop is used when you are iterating over the entire file.

Step 5   With line-oriented input, extract the required data.

We can split the input line into the five parts using the `split` method because none of the names contain spaces such as "Mary Jane". When extracting the rank and percentages, the rank has to be converted to an integer and the percentages have to be converted to floating-point values. We also need to strip the percent sign from the percentage string before converting it to a floating-point value.

Step 6   Use functions to factor out common tasks.

In the pseudocode, we wrote *Repeat for girl part.* Clearly, there is a common task that calls for a helper function. It involves two tasks:

Print the name if the total is less than 50 percent.
Add the percentage to the total.

The last task poses a technical problem. In Python, it is not possible for a function to update a number parameter. Therefore, our function will receive a total and return the updated value. The updated value is then stored, like this:

```
boyTotal = processName(boyName, boyPercent, boyTotal)
girlTotal = processName(girlName, girlPercent, girlTotal)
```

As you can see, the function also needs to receive the name and percentage. Here is the code of the function:

```
## Prints the name if total < LIMIT and adjusts the total.
#   @param name the boy or girl name
#   @param percent the percentage for this name
#   @param total the total percentage processed
#   @return the adjusted total
#
def processName(name, percent, total) :
    if total < LIMIT :
        print("%-15s" % name, end="")
```

```
      else :
         print("%-15s" % "", end="")
      total = total + percent
      return total
```

The complete program is shown below. Have a look at the program output. Remarkably, only 141 boy names and 324 girl names account for half of all births. That's good news for those who are in the business of producing personalized doodads. Exercise •• P7.10 asks you to study how this distribution changed over the years.

worked_example_1/babynames.py

```
1  ##
2  #  This program displays the most common baby names. Half of boys and girls in
3  #  the United States were given these names in 2011.
4  #
5
6  # The percentage limit to be extracted.
7  LIMIT = 50.0
8
9  def main() :
10     inputFile = open("babynames.txt", "r")
11
12     boyTotal = 0.0
13     girlTotal = 0.0
14     while boyTotal < LIMIT or girlTotal < LIMIT :
15        # Extract the data from the next line and split it.
16        line = inputFile.readline()
17        dataFields = line.split()
18
19        # Extract the individual field values.
20        rank = int(dataFields[0])
21        boyName = dataFields[1]
22        boyPercent = float(dataFields[2].rstrip("%"))
23        girlName = dataFields[3]
24        girlPercent = float(dataFields[4].rstrip("%"))
25
26        # Process the data.
27        print("%3d " % rank, end="")
28        boyTotal = processName(boyName, boyPercent, boyTotal)
29        girlTotal = processName(girlName, girlPercent, girlTotal)
30        print()
31
32     inputFile.close()
33
34  ## Prints the name if total < LIMIT and adjusts the total.
35  #  @param name the boy or girl name
36  #  @param percent the percentage for this name
37  #  @param total the total percentage processed
38  #  @return the adjusted total
39  #
40  def processName(name, percent, total) :
41     if total < LIMIT :
42        print("%-15s " % name, end="")
43     else :
44        print("%-15s " % "", end="")
45
46     total = total + percent
47     return total
48
```

```
49  # Start the program.
50  main()
```

Program Run

```
  1 Jacob        Sophia
  2 Mason        Isabella
  3 William      Emma
  4 Jayden       Olivia
  5 Noah         Ava
  6 Michael      Emily
  7 Ethan        Abigail
  8 Alexander    Madison
  9 Aiden        Mia
 10 Daniel       Chloe
...
140 Jaxson       Izabella
141 Jesse        Laila
142              Alice
143              Amy
...
321              Selena
322              Maddison
323              Giuliana
324              Emilia
```

TOOLBOX 7.2

Working with Files and Directories

The operating system is responsible for managing the file systems on your computer. When your program opens a file, Python uses tools provided by the operating system to handle that operation. Sometimes, you may need to do more than simply open a file. For example, suppose you want to obtain the contents of a directory or determine whether a file exists. In this Toolbox, you will learn to do this and more using the operating system tools provided by the os module in the Python standard library.

When you open a file in Python, the operating system looks for the file in the directory that contains your program. This is known as the *current working directory*. Sometimes it can be helpful to provide the user of your program with the name of the directory from which input and output files are going to be accessed. To get the name of the current working directory, use the function call

```
name = os.getcwd()
```

If the data files used by your program are stored in a different directory, such as reports, you can change the program's current working directory before opening a file:

```
subdir = "reports"
os.chdir(subdir)
```

As you learned earlier in the chapter, when a file is opened for input, it must exist or an exception is raised. You can test to see whether a file exists without first opening it. The exists function takes the name of a file as its argument and returns a Boolean indicating whether the file exists:

```
filename = "scores.txt"
if os.path.exists(filename) :
    inputFile = open(filename)
```

This function comes in handy when prompting the user for the name of an input file. You can use it with a loop to repeatedly prompt for a file name until the name of an existing file is entered.

```
filename = input("Enter data file name: ")
while not os.path.exists(filename) :
    print("Error: invalid file name!")
    filename = input("Enter data file name: ")
```

You can further improve the usability of your programs by providing a list of the contents of the current directory before prompting for a file name. The listdir function

```
contents = os.listdir()
```

returns a list of strings, one for each file in the current directory. After obtaining the list of file names, you can iterate over the list and print the strings

```
for filename in contents :
    print(filename)
```

To obtain a list of the files in a different directory, you pass the name of the directory as an argument to the listdir function:

```
contents = os.listdir("reports")
```

The listdir function not only returns the names of the files in a directory, but also the names of any subdirectories. When displaying a list of file names from which the user should choose, you would not typically include the names of directories.

You can test to see whether a string in the list is the name of a file

```
if os.path.isfile(filename) :
    print(filename, "is a file.")
```

or of a directory

```
if os.path.isdir(filename) :
    print(filename, "is a directory.")
```

Table 6 lists other useful functions for working with files. Almost all of them are in the os and os.path modules. However, the function for copying a file is in the shutil module.

The following program prints the names of all GIF image files in the current directory and its subdirectories. Traversing the contents of an entire file system or multiple directory levels is more advanced and requires the use of recursion (see Worked Example 11.1).

toolbox_2/listgifs.py

```
1  ##
2  #   This program prints the names of all GIF image files in the current directory
3  #   and the subdirectories of the current directory.
4  #
5
6  import os
7
8  print("Image Files:")
9
10 # Get the contents of the current directory.
11 dirName = os.getcwd()
12 contents = os.listdir()
13 for name in contents :
14     # If the entry is a directory, repeat on its contents.
15     if os.path.isdir(name) :
16         for name2 in os.listdir(name) :
```

```
17        entry = os.path.join(name, name2)
18        # If it is a file ending in .gif, print it.
19        if os.path.isfile(entry) and name2.endswith(".gif") :
20            print(os.path.join(dirName, entry))
21
22    # Otherwise, it's a file. If the name ends in .gif, print it.
23    elif name.endswith(".gif") :
24        print(os.path.join(dirName, name))
```

Table 6 Functions in the os, os.path, and shutil Modules

Function	Description
os.chdir(*dirname*)	Changes the current working directory.
os.getcwd()	Returns the name of the current working directory.
os.listdir() os.listdir(*dirname*)	Returns a list containing the names of the files and directories in the current working directory or the specified directory.
os.rename(*source*, *dest*)	Renames a file. The *source* is renamed to *dest*.
os.remove(*filename*)	Deletes an existing file.
os.path.exists(*name*)	Returns a Boolean indicating whether a file or directory exists.
os.path.isdir(*name*)	Returns a Boolean indicating whether the given *name* is that of a directory.
os.path.isfile(*name*)	Returns a Boolean indicating whether the given *name* is that of a file.
os.path.join(*path*, *name*)	Returns a string that results from appending a file name to a directory name, including the appropriate path separator.
shutil.copy(*source*, *dest*)	Copies the file whose name is given in the string *source* to the directory or file whose name is given in *dest*.

Computing & Society 7.1 Encryption Algorithms

This chapter's exercise section gives a few algorithms for encrypting text. Don't actually use any of those methods to send secret messages to your lover. Any skilled cryptographer can *break* these schemes in a very short time—that is, reconstruct the original text without knowing the secret keyword.

In 1978, Ron Rivest, Adi Shamir, and Leonard Adleman introduced an encryption method that is much more powerful. The method is called *RSA encryption*, after the last names of its inventors. The exact scheme is too complicated to present here, but it is not actually difficult to follow. You can find the details in https://people. csail.mit.edu/rivest/Rsapaper.pdf.

RSA is a remarkable encryption method. There are two keys: a public key and a private key (see the figure below). You can print the public key on your business card (or in your e-mail signature block) and give it to anyone. Then anyone can send you messages that only you can decrypt. Even though everyone else knows the public key, and even if they intercept all the messages coming to you, they cannot break the scheme and actually read the messages. With today's technology, the RSA algorithm is expected to be unbreakable provided that the keys are long enough. However, it is possible that "quantum computers" may be able to crack RSA in the future.

The inventors of the algorithm obtained a *patent* for it. A patent is a deal that society makes with an inventor. For a period of 20 years, the inventor has an exclusive right to its commercialization, may collect royalties from others wishing to manufacture the invention, and may even stop competitors from using it altogether. In return, the inventor must publish the invention, so that others may learn from it, and must relinquish all claim to it after the monopoly period ends. The presumption is that in the absence of patent law, inventors would be reluctant to go through the trouble of inventing, or they would try to cloak their techniques to prevent others from copying their devices.

There has been some controversy about the RSA patent. Had there not been patent protection, would the inventors have published the method anyway, thereby giving the benefit to society without the cost of the 20-year monopoly? In this case, the answer is probably yes. The inventors were academic researchers, who live on salaries rather than sales receipts and are usually rewarded for their discoveries by a boost in their reputation and careers. Would their followers have been as active in discovering (and patenting) improvements? There is no way of knowing, of course. Is an algorithm even patentable, or is it a mathematical fact that belongs to nobody? The patent office took the latter attitude for a long time. The RSA inventors and many others described their inventions in terms of imaginary electronic devices, rather than algorithms, to circumvent that restriction. Nowadays, the patent office will award software patents.

The existence of strong encryption methods bothers governments to no end. Criminals and foreign agents can send communications that the police and intelligence agencies cannot decipher. Devices such as cell phones use encryption so that thieves cannot read the information if the device is stolen. However, neither can government organizations. There have been serious proposals to make it illegal for private citizens to use these encryption methods, or to compel hardware and software makers to provide "back doors" that allow law enforcement access.

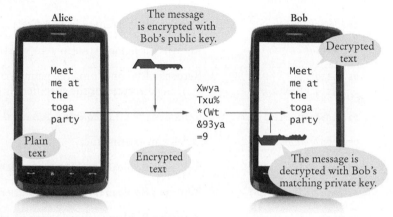

(mobile phone) © Anna Khomulo/iStockphoto.

Public-Key Encryption

7.4 Binary Files and Random Access (Optional)

In the following sections, you will learn how to process files that contain data other than text. You will also see how to read and write data at arbitrary positions in a file. As an application, we show you how to edit image files.

7.4.1 Reading and Writing Binary Files

There are two fundamentally different ways to store data: in text format or binary format. In text format, data items are represented in human-readable form as a sequence of characters. For example, in text form, the integer 12,345 is stored as the sequence of five characters:

```
"1" "2" "3" "4" "5"
```

In binary form, data items are represented in bytes. A byte is composed of 8 bits, each of which can be 0 or 1. A byte can denote one of 256 values ($256 = 2^8$). To represent larger values, one uses sequences of bytes. Integers are frequently stored as a sequence of four bytes. For example, the integer 123,456 can be stored as

```
64 226 1 0
```

(because $123{,}456 = 64 + 226 \cdot 256 + 1 \cdot 256^2 + 0 \cdot 256^3$). Files containing images and sounds usually store their information in binary format. **Binary files** save space: as you can see from our example, it takes fewer bytes than digits to store an integer.

If you load a binary file into a text editor, you will not be able to view its contents. Processing binary files requires programs written explicitly for reading or writing the binary data. We will use binary files that store images to illustrate the processing steps.

We have to cover a few technical issues about binary files. To open a binary file for reading, use the following command:

```
infile = open(filename, "rb")
```

> To open a binary file for reading, use the mode string "rb"; to open it for writing, use the mode string "wb".

Remember, the second argument to the open function indicates the mode in which the file will be opened. In this example, the mode string indicates that we are opening a binary file for reading. To open a binary file for writing, you would use the mode string "wb":

```
outfile = open(filename, "wb")
```

With a binary file, you don't read strings of text but rather the individual bytes. For example, you read four bytes with the call

```
theBytes = infile.read(4)
```

The byte value returned by this function is stored in a bytes sequence type. The elements in a bytes sequence are integer values between 0 and 255. To use the byte value itself, you must retrieve it from the bytes sequence using the subscript operator (just as if it were stored in a list):

```
value = theBytes[0]
```

If you want to read a single byte, you can combine these two steps into a single operation:

```
value = infile.read(1)[0]
```

You write one or more bytes to a binary file using the write method. The method requires a bytes sequence as its argument. To create the sequence, you use the bytes function with a list argument that contains the individual values:

```
theBytes = bytes([64, 226, 1, 0])
outfile.write(theBytes)
```

7.4.2 Random Access

> You can access any position in a random access file by moving the *file marker* prior to a read or write operation.

So far, you've read from a file one string at a time and written to a file one string at a time, without skipping forward or backward. That access pattern is called **sequential access**. In many applications, we would like to access specific items in a file without first having to first read all preceding items. This access pattern is called **random access**.

© Dominik Pabis/Getty Images, Inc.

At a sit-down dinner, food is served sequentially.
At a buffet, you have "random access" to all food items.

Figure 2
Sequential and Random Access

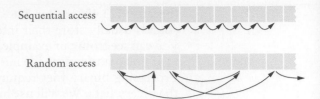

There is nothing "random" about random access—the term means that you can read and modify any item stored at any location in the file (see Figure 2).

Each file has a special marker that indicates the current position within the file. This marker is used to determine where the next string is read or written. You can move the file marker to a specific position within the file. To position the marker relative to the beginning of the file, you use the method call

```
infile.seek(position)
```

You can also move the marker relative to its current position. For example, to move the marker forward four bytes, you use a second version of the seek method, in which the second argument is SEEK_CUR, a constant defined in the io module.

```
infile.seek(4, SEEK_CUR)    # Move forward four bytes.
```

You can also move the marker backward using a negative value for the first argument:

```
infile.seek(-3, SEEK_CUR)    # Move backward three bytes.
```

To determine the current position of the file marker (counted from the beginning of the file), use

```
position = infile.tell()    # Get current position.
```

7.4.3 Image Files

Different types of image files use different layouts for the image information and pixel values.

In this section, you will learn about the file format for BMP image files. Unlike the more common GIF, PNG, and JPEG formats, the BMP format is quite simple because it does not use data compression. As a consequence, BMP files are huge and you will rarely find them in the wild. However, image editors can convert any image into BMP format.

There are different versions of the BMP format; we will only cover the simplest and most common one, sometimes called the 24-bit true color format. In this format, each pixel is represented as a sequence of three bytes, one each for the blue, green, and red value. For example, the color cyan (a mixture of blue and green) is 255 255 0, red is 0 0 255, and medium gray is 128 128 128.

A BMP file starts with a header that contains various pieces of information. We only need the following items:

Position	Item
2	The size of this file in bytes
10	The start of the image data
18	The width of the image in pixels
22	The height of the image in pixels

To read an integer from a BMP file, you need to read four bytes (b_0, b_1, b_2, b_3) and combine them into a single integer value using the equation

$$b_0 + b_1 \cdot 256 + b_2 \cdot 256^2 + b_3 \cdot 256^3$$

The Python code for this task is:

```python
theBytes = infile.read(4)   # Read the 4 bytes.
result = 0   # Store the resulting integer.
base = 1
# Iterate through the bytes sequence and compute the integer.
for i in range(4) :
    result = result + theBytes[i] * base
    base = base * 256
```

(Note that b_0 is the coefficient of 1 and b_3 is the coefficient of 256^3. This is called the "little-endian" byte order. Some file formats use the opposite byte order, called "big-endian", where the first byte is the coefficient of the highest power of 256. When processing a binary file, you have to find out which byte ordering is used.)

The image is stored as a sequence of pixel rows, starting with the pixels in the bottommost row of the image. Each pixel row contains a sequence of blue/green/red triplets. The end of the row is padded with additional bytes so that the number of bytes in the row is divisible by 4 (see Figure 3.) For example, if a row consisted of merely three pixels, one cyan, one red, and one medium gray, the row would be encoded as

255 255 0 0 0 255 128 128 128 x y z

where x y z are padding bytes to bring the row length up to 12, a multiple of 4. It is these little twists that make working with real-life file formats such a joyful experience.

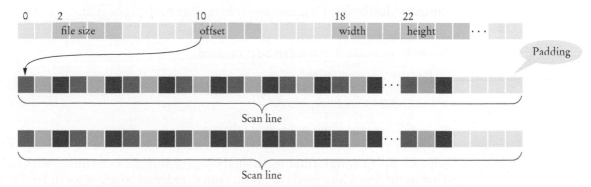

Figure 3   The BMP File Format for 24-bit True Color Images

7.4.4   Processing BMP Files

To illustrate the processing of a binary file, we will create a Python program that can be used to edit a BMP image file.

Up to this point, we have opened files for either reading or writing. But a file can be opened for both reading and writing using the open function with a plus (+) character in the mode string:

A file can be opened for both reading and writing.

```python
imgFile = open(filename, "rb+")
```

By opening a file for both reading and writing, you can read data from a file, process or manipulate it, and write it back to the file, generally to the same location from which it was read. This is a common task when working with image files.

Once the file is opened, extract the image dimensions and the start of the pixel storage from the header:

```
# Extract the image information.
fileSize = readInt(imgFile, 2)
start = readInt(imgFile, 10)
width = readInt(imgFile, 18)
height = readInt(imgFile, 22)
```

The readInt function is a version of the algorithm introduced earlier for converting four successive bytes to an integer:

```
def readInt(imgFile, offset) :
    # Move the file pointer to the given byte within the file.
    imgFile.seek(offset)

    # Read the 4 individual bytes and build an integer.
    theBytes = imgFile.read(4)
    result = 0
    base = 1
    for i in range(4) :
        result = result + theBytes[i] * base
        base = base * 256

    return result
```

The only difference is that we use the seek method to first move the file marker to the position where the related information is stored in the BMP file.

The start value indicates the location of the first byte of the first pixel. To extract the individual bytes, we must move the marker to that position.

```
imgFile.seek(start)
```

Now the individual pixels can be processed.

```
for row in range(height) :
    for col in range(width) :
        Process the pixel.

    # Skip the padding at the end of the row.
    imgFile.seek(padding, SEEK_CUR)   # The padding is calculated in lines 20-25
```

We will apply a simple filter to a digital image that replaces an image with its negative. That is, turning white pixels to black, cyan to red, and so on, as we did in Section 4.10.

To create the negative of a BMP image, first extract the blue/green/red component values for each pixel:

```
theBytes = imgFile.read(3)
blue = theBytes[0]
green = theBytes[1]
red = theBytes[2]
```

Then adjust the values using the equations:

```
newBlue = 255 - blue
newGreen = 255 - green
newRed = 255 - red
```

Courtesy of Cay Horstmann.

An Image and its Negative

After the pixels have been adjusted, the new values have to be written back to the same location in the file from which they were read:

```
imgFile.seek(-3, SEEK_CUR)    # Go back 3 bytes to the start of the pixel.
imgFile.write(bytes([newBlue, newGreen, newRed]))
```

The complete program that converts a BMP image to its negative follows. Unlike the programs in Section 4.10, this program does not display the image. Instead, it reads and updates the file in which the image is stored. Exercises • P7.24 and • P7.25 ask you to produce more interesting effects.

sec04/imageproc.py

```
1   ##
2   #   This program processes a digital image by creating a negative of a BMP image.
3   #
4
5   from io import SEEK_CUR
6   from sys import exit
7
8   def main() :
9       filename = input("Please enter the file name: ")
10
11      # Open as a binary file for reading and writing.
12      imgFile = open(filename, "rb+")
13
14      # Extract the image information.
15      fileSize = readInt(imgFile, 2)
16      start = readInt(imgFile, 10)
17      width = readInt(imgFile, 18)
18      height = readInt(imgFile, 22)
19
20      # Scan lines must occupy multiples of four bytes.
21      scanlineSize = width * 3
22      if scanlineSize % 4 == 0 :
23          padding = 0
24      else :
25          padding = 4 - scanlineSize % 4
26
27      # Make sure this is a valid image.
28      if fileSize != (start + (scanlineSize + padding) * height) :
29          sys.exit("Not a 24-bit true color image file.")
30
31      # Move to the first pixel in the image.
32      imgFile.seek(start)
33
34      # Process the individual pixels.
35      for row in range(height) :    # For each scan line
36          for col in range(width) :    # For each pixel in the line
37              processPixel(imgFile)
38
39          # Skip the padding at the end.
40          imgFile.seek(padding, SEEK_CUR)
41
42      imgFile.close()
43
44  ## Processes an individual pixel.
45  #   @param imgFile the binary file containing the BMP image
46  #
```

```
47  def processPixel(imgFile) :
48      # Read the pixel as individual bytes.
49      theBytes = imgFile.read(3)
50      blue = theBytes[0]
51      green = theBytes[1]
52      red = theBytes[2]
53
54      # Process the pixel.
55      newBlue = 255 - blue
56      newGreen = 255 - green
57      newRed = 255 - red
58
59      # Write the pixel.
60      imgFile.seek(-3, SEEK_CUR)    # Go back 3 bytes to the start of the pixel.
61      imgFile.write(bytes([newBlue, newGreen, newRed]))
62
63  ## Gets an integer from a binary file.
64  #   @param imgFile  the file
65  #   @param offset  the offset at which to read the integer
66  #   @return  the integer starting at the given offset
67  #
68  def readInt(imgFile, offset) :
69      # Move the file pointer to the given byte within the file.
70      imgFile.seek(offset)
71
72      # Read the 4 individual bytes and build an integer.
73      theBytes = imgFile.read(4)
74      result = 0
75      base = 1
76      for i in range(4) :
77          result = result + theBytes[i] * base
78          base = base * 256
79
80      return result
81
82  # Start the program.
83  main()
```

WORKED EXAMPLE 7.2

Graphics: Displaying a Scene File

Some drawing applications allow you to create and save a scene that consists of various objects that can later be changed by editing the individual objects. To save the scene, the program creates a data file that stores each object in the scene and its corresponding characteristics.

Problem Statement Develop a graphics program using the ezgraphics library that can read the scene description from a text file and draw the scene in a graphics window.

Step 1 Understand the processing task.

To extract the scene data, you must first understand the format used for storing it.

Our file format stores data related to the canvas on multiple lines, and stores data for each object on a single line.

For example, the following text file holds the data for the simple scene of a lamp post shown to the right.

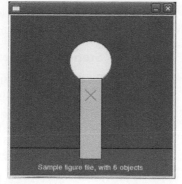

```
# Lamp post scene
300
300
blue
# The grass area is a green rectangle.
rect, 0, 250, dark green, dark green, 300, 50
# The fixture is a yellow circle.
oval, 112, 50, yellow, yellow, 75, 75
# The lamp post is a rectangle with a big X for decoration.
rect, 130, 120, black, gray, 40, 150
line, 140, 140, red, 160, 160
line, 140, 160, red, 160, 140
# Text drawn at the bottom of the scene.
text, 52, 285, white, Sample figure file, with 6 objects
```

The format assumes that there are no blank lines in the file, and a line beginning with a hash symbol (#) is a comment to be ignored. All non-comment lines contain data related to the scene. The first three lines, which are required, contain parameters related to the canvas: the width and height of the canvas, and the background color. Each additional non-comment line contains the parameters necessary to draw one of four objects: a line, rectangle, oval, or text.

The data fields for each object are on a single line, separated by commas. The first four fields are the same for all objects and include:

• the type of object,
• the *x*-and *y*-position as defined by the various canvas methods, and
• the outline color.

The type of object is indicated by one of the following strings: "line", "rect", "oval", or "text". Outline and fill colors must be specified by name.

The optional fields depend on the specific object. For a text object, there is one additional field, which is the text to be drawn. For a rectangle and an oval, there are three additional fields: the fill color and two integers that specify the width and height of the rectangle or the bounding box of the oval. The line object's two additional fields specify the *x*- and *y*-coordinates of the line's end point.

Step 2 Design the algorithm using a top-down approach.

At the top level, the solution algorithm is rather simple:

> *Open the scene file.*
> *Read the canvas parameters and configure the window.*
> *For each object in the scene*
> *Read the object description and draw the object.*

For simplicity, we specify the name of the file directly in the program. To make the program more useful, the name of the file should be obtained from the user either by way of a prompt or from the command line. We will create functions for the three main tasks of configuring the window, reading an object description, and drawing an object.

The main function implements this algorithm as follows:

```
def main() :
    infile = open("lamppost.fig", "r")

    win = configureWindow(infile)
    canvas = win.canvas()

    objData = extractNextLine(infile)
```

```
                           while objData != "" :
                               drawObject(objData, canvas)
                               objData = extractNextLine(infile)

                           win.wait()
```

Step 3   Create and configure the graphics window.

This is simply a matter of extracting the first three values from the input file and using them to create and configure the graphics window:

```
def configureWindow(infile) :
    # Extract the window size.
    width = int(extractNextLine(infile))
    height = int(extractNextLine(infile))

    # Extract the background color.
    color = extractNextLine(infile)
    color = color.strip()

    # Create the window and set the background color.
    win = GraphicsWindow(width, height)
    canvas = win.canvas()
    canvas.setBackground(color)

    # Return the window object.
    return win
```

The difficult part is the actual extraction of the data from the input file, which is described in the next step.

Step 4   Extract a non-comment line from the file.

Any line of the file that begins with a hash symbol is considered a comment. Extracting a single value or line of data is no longer as simple as reading a line from the file. Instead, we have to skip over any comments and extract the first non-comment line. Because this has to be done every time we read from the file, we will create a helper function to perform the task.

To skip over the comments, we read a line from the file and test to see whether the first character is a hash symbol. If it is not, the line is returned. If it is a hash symbol, we read and test another line until we find a non-comment line or the end of file is reached:

```
## Extracts a single non-comment line from the text file.
#  @param infile  the text file containing the scene description
#  @return the next non-comment line as a string or the empty string if the
#  end of file was reached
#
def extractNextLine(infile) :
    line = infile.readline()
    while line != "" and line[0] == "#" :
        line = infile.readline()

    return line
```

Step 5   Read an object description and draw the object.

Each non-comment line of the data file (other than the three canvas parameters) contains an object description. After reading the line, it can be split into five parts—the first four fields shared by all of the objects and the remaining fields in the fifth part of the split. We do this because the last field of a text object contains the string to be drawn and that string may contain a comma. To prevent the comma from resulting in an additional split, we limit the number of splits to four and keep the string for the text object intact.

After splitting the original string, we set the outline color for the object, because all objects have an outline color. Next, we check the type of object being drawn. If the object is a text object, we simply draw the string in the last part of the split. For the other object types, the string will contain two or three values. These will be the *x*- and *y*-coordinates for the end point of the line or the fill color, width, and height of the rectangle or oval. We split the string again to retrieve these values. The function for reading the description and drawing the objects is:

```python
## Draws a single object on the canvas based on the description extracted
#  from a scene file.
#  @param objData a string containing the description of an object
#  @param canvas  the canvas on which to draw
#
def drawObject(objData, canvas) :
    # Extract the object data. All objects share the first 4 fields.
    parts = objData.split(",", 4)    # Split into 5 parts.
    objType = parts[0].strip()
    x = int(parts[1])
    y = int(parts[2])
    outline = parts[3].strip()
    params = parts[4].strip()

    # Set the object color. All objects have an outline color.
    canvas.setOutline(outline)

    # The last substring from the split contains the parameters for the
    # given object, which depends on the type of the object.
    if objType == "text" :
        canvas.drawText(x, y, params)
    else :
        values = params.split(",")
        if objType == "line" :
            endX = int(values[0])
            endY = int(values[1])
            canvas.drawLine(x, y, endX, endY)
        else :
            # Extract the fill color and set the canvas to use it.
            fill = values[0].strip()
            canvas.setFill(fill)

            # Extract the width and height and use them to draw the object.
            width = int(values[1])
            height = int(values[2])
            if objType == "rect" :
                canvas.drawRect(x, y, width, height)
            elif objType == "oval" :
                canvas.drawOval(x, y, width, height)
```

Step 6   Put all of the functions together in a single Python source file.

EXAMPLE CODE   See worked_example_2/drawscene.py in your eText or companion code for the complete program.

7.5 Exception Handling

There are two aspects to dealing with program errors: *detection* and *handling*. For example, the open function can detect an attempt to read from a non-existent file.

However, it cannot handle that error. A satisfactory way of handling the error might be to terminate the program, or to ask the user for another file name. The open function cannot choose between these alternatives. It needs to report the error to another part of the program.

In Python, *exception handling* provides a flexible mechanism for passing control from the point of error detection to a handler that can deal with the error. In the following sections, we will look into the details of this mechanism.

7.5.1 Raising Exceptions

> To signal an exceptional condition, use the raise statement to raise an exception object.

When you detect an error condition, your job is really easy. You just *raise* an appropriate exception, and you are done. For example, suppose someone tries to withdraw too much money from a bank account.

```
if amount > balance :
    # Now what?
```

First look for an appropriate exception. The Python library provides a number of standard exceptions to signal all sorts of exceptional conditions. Figure 4 shows the most useful ones. (The exceptions are arranged as a tree-shaped hierarchy, with more specialized exceptions at the bottom of the tree. We will discuss such hierarchies in more detail in Chapter 10.)

Look around for an exception type that might describe your situation. How about the ArithmeticError exception? Is it an arithmetic error to have a negative balance? No, Python can deal with negative numbers. Is

© Lisa F. Young/iStockphoto.

When you raise an exception, the normal control flow is interrupted. This is similar to a circuit breaker that cuts off the flow of electricity in a dangerous situation.

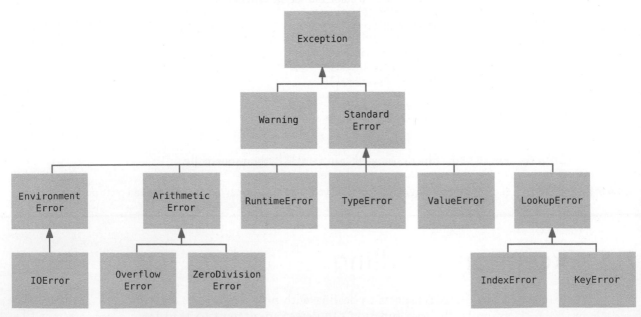

Figure 4 A Part of the Hierarchy of Exception Classes

the amount to be withdrawn an illegal value? Indeed it is. It is just too large. Therefore, let's raise a ValueError exception.

```
if amount > balance :
    raise ValueError("Amount exceeds balance")
```

When you raise an exception, execution does not continue with the next statement but with an **exception handler**. That is the topic of the next section.

Syntax 7.2 Raising an Exception

| Syntax | raise *exceptionObject* |

This message provides detailed information about the exception.

A new exception object is constructed, then raised.

```
if amount > balance :
    raise ValueError("Amount exceeds balance")

balance = balance - amount
```

This line is not executed when the exception is raised.

7.5.2 Handling Exceptions

Every exception should be handled somewhere in your program. If an exception has no handler, an error message is printed, and your program terminates. Of course, such an unhandled exception is confusing to program users.

You handle exceptions with the try/except statement. Place the statement into a location of your program that knows how to handle a particular exception. The try block contains one or more statements that may cause an exception of the kind that you are willing to handle. Each except clause contains the handler for an exception type.

Here is an example:

```
try :
    filename = input("Enter filename: ")
    infile = open(filename, "r")
    line = infile.readline()
    value = int(line)
    . . .
except IOError :
    print("Error: file not found.")

except ValueError as exception :
    print("Error:", str(exception))
```

Two exceptions may be raised in this try block:

- The open function can raise an IOError exception if the file with the given name cannot be opened.
- The int function can raise a ValueError exception if the string contains any characters that cannot be part of an integer literal.

If either of these exceptions is actually raised, then the rest of the instructions in the try block are skipped. Here is what happens for the various exception types:

- If an IOError exception is raised, then the except clause for the IOError exception is executed.
- If a ValueError exception occurs, then the second except clause is executed.
- If any other exception is raised, it will not be handled by any of the except clauses of this try block. It remains raised until it is handled by another try block.

Each except clause contains a handler. When the body of the except IOError clause is executed, then some function in the try block failed with an IOError exception. In this handler, we simply print an error message indicating that the file cannot be found.

Now look again at the second exception handler:

```
except ValueError as exception :
    print("Error:", str(exception))
```

When the body of this handler is executed, it prints the message included with the exception. The int function raises a ValueError exception when it cannot convert a string to an integer value. The function includes a message as part of the exception, which contains the string that it was unable to convert. For example, if the string passed to the int function was "35x2", then the message included with the exception will be

```
invalid literal for int() with base 10: '35x2'
```

Syntax 7.3   Handling Exceptions

Syntax

```
try :
    statement
    statement
    . . .
except ExceptionType :
    statement
    statement
    . . .
except ExceptionType as varName :
    statement
    statement
    . . .
```

This function can raise an IOError exception.

```
try :
    infile = open("input.txt", "r")

    line = infile.readline()
    process(line)

except IOError :
    print("Could not open input file.")

except Exception as exceptObj :
    print("Error:", str(exceptObj))
```

When an IOError is raised, execution resumes here.

This is the exception object that was raised.

Additional except clauses can appear here. Place more specific exceptions before more general ones.

To obtain the message, we must have access to the exception object itself. You can store the exception object in a variable with the as syntax:

```
except ValueError as exception :
```

When the handler for ValueError is executed, exception is set to the exception object. In our code, we then obtain the message string by calling str(exception). You can think of this operation as converting the exception object to a string.

When you raise an exception, you can provide your own message string. For example, when you call

```
raise ValueError("Amount exceeds balance")
```

the message of the exception is the string provided as the argument to the constructor.

In these sample except clauses, we merely inform the user of the source of the problem. Often, it is better to give the user another chance to provide a correct input; see Section 7.6 for a solution.

7.5.3 The finally Clause

Once a try block is entered, the statements in a finally clause are guaranteed to be executed, whether or not an exception is raised.

Occasionally, you need to take some action whether or not an exception is raised. The finally construct is used to handle this situation. Here is a typical situation.

It is important to close an output file to ensure that all output is written to the file. In the following code segment, we open an output file, call one or more functions, and then close the file:

```
outfile = open(filename, "w")
writeData(outfile)
outfile.close()    # May never get here.
```

Now suppose that one of the methods or functions before the last line raises an exception. Then the call to close is never executed! You solve this problem by placing the call to close inside a finally clause:

```
outfile = open(filename, "w")
try :
    writeData(outfile)

finally :
    outfile.close()
```

In a normal case, there will be no problem. When the try block is completed, the finally clause is executed, and the file is closed. However, if an exception occurs, the finally clause is also executed before the exception is passed to its handler.

Use the finally clause whenever you need to do some clean up, such as closing a file, to ensure that clean up happens no matter how the function or method exits.

All visitors to a foreign country have to go through passport control, no matter what happened on their trip. Similarly, the code in a finally clause is always executed, even when an exception has occurred.   © archives/iStockphoto.

Syntax 7.4 The finally Clause

```
Syntax    try :
              statement
              statement
              . . .
          finally :
              statement
              statement
              . . .
```

This code may raise exceptions.

```
                         outfile = open(filename, "w")
                         try :
                             writeData(outfile)
                             . . .
                         finally :
                             outfile.close()
                             . . .
```

The file must be opened outside the try *block in case it fails. Otherwise, the* finally *clause would try to close an unopened file.*

This code is always executed, even if an exception is raised in the try *block.*

Programming Tip 7.1
Raise Early, Handle Late

Raise an exception as soon as a problem is detected. Handle it only when the problem can be handled.

When a function detects a problem that it cannot solve, it is better to raise an exception rather than try to come up with an imperfect fix. For example, suppose a function expects to read a number from a file, and the file doesn't contain a number. Simply using a zero value would be a poor choice because it hides the actual problem and perhaps causes a different problem elsewhere.

Conversely, a function should only handle an exception if it can really remedy the situation. Otherwise, the best remedy is simply to have the exception propagate to its caller, allowing it to be caught by a competent handler.

These principles can be summarized with the slogan "raise early, handle late".

Programming Tip 7.2
Do Not Use except and finally in the Same try Statement

It is possible to have a finally clause following one or more except clauses. Then the code in the finally clause is executed whenever the try block is exited in any of three ways:

1. After completing the last statement of the try block.
2. After completing the last statement of an except clause, if this try block caught an exception.
3. When an exception was raised in the try block and not caught.

It is tempting to combine except and finally clauses, but the resulting code can be hard to understand, and it is often incorrect. Instead, use two statements:

- a try/finally statement to close resources
- a separate try/except statement to handle errors

For example,

```
try :
    outfile = open(filename, "w")
    try :
        Write output to outfile.
    finally :
        outfile.close()

except IOError :
    Handle exception.
```

The nested statements work correctly if the open function raises an exception. (Work through Exercise •• R7.17 to see why you can't use a single try statement.)

Special Topic 7.4

The with Statement

Because a try/finally statement for opening and closing files is so common, Python has a special shortcut:

```
with open(filename, "w") as outfile :
    Write output to outfile.
```

This with statement opens the file with the given name, sets outfile to the file object, and closes the file object when the end of the statement has been reached or an exception was raised.

TOOLBOX 7.3

Reading Web Pages

The Python standard library contains tools for working with Internet protocols. In this Toolbox, we will use a few from Python's urllib library to open and read pages from the Web.

To get started, you need the URL (universal resource locator) of the page. That is an address starting with http://, followed by the web site location. To open the page, use the urlopen function from the urllib.request module, like this:

```
import urllib.request
address = "http://horstmann.com/index.html"
response = urllib.request.urlopen(address)
```

You get a "response" object from which you can read the data to which the URL refers. This might be binary data (such as an image) or text (such as a web page). The read method yields all response object data in bytes:

```
theBytes = response.read()
```

If you know the web page is text, turn the binary data into a string with the decode method:

```
text = theBytes.decode()
```

This method call assumes that the text uses the UTF-8 character encoding (see Special Topic 7.3). If it doesn't, you can specify the name of the encoding as an argument to the decode method.

If you'd like to look at the text one line at a time, use this loop:

```
for line in text.splitlines() :
    Process line.
```

Alternatively, you can simply keep the text as a string and search it for information.

For example, we may want to find all links to other web pages. Web pages are written in a language called HTML (Hypertext Markup Language). A link to another page has the form

```
<a href="link URL">
```

This loop searches for all occurrences of the term href. For each occurrence, we locate the string enclosed in quotes that follows it, and print it.

```
i = text.find("href")
while i != -1 :
    start = text.find("\"", i)
    end = text.find("\"", start + 1)
    print(text[start + 1 : end])
    i = text.find("href", end + 1)
```

As you can see, for this search, there was no need to break the text into lines. In fact, it would not have been a good idea to do so because we might have missed a link if a line break had fallen between href and the link.

Note the use of the second argument passed to the string method find. Instead of searching an entire source string for the position of a substring, you can use the second argument to specify the position in the source string where the search should begin.

If you are familiar with HTML, you will realize that this search is a bit simplistic, and it might miss some links. See Exercise • Toolbox P7.49 for an improvement.

But that is a minor detail. You now know how to gather all links from a web page. If you followed each of them in turn, you could map out a portion of the World Wide Web. That's what a search engine such as Google does. In Chapter 11, you will see how you can do the same on a smaller scale.

After reading the contents of a web page, close the connection by calling the close method on the response object.

```
response.close()
```

EXAMPLE CODE   See toolbox_3/websearch.py in your eText or companion code for a complete program that reads and searches the contents of a web page.

7.6 Application: Handling Input Errors

This section walks through an example program that includes exception handling. The program, analyzedata.py, asks the user for the name of a file. The file is expected to contain data values. The first line of the file should contain the total number of values, and the remaining lines contain the data. A typical input file looks like this:

```
3
1.45
-2.1
0.05
```

What can go wrong? There are two principal risks.

When designing a program, ask yourself what kinds of exceptions can occur.

- The file might not exist.

- The file might have data in the wrong format.

Who can detect these faults? The open function will raise an exception when the file does not exist. The functions that process the input values need to raise an exception when they find an error in the data format.

What exceptions can be raised? The open function raises an IOError exception when the file does not exist, which is appropriate in our situation. When there are fewer data items than expected, or when the file doesn't start with the count of values, the program will raise a ValueError exception.

Finally, when there are more inputs than expected, a RuntimeError exception with an appropriate message should be raised.

Who can remedy the faults that the exceptions report? Only the main function of the analyzedata.py program interacts with the user, so it handles the exceptions, prints appropriate error messages, and gives the user another chance to enter a correct file:

For each exception, you need to decide which part of your program can competently handle it.

```
done = False
while not done :
    try :
        Prompt user for file name.
        data = readFile(filename)
        Process data.
        done = True

    except IOError :
        print("Error: file not found.")

    except ValueError :
        print("Error: file contents invalid.")

    except RuntimeError as error :
        print("Error:", str(error))
```

The first two except clauses in the main function give a human-readable error report if bad data was encountered or the file was not found. The third except clause prints the error report when there are more values in the file than expected. Because there is no standard exception that can be used for this type of error, we will use the generic RuntimeError exception. Generally, that exception is used for multiple types of errors. When handling this exception, the program should print the message that was supplied when it was raised. This requires accessing the exception object with the as operator and converting it to a string.

If a different exception is raised from those caught in the main function, the program will abort and print the exception message along with the line number at which the exception was raised. In addition, the printout will contain the chain of function calls that led to the exception and the line number at which the call was made. This allows the programmer to diagnose the problem.

The following readFile function creates the file object and calls the readData function. It does not handle any exceptions. If there is a problem with the input file, either because it does not exist or it contains invalid data, the function simply passes the exception to its caller.

```
def readFile(filename) :
    infile = open(filename, "r")
    try :
        return readData(infile)
    finally :
        infile.close()
```

Note how the finally clause ensures that the file is closed even when an exception occurs.

The readData function reads the number of values, creates a list, and fills it with the data values.

```
def readData(infile) :
    line = infile.readline()
    numberOfValues = int(line)    # May raise a ValueError exception.
    data = []

    for i in range(numberOfValues) :
        line = infile.readline()
        value = float(line)    # May raise a ValueError exception.
        data.append(value)

    # Make sure there are no more values in the file.
    line = infile.readline()
    if line != "" :
        raise RuntimeError("End of file expected.")

    return data
```

There are three potential errors:

- The file might not start with an integer.
- There might not be a sufficient number of data values.
- There might be additional input after reading all data values.

In the first case, the int function raises a ValueError exception when we attempt to convert the input string to an integer value. Likewise, the float function does the same in the second case. Because these functions do not know what to do in these cases, they allow the exception to be sent to a handler elsewhere. When we find that there is additional unexpected input, we raise a RuntimeError exception and specify an appropriate message.

To see the exception handling at work, look at a specific error scenario:

1. main calls readFile.
2. readFile calls readData.
3. readData calls int.
4. There is no integer in the input, and int raises a ValueError exception.
5. readData has no except clause. It terminates immediately.
6. readFile has no except clause. It terminates immediately after executing the finally clause and closing the file.
7. The first except clause in main is for an IOError exception. The exception that is currently being raised is a ValueError, and this handler doesn't apply.
8. The next except clause is for a ValueError exception, and execution resumes here. That handler prints a message to the user. Afterward, the user is given another chance to enter a file name. Note that the statements for processing the data have been skipped.

This example shows the separation between error detection (in the readData function) and error handling (in the main function). In between the two is the readFile function, which simply passes the exceptions along.

sec06/analyzedata.py

```
1  ##
2  #   This program processes a file containing a count followed by data values.
3  #   If the file doesn't exist or the format is incorrect, you can specify another file.
4  #
```

```
5
6  def main() :
7     done = False
8     while not done :
9        try :
10          filename = input("Please enter the file name: ")
11          data = readFile(filename)
12
13          # As an example for processing the data, we compute the sum.
14          total = 0
15          for value in data :
16             total = total + value
17
18          print("The sum is", total)
19          done = True
20
21       except IOError :
22          print("Error: file not found.")
23
24       except ValueError :
25          print("Error: file contents invalid.")
26
27       except RuntimeError as error :
28          print("Error:", str(error))
29
30  ## Opens a file and reads a data set.
31  #  @param filename the name of the file holding the data
32  #  @return a list containing the data in the file
33  #
34  def readFile(filename) :
35     infile = open(filename, "r")
36     try :
37        return readData(infile)
38     finally :
39        infile.close()
40
41  ## Reads a data set.
42  #  @param infile the input file containing the data
43  #  @return the data set in a list
44  #
45  def readData(infile) :
46     line = infile.readline()
47     numberOfValues = int(line)    # May raise a ValueError exception.
48     data = []
49
50     for i in range(numberOfValues) :
51        line = infile.readline()
52        value = float(line)          # May raise a ValueError exception.
53        data.append(value)
54
55     # Make sure there are no more values in the file.
56     line = infile.readline()
57     if line != "" :
58        raise RuntimeError("End of file expected.")
59
60     return data
61
62  # Start the program.
63  main()
```

TOOLBOX 7.4
Statistical Analysis

Python is commonly used for data analysis, and many statistical functions are readily available. The standard library has functions for computing the mean, median, and standard deviation. In addition, the scipy.stats module has many functions for testing relationships between statistical variables. In this Toolbox, you will see several interesting sample applications of these functions. (Refer to Toolbox 2.1 on page 68 if you have not already installed the SciPy library.)

Basic Statistical Measurements

The statistics module of the standard library offers functions to compute the mean, median, and standard deviation of a list of values:

```
mean = statistics.mean(data)
median = statistics.median(data)
stdev = statistics.stdev(data)
```

For example, when data contains the populations of the world's countries, the mean is about 30 million, whereas the median is about 4.6 million. A small number of very populous countries greatly pull up the mean. In this situation, the standard deviation (about 122 million) is not very useful.

To see a more useful example of the standard deviation, consider data that follows the normal or "bell curve" distribution. Common examples of normal distributions are the sizes of individuals within a species. With normally-distributed data, one expects about 68 percent of the population to be within one standard deviation of the mean, and about 96 percent of the population within two standard deviations. As shown in the example program in your companion code, the heights of the American presidents have a mean of 180 cm (5'11") and a standard deviation of about 7 cm. Thus, the probability of the occupant of the White House being shorter than 166 cm (5'5") or taller than 194 cm (6'4") is less than 4 percent.

EXAMPLE CODE   See toolbox_4/basic/stats.py in your eText or companion code for the sample program.

The Chi-Square Test

One common use of statistics is to test whether there is a significant difference between two variables. For example, we may want to find out whether test scores vary between male and female students, or whether they are influenced by family income. One distinguishes between *categorical* and *continuous* variables. A categorical variable has a fixed number of possible values without a numeric value attached to each, such as male/female or racial classifications. A continuous variable (such as a test score, income, or height) can assume a continuous range of numerical values.

The chi-square test analyzes a relationship between categorical variables. For example, the U.S. Census Bureau publishes data on multiple births by race and Hispanic origin—see Table 7.

Table 7 **2008 Births**			
	White	Black	Hispanic
Single	2,184,914	599,536	1,017,139
Twin	82,903	22,924	23,266
Multiple	4,493	569	834

Intuitively, it seems that the likelihood of twins and triplets should not depend on the race or ethnicity of the parents. But it is odd that the numbers for Hispanic and Black twins are similar, even though there were 70 percent more Hispanic children. Of course, in any observations, you expect some random fluctuation. The chi-square test measures the probability that two variables are independent when given a particular matrix of values.

For this kind of statistical analysis, you need the `scipy.stats` module from the `scipy` library. Import the `scipy.stats` module and call the `chi2_contingency` function. The function returns a tuple of several values, of which only the second value is of interest for a basic analysis. It is the probability that the variation in the individual cells could have occurred by chance.

```
data = [
    [ 2184914, 599536,  1017139 ],
    [ 82903,  22924,  23266 ],
    [ 4493, 569, 834 ]
]

p = scipy.stats.chi2_contingency(data)[1]  # Yields 0
```

In this case, p is zero, indicating the difference is not due to chance, and the hypothesis that multiple births are independent of race should be rejected. There must be some reason other than chance that Hispanic twins are less common.

Another statistic (shown in Table 8) lists vaginal and caesarean deliveries by race and Hispanic origin. One might wonder whether caesarean delivery is less common among disadvantaged groups due to the expense of the procedure. However, in this case, the chi-square test reports a probability of 0.68 that this distribution might happen by chance, so we cannot conclude that there is a difference between the groups.

Table 8 2008 Deliveries by Race and Hispanic Origin (in thousands)		
	White	Black	Hispanic
Vaginal	1,527	406	717
Caesarean	733	214	322
Not stated	8	2	3

EXAMPLE CODE   See `toolbox_4/chi2/chi2.py` in your eText or companion code for the complete program for analyzing birth data.

Analysis of Variance

Analysis of variance (commonly abbreviated ANOVA) is used to determine a dependency between a categorical and a continuous variable. For example, you can use it to determine whether test scores differ significantly among groups of students.

The Programme for International Assessment (PISA) is administered every three years in more than 70 countries, to evaluate performance of 15-year old students. (See `http://www.oecd.org/pisa/aboutpisa/` for a detailed description of the test.) Raw data files for many nations are available. We will analyze the 2012 student data from the United States. The data set provides anonymized records for each of the almost 5,000 students who took the test, with demographic data and answers to attitudinal questions.

One set of questions asks students about the amount of English instruction per week. (There are two questions, one asking for minutes per class period, and another for class periods per week.) Suppose we want to check whether different racial groups reported having received the same amount of instruction.

The data file is voluminous but easy to process with the tools of this chapter. Each student record occupies one line. The offset and length of each field is documented, which allows us to extract the gender, race, and hours of instruction.

Here is the code that extracts the hours of instruction and adds it to the appropriate group:

```python
white = []
black = []
asian = []

infile = open("US_ST12.TXT")
for line in infile :
    race = line[2331 : 2332]
    minPerPeriod = int(line[248 : 252])
    periodsPerWeek = int(line[260 : 264])

    if minPerPeriod > 0 and minPerPeriod < 1000 and \
        periodsPerWeek > 0 and periodsPerWeek < 1000 :
        hours = minPerPeriod * periodsPerWeek / 60
        if race == "1" :
            white.append(hours)
        elif race == "2" :
            black.append(hours)
        elif race == "3" :
            asian.append(hours)
infile.close()
```

Then we print the size and mean of each group:

```
White: 1589 responses, mean 4.463184
Black: 379 responses, mean 4.168162
Asian: 699 responses, mean 4.231354
```

As you can see, the means differ by group, and the average for Blacks is almost 30 minutes less than that for Whites. Is the difference significant or could it have occurred randomly? That is what ANOVA tests. The stats.f_oneway function computes, from the lists passed to it, the probability that the data distribution might have been the result of chance. The function returns a tuple, with that probability as the second element. In our application, we compute

```python
p = scipy.stats.f_oneway(white,black,asian)[1]
```

In our case, p is 0.027774, or just under 3 percent, so one would conclude that it's unlikely the data distribution was the result of chance.

As a check, let us also group the hours of English instruction by gender. The program yields this information:

```
Boys: 1500 responses, mean 4.397800
Girls: 1532 responses, mean 4.339001
p = 0.500792
```

The means are quite similar, and the ANOVA test says that there is a probability of over 50 percent that the distributions are the same. This is not surprising, because in American schools, boys and girls don't usually take different English classes.

EXAMPLE CODE   See toolbox_4/anova/anova.py in your eText or companion code for the complete program.

Linear Regression

In the preceding section, we analyzed the relationship between a categorical and a continuous variable. When both variables are continuous, you can use a different test, called *linear regression*, to test whether there is a linear dependence between the variables.

As a source of data, we extracted statistical indicators for various industrialized countries from the OECD Factbook (http://www.oecd-ilibrary.org/economics/oecd-factbook_18147364) and saved it in CSV format.

Each row lists the values for a particular country:

```
Country,Per capita income,Life expectancy,% tertiary education,Health
    expenditures,Per capita GDP,GINI
Australia,43372,82.0,38.3,8.9,44407,0.33
Austria,43869,81.1,19.3,10.8,44141,0.27
. . .
```

Let us study the relationship between health expenditures and life expectancy. Does higher spending buy the citizens of a country a longer life?

We use a CSV reader to read the data, and append the values for the life expectancy and health expenditure columns to two lists.

```
lifeexp = []
healthex = []

reader = csv.reader(open("oecd.csv"))
next(reader) # Skip header row
for row in reader :
    lifeexp.append(float(row[2]))
    healthex.append(float(row[4]))
```

Now we can compute the *linear correlation coefficient*, a value between −1 and 1 that signifies how closely the data follow a linear relationship—see Figure 5. A correlation close to +1 or −1 indicates that corresponding data points fall along a line. A correlation of zero means that the points form a shape that is not at all linear.

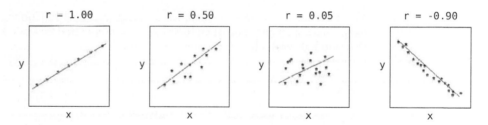

Figure 5   Sample Linear Correlation Coefficients

The function scipy.stats.linregress computes the linear correlation coefficient as well as the slope and *x*-intercept of the regression line—the line that best fits through the data points. Again, the result is a tuple, and the slope, intercept, and correlation are its first three elements.

```
r = scipy.stats.linregress(healthex, lifeexp)
slope = r[0]
intercept = r[1]
correlation = r[2]
```

In our case, the correlation is 0.358864, which is quite weak. Let's plot the data points and the regression line:

```
matplotlib.pyplot.scatter(healthex, lifeexp)

x1 = min(healthex)
y1 = intercept + slope * x1
x2 = max(healthex)
y2 = intercept + slope * x2
matplotlib.pyplot.plot([x1,x2],[y1,y2])
matplotlib.pyplot.show()
```

Figure 6 shows the result.

Figure 6 Correlating Health
Expenditure and Longevity

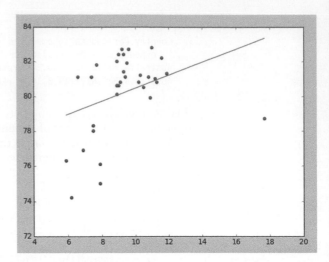

It seems that there is one outlier, a country that spends far more than all others on health-care without getting a commensurate return in terms of longevity. Yes, that would be the United States of America. Removing the outlying data point yields a correlation of about 0.61 (see Exercise • Toolbox P7.40).

EXAMPLE CODE   See `toolbox_4/regression/regression.py` in your eText or companion code for the complete program.

You have now seen several examples of using statistical functions for analyzing real-world data. There are many more such functions, and it is a good idea to take a course in statistics so that you know which ones are appropriate for different circumstances. We hope that you feel inspired to use Python when you are faced with analyzing data in your field of study.

WORKED EXAMPLE 7.3

Creating a Bubble Chart

A bubble chart illustrates the relationship between *three-dimensional data*, that is, each data point is made of three values (*x*, *y*, *z*). The individual data points are plotted as a circle, or "bubble". The center of the bubble is positioned horizontally and vertically on the graph based on the *x*- and *y*-values, and the *z*-value specifies the size of the bubble.

Problem Statement Your task is to create a bubble chart illustrating the relationship between a country's annual education spending and student test scores in math and science using the `matplotlib` library. (See Toolbox 2.1 if you have not installed this library.) The data are stored in a text file.

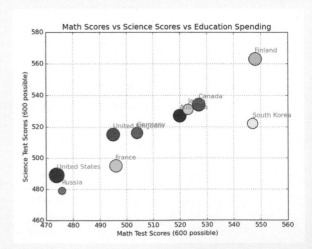

Step 1   Decompose the task into steps.

This problem can be split into three steps:

> *Load the data from the text file.*
> *Plot the data.*
> *Improve the appearance of the graph.*

Step 2   Understand the processing task.

To load the data from the file, you need to understand the format in which it was stored. Here are the contents of the education.txt file:

```
Australia
5766 520 527
Canada
5749 527 534
Germany
4682 504 516
. . .
```

Each record has four pieces of information, spread across two lines. The first line identifies the country. The second line contains the country's per capita spending on education (in dollars), followed by the average math score and the average science score earned by students who completed secondary education in that country. Both scores have a maximum of 600 points.

To get the country name, you can simply read the first line. To obtain the three values associated with each country, split the second line and convert the three strings to their respective types:

```
parts = line.split()
dollars = int(parts[0])
math = int(parts[1])
science = int(parts[2])
```

Step 3   Choose between iterating over the file or reading individual lines.

Because each record has two lines in the file, we need to read pairs of lines for each record.

```
done = False
while not done :
    country = infile.readline()
    if country == "" :
        done = True
    else :
        line = infile.readline()
        . . .
```

Step 4   Choose how to store the data.

The bubble chart will be constructed using the scatter function from the pyplot module. That function takes the data as three lists, one for each of the three values associated with each data point. So we want to store the *x*-values (math scores) in one list, the *y*-values (science scores) in another, and the *z*-values (spending) in a third. Thus, the corresponding elements of each list will contain the values for a single data point.

We also want to label each bubble, so we will store the country names in a fourth list.

Step 5   Load the graph data.

The algorithm for loading the data is:

> *Create empty lists to store the data.*
> *Open the file.*

> *Repeat while there are records in the file*
>   *Read the first line of the record.*
>   *Append to the countries list.*
>   *Read the second line of the record.*
>   *Split the line into three parts.*
>   *Store the parts in lists for math scores, science scores, and spending.*

Step 6   Plot the data.

The scatter function in the pyplot module requires four arguments: the list of *x*-values, the list of *y*-values, the list of *z*-values, and the colors.

In our case, we don't care what the colors of the bubbles are. We just want each bubble to have a different color. Python will assign a random color, but we will pass a list of different integers (which are indexes into a default color table) to be sure each is different.

```python
pyplot.scatter(mathScores, sciScores, spending, range(0, len(countries)))
```

We also want to label each bubble. This is done by looping over the countries and placing a label for each country at the position of the bubble:

```python
for i in range(len(countries)) :
    pyplot.text(mathScores[i], sciScores[i], countries[i], color="gray")
```

Step 7   Improve the appearance of the graph.

The final step is to improve the appearance of the graph by adding a title and labeling the axes. For easier viewing, you can also turn on the grid. The complete program is shown below.

worked_example_3/bubblechart.py

```python
1  ##
2  #   This program constructs a bubble chart that illustrates the relationship between
3  #   annual education spending and math and science test scores.
4  #
5
6  from matplotlib import pyplot
7
8  # Load the data from the text file.
9  infile = open("education.txt")
10 countries = []
11 mathScores = []
12 sciScores = []
13 spending = []
14
15 done = False
16 while not done :
17    country = infile.readline()
18    if country == "" :
19       done = True
20    else :
21       line = infile.readline()
22       countries.append(country)
23       parts = line.split()
24
25       dollars = int(parts[0])
26       math = int(parts[1])
27       science = int(parts[2])
28
29       spending.append(dollars / 10)   # Scaling the bubbles so they don't overlap
30       mathScores.append(math)
31       sciScores.append(science)
32
33 infile.close()
```

```
34
35  # Construct the bubble chart.
36  pyplot.scatter(mathScores, sciScores, spending,
37     range(0, len(countries)))
38
39  # Label each bubble.
40  for i in range(len(countries)) :
41     pyplot.text(mathScores[i], sciScores[i],
42         countries[i], color="gray")
43
44  pyplot.grid("on")
45  pyplot.xlabel("Math Test Scores (600 possible)")
46  pyplot.ylabel("Science Test Scores (600 possible)")
47  pyplot.title("Math Scores vs Science Scores vs Education Spending")
48
49  pyplot.show()
```

Computing & Society 7.2   The Ariane Rocket Incident

The European Space Agency (ESA), Europe's counterpart to NASA, had successfully launched many satellites and scientific experiments into space. However, when a new rocket version, the Ariane 5, was launched on June 4, 1996, from ESA's launch site in Kourou, French Guiana, the rocket veered off course about 40 seconds after liftoff. Flying at an angle of more than 20 degrees, rather than straight up, exerted such an aerodynamic force that the boosters separated, which triggered the automatic self-destruction mechanism. The rocket blew itself up.

The ultimate cause of this accident was an unhandled exception! The rocket contained two identical devices (called inertial reference systems) that processed flight data from measuring devices and turned the data into information about the rocket position. The onboard computer used the position information for controlling the boosters. The same inertial reference systems and computer software had worked fine on the Ariane 4.

However, due to design changes to the rocket, one of the sensors measured a larger acceleration force than had been encountered in the Ariane 4. That value, expressed as a floating-point value, was stored in a 16-bit integer. The Ada language, used for the device software, generates an exception if a floating-point number is too large to be converted to an integer. Unfortunately, the programmers of the device had decided that this situation would never happen and didn't provide an exception handler.

When the overflow did happen, the exception was triggered and, because there was no handler, the device shut itself off. The onboard computer sensed the failure and switched over to the backup device. However, that device had shut itself off for exactly the same reason, something that the designers of the rocket had not expected. They figured that the devices might fail for mechanical reasons, and the chance of two devices having the same mechanical failure was considered remote. At that point, the rocket was without reliable position information and went off course.

Perhaps it would have been better if the software hadn't been so thorough? If it had ignored the overflow, the device wouldn't have been shut off. It would have computed bad data. But then the device would have reported wrong position data, which could have been just as fatal. Instead, a correct implementation should have caught overflow exceptions and come up with some strategy to recompute the flight data. Clearly, giving up was not a reasonable option in this context.

The advantage of the exception-handling mechanism is that it makes these issues explicit to programmers.

© AP/Wide World Photos.

The Explosion of the Ariane Rocket

CHAPTER SUMMARY

Develop programs that read and write files.

- To open a file, supply the name of the file stored on disk and the mode in which the file is to be opened.
- Close all files when you are done processing them.
- Use the `readline` method to obtain lines of text from a file.
- Write to a file using the `write` method or the `print` function.

Be able to process text in files.

- You can iterate over a file object to read the lines of text in the file.
- Use the `rstrip` method to remove the newline character from a line of text.
- Use the `split` method to split a string into individual words.
- Read one or more characters with the `read` method.

Process the command line arguments of a program.

- Programs that start from the command line receive the command line arguments in the `argv` list defined in the `sys` module.

Develop programs that read and write binary files.

- To open a binary file for reading, use the mode string `"rb"`; to open it for writing, use the mode string `"wb"`.
- You can access any position in a random access file by moving the *file marker* prior to a read or write operation.
- Different types image of files use different layouts for the image information and pixel values.
- A file can be opened for both reading and writing.

Use exception handling to transfer control from an error location to an error handler.

- To signal an exceptional condition, use the `raise` statement to raise an exception object.
- When you raise an exception, processing continues in an exception handler.
- Place the statements that can cause an exception inside a `try` block, and the handler inside an `except` clause.
- Once a `try` block is entered, the statements in a `finally` clause are guaranteed to be executed, whether or not an exception is raised.
- Raise an exception as soon as a problem is detected. Handle it only when the problem can be handled.

Use exception handling in a program that processes input.

- When designing a program, ask yourself what kinds of exceptions can occur.
- For each exception, you need to decide which part of your program can competently handle it.

REVIEW EXERCISES

■■ R7.1 What happens if you try to open a file for reading that doesn't exist? What happens if you try to open a file for writing that doesn't exist?

■■ R7.2 What happens if you try to open a file for writing, but the file or device is write-protected (sometimes called read-only)? Try it out with a short test program.

■ R7.3 How do you open a file whose name contains a backslash, like `c:\temp\output.dat`?

■ R7.4 If a program Woozle is started with the command

```
python woozle.py -Dname=piglet -Ieeyore -v heff.txt a.txt lump.txt
```

what are the values of `argv[0]`, `argv[1]`, and so on?

■ R7.5 What is the difference between raising an exception and handling an exception?

■■ R7.6 When your program executes a `raise` statement, which statement is executed next?

■■ R7.7 What happens if an exception does not have a matching `except` clause?

■■ R7.8 What can your program do with the exception object that an `except` clause receives?

■ R7.9 What is the difference between sequential access and random access?

■ R7.10 What is the difference between a text file and a binary file?

■ R7.11 What is the file marker? How do you move it? How do you determine its current position?

■■ R7.12 What happens if you try to move the file marker past the end of a file? Try it out and report your results.

■ R7.13 Give an output statement to write a date and time in ISO 8601 format, such as

```
2018-03-01 09:35
```

Assume that the date and time are given in five integer variables named `year`, `month`, `day`, `hour`, `minute`.

■ R7.14 Give an output statement to write one line of a table containing a product description, quantity, unit price, and total price in dollars and cents. You want the columns to line up, like this:

Item	Qty	Price	Total
Toaster	3	$29.95	$89.85
Hair Dryer	1	$24.95	$24.95
Car Vacuum	2	$19.99	$39.98

■ R7.15 What is a command line? How can a program read its command line?

■ R7.16 What is the purpose of the `finally` clause used with a `try/except` block? Give an example of how it can be used.

■■ **R7.17** Programming Tip 7.2 suggests that you use a try/except block to handle exceptions and a separate try/finally block to close a file. What would happen if you combined the two into a single block, as below, and the open function raised an exception?

```
try :
    outfile = open(filename, "w")
    Write output.
except IOError :
    Handle exception.
finally :
    outfile.close()
```

You could overcome this problem by moving the call to open outside the try block. What problem do you then have?

■■ **R7.18** What happens when an exception is raised, the code of a finally clause executes, and that code raises an exception of a different kind than the original one? Which one is caught by a surrounding clause? Write a sample program to try it out.

■■ **R7.19** Suppose the program in Section 7.6 reads a file containing the following values:

```
1
2
3
4
```

What is the outcome? How could the program be improved to give a more accurate error report?

■■■ **Toolbox R7.20** The file exercises/deductions.csv in your companion code (from web site http://www.irs.gov/uac/Tax-Stats-2) contains information about many tax deductions. Write a Python program that analyzes the deduction for home mortgage interest. What is the average deduction for taxpayers in each of the listed income groups? How much more would the treasury collect if the deduction was eliminated for the top n groups?

■ **Toolbox R7.21** How can you print the names of only those files in the current directory that have an extension of .txt?

■■ **Toolbox R7.22** The parent directory of the current working directory is specified by a string containing two periods, "..". How would you list the contents of the parent directory, excluding the current working directory?

■ **Toolbox R7.23** How would you compute the mean and standard deviation of the lengths of all words in a file?

■ **Toolbox R7.24** Suppose the rows and columns in Table 7 were flipped. What would be the effect on the chi-square test?

■ **Toolbox R7.25** When the ANOVA test in Toolbox 7.4 is restricted to only Black and Asian students, a probability of 0.725968 is reported. What does that mean?

■ **Toolbox R7.26** When the outlier in the linear regression example in Toolbox 7.4 is removed, what is the effect on the slope of the regression line?

■ **Toolbox R7.27** Why is the linear correlation coefficient not equal to 1 after removing the outlier in in the linear regression example in Toolbox 7.4?

PROGRAMMING EXERCISES

▪ P7.1 Write a program that carries out the following tasks:

> *Open a file with the name hello.txt.*
> *Store the message "Hello, World!" in the file.*
> *Close the file.*
> *Open the same file again.*
> *Read the message into a string variable and print it.*

▪ P7.2 Write a program that reads a file containing text. Read each line and send it to the output file, preceded by *line numbers*. If the input file is

```
Mary had a little lamb
Whose fleece was white as snow.
And everywhere that Mary went,
The lamb was sure to go!
```

then the program produces the output file

```
/* 1 */ Mary had a little lamb
/* 2 */ Whose fleece was white as snow.
/* 3 */ And everywhere that Mary went,
/* 4 */ The lamb was sure to go!
```

© Chris Price/iStockphoto.

Prompt the user for the input and output file names.

▪ P7.3 Repeat Exercise • P7.2, but allow the user to specify the file name on the command line. If the user doesn't specify any file name, then prompt the user for the name.

▪ P7.4 Write a program that reads a file containing two columns of floating-point numbers. Prompt the user for the file name. Print the average of each column.

▪▪ P7.5 Write a program that asks the user for a file name and prints the number of characters, words, and lines in that file.

▪▪ P7.6 Write a program find.py that searches all files specified on the command line and prints out all lines containing a specified word. For example, if you call

```
python find.py ring report.txt address.txt homework.py
```

then the program might print

```
report.txt: has broken up an international ring of DVD bootleggers that
address.txt: Kris Kringle, North Pole
address.txt: Homer Simpson, Springfield
homework.py: string = "text"
```

The specified word is always the first command line argument.

▪▪ P7.7 Write a program that checks the spelling of all words in a file. It should read each word of a file and check whether it is contained in a word list. A word list is available on most Linux systems in the file /usr/share/dict/words. (If you don't have access to a Linux system, use ch08/sec01/words in your companion code.) The program should print out all words that it cannot find in the word list.

▪▪ P7.8 Write a program that replaces each line of a file with its reverse. For example, if you run

```
python reverse.py hello.py
```

then the contents of hello.py are changed to

```
.margorp nohtyP tsrif yM #
)"!dlroW ,olleH"(tnirp
```

Of course, if you run Reverse twice on the same file, you get back the original file.

■■ **P7.9** Write a program that reads each line in a file, reverses its lines, and writes them to another file. For example, if the file input.txt contains the lines

```
Mary had a little lamb
Its fleece was white as snow
And everywhere that Mary went
The lamb was sure to go.
```

and you run

```
reverse input.txt output.txt
```

then output.txt contains

```
The lamb was sure to go.
And everywhere that Mary went
Its fleece was white as snow
Mary had a little lamb
```

■■ **P7.10** Get the data for baby names in prior years from the Social Security Administration. Paste the table data in files named babynames2010.txt, etc. Modify the babynames.py program so that it prompts the user for a file name. Can you spot a trend in the frequencies?

■■ **P7.11** Write a program that reads in worked_example_1/babynames.txt and produces two files, boynames.txt and girlnames.txt, separating the data for the boys and girls.

■■■ **P7.12** Write a program that reads a file in the same format as worked_example_1/babynames.txt and prints all names that are both boy and girl names (such as Alexis or Morgan).

■■ **P7.13** Write a program that asks the user to input a set of floating-point values. When the user enters a value that is not a number, give the user a second chance to enter the value. After two chances, quit reading input. Add all correctly specified values and print the sum when the user is done entering data. Use exception handling to detect improper inputs.

■■ **Toolbox P7.14** Using the mechanism described in Toolbox 7.3, write a program that reads all data from a web page and writes them to a file. Prompt the user for the web page URL and the file.

■■ **Toolbox P7.15** Using the mechanism described in Toolbox 7.3, write a program that reads all data from a web page and prints all hyperlinks of the form

```
<a href="link">link text</a>
```

Extra credit if your program can follow the links that it finds and find links in those web pages as well. (This is the method that search engines such as Google use to find web sites.)

■■■ **Toolbox P7.16** In order to read a web page (Toolbox 7.3), you need to know its character encoding (Special Topic 7.3). Write a program that has the URL of a web page as a command-line argument and that fetches the page contents in the proper encoding. Determine the encoding as follows:

1. After calling `urlopen`, call `input.headers["content-type"]`. You may get a string such as `"text/html; charset=windows-1251"`. If so, use the value of the `charset` attribute as the encoding.

2. Read the first line using the `"latin_1"` encoding. If the first two bytes of the file are 254 255 or 255 254, the encoding is `"utf-16"`. If the first three bytes of the file are 239 187 191, the encoding is `"utf-8"`.

3. Continue reading the page using the `"latin_1"` encoding and look for a string of the form

    encoding=. . .

or

    charset=. . .

If you found a match, extract the character encoding (discarding any surrounding quotation marks) and re-read the document with that encoding. If none of these applies, write an error message that the encoding could not be determined.

■■ **P7.17** Write a program that reads the country data in the file `how_to_1/worldpop.txt`. Do not edit the file. Use the following algorithm for processing each line: Add non-white space characters to the country name. When you encounter a white space, locate the next non-white space character. If it is not a digit, add a space and that character to the country name. Otherwise, read the rest of the number as a string, add the first digit, and convert to a number. Print the total of all country populations (excepting the entry for "European Union").

■ **P7.18** Write a program `copyfile` that copies one file to another. The file names are specified on the command line. For example,

    copyfile report.txt report.sav

■■ **P7.19** Write a program that concatenates the contents of several files into one file. For example,

    catfiles chapter1.txt chapter2.txt chapter3.txt book.txt

makes a long file `book.txt` that contains the contents of the files `chapter1.txt`, `chapter2.txt`, and `chapter3.txt`. The target file is always the last file specified on the command line.

■■ **P7.20** *Random monoalphabet cipher.* The Caesar cipher, which shifts all letters by a fixed amount, is far too easy to crack. Here is a better idea. As the key, don't use numbers but words. Suppose the key word is FEATHER. Then first remove duplicate letters, yielding FEATHR, and append the other letters of the alphabet in reverse order:

    F E A T H R Z Y X W V U S Q P O N M L K J I G D C B

Now encrypt the letters as follows:

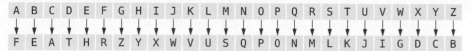

Write a program that encrypts or decrypts a file using this cipher. For example,

    crypt -d -kFEATHER encrypt.txt output.txt

decrypts a file using the keyword FEATHER. It is an error not to supply a keyword.

■ P7.21   *Letter frequencies.* If you encrypt a file using the cipher of Exercise ●● P7.20, it will have all of its letters jumbled up, and will look as if there is no hope of decrypting it without knowing the keyword. Guessing the keyword seems hopeless too. There are just too many possible keywords. However, someone who is trained in decryption will be able to break this cipher in no time at all. The average letter frequencies of English letters are well known. The most common letter is E, which occurs about 13 percent of the time. Here are the average frequencies of the letters.

A	8%	F	3%	K	<1%	P	3%	U	3%	X	<1%
B	<1%	G	2%	L	4%	Q	<1%	V	1%	Y	2%
C	3%	H	4%	M	3%	R	8%	W	2%	Z	<1%
D	4%	I	7%	N	8%	S	6%				
E	13%	J	<1%	O	7%	T	9%				

Write a program that reads an input file and displays the letter frequencies in that file. Such a tool will help a code breaker. If the most frequent letters in an encrypted file are H and K, then there is an excellent chance that they are the encryptions of E and T.

Show the result in a table such as the one above, and make sure the columns line up.

■■ P7.22   *Vigenère cipher.* In order to defeat a simple letter frequency analysis, the Vigenère cipher encodes a letter into one of several cipher letters, depending on its position in the input document. Choose a keyword, for example TIGER. Then encode the first letter of the input text like this:

The encoded alphabet is just the regular alphabet shifted to start at T, the first letter of the keyword TIGER. The second letter is encrypted according to the following map.

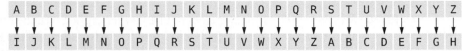

The third, fourth, and fifth letters in the input text are encrypted using the alphabet sequences beginning with characters G, E, and R, and so on. Because the key is only five letters long, the sixth letter of the input text is encrypted in the same way as the first.

Write a program that encrypts or decrypts an input text according to this cipher.

■■ P7.23   *Playfair cipher.* Another way of thwarting a simple letter frequency analysis of an encrypted text is to encrypt *pairs* of letters together. A simple scheme to do this is the Playfair cipher. You pick a keyword and remove duplicate letters from it. Then you fill the keyword, and the remaining letters of the alphabet, into a 5 × 5 square. (Because there are only 25 squares, I and J are considered the same letter.)

Here is such an arrangement with the keyword PLAYFAIR.

```
P L A Y F
I R B C D
E G H K M
N O Q S T
U V W X Z
```

To encrypt a letter pair, say AM, look at the rectangle with corners A and M:

```
P L A Y F
I R B C D
E G H K M
N O Q S T
U V W X Z
```

The encoding of this pair is formed by looking at the other two corners of the rectangle, in this case, FH. If both letters happen to be in the same row or column, such as GO, simply swap the two letters. Decryption is done in the same way.

Write a program that encrypts or decrypts an input text according to this cipher.

■ **P7.24** Write a program using the techniques in Section 7.4 that edits an image file and reduces the blue and green values by 30 percent, giving it a "sunset" effect.

Courtesy of Cay Horstmann.

■ **P7.25** Write a program that edits an image file, using the techniques in Section 7.4, turning it into a grayscale image.

Replace each pixel with a pixel that uses the same grayness level for its blue, green, and red components. A pixel's grayness level is computed by adding 30 percent of the pixel's red level, 59 percent of its green level, and 11 percent of its blue level. (The color-sensing cone cells in the human eye differ in their sensitivity for red, green, and blue light.)

Courtesy of Cay Horstmann.

■■ **P7.26** *Junk mail*. Write a program that reads in two files: a *template* and a *database*. The template file contains text and tags. The tags have the form |1| |2| |3|... and need to be replaced with the first, second, third, ... field in the current database record.

A typical database looks like this:

```
Mr.|Harry|Morgan|1105 Torre Ave.|Cupertino|CA|95014
Dr.|John|Lee|702 Ninth Street Apt. 4|San Jose|CA|95109
Miss|Evelyn|Garcia|1101 S. University Place|Ann Arbor|MI|48105
```

And here is a typical form letter:

```
To:
|1| |2| |3|
|4|
|5|, |6| |7|

Dear |1| |3|:

You and the |3| family may be the lucky winners of $10,000,000 in the Python
clearinghouse sweepstakes! . . .
```

■■ **P7.27** Write a program that queries information from three files. The first file contains the names and telephone numbers of a group of people. The second file contains the names and Social Security numbers of a group of people. The third file contains the Social Security numbers and annual income of a group of people. The groups of people should overlap but need not be completely identical. Your program should ask the user for a telephone number and then print the name, Social Security number, and annual income, if it can determine that information.

■■ **P7.28** Write a program that prints out a student grade report. Assume there is a file, classes.txt, that contains the names of all classes taught at a college, such as

classes.txt

```
CSC1
CSC2
CSC46
CSC151
MTH121
. . .
```

For each class, there is a file with student ID numbers and grades:

CSC2.txt

```
11234 A-
12547 B
16753 B+
21886 C
. . .
```

Write a program that asks for a student ID and prints out a grade report for that student, by searching all class files. Here is a sample report

```
Student ID 16753
CSC2 B+
MTH121 C+
CHN1 A
PHY50 A-
```

■■ **Business P7.29** A hotel salesperson enters sales in a text file. Each line contains the following, separated by semicolons: The name of the client, the service sold (such as Dinner, Conference, Lodging, and so on), the amount of the sale, and the date of that event. Write a program that reads such a file and displays the total amount for each service category. Display an error if the file does not exist or the format is incorrect.

■■ **Business P7.30** Write a program that reads a text file as described in Exercise ●● Business P7.29, and that writes a separate file for each service category, containing the entries for that category. Name the output files Dinner.txt, Conference.txt, and so on.

•• Business P7.31 A store owner keeps a record of daily cash transactions in a text file. Each line contains three items: The invoice number, the cash amount, and the letter P if the amount was paid or R if it was received. Items are separated by spaces. Write a program that prompts the store owner for the amount of cash at the beginning and end of the day, and the name of the file. Your program should check whether the actual amount of cash at the end of the day equals the expected value.

••• Science P7.32 After the switch in the figure below closes, the voltage (in volts) across the capacitor is represented by the equation

$$v(t) = B\left(1 - e^{-t/(RC)}\right)$$

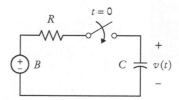

Suppose the parameters of the electric circuit are $B = 12$ volts, $R = 500\ \Omega$, and $C = 0.25\ \mu F$. Consequently

$$v(t) = 12\left(1 - e^{-0.008t}\right)$$

where t has units of μs. Read the exercises/params.txt file (found in your companion code) containing the values for B, R, C, and the starting and ending values for t. Write a file rc.txt of values for the time t and the corresponding capacitor voltage $v(t)$, where t goes from the given starting value to the given ending value in 100 steps. In our example, if t goes from 0 to 1,000 μs, the twelfth entry in the output file would be:

```
110   7.02261
```

••• Science P7.33 The figure below shows a plot of the capacitor voltage from the circuit shown in Exercise ••• Science P7.32. The capacitor voltage increases from 0 volts to B volts. The "rise time" is defined as the time required for the capacitor voltage to change from $v_1 = 0.05 \times B$ to $v_2 = 0.95 \times B$.

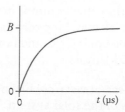

The exercises/rc.txt file in your companion code contains a list of values of time t and the corresponding capacitor voltage $v(t)$. A time in μs and the corresponding voltage in volts are printed on the same line. For example, the line

```
110   7.02261
```

indicates that the capacitor voltage is 7.02261 volts when the time is 110 μs. The time is increasing in the data file.

Write a program that reads the file rc.txt and uses the data to calculate the rise time. Approximate B by the voltage in the last line of the file, and find the data points that are closest to $0.05 \times B$ and $0.95 \times B$.

■■ Science P7.34 Suppose a file contains bond energies and bond lengths for covalent bonds in the following format:

© Chris Dascher/iStockphoto.

Single, double, or triple bond	Bond energy (kJ/mol)	Bond length (nm)
C|C	370	0.154
C||C	680	0.13
C|||C	890	0.12
C|H	435	0.11
C|N	305	0.15
C|O	360	0.14
C|F	450	0.14
C|Cl	340	0.18
O|H	500	0.10
O|O	220	0.15
O|Si	375	0.16
N|H	430	0.10
N|O	250	0.12
F|F	160	0.14
H|H	435	0.074

Write a program that accepts data from one column and returns the corresponding data from the other columns in the stored file. If input data matches different rows, then return all matching row data. For example, a bond length input of 0.12 should return triple bond C\|\|\|C and bond energy 890 kJ/mol *and* single bond N\|O and bond energy 250 kJ/mol.

■ Toolbox P7.35 The exercises/planets.csv file in the book's companion code has information about the planets of the solar system. Write a program that reads in the spreadsheet data from the file and makes a plot of the masses of the planets.

■■ Toolbox P7.36 The exercises/census.csv file in the book's companion code (from the web site https://www.census.gov/programs-surveys/popest/data/data-sets.html) contains a data set of the population for all U.S. states, as determined by the last census, as well as a large amount of additional information. Write a program that reads in the CSV file and produces a file with just the state names and populations.

■■ Toolbox P7.37 Modify the program of Toolbox 7.4 to analyze the hours of instruction in mathematics and science in the PISA data.

■■ Toolbox P7.38 Five questions in the PISA questionnaire in Toolbox 7.4 are concerned with "math anxiety". They are in positions 147, 149, 151, 154, and 156, with responses from 1 (not anxious) to 5 (very anxious). Form an anxiety score by averaging all responses, and analyze whether math anxiety depends on race or gender. Consider only students who responded to all five questions.

■■■ Toolbox P7.39 One of the questions in the PISA questionnaire in Toolbox 7.4 is:

How many books are there in your home?

There are usually about 15 books per foot of shelving. Do not include magazines, newspapers, or your schoolbooks.

1. 0–10 books
2. 11–25 books
3. 26–100 books
4. 101–200 books
5. 201–500 books
6. More than 500 books

Modify the program of Toolbox 7.4 to analyze the response to this question (which is in column 124 of the input) by race. Note that you cannot use an ANOVA test because you don't have the actual number of books, only the six categories.

■ Toolbox P7.40 Modify the regression.py program of Toolbox 7.4 to remove the data point for the United States. Draw the regression line and print the correlation.

■ Toolbox P7.41 Using the OECD data set from Toolbox 7.4, determine the correlation between per capita income and the other indicators.

■■ Toolbox P7.42 Using the data from How To 7.1 and the tools in Toolbox 7.4, determine the correlation between country size and population.

■■■ Toolbox P7.43 The National UFO Reporting Center Online Database at http://www.nuforc.org/webreports.html contains reports of UFO sightings. How well does the number of sightings per state correlate with the population of the U.S. states?

■■■ Toolbox P7.44 You can find data about vote counts of the 2000 U.S. presidential election in Florida at http://lib.stat.cmu.edu/datasets/fl2000.txt. At the time, it was suspected that different voting machine technologies might make voters accidentally vote for unintended candidates. In some otherwise left-leaning districts, Mr. Buchanan got a surprising number of votes. Moreover, a good number of ballots had too many or no selections. Investigate whether the ratios of votes Nader : Gore and Buchanan : Bush and over- and undervote rates depend on the type of the voting machine used.

■ Toolbox P7.45 When saving a file, many programs make a backup copy of the existing file before writing the new contents. Write a function named backup that will create a backup of a file by appending the extension .bak to the file name. Note that if a backup file already exists, it should first be deleted.

■■■ Toolbox P7.46 Write a function saveWithBackup(data, file) that writes the string data to a file (replacing what was there before), but first makes a backup of the old file *if the old contents was different*.

■ ■ **Toolbox P7.47** Write a program that makes a backup of all files in a directory that are not already backup files. Append the extension .bak to all backed-up files. Be sure to skip directories.

■ ■ ■ **Toolbox P7.48** Write a program that checks whether two directories contain exactly the same files. Note that they may be listed in different order.

■ **Toolbox P7.49** Improve the link search program of Toolbox 7.3. The word href might be in upper-case. Check that it is preceded by white space and followed by an = symbol, possibly surrounded by white space. The link might be enclosed in either single or double quotes, or in no quotes at all (in which case it extends to the next white space or >).

■ **Toolbox P7.50** The list of color names that can be used when drawing shapes on an ezgraphics canvas are provided in a text file at http://ezgraphics.org/data/colornames.txt. Each line contains the name and the corresponding RGB values for a single color, separated by blank spaces. The first six lines of the file are shown below:

```
alice blue 240 248 255
AliceBlue 240 248 255
antique white 250 235 215
AntiqueWhite 250 235 215
AntiqueWhite1 255 239 219
AntiqueWhite2 238 223 204
```

The urllib module from Toolbox 7.3 can be used to read data from files stored on the Web. The response object returned from the statement dataFile = urllib.request.urlopen(address) can be used in the same fashion as a text file object:

```
dataFile = urllib.request.urlopen(address)
for line in dataFile :
    Process the line.
```

Write a program using the urllib module that prompts the user for a string (such as "yellow") and that prints all lines of the file that contain that string.

■ **Toolbox P7.51** As in Exercise • Toolbox P7.50, read the colornames.txt file, but now search for colors that are "close" to a color that the user specified. You should prompt the user for red, green, and blue values and print lines whose red, green, and blue values differ by less than 10 from those supplied by the user.

■ **Toolbox P7.52** Design and implement a program that prints a list of the airport names obtained from a remote data file that contains information on thousands of international airports. The file is located at

https://github.com/jpatokal/openflights/blob/master/data/airlines.dat

■ **Toolbox P7.53** The file exercises/google.csv contains the 2014 daily stock data for Google, Inc.

	A	B	C	D	E	F
1	Google Stock Data					
2						
3	Date	Open	Maximum	Minimum	Closing	Shares
4	2014-12-31	531.25	532.6	525.8	526.4	1364500
5	2014-12-30	528.37	531.07	527.3	530.39	30100
6	2014-12-29	532.19	535.48	530.01	530.33	2272300
7	2014-12-26	528.77	534.25	527.31	534.03	1033200
8	2014-12-24	530.51	531.76	527.02	528.77	704000
9	2014-12-23	527	534.56	526.29	530.59	2145800
10	2014-12-22	516.08	526.46	516.08	524.87	2716300
11	2014-12-19	511.51	517.72	506.91	516.35	3566200

Write a program that reads data from the CSV file and writes all data except the maximum and minimum columns to a new CSV file.

• Toolbox P7.54 Write a program that reads the exam grades for multiple students from a text file (exercises/grades.txt) that is formatted as follows,

```
Luigi
80 69 75
Spiny
85 89 92
Gumby
78 87 82
Arthur
89 94 91
```

and creates a CSV file that can be used to create the spreadsheet shown here.

	A	B	C	D	E
1	Basket Weaving 101				
2					
3	Student	Exam 1	Exam 2	Exam 3	Average
4	Luigi	80	69	75	74.67
5	Spiny	85	89	92	88.67
6	Gumby	78	87	82	82.33
7	Arthur	89	94	91	91.33

## CHAPTER 8

SETS AND DICTIONARIES

© nicholas belton/iStockphoto.

CHAPTER GOALS

To build and use a set container

To learn common set operations for processing data

To build and use a dictionary container

To work with a dictionary for table lookups

To work with complex data structures

CHAPTER CONTENTS

When you need to organize multiple values in your program, you can place them into a *container*. The list container that was introduced earlier is one of several containers provided by Python. In this chapter, you will learn about two additional built-in containers, the set and the dictionary. We then show you how to combine containers to model complex structures.

8.1 Sets

A set stores a collection of unique values.

A **set** is a container that stores a collection of unique values. Unlike list elements, the elements or members of the set are not stored in any particular order and cannot be accessed by position. The operations available for use with a set, which we explore in this section, are the same as the operations performed on sets in mathematics. Because sets need not maintain a particular order, set operations are much faster than the equivalent list operations (see Programming Tip 8.1).

© parema/iStockphoto.

Set elements are not stored in any particular order.

Figure 1 shows three sets of colors—the colors of the British, Canadian, and Italian flags. In each set, the order does not matter, and the colors are not duplicated.

Figure 1
Sets of Flag Colors

8.1.1 Creating and Using Sets

To create a set with initial elements, you can specify the elements enclosed in braces, just like in mathematics:

```
cast = { "Luigi", "Gumbys", "Spiny" }
```

Alternatively, you can use the set function to convert any sequence into a set:

```
names = ["Luigi", "Gumbys", "Spiny"]
cast = set(names)
```

```
vowels = set("AEIOU")
```

For historical reasons, you cannot use {} to make an empty set in Python. Instead, use the set function with no arguments:

```
cast = set()
```

As with any container, you can use the len function to obtain the number of elements in a set:

```
numberOfCharacters = len(cast)
```

To determine whether an element is contained in the set, use the in operator or its inverse, the not in operator:

```
if "Luigi" in cast :
    print("Luigi is a character in Monty Python's Flying Circus.")
else :
    print("Luigi is not a character in the show.")
```

Because sets are unordered, you cannot access the elements of a set by position as you can with a list. Instead, use a for loop to iterate over the individual elements:

```
print("The cast of characters includes:")
for character in cast :
    print(character)
```

Note that the order in which the elements of the set are visited depends on how they are stored internally. For example, the loop above displays the following:

```
The cast of characters includes:
Gumbys
Spiny
Luigi
```

Note that the order of the elements in the output is different from the order in which the set was created. (See Special Topic 8.1 for more information on the ordering used by sets.)

The fact that sets do not retain the initial ordering is not a problem when working with sets. In fact, the lack of an ordering makes it possible to implement set operations very efficiently.

However, you usually want to display the elements in sorted order. Use the sorted function, which returns a list (not a set) of the elements in sorted order. The following loop prints the cast in sorted order:

```
for character in sorted(cast) :
    print(character)
```

8.1.2 Adding and Removing Elements

Like lists, sets are mutable containers, so you can add and remove elements.

A set is created using a set literal or the set function.

The in operator is used to test whether an element is a member of a set.

New elements can be added using the add method.

For example, suppose we need to add more characters to the set cast created in the previous section. Use the add method to add elements:

```
cast = {"Luigi", "Gumbys", "Spiny"} ❶
cast.add("Arthur") ❷
```

If the element being added is not already contained in the set, it will be added to the set and the size of the set increased by one. Remember, however, that a set cannot contain duplicate elements. If you attempt to add an element that is already in the set, there is no effect and the set is not changed (see Figure 2):

```
cast.add("Spiny") ❸
```

Use the discard method to remove elements from a set.

There are two methods that can be used to remove individual elements from a set. The discard method removes an element if the element exists (see Figure 2):

```
cast.discard("Arthur") ❹
```

but has no effect if the given element is not a member of the set:

```
cast.discard("The Colonel")    # Has no effect
```

The remove method, on the other hand, removes an element if it exists, but raises an exception if the given element is not a member of the set:

```
cast.remove("The Colonel")    # Raises an exception
```

Finally, the clear method removes *all* elements of a set, leaving the empty set:

```
cast.clear()    # cast now has size 0
```

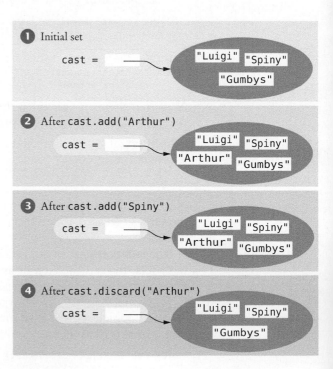

Figure 2
Adding and Discarding
Set Elements

8.1.3 Subsets

A set is a *subset* of another set if and only if every element of the first set is also an element of the second set. For example, in Figure 3, the Canadian colors are a subset of the British colors, but the Italian colors are not. (The British set does not contain green.)

The issubset method returns True or False to report whether one set is a subset of another:

```
canadian = { "Red", "White" }
british = { "Red", "Blue", "White" }
italian = { "Red", "White", "Green" }

if canadian.issubset(british) :
   print("All Canadian flag colors occur in the British flag.")
if not italian.issubset(british) :
   print("At least one of the colors in the Italian flag does not.")
```

You can also test for equality between two sets using the == and != operators. Two sets are equal if and only if they have exactly the same elements.

```
french = { "Red", "White", "Blue" }
if british == french :
   print("The British and French flags use the same colors.")
```

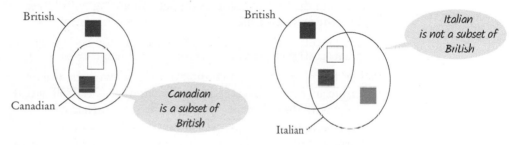

Figure 3 A Set is a Subset If It is Contained Entirely Within Another Set

8.1.4 Set Union, Intersection, and Difference

The *union* of two sets contains all of the elements from both sets, with duplicates removed (see Figure 4).

Use the union method to create the union of two sets in Python. For example:

```
inEither = british.union(italian)    # The set {"Blue", "Green", "White", "Red"}
```

Both the british and italian sets contain the colors "Red" and "White", but the union is a set and therefore contains only one instance of each color.

Note that the union method returns a new set. It does not modify either of the sets in the call.

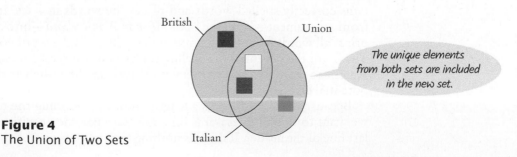

Figure 4
The Union of Two Sets

The intersection
method produces
a new set with
the elements that
are contained in
both sets.

The *intersection* of two sets contains all of the elements that are in *both* sets (see Figure 5).

To create the intersection of two Python sets, use the `intersection` method:

```
inBoth = british.intersection(italian))   # The set {"White", "Red"}
```

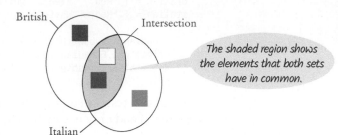

Figure 5
The Intersection of Two Sets

The difference
method produces
a new set with the
elements that belong
to the first set but
not the second.

Finally, the *difference* of two sets results in a new set that contains those elements in the first set that are not in the second set. For example, the difference between the Italian and the British colors is the set containing only `"Green"` (see Figure 6).

Use the `difference` method to find the set difference:

```
print("Colors that are in the Italian flag but not the British:")
print(italian.difference(british))   # Prints {'Green'}
```

When forming the union or intersection of two sets, the order does not matter. For example, `british.union(italian)` is the same set as `italian.union(british)`. But the order matters with the `difference` method. The set returned by

```
british.difference(italian)
```

is `{"Blue"}`.

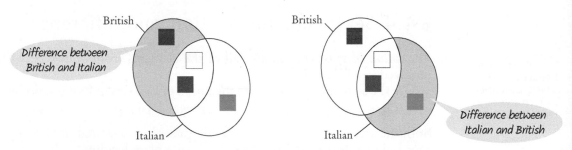

Figure 6   The Difference of Two Sets

The following program shows a practical application of sets. It reads a file that contains correctly spelled words and places the words in a set. It then reads all words from a document—here, the book *Alice in Wonderland*—into a second set. Finally, it prints all words from the document that are not in the set of correctly spelled words. These are the potential misspellings. (As you can see from the output, we used an American word list, and words with British spelling, such as *clamour*, are flagged as potential errors.)

Because the book file has a lengthy header describing the distribution rights that we want to skip, the `readWords` function has a parameter with a string that marks the last line of the header. If there is nothing to skip, pass an empty string.

Table 1 Common Set Operations	
Operation	Description
s = set() s = set(*seq*) s = {e_1, e_2, ..., e_n}	Creates a new set that is either empty, a duplicate copy of sequence *seq*, or that contains the initial elements provided.
len(s)	Returns the number of elements in set *s*.
element in s element not in s	Determines whether *element* is in the set.
s.add(*element*)	Adds a new element to the set. If the element is already in the set, no action is taken.
s.discard(*element*) s.remove(*element*)	Removes an element from the set. If the element is not a member of the set, discard has no effect, but remove will raise an exception.
s.clear()	Removes all elements from a set.
s.issubset(t)	Returns a Boolean indicating whether set *s* is a subset of set *t*.
s == t s != t	Returns a Boolean indicating whether set *s* is equal or not equal to set *t*.
s.union(t)	Returns a new set that contains all elements in set *s* and set *t*.
s.intersection(t)	Returns a new set that contains elements that are in *both* set *s* and set *t*.
s.difference(t)	Returns a new set that contains elements in *s* that are not in set *t*.

sec01/spellcheck.py

```
 1  ##
 2  #   This program checks which words in a file are not present in a list of
 3  #   correctly spelled words.
 4  #
 5
 6  #   Import the split function from the regular expression module.
 7  from re import split
 8
 9  def main() :
10      # Read the word list and the document.
11      correctlySpelledWords = readWords("words", "")
12      documentWords = readWords("alice30.txt", "*END*")   # Skip the prefix
13
14      # Print all words that are in the document but not the word list.
15      misspellings = documentWords.difference(correctlySpelledWords)
16      for word in sorted(misspellings) :
17          print(word)
18
19  ## Reads all words from a file.
20  #   @param filename  the name of the file
21  #   @param skipUntil  skip all lines until a line starts with a string
22  #   @return  a set with all lowercased words in the file. Here, a word is a
23  #   sequence of upper- and lowercase letters
```

```
24  #
25  def readWords(filename, skipUntil) :
26     wordSet = set()
27     inputFile = open(filename, "r")
28     skip = True
29
30     for line in inputFile :
31        line = line.strip()
32        if not skip :
33           # Use any character other than a-z or A-Z as word delimiters.
34           parts = split("[^a-zA-Z]+", line)
35           for word in parts :
36              if len(word) > 0 :
37                 wordSet.add(word.lower())
38        elif line.find(skipUntil) >= 0 :
39           skip = False
40
41     inputFile.close()
42     return wordSet
43
44  # Start the program.
45  main()
```

Program Run

```
...
centre
chatte
clamour
comfits
conger
croqueted
croqueting
daresay
dinn
draggled
dutchess
...
```

WORKED EXAMPLE 8.1

Counting Unique Words

Problem Statement Determine the number of unique words contained in a text document. For example, the nursery rhyme "Mary had a little lamb" contains 57 unique words. Your task is to write a program that reads a text document and determines the number of unique words in it.

Step 1 Understand the processing task.

To count the number of unique words in a text document, we need to process each word and determine whether the word has been encountered earlier in the document. Only the first occurrence of a word should be counted as being unique.

The easiest way to solve this task is to read each word from the file and add it to a set. Because a set cannot contain duplicates, the add method will prevent a word that was encountered earlier from being added to the set. After processing every word in the document, the size of the set will be the number of unique words contained in the document.

Step 2   Decompose the task into steps.

This problem can be split into several simple steps:

> *Create an empty set.*
> *For each word in the text document*
> *   Add the word to the set.*
> *number of unique words = size of the set*

Creating an empty set, adding an element to a set, and determining the size of a set after each word has been added are standard set operations. Reading the words in the file can be handled as a separate task.

Step 3   Build the set of unique words.

To build the set of unique words, we must read individual words from the file. For simplicity, we use a literal file name. For a more useful program, however, the file name should be obtained from the user.

```
inputFile = open("nurseryrhyme.txt", "r")
for line in inputFile :
    theWords = line.split()
    for word in theWords :
        Process word.
```

Here processing a word involves adding it to a set of words. In counting unique words, however, a word cannot contain any characters that are not letters. In addition, the capitalized version of a word must be counted as being the same as the non-capitalized version. To aid in handling these special cases, let's design a separate function that can be used to "clean" the word before it's added to the set.

Step 4   Clean the words.

To strip out all characters that are not letters, we can iterate through the string, one character at a time, and build a new clean word using the lowercase version of the character:

```
def clean(string) :
    result = ""
    for char in string :
        if char.isalpha() :
            result = result + char.lower()

    return result
```

Step 5   Combine the functions into a single program.

Implement the main function and combine it with the other function definitions in a single file. Here is the complete program.

worked_example_1/countwords.py

```
1  ##
2  #   This program counts the number of unique words contained in a text document.
3  #
4
5  def main() :
6      uniqueWords = set()
```

```
7
8     filename = input("Enter filename (default: nurseryrhyme.txt): ")
9     if len(filename) == 0 :
10       filename = "nurseryrhyme.txt"
11    inputFile = open(filename, "r")
12
13    for line in inputFile :
14       theWords = line.split()
15       for word in theWords :
16          cleaned = clean(word)
17          if cleaned != "" :
18             uniqueWords.add(cleaned)
19
20    print("The document contains", len(uniqueWords), "unique words.")
21
22 ## Cleans a string by making letters lowercase and removing characters
23 #    that are not letters.
24 #    @param string the string to be cleaned
25 #    @return the cleaned string
26 #
27 def clean(string) :
28    result = ""
29    for char in string :
30       if char.isalpha() :
31          result = result + char.lower()
32
33    return result
34
35 # Start the program.
36 main()
```

Program Run

```
Enter filename (default: nurseryrhyme.txt):
The document contains 57 unique words.
```

Programming Tip 8.1

Use Python Sets, Not Lists, for Efficient Set Operations

When you write a program that manages a collection of unique items, sets are far more efficient than lists. Some programmers prefer to use the familiar lists, replacing

```
itemSet.add(item)
```

with

```
if (item not in itemList) :
    itemList.append(item)
```

However, the resulting program is much slower.

EXAMPLE CODE   Try out programming_tip_1/countwords2.py in your companion code, a list version of the program in Worked Example 8.1, with the file war-and-peace.txt. It takes 45 seconds on our test machine, whereas the set version takes 4 seconds.

Special Topic 8.1

Hashing

To check whether a list contains a particular value, you need to traverse the list until you have found a match or reached the end. If the list is long, that is a time-consuming operation. Sets can find elements much faster because they aren't required to maintain the order of the elements. Internally, Python sets use a data structure called a *hash table*.

The basic idea of a hash table is simple. Set elements are grouped into smaller collections of elements that share the same characteristic. You can imagine a hash table of books as having a group for each color, so that books of the same color are in the same group. To find whether a book is already present, you don't compare it against all books, but only against the books in the same color group.

> Set implementations arrange the elements so that they can be located quickly.

On this shelf, books of the same color are grouped together. Similarly, in a hash table, objects with the same hash code are placed in the same group. © Alfredo Ragazzoni/iStockphoto.

Actually, hash tables don't use colors, but integer values (called *hash codes*) that can be computed from the elements. In Python, the hash function computes hash codes. Here is an interactive session that shows several hash codes:

```
>>> hash(42)
42
>>> hash(4.2)
461168601842739204
>>> hash("Gumby")
1811778348220604920
```

To check whether a value is in a set, one computes hash(*value*) and then compares the value with those elements that have the same hash code. It is possible that there are multiple elements with the same hash code, but there won't be very many.

A hash function produces different hash codes for most values so that they are scattered about in a hash table. © one clear vision/iStockphoto.

In Python, you can only form sets from values that can be hashed. Numbers and strings can be included in sets. But it is not possible to hash a mutable value (such as a list or set). Therefore, you cannot form sets of sets in Python. If you need to collect sequences, use a set of tuples (see Special Topic 6.5).

Computing & Society 8.1 Standardization

You encounter the benefits of standardization every day. When you buy a light bulb, you can be assured that it fits the socket without having to measure the socket at home and the light bulb in the store. In fact, you may have experienced how painful the lack of standards can be if you have ever purchased a flashlight with nonstandard bulbs. Replacement bulbs for such a flashlight can be difficult and expensive to obtain.

© Denis Vorob'yev/iStockphoto.

Programmers have a similar desire for standardization. When you write a Python program, you want it to work the same way on every computer that executes Python code. And it shouldn't matter who wrote the Python implementation. For example, there is a version of Python that runs on the Java virtual machine, and one expects it to work correctly. For this to work, the behavior of the Python language has to be strictly defined, and all interested parties need to agree on that definition. A formal definition of the behavior of a technical artifact, detailed enough to ensure interoperability, is called a *standard*.

Who creates standards? Some of the most successful standards have been created by volunteer groups such as the Internet Engineering Task Force (IETF) and the World Wide Web Consortium (W3C). The IETF standardizes protocols used in the Internet, such as the protocol for exchanging e-mail messages. The W3C standardizes the Hypertext Markup Language (HTML), the format for web pages. These standards have been instrumental in the creation of the World Wide Web as an open platform that is not controlled by any one company.

Many programming languages, such as C++ and Scheme, have been standardized by independent standards organizations, such as the American National Standards Institute (ANSI) and the International Organization for Standardization—called ISO for short (not an acronym; see https://www.iso.org/about-us.html). ANSI and ISO are associations of industry professionals who develop standards for everything from car tires to credit card shapes to programming languages.

The inventors of a new technology often have an interest in its invention becoming a standard, so that other vendors produce tools that work with the invention and thus increase its likelihood of success. On the other hand, by handing over the invention to a standards committee, the inventors may lose control over the standard.

The Python language was never standardized by an independent standards organization, relying instead on an informal community under the leadership of its founder, the "benevolent dictator for life", Guido van Rossum. The absence of a standard limits the appeal of the language. For example, a government may not want to use Python for a project that lasts twenty years. After all, the benevolent dictator may not always be present, or may cease to be benevolent. Governments and large companies often insist on using standardized products.

Unfortunately, not all standards are created equal. Most standards committees try to codify best practices and create standards that are useful for a long time. Sometimes, the process breaks down and a self-interested vendor manages to standardize their product, warts and all. This happened with the OOXML standard for office documents that lists, in over 5,000 pages, the often arbitrary and inconsistent minutiae of Microsoft's office format. In theory, a very diligent vendor should be able to develop interoperable products, but several years after its publication, not even Microsoft has managed to do so.

As a computer professional, there will be many times in your career when you need to make a decision whether to support a particular standard. For example, when you need to generate documents, you may need to choose between HTML or OOXML. Or consider a simpler example. In this chapter, you are learning about the container classes in the Python library. It is possible to implement these containers more efficiently. Should you use the library containers in your own code, or should you implement better containers yourself? Most software engineers would "roll their own" only if there was a very significant reason to deviate from the standard implementation.

8.2 Dictionaries

A dictionary keeps associations between keys and values.

A **dictionary** is a container that keeps associations between *keys* and *values*. Every key in the dictionary has an associated value. Keys are unique, but a value may be associated with several keys. Figure 7 gives a typical example: a dictionary that associates names with colors might describe the favorite colors of various people. The dictionary structure is also known as a *map* because it maps a unique key to a value. It stores the keys, values, and the associations between them.

Syntax 8.1 **Set and Dictionary Literals**

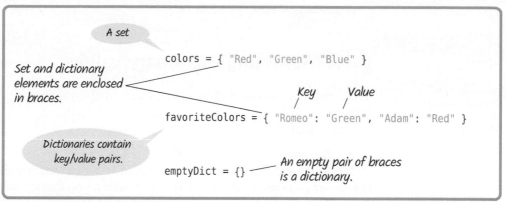

In Figure 7, we show the dictionary object for a collection of items in which the mapping between the key and value is indicated by an arrow.

Each bar code (key) is associated with a book (value). In Python, you can store the key/value pairs in a dictionary.

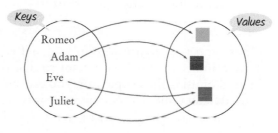

Figure 7 A Dictionary

8.2.1 Creating Dictionaries

Suppose you need to write a program that looks up the phone number for a person in your mobile phone's contact list. You can use a dictionary where the names are keys and the phone numbers are values. The dictionary also allows you to associate more than one person with a given number.

Here we create a small dictionary for a contact list that contains four items (see Figure 8):

```
contacts = { "Fred": 7235591, "Mary": 3841212, "Bob": 3841212, "Sarah": 2213278 }
```

Each key/value pair is separated by a colon. You enclose the key/value pairs in braces, just as you would when forming a set. When the braces contain key/value pairs, they denote a dictionary, not a set. The only ambiguous case is an empty {}. By convention, it denotes an empty dictionary, not an empty set.

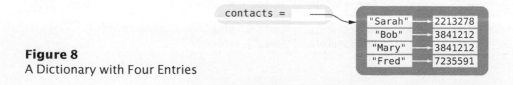

Figure 8
A Dictionary with Four Entries

You can create a duplicate copy of a dictionary using the dict function:

```
oldContacts = dict(contacts)
```

8.2.2 Accessing Dictionary Values

Use the [] operator to access the value associated with a key.

The subscript operator [] is used to return the value associated with a key. The statement

```
print("Fred's number is", contacts["Fred"])
```

prints 7235591.

Note that the dictionary is not a sequence-type container like a list. Even though the subscript operator is used with a dictionary, you cannot access the items by index or position. A value can only be accessed using its associated key.

The in operator is used to test whether a key is in a dictionary.

The key supplied to the subscript operator must be a valid key in the dictionary or a KeyError exception will be raised. To find out whether a key is present in the dictionary, use the in (or not in) operator:

```
if "John" in contacts :
    print("John's number is", contacts["John"])
else :
    print("John is not in my contact list.")
```

Often, you want to use a default value if a key is not present. For example, if there is no number for Fred, you want to dial the directory assistance number instead. Instead of using the in operator, you can simply call the get method and pass the key and a default value. The default value is returned if there is no matching key.

```
number = contacts.get("Fred", 411)
print("Dial " + number)
```

8.2.3 Adding and Modifying Items

New items can be added or modified using the [] operator.

A dictionary is a mutable container. That is, you can change its contents after it has been created. You can add a new item using the subscript operator [] much as you would with a list (see Figure 9):

```
contacts["John"] = 4578102
```
❶

To change the value associated with a given key, set a new value using the [] operator on an existing key:

```
contacts["John"] = 2228102
```
❷

Sometimes you may not know which items will be contained in the dictionary when it's created. You can create an empty dictionary like this:

```
favoriteColors = {}
```

and add new items as needed:

```
favoriteColors["Juliet"] = "Blue"
favoriteColors["Adam"] = "Red"
favoriteColors["Eve"] = "Blue"
favoriteColors["Romeo"] = "Green"
```

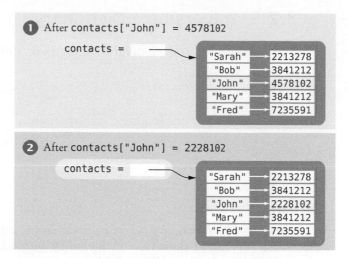

Figure 9 Adding and Modifying Dictionary Entries

8.2.4 Removing Items

To remove an item from a dictionary, call the pop method with the key as the argument:

```
contacts.pop("Fred")
```

This removes the entire item, both the key and its associated value (see Figure 10). The pop method returns the value of the item being removed, so you can use it or store it in a variable:

```
fredsNumber = contacts.pop("Fred")
```

If the key is not in the dictionary, the pop method raises a KeyError exception. To prevent the exception from being raised, you can test for the key in the dictionary:

```
if "Fred" in contacts :
    contacts.pop("Fred")
```

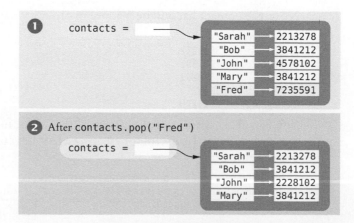

Figure 10 Removing a Dictionary Entry

8.2.5 Traversing a Dictionary

You can iterate over the individual keys in a dictionary using a for loop:

```
print("My Contacts:")
for key in contacts :
    print(key)
```

The result of this code fragment is shown below:

```
My Contacts:
Sarah
Bob
John
Mary
Fred
```

Note that the dictionary stores its items in an order that is optimized for efficiency, which may not be the order in which they were added. (Like a set, a dictionary uses a hash table—see Special Topic 8.1.)

To access the value associated with a key in the body of the loop, you can use the loop variable with the subscript operator. For example, these statements print both the name and phone number of your contacts:

```
print("My Contacts:")
for key in contacts :
    print("%-10s %d" % (key, contacts[key]))
```

in this format:

```
My Contacts:
Sarah      2213278
Bob        3841212
John       4578102
Mary       3841212
Fred       7235591
```

The order in which the keys are visited is based on the order in which the items are stored internally. To iterate through the keys in sorted order, you can use the sorted function as part of the for loop:

```
print("My Contacts:")
for key in sorted(contacts) :
    print("%-10s %d" % (key, contacts[key]))
```

Now, the contact list will be printed in order by name:

```
My Contacts:
Bob        3841212
Fred       7235591
John       4578102
Mary       3841212
Sarah      2213278
```

You can also iterate over the *values* of the items, instead of the keys, using the values method. This can be useful for creating a list that contains all of the phone numbers in our dictionary:

```
phoneNumbers = []    # Create an empty list.
for number in contacts.values() :
    phoneNumbers.append(number)
```

Table 2 Common Dictionary Operations

Operation	Description
d = dict() d = dict(c)	Creates a new empty dictionary or a duplicate copy of dictionary c.
d = {} d = {k_1: v_1, k_2: v_2, ..., k_n: v_n}	Creates a new empty dictionary or a dictionary that contains the initial items provided. Each item consists of a key (k) and a value (v) separated by a colon.
len(d)	Returns the number of items in dictionary d.
key in d *key* not in d	Determines if the key is in the dictionary.
$d[key]$ = *value*	Adds a new *key*/*value* item to the dictionary if the *key* does not exist. If the key does exist, it modifies the value associated with the key.
x = $d[key]$	Returns the value associated with the given key. The key must exist or an exception is raised.
d.get(*key*, *default*)	Returns the value associated with the given key, or the default value if the key is not present.
d.pop(*key*)	Removes the key and its associated value from the dictionary and returns the value. Raises an exception if the key is not present.
d.values()	Returns a sequence containing all values in the dictionary.

As an alternative, you can pass the result of the values method to the list function to create the same list:

```
phoneNumbers = list(contacts.values())
```

A simple example to illustrate the use of a dictionary is a telephone database in which names are associated with telephone numbers. In the sample program below, the find-Names function searches the dictionary for all names associated with a given number. The printAll function produces an alphabetical listing of all items.

sec02/telephone.py

```
 1  ##
 2  #   This program maintains a dictionary of name/phone number pairs.
 3  #
 4
 5  def main() :
 6      myContacts = {"Fred": 7235591, "Mary": 3841212,
 7                    "Bob": 3841212, "Sarah": 2213278 }
 8
 9      # See if Fred is in the list of contacts.
10      if "Fred" in myContacts :
11          print("Number for Fred:", myContacts["Fred"])
12      else :
13          print("Fred is not in my contact list.")
14
15      # Get and print a list of every contact with a given number.
16      nameList = findNames(myContacts, 3841212)
```

```
17      print("Names for 384-1212: ", end="")
18      for name in nameList :
19         print(name, end=" ")
20      print()
21
22      # Print a list of all names and numbers.
23      printAll(myContacts)
24
25   ## Find all names associated with a given telephone number.
26   #    @param contacts the dictionary
27   #    @param number the telephone number to be searched
28   #    @return the list of names
29   #
30   def findNames(contacts, number) :
31      nameList = []
32      for name in contacts :
33         if contacts[name] == number :
34            nameList.append(name)
35
36      return nameList
37
38   ## Print an alphabetical listing of all dictionary items.
39   #    @param contacts the dictionary
40   #
41   def printAll(contacts) :
42      print("All names and numbers:")
43      for key in sorted(contacts) :
44         print("%-10s %d" % (key, contacts[key]))
45
46   # Start the program.
47   main()
```

Program Run

```
Number for Fred: 7235591
Names for 384-1212: Bob Mary
All names and numbers:
Bob         3841212
Fred        7235591
Mary        3841212
Sarah       2213278
```

Special Topic 8.2

Iterating over Dictionary Items

Python allows you to iterate over the items in a dictionary using the items method. This is a bit more efficient than iterating over the keys and then looking up the value of each key.

The items method returns a sequence of tuples that contain the keys and values of all items. (See Special Topic 6.5 for more information about tuples.) For example,

```
for item in contacts.items() :
   print(item[0], item[1])
```

Here the loop variable item will be assigned a tuple that contains the key in the first slot and the value in the second slot.

Alternatively, you can use tuple assignment:

```
for (key, value) in contacts.items() :
   print(key, value)
```

Special Topic 8.3

Storing Data Records

Data records, in which each record consists of multiple fields, are very common. In Chapter 7, you learned how to extract data records from text files using different file formats. In some instances, the individual fields of the record were stored in a list to simplify the storage. But this requires remembering in which element of the list each field is stored. This can introduce run-time errors into your program if you use the wrong list element when processing the record.

In Python, it is common to use a dictionary to store a data record. You create an item for each data record in which the key is the field name and the value is the data value for that field. For example, this dictionary named `record` stores a single student record with fields for ID, name, class, and GPA:

```
record = { "id": 100, "name": "Sally Roberts", "class": 2, "gpa": 3.78 }
```

To extract records from a file, we can define a function that reads a single record and returns it as a dictionary. In this example, the file to be read contains records made up of country names and population data separated by a colon:

```python
def extractRecord(infile) :
    record = {}
    line = infile.readline()
    if line != "" :
        fields = line.split(":")
        record["country"] = fields[0]
        record["population"] = int(fields[1])
    return record
```

The dictionary `record` that is returned has two items, one with the key "country" and the other with the key "population". This function's result can be used to print all of the records to the terminal. With a dictionary, you can access the data fields by name (instead of by position as you would with a list):

```python
infile = open("populations.txt", "r")
record = extractRecord(infile)
while len(record) > 0 :
    print("%-20s %10d" % (record["country"], record["population"]))
    record = extractRecord(infile)
```

WORKED EXAMPLE 8.2

Translating Text Messages

Problem Statement Instant messaging (IM) and texting on portable devices has resulted in a set of common abbreviations useful for brief messages. However, some individuals may not understand these abbreviations. Write a program that reads a one-line text message containing common abbreviations and translates the message into English using a set of translations stored in a file. For example, if the user enters the text message

```
y r u l8?
```

the program should print

```
why are you late?
```

Step 1   Decompose the task into steps.

This problem can be split into several simple steps:

> *Load standard translations into a dictionary.*
> *Get message from user.*
> *Split the message into parts.*
> *Build a translation for each part.*
> *Print the translated message.*

We know how to read the message and split it into parts using the split function. Printing the resulting translation is also clear. Loading the translations and translating the parts are explored in the following steps.

Step 2   Load the standard translations.

The standard translations are stored in a text file with each abbreviation/translation pair on its own line and separated by a colon:

```
r:are
y:why
u:you
ttyl:talk to you later
l8:late
...
```

To read the file entries and build the dictionary, we add one item for each abbreviation to the transMap dictionary. The abbreviation is the key and the translation is the value:

```
transMap = {}
infile = open(filename, "r")
for line in infile :
    parts = line.split(":")
    transMap[parts[0]] = parts[1].rstrip()
```

Step 3   Translate a single abbreviation.

We separate out the task of translating a single abbreviation into the translateAbbr function because the processing is fairly complex.

If the abbreviation ends with a punctuation symbol (. ? ! , ; :), we must remove the punctuation, translate the abbreviation, and add the punctuation back.

If the abbreviation is not known, we use the original as the translation.

> *If abbrv ends in punctuation*
>   *lastChar = punctuation*
>   *abbrv = abbrv with punctuation removed*
> *Else*
>   *lastChar = ""*
> *If abbrv in dictionary*
>   *translated = translation[abbrv]*
> *Else*
>   *translated = abbrv*
> *translated = translated + lastChar*

Step 4   Combine the translations of the parts.

After getting a message from the user, we split it into words. Then we translate it one abbreviation at a time and build a string that contains the final translation:

```
theParts = message.split()
translation = ""
for abbrv in theParts :
    translation = translation + translateAbbrv(transMap, abbrv) + " "
```

Step 5 Combine the functions into a single program.

The following program shows the implementation of the main function and all the helper functions in a single file.

worked_example_2/translate.py

```
1  ##
2  #    This program translates a single line of text from text messaging
3  #    abbreviations to English.
4  #
5
6  def main() :
7      transMap = buildMapping("textabbv.txt")
8
9      print("Enter a message to be translated:")
10     message = input("")
11     theParts = message.split()
12
13     translation = ""
14     for abbrv in theParts :
15         translation = translation + translateAbbrv(transMap, abbrv) + " "
16
17     print("The translated text is:")
18     print(translation)
19
20  ## Extracts abbreviations and their corresponding English phrases from a
21  #  file and builds a translation mapping.
22  #  @param filename  name of the file containing the translations
23  #  @return a dictionary associating abbreviations with phrases
24  #
25  def buildMapping(filename) :
26      transMap = {}
27      infile = open(filename, "r")
28      for line in infile :
29          parts = line.split(":")
30          transMap[parts[0]] = parts[1].rstrip()
31
32      infile.close()
33      return transMap
34
35  ## Translates a single abbreviation using the translation map. If the abbre-
36  #  viation ends with a punctuation mark, it remains part of the translation.
37  #  @param transMap  a dictionary containing the common translations
38  #  @param abbrv  a string that contains the abbreviation to be translated
39  #  @return the word or phrase corresponding to the abbreviation. If the
40  #  abbreviation cannot be translated, it is returned unchanged
41  #
42  def translateAbbrv(transMap, abbrv) :
43      # Determine if the word ends with a punctuation mark.
44      lastChar = abbrv[len(abbrv) - 1]
45      if lastChar in ".?!,;:" :
46          abbrv = abbrv.rstrip(lastChar)
47      else :
48          lastChar = ""
49
50      # Translate the abbrv.
51      if abbrv in transMap :
52          word = transMap[abbrv]
```

```
53      else :
54          word = abbrv
55
56      # Return the translated word and the original punctuation mark.
57      return word + lastChar
58
59  # Start the program.
60  main()
```

Program Run

```
Enter a message to be translated:
y r u l8?
The translated text is:
why are you late?
```

8.3 Complex Structures

Complex structures can help to better organize data for processing.

Containers are very useful for storing collections of values. Some data collections, however, may require more complex structures. In Chapter 6, we used a list of lists to create a two-dimensional structure that could be used to store tabular data. In Python, the list and dictionary containers can contain any type of data, including other containers. In this section, we explore problems that require the use of a complex structure.

8.3.1 A Dictionary of Sets

The index of a book specifies on which pages each term occurs. Suppose you are assigned the task of building a book index from page numbers and terms contained in a text file with the following format:

```
6:type
7:example
7:index
7:program
8:type
10:example
11:program
20:set
...
```

The file includes every occurrence of every term to be included in the index and the page on which the term occurs. When building an index, if a term occurs on the same page more than once, the index includes the page number only once.

The output of the program should be a list of terms in alphabetical order followed by the page numbers on which the term occurs, separated by commas, like this:

```
example 7, 10
index 7
program 7, 11
set 20
type 6, 8
```

What type of container or structure would be appropriate for this problem?

The most practical would be a dictionary of sets. Each key can be a term and its corresponding value a set of the page numbers where it occurs (see Figure 11).

The use of this structure ensures that we satisfy several requirements:

© Neil Kurtzman/iStockphoto.

In a dictionary of sets, each key is associated with a set of values.

- The terms in the index must be unique. By making each term a dictionary key, there will be only one instance of each term.

- The index listing must be provided in alphabetical order by term. We can iterate over the keys of the dictionary in sorted order to produce the listing.

- Duplicate page numbers for a term should only be included once. By adding each page number to a set, we ensure that no duplicates will be added.

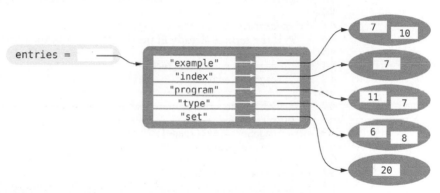

Figure 11   A Dictionary of Sets for Creating an Index

A complete solution for this problem is provided below.

sec03_01/buildindex.py

```
1   ##
2   #  This program builds the index of a book from terms and page numbers.
3   #
4
5   def main() :
6      # Create an empty dictionary.
7      indexEntries = {}
8
9      # Extract the data from the text file.
10     infile = open("indexdata.txt", "r")
11     fields = extractRecord(infile)
12     while len(fields) > 0 :
13        addWord(indexEntries, fields[1], fields[0])
14        fields = extractRecord(infile)
15
16     infile.close()
```

```
17
18      # Print the index listing.
19      printIndex(indexEntries)
20
21  ## Extract a single record from the input file.
22  #   @param infile the input file object
23  #   @return a list containing the page number and term or an empty list if
24  #   the end of file was reached
25  #
26  def extractRecord(infile) :
27      line = infile.readline()
28      if line != "" :
29          fields = line.split(":")
30          page = int(fields[0])
31          term = fields[1].rstrip()
32          return [page, term]
33      else :
34          return []
35
36  ## Add a word and its page number to the index.
37  #   @param entries  the dictionary of index entries
38  #   @param term the term to be added to the index
39  #   @param page the page number for this occurrence of the term
40  #
41  def addWord(entries, term, page) :
42      # If the term is already in the dictionary, add the page to the set.
43      if term in entries :
44          pageSet = entries[term]
45          pageSet.add(page)
46
47      # Otherwise, create a new set that contains the page and add an entry.
48      else :
49          pageSet = set([page])
50          entries[term] = pageSet
51
52  ## Print the index listing.
53  #   @param entries a dictionary containing the entries of the index
54  #
55  def printIndex(entries) :
56      for key in sorted(entries) :
57          print(key, end=" ")
58          pageSet = entries[key]
59          first = True
60          for page in sorted(pageSet) :
61              if first :
62                  print(page, end="")
63                  first = False
64              else :
65                  print(",", page, end="")
66
67          print()
68
69  # Start the program.
70  main()
```

8.3.2 A Dictionary of Lists

As you have seen, dictionary values, which are associated with unique keys, can be any data type, including a container. A common use of dictionaries in Python is to store a collection of lists in which each list is associated with a unique name or key. For example, consider the problem of extracting data from a text file that represents the yearly sales of different ice cream flavors in multiple stores of a retail ice cream company.

© fotofrog/iStockphoto.

```
vanilla:8580.0:7201.25:8900.0
chocolate:10225.25:9025.0:9505.0
rocky road:6700.1:5012.45:6011.0
strawberry:9285.15:8276.1:8705.0
cookie dough:7901.25:4267.0:7056.5
```

The data is to be processed to produce a report similar to the following:

```
chocolate       10225.25    9025.00    9505.00    28755.25
cookie dough     7901.25    4267.00    7056.50    19224.75
rocky road       6700.10    5012.45    6011.00    17723.55
strawberry       9285.15    8276.10    8705.00    26266.25
vanilla          8580.00    7201.25    8900.00    24681.25
                42691.75   33781.80   40177.50
```

The report includes the sales of each flavor of ice cream in each store with the flavors listed in alphabetical order. The total sales by flavor and by store are also included.

Because the records of the report have to be listed in alphabetical order by flavor, we must read all of the records before the report can be generated.

This sales data is an example of tabular data that consists of rows and columns. In Chapter 6, we created a list of lists to store tabular data. But that structure is not the best choice because the entries consist of strings and floating-point values, and they have to be sorted by the flavor name.

We can still store the data in tabular form, but instead of using a list of lists, we will use a dictionary of lists (see Figure 12). With this structure, each row of the table is an item in the dictionary. The name of the ice cream flavor is the key used to identify a particular row in the table. The value for each key is a list that contains the sales, by store, for that flavor of ice cream.

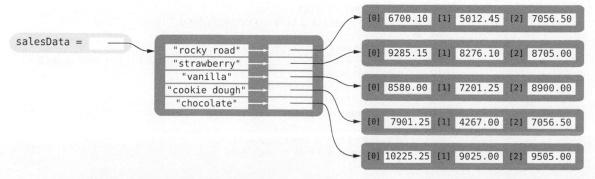

Figure 12 A Dictionary of Lists for Tabular Data

A complete solution that prints the data in the tabular format above is provided below.

sec03_02/icecreamsales.py

```python
1   ##
2   #   This program processes a collection of sales data for flavors of ice cream
3   #   and prints a report sorted by flavor.
4   #
5
6   def main() :
7       salesData = readData("icecream.txt")
8       printReport(salesData)
9
10  ## Reads the tabular data.
11  #   @param filename  name of the input file
12  #   @return a dictionary whose keys are ice cream flavors and
13  #   whose values are sales data
14  #
15  def readData(filename) :
16      # Create an empty dictionary.
17      salesData = {}
18
19      infile = open(filename, "r")
20
21      # Read each record from the file.
22      for line in infile :
23          fields = line.split(":")
24          flavor = fields[0]
25          salesData[flavor] = buildList(fields)
26
27      infile.close()
28      return salesData
29
30  ## Builds a list of store sales contained in the fields split from a string.
31  #   @param fields  a list of strings comprising the record fields
32  #   @return a list of floating-point values
33  #
34  def buildList(fields) :
35      storeSales = []
36      for i in range(1, len(fields)) :
37          sales = float(fields[i])
38          storeSales.append(sales)
39
40      return storeSales
41
42  ## Prints a sales report.
43  #   @param salesData  a table composed of a dictionary of lists
44  #
45  def printReport(salesData) :
46      # Find the number of stores as the length of the longest store sales list.
47      numStores = 0
48      for storeSales in salesData.values() :
49          if len(storeSales) > numStores :
50              numStores = len(storeSales)
51
52      # Create a list of store totals.
53      storeTotals = [0.0] * numStores
54
```

```
55    # Print the flavor sales.
56    for flavor in sorted(salesData) :
57        print("%-15s" % flavor, end="")
58
59        flavorTotal = 0.0
60        storeSales = salesData[flavor]
61        for i in range(len(storeSales)) :
62            sales = storeSales[i]
63            flavorTotal = flavorTotal + sales
64            storeTotals[i] = storeTotals[i] + sales
65            print("%10.2f" % sales, end="")
66
67        print("%15.2f" % flavorTotal)
68
69    # Print the store totals.
70    print("%15s" % " ", end="")
71    for i in range(numStores) :
72        print("%10.2f" % storeTotals[i], end="")
73    print()
74
75  # Start the program.
76  main()
```

Special Topic 8.4
User Modules

When you write small programs, you can place all of your code into a single source file. When your programs get larger or you work in a team, that situation changes. You will want to structure your code by splitting it into separate source files.

There are two reasons why this split becomes necessary. First, large programs can consist of hundreds of functions that become difficult to manage and debug if they are all in one source file. By distributing the functions over several source files and grouping related functions together, it becomes easier to test and debug the various functions. The second reason becomes apparent when you work with other programmers in a team. It would be very difficult for multiple programmers to edit a single source file simultaneously. Therefore, the program code is broken up so that each programmer is solely responsible for a separate set of files.

The code of complex programs is distributed over multiple files.

Large Python programs typically consist of a **driver module** and one or more supplemental modules. The driver module contains the main function or the first executable statement if no main function is used. The supplemental modules contain supporting functions and constant variables.

For example, we can split up the program of Section 8.3.2 into two modules. The tabulardata.py module contains functions for reading the data from a file and printing a dictionary of lists with row and column totals. The salesreport.py module is the driver (or main) module that contains the main function. By splitting the program into two modules, the functions in the tabulardata.py module can be reused in another program that needs to process named lists of numbers.

To call a function or use a constant variable that is defined in a user module, you can first import the module in the same way that you imported a standard library module:

```
from tabulardata import readData, printReport
```

However, if a module defines many functions, it is easier to use the form

```
import tabulardata
```

With this form, you must prepend the name of the module to the function name:

```
tabulardata.printReport(salesData)
```

We provide the two modules in the book's companion code. To run the program, you execute the driver module either from the command line

```
python salesreport.py
```

or using your integrated development environment.

EXAMPLE CODE   See special_topic_4/salesreport.py and tabulardata.py in your companion code for the modules.

WORKED EXAMPLE 8.3
Graphics: Pie Charts

Pie charts are commonly used to graphically illustrate the distribution of data among various categories. The circular pie is divided into slices with each slice's size representing a proportion of the whole. A brief description of the category and the proportion of each slice is commonly shown as part of the chart, often as a legend that maps the information to a specific slice using the slice color.

Problem Statement   Design and implement a program that draws a pie chart and its corresponding legend illustrating the distribution of an individual's investments among several categories.

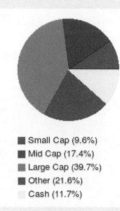

■ Small Cap (9.6%)
■ Mid Cap (17.4%)
■ Large Cap (39.7%)
■ Other (21.6%)
□ Cash (11.7%)

We'll use a modular design and divide the solution into three parts: drawing the pie chart, creating the chart data, and drawing the legend.

Pie Chart and Legend

A pie chart can be constructed by drawing multiple arcs of a circle, each one a slice for one category of the chart. You can draw an arc using the canvas method drawArc in the ezgraphics module.

```
canvas.drawArc(x, y, diameter, startAngle, extent)
```

To draw an arc, you specify the *x*- and *y*-coordinates of the bounding square, as with an oval, followed by the diameter of the circle. You must also indicate the angle in degrees (0–360) where the arc begins on the circle, and the angular extent, or size, of the arc.

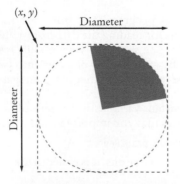

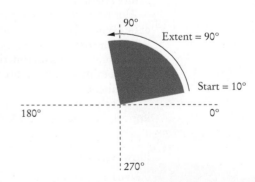

To draw the pie chart, we can implement a generic drawing function that can be used to draw a chart for any type of data. The information needed to draw a pie chart includes: the size of the pie (or circle), the (x, y) coordinates of the upper-left corner of the circle's bounding square, the canvas on which to draw the chart, the proportion (percentage) of each slice to the whole, and the color of each slice.

Because we need multiple data values for each slice, we can supply this information as a list of dictionaries. Each dictionary in the list will contain three entries, the "size", "color", and "label" of a slice. We use the data field names as the keys in the dictionary so we can access the fields by name. That way, we don't have to remember which position each field occupies, as we would with a list.

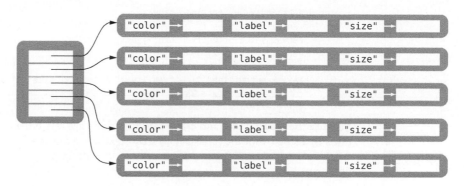

Each slice of the pie is drawn as an individual arc. Because the data for each slice is stored in a separate dictionary, we can iterate over the list of dictionaries and draw each slice in turn.

The size of the arc will be the proportion of the slice to the whole pie. A circle has an angle of 360 degrees, so the extent of an individual slice can be computed as

slice extent = 360 x slice proportion

where the slice proportion is specified as a percentage. For simplicity, we start the first slice at an angle of 0 degrees (the positive x-axis). The angle at which each succeeding slice begins is the angle where the previous slice ended. The ending angle of a slice is simply the starting angle plus the slice extent. Before a slice is drawn, the outline and fill color must be set to the color specified for that slice. The implementation of this task is provided below:

```
## Draws a pie chart on a canvas inside an invisible bounding square.
#  @param x x-coord of the upper-left corner of the bounding square
#  @param y y-coord of the upper-left corner of the bounding square
#  @param diameter the diameter of the bounding square
#  @param slices a list of dictionaries that specify the "size" and
#  "color" of each slice
#  @param canvas the canvas on which to draw the pie chart
#
def drawPieChart(x, y, diameter, slices, canvas) :
    startAngle = 0
    for piece in slices :
        extent = 360 * piece["size"]
        canvas.setColor(piece["color"])
        canvas.drawArc(x, y, diameter, startAngle, extent)
        startAngle = startAngle + extent
```

We also want to include a legend with the pie chart to indicate the category and proportion of each slice. Our legend will include a small colored box and a short label for each slice. The legend entries will be stacked to provide a neatly organized view.

To draw a legend on the canvas we again implement a generic function that can be used with any type of chart. For this function, we need the (x, y) coordinates of the upper-left corner of a bounding box, the canvas on which to draw the legend, and the color, label, and size of each slice. Because a legend will most likely be used with a pie chart, we will pass the slice information to the drawLegend function as a list of dictionaries. This allows us to use the same structure with both draw functions. To draw the legend, each dictionary needs three entries, the `"size"`, `"color"`, and `"label"`. The implementation of the `drawLegend` function is provided below:

```
## Draws a legend, consisting of a colored box and text, on a canvas.
#  @param x x-coord of the starting position of the entries
#  @param y y-coord of the top position of the first entry
#  @param entries a list of dictionaries that specify the information
#  for each entry: "color", "label", "size"
#  @param canvas the canvas on which to draw the legend
#
def drawLegend(x, y, entries, canvas) :
    for entry in entries :
        canvas.setColor(entry["color"])
        canvas.drawRect(x, y, 10, 10)
        canvas.setColor("black")
        text = entry["label"] + " (%.1f%%)" % (entry["size"] * 100)
        canvas.drawText(x + 15, y, text)
        y = y + 20
```

Because the `drawPieChart` and `drawLegend` functions are related, we can place both implementations in a single module (`piechart.py`). By separating out these two functions from the rest of the program, we can easily reuse one or both in another program that needs to draw a pie chart or legend.

Stock Portfolio

The second module for this program will contain the functions needed to extract the stock portfolio from a text file and to build the list of dictionaries needed by the two draw functions. For simplicity, we assume a text file that contains stock allocations in the following format:

```
PETS small 8250.0
BBY mid 6535.0
NVDA mid 5500.0
LXK mid 2825.0
LOW large 5800.0
COP large 9745.0
TGT large 6200.0
VZ large 12185.0
bonds misc 18500.0
cash cash 10000.0
```

Each line contains a single record made of three fields: the stock symbol, the category of stock, and the dollar amount owned of that stock.

To illustrate the distribution of stocks by category, we need to accumulate the total amount owned in each category. We'll use a dictionary in which each key is a category and the corresponding value is the total amount of the stocks in that category. As each record is extracted from the file, we check the dictionary to see if the category is already in the dictionary. If not, we add a new entry along with the amount from the current record. If the category is in the dictionary, then we increment its value by the amount of this record. After all of the records have been extracted, the function returns the dictionary:

```
## Loads the category allocations from a stock portfolio.
#  @param filename name of the file containing the portfolio
#  @return a dictionary consisting of category codes and total per category
#
def loadAllocations(filename) :
    # Open the stock portfolio file.
    infile = open("stocks.txt", "r")

    # Extract the stocks and accumulate the category sums.
    allocations = {}
```

```
    for line in infile :
        fields = line.split()
        cat = fields[1]
        amount = float(fields[2])
        if cat in allocations :
            allocations[cat] = allocations[cat] + amount
        else :
            allocations[cat] = amount

    infile.close()
    return allocations
```

To draw the pie chart and legend, we must take the category allocations returned by the `load-Allocations` function and build the list of dictionaries needed by the `drawPieChart` and `drawLegend` functions. The function for this task needs to compute the stock allocation percentages by category, but the colors and descriptions of each category can be hard coded.

The implementation of the function for this task is provided below:

```
## Builds a list of dictionaries that contain the categories, allocation
#  percentages, and slice colors.
#  @param allocations a dictionary containing the stock allocations by category
#  @return a list of dictionaries containing the pie chart and legend information
#
def buildChartData(allocations) :
    categories = [
        {"cat": "small", "color": "blue", "text": "Small Cap"},
        {"cat": "mid", "color": "red", "text": "Mid Cap"},
        {"cat": "large", "color": "green", "text": "Large Cap"},
        {"cat": "misc", "color": "magenta", "text": "Other"},
        {"cat": "cash", "color": "yellow", "text": "Cash"}
    ]

    # Compute the total allocations.
    total = sum(allocations.values())

    # Compute the percentages per category and build a list of categories.
    slices = []
    for info in categories :
        category = info["cat"]
        info["size"] = allocations[category] / total
        slices.append(info)

    return slices
```

Driver Module

The driver module imports our two user-defined modules, `piechart` and `portfolio`, in addition to the `ezgraphics` module, and provides the `main` function:

Load the stock allocations.
Build the structure for use with the draw routines.
Create a graphics window.
Draw the pie chart and legend on the canvas.

The Python code that implements these simple steps is shown below. To allow for a pie chart of any size, we define a constant variable for its width. This variable is used to calculate the size of the window and the position of the legend.

```
from ezgraphics import GraphicsWindow
from piechart import drawPieChart, drawLegend
from portfolio import loadAllocations, buildChartData
```

```
PIE_SIZE = 150

# Load the stock allocations and compute the percentages.
allocations = loadAllocations("stocks.txt")
slices = buildChartData(allocations)

# Create the graphics window and draw the pie chart and legend.
height = PIE_SIZE + 75 + len(slices) * 20

win = GraphicsWindow(PIE_SIZE + 100, height)
canvas = win.canvas()
drawPieChart(50, 25, PIE_SIZE, slices, canvas)
drawLegend(50, PIE_SIZE + 50, slices, canvas)
win.wait()
```

EXAMPLE CODE   See `worked_example_3` in your eText or companion code for the complete stock allocation program.

TOOLBOX 8.1

Harvesting JSON Data from the Web

Many web applications provide data that can be used in other programs. A web application is a program that is executed by a web server when a connection is made to a designated URL. Some web applications build a web page for display in a browser; others can return data. To obtain data from a web application, you access its web site through its **application programming interface (API)**. The API specifies the web address and any arguments that must be provided in order for it to produce the desired results.

To share or exchange data, web applications commonly use the JSON (JavaScript Object Notation) format. JSON is a standard data format that allows for the exchange of data between applications with no more than plain text. It is especially useful for data that has large records with multiple data fields.

In this section you will learn how to use Python's json module to work with web data in the JSON format.

Suppose you want to know the current weather conditions in London. You can write a program that downloads this information from the openweathermap.org web site. To obtain the data, you obtain the web address

```
address = "http://api.openweathermap.org/data/2.5/weather"
```

and append the name of the city and the units of measurement as arguments before opening the web connection:

```
url = address + "?" + "q=London,UK&units=imperial"
webData = urllib.request.urlopen(url)
```

The data is then read in one large chunk and converted to a string:

```
results = webData.read().decode()
```

The string contains the data stored in the JSON format (shown here neatly organized for readability):

```
{
    "coord": {"lon": -0.13,"lat": 51.51},
```

```
      "sys": {
         "type": 3,
         "id": 186527,
         "message": 1.2806,
         "country": "GB",
         "sunrise": 1427348916,
         "sunset": 1427394217
      },
      "weather": [
         {  "id": 800,
            "main: "Clear",
            "description": "Sky is Clear",
            "icon": "01d"
         }
      ],
      "base": "stations",
      "main": {
         "temp": 50.77,
         "humidity": 59,
         "pressure": 999.658,
         "temp_min": 48.99,
         "temp_max": 53.01
      },
      "wind": {"speed": 13.63, "deg": 308},
      "rain": {"3h": 0},
      "clouds": {"all": 0},
      "dt": 1427392093,
      "id": 2643743,
      "name": "London",
      "cod": 200
   }
```

As you can see, JSON uses the same notation for lists and dictionaries as Python.

To use the data in your program, it has to be converted from the JSON format to a dictionary. Use the loads function from the json module to convert it:

```
data = json.loads(results)
```

As part of the conversion, each data value is converted to its appropriate data type based on the definition of the JSON format (strings must be enclosed within double quotes and numbers follow the same rules as in Python). Thus, the data is ready for use without having to convert any of the data fields further:

```
current = data["main"]
degreeSym = chr(176)
print("Temperature: %d%sF" % (current["temp"], degreeSym))  # F for Fahrenheit
print("Humidity: %d%%" % current["humidity"])
print("Pressure: %d" % current["pressure"])
```

As indicated earlier, you may have to provide information to the web application as arguments in the URL when opening the connection. The openweathermap.org web application requires at least the name of the city, but we also supplied the units in which the temperature and wind data was to be provided.

Sometimes, the data passed as arguments may contain blank spaces or special characters. But a valid URL cannot contain such characters. To help produce a valid URL, you can use the urlencode function from the urllib.parse module and let Python do the work for you.

First, create a dictionary in which each parameter is stored as a key and the argument for the parameter is stored as the key's value:

```
params = {"q": "London, UK", "units": "imperial" }
```

Then, create a URL-encoded string from the dictionary and append it to the web address separated by a "?":

```
arguments = urllib.parse.urlencode(params)
url = address + "?" + arguments
```

The following is a complete program that obtains current weather information for a user-specified location.

toolbox_1/weather.py

```
 1  ##
 2  #   This program prints information about the current weather in a user-chosen city.
 3  #
 4
 5  import urllib.request
 6  import urllib.parse
 7  import json
 8
 9  # Get the location information from the user.
10  city = input("Enter the location: ")
11
12  # Build and encode the URL parameters.
13  params = {"q": city, "units": "imperial" }
14  arguments = urllib.parse.urlencode(params)
15
16  # Get the weather information.
17  address = "http://api.openweathermap.org/data/2.5/weather"
18  url = address + "?" + arguments
19
20  webData = urllib.request.urlopen(url)
21  results = webData.read().decode
22  webData.close()
23
24  # Convert the json result to a dictionary.
25  data = json.loads(results)
26
27  # Print the results.
28  current = data["main"]
29  degreeSym = chr(176)
30  print("Temperature: %d%sF" % (current["temp"], degreeSym))
31  print("Humidity: %d%%" % current["humidity"])
32  print("Pressure: %d" % current["pressure"])
```

CHAPTER SUMMARY

Understand how to use the operations from set theory with Python sets.

- A set stores a collection of unique values.
- A set is created using a set literal or the set function.
- The in operator is used to test whether an element is a member of a set.
- New elements can be added using the add method.
- Use the discard method to remove elements from a set.
- The issubset method tests whether one set is a subset of another set.
- The union method produces a new set that contains the elements in both sets.
- The intersection method produces a new set with the elements that are contained in both sets.
- The difference method produces a new set with the elements that belong to the first set but not the second.
- Set implementations arrange the elements so that they can be located quickly.

Work with Python dictionaries.

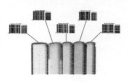

- A dictionary keeps associations between keys and values.
- Use the [] operator to access the value associated with a key.
- The in operator is used to test whether a key is in a dictionary.
- New entries can be added or modified using the [] operator.
- Use the pop method to remove a dictionary entry.

Combine containers to model data with complex structure.

- Complex structures can help to better organize data for processing.
- The code of complex programs is distributed over multiple files.

REVIEW EXERCISES

- **R8.1** A school web site keeps a collection of web sites that are blocked on student computers. Should the program that checks for blocked sites use a list, set, or dictionary for storing the site addresses? Explain your answer.

- **R8.2** A library wants to track which books are checked out to which patrons. Which type of container should they use?

- **R8.3** What is the difference between a set and a list?

- **R8.4** What is the difference between a list and a dictionary?

- **R8.5** An invoice contains a collection of purchased items. Should that collection be implemented as a list, set, or dictionary? Explain your answer.

- **R8.6** Consider a program that manages a schedule of classes. Should it place the meeting information into a list, set, or dictionary? Explain your answer.

- **R8.7** One way of implementing a calendar is as a dictionary that maps dates to event descriptions. However, that only works if there is a single event for a given date. What type of complex structure can you use to allow for multiple events on a given date?

- **R8.8** It is customary to represent a month of the year as an integer value. Suppose you need to write a program that prints the month name instead of the month number for a collection of dates. Instead of using a big if/elif/else statement to select the name for a given month, you can store the names in a structure. Should the names be stored in a list, set, or dictionary? Explain your answer.

  Suppose you frequently need to carry out the opposite conversion, from month names to integers. Would you use a list, set, or dictionary? Explain your answer.

- **R8.9** If Python did not provide the set container, but you needed one in your program, what type of container could you use instead? Explain your answer.

- **R8.10** Assume that Python does not provide the set container and, using the container from Exercise • R8.9, implement a function that performs the set intersection operation.

- **R8.11** Can a dictionary have two keys with the same value? Two values with the same key?

- **R8.12** Define a dictionary that maps month name abbreviations to month names.

- **R8.13** Define a dictionary with five entries that maps student identification numbers to their full names.

- **R8.14** Define a dictionary that maps the course numbers of the courses you are currently taking to their corresponding course titles.

- **R8.15** Define a dictionary that maps the ISBN number of your textbooks to their titles.

- **R8.16** Write a function that takes a string argument and returns
    - **a.** the most common letter in the string.
    - **b.** a set consisting of the lowercase letters not contained in the string.
    - **c.** a dictionary containing the number of times each letter occurs in the string.

- **R8.17** Write a function that takes two string arguments and returns

  a. a set consisting of the upper- and lowercase letters that are contained in both strings.

  b. a set consisting of the upper- and lowercase letters that are not contained in either string.

  c. a set consisting of all non-letter characters contained in both strings.

- **R8.18** Given a dictionary

  ```
  gradeCounts = { "A": 8, "D": 3, "B": 15, "F": 2, "C": 6 }
  ```

  write the Python statement(s) to print:

  a. all the keys.

  b. all the values.

  c. all the key and value pairs.

  d. all of the key and value pairs in key order.

  e. the average value.

  f. a chart similar to the following in which each row contains a key followed by a number of asterisks equal to the key's data value. The rows should be printed in key order, as shown below.

  ```
  A: ********
  B: ***************
  C: ******
  D: ***
  F: **
  ```

- **R8.19** Given the set definitions below, answer the following questions:

  ```
  set1 = { 1, 2, 3, 4, 5 }
  set2 = { 2, 4, 6, 8 }
  set3 = { 1, 5, 9, 13, 17 }
  ```

  a. Is set1 a subset of set2?

  b. Is the intersection of set1 and set3 empty?

  c. What is the result of performing set union on set1 and set2?

  d. What is the result of performing set intersection on set2 and set3?

  e. What is the result of performing set intersection on all three sets?

  f. What is the result of performing the set difference on set1 and set2 (set1 – set2)?

  g. What is the result of the instruction set1.discard(5)?

  h. What is the result of the instruction set2.discard(5)?

- ■■ **R8.20** Given three sets, set1, set2, and set3, write Python statement(s) to perform the following actions:

  a. Create a new set of all elements that are in set1 or set2, but not both.

  b. Create a new set of all elements that are in only one of the three sets set1, set2, and set3.

  c. Create a new set of all elements that are in exactly two of the sets set1, set2, and set3.

d. Create a new set of all integer elements in the range 1 through 25 that are not in set1.

e. Create a new set of all integer elements in the range 1 through 25 that are not in any of the three sets set1, set2, or set3.

f. Create a new set of all integer elements in the range 1 through 25 that are not in all three sets set1, set2, and set3.

PROGRAMMING EXERCISES

■ **P8.1** Write a new version of the program intname.py from Chapter 5 that uses a dictionary instead of if statements.

■ **P8.2** Write a program that counts how often each word occurs in a text file.

■■ **P8.3** Enhance the program from Exercise • P8.2 to print the 100 most common words.

■■ **P8.4** Implement the *sieve of Eratosthenes:* a function for computing prime numbers, known to the ancient Greeks. Choose an integer n. This function will compute all prime numbers up to n. First insert all numbers from 1 to n into a set. Then erase all multiples of 2 (except 2); that is, 4, 6, 8, 10, 12, ... Erase all multiples of 3, that is, 6, 9, 12, 15, ... Go up to $\sqrt{n}$. The remaining numbers are all primes.

■■ **P8.5** Write a program that keeps a dictionary in which both keys and values are strings—names of students and their course grades. Prompt the user of the program to add or remove students, to modify grades, or to print all grades. The printout should be sorted by name and formatted like this:

© martin mcelligott/iStockphoto.

```
Carl: B+
Joe: C
Sarah: A
Francine: A
```

■■■ **P8.6** Write a program that reads a Python source file and produces an index of all identifiers in the file. For each identifier, print all lines in which it occurs. For simplicity, consider any string consisting only of letters, numbers, and underscores an identifier.

■■■ **P8.7** Write a program that can store a polynomial such as

$$p(x) = 5x^{10} + 9x^7 - x - 10$$

as a list of terms. A term contains the coefficient and the power of x. For example, you would store $p(x)$ as

$$(5,10),(9,7),(-1,1),(-10,0)$$

Supply functions to add, multiply, and print polynomials. Supply a function that makes a polynomial from a single term. For example, the polynomial p can be constructed as

```
p = newPolynomial(-10, 0)
addTerm(p, -1, 1)
addTerm(p, 9, 7)
addTerm(p, 5, 10)
```

Then compute $p(x) \times p(x)$.

```
q = multiply(p, p)
printPolynomial(q)
```

Provide a module for the polynomial functions and import it into the driver module.

■■■ **P8.8** Repeat Exercise ●●● P8.7, but use a dictionary for the coefficients.

■■ **P8.9** Write a program that asks a user to type in two strings and that prints
- the characters that occur in both strings.
- the characters that occur in one string but not the other.
- the letters that don't occur in either string.

Use the set function to turn a string into a set of characters.

■■ **P8.10** Write a program that reads in two text files and prints out, in sorted order, all words that are common to both of them.

■■■ **P8.11** Write a program that reads in a text file, converts all words to lowercase, and prints out all words in the file that contain the letter a, the letter b, and so on. Build a dictionary whose keys are the lowercase letters, and whose values are sets of words containing the given letter.

■■■ **P8.12** Write a program that reads in a text file and builds up a dictionary as in Exercise ●●● P8.11. Then prompt the user for a word and print all words in the file containing all characters of that word. For example, if the program reads an English dictionary (such as /usr/share/dict/words on UNIX-like systems, or ch08/sec01/words in *your companion code*) and the user types in the word hat, your program should print all words containing these three letters: hat, that, heat, theater, and so on.

■■■ **P8.13** A multiset is a collection in which each item occurs with a frequency. You might have a multiset with two bananas and three apples, for example. A multiset can be implemented as a dictionary in which the keys are the items and the values are the frequencies. Write Python functions union, intersection, and difference that take two such dictionaries and return a dictionary representing the multiset union, intersection, and difference. In the union, the frequency of an item is the sum of the frequencies in both sets. In the intersection, the frequency of an item is the minimum of the frequencies in both sets. In the difference, the frequency of an item is the difference of the frequencies in both sets, but not less than zero.

■■ **P8.14** Write a "censor" program that first reads a file with "bad words" such as "sex", "drugs", "C++", and so on, places them in a set, and then reads an arbitrary text file. The program should write the text to a new text file, replacing each letter of any bad word in the text with an asterisk.

■■ **P8.15** Modify the program in Worked Example 8.2 so that, instead of reading a file with specific abbreviations, it reads a file with patterns such as

```
8:ate
2:to
2:too
4:for
@:at
&:and
```

Place these patterns in a dictionary. Read in a text and replace any occurrences of the words on the right with those on the left. For example, "fortunate" becomes "4tun8" and "tattoo" becomes "t@2".

■■ **P8.16** Modify the program in Section 8.3.2 so that the first line of the input file contains a sequence of column headers, separated by colons, such as

```
Downtown Store:Pleasantville Mall:College Corner
```

■■ **P8.17** Write a program that reads the data from https://www.cia.gov/library/publications/the-world-factbook/rankorder/rawdata_2004.txt into a dictionary whose keys are country names and whose values are per capita incomes. Then the program should prompt the user to enter country names and print the corresponding values. Stop when the user enters quit.

■■ **P8.18** The program of Exercise ●● P8.17 is not very user-friendly because it requires the user to know the exact spelling of the country name. As an enhancement, whenever a user enters a single letter, print all countries that start with that letter. Use a dictionary whose keys are letters and whose values are sets of country names.

■ **P8.19** A useful application for a dictionary is to remember, or cache, previously obtained results so that they can be retrieved from the cache when they are requested anew. Modify the word count program in Exercise ● P8.2 so that the user can repeatedly enter file names. If the user enters the same file name more than once, look up the answer from a dictionary instead of counting the words in the file again.

■■■ **P8.20** Write a program that reads a text file containing the image of maze such as

```
* *******
*   * * *
* ***** *
* * *   *
* * *** *
*   *   *
***** * *
*     * *
******* *
```

Here, the * are walls and the spaces are corridors. Produce a dictionary whose keys are tuples (row, column) of corridor locations and whose values are sets of neighboring corridor locations. In the example above, (1, 1) has neighbors { (1, 2), (0, 1), (2, 1) }. Print the dictionary.

■■■ **P8.21** Continue the program from Exercise ●●● P8.20 by finding an escape path from any point in the maze. Make a new dictionary whose keys are the corridor locations and whose values are the string "?". Then traverse the keys. For any key that is at the boundary of the maze, replace the "?" with a value "N", "E", "S", "W", indicating the compass direction of the escape path. Now repeatedly traverse the keys whose values are "?" and check if their neighbors are not "?", using the first dictionary to locate the neighbors. Whenever you have found such a neighbor, replace the "?" with the compass direction to the neighbor. Stop if you were unable to make any such replacement in a given traversal. Finally, print the maze, with the compass directions to the next escape location in each corridor location. For example,

```
*N*******
*NWW*?*S*
*N*****S*
*N*S*EES*
*N*S***S*
*NWW*EES*
*****N*S*
*EEEEN*S*
*******S*
```

■ ■ P8.22 A sparse array is a sequence of numbers in which most entries are zero. An efficient way of storing a sparse array is a dictionary in which the keys are the positions with nonzero values, and the values are the corresponding values in the sequence. For example, the sequence 0 0 0 0 0 4 0 0 0 2 9 would be represented with the dictionary { 5: 4, 9: 2, 10: 9 }. Write a function sparseArraySum, whose arguments are two such dictionaries a and b, that produces a sparse array that is the *vector sum*; that is, the result's value at position i is the sum of the values of a and b at position i.

■ Toolbox P8.23 The http://openweathermap.org web site also allows you to obtain the current weather information for a geographic location specified by its latitude and longitude (URL arguments lat=#&lon=#). Modify the toolbox_1/weather.py program to allow the user to provide the latitude and longitude of a location instead of its name.

■ Toolbox P8.24 When you connect to a web server with the call (as described in Toolbox 7.3)

```
response = urllib.request.urlopen(url)
```

you can query the "response headers", by calling

```
dict = response.getheaders()
```

The result is a dictionary that identifies, among other things, the web server, the date when the document was last modified, and the content type of the resource stored at that URL.

Write a program that prints this dictionary for a given URL, and test the program with a number of different URLs.

■ ■ Toolbox P8.25 Many CSV files (see Toolbox 7.1) start out with a header row that names the columns, as in

```
id,name,score,grade
1729,"Harry Smith",48,F
2358,"Susan Lee",99,A
4928,"Sammy Davis, Jr",78,C
```

If you have such a file, you can use the DictReader in the csv module to read each line as a dictionary, mapping the column names to the values. That is nicer than accessing the columns by their integer index. Here is the code outline:

```
reader = csv.DictReader(open(filename))
for row in reader :
    Process the dictionary row.
```

Write a program that uses this technique to read a CSV file such as the one given above. Display the IDs and names of the students with the highest and lowest scores.

CHAPTER 9

OBJECTS AND CLASSES

CHAPTER GOALS

To understand the concepts of classes, objects, and encapsulation

To implement instance variables, methods, and constructors

To be able to design, implement, and test your own classes

To understand the behavior of object references

CHAPTER CONTENTS

This chapter introduces you to object-oriented programming, an important technique for writing complex programs. In an object-oriented program, you don't simply manipulate numbers and strings, but you work with objects that are meaningful for your application. Objects with the same behavior (such as the windmills to the left) are grouped into classes. A programmer provides the desired behavior by specifying and implementing methods for these classes. In this chapter, you will learn how to discover, specify, and implement your own classes, and how to use them in your programs.

9.1 Object-Oriented Programming

You have learned how to structure your programs by decomposing tasks into functions. This is an excellent practice, but experience shows that it does not go far enough. It is difficult to understand and update a program that consists of a large collection of functions.

To overcome this problem, computer scientists invented **object-oriented programming**, a programming style in which tasks are solved by collaborating objects. Each object has its own set of data, together with a set of methods that act upon the data.

You have already experienced this programming style when you used strings, lists, and file objects. Each of these objects has a set of methods. For example, you can use the insert or remove methods to operate on list objects.

When you develop an object-oriented program, you create your own objects that describe what is important in your application. For example, in a student database you might work with Student and Course objects. Of course, then you must supply methods for these objects.

In Python, a **class** describes a set of objects with the same behavior. For example, the str class describes the behavior of all strings. The class specifies how a string stores its characters, which methods can be used with strings, and how the methods are implemented.

A class describes a set of objects with the same behavior.

A Car *class describes passenger vehicles that can carry 4–5 people and a small amount of luggage.* © Media Bakery.

You can drive a car by operating the steering wheel and pedals, without knowing how the engine works. Similarly, you use an object through its methods. The implementation is hidden.

© Damir Cudic/iStockphoto.

In contrast, the list class describes the behavior of objects that can be used to store a collection of values. You have seen in Chapter 6 how to create and use lists.

Each class defines a specific set of methods that you can use with its objects. For example, when you have a str object, you can invoke the upper method:

```
"Hello, World".upper()
```

We say that the upper method is a method of the str class. The list class has a different set of methods. For example, the call

```
["Hello", "World"].upper()
```

would be illegal—the list class has no upper method. However, list has a pop method, and the call

```
["Hello", "World"].pop()
```

is legal.

Every class has a public interface: a collection of methods through which the objects of the class can be manipulated.

The set of all methods provided by a class, together with a description of their behavior, is called the **public interface** of the class.

Encapsulation is the act of providing a public interface and hiding the implementation details.

When you work with an object of a class, you do not know how the object stores its data, or how the methods are implemented. You need not know how a str object organizes a character sequence, or how a list stores its elements. All you need to know is the public interface—which methods you can apply, and what these methods do. The process of providing a public interface, while hiding the implementation details, is called **encapsulation**.

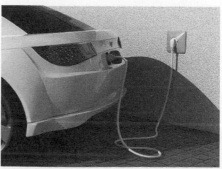

A driver of an electric car doesn't have to learn new controls even though the car's engine is very different. Neither does the programmer who uses an object with an improved implementation—as long as the same methods are provided.

© iStockphoto.com/Christian Waadt.

When you design your own classes, you will use encapsulation. That is, you will specify a set of public methods and hide the implementation details. Other programmers on your team can then use your classes without having to know their implementations, just as you are able to make use of the str and list classes.

If you work on a program that is being developed over a long period of time, it is common for implementation details to change, usually to make objects more efficient or more capable. Encapsulation is crucial to enabling these changes. When the implementation is hidden, the improvements do not affect the programmers who use the objects.

9.2 Implementing a Simple Class

In this section, we look at the implementation of a very simple class. You will see how objects store their data, and how methods access the data of an object. Knowing how a very simple class operates will help you design and implement more complex classes later in this chapter.

Our first example is a class that models a *tally counter*, a mechanical device that is used to count people—for example, to find out how many people attend a concert or board a bus (see Figure 1).

Whenever the operator pushes a button, the counter value advances by one. We model this operation with a click method. A physical counter has a display to show the current value. In our simulation, we use a getValue method instead.

Here is an example of using the Counter class. First, we construct an object of the class:

© Jasmin Awad/iStockphoto.

Figure 1 A Tally Counter

```
tally = Counter()
```

We will discuss object construction in detail in Section 9.5.

Next, we invoke methods on our object. First, we reset the counter to 0 by invoking the reset method. Then we invoke the click method twice, simulating two button pushes. Finally, we invoke the getValue method to check how many times the button was pushed.

```
tally.reset()
tally.click()
tally.click()
result = tally.getValue()    # Sets result to 2
```

We can invoke the methods again, and the result will be different:

```
tally.click()
result = tally.getValue()    # Sets result to 3
```

As you can see, the tally object remembers the effects of prior method calls.

When implementing the Counter class, we need to specify how each Counter object stores its data. In this simple example, that is very straightforward. Each counter needs a variable that keeps track of how many times the counter has been advanced.

An object stores its data in **instance variables**. An *instance* of a class is an object of the class. Thus, an instance variable is a storage location that is present in each object of the class. In our example, each Counter object has a single instance variable named

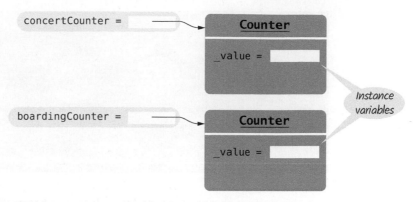

Figure 2 Instance Variables

_value. By convention, instance variables in Python start with an underscore to indicate that they should be private. Instance variables are part of the implementation details that should be hidden from the user of the class. An instance variable should only be accessed by the methods of its own class. The Python language does not enforce this restriction. However, the underscore indicates to class users that they should not directly access the instance variables.

> Each object of a class has its own set of instance variables.

Each object of a class has its own set of instance variables. For example, if concertCounter and boardingCounter are two objects of the Counter class, then each object has its own _value variable (see Figure 2).

Next, let us have a quick look at the implementation of the Counter class. A class is implemented using the class statement:

```
class Counter :
    . . .
```

The methods provided by the class are defined in the class body.

The click method advances the _value instance variable by 1.

```
def click(self) :
    self._value = self._value + 1
```

A method definition is very similar to a function with these exceptions:

- A method is defined as part of a class definition.
- The first parameter variable of a method is called self.

> A method can access the instance variables of the object on which it acts.

We will cover the syntax of the method header and the use of the special self parameter variable in the following sections. For now, it is sufficient to note that instance variables must be referenced within a method using the self parameter (self._value).

Note how the click method increments the instance variable _value. *Which* instance variable? The one belonging to the object on which the method is invoked. For example, consider the call

```
concertCounter.click()
```

This call advances the _value variable of the concertCounter object. No argument was provided to the click method even though the definition includes the self parameter variable. The self parameter variable refers to the object on which the method was invoked — concertCounter in this example.

© Mark Evans/iStockphoto.

These clocks have common behavior, but each of them has a different state. Similarly, objects of a class can have their instance variables set to different values.

Let us look at the other methods of the Counter class. The getValue method returns the current _value:

```
def getValue(self) :
    return self._value
```

This method is provided so that users of the Counter class can find out how many times a particular counter has been clicked. A class user should not directly access any instance variables. Restricting access to instance variables is an essential part of encapsulation. This allows a programmer to hide the implementation of a class from a class user.

The reset method resets the counter:

```
def reset(self) :
    self._value = 0
```

In Python, you don't explicitly declare instance variables. Instead, when one first assigns a value to an instance variable, the instance variable is created. In our sample program, we call the reset method before calling any other methods, so that the _value instance variable is created and initialized. (You will see a more convenient, and preferred, way of creating instance variables in Section 9.5.)

The complete Counter class and a driver module are provided below.

sec02/counterdemo.py

```
 1  ##
 2  #   This program demonstrates the Counter class.
 3  #
 4
 5  # Import the Counter class from the counter module.
 6  from counter import Counter
 7
 8  tally = Counter()
 9  tally.reset()
10  tally.click()
11  tally.click()
12
13  result = tally.getValue()
14  print("Value:", result)
15
```

```
16  tally.click()
17  result = tally.getValue()
18  print("Value:", result)
```

sec02/counter.py

```
 1  ##
 2  #   This module defines the Counter class.
 3  #
 4
 5  ## Models a tally counter whose value can be incremented, viewed, or reset.
 6  #
 7  class Counter :
 8      ## Gets the current value of this counter.
 9      #   @return the current value
10      #
11      def getValue(self) :
12          return self._value
13
14      ## Advances the value of this counter by 1.
15      #
16      def click(self) :
17          self._value = self._value + 1
18
19      ## Resets the value of this counter to 0.
20      #
21      def reset(self) :
22          self._value = 0
```

Program Run

```
Value: 2
Value: 3
```

9.3 Specifying the Public Interface of a Class

When designing a class, you start by specifying its **public interface**. The public interface of a class consists of all methods that a user of the class may want to apply to its objects.

Let's consider a simple example. We want to use objects that simulate cash registers. A cashier who rings up a sale presses a key to start the sale, then rings up each item. A display shows the amount owed as well as the total number of items purchased.

In our simulation, we want to call the following methods on a cash register object:

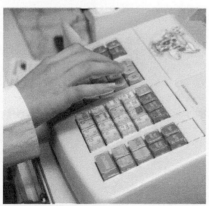

© James Richey/iStockphoto.

- Add the price of an item.
- Get the total amount owed, and the count of items purchased.
- Clear the cash register to start a new sale.

Here is an outline of the CashRegister class. We supply comments for all of the methods to document their purpose.

> You can use method headers and method comments to specify the public interface of a class.

```
## A simulated cash register that tracks the item count and the total amount due.
#
class CashRegister :
   ## Adds an item to this cash register.
   # @param price the price of this item
   #
   def addItem(self, price) :
      implementation—see Section 9.6

   ## Gets the price of all items in the current sale.
   # @return the total price
   #
   def getTotal(self) :
      implementation—see Section 9.6

   ## Gets the number of items in the current sale.
   #  @return the item count
   #
   def getCount(self) :
      implementation—see Section 9.6

   ## Clears the item count and the total.
   #
   def clear(self) :
      implementation—see Section 9.6
```

The method definitions and comments make up the *public interface* of the class. The data and the method bodies make up the *private implementation* of the class.

To see a method in action, we first need to construct an object:

```
register1 = CashRegister()
   # Constructs a CashRegister object.
```

This statement defines the register1 variable and initializes it with a reference to a new CashRegister object—see Figure 3. (We discuss the process of object construction in Section 9.5 and object references in Section 9.10.)

Once the object has been constructed, we are ready to invoke a method:

```
register1.addItem(1.95)    # Invokes a method.
```

> A mutator method changes the object on which it operates.

When you look at the public interface of a class, it is useful to classify its methods as *mutators* and *accessors*. A **mutator** method modifies the object on which it operates. The CashRegister class has two mutators: addItem and clear. After you call either of these methods, the object has changed. You can observe that change by calling the getTotal or getCount methods.

An **accessor** method queries the object for some information without changing it. The CashRegister class has two accessors: getTotal and getCount. Applying either of

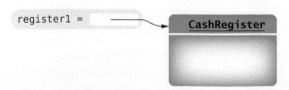

Figure 3 An Object Reference and an Object

An accessor method does not change the object on which it operates.

these methods to a CashRegister object simply returns a value and does not modify the object. For example, the following statement prints the current total and count:

```
print(register1.getTotal(), register1.getCount())
```

Now we know *what* a CashRegister object can do, but not *how* it does it. Of course, to use CashRegister objects in our programs, we don't need to know.

In the next sections, you will see how the CashRegister class is implemented.

9.4 Designing the Data Representation

An object stores its data in **instance variables**. These are variables that are declared inside the class.

When implementing a class, you have to determine which data each object needs to store. The object needs to have all the information necessary to carry out any method call.

Go through all methods and consider their data requirements. It is a good idea to start with the accessor methods. For example, a CashRegister object must be able to return the correct value for the getTotal method. That means it must either store all entered prices and compute the total in the method call, or it must store the total.

© migin/iStockphoto.

Like a wilderness explorer who needs to carry all items that may be needed, an object needs to store the data required for any method calls.

For each accessor method, an object must either store the result or the data necessary to compute the result.

Now apply the same reasoning to the get-Count method. If the cash register stores all entered prices, it can count them in the get-Count method. Otherwise, you need to have a variable for the count.

The addItem method receives a price as an argument, and it must record the price. If the CashRegister object stores a list of entered prices, then the addItem method appends the price. On the other hand, if we decide to store just the item total and count, then the addItem method updates these two variables.

Finally, the clear method must prepare the cash register for the next sale, either by emptying the list of prices or by setting the total and count to zero.

Commonly, there is more than one way of representing the data of an object, and you must make a choice.

We have now discovered two different ways of representing the data that the object needs. Either of them will work, and we have to make a choice. We will choose the simpler one: instance variables _totalPrice and _itemCount for the total price and the item count. (Other options are explored in Exercises •• Business P9.19 and •• Business P9.20.)

Note that method calls can come in any order. For example, consider the Cash-Register class. After calling

```
register1.getTotal()
```

a program can make another call to

```
register1.addItem(1.95)
```

> **Be sure that your data representation supports method calls in any order.**

You should not assume that you can clear the sum in a call to getTotal. Your data representation should allow for method calls that come in arbitrary order, in the same way that occupants of a car can push the various buttons and levers in any order they choose.

Programming Tip 9.1

Make All Instance Variables Private, Most Methods Public

All instance variables should be private and most methods should be public. Although most object-oriented languages provide a mechanism to explicitly hide or protect private members from outside access, Python does not. Instead, the designer of a class has to indicate which instance variables and methods are supposed to be private. It's then the responsibility of the class user not to violate the privacy.

It is common practice among Python programmers to use names that begin with a single underscore for private instance variables and methods. The single underscore serves as a flag to the class user that those members are private. You then must trust that the class user will not attempt to access these items directly. This technique is recognized by documentation generator tools that flag private instance variables and methods in the documentation.

You should always use encapsulation, in which all instance variables are private and are only manipulated with methods.

Typically, methods are public. However, sometimes you have a method that is used only as a helper method by other methods. In that case, you should make the helper method private by using a name that begins with a single underscore.

9.5 Constructors

> **A constructor initializes the instance variables of an object.**

A **constructor** defines and initializes the instance variables of an object. The constructor is automatically called whenever an object is created.

To create an instance of a class, you use the name of the class as if it were a function along with any arguments required by the constructor. To create an instance of the CashRegister class, we use the command:

```
register = CashRegister()
```

A constructor is like a set of assembly instructions for an object.

© Ann Marie Kurtz/iStockphoto.

Syntax 9.1   Constructor

Syntax   class *ClassName* :
      def __init__(self, *parameterName*$_1$, *parameterName*$_2$, . . .) :
        constructor body

The special name __init__
is used to define a constructor. ——
                 class BankAccount :
                    def __init__(self) :
                       self._balance = 0.0
                    . . .

> There can be only one constructor per class. But a constructor can contain default arguments to provide alternate forms for creating objects.

A constructor defines
and initializes the
instance variables. ◀——
                 class BankAccount :
                    def __init__(self, initialBalance = 0.0) :
                      self._balance = initialBalance
                    . . .

> **The constructor is automatically called when an object is created.**

Here an object is created and the constructor of the CashRegister class is automatically called. This particular constructor needs no arguments.

The constructor is responsible for defining and initializing all of the instance variables that are to be contained in the object. After the constructor completes its work, a reference to the newly created and initialized object is returned. The reference is saved in a variable so we can later call methods on the object.

> **The constructor is defined using the special method name __init__.**

Python uses the special name __init__ for the constructor because its purpose is to initialize an instance of the class:

```python
def __init__(self) :
    self._itemCount = 0
    self._totalPrice = 0.0
```

Note the self parameter variable in the constructor definition. The first parameter variable of every constructor must be self. When the constructor is invoked to construct a new object, the self parameter variable is set to the object that is being initialized.

When you first refer to an instance variable in the constructor, that instance variable is created. For example,

```python
self._itemCount = 0
```

creates an _itemCount instance variable in the newly created object and initializes it with zero.

Sometimes, it can be useful to allow objects to be created in different ways. For example, we can create an empty list using the list constructor in this form

```python
empty = list()
```

or create a duplicate copy of an existing list using another version of the list constructor

```python
duplicate = list(values)
```

> **Default arguments can be used with a constructor to provide different ways of creating an object.**

Python allows you to define only one constructor per class. But you can define a constructor with *default argument values* (see Special Topic 9.1) that simulate multiple definitions. Consider, for example, a BankAccount class that needs two forms for the constructor: one that accepts an argument for the initial balance and another that uses a default initial balance of 0. This can be achieved by including a default argument for the initialBalance parameter variable,

```
class BankAccount :
   def __init__(self, initialBalance = 0.0) :
      self._balance = initialBalance
```

The user of the class can choose which form to use when creating an object. If no value is passed to the constructor when a BankAccount object is created,

```
joesAccount = BankAccount()
```

the default value will be used. If a value is passed to the constructor

```
joesAccount = BankAccount(499.95)
```

that value will be used instead of the default one.

Common Error 9.1

Trying to Call a Constructor

The constructor is automatically called when an object is created:

```
register1 = CashRegister()
```

After an object has been constructed, you should not directly call the constructor on that object again:

```
register1.__init__()   # Bad style
```

It's true that the constructor can set a new CashRegister object to the cleared state, but you should not call the constructor on an existing object. Instead, replace the object with a new one:

```
register1 = CashRegister()   # OK
```

In general, you should never call a Python method that starts with a double underscore. All these methods are intended for specific internal purposes (in this case, to initialize a newly created object).

Special Topic 9.1

Default and Named Arguments

In the preceding section, you saw how default arguments make it possible to initialize an object in more than one way. This feature is not limited to constructors. In Python, you can specify default values for the parameter variables of any function or method. For example,

```
def readIntBetween(prompt, low = 0, high = 100) :
```

When you call this function as readIntBetween("Temperature:"), the default arguments are provided automatically, as if you had called readIntBetween("Temperature:", 0, 100). You can override some or all of the defaults. For example, readIntBetween("Percent:", 10) is the same as readIntBetween("Percent", 10, 100).

The arguments specified in a function or method call are passed to the parameter variables of the function or method in the order they were specified. But you can pass arguments in any order, provided you use *named arguments*, like this:

```
temp = readIntBetween(low=-50, high=50, prompt="Temperature:")
```

You have already seen an example of a named argument: the print function's end argument.

When using named arguments, you don't have to name every argument. Only the arguments for parameter variables that are specified out of order have to be named. For example,

```
temp = readIntBetween("Price:", high=1000)
```

Here, the prompt parameter variable is set to "Price:", low is set to its default, and high is set to 1000.

9.6 Implementing Methods

When implementing a class, you need to provide the bodies for all methods. Implementing a method is very similar to implementing a function, with one essential difference: You access the instance variables of the object in the method body.

For example, here is the implementation of the addItem method of the CashRegister class. (You can find the remaining methods at the end of this section.)

```
def addItem(self, price) :
    self._itemCount = self._itemCount + 1
    self._totalPrice = self._totalPrice + price
```

The object on which a method is applied is automatically passed to the self parameter variable of the method.

As with the constructor, every method must include the special self parameter variable, and it must be listed first. When a method is called,

```
register1.addItem(2.95)
```

a reference to the object on which the method was invoked (register1) is automatically passed to the self parameter variable (see Figure 4). The remaining parameter

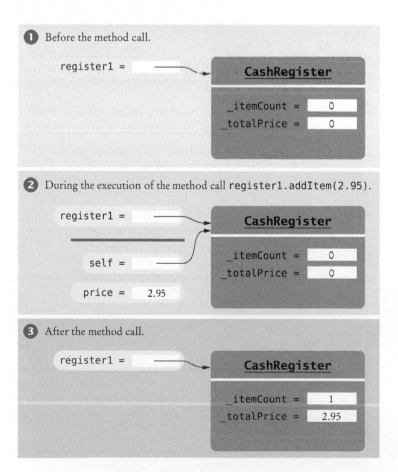

1 Before the method call.

register1 =

CashRegister

_itemCount = 0
_totalPrice = 0

2 During the execution of the method call `register1.addItem(2.95)`.

register1 =

CashRegister

self =

_itemCount = 0
_totalPrice = 0

price = 2.95

3 After the method call.

register1 =

CashRegister

_itemCount = 1
_totalPrice = 2.95

Figure 4
Assignment of the
self Reference

When an item is added, it affects the instance variables of the cash register object on which the method is invoked.

© Glow Images/Getty Images, Inc.

variables must be supplied as arguments of the method call. In the preceding example, the price parameter variable is set to 2.95.

In a method, you access instance variables through the self parameter variable.

To access an instance variable, such as _itemCount or _totalPrice, in a method, you must access the variable name through the self reference. This indicates that you want to access the instance variables of the object on which the method is invoked, and not those of some other CashRegister object.

The first statement in the addItem method is

```
self._itemCount = self._itemCount + 1
```

Which _itemCount is incremented? In this call, it is the _itemCount of the register1 object. (See Figure 4.)

When one method needs to call another method *on the same object*, you invoke the method on the self parameter. Suppose we want to provide a CashRegister method that adds multiple instances of the same item. An easy way to implement this method is to repeatedly call the addItem method:

```
def addItems(self, quantity, price) :
    for i in range(quantity) :
        self.addItem(price)
```

Syntax 9.2 Method Definition

Syntax

```
class ClassName :
    . . .
    def methodName(self, parameterName₁, parameterName₂, . . .) :
        method body
    . . .
```

```
class CashRegister :
    . . .
    def addItem(self, price) :
        self._itemCount = self._itemCount + 1
        self._totalPrice = self._totalPrice + price
    . . .
```

Every method must include the special self parameter variable. It is automatically assigned a value when the method is called.

Instance variables are referenced using the self parameter.

Local variable

Here, the addItem method is invoked on the object referenced by self. That is the object on which the addItems method was invoked. For example, in the call

```
register1.addItems(6, 0.95)
```

the addItem method is invoked six times on the register1 object.

You have now encountered all concepts that are necessary to implement the CashRegister class. The complete code for the class is given here. In the next section, you will see how to test the class.

sec06/cashregister.py

```
1   ##
2   #   This module defines the CashRegister class.
3   #
4
5   ## A simulated cash register that tracks the item count and the total amount due.
6   #
7   class CashRegister :
8       ## Constructs a cash register with cleared item count and total.
9       #
10      def __init__(self) :
11          self._itemCount = 0
12          self._totalPrice = 0.0
13
14      ## Adds an item to this cash register.
15      #   @param price the price of this item
16      #
17      def addItem(self, price) :
18          self._itemCount = self._itemCount + 1
19          self._totalPrice = self._totalPrice + price
20
21      ## Gets the price of all items in the current sale.
22      #   @return the total price
23      #
24      def getTotal(self) :
25          return self._totalPrice
26
27      ## Gets the number of items in the current sale.
28      #   @return the item count
29      #
30      def getCount(self) :
31          return self._itemCount
32
33      ## Clears the item count and the total.
34      #
35      def clear(self) :
36          self._itemCount = 0
37          self._totalPrice = 0.0
```

Programming Tip 9.2

Define Instance Variables Only in the Constructor

Python is a dynamic language in which all variables, including instance variables, are created at run time. As such, there is nothing to prevent you from creating instance variables in any method of a class. For example, in Section 9.2, we called the reset method to create the _value instance variable. That was just a temporary solution because constructors had not yet been covered.

You know that the constructor is invoked before any method can be called, so any instance variables that were created in the constructor are sure to be available in all methods. In contrast, creating instance variables in methods is dangerous. Consider the code in Section 9.2. If a programmer calls the click method on a newly created object, without having called the reset method, a run-time error will occur when the click method attempts to increment the nonexistent _value variable.

Therefore, you should make it a habit to create all instance variables in the constructor.

Special Topic 9.2
Class Variables

Sometimes, a value properly belongs to a class, not to any object of the class. You use a **class variable** for this purpose. (Class variables are often called "static variables"—a term that originated in the C++ language.)

Here is a typical example: We want to assign bank account numbers sequentially. That is, we want the bank account constructor to construct the first account with number 1001, the next with number 1002, and so on. To solve this problem, we need to have a single value of _lastAssignedNumber that is a property of the *class*, not any object of the class. Class variables are declared at the same level as methods. (In contrast, instance variables are created in the constructor.)

```
class BankAccount :
   _lastAssignedNumber = 1000   # A class variable

   def __init__(self) :
      self._balance = 0.0
      BankAccount._lastAssignedNumber = BankAccount._lastAssignedNumber + 1
      self._accountNumber = BankAccount._lastAssignedNumber

      . . .
```

Every BankAccount object has its own _balance and _accountNumber instance variables, but there is only a single copy of the _lastAssignedNumber variable. That variable is stored in a separate location, outside any BankAccount objects.

Note that you reference the class variable as BankAccount._lastAssignedNumber.

Like instance variables, class variables should always be private to ensure that methods of other classes do not change their values. However, class *constants* can be public. For example, the BankAccount class can define a public constant value, such as

> A class variable belongs to the class, not to any instance of the class.

```
class BankAccount :
   OVERDRAFT_FEE = 29.95
   . . .
```

Methods from any class can refer to such a constant as BankAccount.OVERDRAFT_FEE.

The term "static" is a holdover from the C++ language that has no relationship to the normal use of the term.

© Diane Diederich/iStockphoto.

9.7 Testing a Class

In the preceding section, we completed the implementation of the CashRegister class. What can you do with it? In the long run, your class may become a part of a larger program that interacts with users, stores data in files, and so on. However, before integrating a class into a program, it is always a good idea to test it in isolation. Testing in isolation, outside a complete program, is called **unit testing**.

© Chris Fertnig/iStockphoto.

An engineer tests a part in isolation. This is an example of unit testing.

A unit test verifies that a class works correctly in isolation, outside a complete program.

To test your class you have two choices. Some interactive development environments provide access to the Python shell (see Programming Tip 1.1) in which individual statements can be executed. You can test a class simply by constructing an object, calling methods, and verifying that you get the expected return values. A sample interactive session that tests the CashRegister class is shown below:

```
>>> from cashregister import CashRegister
>>> reg = CashRegister()
>>> reg.addItem(1.95)
>>> reg.addItem(0.95)
>>> reg.addItem(2.50)
>>> print(reg.getCount())
3
>>> print(reg.getTotal())
5.4
>>>
```

To test a class, use an environment for interactive testing, or write a tester program to execute test instructions.

Interactive testing is quick and convenient but it has a drawback. When you find and fix a mistake, you need to type in the tests again.

As your classes get more complex, you should write *tester programs*. A tester program is a driver module that imports the class and contains statements to run methods of your class. A tester program typically carries out the following steps:

1. Construct one or more objects of the class that is being tested.

2. Invoke one or more methods.

3. Print out one or more results.

4. Print the expected results.

Here is a program to run methods of the CashRegister class. It constructs an object of type CashRegister, invokes the addItem method three times, and displays the result of the getCount and getTotal methods.

sec07/registertester.py

```
1  ##
2  #   This program tests the CashRegister class.
3  #
4
5  from cashregister import CashRegister
6
```

```
 7  register1 = CashRegister()
 8  register1.addItem(1.95)
 9  register1.addItem(0.95)
10  register1.addItem(2.50)
11  print(register1.getCount())
12  print("Expected: 3")
13  print("%.2f" % register1.getTotal())
14  print("Expected: 5.40")
```

Program Run

```
3
Expected: 3
5.40
Expected: 5.40
```

In our sample program, we add three items totaling $5.40. When displaying the method results, we also display messages that describe the values we expect to see.

> Determining the expected result in advance is an important part of testing.

This is a very important step. You want to spend some time thinking about what the expected result is before you run a test program. This thought process will help you understand how your program should behave, and it can help you track down errors at an early stage.

You need to import the class you are testing (here, the CashRegister class) into the driver module:

```
from cashregister import CashRegister
```

The specific details for running the program depend on your development environment, but in most environments, both modules must reside in the same directory.

HOW TO 9.1

Implementing a Class

A very common task is to implement a class whose objects can carry out a set of specified actions. This How To walks you through the necessary steps.

As an example, consider a class Menu. An object of this class can display a menu such as

```
1) Open new account
2) Log into existing account
3) Help
4) Quit
```

© Mark Evans/iStockphoto.

Then the menu waits for the user to supply a value. If the user does not supply a valid value, the menu is redisplayed, and the user can try again.

Step 1 Get an informal list of the responsibilities of your objects.

Be careful that you restrict yourself to features that are actually required in the problem. With real-world items, such as cash registers or bank accounts, there are potentially dozens of features that might be worth implementing. But your job is not to faithfully model the real world. You need to determine only those responsibilities that you need for solving your specific problem.

In the case of the menu, you need to

Display the menu.
Get user input.

Now look for hidden responsibilities that aren't part of the problem description. How do objects get created? Which mundane activities need to happen, such as clearing the cash register at the beginning of each sale?

In the menu example, consider how a menu is produced. The programmer creates an empty menu object and then adds options "Open new account", "Help", and so on. That is another responsibility:

Add an option.

Step 2   Specify the public interface.

Turn the list in Step 1 into a set of methods, with specific parameter variables and return values. Many programmers find this step simpler if they write out method calls that are applied to a sample object, like this:

```
mainMenu = Menu()
mainMenu.addOption("Open new account")
# Add more options
input = mainMenu.getInput()
```

Now we have a specific list of methods.

- `addOption(option)`
- `getInput()`

What about displaying the menu? There is no sense in displaying the menu without also asking the user for input. However, getInput may need to display the menu more than once if the user provides a bad input. Thus, display is a good candidate for a helper method. In our case, our display will be simple enough that we don't need a helper.

To complete the public interface, you need to specify the constructor. Ask yourself what information you need in order to construct an object of your class. If you need user-supplied values, then the constructor must specify one or more parameter variables.

In the case of the menu example, we can get by with a constructor that requires no arguments.

Here is the public interface:

```
class Menu :
   def __init__(self) :
      . . .
   def addOption(self, option) :
      . . .
   def getInput(self) :
      . . .
```

Step 3   Document the public interface.

Supply a documentation comment for the class, then comment each method.

```
## A menu that is displayed in the terminal window.
#
class Menu :
   ## Constructs a menu with no options.
   #
   def __init__(self) :

   ## Adds an option to the end of this menu.
   #  @param option the option to add
   #
   def addOption(self, option) :
```

```
## Displays the menu, with options numbered starting with 1, and prompts
#  the user for input. Repeats until a valid input is supplied.
#  @return the number that the user supplied
#
def getInput(self) :
```

Step 4   Determine instance variables.

Ask yourself what information an object needs to store to do its job. The object needs to be able to process every method using just its instance variables and the method arguments.

Go through each method, perhaps starting with a simple one or an interesting one, and ask yourself what the object needs in order to carry out the method's task. Which data items are required in addition to the method arguments? Make instance variables for those data items.

In our example, let's start with the addOption method. We clearly need to store the added menu option so that it can be displayed later as part of the menu. How should we store the options? As a list of strings? As one long string? Both approaches can be made to work. We will use a list here. Exercise ••• P9.3 asks you to implement the other approach.

Now consider the getInput method. It shows the stored options and reads an integer. When checking whether the input is valid, we need to know the number of menu items. Because we store them in a list, the number of menu items is simply the size of the list. If you stored the menu items in one long string, you might want to keep another instance variable to store the item count.

Step 5   Implement the constructor.

Implement the constructor of your class, which defines and initializes the instance variables. In this case, _options is set to an empty list.

```
def __init__(self) :
    self._options = []
```

Step 6   Implement the methods.

Implement the methods in your class, one at a time, starting with the easiest ones. For example, here is the implementation of the addOption method:

```
def addOption(self, option) :
    self._options.append(option)
```

Here is the getInput method. This method is a bit more sophisticated. It loops until a valid input has been obtained, displaying the menu options before reading the input:

```
def getInput(self) :
    done = False
    while not done :
        for i in range(len(self._options)) :
            print("%d %s" % (i + 1, self._options[i]))

        userChoice = int(input())
        if userChoice >= 1 and userChoice < len(self._options) :
            done = True

    return userChoice
```

If you find that you have trouble with the implementation of some of your methods, you may need to rethink your choice of instance variables. It is common for a beginner to start out with a set of instance variables that cannot accurately describe the state of an object. Don't hesitate to go back and rethink your implementation strategy.

Step 7   Test your class.

Write a short tester program and execute it. The tester program should call the methods that you found in Step 2.

how_to_1/menutester.py

```
1   ##
2   #   This program tests the Menu class.
3   #
4
5   from menu import Menu
6
7   mainMenu = Menu()
8   mainMenu.addOption("Open new account")
9   mainMenu.addOption("Log into existing account")
10  mainMenu.addOption("Help")
11  mainMenu.addOption("Quit")
12  choice = mainMenu.getInput()
13  print("Input:", choice)
```

Program Run

```
1) Open new account
2) Log into existing account
3) Help
4) Quit
5
1) Open new account
2) Log into existing account
3) Help
4) Quit
1
Input: 1
```

The complete Menu class is provided below.

how_to_1/menu.py

```
1   ##
2   #   This module defines the Menu class.
3   #
4
5   ## A menu that is displayed in the terminal window.
6   #
7   class Menu :
8      ## Constructs a menu with no options.
9      #
10     def __init__(self) :
11        self._options = []
12
13     ## Adds an option to the end of this menu.
14     #  @param option the option to add
15     #
16     def addOption(self, option) :
17        self._options.append(option)
18
19     ## Displays the menu, with options numbered starting with 1, and prompts
20     #  the user for input. Repeats until a valid input is supplied.
21     #  @return the number that the user supplied
22     #
23     def getInput(self) :
24        done = False
25        while not done :
26           for i in range(len(self._options)) :
27              print("%d %s" % (i + 1, self._options[i]))
28
```

```
29        userChoice = int(input())
30        if userChoice >= 1 and userChoice < len(self._options) :
31            done = True
32
33    return userChoice
```

WORKED EXAMPLE 9.1

Implementing a Bank Account Class

Problem Statement Your task is to write a class that simulates a bank account. Customers can deposit and withdraw funds. If sufficient funds are not available for withdrawal, a $10 overdraft penalty is charged. At the end of the month, interest is added to the account. The interest rate can vary every month.

Step 1   Get an informal list of the responsibilities of your objects.

The following responsibilities are mentioned in the problem statement:

> *Deposit funds.*
> *Withdraw funds.*
> *Add interest.*

There is a hidden responsibility as well. We need to be able to find out how much money is in the account.

> *Get balance.*

Step 2   Specify the public interface.

We need to supply parameter variables and determine which methods are accessors and mutators. To deposit or withdraw money, one needs to know the amount of the deposit or withdrawal:

```
def deposit(self, amount) :
def withdraw(self, amount) :
```

To add interest, one needs to know the interest rate that is to be applied:

```
def addInterest(self, rate) :
```

Clearly, all these methods are mutators because they change the balance.
Finally, we have

```
def getBalance(self) :
```

This method is an accessor because inquiring about the balance does not change it.

Now we move on to the constructor. The constructor should accept the initial balance of the account. But it can also be useful to allow for an initial zero balance using a default argument (see Special Topic 9.1).

Here is the complete public interface:

- Constructor

```
def __init__(self, initialBalance = 0.0) :
```

- Mutators

```
def deposit(self, amount) :
def withdraw(self, amount) :
def addInterest(self, rate) :
```

- Accessors

```
def getBalance(self) :
```

Step 3 Document the public interface.

```
## A bank account has a balance that can be changed by deposits and withdrawals.
#
class BankAccount :
   ## Constructs a bank account with a given balance.
   # @param initialBalance the initial account balance (default = 0.0)
   #
   def __init__(self, initialBalance = 0.0) :

   ## Deposits money into this account.
   # @param amount the amount to deposit
   #
   def deposit(self, amount) :

   ## Makes a withdrawal from this account, or charges a penalty if
   #    sufficient funds are not available.
   #    @param amount the amount of the withdrawal
   #
   def withdraw(self, amount) :

   ## Adds interest to this account.
   #    @param rate the interest rate in percent
   #
   def addInterest(self, rate) :

   ## Gets the current balance of this account.
   #    @return the current balance
   #
   def getBalance(self) :
```

Step 4 Determine instance variables.

Clearly we need to store the bank balance:

```
self._balance = initialBalance
```

Do we need to store the interest rate? No—it varies every month, and is supplied as an argument to addInterest. What about the withdrawal penalty? The problem description states that it is a fixed $10, so we need not store it. If the penalty could vary over time, as is the case with most real bank accounts, we would need to store it somewhere (perhaps in a Bank object), but it is not our job to model every aspect of the real world.

Step 5 Implement the constructor and methods.

Let's start with a simple one:

```
def getBalance(self) :
   return self._balance
```

The deposit method is a bit more interesting:

```
def deposit(self, amount) :
   self._balance = self._balance + amount
```

The withdraw method needs to charge a penalty if sufficient funds are not available:

```
def withdraw(self, amount) :
   PENALTY = 10.0
   if amount > self._balance :
      self._balance = self._balance - PENALTY
   else :
      self._balance = self._balance - amount
```

Finally, here is the addInterest method. We compute the interest and then add it to the balance:

```
def addInterest(self, rate) :
    amount = self._balance * rate / 100.0
    self._balance = self._balance + amount
```

The constructor is once again quite simple:

```
def __init__(self, initialBalance = 0.0) :
    self._balance = initialBalance
```

This finishes the implementation.

Step 6   Test your class.

Here is a simple tester program that exercises all methods.

```
from bankaccount import BankAccount

harrysAccount = BankAccount(1000.0)
harrysAccount.deposit(500.0)    # Balance is now $1500
harrysAccount.withdraw(2000.0)   # Balance is now $1490
harrysAccount.addInterest(1.0)    # Balance is now $1490 + 14.90
print("%.2f" % harrysAccount.getBalance())
print("Expected: 1504.90")
```

Program Run

```
1504.90
Expected: 1504.90
```

EXAMPLE CODE   See worked_example_1/bankaccount.py in your eText or companion code for the completed class.

9.8 Problem Solving: Tracing Objects

You have seen how the technique of hand-tracing is useful for understanding how a program works. When your program contains objects, it is useful to adapt the technique so that you gain a better understanding of object data and encapsulation.

Use an index card or a sticky note for each object. On the front, write the methods that the object can execute. On the back, make a table for the values of the instance variables.

Write the methods on the front of a card, and the instance variables on the back.

Here is a card for a CashRegister object:

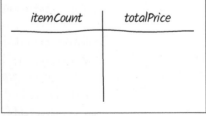

In a small way, this gives you a feel for encapsulation. An object is manipulated through its public interface (on the front of the card), and the instance variables are hidden on the back. (Here, we don't add the underscores to the variable names. That's an implementation detail in Python.)

When an object is constructed, fill in the initial values of the instance variables:

itemCount	totalPrice
0	0

Whenever a mutator method is executed, cross out the old values and write the new ones below. Here is what happens after a call to the addItem method:

itemCount	totalPrice
~~0~~	~~0~~
1	19.95

If you have more than one object in your program, you will have multiple cards, one for each object:

itemCount	totalPrice
~~0~~	~~0~~
1	19.95

itemCount	totalPrice
~~0~~	~~0~~
1	19.95
2	34.95

These diagrams are also useful when you design a class. Suppose you are asked to enhance the CashRegister class to compute the sales tax. Add a method getSalesTax to the front of the card. Now turn the card over, look over the instance variables, and ask yourself whether the object has sufficient information to compute the answer. Remember that each object is an autonomous unit. Any data value that can be used in a computation must be

- An instance variable.
- A method argument.

To compute the sales tax, we need to know the tax rate and the total of the taxable items. (In many states, food items are not subject to sales tax.) We don't have that information available. Let us introduce additional instance variables for the tax rate and the taxable total. The tax rate can be set in the constructor (assuming it stays fixed for the lifetime of the object). When adding an item, we need to be told whether the item is taxable. If so, we add its price to the taxable total.

For example, consider the following statements.

```
register2 = CashRegister(7.5)      # 7.5 percent sales tax
register2.addItem(3.95, False)     # Not taxable
register2.addItem(19.95, True)     # Taxable
```

Update the values of the instance variables when a mutator method is called.

When you record the effect on a card, it looks like this:

itemCount	totalPrice	taxableTotal	taxRate
~~0~~	~~0~~	~~0~~	7.5
~~1~~	~~3.95~~		
2	23.90	19.95	

With this information, it becomes easy to compute the tax. It is *taxableTotal x taxRate / 100*. Tracing the object helped us understand the need for additional instance variables. An enhanced CashRegister class that computes the sales tax is provided below.

sec08/cashregister2.py

```python
1   ##
2   #   This module defines the CashRegister class.
3   #
4
5   ## A simulated cash register that tracks the item count and the total amount due.
6   #
7   class CashRegister :
8       ## Constructs a cash register with cleared item count and total.
9       #  @param taxRate the tax rate to use with this cash register
10      #
11      def __init__(self, taxRate) :
12          self._itemCount = 0
13          self._totalPrice = 0.0
14          self._taxableTotal = 0.0
15          self._taxRate = taxRate
16
17      ## Adds an item to this cash register.
18      #  @param price the price of this item
19      #  @param taxable True if this item is taxable
20      #
21      def addItem(self, price, taxable) :
22          self._itemCount = self._itemCount + 1
23          self._totalPrice = self._totalPrice + price
24          if taxable :
25              self._taxableTotal = self._taxableTotal + price
26
27      ## Gets the price of all items in the current sale.
28      #  @return the total price
29      #
30      def getTotal(self) :
31          return self._totalPrice + self._taxableTotal * self._taxRate / 100
32
33      ## Gets the number of items in the current sale.
34      #  @return the item count
35      #
36      def getCount(self) :
37          return self._itemCount
38
39      ## Clears the item count and the total.
40      #
41      def clear(self) :
```

```
42        self._itemCount = 0
43        self._totalPrice = 0.0
44        self._taxableTotal = 0.0
```

sec08/registertester2.py

```
1  ##
2  #   This program tests the enhanced CashRegister class.
3  #
4
5  from cashregister2 import CashRegister
6
7  register1 = CashRegister(7.5)
8  register1.addItem(3.95, False)
9  register1.addItem(19.95, True)
10 print(register1.getCount())
11 print("Expected: 2")
12 print("%.2f" % register1.getTotal())
13 print("Expected: 25.40")
```

9.9 Problem Solving: Patterns for Object Data

When you design a class, you first consider the needs of the programmers who use the class. You provide the methods that the users of your class will call when they manipulate objects. When you implement the class, you need to come up with the instance variables for the class. It is not always obvious how to do this. Fortunately, there is a small set of recurring patterns that you can adapt when you design your own classes. We introduce these patterns in the following sections.

9.9.1 Keeping a Total

Many classes need to keep track of a quantity that can go up or down as certain methods are called. Examples:

- A bank account has a balance that is increased by a deposit, decreased by a withdrawal.
- A cash register has a total that is increased when an item is added to the sale, cleared after the end of the sale.
- A car has gas in the tank, which is increased when fuel is added and decreased when the car drives.

In all of these cases, the implementation strategy is similar. Keep an instance variable that represents the current total. For example, for the cash register we defined the _totalPrice instance variable.

> An instance variable for the total is updated in methods that increase or decrease the total amount.

Locate the methods that affect the total. There is usually a method to increase it by a given amount:

```
def addItem(self, price) :
    self._totalPrice = self._totalPrice + price
```

Depending on the nature of the class, there may be a method that reduces or clears the total. In the case of the cash register, there is a `clear` method:

```
def clear(self) :
    self._totalPrice = 0.0
```

There is usually a method that yields the current total. It is easy to implement:

```
def getTotal(self) :
    return self._totalPrice
```

All classes that manage a total follow the same basic pattern. Find the methods that affect the total and provide the appropriate code for increasing or decreasing it. Find the methods that report or use the total, and have those methods read the current total.

9.9.2 Counting Events

You often need to count how often certain events occur in the life of an object. For example:

- In a cash register, you want to know how many items have been added in a sale.
- A bank account charges a fee for each transaction; you need to count them.

Keep a counter, such as `_itemCount`.

A counter that counts events is incremented in methods that correspond to the events.

Increment the counter in those methods that correspond to the events that you want to count:

```
def addItem(self, price) :
    self._totalPrice = self._totalPrice + price
    self._itemCount = self._itemCount + 1
```

You may need to clear the counter, for example at the end of a sale or a statement period:

```
def clear(self) :
    self._totalPrice = 0.0
    self._itemCount = 0
```

There may or may not be a method that reports the count to the class user. The count may only be used to compute a fee or an average. Find out which methods in your class make use of the count, and read the current value in those methods.

9.9.3 Collecting Values

Some objects collect numbers, strings, or other objects. For example, each multiple-choice question has a number of choices. A cash register may need to store all prices of the current sale.

An object can collect other objects in a list.

Use a list to store the values. In the constructor, define the instance variable and initialize it to an empty container:

```
def __init__(self) :
    self._choices = []    # An empty list.
```

A shopping cart object needs to manage a collection of items. © paul prescott/iStockphoto.

You need to supply some mechanism for adding values. It is common to provide a method for appending a value to the collection:

```
def addChoice(self, choice) :
    self._choices.append(choice)
```

The user of a multiple-choice Question object can call this method multiple times to add the various choices.

9.9.4 Managing Properties of an Object

An object property can be accessed with a getter method and changed with a setter method.

A property is a value of an object that a user of that object can set and retrieve. For example, a Student object may have a name and an ID.

Provide an instance variable to store the property's value and write methods to get and set it.

```
class Student :
    def __init__(self) :
        self._name = ""

    def getName(self) :
        return self._name

    def setName(self, newName) :
        self._name = newName
```

It is common to add error checking to the setter method. For example, we may want to reject a blank name:

```
def setName(self, newName) :
    if len(newName) > 0 :
        self._name = newName
```

Some properties should not change after they have been set in the constructor. For example, a student's ID may be fixed (unlike the student's name, which may change). In that case, don't supply a setter method.

```
class Student :
    def __init__(self, anId) :
        self._id = anId

    def getId(self) :
        return self._id

    # No setId method
    . . .
```

9.9.5 Modeling Objects with Distinct States

If your object can have one of several states that affect the behavior, supply an instance variable for the current state.

Some objects have behavior that varies depending on what has happened in the past. For example, a Fish object may look for food when it is hungry and ignore food after it has eaten. Such an object would need to remember whether it has recently eaten.

If a fish is in a hungry state, its behavior changes. © John Alexander/iStockphoto.

Supply an instance variable that models the state, together with some constants for the state values.

```
class Fish :
   # Constant state values.
   NOT_HUNGRY = 0
   SOMEWHAT_HUNGRY = 1
   VERY_HUNGRY = 2

   def __init__(self) :
      self._hungry = Fish.NOT_HUNGRY
   . . .
```

Determine which methods change the state. In this example, a fish that has just eaten food won't be hungry. But as the fish moves, it will get hungrier.

```
def eat(self) :
   self._hungry = Fish.NOT_HUNGRY
   . . .

def move(self) :
   . . .
   if self._hungry < Fish.VERY_HUNGRY :
      self._hungry = self._hungry + 1
```

Finally, determine where the state affects behavior. A fish that is very hungry will want to look for food first.

```
def move(self) :
   if self._hungry == Fish.VERY_HUNGRY :
      Look for food.
   . . .
```

9.9.6 Describing the Position of an Object

Some objects move around during their lifetime, and they remember their current position. For example,

- A train drives along a track and keeps track of the distance from the terminus.
- A simulated bug living on a grid crawls from one grid location to the next, or makes 90 degree turns to the left or right.
- A cannonball is shot into the air, then descends as it is pulled by the gravitational force.

Such objects need to store their position. Depending on the nature of their movement, they may also need to store their orientation or velocity.

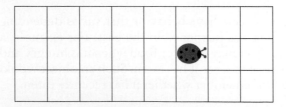

A bug in a grid needs to store its row, column, and direction.

To model a moving object, you need to store and update its position.

If the object moves along a line, you can represent the position as a distance from a fixed point.

```
self._distanceFromTerminus = 0.0
```

If the object moves in a grid, remember its current location and direction in the grid:

```
self._row = 0
self._column = 0
self._direction = "N"
```

When you model a physical object such as a cannonball, you need to track both the position and the velocity, possibly in two or three dimensions. Here we model a cannonball that is shot straight upward into the air, so that we only need to track its height, not its *x*- or *y*-position. (Don't try this at home.)

```
self._zPosition = 0.0
self._zVelocity = 0.0
```

There will be methods that update the position. In the simplest case, you may be told by how much the object moves:

```
def move(self, distanceMoved) :
    self._distanceFromTerminus = self._distanceFromTerminus + distanceMoved
```

If the movement happens in a grid, you need to update the row or column, depending on the current orientation:

```
def moveOneUnit(self) :
    if self._direction == "N" :
        self._row = self._row - 1
    elif self._direction == "E" :
        self._column = self._column + 1
    . . .
```

Exercise ••• Science P9.28 shows you how to update the position of a physical object with known velocity.

Whenever you have a moving object, keep in mind that your program will simulate the actual movement in some way. Find out the rules of that simulation, such as movement along a line or in a grid with integer coordinates. Those rules determine how to represent the current position. Then locate the methods that move the object, and update the positions according to the rules of the simulation.

9.10 Object References

In Python, a variable does not actually hold an object. It merely holds the *memory location* of an object. The object itself is stored elsewhere (see Figure 5).

Figure 5
An Object Variable
Containing an Object Reference

An object reference specifies the location of an object.

We use the technical term **object reference** to denote the memory location of an object. When a variable contains the memory location of an object, we say that it *refers* to an object. For example, after the statement

```
reg1 = CashRegister()
```

the variable reg1 refers to the CashRegister object that was constructed. Technically speaking, the constructor returns a reference to the new object, and that reference is stored in the reg1 variable.

9.10.1 Shared References

Multiple object variables can contain references to the same object.

You can have two (or more) variables that store references to the same object, for example by assigning one to the other.

```
reg2 = reg1
```

Now you can access the same CashRegister object both as reg1 and as reg2, as shown in Figure 6.

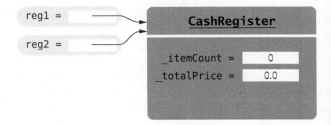

Figure 6
Two Object Variables
Referring to the Same Object

When you copy an object reference, both the original and the copy are references to the same object (see Figure 7):

```
reg1 = CashRegister()   ❶
reg2 = reg1   ❷
reg2.addItem(2.95)   ❸
```

Because reg1 and reg2 refer to the same cash register after step ❷, both variables now refer to a cash register with item count 1 and total price 2.95. Two variables that refer to the same object are known as *aliases*.

You can test whether two variables are aliases using the is (or the inverse is not) operator:

```
if reg1 is reg2 :
    print("The variables are aliases.")

if reg1 is not reg2 :
    print("The variables refer to different objects.")
```

Use the is and is not operators to test whether two variables are aliases.

The is and is not operators do not check whether the data contained in the objects are equal, but whether two variables refer to the same object. Objects that contain the same data may or may not be referenced by the same variable.

For example, if we create a third cash register and add an item to it

```
reg3 = CashRegister()
reg3.addItem(2.95)
```

Figure 7
Copying Object
References

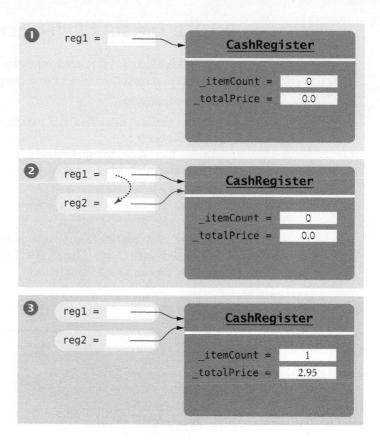

reg3 will have the same data as reg1, but the variables are not aliases because they refer to different objects.

9.10.2 The None Reference

An object reference can have the special value None if it refers to no object at all. It is common to use the None value to indicate that a value has never been set. For example,

```
middleInitial = None    # No middle initial
```

You use the is operator (and not ==) to test whether an object reference is None:

```
if middleInitial is None :
    print(firstName, lastName)
else :
    print(firstName, middleInitial + ".", lastName)
```

Note that the None reference is not the same as the empty string "". The empty string is a valid string of length 0, whereas None indicates that a variable refers to nothing at all. It is an error to invoke a method on a None reference. For example,

```
reg = None
print(reg.getTotal())    # Error – cannot invoke a method on a None reference.
```

This code causes an AttributeError exception at run time:

```
AttributeError:  'NoneType' object has no attribute 'getTotal'.
```

> The None reference refers to no object.

9.10.3 The self Reference

The self parameter variable refers to the object on which a method was invoked.

Every method has a reference to the object on which the method was invoked, stored in the self parameter variable. For example, consider the method call

```
reg1.addItem(2.95) :
```

When the method is called, the parameter variable self refers to the same object as reg1 (see Figure 8).

As you have seen, the self reference is used to access instance variables of the object on which the method is invoked. For example, consider the method

```
def addItem(self, price) :
    self._itemCount = self._itemCount + 1
    self._totalPrice = self._totalPrice + price
```

In the call reg1.addItem(2.95), self is initialized with the reference reg1, and price is initialized with 2.95. Then self._itemCount and self._totalPrice are the same as reg1._itemCount and reg1._totalPrice.

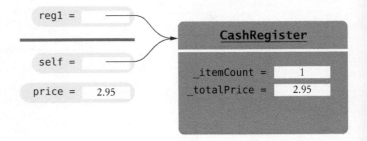

Figure 8
The self Parameter
Variable of a Method Call

You can also invoke a method on self. For example, we could implement the constructor as

```
def __init__(self) :
    self.clear()
```

In a constructor, self is a reference to the object that is being constructed. The clear method is invoked on that object.

Finally, you sometimes pass self to another method. Suppose, for example, you have a Person class with a method likes(self, other) that checks, perhaps from a social network, whether a person likes another. Then you can define a method

```
def isFriend(self, other) :
    return self.likes(other) and other.likes(self)
```

Note how in the last method call, self was passed to the likes method.

9.10.4 The Lifetime of Objects

When you construct an object with a constructor, the object is created, and the self variable of the constructor is set to the memory location of the object. Initially, the object contains no instance variables. As the constructor executes statements such as

```
self._itemCount = 0
```

instance variables are added to the object. Finally, when the constructor exits, it returns a reference to the object, which is usually captured in a variable:

```
reg1 = CashRegister()
```

The object, and all of its instance variables, stays alive as long as there is at least one reference to it. When an object is no longer referenced at all, it is eventually removed by a part of the virtual machine called the "garbage collector".

Computing & Society 9.1   Electronic Voting

In the 2000 presidential election in the United States, votes were tallied by a variety of machines. Some machines processed cardboard ballots into which voters punched holes to indicate their choices (see below). When voters were not careful, remains of paper—the now infamous "chads"—were partially stuck in the punch cards, causing votes to be miscounted. A manual recount was necessary, but it was not carried out everywhere due to time constraints and procedural wrangling. The election was very close, and there remain doubts in the minds of many people whether the election outcome would have been different if the voting machines had accurately counted the intent of the voters.

Subsequently, voting machine manufacturers have argued that electronic voting machines would avoid the problems caused by punch cards or optically scanned forms. In an electronic voting machine, voters indicate their preferences by pressing buttons or touching icons on a computer screen. Typically, each voter is presented with a summary screen for review before casting the ballot. The process is very similar to using a bank's automated teller machine.

It seems plausible that these machines make it more likely that a

vote is counted in the way that the voter intends. However, there has been significant controversy surrounding some types of electronic voting machines. If a machine simply records the votes and reports the totals after the election has been completed, then how do you know that the machine worked correctly? Inside the machine is a computer that executes a program, and, as you may know from your own experience, programs can have bugs.

In fact, some electronic voting machines do have bugs. There is also increasing fear that the machines can be attacked remotely. When a machine reports far more or far fewer votes than voters, then it is clear that it malfunctioned. Unfortunately, it is then impossible to find out the actual votes. More insidiously, if the results are plausible, nobody may ever investigate.

Many computer scientists have spoken out on this issue and confirmed that it is impossible, with today's technology, to tell that software is error free and has not been tampered with. Many of them recommend that electronic voting machines should employ a *voter-verifiable audit trail*. (A good source of information is http://verifiedvoting.org.) Typically, a voter-verifiable machine prints out a ballot. Each voter has a chance to review the printout, and then deposits it in an old-fashioned ballot box. If there is a problem with the electronic equipment, the printouts can be scanned or counted by hand.

Some states require random manual audits in which a small percentage of the votes is hand-tallied and compared with the electronic results. Naturally, this process, recommended as a best practice by security experts, is only meaningful when paper ballots are available. Elections that take place over the Internet have so many

© Lisa F. Young/iStockphoto.

Touch Screen Voting Machine

security concerns that most experts strongly advise against them.

What do you think? You probably use an automated bank teller machine to get cash from your bank account. Do you review the paper record that the machine issues? Do you check your bank statement? Even if you don't, do you put your faith in other people who double-check their balances, so that the bank won't get away with widespread cheating?

Is the integrity of banking equipment more important or less important than that of voting machines? Won't every voting process have some room for error and fraud anyway? Is the added cost for equipment, paper, and staff time reasonable to combat a potentially slight risk of malfunction and fraud? Computer scientists cannot answer these questions—an informed society must make these decisions. But, like all professionals, they have an obligation to speak out and give accurate testimony about the capabilities and limitations of computing equipment.

© Peter Nguyen/iStockphoto.

Punch Card Ballot

9.11 Application: Writing a Fraction Class

We have worked with floating-point numbers throughout this book. But computers store binary values, so not all real numbers can be represented precisely. In applications where the precision of real numbers is important, we can use *rational numbers* to store exact values. This helps to reduce or eliminate round-off errors that can occur when performing arithmetic operations.

A rational number is a number that can be expressed as a ratio of two integers: 7/8. The top value is called the *numerator* and the bottom value, which cannot be zero, is called the *denominator*. In this section, we walk through the design and implementation of a Fraction class that models a rational number.

9.11.1 Fraction Class Design

As you learned in Section 9.3, the first step in designing a class is to specify its public interface. We want to use our rational numbers as we would use integers and floating-point values. Thus, our Fraction class must perform the following operations:

- Create a rational number.
- Access the numerator and denominator values, individually.
- Determine if the rational number is negative or zero.
- Perform normal mathematical operations on two rational numbers (addition, subtraction, multiplication, division, exponentiation).
- Logically compare two rational numbers.
- Produce a string representation of the rational number.

The objects of the Fraction class will be immutable because none of the operations modify the objects' instance variables. This is similar to the immutable int and float types used by Python.

After specifying the operations, we need to determine what data must be stored in a Fraction object. Because a rational number consists of two integers, we need two instance variables to store those values:

```
self._numerator = 0
self._denominator = 1
```

At no time should the rational number be converted to a floating-point value or we will lose the precision gained from working with rational numbers. All operations can be performed using the numerator and denominator integer values.

How much is 1/6 + 1/3? That's 1/6 + 2/6 = 3/6 = 1/2.
The add method of the Fraction class makes this calculation for us. © Debbi Smirnoff/Getty Images, Inc.

A rational number that is equal to 0 can be represented by many different fractions—specifically, any rational number whose numerator is zero and whose denominator is nonzero. To simplify some of the operations in our Fraction class, we will set the numerator to zero and the denominator to 1 for a zero value.

Negative and positive rational numbers each have two forms that can be used to specify the corresponding value. Positive values can be indicated as 1/2 or –1/–2, and negative values as –2/5 or 2/–5. When performing an arithmetic operation or logically comparing two rational numbers, it will be much easier if we have a single way to represent a negative value. For simplicity, we choose to set only the numerator to a negative value when the rational number is negative, and both the numerator and denominator will be positive integers when the rational number is positive.

Finally, a rational number can be written in many different forms. For example, 1/4 can be written as 1/4, 2/8, 16/64, or 123/492. When logically comparing two rational numbers or producing a string representation of a rational number, it will be much easier to perform the operation if the number is stored in reduced form.

9.11.2 The Constructor

To implement the Fraction class, we will begin with the constructor. Because Fraction objects are immutable, their values must be set when they are created. This requires parameter variables for both the numerator and denominator.

```
def __init__(self, numerator, denominator) :
```

We assume that the user of the class will pass integer arguments to the constructor. But what if they pass a zero for the denominator? Remember, a rational number cannot have a zero denominator. To prevent this from occurring, we can check the value and raise a ZeroDivisionError if necessary.

After verifying that the denominator is not zero, we need to check whether the rational number is zero or negative. If the rational number is zero, it has to be stored with the numerator set to zero and the denominator set to 1.

A negative rational number will be stored with the numerator set to a negative integer. For a non-zero rational number, it must be stored in the smallest form possible. To reduce a rational number, we must find the greatest common divisor of the numerator and denominator.

To compute the greatest common divisor, we use an algorithm that was published by Euclid around 300 b.c.e. Given two positive integers greater than zero, a and b, compute the remainder of the larger number by the smaller number and then repeat this computation, using the smaller number and the remainder, until one of the numbers is 0. Then the other number is the greatest common divisor of a and b.

Here is the implementation of the constructor:

```
class Fraction :
    ## Constructs a rational number initialized to zero or a user specified value.
    #  @param numerator the numerator of the fraction (default is 0)
    #  @param denominator the denominator of the fraction (cannot be 0)
    #
    def __init__(self, numerator = 0, denominator = 1) :
        # The denominator cannot be zero.
        if denominator == 0 :
            raise ZeroDivisionError("Denominator cannot be zero.")
```

```
# If the rational number is zero, set the denominator to 1.
if numerator == 0 :
    self._numerator = 0
    self._denominator = 1

# Otherwise, store the rational number in reduced form.
else :
    # Determine the sign.
    if (numerator < 0 and denominator >= 0 or
        numerator >= 0 and denominator < 0) :
        sign = -1
    else :
        sign = 1

    # Reduce to smallest form.
    a = abs(numerator)
    b = abs(denominator)
    while a % b != 0 :
        tempA = a
        tempB = b
        a = tempB
        b = tempA % tempB

    self._numerator = abs(numerator) // b * sign
    self._denominator = abs(denominator) // b
```

To illustrate the use of our `Fraction` class, we create several objects with various numerators and denominators:

```
frac1 = Fraction(1, 8)     # Stored as 1/8
frac2 = Fraction(-2, -4)   # Stored as 1/2
frac3 = Fraction(-2, 4)    # Stored as –1/2
frac4 = Fraction(3, -7)    # Stored as –3/7
frac5 = Fraction(0, 15)    # Stored as 0/1
frac6 = Fraction(8, 0)     # Error! exception is raised.
```

9.11.3 Special Methods

To use a standard operator with objects, define the corresponding special method.

In Python, we can define and implement methods that will be called automatically when a standard Python operator (such as +, *, ==, <) is applied to an instance of the class. This allows for a more natural use of the objects than calling methods by name. For example, to test whether two fractions are equal, we could implement a method `isequal` and use it as follows:

```
if frac1.isequal(frac2) :
    print("The fractions are equal.")
```

Of course, we would prefer to use the operator ==. This is achieved by defining the special method `__eq__`:

```
def __eq__(self, rhsValue) :  # rhs = right-hand side
    return (self._numerator == rhsValue._numerator and
            self._denominator == rhsValue._denominator)
```

This method is called automatically when we compare two `Fraction` objects using the == operator:

```
if frac1 == frac2 :  # Calls frac1.__eq__(frac2)
    print("The fractions are equal.")
```

Table 1 Common Special Methods			
Expression	Method Name	Returns	Description
$x + y$	`__add__(self, y)`	object	Addition
$x - y$	`__sub__(self, y)`	object	Subtraction
$x * y$	`__mul__(self, y)`	object	Multiplication
x / y	`__truediv__(self, y)`	object	Real division
$x // y$	`__floordiv__(self, y)`	object	Floor division
$x \% y$	`__mod__(self, y)`	object	Modulus
$x ** y$	`__pow__(self, y)`	object	Exponentiation
$x == y$	`__eq__(self, y)`	Boolean	Equal
$x != y$	`__ne__(self, y)`	Boolean	Not equal
$x < y$	`__lt__(self, y)`	Boolean	Less than
$x <= y$	`__le__(self, y)`	Boolean	Less than or equal
$x > y$	`__gt__(self, y)`	Boolean	Greater than
$x >= y$	`__ge__(self, y)`	Boolean	Greater than or equal
x	`__neg__(self)`	object	Unary minus
`abs(`x`)`	`__abs__(self)`	object	Absolute value
`float(`x`)`	`__float__(self)`	float	Convert to a floating-point value
`int(`x`)`	`__int__(self)`	integer	Convert to an integer value
`str(`x`)` `print(`x`)`	`__repr__(self)`	string	Convert to a readable string
x = *ClassName*`()`	`__init__(self)`	object	Constructor

Some special methods are called when an instance of the class is passed to a built-in function. For example, suppose you attempt to convert a `Fraction` object to a floating-point number using the `float` function:

```
x = float(frac1)
```

Then the `__float__` special method is called. Here is a definition of that method:

```
def __float__(self) :
    return self._numerator / self._denominator
```

Similarly, when an object is printed or otherwise converted to a string, Python will automatically call the special method `__repr__` on the object. This method is supposed to build and return a meaningful string representation of the object's value. For the Fraction class, we can have the method return a string containing the rational number in the form "#/#"

```
def __repr__(self) :
    return str(self._numerator) + "/" + str(self._denominator)
```

Special methods can be defined for any of Python's operators (see Table 1). The special methods are indicated with names that begin and end with two underscores. You should not directly call the special methods, but instead use the corresponding operator or function and let Python call the method for you.

It can be tempting to define operators for every class that you create, but you should only do so when the operator has a meaningful purpose. For the Fraction class, it makes sense to define special methods for the arithmetic operations +, –, *, /, **, and the logical operations ==, !=, <, <=, >, >=. In the following sections, we implement some of these and leave the others as an exercise.

9.11.4 Arithmetic Operations

All of the arithmetic operations that can be performed on a Fraction object should return the result in a new Fraction object. For example, when the statement

```
newFrac = frac1 + frac2
```

is executed, frac1 should be added to frac2 and the result returned as a new Fraction object that is assigned to the newFrac variable.

Let's start with addition, which requires that we implement the __add__ special method:

```
def __add__(self, rhsValue) :
```

From elementary arithmetic, you know that two fractions must have a common denominator in order to add them. If they do not have a common denominator, we can still add them using the formula

$$\frac{a}{b} + \frac{c}{d} = \frac{d \cdot a + b \cdot c}{b \cdot d}$$

In Python code, the numerator and denominator are computed using the instance variables from the two objects referenced by self and rhsValue:

```
num = (self._numerator * rhsValue._denominator +
       self._denominator * rhsValue._numerator)
den = self._denominator * rhsValue._denominator
```

After computing the numerator and denominator, we must create and return a new Fraction object from these values

```
return Fraction(num, den)
```

We do not have to worry about converting the rational number resulting from the addition to the reduced form because this will be taken care of in the constructor when the new object is created.

The complete addition method is shown below

```
## Adds a fraction to this fraction.
#  @param rhsValue the right-hand side fraction
#  @return a new Fraction object resulting from the addition
#
```

```
def __add__(self, rhsValue) :
    num = (self._numerator * rhsValue._denominator +
           self._denominator * rhsValue._numerator)
    den = self._denominator * rhsValue._denominator
    return Fraction(num, den)
```

Subtraction of two rational numbers is very similar to addition:

```
## Subtracts a fraction from this fraction.
#  @param rhsValue the right-hand side fraction
#  @return a new Fraction object resulting from the subtraction
#
def __sub__(self, rhsValue) :
    num = (self._numerator * rhsValue._denominator -
           self._denominator * rhsValue._numerator)
    den = self._denominator * rhsValue._denominator
    return Fraction(num, den)
```

The implementations of the remaining arithmetic operations are left as an exercise.

9.11.5 Logical Operations

In Python, two objects can be compared logically if the class implements the comparison operators (==, !=, <, <=, >, >=). Earlier, we implemented the `__eq__` method for testing whether two rational numbers are equal.

Next, let us determine which rational number is less than the other. Note that $a/b < c/d$ when $d \cdot a < b \cdot c$. (Multiply both sides with $b \cdot d$.)

Based on this observation, the less than operation is implemented by the `__lt__` method as follows:

```
## Determines if this fraction is less than another fraction.
#  @param rhsValue the right-hand side fraction
#  @return True if this fraction is less than the other
#
def __lt__(self, rhsValue) :
    return (self._numerator * rhsValue._denominator <
            self._denominator * rhsValue._numerator)
```

From these two relations, you can define the other four because

- $x > y$ when $y < x$
- $x \geq y$ when x is not less than y
- $x \leq y$ when y is not less than x
- $x \neq y$ when x is not equal to y

The implementation of the Fraction class is provided below.

sec11/fraction.py

```
1  ##
2  #   This module defines the Fraction class.
3  #
4
5  ## Defines an immutable rational number with common arithmetic operations.
6  #
7  class Fraction :
8      ## Constructs a rational number initialized to zero or a user specified value.
9      #  @param numerator the numerator of the fraction (default is 0)
```

```
10      #   @param denominator the denominator of the fraction (cannot be 0)
11      #
12      def __init__(self, numerator = 0, denominator = 1) :
13         # The denominator cannot be zero.
14         if denominator == 0 :
15            raise ZeroDivisionError("Denominator cannot be zero.")
16
17         # If the rational number is zero, set the denominator to 1.
18         if numerator == 0 :
19            self._numerator = 0
20            self._denominator = 1
21
22         # Otherwise, store the rational number in reduced form.
23         else :
24            # Determine the sign.
25            if (numerator < 0 and denominator >= 0 or
26                  numerator >= 0 and denominator < 0) :
27               sign = -1
28            else :
29               sign = 1
30
31            # Reduce to smallest form.
32            a = abs(numerator)
33            b = abs(denominator)
34            while a % b != 0 :
35               tempA = a
36               tempB = b
37               a = tempB
38               b = tempA % tempB
39
40            self._numerator = abs(numerator) // b * sign
41            self._denominator = abs(denominator) // b
42
43      ## Adds a fraction to this fraction.
44      #   @param rhsValue the right-hand side fraction
45      #   @return a new Fraction object resulting from the addition
46      #
47      def __add__(self, rhsValue) :
48         num = (self._numerator * rhsValue._denominator +
49               self._denominator * rhsValue._numerator)
50         den = self._denominator * rhsValue._denominator
51         return Fraction(num, den)
52
53      ## Subtracts a fraction from this fraction.
54      #   @param rhsValue the right-hand side fraction
55      #   @return a new Fraction object resulting from the subtraction
56      #
57      def __sub__(self, rhsValue) :
58         num = (self._numerator * rhsValue._denominator -
59               self._denominator * rhsValue._numerator)
60         den = self._denominator * rhsValue._denominator
61         return Fraction(num, den)
62
63      ## Determines if this fraction is equal to another fraction.
64      #   @param rhsValue the right-hand side fraction
65      #   @return True if the fractions are equal
66      #
67      def __eq__(self, rhsValue) :
68         return (self._numerator == rhsValue._numerator and
69               self._denominator == rhsValue._denominator)
```

```
70
71      ## Determines if this fraction is less than another fraction.
72      #   @param rhsValue the right-hand side fraction
73      #   @return True if this fraction is less than the other
74      #
75      def __lt__(self, rhsValue) :
76         return (self._numerator * rhsValue._denominator <
77                 self._denominator * rhsValue._numerator)
78
79      ## Determines if this fraction is not equal to another fraction.
80      #   @param rhsValue the right-hand side fraction
81      #   @return True if the fractions are not equal
82      #
83      def __ne__(self, rhsValue) :
84         return not self == rhsValue
85
86      ## Determines if this fraction is less than or equal to another fraction.
87      #   @param rhsValue the right-hand side fraction
88      #   @return True if this fraction is less than or equal to the other
89      #
90      def __le__(self, rhsValue) :
91         return not rhsValue < self
92
93      ## Determines if this fraction is greater than another fraction.
94      #   @param rhsValue the right-hand side fraction
95      #   @return True if this fraction is greater than the other
96      #
97      def __gt__(self, rhsValue) :
98         return rhsValue < self
99
100     ## Determines if this fraction is greater than or equal to another fraction.
101     #   @param rhsValue the right-hand side fraction
102     #   @return True if this fraction is greater than or equal to the other
103     #
104     def __ge__(self, rhsValue) :
105        return not self < rhsValue
106
107     ## Converts a fraction to a floating-point number.
108     #   @return the floating-point value of this fraction
109     #
110     def __float__(self) :
111        return self._numerator / self._denominator
112
113     ## Gets a string representation of the fraction.
114     #   @return a string in the format #/#
115     #
116     def __repr__(self) :
117        return str(self._numerator) + "/" + str(self._denominator)
```

Special Topic 9.3

Object Types and Instances

As we have defined functions or methods, we have assumed that the user will supply arguments of the correct data type. To ensure that, Python provides the built-in isinstance function that can be used to check the type of object referenced by a variable. For example, the constructor for the Fraction class in Section 9.11.2 requires two integers. We can use the isinstance function to check the types and raise an exception if necessary:

```python
class Fraction :
    def __init__(self, numerator, denominator) :
        if (not isinstance(numerator, int) or
                not isinstance(denominator, int)) :
            raise TypeError("The numerator and denominator must be integers.")
```

The isinstance function returns True if the object referenced by the first argument (numerator) is an instance of the data type indicated by the second argument (int). If the object is of a different type, the function returns False. The data type used as the second argument can be any built-in type (int, float, str, list, dict, set) or the name of a user-defined class.

The isinstance function can also be used in a function or method to allow for different actions depending on the type of data passed as an argument. For example, in the following code, we want to add an integer to a rational number:

```python
frac = Fraction(2, 3)
newFrac = frac + 5
```

When an operator is used, Python invokes the special method associated with that operator for the object on the left-hand side. In this example, the __add__ method will be invoked on the Fraction object referenced by frac. The value or object on the right-hand side of the operator is passed as an argument. Our implementation of the __add__ method assumes the right-hand side argument will be also be a Fraction object. To allow an integer to be added to a rational number, we can check the type of argument using the isinstance function and take the appropriate action based on the type:

```python
class Fraction :
    . . .
    def __add__(self, rhsValue) :
        if isinstance(rhsValue, int) :
            rhsFrac = Fraction(rhsValue, 1)
        elif isinstance(rhsValue, Fraction) :
            rhsFrac = rhsValue
        else :
            raise TypeError("Argument must be an int or Fraction object.")

        num = (self._numerator * rhsFrac._denominator +
                self._denominator * rhsFrac._numerator)
        den = self._denominator * rhsFrac._denominator
        return Fraction(num, den)
```

WORKED EXAMPLE 9.2

Graphics: A Die Class

In Worked Example 5.4, we developed a graphical program that simulated the rolling of five dice. In that program, we used a top-down design and divided each task into separate functions. But one part of the program is a prime candidate for implementation as a class.

Problem Statement　Define and implement a class to model a six-sided die that can be rolled and drawn on a canvas. This class can then be used in other programs that call for rolling or drawing a die.

Class Design

The common die is a six-sided object and each side (or face) contains from one to six dots. The number of dots indicates the face value. When a die is rolled, one of the six faces ends up on top. This is the value of the die after the roll.

We want to design a class that models a six-sided die that, when rolled, can display a graphical representation of the top face on a canvas. To use an instance of a Die in this fashion, as was done in the rolldice program developed in Worked Example 5.4, the class must define the following operations:

- Create a die whose position and size is provided by the user.
- Access the position and size of the die.
- Roll the die.
- Access the value of the face shown on top of the die.
- Set the color used to draw the die.
- Draw the die on a canvas.

After specifying the operations, we need to determine what data must be stored in a Die object. To draw the die on a canvas requires the *x*- and *y*-coordinates of the upper-left corner of the die and the size of the die. In the earlier program, there were three colors needed to draw the die: the fill and outline colors of the face and the color of the dots. When a die is rolled, the top face will have one of the six values. This value must be stored as an instance variable. In total, we will need seven instance variables: _x, _y, _size, _value, _fillColor, _outlineColor, _dotColor.

Class Implementation

To begin the implementation of the Die class, we start with the constructor. To make it as portable as possible, we allow the user to specify the size of the die and the coordinates where the upper-left corner of the die will be drawn. We specify a default size of 60 pixels to match what was used in the earlier program. By default, the die will be drawn with a white face, black frame, and black dots.

```
## A simulated 6-sided die that can be rolled and drawn on a canvas.
#
class Die :
   ## Constructs the die.
   #  @param x the upper-left x-coordinate of the die
   #  @param y the upper-left y-coordinate of the die
   #  @param size the size of the die
   #
   def __init__(self, x, y, size = 60) :
      self._x = x
      self._y = y
      self._size = size
      self._value = 1
      self._fillColor = "white"
      self._outlineColor = "black"
      self._dotColor = "black"
```

Several basic operations specified for the Die class will be accessor methods. These simply return the values of the instance variables:

```
## Get the face value of the die.
#  @return the face value
#
def faceValue(self) :
   return self._value
```

```
## Get the upper-left x-coordinate of the die.
# @return the x-coordinate
#
def getX(self) :
   return self._x
```

```
## Get the upper-left y-coordinate of the die.
# @return the y-coordinate
#
def getY(self) :
   return self._y
```

```
## Get the size of the die.
# @return the die size
#
def getSize(self) :
   return self._size
```

When a Die object is created, its default colors are set by the constructor. But we want the user to be able to change the colors used to draw the dice, so we create two mutator methods:

```
## Set the fill and outline colors of the die face.
# @param fill the fill color
# @param outline the outline color
#
def setFaceColor(self, fill, outline) :
   self._fillColor = fill
   self._outlineColor = outline
```

```
## Set the color used to draw the dots on the die face.
# @param color the dot color
#
def setDotColor(self, color) :
   self._dotColor = color
```

To simulate the rolling of a die, we again use the random number generator to produce a number between 1 and 6, which is assigned to the _value instance variable:

```
## Simulates the rolling of the die using the random number generator.
#
def roll(self) :
   self._value = randint(1, 6)
```

Finally, drawing the face of the die on a canvas is identical to the approach used in Worked Example 5.4. The only difference is that the parameters used to specify the position, size, and color can be extracted from the instance variables:

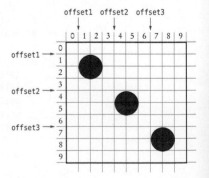

```
## Draws the die on the canvas.
# @param canvas the graphical canvas on which
#   to draw the die
#
def draw(self, canvas) :
   # The size of the dot and positioning will be
   # based on the size of the die.
   dotSize = self._size // 5
   offset1 = dotSize // 2
   offset2 = dotSize // 2 * 4
   offset3 = dotSize // 2 * 7
```

```
# Draw the rectangle for the die.
canvas.setFill(self._fillColor)
canvas.setOutline(self._outlineColor)
canvas.setLineWidth(2)
canvas.drawRect(self._x, self._y, self._size, self._size)

# Set the color used for the dots.
canvas.setColor(self._dotColor)
canvas.setLineWidth(1)

# Draw the center dot or middle row of dots, if needed.
if self._value == 1 or self._value == 3 or self._value == 5 :
    canvas.drawOval(self._x + offset2, self._y + offset2, dotSize, dotSize)
elif self._value == 6 :
    canvas.drawOval(self._x + offset1, self._y + offset2, dotSize, dotSize)
    canvas.drawOval(self._x + offset3, self._y + offset2, dotSize, dotSize)

# Draw the upper-left and lower-right dots, if needed.
if self._value >= 2 :
    canvas.drawOval(self._x + offset1, self._y + offset1, dotSize, dotSize)
    canvas.drawOval(self._x + offset3, self._y + offset3, dotSize, dotSize)

# Draw the lower-left and upper-right dots, if needed.
if self._value >= 4 :
    canvas.drawOval(self._x + offset1, self._y + offset3, dotSize, dotSize)
    canvas.drawOval(self._x + offset3, self._y + offset1, dotSize, dotSize)
```

EXAMPLE CODE   See the `worked_example_2/die.py` module in your companion code for the complete implementation of the `Die` class and the `rolldice.py` program that uses the class to simulate the rolling of five dice.

Computing & Society 9.2   Open Source and Free Software

Most companies that produce software regard the source code as a trade secret. After all, if customers or competitors had access to the source code, they could study it and create similar programs without paying the original vendor. For the same reason, customers dislike secret source code. If a company goes out of business or decides to discontinue support for a computer program, its users are left stranded. They are unable to fix bugs or adapt the program to a new operating system. Fortunately, many software packages are distributed as "open source software", giving its users the right to see, modify, and redistribute the source code of a program.

Having access to source code is not sufficient to ensure that software serves the needs of its users. Some companies have created software that spies on users or restricts access to previously purchased books, music, or videos. If that software runs on a server or in an embedded device, the user cannot change its behavior. In the article http://www.gnu.org/philosophy/free-software-even-more-important.en.html, Richard Stallman, a famous computer scientist and winner of a MacArthur "genius" grant, describes the "free software movement" that champions the right of users to control what their software does. This is an ethical position that goes beyond using open source for reasons of convenience or cost savings.

Stallman is the originator of the GNU project (http://gnu.org/gnu/the-gnu-project.html) that has produced an entirely free version of a UNIX-compatible operating system: the GNU operating system. All programs of the GNU project are licensed under the GNU General Public License (GNU GPL). The license allows you to make as many copies as you wish, make any modifications to the source, and redistribute the original and modified programs, charging nothing at all or whatever the market will bear. In return, you must agree that your modifications also fall under the license. You must give out the source code to any changes that you distribute, and anyone else can distribute them under the same conditions. The GNU GPL forms a social contract. Users of the software enjoy the freedom to use and modify the software, and in return they are obligated to share any improvements that they make available.

Some commercial software vendors have attacked the GPL as "viral" and "undermining the commercial software sector". Other companies have a more nuanced strategy, producing free or open source software, but charging for support or proprietary extensions. For example, the Java Development Kit is available under the GPL, but companies that need security updates for old versions or other support must pay Oracle.

Open source software sometimes lacks the polish of commercial software because many of the programmers are volunteers who are interested in solving their own problems, not in making a product that is easy to use by everyone. Open source software has been particularly successful in areas that are of interest to programmers, such as the Linux kernel, web servers, and programming tools.

The open source software community can be very competitive and creative. It is quite common to see several competing projects that take ideas from each other, all rapidly becoming more capable. Having many programmers involved, all reading the source code, often means that bugs tend to get squashed quickly. Eric Raymond describes open source development in his famous article "The Cathedral and the Bazaar" (http://catb.org/~esr/writings/cathedral-bazaar/cathedral-bazaar/index.html). He writes "Given enough eyeballs, all bugs are shallow".

Richard Stallman, a pioneer of the free source movement.

CHAPTER SUMMARY

Understand the concepts of classes, objects, and encapsulation.

- A class describes a set of objects with the same behavior.
- Every class has a public interface: a collection of methods through which the objects of the class can be manipulated.
- Encapsulation is the act of providing a public interface and hiding the implementation details.
- Encapsulation enables changes in the implementation without affecting users of a class.

Understand instance variables and method implementations of a simple class.

- An object's instance variables store the data required for executing its methods.
- Each object of a class has its own set of instance variables.
- A method can access the instance variables of the object on which it acts.

Write method headers that describe the public interface of a class.

- You can use method headers and method comments to specify the public interface of a class.
- A mutator method changes the object on which it operates.
- An accessor method does not change the object on which it operates.

Choose an appropriate data representation for a class.

- For each accessor method, an object must either store the result or the data necessary to compute the result.
- Commonly, there is more than one way of representing the data of an object, and you must make a choice.
- Be sure that your data representation supports method calls in any order.

Design and implement constructors.

- A constructor initializes the instance variables of an object.
- The constructor is automatically called when an object is created.
- The constructor is defined using the special method name __init__ .
- Default arguments can be used with a constructor to provide different ways of creating an object.

Provide the implementation of instance methods for a class.

- The object on which a method is applied is automatically passed to the self parameter variable of the method.
- In a method, you access instance variables through the self parameter variable.
- A class variable belongs to the class, not to any instance of the class.

Write tests that verify that a class works correctly.

- A unit test verifies that a class works correctly in isolation, outside a complete program.
- To test a class, use an environment for interactive testing, or write a tester program to execute test instructions.
- Determining the expected result in advance is an important part of testing.

Use the technique of object tracing for visualizing object behavior.

- Write the methods on the front of a card, and the instance variables on the back.
- Update the values of the instance variables when a mutator method is called.

Use patterns to design the data representation of a class.

- An instance variable for the total is updated in methods that increase or decrease the total amount.
- A counter that counts events is incremented in methods that correspond to the events.
- An object can collect other objects in a list.
- An object property can be accessed with a getter method and changed with a setter method.
- If your object can have one of several states that affect the behavior, supply an instance variable for the current state.
- To model a moving object, you need to store and update its position.

Describe the behavior of object references.

- An object reference specifies the location of an object.
- Multiple object variables can contain references to the same object.
- Use the is and is not operators to test whether two variables are aliases.
- The None reference refers to no object.
- The self parameter variable refers to the object on which a method was invoked.

Define special methods to allow class users to use operators with objects.

- To use a standard operator with objects, define the corresponding special method.
- Define the special __repr__ method to create a string representation of an object.

REVIEW EXERCISES

- **R9.1** What is encapsulation? Why is it useful?

- **R9.2** What values are returned by the calls `reg1.getCount()`, `reg1.getTotal()`, `reg2.getCount()`, and `reg2.getTotal()` after these statements?

  ```
  reg1 = CashRegister()
  reg1.addItem(3.25)
  reg1.addItem(1.95)
  reg2 = CashRegister()
  reg2.addItem(3.25)
  reg2.clear()
  ```

- **R9.3** Consider the `Menu` class in How To 9.1. What is displayed when the following calls are executed?

  ```
  simpleMenu = Menu()
  simpleMenu.addOption("Ok")
  simpleMenu.addOption("Cancel")
  response = simpleMenu.getInput()
  ```

- **R9.4** What is the *public interface* of a class? How does it differ from the *implementation* of a class?

- ■■ **R9.5** Consider the data representation of a cash register that keeps track of sales tax in Section 9.8. Instead of tracking the taxable total, track the total sales tax. Redo the walkthrough with this change.

- ■■■ **R9.6** Suppose the `CashRegister` needs to support a method `undo()` that undoes the addition of the preceding item. This enables a cashier to quickly undo a mistake. What instance variables should you add to the `CashRegister` class to support this modification?

- **R9.7** What is a mutator method? What is an accessor method?

- **R9.8** What is a constructor?

- **R9.9** How many constructors can a class have? Can you have a class with no constructors?

- **R9.10** Using the object tracing technique described in Section 9.8, trace the program at the end of Section 9.7.

- ■■ **R9.11** Using the object tracing technique described in Section 9.8, trace the program in Worked Example 9.1.

- ■■■ **R9.12** Design a modification of the `BankAccount` class in Worked Example 9.1 in which the first five transactions per month are free and a $1 fee is charged for every additional transaction. Provide a method that deducts the fee at the end of a month. What additional instance variables do you need? Using the object tracing technique described in Section 9.8, trace a scenario that shows how the fees are computed over two months.

- **R9.13** Instance variables should be "hidden" by using an underscore as the first character of their names, but they aren't hidden very well at all. What happens in Python when you try accessing an instance variable of a class from somewhere other than a method of the class?

■■■ **R9.14** You can read the _itemCount instance variable of the CashRegister class with the get-Count accessor method. Should there be a setCount mutator method to change it? Explain why or why not.

■■ **R9.15** What is the self reference? Why would you use it?

■■ **R9.16** What is the difference between the number zero, the None reference, the value False, and the empty string?

PROGRAMMING EXERCISES

■ **P9.1** We want to add a button to the tally counter in Section 9.2 that allows an operator to undo an accidental button click. Provide a method

```
def undo(self)
```

that simulates such a button. As an added precaution, make sure that the operator cannot click the undo button more often than the click button.

■ **P9.2** Simulate a tally counter that can be used to admit a limited number of people. First, the limit is set with a call to

```
def setLimit(self, maximum)
```

If the click button is clicked more often than the limit, simulate an alarm by printing out a message "Limit exceeded".

■■■ **P9.3** Reimplement the Menu class in How To 9.1 so that it stores all menu items in one long string. *Hint:* Keep a separate counter for the number of options. When a new option is added, append the option count, the option, and a newline character.

■■ **P9.4** Implement a class Address. An address has a house number, a street, an optional apartment number, a city, a state, and a postal code. Define the constructor such that an object can be created in one of two ways: with an apartment number or without. Supply a print method that prints the address with the street on one line and the city, state, and postal code on the next line. Supply a method def comesBefore(self, other) that tests whether this address comes before other when compared by postal code.

■ **P9.5** Implement a class SodaCan with methods getSurfaceArea() and getVolume(). In the constructor, supply the height and radius of the can.

■■ **P9.6** Implement a class Car with the following properties. A car has a certain fuel efficiency (measured in miles/gallon) and a certain amount of fuel in the gas tank. The efficiency is specified in the constructor, and the initial fuel level is 0. Supply a method drive that simulates driving the car for a certain distance, reducing the fuel level in the gas tank, and methods getGasLevel, to return the current fuel level, and addGas, to tank up. Sample usage:

```
myHybrid = Car(50)        # 50 miles per gallon
myHybrid.addGas(20)       # Tank 20 gallons
myHybrid.drive(100)       # Drive 100 miles
print(myHybrid.getGasLevel())    # Print fuel remaining
```

© Miklos Voros/
iStockphoto.

■■ P9.7 Implement a class Student. For the purpose of this exercise, a student has a name and a total quiz score. Supply an appropriate constructor and methods getName(), addQuiz(score), getTotalScore(), and getAverageScore(). To compute the latter, you also need to store the *number of quizzes* that the student took.

■■ P9.8 Modify the Student class of Exercise ●● P9.7 to compute grade point averages. Methods are needed to add a grade and get the current GPA. Specify grades as elements of a class Grade. Supply a constructor that constructs a grade from a string, such as "B+". You will also need a method that translates grades into their numeric values (for example, "B+" becomes 3.3).

■■■ P9.9 Implement a class ComboLock that works like the combination lock in a gym locker, as shown here. The lock is constructed with a combination—three numbers between 0 and 39. The reset method resets the dial so that it points to 0. The turnLeft and turnRight methods turn the dial by a given number of ticks to the left or right. The open method attempts to open the lock. The lock opens if the user first turned it right to the first number in the combination, then left to the second, and then right to the third.

© pixhook/iStockphoto.

```
class ComboLock :
    def ComboLock(self, secret1, secret2, secret3) :
        . . .
    def reset(self) :
        . . .
    def turnLeft(self, ticks) :
        . . .
    def turnRight(self, ticks) :
        . . .
    def open(self) :
        . . .
```

■■ P9.10 Implement a VotingMachine class that can be used for a simple election. Have methods to clear the machine state, to vote for a Democrat, to vote for a Republican, and to get the tallies for both parties.

■■ P9.11 Provide a class Letter for authoring a simple letter. In the constructor, supply the names of the sender and the recipient:

```
def __init__(self, letterFrom, letterTo)
```

Supply a method

```
def addLine(self, line)
```

to add a line of text to the body of the letter. Supply a method

```
def getText(self)
```

that returns the entire text of the letter. The text has the form:

```
Dear recipient name:
blank line
first line of the body
second line of the body
. . .
last line of the body
blank line
Sincerely,
blank line
sender name
```

Also supply a driver program that prints the following letter.

```
Dear John:

I am sorry we must part.
I wish you all the best.

Sincerely,

Mary
```

Construct an object of the Letter class and call addLine twice.

■■ **P9.12** Write a class Bug that models a bug moving along a horizontal line. The bug moves either to the right or left. Initially, the bug moves to the right, but it can turn to change its direction. In each move, its position changes by one unit in the current direction. Provide a constructor

```
def __init__(self, initialPosition)
```

and methods

- def turn(self)
- def move(self)
- def getPosition(self)

Sample usage:

```
bugsy = Bug(10)
bugsy.move()    # Now the position is 11
bugsy.turn()
bugsy.move()    # Now the position is 10
```

Your driver program should construct a bug, make it move and turn a few times, and print the actual and expected positions.

■■ **P9.13** Implement a class Moth that models a moth flying in a straight line. The moth has a position, the distance from a fixed origin. When the moth moves toward a point of light, its new position is halfway between its old position and the position of the light source. Supply a constructor

```
def __init__(self, initialPosition)
```

and methods

- def moveToLight(self, lightPosition)
- def getPosition(self)

Your driver program should construct a moth, move it toward a couple of light sources, and check that the moth's position is as expected.

■■■ **P9.14** Write functions

- def sphereVolume(r)
- def sphereSurface(r)
- def cylinderVolume(r, h)
- def cylinderSurface(r, h)
- def coneVolume(r, h)
- def coneSurface(r, h)

that compute the volume and surface area of a sphere with a radius r, a cylinder with a circular base with radius r and height h, and a cone with a circular base with radius r and height h. Place them into a geometry module. Then write a program that prompts the user for the values of r and h, calls the six functions, and prints the results.

■■ **P9.15** Solve Exercise ●●● P9.14 by implementing classes Sphere, Cylinder, and Cone. Which approach is more object-oriented?

■ **P9.16** Implement multiplication and division for the Fraction class in Section 9.11.5.

■ **P9.17** Add a unary minus operator to the Fraction class in Section 9.11.5. Reimplement the binary minus operator to call self + (-rhsValue).

■ **P9.18** In the Fraction class of Section 9.11.5, reimplement the __eq__ method, using the fact that two numbers are equal if neither is less than the other.

■■ **Business P9.19** Reimplement the CashRegister class so that it keeps track of the price of each added item in a list. Remove the _itemCount and _totalPrice instance variables. Reimplement the clear, addItem, getTotal, and getCount methods. Add a method displayAll that displays the prices of all items in the current sale.

■■ **Business P9.20** Reimplement the CashRegister class so that it keeps track of the total price as an integer: the total cents of the price. For example, instead of storing 17.29, store the integer 1729. Such an implementation is commonly used because it avoids the accumulation of roundoff errors. Do not change the public interface of the class.

■■ **Business P9.21** After closing time, the store manager would like to know how much business was transacted during the day. Modify the CashRegister class to enable this functionality. Supply methods getSalesTotal and getSalesCount to get the total amount of all sales and the number of sales. Supply a method resetSales that resets any counters and totals so that the next day's sales start from zero.

■■ **Business P9.22** Implement a class Portfolio. This class has two objects, checking and savings, of the type BankAccount that was developed in Worked Example 9.1 (worked_example_1/bank-account.py in your companion code). Implement four methods:

- def deposit(self, amount, account)
- def withdraw(self, amount, account)
- def transfer(self, amount, account)
- def getBalance(self, account)

Here the account string is "S" or "C". For the deposit or withdrawal, it indicates which account is affected. For a transfer, it indicates the account from which the money is taken; the money is automatically transferred to the other account.

■■ **Business P9.23** Design and implement a class Country that stores the name of the country, its population, and its area. Then write a program that reads in a set of countries and prints

- The country with the largest area.
- The country with the largest population.
- The country with the largest population density (people per square kilometer (or mile)).

■■ **Business P9.24** Design a class Message that models an e-mail message. A message has a recipient, a sender, and a message text. Support the following methods:

- A constructor that takes the sender and recipient
- A method append that appends a line of text to the message body
- A method toString that makes the message into one long string like this: "From: Harry Morgan\nTo: Rudolf Reindeer\n . . ."

Write a program that uses this class to make a message and print it.

■■ **Business P9.25** Design a class Mailbox that stores e-mail messages, using the Message class of Exercise •• Business P9.24. Implement the following methods:

- def addMessage(self, message)
- def getMessage(self, index)
- def removeMessage(self, index)

■■ **Business P9.26** Design a Customer class to handle a customer loyalty marketing campaign. After accumulating $100 in purchases, the customer receives a $10 discount on the next purchase. Provide methods

- def makePurchase(self, amount)
- def discountReached(self)

Provide a test program and test a scenario in which a customer has earned a discount and then made over $90, but less than $100 in purchases. This should not result in a second discount. Then add another purchase that results in the second discount.

■■■ **Business P9.27** The Downtown Marketing Association wants to promote downtown shopping with a loyalty program similar to the one in Exercise •• Business P9.26. Shops are identified by a number between 1 and 20. Add a new parameter variable to the makePurchase method that indicates the shop. The discount is awarded if a customer makes purchases in at least three different shops, spending a total of $100 or more.

© ThreeJays/iStockphoto.

■■■ **Science P9.28** Design a class Cannonball to model a cannonball that is fired into the air. A ball has

- An x- and a y-position.
- An x- and a y-velocity.

Supply the following methods:

- A constructor with an x-position (the y-position is initially 0)
- A method move(sec) that moves the ball to the next position (First compute the distance traveled in sec seconds, using the current velocities, then update the x- and y-positions; then update the y-velocity by taking into account the gravitational acceleration of -9.81 m/sec^2; the x-velocity is unchanged.)
- Methods getX and getY that get the current location of the cannonball
- A method shoot whose arguments are the angle α and initial velocity v (Compute the x-velocity as $v \cos \alpha$ and the y-velocity as $v \sin \alpha$; then keep calling move

with a time interval of 0.1 seconds until the *y*-position is approximately 0; call getX and getY after every move and display the position.)

Use this class in a program that prompts the user for the starting angle and the initial velocity. Then call shoot.

■■ **Science P9.29** The colored bands on the top-most resistor shown in the photo at right indicate a resistance of 6.2 kΩ ±5 percent. The resistor tolerance of ±5 percent indicates the acceptable variation in the resistance. A 6.2 kΩ ±5 percent resistor could have a resistance as small as 5.89 kΩ or as large as 6.51 kΩ. We say that 6.2 kΩ is the *nominal value* of the resis-

© Maria Toutoudaki/iStockphoto.

tance and that the actual value of the resistance can be any value between 5.89 kΩ and 6.51 kΩ.

Write a program that represents a resistor as a class. Provide a single constructor that accepts values for the nominal resistance and tolerance and then determines the actual value randomly. The class should provide public methods to get the nominal resistance, tolerance, and the actual resistance.

Write a main function for the program that demonstrates that the class works properly by displaying actual resistances for ten 330 Ω ±10 percent resistors.

■■ **Science P9.30** In the Resistor class from Exercise ●● Science P9.29, supply a method that returns a description of the "color bands" for the resistance and tolerance. A resistor has four color bands:

- The first band is the first significant digit of the resistance value.
- The second band is the second significant digit of the resistance value.
- The third band is the decimal multiplier.
- The fourth band indicates the tolerance.

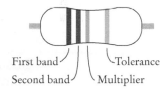

First band — Tolerance
Second band — Multiplier

Color	Digit	Multiplier	Tolerance
Black	0	$\times 10^0$	—
Brown	1	$\times 10^1$	±1%
Red	2	$\times 10^2$	±2%
Orange	3	$\times 10^3$	—
Yellow	4	$\times 10^4$	—
Green	5	$\times 10^5$	±0.5%
Blue	6	$\times 10^6$	±0.25%
Violet	7	$\times 10^7$	±0.1%

Color	Digit	Multiplier	Tolerance
Gray	8	$\times 10^8$	±0.05%
White	9	$\times 10^9$	—
Gold	—	$\times 10^{-1}$	±5%
Silver	—	$\times 10^{-2}$	±10%
None	—	—	±20%

For example (using the values from the table as a key), a resistor with red, violet, green, and gold bands (left to right) will have 2 as the first digit, 7 as the second digit, a multiplier of 10^5, and a tolerance of ±5 percent, for a resistance of 2,700 kΩ, plus or minus 5 percent.

■■■ **Science P9.31** The figure below shows a frequently used electric circuit called a "voltage divider". The input to the circuit is the voltage v_i. The output is the voltage v_o. The output of a voltage divider is proportional to the input, and the constant of proportionality is called the "gain" of the circuit. The voltage divider is represented by the equation

$$G = \frac{v_o}{v_i} = \frac{R_2}{R_1 + R_2}$$

where G is the gain and R_1 and R_2 are the resistances of the two resistors that comprise the voltage divider.

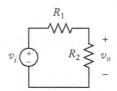

Manufacturing variations cause the actual resistance values to deviate from the nominal values, as described in Exercise ●● Science P9.29. In turn, variations in the resistance values cause variations in the values of the gain of the voltage divider. We calculate the *nominal value of the gain* using the nominal resistance values and the *actual value of the gain* using actual resistance values.

Write a program that contains two classes, VoltageDivider and Resistor. The Resistor class is described in Exercise ●● Science P9.29. The VoltageDivider class should have two instance variables that are objects of the Resistor class. Provide a single constructor that accepts two Resistor objects, nominal values for their resistances, and the resistor tolerance. The class should provide public methods to get the nominal and actual values of the voltage divider's gain.

Write a driver program that demonstrates that the class works properly by displaying nominal and actual gain for ten voltage dividers each consisting of 5 percent resistors having nominal values $R_1 = 250 \; \Omega$ and $R_2 = 750 \; \Omega$.

## CHAPTER 10

INHERITANCE

Jason Hosking/Getty Images, Inc.

CHAPTER GOALS

To learn about inheritance

To implement subclasses that inherit and override superclass methods

To understand the concept of polymorphism

CHAPTER CONTENTS

Objects from related classes usually share common characteristics and behavior. For example, cars, buses, and motorcycles all have wheels, require a fuel source, and can transport people. In this chapter, you will learn how the notion of inheritance expresses the relationship between specialized and general classes. By using inheritance, you will be able to share code between classes and provide services that can be used by multiple classes.

10.1 Inheritance Hierarchies

A subclass inherits data and behavior from a superclass.

In object-oriented design, **inheritance** is a relationship between a more general class (called the **superclass**) and a more specialized class (called the **subclass**). The subclass inherits data and behavior from the superclass. For example, consider the relationships between different kinds of vehicles depicted in Figure 1.

Every car *is a* vehicle. Cars share the common traits of all vehicles, such as the ability to transport people from one place to another. We say that the class Car inherits from the class Vehicle. In this relationship, the Vehicle class is the superclass and the Car class is the subclass. In Figure 2, the superclass and subclass are joined with an arrow that points to the superclass.

You can always use a subclass object in place of a superclass object.

Suppose we have an algorithm that manipulates a Vehicle object. Because a car is a special kind of vehicle, we can use a Car object in such an algorithm, and it will work correctly. The **substitution principle** states that you can always use a subclass object when a superclass object is expected. For example, consider a function that takes an argument of type Vehicle:

```
processVehicle(vehicle)
```

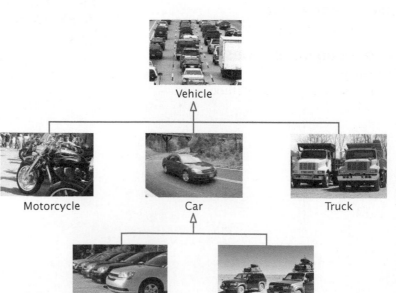

Figure 1 An Inheritance Hierarchy of Vehicle Classes

© Richard Stouffer/iStockphoto (vehicle); © Ed Hidden/iStockphoto (motorcycle); © Yin Yang/iStockphoto (car); © Robert Pernell/iStockphoto (truck); nicholas belton/iStockphoto (sedan); © Cezary Wojtkowski/Age Fotostock America (SUV).

Figure 2
An Inheritance Diagram

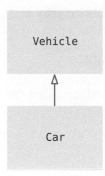

Because Car is a subclass of Vehicle, you can call that function with a Car object:

```
myCar = Car(. . .)
processVehicle(myCar)
```

Why provide a function that processes Vehicle objects instead of Car objects? That function is more useful because it can handle *any* kind of vehicle (including Truck and Motorcycle objects). In general, when we group classes into an inheritance hierarchy, we can share common code among the classes.

In this chapter, we will consider a simple hierarchy of classes representing questions. Most likely, you have taken computer-graded quizzes. A quiz consists of questions, and there are different kinds of questions:

© paul kline/iStockphoto.

We will develop a simple but flexible quiz-taking program to illustrate inheritance.

- Fill-in-the-blank
- Choice (single or multiple)
- Numeric (where an approximate answer is ok; e.g., 1.33 when the actual answer is 4/3)
- Free response

Figure 3 shows an inheritance hierarchy for these question types.

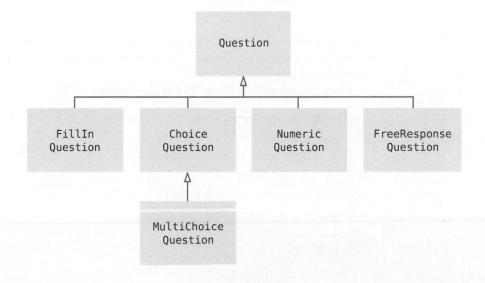

Figure 3
Inheritance Hierarchy
of Question Types

At the root of this hierarchy is the Question type. A question can display its text, and it can check whether a given response is a correct answer.

sec01/questions.py

```
1   ##
2   #    This module defines a class that models exam questions.
3   #
4
5   ## A question with a text and an answer.
6   #
7   class Question :
8      ## Constructs a question with empty question and answer strings.
9      #
10     def __init__(self) :
11        self._text = ""
12        self._answer = ""
13
14     ## Sets the question text.
15     #  @param questionText the text of this question
16     #
17     def setText(self, questionText) :
18        self._text = questionText
19
20     ## Sets the answer for this question.
21     #  @param correctResponse the answer
22     #
23     def setAnswer(self, correctResponse) :
24        self._answer = correctResponse
25
26     ## Checks a given response for correctness.
27     #  @param response the response to check
28     #  @return True if the response was correct, False otherwise
29     #
30     def checkAnswer(self, response) :
31        return response == self._answer
32
33     ## Displays this question.
34     #
35     def display(self) :
36        print(self._text)
```

This question class is very basic. It does not handle multiple-choice questions, numeric questions, and so on. In the following sections, you will see how to form subclasses of the Question class.

Here is a simple test program for the Question class.

sec01/questiondemo1.py

```
1   ##
2   #    This program shows a simple quiz with one question.
3   #
4
5   from questions import Question
6
7   # Create the question and expected answer.
8   q = Question()
9   q.setText("Who is the inventor of Python?")
```

```
10  q.setAnswer("Guido van Rossum")
11
12  # Display the question and obtain user's response.
13  q.display()
14  response = input("Your answer: ")
15  print(q.checkAnswer(response))
```

Program Run

```
Who was the inventor of Python?
Your answer: Guido van Rossum
True
```

Programming Tip 10.1

Use a Single Class for Variation in Values, Inheritance for Variation in Behavior

The purpose of inheritance is to model objects with different *behavior*. When students first learn about inheritance, they have a tendency to overuse it, creating multiple classes even though the variation could be expressed with a simple instance variable.

Consider a program that tracks the fuel efficiency of a fleet of cars by logging the distance traveled and the refueling amounts. Some cars in the fleet are hybrids. Should you create a subclass HybridCar? Not in this application. Hybrids don't behave any differently than other cars when it comes to driving and refueling. They just have better fuel efficiency. A single Car class with an instance variable

```
milesPerGallon
```

that stores a floating-point value is entirely sufficient.

However, if you write a program that shows how to repair different kinds of vehicles, then it makes sense to have a separate class HybridCar. When it comes to repairs, hybrid cars behave differently from other cars.

Special Topic 10.1

The Cosmic Superclass: object

In Python, every class that is declared without an explicit superclass automatically extends the class object. That is, the class object is the direct or indirect superclass of every class in Python (see Figure 4). The object class defines several very general methods, including the __repr__ method.

The __repr__ method returns a string representation for each object. By default, this includes the name of the class from which the object was created and the name of the module in which the class was defined. For example, we can create two Question objects and print the string representation of each:

```
first = Question()
second = Question()
print(first)
print(second)
```

which results in the output

```
<questions.Question object at 0xb7498d2c>
<questions.Question object at 0xb7498d4c>
```

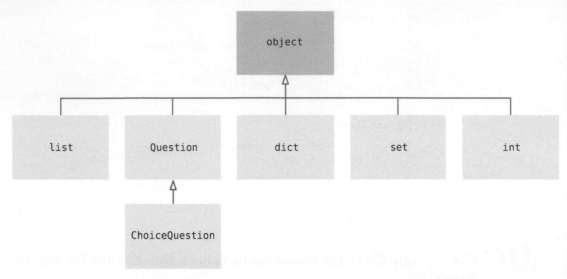

Figure 4 The object Class is a Superclass of Every Python Class

As you learned in Section 9.11.3, the __repr__ method can be overridden in a user-defined class to provide a more meaningful representation of the object. For example, in the Fraction class, we defined the __repr__ method to return the string representation of a rational number in the form #/#.

The __repr__ method is often overridden in subclasses for use in debugging. For example, we can override the __repr__ method in the Question class to return both the question and correct answer:

```
class Question :
    . . .
    def __repr__(self) :
        return "Question[%s, %s]" % (self._text, self._answer)
```

When testing our implementation of the Question class, we can create test objects and print them to verify that they contain the correct data:

```
q = Question()
print("Created object:", q)
q.setText("Who was the inventor of Python?")
print("Added the text:", q)
q.setAnswer("Guido van Rossum")
print("Added the answer:", q)
```

which produces the following output

```
Created object: Question[, ]
Added the text: Question[Who was the inventor of Python?, ]
Added the answer: Question[Who was the inventor of Python?, Guido van Rossum]
```

When debugging your code, knowing the state or contents of an object after an operation is performed is more meaningful than simply knowing the module and class name of the object.

10.2 Implementing Subclasses

In this section, you will see how to form a subclass and how a subclass automatically inherits functionality from its superclass.

Suppose you want to write a program that handles questions such as the following:

```
In which country was the inventor of Python born?
1. Australia
2. Canada
3. Netherlands
4. United States
```

You could write a ChoiceQuestion class from scratch, with methods to set up the question, display it, and check the answer. But you don't have to. Instead, use inheritance and implement ChoiceQuestion as a subclass of the Question class (see Figure 5). This will allow the ChoiceQuestion subclass to inherit the characteristics and behavior of the Question class that are shared by both.

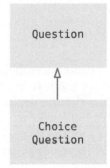

Figure 5
The ChoiceQuestion Class Is a Subclass of the Question Class

In Python, you form a subclass by specifying what makes the subclass different from its superclass.

Subclass objects automatically have the instance variables that are declared in the superclass. You declare only instance variables that are not part of the superclass objects.

> A subclass inherits all methods that it does not override.

The subclass inherits all methods from the superclass. You define any methods that are *new* to the subclass, and *change* the implementation of inherited methods if the inherited behavior is not appropriate. When you supply a new implementation for an inherited method, you **override** the method.

Like the manufacturer of a stretch limo, who starts with a regular car and modifies it, a programmer makes a subclass by modifying another class.

Media Bakery.

A ChoiceQuestion object differs from a Question object in three ways:

- Its objects store the various choices for the answer.
- There is a method for adding answer choices.
- The display method of the ChoiceQuestion class shows these choices so that the respondent can choose one of them.

When the ChoiceQuestion class inherits from the Question class, it needs to spell out these three differences:

```python
class ChoiceQuestion(Question) :
    # The subclass has its own constructor.
    def __init__(self) :
        . . .
        # This instance variable is added to the subclass.
        self._choices = []

    # This method is added to the subclass.
    def addChoice(self, choice, correct) :
        . . .

    # This method overrides a method from the superclass.
    def display(self) :
        . . .
```

The class name inside parentheses in the class header denotes inheritance.

Figure 6 shows the layout of a ChoiceQuestion object. It has the _text and _answer instance variables that are declared in the Question superclass, and it adds an additional instance variable, _choices.

The addChoice method is specific to the ChoiceQuestion class. You can only apply it to ChoiceQuestion objects, not general Question objects.

In contrast, the display method is a method that already exists in the superclass. The subclass overrides this method, so that the choices can be properly displayed.

All other methods of the Question class are automatically inherited by the Choice-Question class.

You can call the inherited methods on a subclass object:

```python
choiceQuestion.setAnswer("2")
```

However, the instance variables of the superclass are private to that class. Only the methods of the superclass should access its instance variables. Note that while Python does not provide a way to protect the instance variables of a superclass, good programming practice dictates that we should enforce this rule ourselves.

In particular, the ChoiceQuestion methods should not directly access the instance variable _answer. These methods must use the public interface of the Question class to access its private data, just like every other function or method.

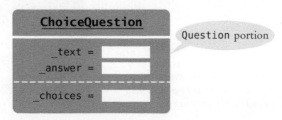

Figure 6 Data Layout of Subclass Object

Syntax 10.1   Subclass Definition

Syntax   class *SubclassName*(*SuperclassName*) :
                      constructor
                      methods

Instance variables   *Subclass*   *Superclass*
can be added to
the subclass.   class ChoiceQuestion(Question) :
                                                def __init__(self) :
                                                      . . .
                                                      self._choices = []
Define methods that are
added to the subclass.   def addChoice(self, choice, correct) :
                                                      . . .

Define methods that
the subclass overrides.   def display(self) :
                                                      . . .

To illustrate this point, let's implement the addChoice method. The method has two arguments: the choice to be added (which is appended to the list of choices), and a Boolean value to indicate whether this choice is correct. For example,

```
question.addChoice("Canada", True)
```

The first argument is added to the _choices instance variable. If the second argument is True, then the _answer instance variable becomes the number of the current choice. For example, if len(self._choices) is 2, then _answer is set to the string "2".

```
def addChoice(self, choice, correct) :
    self._choices.append(choice)
    if correct :
        # Convert the length of the list to a string.
        choiceString = str(len(self._choices))
        self.setAnswer(choiceString)
```

You should not access the _answer variable in the superclass. Fortunately, the Question class has a setAnswer method. You can call that method. On which object? The question that you are currently modifying—that is, the object on which the addChoice method was called. As you learned in Chapter 9, a reference to the object on which a method is called is automatically passed to the self parameter variable of the method. Thus, to call the setAnswer method on that object, use the self reference:

```
self.setAnswer(choiceString)
```

Common Error 10.1

Confusing Super- and Subclasses

If you compare an object of type ChoiceQuestion with an object of type Question, you find that

- The ChoiceQuestion object is larger; it has an added instance variable, _choices.
- The ChoiceQuestion object is more capable; it has an addChoice method.

It seems a superior object in every way. So why is ChoiceQuestion called the *subclass* and Question the *superclass*?

The *super/sub* terminology comes from set theory. Look at the set of all questions. Not all of them are ChoiceQuestion objects; some of them are other kinds of questions. Therefore, the set of ChoiceQuestion objects is a *subset* of the set of all Question objects, and the set of Question objects is a *superset* of the set of ChoiceQuestion objects. The more specialized objects in the subset have a richer state and more capabilities.

10.3 Calling the Superclass Constructor

Consider the process of constructing a subclass object. A subclass constructor can only define the instance variables of the subclass. But the superclass instance variables also need to be defined.

The superclass is responsible for defining its own instance variables. Because this is done within its constructor, the constructor of the subclass must explicitly call the superclass constructor. To call the superclass constructor, you use the __init__ special method. But the constructors of both classes have the same name. To distinguish between the constructor of the superclass and that of the subclass, you must use the super function in place of the self reference when calling the constructor:

> The superclass is responsible for defining its own instance variables.

> The subclass constructor must explicitly call the superclass constructor.

```
class ChoiceQuestion(Question) :
    def __init__(self) :
        super().__init__()
        self._choices = []
```

The superclass constructor should be called *before* the subclass defines its own instance variables. Note that the self reference must still be used to define the instance variables of the subclass.

> Use the super function to call the superclass constructor.

If a superclass constructor requires arguments, you must provide those as arguments to the __init__ method. For example, suppose the constructor of the Question superclass accepted an argument for setting the question text. Here is how a subclass constructor would call that superclass constructor:

```
class ChoiceQuestion(Question) :
    def __init__(self, questionText) :
        super().__init__(questionText)
        self._choices = []
```

Syntax 10.2 Subclass Constructor

Syntax
```
class SubclassName(SuperclassName) :
    def __init__(self, parameterName₁, parameterName₂, . . .) :
        super().__init__(arguments)
        constructor body
```

The super *function is used to refer to the superclass.*

The subclass constructor body can contain additional statements.

```
class ChoiceQuestion(Question) :
    def __init__(self, questionText) :
        super().__init__(questionText)
        self._choices = []
```

The superclass constructor is called first.

As another example, suppose we have defined a Vehicle class and the constructor requires an argument:

```
class Vehicle :
    def __init__(self, numberOfTires) :
        self._numberOfTires = numberOfTires
    . . .
```

We can extend the Vehicle class by defining a Car subclass:

```
class Car(Vehicle) :
    def __init__(self) :  ❶
        # Call the superclass constructor to define its instance variable.
        super().__init__(4)  ❷

        # This instance variable is set by the subclass.
        self._plateNumber = "??????"  ❸
    . . .
```

When a Car object is constructed,

```
aPlainCar = Car()
```

the constructor of the Car subclass calls the constructor of the superclass and passes the value 4 as the argument (because a standard car has four tires). The Vehicle superclass uses that value to initialize its _numberOfTires instance variable. Figure 7 illustrates the steps involved in constructing a Car object.

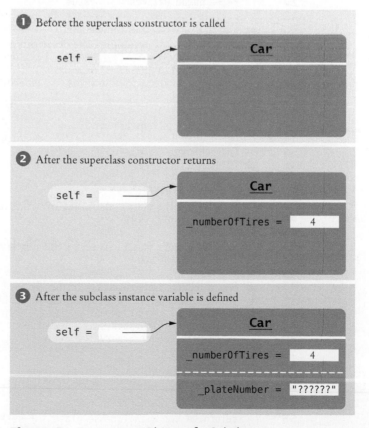

Figure 7   Creating an Object of a Subclass

Following are the complete `Vehicle` and `Car` classes and a simple test program.

sec03/car.py

```
1   ##
2   #  This module defines classes that model vehicle classes.
3   #
4
5   ## A generic vehicle superclass.
6   #
7   class Vehicle :
8      ## Constructs a vehicle object with a given number of tires.
9      #  @param numberOfTires  the number of tires on the vehicle
10     #
11     def __init__(self, numberOfTires) :
12        self._numberOfTires = numberOfTires
13
14     ## Gets the number of tires on the vehicle.
15     #  @return  number of tires
16     #
17     def getNumberOfTires(self) :
18        return self._numberOfTires
19
20     ## Changes the number of tires on the vehicle.
21     #  @param newValue  the number of tires
22     #
23     def setNumberOfTires(self, newValue) :
24        self._numberOfTires = newValue
25
26     ## Gets a description of the vehicle.
27     #  @return  a string containing the description
28     #
29     def getDescription(self) :
30        return "A vehicle with " + self._numberOfTires + " tires"
31
32
33   ## A specific type of vehicle - car.
34   #
35   class Car(Vehicle) :
36      ## Constructs a car object.
37      #
38      def __init__(self) :
39         # Call the superclass constructor to define its instance variables.
40         super().__init__(4)
41
42         # This instance variable is set by the subclass.
43         self._plateNumber = "??????"
44
45      ## Sets the license plate number of the car.
46      #  @param newValue  a string containing the number
47      #
48      def setLicensePlateNumber(self, newValue) :
49         self._plateNumber = newValue
50
51      ## Gets a description of the car.
52      #  @return  a string containing the description
53      #
54      def getDescription(self) :
55         return "A car with license plate " + self._plateNumber
```

sec03/cardemo.py

```
1  ##
2  #  This program provides a simple test of the Car class.
3  #
4
5  from car import Car
6
7  def main() :
8     aPlainCar = Car()
9     printInfo(aPlainCar)
10
11    aLimo = Car()
12    aLimo.setLicensePlateNumber("W00H00")
13    aLimo.setNumberOfTires(8)
14    printInfo(aLimo)
15
16  def printInfo(car) :
17     print(car.getDescription())
18     print("Tires:", car.getNumberOfTires())
19
20  # Start the program
21  main()
```

Program Run

```
A car with license plate ??????
Tires: 4
A car with license plate W00H00
Tires: 8
```

10.4 Overriding Methods

The subclass inherits the methods in the superclass. If you are not satisfied with the behavior of an inherited method, you *override* it by specifying a new implementation in the subclass.

Consider the display method of the ChoiceQuestion class. It overrides the superclass display method in order to show the choices for the answer. This method *extends* the functionality of the superclass version. This means that the subclass method carries out the action of the superclass method (in our case, displaying the question text), and it also does some additional work (in our case, displaying the choices). In other cases,

An overriding method can extend or replace the functionality of the superclass method.

Should you extend a house or replace it? You face the same question when overriding a superclass method.

© Andrew Howe/iStockphoto.

a subclass method *replaces* the functionality of a superclass method, implementing an entirely different behavior.

Let us turn to the implementation of the display method of the ChoiceQuestion class. The method needs to

- *Display the question text.*
- *Display the answer choices.*

The second part is easy because the answer choices are an instance variable of the subclass.

```python
class ChoiceQuestion(Question) :
    . . .
    def display(self) :
        # Display the question text.
        . . .
        # Display the answer choices.
        for i in range(len(self._choices)) :
            choiceNumber = i + 1
            print("%d: %s" % (choiceNumber, self._choices[i]))
```

But how do you get the question text? You can't access the text variable of the superclass directly because it is private.

> Use the super function to call a superclass method.

Instead, you can call the display method of the superclass, using the super function:

```python
def display(self) :
    # Display the question text.
    super().display()    # OK
    # Display the answer choices.
    . . .
```

If you use the self reference instead of the super function, then the method will not work as intended.

```python
def display(self) :
    # Display the question text.
    self.display()    # Error—invokes display() of ChoiceQuestion.
    . . .
```

Because the self parameter references an object of type ChoiceQuestion, and there is a method named display in the ChoiceQuestion class, that method will be called—but that is the method you are currently writing! Written that way, the method would call itself over and over.

Here is a program that lets you take a quiz consisting of two ChoiceQuestion objects. We construct both objects and pass each, in turn, to a function presentQuestion. That function displays the question to the user and checks whether the user response is correct. (questions.py is unchanged from Section 10.1.)

sec04/questiondemo2.py

```python
1  ##
2  #  This program shows a simple quiz with two choice questions.
3  #
4
5  from choicequestions import ChoiceQuestion
6
7  def main() :
8      first = ChoiceQuestion()
9      first.setText("In what year was the Python language first released?")
```

```
10      first.addChoice("1991", True)
11      first.addChoice("1995", False)
12      first.addChoice("1998", False)
13      first.addChoice("2000", False)
14
15      second = ChoiceQuestion()
16      second.setText("In which country was the inventor of Python born?")
17      second.addChoice("Australia", False)
18      second.addChoice("Canada", False)
19      second.addChoice("Netherlands", True)
20      second.addChoice("United States", False)
21
22      presentQuestion(first)
23      presentQuestion(second)
24
25  ## Presents a question to the user and checks the response.
26  #   @param q the question
27  #
28  def presentQuestion(q) :
29      q.display()
30      response = input("Your answer: ")
31      print(q.checkAnswer(response))
32
33  # Start the program.
34  main()
```

sec04/choicequestions.py

```
1   ##
2   #   This module defines a class that extends the base Question class.
3   #
4
5   from questions import Question
6
7   ## A question with multiple choices.
8   #
9   class ChoiceQuestion(Question) :
10      # Constructs a choice question with no choices.
11      def __init__(self) :
12          super().__init__()
13          self._choices = []
14
15      ## Adds an answer choice to this question.
16      #   @param choice the choice to add
17      #   @param correct True if this is the correct choice, False otherwise
18      #
19      def addChoice(self, choice, correct) :
20          self._choices.append(choice)
21          if correct :
22              # Convert len(choices) to string.
23              choiceString = str(len(self._choices))
24              self.setAnswer(choiceString)
25
26      # Override Question.display().
27      def display(self) :
28          # Display the question text.
29          super().display()
30
31          # Display the answer choices.
```

```
32        for i in range(len(self._choices)) :
33            choiceNumber = i + 1
34            print("%d: %s" % (choiceNumber, self._choices[i]))
```

Program Run

```
In what year was the Python language first released?
1: 1991
2: 1995
3: 1998
4: 2000
Your answer: 2
False
In which country was the inventor of Python born?
1: Australia
2: Canada
3: Netherlands
4: United States
Your answer: 3
True
```

Common Error 10.2

Forgetting to Use the super Function When Invoking a Superclass Method

A common error in extending the functionality of a superclass method is to forget the super function. For example, to compute the salary of a manager, get the salary of the underlying Employee object and add a bonus:

```
class Manager(Employee) :
    . . .
    def getSalary(self) :
        base = self.getSalary()    # Error: should be super().getSalary()
        return base + self._bonus
```

Here self refers to an object of type Manager and there is a getSalary method in the Manager class. Calling that method is a recursive call, which will never stop. Instead, you must explicitly invoke the superclass method:

```
class Manager(Employee) :
    . . .
    def getSalary(self) :
        base = super().getSalary()
        return base + self._bonus
```

Whenever you call a superclass method from a subclass method with the same name, be sure to use the super function in place of the self reference.

10.5 Polymorphism

In this section, you will learn how to use inheritance for processing objects of different types in the same program.

Consider our first sample program. It presented two Question objects to the user. The second sample program presented two ChoiceQuestion objects. Can we write a program that shows a mixture of both question types?

With inheritance, this goal is very easy to realize. In order to present a question to the user, we need not know the exact type of the question. We just display the question and check whether the user supplied the correct answer. The Question superclass has methods for this purpose. Therefore, we can define the presentQuestion function to expect a Question type object:

```
def presentQuestion(q) :
    q.display()
    response = input("Your answer: ")
    print(q.checkAnswer(response))
```

That is, we can call any method on the q parameter variable that is defined by the Question class.

As discussed in Section 10.1, we can substitute a subclass object whenever a superclass object is expected:

> A subclass reference can be used when a superclass reference is expected.

```
second = ChoiceQuestion()
presentQuestion(second)    # OK to pass a ChoiceQuestion
```

But you cannot substitute a superclass object when a subclass object is expected. For example, suppose we define the function addAllChoices to add the strings from a list to a ChoiceQuestion object as the choices from which to choose:

```
def addAllChoices(q, choices, correct) :
    for i in range(len(choices)) :
        if i == correct :
            q.addChoice(choices[i], True)
        else :
            q.addChoice(choices[i], False)
```

This function works correctly if we pass a ChoiceQuestion object as the first argument:

```
text = "In which year was Python first released?"
answers = ["1991", "1995", "1998", "2000"]
correct = 1

first = ChoiceQuestion()
first.setText(text)
addAllChoices(first, answers, correct)
```

When the addAllChoices function executes, the q parameter variable refers to a ChoiceQuestion object. But if we create a Question object and pass it to the addAllChoices function instead:

```
. . .
first = Question()
first.setText(text)
addAllChoices(first, answers, correct)
```

an AttributeError exception will be raised. That is as it should be. The q parameter variable refers to a Question object, but the Question class does not define the addChoice method. You cannot invoke a method on an object that has not been defined by that object's class.

Now let's have a closer look inside the presentQuestion function. It starts with the call

```
q.display()    # Does it call Question.display or ChoiceQuestion.display?
```

Which display method is called? If you look at the output following the program below, you will see that the method called depends on the contents of the parameter variable q. In the first case, q refers to a Question object, so the Question.display method is called. But in the second case, q refers to a ChoiceQuestion, so the ChoiceQuestion.display method is called, showing the list of choices.

Method calls *are always determined at run time based on the type of the actual object*. This is called **dynamic method lookup**. Dynamic method lookup allows us to treat objects of different classes in a uniform way. This feature is called **polymorphism**. We ask multiple objects to carry out a task, and each object does so in its own way.

Polymorphism makes programs *easily extensible*. Suppose we want to have a new kind of question for calculations where we are willing to accept an approximate answer. All we need to do is to define a new class NumericQuestion that extends Question, with its own checkAnswer method. Then we can call the presentQuestion function with a mixture of plain questions, choice questions, and numeric questions. The presentQuestion function need not be changed at all! Thanks to dynamic method lookup, calls to the display and checkAnswer methods automatically select the method of the correct class.

> Polymorphism ("having multiple shapes") allows us to manipulate objects that share a set of tasks, even though the tasks are executed in different ways.

© Alpophoto/iStockphoto.

In the same way that vehicles can differ in their method of locomotion, polymorphic objects carry out tasks in different ways.

sec05/questiondemo3.py

```
1  ##
2  #   This program shows a simple quiz with two question types.
3  #
4
5  from questions import Question
6  from choicequestions import ChoiceQuestion
7
8  def main() :
9      first = Question()
10     first.setText("Who was the inventor of Python?")
11     first.setAnswer("Guido van Rossum")
12
13     second = ChoiceQuestion()
14     second.setText("In which country was the inventor of Python born?")
15     second.addChoice("Australia", False)
16     second.addChoice("Canada", False)
17     second.addChoice("Netherlands", True)
18     second.addChoice("United States", False)
19
20     presentQuestion(first)
21     presentQuestion(second)
22
23  ## Presents a question to the user and checks the response.
24  #   @param q the question
25  #
26  def presentQuestion(q) :
27      q.display()    # Uses dynamic method lookup.
28      response = input("Your answer: ")
29      print(q.checkAnswer(response))    # checkAnswer uses dynamic method lookup.
30
31  # Start the program.
32  main()
```

Program Run

```
Who was the inventor of Python?
Your answer: Bjarne Stroustrup
False
In which country was the inventor of Python born?
1: Australia
2: Canada
3: Netherlands
4: United States
Your answer: 3
True
```

Special Topic 10.2

Subclasses and Instances

In Special Topic 9.3 you learned that the isinstance function can be used to determine if an object is an instance of a specific class. But the isinstance function can also be used to determine if an object is an instance of a subclass. For example, the function call

```
isinstance(q, Question)
```

will return True if q is an instance of the Question class or of any subclass that extends the Question class. Otherwise, it returns False.

A common use of the isinstance function is to verify that the arguments passed to a function or method are of the correct type. Consider the presentQuestion function. It requires an object that is an instance of the Question class or one of its subclasses. To verify the correct type of the object supplied, we can use the isinstance function:

```
def presentQuestion(q) :
    if not isintance(q, Question) :
        raise TypeError("The argument is not a Question or one of its subclasses.")
    q.display()
    response = input("Your answer: ")
    print(q.checkAnswer(response))
```

When the function is called, we check the type of the argument. If an invalid object type is passed to the function, a TypeError exception is raised.

```
first = Question()
second = ChoiceQuestion()
. . .
presentQuestion(first)    # OK
presentQuestion(second)    # OK—subclass of Question.
presentQuestion(5)    # Error—an integer is not a subclass of Question.
```

Special Topic 10.3

Dynamic Method Lookup

Suppose we add presentQuestion as a method of the Question class itself:

```
class Question :
    . . .
    def presentQuestion(self) :
        self.display()
        response = input("Your answer: ")
        print(self.checkAnswer(response))
```

Now consider the call

```
cq = ChoiceQuestion()
cq.setText("In which country was the inventor of Python born?")
. . .
cq.presentQuestion()
```

Which `display` and `checkAnswer` method will the `presentQuestion` method call? If you look at the code of the `presentQuestion` method, you can see that these methods are executed on the `self` reference parameter.

Remember, the `self` reference parameter is a reference to the object on which the method was invoked. In this case, `self` refers to an object of type `ChoiceQuestion`. Because of dynamic method lookup, the `ChoiceQuestion` versions of the `display` and `checkAnswer` methods are called automatically. This happens even though the `presentQuestion` method is declared in the `Question` class, which has no knowledge of the `ChoiceQuestion` class.

As you can see, polymorphism is a very powerful mechanism. The `Question` class supplies a `presentQuestion` method that specifies the common nature of presenting a question, namely to display it and check the response. How the displaying and checking are carried out is left to the subclasses.

Special Topic 10.4

Abstract Classes

When you extend an existing class, you have the choice whether or not to override the methods of the superclass. Sometimes, it is desirable to force programmers to override a method. That happens when there is no good default for the superclass, and only the subclass programmer can know how to implement the method properly. Here is an example: Suppose the First National Bank of Python decides that every account type must have some monthly fees. Therefore, a `deductFees` method should be added to the `Account` class:

```
class Account :
    . . .
    def deductFees(self) :
        . . .
```

But what should this method do? Of course, we could have the method do nothing. But then a programmer implementing a new subclass might simply forget to implement the `deductFees` method, and the new account would inherit the do-nothing method of the superclass. There is a better way—specify that the `deductFees` method is an **abstract method**. An abstract method has no implementation. This forces the implementors of subclasses to specify concrete implementations of this method. (Of course, some subclasses might decide to implement a do-nothing method, but then that is their choice—not a silently inherited default.)

A class that contains at least one abstract method is known as an **abstract class**. A class that contains no abstract methods is sometimes called a **concrete class**.

In Python, there is no explicit way to specify that a method is an abstract method. Instead, the common practice among Python programmers is to have the method raise a `NotImplementedError` exception as its only statement:

> An abstract method is a method whose implementation is not specified.

```
class Account :
    . . .
    def deductFees(self) :
        raise NotImplementedError
```

That way, if the user of the class attempts to invoke the method of the superclass, the exception will be raised to flag the missing implementation.

Although this allows you to create an object of the superclass or subclass, fully testing the implementation should discover any abstract methods that are not properly implemented. In other object-oriented languages, the missing implementation is discovered at compile time because you are not allowed to create an instance of a class that contains an abstract method.

The reason for using abstract classes is to force programmers to create subclasses. By specifying certain methods as abstract, you avoid the trouble of coming up with useless default methods that others might inherit by accident.

Common Error 10.3

Don't Use Type Tests

Some programmers use specific type tests in order to implement behavior that varies with each class:

```
if isinstance(q, ChoiceQuestion) :    # Don't do this.
    # Do the task the ChoiceQuestion way.
elif isinstance(q, Question) :
    # Do the task the Question way.
```

This is a poor strategy. If a new class such as NumericQuestion is added, then you need to revise all parts of your program that make a type test, adding another case:

```
elif isinstance(q, NumericQuestion) :
    # Do the task the NumericQuestion way.
```

In contrast, consider the addition of a class NumericQuestion to our quiz program. Nothing needs to change in that program because it uses polymorphism, not type tests.

Whenever you find yourself trying to use type tests in a hierarchy of classes, reconsider and use polymorphism instead. Declare a method doTheTask in the superclass, override it in the subclasses, and call

```
q.doTheTask()
```

HOW TO 10.1

Developing an Inheritance Hierarchy

When you work with a set of classes, some of which are more general and others more specific, you want to organize them into an inheritance hierarchy. This enables you to process objects of different classes in a uniform way.

Problem Statement Simulate a bank that offers customers the following account types:

- A savings account that earns interest. The interest compounds monthly and is computed on the minimum monthly balance.
- A checking account that has no interest, gives you three free withdrawals per month, and charges a $1 transaction fee for each additional withdrawal.

The program will manage a set of accounts of both types, and it should be structured so that other account types can be added without affecting the main processing loop. Supply a menu

```
D)eposit  W)ithdraw  M)onth end  Q)uit
```

For deposits and withdrawals, query the account number and amount. Print the balance of the account after each transaction.

In the "Month end" command, accumulate interest or clear the transaction counter, depending on the type of the bank account. Then print the balance of all accounts.

Step 1   List the classes that are part of the hierarchy.

In our case, the problem description yields two classes: SavingsAccount and CheckingAccount. Of course, you could implement each of them separately. But that would not be a good idea because the classes would have to repeat common functionality, such as updating an account balance. We need another class that can be responsible for that common functionality. The problem statement does not explicitly mention such a class. Therefore, we need to discover it. Of course, in this case, the solution is simple. Savings accounts and checking accounts are special cases of a bank account. Therefore, we will introduce a common superclass BankAccount.

Step 2   Organize the classes into an inheritance hierarchy.

Draw an inheritance diagram that shows super- and subclasses. Here is one for our example:

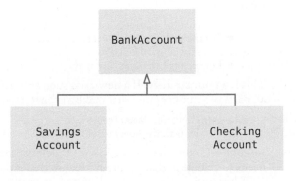

Step 3   Determine the common responsibilities.

In Step 2, you will have identified a class at the base of the hierarchy. That class needs to have sufficient responsibilities to carry out the tasks at hand. To find out what those tasks are, write pseudocode for processing the objects.

For each user command
   If it is a deposit or withdrawal
      Deposit or withdraw the amount from the specified account.
      Print the balance.
   If it is month end processing
      For each account
         Call month end processing.
         Print the balance.

From the pseudocode, we obtain the following list of common responsibilities that every bank account must carry out:

Deposit money.
Withdraw money.
Get the balance.
Carry out month end processing.

Step 4   Decide which methods are overridden in subclasses.

For each subclass and each of the common responsibilities, decide whether the behavior can be inherited or whether it needs to be overridden. Be sure to declare any methods that are inherited or overridden in the base of the hierarchy.

```
## A bank account has a balance and a mechanism for applying interest or fees at
#    the end of the month.
#
```

```
class BankAccount :
    ## Constructs a bank account with zero balance.
    #
    def __init__(self) :
        . . .


    ## Makes a deposit into this account.
    #  @param amount  the amount of the deposit
    #
    def deposit(self, amount) :
        . . .


    ## Makes a withdrawal from this account, or charges a penalty if
    #  sufficient funds are not available.
    #  @param amount  the amount of the withdrawal
    #
    def withdraw(self, amount) :
        . . .


    ## Carries out the end of month processing that is appropriate
    #  for this account.
    #
    def monthEnd(self) :
        . . .


    ## Gets the current balance of this bank account.
    #  @return the current balance
    #
    def getBalance(self) :
        . . .
```

The SavingsAccount and CheckingAccount classes both override the monthEnd method. The SavingsAccount class must also override the withdraw method to track the minimum balance. The CheckingAccount class must update a transaction count in the withdraw method.

Step 5   Define the public interface of each subclass.

Typically, subclasses have responsibilities other than those of the superclass. List those, as well as the methods that need to be overridden. You also need to specify how the objects of the subclasses should be constructed.

In this example, we need a way of setting the interest rate for the savings account. In addition, we need to specify constructors and overridden methods.

```
## A savings account earns interest on the minimum balance.
#
class SavingsAccount(BankAccount) :
    ## Constructs a savings account with a zero balance.
    #
    def __init__(self) :
        . . .


    ## Sets the interest rate for this account.
    #  @param rate  the monthly interest rate in percent
    #
    def setInterestRate(self, rate) :
        . . .


    # These methods override superclass methods.
    def withdraw(self, amount) :
        . . .
```

```
         def monthEnd(self) :
            . . .


## A checking account has a limited number of free deposits and withdrawals.
#
class CheckingAccount(BankAccount) :
   ## Constructs a checking account with a zero balance.
   #
   def __init__(self) :
      . . .

   # These methods override superclass methods.
   def withdraw(self, amount) :
      . . .

   def monthEnd(self) :
      . . .
```

Step 6   Identify instance variables.

List the instance variables for each class. If you find an instance variable that is common to all classes, be sure to define it in the base of the hierarchy.

All accounts have a balance. We define an instance variable _balance in the BankAccount superclass that stores that value as a float.

The SavingsAccount class needs to store the interest rate. It also needs to store the minimum monthly balance, which must be updated by all withdrawals. These will be stored as floating-point values in the instance variables _interestRate and _minBalance.

The CheckingAccount class needs to count the withdrawals, so that the charge can be applied after the free withdrawal limit is reached. We define the instance variable _withdrawals in the CheckingAccount subclass for that value.

Step 7   Implement constructors and methods.

The methods of the BankAccount class update or return the balance.

```
class BankAccount :
   def __init__(self) :
      self._balance = 0.0

   def deposit(self, amount) :
      self._balance = self._balance + amount

   def withdraw(self, amount) :
      self._balance = self._balance - amount

   def getBalance(self) :
      return self._balance
```

At the level of the BankAccount superclass, we can say nothing about end of month processing because it depends on the type of account. Thus, this method will have to be implemented by each subclass to carry out the processing appropriate for that type of account. We choose to make that method do nothing:

```
def monthEnd(self) :
   return
```

It would also be appropriate to have this method raise the NotImplementedError exception. That would indicate that the method is abstract (see Special Topic 10.4) and should be overridden in a subclass:

```
    def monthEnd(self) :
        raise NotImplementedError
```

In the `withdraw` method of the `SavingsAccount` class, the minimum balance is updated. Note the call to the superclass method:

```
def withdraw(self, amount) :
    super().withdraw(amount)
    balance = self.getBalance()
    if balance < self._minBalance :
        self._minBalance = balance
```

In the `monthEnd` method of the `SavingsAccount` class, the interest is deposited into the account. We must call the `deposit` method because we have no direct access to the `_balance` instance variable. The minimum balance is reset for the next month.

```
def monthEnd(self) :
    interest = self._minBalance * self._interestRate / 100
    self.deposit(interest)
    self._minBalance = self.getBalance()
```

The `withdraw` method of the `CheckingAccount` class needs to check the withdrawal count. If there have been too many withdrawals, a charge is applied. Again, note how the method invokes the superclass method:

```
def withdraw(self, amount) :
    FREE_WITHDRAWALS = 3
    WITHDRAWAL_FEE = 1

    super().withdraw(amount)
    self._withdrawals = self._withdrawals + 1
    if self._withdrawals > FREE_WITHDRAWALS :
        super().withdraw(WITHDRAWAL_FEE)
```

End of month processing for a checking account simply resets the withdrawal count:

```
def monthEnd(self) :
    self._withdrawals = 0
```

Step 8 Construct objects of different subclasses and process them.

In our sample program, we allocate five checking accounts and five savings accounts and store their addresses in a list of bank accounts. Then we accept user commands and execute deposits, withdrawals, and monthly processing.

```
# Create accounts.
accounts = []
. . .

# Execute commands.
done = False
while not done :
    action = input("D)eposit W)ithdraw M)onth end Q)uit: ")
    action = action.upper()
    if action == "D" or action == "W" :    # Deposit or withdrawal.
        num = int(input("Enter account number: "))
        amount = float(input("Enter amount: "))

        if action == "D" :
            accounts[num].deposit(amount)
        else :
            accounts[num].withdraw(amount)

        print("Balance:", accounts[num].getBalance())
```

```
          elif action == "M" :    # Month end processing.
             for n in range(len(accounts)) :
                accounts[n].monthEnd()
                print(n, accounts[n].getBalance())
          elif action == "Q" :
             done = True
```

EXAMPLE CODE   The complete program is available in your eText or companion code. It includes the test program (how_to_1/accountdemo.py) and the class definitions (how_to_1/accounts.py).

WORKED EXAMPLE 10.1

Implementing an Employee Hierarchy for Payroll Processing

Problem Statement   Your task is to implement payroll processing for different kinds of employees.

- *Hourly employees get paid an hourly rate, but if they work more than 40 hours per week, the excess is paid at "time and a half".*
- *Salaried employees get paid their salary, no matter how many hours they work.*
- *Managers are salaried employees who get paid a salary and a bonus.*

Jose Luis Pelaez Inc./Getty Images, Inc.

Your program should compute the pay for a collection of employees. For each employee, ask for the number of hours worked in a given week, then display the wages earned.

Step 1   List the classes that are part of the hierarchy.

In our case, the problem description lists three classes: HourlyEmployee, SalariedEmployee, and Manager. We need a class that expresses the commonality among them: Employee.

Step 2   Organize the classes into an inheritance hierarchy.

Here is the inheritance diagram for our classes.

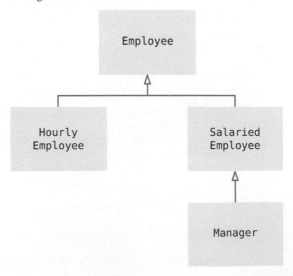

Step 3 Determine the common responsibilities of the classes.

In order to discover the common responsibilities, write pseudocode for processing the objects.

> *For each employee*
> *Print the name of the employee.*
> *Read the number of hours worked.*
> *Compute the wages due for those hours.*

We conclude that the `Employee` superclass has these responsibilities:

> *Get the name.*
> *Compute the wages due for a given number of hours.*

Step 4 Decide which methods are overridden in subclasses.

In our example, there is no variation in getting the employee's name, but the salary is computed differently in each subclass, so `weeklyPay` will be overridden in each subclass.

```
## An employee has a name and a mechanism for computing weekly pay.
#
class Employee :
    . . .

    ## Gets the name of this employee.
    #  @return the name
    #
    def getName(self) :
        . . .

    ## Computes the pay for one week of work.
    #  @param hoursWorked the number of hours worked in the week
    #  @return the pay for the given number of hours
    #
    def weeklyPay(self, hoursWorked) :
        . . .
```

Step 5 Declare the public interface of each class.

We will construct employees by supplying their name and salary information.

```
class HourlyEmployee(Employee) :
    ## Constructs an hourly employee with a given name and hourly wage.
    #  @param name the name of this employee
    #  @param wage the hourly wage
    #
    def __init__(self, name, wage) :
        . . .

class SalariedEmployee(Employee) :
    ## Constructs a salaried employee with a given name and annual salary.
    #  @param name the name of this employee
    #  @param salary the annual salary
    #
    def __init__(self, name, salary) :
        . . .

class Manager(SalariedEmployee) :
    ## Constructs a manager with a given name, annual salary, and weekly bonus.
    #  @param name the name of this employee
    #  @param salary the annual salary
    #  @param bonus the weekly bonus
    #
    def __init__(self, name, salary, bonus) :
        . . .
```

These constructors need to set the name of the Employee object. We will define the constructor of the Employee class to require that the name be specified as an argument:

```
class Employee :
    ## Constructs an employee with a given name.
    #  @param name  the name of the employee
    #
    def __init__(self, name) :
        self._name = name
```

Of course, each subclass needs a method for computing the weekly wages:

```
# This method overrides the superclass method.
def weeklyPay(self, hoursWorked) :
    . . .
```

In this simple example, no further methods are required.

Step 6 Identify instance variables.

All employees have a name. Therefore, the Employee class should have an instance variable _name. (See the revised hierarchy below.)

What about the salaries? Hourly employees have an hourly wage, whereas salaried employees have an annual salary. While it would be possible to store these values in an instance variable of the superclass, it would not be a good idea. The resulting code, which would need to make sense of what that number means, would be complex and error-prone.

Instead, HourlyEmployee objects will store the hourly wage and SalariedEmployee objects will store the annual salary. Manager objects need to store the weekly bonus.

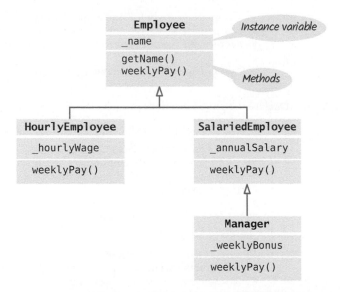

Step 7 Implement constructors and methods.

In a subclass constructor, we need to remember to set the instance variables of the superclass. Because the superclass is responsible for initializing its own instance variables, we pass the employee name to the superclass constructor.

```
class HourlyEmployee(Employee) :
    def __init__(self, name, wage) :
        super().__init__(name)
        self._hourlyWage = wage
    . . .
```

```
class SalariedEmployee(Employee) :
   def __init__(self, name, salary) :
      super().__init__(name)
      self._annualSalary = salary
   . . .
class Manager(SalariedEmployee) :
   def __init__(self, name, salary, bonus) :
      super().__init__(name, salary)
      self._weeklyBonus = bonus
   . . .
```

The weekly pay needs to be computed as specified in the problem description:

```
class HourlyEmployee(Employee) :
   . . .
   def weeklyPay(self, hoursWorked) :
      pay = hoursWorked * self._hourlyWage
      if hoursWorked > 40 :
         # Add overtime.
         pay = pay + ((hoursWorked - 40) * 0.5) * self._hourlyWage
      return pay

class SalariedEmployee(Employee) :
   . . .
   def weeklyPay(self, hoursWorked) :
      WEEKS_PER_YEAR = 52
      return self._annualSalary / WEEKS_PER_YEAR
```

In the case of the Manager, we need to call the version from the SalariedEmployee superclass:

```
class Manager(SalariedEmployee) :
   . . .
   def weeklyPay(self, hoursWorked) :
      return super().weeklyPay(hoursWorked) + self._weeklyBonus
```

Step 8   Construct objects of different subclasses and process them.

In our sample program, we populate a list of employees and compute the weekly salaries:

```
staff = []
staff.append(HourlyEmployee("Morgan, Harry", 30.0))
staff.append(SalariedEmployee("Lin, Sally", 52000.0))
staff.append(Manager("Smith, Mary", 104000.0, 50.0))

for employee in staff :
   hours = int(input("Hours worked by " + employee.getName() + ": "))
   pay = employee.weeklyPay(hours)
   print("Salary: %.2f" % pay)
```

EXAMPLE CODE   The complete program is contained in the files worked_example_1/salarydemo.py and worked_example_1/
employees.py of your companion code.

10.6 Application: A Geometric Shape Class Hierarchy

In Chapter 2 you learned how to draw geometric shapes using the ezgraphics module. You used the methods of the Canvas class to draw the various shapes. To create complex scenes, however, you may need a large number of shapes that vary in color, size, or location. Rather than calling the various methods again and again, it would be useful to have classes that model the various geometric shapes. The user could then design a scene by creating and manipulating the appropriate objects.

In this section, we will design and implement a class hierarchy for geometric shapes. Using shape classes, a programmer can create a shape object with specific characteristics, then use the same object to draw multiple instances of the shape with only minor changes. For example, we could define a red rectangle object with its upper-left corner at position (0, 0). To draw another red rectangle of the same size at position (100, 200), we can change the rectangle object's position and redraw it.

> The GeometricShape class provides methods that are common to all shapes.

The base class of our shape class hierarchy will define and manage the characteristics and operations common to all shapes. Each subclass will define and manage the characteristics and operations specific to an individual shape.

Our class hierarchy design includes all of the shape classes shown in Figure 8. We will discuss the design and implementation of a few and leave the others to be implemented in the exercises.

10.6.1 The Base Class

We start with the design and implementation of the class at the base of the hierarchy. The GeometricShape class should provide the functionality that is common among the various subclasses.

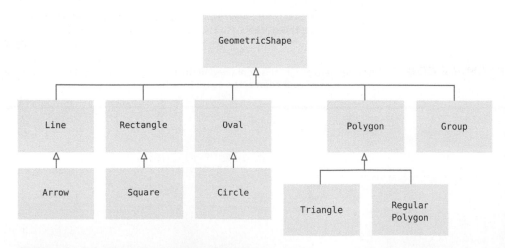

Figure 8 Inheritance Diagram of Geometric Shapes

These include:

- Setting the colors used to draw the shape.
- Getting and setting the coordinates for the upper-left corner of a bounding box.
- Computing the width and height of the shape (or the bounding box used to define the shape).
- Drawing the shape on a canvas.

Each subclass of GeometricShape must override the draw method.

All subclasses will have to override the draw method. The base class cannot possibly know how to draw every shape and must rely on the subclasses to handle this operation. Similarly, the methods for computing the width and height must be provided in the subclasses.

After identifying the common operations and those to be overridden, we need to determine instance variables for the base class. We need instance variables _fill and _outline to store the fill and outline colors used by the shapes. We also supply instance variables _x and _y for the top-left corner of the bounding box.

The constructor of the GeometricShape base class needs to define the common instance variables. We pass the x- and y-coordinates as arguments to the constructor:

```python
class GeometricShape :
    ## Construct a basic geometric shape.
    #  @param x the x-coordinate of the shape
    #  @param y the y-coordinate of the shape
    #
    def __init__(self, x, y) :
        self._x = x
        self._y = y
        self._fill = None
        self._outline = "black"
```

Next, we implement the accessor methods, which return the values stored in the instance variables:

```python
## Gets the leftmost x-position of the shape.
#  @return the x-coordinate
#
def getX(self) :
    return self._x

## Gets the topmost y-position of the shape.
#  @return the y-coordinate
#
def getY(self) :
    return self._y
```

The getWidth and getHeight methods return zero. These methods should be overridden by subclasses.

```python
## Gets the width of the shape.
#  @return the width
#
def getWidth(self) :
    return 0

## Gets the height of the shape.
#  @return the height
#
def getHeight(self) :
    return 0
```

We define three mutator methods for setting the colors. Two methods set the outline or fill color individually, and the third method sets both to the same color:

```
## Sets the fill color.
#  @param color the fill color
#
def setFill(self, color = None) :
   self._fill = color

## Sets the outline color.
#  @param color the outline color
#
def setOutline(self, color = None) :
   self._outline = color

## Sets both the fill and outline colors to the same color.
#  @param color the new color
#
def setColor(self, color) :
   self._fill = color
   self._outline = color
```

Note the use of the default argument in the setFill and setOutline methods. A value of None is used when no color is to be used. We specify it here to allow these methods to be used in the same fashion as the corresponding GraphicsCanvas methods; the call canvas.setFillColor() (with no argument) sets the fill color to None.

The following method moves the shape by a given amount:

```
## Moves the shape to a new position by adjusting its (x, y) coordinates.
#  @param dx the amount to move in x-direction
#  @param dy the amount to move in y-direction
#
def moveBy(self, dx, dy) :
   self._x = self._x + dx
   self._y = self._y + dy
```

Finally, we define the draw method that will be used to draw an individual shape. As indicated earlier, this method has to be overridden for each subclass's specific shape. But there is a common operation that all subclasses have to perform before drawing: setting the drawing colors. Thus, we define the base class's draw method to set the colors. You will see how it is called by the draw method in each subclass in the next section.

```
## Draws the shape on a canvas.
#  @param canvas the graphical canvas on which to draw the shape
#
def draw(self, canvas) :
   canvas.setFill(self._fill)
   canvas.setOutline(self._outline)
```

10.6.2 Basic Shapes

The class hierarchy contains a number of subclasses for drawing shapes. In this section we limit our focus to only three: the Rectangle, Square, and Line.

A rectangle is a geometric shape that is specified by its upper-left corner, width, and height. The Rectangle class inherits from GeometricShape. The constructor passes the upper-left corner to the superclass and stores the width and height.

```
class Rectangle(GeometricShape) :
   ## Constructs a width × height rectangle with the upper-left corner at (x, y).
   #  @param x  the x-coordinate of the upper-left corner
   #  @param y  the y-coordinate of the upper-left corner
   #  @param width  the horizontal size
   #  @param height  the vertical size
   #
   def __init__(self, x, y, width, height) :
      super().__init__(x, y)
      self._width = width
      self._height = height
```

The draw method is overridden in the Rectangle subclass to include the call to the appropriate canvas method:

```
# Overrides the superclass method to draw the rectangle.
def draw(self, canvas) :
   super().draw(canvas)
   canvas.drawRect(self.getX(), self.getY(), self._width, self._height)
```

Note that the draw method of the GeometricShape superclass is called to set the colors used to draw the rectangle.

We also need to supply methods that yield the width and the height, to override the superclass methods that return zero:

```
def getWidth(self) :
   return self._width

def getHeight(self) :
   return self._height
```

The Square subclass is an example of a **wrapper class**. A wrapper class wraps or encapsulates the functionality of another class to provide a more convenient interface. For example, we could draw a square using the Rectangle subclass. But it requires that we supply both the width and height. Because a square is a special case of a rectangle, we can define a Square subclass that extends, or *wraps*, the Rectangle class and only requires one value, the length of a side.

```
class Square(Rectangle) :
   ## Constructs a square of the given size positioned at (x, y).
   #  @param x  the x-coordinate of the upper-left corner
   #  @param y  the y-coordinate of the upper-left corner
   #  @param size  the length of a side
   #
   def __init__(self, x, y, size) :
      super().__init__(x, y, size, size)
```

Now we move on to implementing the Line class. A line is specified by its start and end points. As you can see from Figure 9, it is possible that neither of these points is the upper-left corner of the bounding box.

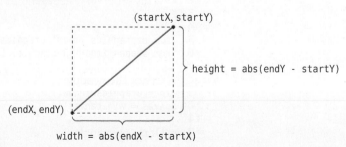

Figure 9
The Bounding Box of a Line

Instead, we need to compute the smaller of the *x*- and *y*-coordinates and pass those values to the superclass constructor. We also need to store the start and end points in instance variables because we need them to draw the line.

```python
class Line(GeometricShape) :
    ## Constructs a line segment.
    #  @param x1 the x-coordinate of the starting point
    #  @param y1 the y-coordinate of the starting point
    #  @param x2 the x-coordinate of the ending point
    #  @param y2 the y-coordinate of the ending point
    #
    def __init__(self, x1, y1, x2, y2) :
        super().__init__(min(x1, x2), min(y1, y2))
        self._startX = x1
        self._startY = y1
        self._endX = x2
        self._endY = y2
```

As always, the draw method has to be overridden:

```python
def draw(self, canvas) :
    super().draw(canvas)
    canvas.drawLine(self._startX, self._startY, self._endX, self._endY)
```

The width and height are the differences between the starting and ending *x*- and *y*-coordinates. However, if the line isn't sloping downward, we need to take the absolute values of the difference (see Figure 9).

```python
def getWidth(self) :
    return abs(self._endX - self._startX)

def getHeight(self) :
    return abs(self._endY - self._startY)
```

Finally, we need to override the moveBy method so that it adjusts the starting and ending points, in addition to the top-left corner.

```python
def moveBy(self, dx, dy) :
    super().moveBy(dx, dy)
    self._startX = self._startX + dx
    self._startY = self._startY + dy
    self._endX = self._endX + dx
    self._endY = self._endY + dy
```

EXAMPLE CODE The program below illustrates the use of the geometric shape classes. See the sec06/shapes.py module in your companion code for the implementation of the geometric shape classes.

sec06_02/testshapes.py

```python
1  ##
2  #   This program tests several of the geometric shape classes.
3  #
4
5  from ezgraphics import GraphicsWindow
6  from shapes import Rectangle, Line
7
8  # Create the window.
9  win = GraphicsWindow()
10 canvas = win.canvas()
11
12 # Draw a rectangle.
```

```
13  rect = Rectangle(10, 10, 90, 60)
14  rect.setFill("light yellow")
15  rect.draw(canvas)
16
17  # Draw another rectangle.
18  rect.moveBy(rect.getWidth(), rect.getHeight())
19  rect.draw(canvas)
20
21  # Draw six lines of different colors.
22  colors = ["red", "green", "blue", "yellow", "magenta", "cyan"]
23
24  line = Line(10, 150, 300, 150)
25
26  for i in range(6) :
27      line.setColor(colors[i])
28      line.draw(canvas)
29      line.moveBy(10, 10)
30
31  win.wait()
```

10.6.3 Groups of Shapes

A Group contains shapes that are drawn and moved together.

The Group subclass in the hierarchy diagram shown in Figure 8 does not actually draw a geometric shape. Instead it is a container of shapes. The Group class can be used to group basic geometric shapes to create a complex shape. For example, suppose you construct a door using a rectangle, a circle for the doorknob, and a circle for the peep hole. The three components can be stored in a Group in which the individual shapes are defined relative to the position of the group. This allows the entire group to be moved to a different position without having to move each individual shape. Once created, the entire group can be drawn with a single call to its draw method. In addition, a Group can store other groups, so you can create even more complex scenes.

As new shapes are added to a Group object, the width and height of the bounding box expands to enclose the new shapes. Figure 10 illustrates the bounding box of a group composed of three shapes.

To create a Group, you provide the coordinates of the upper-left corner of its bounding box. The class defines an instance variable that stores the shapes in a list.

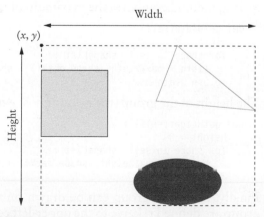

Figure 10 A Group's Bounding Box

```
class Group(GeometricShape) :
    ## Constructs the group with its bounding box positioned at (x, y).
    #  @param x the x-coordinate of the upper-left corner of the bounding box
    #  @param y the y-coordinate of the upper-left corner of the bounding box
    #
    def __init__(self, x = 0, y = 0) :
        super().__init__(x, y)
        self._shapeList = []
```

Adding a shape to the group involves several steps. First, the shape has to be appended to the list:

```
## Adds a shape to the group.
#  @param shape the shape to be added
#
def add(self, shape) :
    self._shapeList.append(shape)
```

The individual shapes are positioned relative to the upper-left corner of the group's bounding box. We must ensure that each shape is positioned below and to the right of this point. If it is not, it must be moved.

```
# Keep the shape within top and left edges of the bounding box.
if shape.getX() < 0 :
    shape.moveBy(-shape.getX(), 0)
if shape.getY() < 0 :
    shape.moveBy(0, -shape.getY())
```

The complete implementation of the add method with the three steps combined is shown below:

```
## Adds a shape to the group.
#  @param shape the shape to be added
#
def add(self, shape) :
    self._shapeList.append(shape)

    # Keep the shape within top and left edges of the bounding box.
    if shape.getX() < 0 :
        shape.moveBy(-shape.getX(), 0)
    if shape.getY() < 0 :
        shape.moveBy(0, -shape.getY())
```

The width of the group is determined by the rightmost extent of any of the group's members. The rightmost extent of a shape is shape.getX() + shape.getWidth(). The following method computes the maximum of these extents.

```
def getWidth(self) :
    width = 0
    for shape in self._shapeList :
        width = max(width, shape.getX() + shape.getWidth())
    return width
```

The height of the group (the bottommost extent) is computed in the same way.

```
def getHeight(self) :
    height = 0
    for shape in self._shapeList :
        height = max(height, shape.getY() + shape.getHeight())
    return height
```

Finally, the entire group can be drawn on the canvas. The shapes contained in the group are defined relative to the upper-left corner of its bounding box. Before a shape can be drawn, it has to be moved to its position relative to the upper-left corner of the group's bounding box. For example, if a rectangle is positioned at (10, 5) and the group is positioned at (100, 25), then the rectangle has to be drawn with its upper-left corner at position (110, 30). After the shape is drawn, it has to be returned to its relative position.

```
## Draws all of the shapes on the canvas.
#   @param canvas the graphical canvas on which to draw the shapes
#
def draw(self, canvas) :
    for shape in self._shapeList :
        shape.moveBy(self.getX(), self.getY())
        shape.draw(canvas)
        shape.moveBy(-self.getX(), -self.getY())
```

To illustrate the use of the Group subclass, we have redesigned the italianflag.py program that was developed in How To 2.2.

sec06/italianflag.py

```
 1  ##
 2  #   This program draws two Italian flags using the geometric shape classes.
 3  #
 4
 5  from ezgraphics import GraphicsWindow
 6  from shapes import Rectangle, Line, Group
 7
 8  # Define constants for the flag size.
 9  FLAG_WIDTH = 150
10  FLAG_HEIGHT = FLAG_WIDTH * 2 // 3
11  PART_WIDTH = FLAG_WIDTH // 3
12
13  # Create the graphics window.
14  win = GraphicsWindow(300, 300)
15  canvas = win.canvas()
16
17  # Build the flag as a group shape.
18  flag = Group()
19
20  part = Rectangle(0, 0, PART_WIDTH, FLAG_HEIGHT)
21  part.setColor("green")
22  flag.add(part)
23
24  part = Rectangle(PART_WIDTH * 2, 0, PART_WIDTH, FLAG_HEIGHT)
25  part.setColor("red")
26  flag.add(part)
27
28  flag.add(Line(PART_WIDTH, 0, PART_WIDTH * 2, 0))
29  flag.add(Line(PART_WIDTH, FLAG_HEIGHT, PART_WIDTH * 2, FLAG_HEIGHT))
30
31  # Draw the first flag in the upper-left area of the canvas.
32  flag.moveBy(10, 10)
33  flag.draw(canvas)
34
35  # Draw the second flag in the bottom-right area of the canvas.
36  flag.moveBy(130, 180)
37  flag.draw(canvas)
38
39  win.wait()
```

TOOLBOX 10.1

Game Programming

Computer programs tend to fall into common categories, such as shopping applications or computer games. Often, someone with expertise in that category has developed a code library that provides the mechanisms that become common to all programs in the particular category. Such libraries can use inheritance to model the shared behavior.

In this Toolbox, you will see how you can use the pygame package to design video games. You will specify what is special about your video game, and you inherit behavior that is common to all games. (If you have not already installed the libraries as explained in Toolbox 2.1, you will need to install the pygame package before you begin.)

The Event Loop

The pygame package is designed for games that manipulate shapes on a two-dimensional grid. It is well suited for implementing classic arcade games.

When you program a game, you need to update the game state whenever the user clicks the mouse or hits a key. You also need to update the positions of the various shapes so that they move across the screen. Finally, when something interesting happens—such as two shapes colliding—you need to update the game state, for example to play a sound, show a visual effect, or add or remove one or more shapes.

Key presses and mouse clicks are called *events*. Another event is "quitting the game", which occurs when the user closes the window in which the game is displayed. In the pygame package, you use a loop in which you listen to events and react to them:

```
while game in progress :
for event in pygame.event.get() :
   if event.type == pygame.QUIT :
      Save the game and quit
   elif event.type == pygame.MOUSEBUTTONDOWN :
      Process a mouse press at event.pos
   elif event.type == pygame.KEYDOWN :
      Process a key press with code event.key
```

The call pygame.event.get() waits until the next event occurs. Then it returns an object that describes the event. You check the instance variable event.type to find the event type as well as additional details about the event.

In Chapter 9, we recommended that you should not access the instance variables of an object directly. However, in the pygame package, few classes use accessor methods. You read the instance variables directly, and you need to know when it is safe to update them.

A mouse event has an instance variable pos that is set to a tuple (x, y) that contains the x- and y-positions of the mouse. A key event has an instance variable key that holds an integer key code describing the key. There are constants such as pygame.K_LEFT and pygame.K_a for each key on the keyboard.

When an event occurs, you will want to update certain parts of your game, and then draw the changes.

The game is drawn on a display object that you obtain as

```
display = pygame.display.set_mode((width, height))
```

Note that you pass a tuple with the width and height in pixels. You will soon see how to draw images on the display.

The pygame library provides several strategies for efficient redrawing of game changes. This is key to producing high-performing games, particularly on less powerful computers. In this example, we will use a simple strategy that is not fast but easy to program.

We first erase the display and redraw everything. The drawing actually happens on an off-screen display, so that the screen does not show an annoying flicker. When we are done with all drawing operations, we tell pygame to update the screen display with the pixels:

```
display.fill(WHITE)
Draw everything
pygame.display.update()
```

A modern computer can update and display the game state very quickly. You need to slow down the event loop so that users have time to observe the display before it changes again. For the human eye to perceive smooth movements, it is sufficient to update the display thirty times per second. This is done with a clock object.

```
clock = pygame.time.Clock()
framesPerSecond = 30
while game in progress :
    Process events
    Update game state
    Draw game state
    clock.tick(framesPerSecond)
```

The tick method waits, in this case for 1/30th of a second from the preceding call to tick. This ensures that the loop carries out 30 iterations per second.

Sprites and Groups

A *sprite* is an image that can be displayed efficiently, sometimes with special support from the graphics hardware. In pygame, the image can come from an image file, or it can be drawn from geometric shapes. In this toolbox, we only look at sprites that are produced from image files.

Some pygame implementations only work with images in an archaic version of the BMP format that does not support transparent pixels. As a workaround, color any pixels that you don't want to have included in an image with a particular color, such as magenta. Then load the image with the following instructions:

```
img = pygame.image.load(filename).convert()
MAGENTA = (255, 0, 255)
img.set_colorkey(MAGENTA)
self.image = img
self.rect = self.image.get_rect()
self.rect.x = x
self.rect.y = y - self.rect.height
```

The pygame package replaces all pixels with the given color key (magenta in our example) with transparent pixels when loading the image.

Next, construct a Sprite object with the image and place the image at the desired position by setting the x- and y-coordinates of the sprite's bounding rectangle.

```
sprite = pygame.sprite.Sprite()
sprite.image = img
sprite.rect = self.image.get_rect()
sprite.rect.x = x
sprite.rect.y = y - self.rect.height    # y is the bottom of the image
```

Note again the liberal use of public instance variables.

A sprite can be placed into one or more *groups*. This is useful for detecting collisions. Suppose you have a ball and want to find out which game elements it is hitting. Place all candidates in a group and use the spritecollideany function:

```
if pygame.sprite.spritecollideany(ball, group) : . . .
```

The function returns the sprite with which the ball collides, or None if there isn't one.

Groups are also useful for drawing and updating a batch of sprites. The call

```
group.draw(display)
```

draws all sprites on the display, placing their images inside their bounding rectangles. If you use the LayeredUpdates subclass of the Group class, then you can control in which *layer* each sprite is drawn. Sprites in a higher layer are drawn above those in a lower layer. You control the layer by setting the _layer instance variable. (Somewhat inconsistently, this instance variable has an underscore even though it is intended for public access.)

The call

```
group.update()
```

calls the update method on each sprite. By default, that method does nothing. That is where inheritance comes in. When you program a game, you provide subclasses of the Sprite class, and you implement the update method to recompute the sprite's state.

For example, we will implement a game in which cars move in a lane of traffic. Here is the update method that moves the car by one pixel to the right or left:

```
class Car(pygame.sprite.Sprite) :
    . . .
    def update(self) :
        if self._lane == 0 :
            self.rect.x = self.rect.x + 1
        else :
            self.rect.x = self.rect.x - 1
```

A Game Framework

The pygame package is suitable for a wide variety of games. For example, there is no requirement that you program an event loop as described earlier. However, for simple games, it is a good idea to follow established practice. We provide a base class from which your games can inherit. Its run method implements the event loop and calls methods mouseButtonDown, keyDown, update, and quit that you can override to achieve the behavior that is specific to your game.

The GameBase class manages a group of sprites. Unlike the pygame implementors, we provide methods for accessing the internal state of the GameBase class. Call the add method to add your sprites. They will then be updated and drawn.

We also provide a tick method that yields the number of elapsed timer ticks. You can use this method if you want to carry out actions at a particular point in time; for example, to periodically add a new sprite.

Here is the code for the GameBase class.

```
class GameBase:
    def __init__(self, width, height) :
        pygame.init()
        self._width = width
        self._height = height

        self._display = pygame.display.set_mode((self._width, self._height))
        self._clock = pygame.time.Clock()
        self._framesPerSecond = 30
        self._sprites = pygame.sprite.LayeredUpdates()
        self._ticks = 0
        pygame.key.set_repeat(1, 120)

    def mouseButtonDown(self, x, y) :
        return

    def keyDown(self, key) :
        return
```

```
    def update(self) :
      self._sprites.update()

    def draw(self) :
      self._sprites.draw(self._display)

    def add(self, sprite) :
      self._sprites.add(sprite)

    def getTicks(self) :
      return self._ticks

    def quit(self) :
      pygame.quit()

    def run(self) :
      while True :
        for event in pygame.event.get() :
          if event.type == pygame.QUIT :
            self.quit()
          elif event.type == pygame.MOUSEBUTTONDOWN :
            self.mouseButtonDown(event.pos[0], event.pos[1])
          elif event.type == pygame.KEYDOWN :
            self.keyDown(event.key)

        self.update()
        WHITE = (255, 255, 255)
        self._display.fill(WHITE)
        self.draw()
        pygame.display.update()
        self._clock.tick(self._framesPerSecond)
        self._ticks = self._ticks + 1
```

We also provide an `ImageSprite` class that handles the tedium of loading an image. You specify an image in the constructor, and you can call its `loadImage` method again to change the image (for example, to reflect a different state of a game character). The `moveBy` method moves the sprite by a given amount.

```
class ImageSprite(
      pygame.sprite.Sprite) :
  def __init__(self, x, y, filename) :
    super().__init__()
    self.loadImage(x, y, filename)

  def loadImage(self, x, y, filename) :
    img = pygame.image.load(filename).convert()
    MAGENTA = (255, 0, 255)
    img.set_colorkey(MAGENTA)
    self.image = img
    self.rect = self.image.get_rect()
    self.rect.x = x
    self.rect.y = y - self.rect.height

  def moveBy(self, dx, dy) :
    self.rect.x = self.rect.x + dx
    self.rect.y = self.rect.y + dy
```

A Sample Game

In the 1980s, Frogger was a popular arcade game. The player controls a frog that must cross a busy highway and then swim on the back of logs, turtles, and alligators to reach a lily pad. We'll implement a part of this game—the freeway crossing. To avoid any copyright issues, and in the Pythonic spirit, a snake will make the crossing to reach its reward on the other side—a tasty frog.

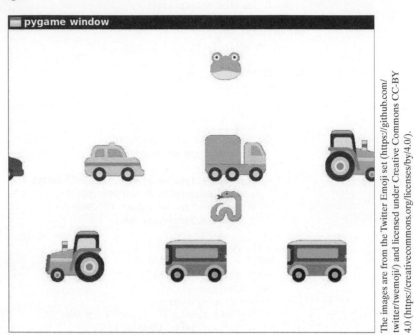

The Snake class is a subclass of our `ImageSprite` convenience class. Provided the snake is alive, it can be moved up, left, down, or right with the keyboard—either the arrow keys or the WASD keys that some game players prefer. When a snake dies, we flip its image horizontally and vertically.

```
class Snake(ImageSprite) :
    def __init__(self, x, y) :
        super().__init__(x, y, "snake.bmp")
        self._alive = True
        self._layer = 2

    def keyDown(self, key) :
        if self._alive :
            distance = 20
            if key == pygame.K_w or key == pygame.K_UP :
                self.moveBy(0, -distance)
            elif key == pygame.K_a  or key == pygame.K_LEFT :
                self.moveBy(-distance, 0)
            elif key == pygame.K_s  or key == pygame.K_DOWN :
                self.moveBy(0, distance)
            elif key == pygame.K_d  or key == pygame.K_RIGHT :
                self.moveBy(distance, 0)

    def die(self) :
        if self._alive :
            self.image = pygame.transform.flip(self.image, True, True)
            self._alive = False
```

The other sprite class is the Car class whose update method you saw earlier. Here we change the superclass to ImageSprite. The car image is randomly chosen from one of ten images of left-facing vehicles. The image is flipped horizontally if the car travels to the right.

```python
class Car(ImageSprite) :
    def __init__(self, x, lane) :
        self._lane = lane
        y = 300 + 200 * lane
        super().__init__(x, y, "car" + str(randint(0, 9)) + ".bmp")

        if lane == 0 :
            self.image = pygame.transform.flip(self.image, True, False)
        self._layer = 1
    . . .
```

The SnakeGame class for our game inherits from the GameBase class. It has instance variables for the snake, frog, and cars (in a sprite group that we will use for collision testing). An addCar helper method adds a new car to a given lane. The car is added to the _cars sprite group and the _sprites group of the superclass by calling its add method.

```python
class SnakeGame(GameBase) :
    def __init__(self) :
        super().__init__(800, 600)
        self._snake = Snake(400, 600)
        self._frog = ImageSprite(400, 100, "frog.bmp")
        self._cars = pygame.sprite.Group()

    def addCar(self, lane) :
        if lane == 0 :
            x = -100
        else:
            x = self._width
        newCar = Car(x, lane)
        self._cars.add(newCar)
        self.add(newCar)
```

When the user hits a key, the event loop of the GameBase superclass calls the keyDown method. We override that method to send the key code to the _snake object.

```python
class SnakeGame(GameBase) :
    . . .
    def keyDown(self, key) :
        self._snake.keyDown(key)
    . . .
```

The update method of the SnakeGame class contains most of the game logic. Every 240 ticks, a new car is added to each lane. Once there are enough cars, the snake and frog appear.

If the snake collides with the cars, it dies. If it collides with the frog, the frog is killed. (The kill method from the Sprite class removes the sprites from all groups.)

```python
class SnakeGame(GameBase) :
    . . .
    def update(self) :
        super().update()

        if self.getTicks() % 240 == 0 : # Add a new car to each lane
            self.addCar(0)
            self.addCar(1)

        if self.getTicks() == 480 :
            self.add(self._snake)
            self.add(self._frog)
```

```
        if pygame.sprite.spritecollideany(self._snake, self._cars) :
            self._snake.die()

        if (pygame.sprite.collide_rect(self._snake, self._frog)) :
            self._frog.kill()
```

Note that the update method invokes the method of the superclass. Otherwise, the cars would not move.

Now you have seen how to implement a very simple game and control the behavior of the game characters. Of course, to be competitive with actual computer games, you would want to make the game more interesting. Exercises • Toolbox P10.28 through •• Toolbox P10.32 provide some suggestions.

EXAMPLE CODE   See toolbox_1 in your companion code for the sample game program.

CHAPTER SUMMARY

Explain the notions of inheritance, superclass, and subclass.

- A subclass inherits data and behavior from a superclass.
- You can always use a subclass object in place of a superclass object.

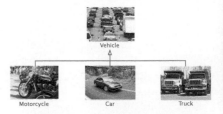

Implement subclasses in Python.

- A subclass inherits all methods that it does not override.
- A subclass can override a superclass method by providing a new implementation.
- A class name inside parentheses in the class header indicates that a class inherits from a superclass.

Understand how and when to call a superclass constructor.

- The superclass is responsible for defining its own instance variables.
- The subclass constructor must explicitly call the superclass constructor.
- Use the super function to call the superclass constructor.

Implement methods that override methods from a superclass.

- An overriding method can extend or replace the functionality of the superclass method.
- Use the super function to call a superclass method.

Use polymorphism for processing objects of related types.

- A subclass reference can be used when a superclass reference is expected.
- Polymorphism ("having multiple shapes") allows us to manipulate objects that share a set of tasks, even though the tasks are executed in different ways.
- An abstract method is a method whose implementation is not specified.

Use inheritance for designing a hierarchy of shapes.

- The GeometricShape class provides methods that are common to all shapes.
- Each subclass of GeometricShape must override the draw method.
- A shape class constructor must call super to initialize the coordinates of its upper-left corner.
- Each shape subclass must override the methods for computing the width and height.
- A Group contains shapes that are drawn and moved together.

REVIEW EXERCISES

- **R10.1** Identify the superclass and subclass in each of the following pairs of classes.

  a. Employee, Manager

  b. GraduateStudent, Student

  c. Person, Student

  d. Employee, Professor

  e. BankAccount, CheckingAccount

  f. Vehicle, Car

  g. Vehicle, Minivan

  h. Car, Minivan

  i. Truck, Vehicle

- **R10.2** Consider a program for managing inventory in a small appliance store. Why isn't it useful to have a superclass SmallAppliance and subclasses Toaster, CarVacuum, TravelIron, and so on?

- **R10.3** Which methods does the ChoiceQuestion class inherit from its superclass? Which methods does it override? Which methods does it add?

- **R10.4** Which methods does the SavingsAccount class in How To 10.1 inherit from its superclass? Which methods does it override? Which methods does it add?

- **R10.5** List the instance variables of a CheckingAccount object from How To 10.1.

- **R10.6** Draw an inheritance diagram that shows the inheritance relationships between these classes.

  - Person
  - Employee
  - Student
  - Instructor
  - Classroom
  - object

- **R10.7** In an object-oriented traffic simulation system, we have the classes listed below. Draw an inheritance diagram that shows the relationships between these classes.

  - Vehicle
  - Car
  - Truck
  - Sedan
  - Coupe
  - PickupTruck
  - SportUtilityVehicle
  - Minivan
  - Bicycle
  - Motorcycle

- **R10.8** What inheritance relationships would you establish among the following classes?

  - Student
  - Professor
  - TeachingAssistant
  - Employee
  - Secretary
  - DepartmentChair
  - Janitor
  - SeminarSpeaker
  - Person
  - Course
  - Seminar
  - Lecture
  - ComputerLab

- **R10.9** The Rectangle class in the class hierarchy in Figure 8 is defined as a subclass of the GeometricShape superclass. But a rectangle is simply a special version of a polygon. Define and implement the Rectangle class as a subclass of the Polygon class instead of the GeometricShape superclass. Assume that the Polygon class is implemented as in Exercise •• Graphics P10.11.

- **Graphics R10.10** Explain the role of polymorphism in the draw method of the Group class (in Section 10.6.3).

- **Graphics R10.11** Can you add a Group object to another Group object? Why or why not?

- **Graphics R10.12** What would happen if you added a Group object to itself?

- **Graphics R10.13** Add two accessor methods, getStartPoint and getEndPoint, to the Line class (in Section 10.6.2) that returns a tuple containing the x- and y-coordinates of the starting or ending point of the line, as appropriate.

- **Graphics R10.14** The GeometricShape class (in Section 10.6.1) defines the _fill and _outline instance variables for specifying the color used to draw a shape. But no methods were defined for accessing these values. Define the accessor methods getFill and getOutline in the GeometricShape hierarchy as appropriate. *Hint:* If a shape class does not use one or both of the colors, no fill or outline value should be returned for instances of that class.

PROGRAMMING EXERCISES

- **P10.1** Add a class NumericQuestion to the question hierarchy of Section 10.1. If the response and the expected answer differ by no more than 0.01, then accept the response as correct.

- **P10.2** Add a class FillInQuestion to the question hierarchy of Section 10.1. Such a question is constructed with a string that contains the answer, surrounded by _ _, for example, "The inventor of Python was _Guido van Rossum_". The question should be displayed as

    The inventor of Python was _____

- **P10.3** Modify the checkAnswer method of the Question class so that it does not take into account different spaces or upper/lowercase characters. For example, the response "GUIDO van Rossum" should match an answer of "Guido van Rossum".

- **P10.4** Add a class AnyCorrectChoiceQuestion to the question hierarchy of Section 10.1 that allows multiple correct choices. The respondent should provide any one of the correct choices. The answer string should contain all of the correct choices, separated by spaces. Provide instructions in the question text.

- **P10.5** Add a class MultiChoiceQuestion to the question hierarchy of Section 10.1 that allows multiple correct choices. The respondent should provide all correct choices, separated by spaces. Provide instructions in the question text.

- **P10.6** Add a method addText to the Question superclass and provide a different implementation of ChoiceQuestion that calls addText rather than storing a list of choices.

- **P10.7** Provide __repr__ methods for the Question and ChoiceQuestion classes.

- **P10.8** Implement a superclass Person. Make two classes, Student and Instructor, that inherit from Person. A person has a name and a year of birth. A student has a major, and an instructor has a salary. Write the class declarations, the constructors, and the `__repr__` method for all classes. Supply a test program that tests these classes and methods.

■ ■ **P10.9** Make a class `Employee` with a name and salary. Make a class `Manager` inherit from `Employee`. Add an instance variable, named `_department`, that stores a string. Supply a method `__repr__` that prints the manager's name, department, and salary. Make a class `Executive` inherit from `Manager`. Supply appropriate `__repr__` methods for all classes. Supply a test program that tests these classes and methods.

■ ■ **Graphics P10.10** A labeled point has x- and y-coordinates and a string label. Provide a subclass `LabeledPoint` of `GeometricShape` with a constructor `LabeledPoint(x, y, label)` and a draw method that draws a small circle and the label text.

■ ■ **Graphics P10.11** Implement the `Polygon` subclass of the `GeometricShape` class. Provide a constructor `__init__(self, vertexList)`, where the vertex list contains a list of points (each of which is a list with an x- and y-coordinate), as in Worked Example 6.4.

■ ■ **Graphics P10.12** Implement the `Polygon` subclass of the `GeometricShape` class with a constructor `__init__(self)` and a method `addVertex(self, x, y)`.

■ ■ **Graphics P10.13** Implement a subclass `RegularPolygon` of the `Polygon` class in Exercise ● ● Graphics P10.11.

■ **Graphics P10.14** Implement a subclass `Diamond` of the `RegularPolygon` class in Exercise ● ● Graphics P10.13.

■ **Graphics P10.15** Implement a subclass `Triangle` of the `Polygon` class in Exercise ● ● Graphics P10.11.

■ ■ **Graphics P10.16** A `Group` object is constructed with the top-left corner of its bounding box. However, the true bounding box may be smaller if no shapes are added that touch the left or top edge. Reimplement the `Group` class so that the constructor takes an anchor point (which need not be the top-left corner of the bounding box). All added shapes are relative to this anchor point. Reimplement the `add` method to update the top-left corner of the bounding box. Note that you no longer need to move a shape in the `add` method.

■ ■ **Graphics P10.17** Reimplement the classes in the shape hierarchy in Section 10.6 so that the top-left corner is not stored in the base class but computed in each subclass.

■ ■ **Graphics P10.18** Implement a subclass `Arrow` of the class `Line` in Section 10.6.2. The draw method should draw the line and two short lines (the arrow tips) at the end point.

■ ■ ■ **Graphics P10.19** Implement a subclass `DashedLine` of the class `Line` (Section 10.6.2). In the constructor, provide arguments for the length of a dash and the length of the gap between dashes.

■ ■ ■ **Graphics P10.20** Add a method `scale(factor)` to the `GeometricShape` class and implement it for each subclass. The method should scale the shape by the given factor. For example, a call `shape.scale(0.5)` makes the bounding box half as large, and moves the top-left corner halfway to the upper-left corner of the canvas.

■ ■ **Business P10.21** Change the `CheckingAccount` class in How To 10.1 so that a $1 fee is levied for deposits or withdrawals in excess of three free monthly transactions. Place the code for computing the fee into a separate method that you call from the deposit and withdraw methods.

■■ **Business P10.22** Implement a superclass Appointment and subclasses Onetime, Daily, and Monthly. An appointment has a description (for example, "see the dentist") and a date. Write a method occursOn(year, month, day) that checks whether the appointment occurs on that date. For example, for a monthly appointment, you must check whether the day of the month matches. Then fill a list of Appointment objects with a mixture of appointments. Have the user enter a date and print out all appointments that occur on that date.

© Pali Rao/iStockphoto.

■■ **Business P10.23** Improve the appointment book program of Exercise •• Business P10.22. Give the user the option to add new appointments. The user must specify the type of the appointment, the description, and the date.

■■■ **Business P10.24** Improve the appointment book program of Exercise •• Business P10.22 and •• Business P10.23 by letting the user save the appointment data to a file and reload the data from a file. The saving part is straightforward: Make a method save. Save the type, description, and date to a file. The loading part is not so easy. First determine the type of the appointment to be loaded, create an object of that type, and then call a load method to load the data.

■■■ **Science P10.25** In this problem, you will model a circuit consisting of an arbitrary configuration of resistors. Provide a superclass Circuit with a method getResistance. Provide a subclass Resistor, representing a single resistor, and subclasses Serial and Parallel, each of which contains a list of Circuit objects. A Serial circuit models a series of circuits, each of which can be a single resistor or another circuit. Similarly, a Parallel circuit models a set of circuits in parallel. For example, the following circuit is a Parallel circuit containing a single resistor and one Serial circuit:

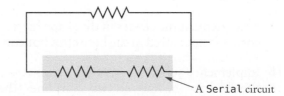
A Serial circuit

Use Ohm's law to compute the combined resistance.

■■ **Science P10.26** Part (a) of the figure below shows a symbolic representation of an electric circuit called an *amplifier*. The input to the amplifier is the voltage v_i and the output is the voltage v_o. The output of an amplifier is proportional to the input. The constant of proportionality is called the "gain" of the amplifier.

Parts (b), (c), and (d) show schematics of three specific types of amplifier: the *inverting amplifier*, *noninverting amplifier*, and *voltage divider amplifier*. Each of these three amplifiers consists of two resistors and an op amp. The value of the gain of each amplifier depends on the values of its resistances. In particular, the gain, g, of the inverting amplifier is given by $g = -\dfrac{R_2}{R_1}$. Similarly, the gains of the noninverting amplifier and voltage divider amplifier are given by $g = 1 + \dfrac{R_2}{R_1}$ and $g = \dfrac{R_2}{R_1 + R_2}$, respectively.

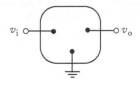

(a) Amplifier

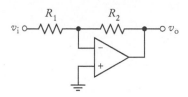

(b) Inverting amplifier

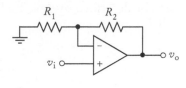

(c) Noninverting amplifier

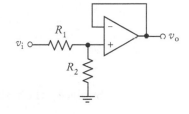

(d) Voltage divider amplifier

Write a Python program that represents the amplifier as a superclass and represents the inverting, noninverting, and voltage divider amplifiers as subclasses. Give the superclass two methods, getGain and a getDescription method that returns a string identifying the amplifier. Each subclass should have a constructor with two arguments, the resistances of the amplifier.

The subclasses need to override the getGain and getDescription methods of the superclass.

Supply a class that demonstrates that the subclasses all work properly for sample values of the resistances.

■■ **Science P10.27** Resonant circuits are used to select a signal (e.g., a radio station or TV channel) from among other competing signals. Resonant circuits are characterized by the frequency response shown in the figure below. The resonant frequency response is completely described by three parameters: the resonant frequency, ω_0, the bandwidth, B, and the gain at the resonant frequency, k.

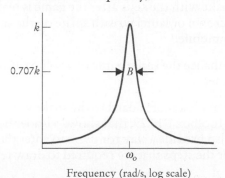

Frequency (rad/s, log scale)

Two simple resonant circuits are shown in the figure below. The circuit in (a) is called a *parallel resonant circuit*. The circuit in (b) is called a *series resonant circuit*. Both resonant circuits consist of a resistor having resistance R, a capacitor having capacitance C, and an inductor having inductance L.

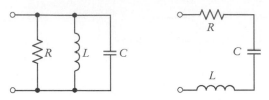

(a) Parallel resonant circuit   (b) Series resonant circuit

These circuits are designed by determining values of R, C, and L that cause the resonant frequency response to be described by specified values of ω_o, B, and k. The design equations for the parallel resonant circuit are:

$$R = k, \quad C = \frac{1}{BR}, \text{ and } \quad L = \frac{1}{\omega_o^2 C}$$

Similarly, the design equations for the series resonant circuit are:

$$R = \frac{1}{k}, \quad L = \frac{R}{B}, \text{ and } \quad C = \frac{1}{\omega_o^2 L}$$

Write a Python program that represents ResonantCircuit as a superclass and represents the SeriesResonantCircuit and ParallelResonantCircuit as subclasses. Give the superclass three instance variables representing the parameters ω_o, B, and k of the resonant frequency response. The superclass should provide public methods to get and set each of these variables. The superclass should also provide a display method that prints a description of the resonant frequency response.

Each subclass should provide a method that designs the corresponding resonant circuit. The subclasses should also override the display method of the superclass to print descriptions of both the frequency response (the values of ω_o, B, and k) and the circuit (the values of R, C, and L).

All classes should provide appropriate constructors.

Supply a program that demonstrates that the subclasses all work properly.

▪ Toolbox P10.28 One drawback of the snake game of Toolbox 10.1 is that you can still move the snake with the keys after the game is over. Add a win method to the snake that places a crown or laurel wreath sprite on the snake after it has won, and that makes it immobile.

▪ Toolbox P10.29 Enhance the snake game of Toolbox 10.1 so that you can play the game multiple times.

▪▪ Toolbox P10.30 Provide a score board to the snake game of Toolbox 10.1, as enhanced in Exercise • Toolbox P10.29, that shows a leader board with the best scores (ticks to victory). Also provide a way for users to enter their initials. Search the pygame documentation for the steps that are required to draw text.

■■■ **Toolbox P10.31**   A leader board, as described in Exercise ●● Toolbox P10.30, would be useful for any kind of game. Add this functionality to the GameBase class. When the game program is quit, save the top ten scores and initials to a file, and restore them when the game is restarted.

■■ **Toolbox P10.32**   In a game that is commonly called "snake", the player uses the arrow keys to turn a snake that is composed of multiple segments and directs it towards a food item (usually an apple). When the snake eats the food, it adds a segment. When it runs against a wall, it dies. Implement this game with the game framework of Toolbox 10.1.

CHAPTER 11

RECURSION

© Nicolae Popovici/iStockphoto.

CHAPTER GOALS

To learn to "think recursively"

To be able to use recursive
   helper functions

To understand the relationship between
   recursion and iteration

To understand when the use of recursion affects the efficiency of an algorithm

To analyze problems that are much easier to solve by recursion than by iteration

To process data with recursive structures using mutual recursion

CHAPTER CONTENTS

The method of recursion is a powerful technique for breaking up complex computational problems into simpler, often smaller, ones. The term "recursion" refers to the fact that the same computation recurs, or occurs repeatedly, as the problem is solved. Recursion is often the most natural way of thinking about a problem, and there are some computations that are very difficult to perform without recursion. This chapter shows you both simple and complex examples of recursion and teaches you how to "think recursively".

11.1 Triangle Numbers Revisited

Chapter 5 contains a simple introduction to writing recursive functions—functions that call themselves with simpler inputs. In that chapter, you saw how to print triangle patterns such as this one:

```
[]
[][]
[][][]
[][][][]
```

The key observation is that you can print a triangle pattern of a given side length, provided you know how to print the smaller triangle pattern that is shown in color.

In this section, we will modify the example slightly and use recursion to compute the area of a triangle shape of side length n, assuming that each [] square has area 1. This value is sometimes called the nth *triangle number*. For example, as you can tell from looking at the above triangle, the third triangle number is 6 and the fourth triangle number is 10.

If the side length of the triangle is 1, then the triangle consists of a single square, and its area is 1. Let's take care of this case first:

```
def triangleArea(sideLength) :
    if sideLength == 1 :
        return 1
    . . .
```

To deal with the general case, suppose you knew the area of the smaller, colored triangle. Then you could easily compute the area of the larger triangle as

```
area = smallerArea + sideLength
```

Using the same method as the one described in this section, you can compute the volume of a Mayan pyramid.

© David Mantel/iStockphoto.

How can you get the smaller area? Call the `triangleArea` function!

```
smallerSideLength = sideLength - 1
smallerArea = triangleArea(smallerSideLength)
```

Now we can complete the `triangleArea` function:

```
def triangleArea(sideLength) :
   if sideLength == 1 :
      return 1
   smallerSideLength = sideLength - 1
   smallerArea = triangleArea(smallerSideLength)
   area = smallerArea + sideLength
   return area
```

Here is an illustration of what happens when we compute the area of a triangle of side length 4:

- The `triangleArea` function executes with the parameter variable `sideLength` set to 4.
- It sets `smallerSideLength` to 3 and calls `triangleArea` with argument `smallerSideLength`.
  - That function call has its own set of parameter and local variables. Its `sideLength` parameter variable is 3, and it sets its `smallerSideLength` variable to 2.
  - The `triangleArea` function is called again, now with argument 2.
    - In that function call, `sideLength` is 2 and `smallerSideLength` is 1.
    - The `triangleArea` function is called with argument 1.
      - That function call returns 1.
    - The returned value is stored in `smallerArea`, and the function returns `smallerArea + sideLength` = 1 + 2 = 3.
  - At this level, `smallerArea` is set to 3, and the function returns `smallerArea + sideLength` = 3 + 3 = 6.
- The function sets `smallerArea` to 6 and returns `smallerArea + sideLength` = 6 + 4 = 10.

As you can see, the function calls itself multiple times, with ever simpler arguments, until a very simple case is reached. Then the recursive function calls return, one by one.

While it is good to understand this pattern of recursive calls, most people don't find it very helpful to think about the call pattern when designing or understanding a recursive solution. Instead, look at the `triangleArea` function one more time. The first part is very easy to understand. If the side length is 1, then of course the area is 1. The next part is just as reasonable. Compute the area of the smaller triangle. Don't worry how that works—treat the function as a black box and simply assume that you will get the correct answer. Then the area of the larger triangle is clearly the sum of the smaller area and the side length.

When a function keeps calling itself, you may wonder how you know that the calls will eventually come to an end. Two conditions need to be fulfilled:

- Every recursive call must simplify the computation in some way.
- There must be special cases (sometimes called *base cases*) to handle the simplest computations directly.

> A recursive computation solves a problem by using the solution to the same problem with simpler inputs.

> For a recursion to terminate, there must be special cases for the simplest inputs.

The `triangleArea` function calls itself again with smaller and smaller values for the side length. Eventually the side length must reach 1, and there is a special case for computing the area of a triangle with side length 1. Thus, the `triangleArea` function always succeeds.

Actually, you have to be careful. What happens when you compute the area of a triangle with side length –1? It computes the area of a triangle with side length –2, which computes the area of a triangle with side length –3, and so on. To avoid this, you should add a condition to the triangleArea function:

```
if sideLength <= 0 :
    return 0
```

Recursion is not really necessary to compute the triangle numbers. The area of a triangle equals the sum

```
1 + 2 + 3 + . . . + sideLength
```

Of course, we can program a simple loop:

```
area = 0.0
for i in range(1, sideLength + 1) :
    area = area + i
```

Many simple recursions can be computed as loops. However, loop equivalents for more complex recursions—such as the ones in Worked Example 11.1 and Section 11.5—can be very difficult to understand.

Actually, in this case, you don't even need a loop to compute the answer. The sum of the first n integers can be computed as

$$1 + 2 + \cdots + n = n \times (n + 1)/2$$

Thus, the area can simply be computed as

```
area = sideLength * (sideLength + 1) / 2
```

Therefore, neither recursion nor a loop is required to solve this problem. The recursive solution is intended as a "warm-up" for the sections that follow.

sec01/trianglenumbers.py

```
1   ##
2   #   This program computes a triangle number using recursion.
3   #
4
5   def main() :
6       area = triangleArea(10)
7       print("Area:", area)
8       print("Expected: 55")
9
10  ## Computes the area of a triangle with a given side length.
11  #  @param sideLength the side length of the triangle base
12  #  @return the area
13  #
14  def triangleArea(sideLength) :
15      if sideLength <= 0 :
16          return 0
17      if sideLength == 1 :
18          return 1
19      smallerSideLength = sideLength - 1
20      smallerArea = triangleArea(smallerSideLength)
21      area = smallerArea + sideLength
22      return area
23
24  # Start the program.
25  main()
```

Program Run

```
Area: 55
Expected: 55
```

Common Error 11.1

Infinite Recursion

A common programming error is an infinite recursion: a function calling itself over and over with no end in sight. The computer needs some amount of memory for bookkeeping for each call. After some number of calls, all memory that is available for this purpose is exhausted. Your program shuts down and reports a "stack overflow".

Infinite recursion happens either because the arguments don't get simpler or because a special terminating case is missing. For example, suppose the triangleArea function was allowed to compute the area of a triangle with side length 0. If it weren't for the special test, the function would construct triangles with side length –1, –2, –3, and so on.

Special Topic 11.1

Recursion with Objects

If you find it confusing that a function can call itself, you may find the following object-oriented variation helpful. Let's implement a Triangle class with a getArea method:

```
class Triangle
    def __init__(self, sideLength) :
        self._sideLength = sideLength

    def getArea(self) :
        . . .
```

We take care of the base case first:

```
def getArea(self) :
    if self._sideLength == 1 :
        return 1
    . . .
```

Now on to the general case. Suppose the area of the smaller triangle was known. Then it would be easy to compute the area of the larger triangle as smallerArea + self._sideLength.

What's my area?
```
[]
[][]
[][][]
[][][][]
```
What's your area?
```
[]
[][]
[][][]
```
My area is 6.
```
[]
[][]
[][][]
[][][][]
```
Then my area is 10.

How can we get the smaller area? Just ask the smaller triangle!

```
smallerTriangle = Triangle(self._sideLength - 1)
smallerArea = smallerTriangle.getArea()
area = smallerArea + self._sideLength
```

Here, we call the getArea method on a different object. To many people, the recursion is less surprising in this setting.

EXAMPLE CODE   See special_topic_1/triangle.py and triangletester.py in your eText or companion code to see this object-oriented variation.

11.2 Problem Solving: Thinking Recursively

How To 5.2 in Chapter 5 told you how to solve a problem recursively by pretending that "someone else" will solve the problem for simpler inputs and by focusing on how to turn the simpler solutions into a solution for the whole problem.

In this section, we walk through these steps with a more complex problem: testing whether a sentence is a *palindrome* — a string that is equal to itself when you reverse all characters. Typical examples are

© Nikada/iStockphoto.

- A man, a plan, a canal — Panama!

- Go hang a salami, I'm a lasagna hog

Thinking recursively is easy if you can recognize a subtask that is similar to the original task.

and, of course, the oldest palindrome of all:

- Madam, I'm Adam

When testing for a palindrome, we ignore the difference between upper- and lower-case letters, as well as spaces and punctuation marks.

We want to implement the following `isPalindrome` function:

```
## Tests whether a string is a palindrome.
#  @param text a string that is being checked
#  @return True if text is a palindrome, False otherwise
#
def isPalindrome(text) :
    . . .
```

Step 1   Consider various ways to simplify inputs.

In your mind, focus on a particular input or set of inputs for the problem that you want to solve. Think how you can simplify the inputs in such a way that the same problem can be applied to the simpler input.

When you consider simpler inputs, you may want to remove just a little bit from the original input — maybe remove one or two characters from a string, or remove a small portion of a geometric shape. But sometimes it is more useful to cut the input in half and then see what it means to solve the problem for both halves.

In the palindrome test problem, the input is the string that we need to test. How can you simplify the input? Here are several possibilities:

- Remove the first character.
- Remove the last character.
- Remove both the first and last characters.
- Remove a character from the middle.
- Cut the string into two halves.

These simpler inputs are all potential inputs for the palindrome test.

Step 2   Combine solutions with simpler inputs into a solution of the original problem.

In your mind, consider the solutions for the simpler inputs that you discovered in Step 1. Don't worry *how* those solutions are obtained. Simply have faith that the solutions are readily available. Just say to yourself: These are simpler inputs, so someone else will solve the problem for me.

Now think how you can turn the solution for the simpler inputs into a solution for the input that you are currently thinking about. Maybe you need to add a small quantity, perhaps related to the quantity that you lopped off to arrive at the simpler input. Maybe you cut the original input in half and have solutions for each half. Then you may need to add both solutions to arrive at a solution for the whole.

Consider the methods for simplifying the inputs for the palindrome test. Cutting the string in half doesn't seem like a good idea. If you cut

```
"Madam, I'm Adam"
```

in half, you get two strings:

```
"Madam, I"
```

and

```
"'m Adam"
```

The first string isn't a palindrome. Cutting the input in half and testing whether the halves are palindromes seems a dead end.

The most promising simplification is to remove the first *and* last characters. Removing the M at the front and the m at the back yields

```
"adam, I'm Ada"
```

Suppose you can verify that the shorter string is a palindrome. Then *of course* the original string is a palindrome—we put the same letter in the front and the back. That's extremely promising. A word is a palindrome if

- The first and last letters match (ignoring letter case), and
- The word obtained by removing the first and last letters is a palindrome.

Again, don't worry how the test works for the shorter string. It just works.

There is one other case to consider. What if the first or last letter of the word is not a letter? For example, the string

```
"A man, a plan, a canal, Panama!"
```

ends in a ! character, which does not match the A in the front. But we should ignore non-letters when testing for palindromes. Thus, when the last character is not a letter but the first character is a letter, it doesn't make sense to remove both the first and the last characters. That's not a problem. Remove only the last character. If the shorter string is a palindrome, then it stays a palindrome when you attach a nonletter.

The same argument applies if the first character is not a letter. Now we have a complete set of cases.

- If the first and last characters are both letters, then check whether they match. If so, remove both and test the shorter string.
- Otherwise, if the last character isn't a letter, remove it and test the shorter string.
- Otherwise, the first character isn't a letter. Remove it and test the shorter string.

In all three cases, you can use the solution to the simpler problem to arrive at a solution to your problem.

Step 3   Find solutions to the simplest inputs.

A recursive computation keeps simplifying its inputs. Eventually it arrives at very simple inputs. To make sure that the recursion comes to a stop, you must deal with the simplest inputs separately. Come up with special solutions for them, which is usually very easy.

However, sometimes you get into philosophical questions dealing with *degenerate* inputs: empty strings, shapes with no area, and so on. Then you may want to investigate a slightly larger input that gets reduced to such a trivial input and see what value you should attach to the degenerate inputs so that the simpler value, when used according to the rules you discovered in Step 2, yields the correct answer.

Let's look at the simplest strings for the palindrome test:

- Strings with two characters
- Strings with a single character
- The empty string

We don't have to come up with a special solution for strings with two characters. Step 2 still applies to those strings—either or both of the characters are removed. But we do need to worry about strings of length 0 and 1. In those cases, Step 2 can't apply. There aren't two characters to remove.

The empty string is a palindrome—it's the same string when you read it backwards. If you find that too artificial, consider a string "mm". According to the rule discovered in Step 2, this string is a palindrome if the first and last characters match and the remainder—that is, the empty string—is also a palindrome. Therefore, it makes sense to consider the empty string a palindrome.

A string with a single letter, such as "I", is a palindrome. How about the case in which the character is not a letter, such as "!"? Removing the ! yields the empty string, which is a palindrome. Thus, we conclude that all strings of length 0 or 1 are palindromes.

Step 4   Implement the solution by combining the simple cases and the reduction step.

Now you are ready to implement the solution. Make separate cases for the simple inputs that you considered in Step 3. If the input isn't one of the simplest cases, then implement the logic you discovered in Step 2.

Here is the isPalindrome function:

```python
def isPalindrome(text) :
   length = len(text)

   # Separate case for shortest strings.
   if length <= 1 :
      return True
   else :
      # Get first and last characters, converted to lowercase.
      first = text[0].lower()
      last = text[length - 1].lower()

      if first.isalpha() and last.isalpha() :
         # Both are letters.
         if first == last :
            # Remove both first and last character.
            shorter = text[1 : length - 1]
            return isPalindrome(shorter)
         else :
            return False
      elif not last.isalpha() :
         # Remove last character.
         shorter = text[0 : length - 1]
         return isPalindrome(shorter)
```

```
        else :
            # Remove first character.
            shorter = text[1 : length]
            return isPalindrome(shorter)
```

EXAMPLE CODE   See sec02/palindromes.py in your eText or companion code for the complete program.

WORKED EXAMPLE 11.1

Finding Files

Problem Statement   Your task is to print the names of all files in a directory tree that end in a given extension.

The top level of a directory tree is called the *root* directory. The "children" of this directory can be files or subdirectories. Each subdirectory's children can also be files or subdirectories. You need to print all files in the root directory and in all subdirectories that have the desired extension.

Because some of these children can themselves be directories, we are naturally led to a recursive algorithm.

Step 1   Consider various ways to simplify inputs.

Our problem has two inputs: the name of a directory and an extension. Clearly, nothing is gained from manipulating the extension. However, there is an obvious way of chopping up the directory tree:

- Consider all children in the root level of the directory tree.
- If a child is a directory, examine that directory in the same way.
- If a child is a file, check whether it has the desired extension.

Step 2   Combine solutions with simpler inputs into a solution of the original problem.

We are asked to simply print the files that we find, so there aren't any results to combine. Had we been asked to produce a list of the found files, we would place all matches from the root directory into a list and add all results from the subdirectories into the same list.

Step 3   Find solutions to the simplest inputs.

The simplest input is a file that isn't a directory. In that case, we simply check whether it ends in the given extension, and if so, print it.

Step 4   Implement the solution by combining the simple cases and the reduction step.

In our case, the reduction step is simply to look at the files and subdirectories:

For each child of dir
    If the child is a directory
        Recursively find files with the given extension in the child.
    Else if the name of child ends in the extension
        Print the name.

To solve this task, you will need to use several functions in the os module that were introduced in Toolbox 7.2. The listdir function takes the path to a directory (such as /home/myname/python-foreveryone) and returns a list of the names of every file and directory in the given directory. These are simple names such as ch01 or hello.py.

To turn a simple name into a full path name, we use the join function and combine the name with the path to the parent. The result is a complete path such as /home/myname/pythonforevery-one/ch01. Finally, the isdir function takes such a path string and determines if it is the name of a directory.

Here is the find function in Python:

```python
## Prints all files whose names end in a given extension.
#  @param dir the starting directory
#  @param extension a file extension (such as ".py")
#
def find(dir, extension) :
    for f in listdir(dir) :
        child = join(dir, f)
        if isdir(child) :
            find(child, extension)
        elif child.endswith(extension) :
            print(child)
```

EXAMPLE CODE   See worked_example_1/filefinder.py in your eText or companion code for the complete solution.

11.3 Recursive Helper Functions

Sometimes it is easier to find a recursive solution if you make a slight change to the original problem.

Sometimes it is easier to find a recursive solution if you change the original problem slightly. Then the original problem can be solved by calling a recursive helper function.

Here is a typical example: Consider the palindrome test of Section 11.2. It is a bit inefficient to construct new string objects in every step. Rather than testing whether the entire sentence is a palindrome, let's check whether a substring is a palindrome:

© gerenme/iStockphoto.

Sometimes, a task can be solved by handing it off to a recursive helper function.

```python
## Recursively tests whether a substring is
#  a palindrome.
#  @param text a string that is being checked
#  @param start the index of the first character of the substring
#  @param end the index of the last character of the substring
#  @return True if the substring is a palindrome
#
def substringIsPalindrome(text, start, end) :
    . . .
```

This function turns out to be even easier to implement than the original test. In the recursive calls, simply adjust the start and end parameter variables to skip over matching letter pairs and characters that are not letters. There is no need to construct new strings to represent the shorter strings.

```python
def substringIsPalindrome(text, start, end) :
    # Separate case for substrings of length 0 and 1.
    if start >= end :
        return True
```

```
    else :
        # Get first and last characters, converted to lowercase.
        first = text[start].lower()
        last = text[end].lower()
        if first.isalpha() and last.isalpha() :
            if first == last :
                # Test substring that doesn't contain the matching letters.
                return substringIsPalindrome(text, start + 1, end - 1)
            else :
                return False
        elif not last.isalpha() :
            # Test substring that doesn't contain the last character.
            return substringIsPalindrome(text, start, end - 1)
        else :
            # Test substring that doesn't contain the first character.
            return substringIsPalindrome(text, start + 1, end)
```

You should still supply a function to solve the whole problem—the user of your function shouldn't have to know about the trick with the substring positions. Simply call the helper function with positions that test the entire string:

```
def isPalindrome(text) :
    return substringIsPalindrome(text, 0, len(text) − 1)
```

Note that this call is not a recursive function call. The isPalindrome function calls the helper function substringIsPalindrome. Use the technique of recursive helper functions whenever it is easier to solve a recursive problem that is equivalent to the original problem—but more amenable to a recursive solution.

EXAMPLE CODE   See sec03/palindromes2.py in your eText or companion code for a complete program that uses the substring version of the palindrome function.

11.4 The Efficiency of Recursion

As you have seen in this chapter, recursion can be a powerful tool for implementing complex algorithms. On the other hand, recursion can lead to algorithms that perform poorly. In this section, we will analyze the question of when recursion is beneficial and when it is inefficient.

Consider the Fibonacci sequence: a sequence of numbers defined by the equations

$$f_1 = 1$$

$$f_2 = 1$$

$$f_n = f_{n-1} + f_{n-2}$$

© pagadesign/iStockphoto.

In most cases, iterative and recursive approaches have comparable efficiency.

That is, each value of the sequence is the sum of the two preceding values. The first ten terms of the sequence are

$$1, 1, 2, 3, 5, 8, 13, 21, 34, 55$$

It is easy to extend this sequence indefinitely. Just keep appending the sum of the last two values of the sequence. For example, the next entry is $34 + 55 = 89$.

We would like to write a function that computes f_n for any value of n. Here we translate the definition directly into a recursive function:

sec04/recursivefib.py

```
1   ##
2   #  This program computes Fibonacci numbers using a recursive function.
3   #
4
5   def main() :
6      n = int(input("Enter n: "))
7      for i in range(1, n + 1) :
8         f = fib(i)
9         print("fib(%d) = %d" % (i, f))
10
11  ## Computes a Fibonacci number.
12  #  @param n an integer
13  #  @return the nth Fibonacci number
14  #
15  def fib(n) :
16     if n <= 2 :
17        return 1
18     else :
19        return fib(n - 1) + fib(n - 2)
20
21  # Start the program.
22  main()
```

Program Run

```
Enter n: 35
fib(1) = 1
fib(2) = 1
fib(3) = 2
fib(4) = 3
fib(5) = 5
fib(6) = 8
fib(7) = 13
. . .
fib(35) = 9227465
```

That is certainly simple, and the function will work correctly. But if you watch the output closely as you run the test program, you will see that the first few calls to the fib function are fast. For larger values, though, the program pauses an amazingly long time between outputs.

That makes no sense. Armed with pencil, paper, and a pocket calculator you could calculate these numbers pretty quickly, so it shouldn't take the computer anywhere near that long.

To see the problem, let us insert **trace messages** into the function:

sec04/recursivefibtracer.py

```
1   ##
2   #  This program prints trace messages that show how often the
3   #  recursive function for computing Fibonacci numbers calls itself.
4   #
5
```

```
 6  def main() :
 7      n = int(input("Enter n: "))
 8      f = fib(n)
 9      print("fib(%d) = %d" % (n, f))
10
11  ## Computes a Fibonacci number.
12  #  @param n an integer
13  #  @return the nth Fibonacci number
14  #
15  def fib(n) :
16      print("Entering fib: n =", n)
17      if n <= 2 :
18          f = 1
19      else :
20          f = fib(n - 1) + fib(n - 2)
21      print("Exiting fib: n =", n, "return value =", f)
22      return f
23
24  # Start the program.
25  main()
```

Program Run

```
Enter n: 6
Entering fib: n = 6
Entering fib: n = 5
Entering fib: n = 4
Entering fib: n = 3
Entering fib: n = 2
Exiting fib: n = 2 return value = 1
Entering fib: n = 1
Exiting fib: n = 1 return value = 1
Exiting fib: n = 3 return value = 2
Entering fib: n = 2
Exiting fib: n = 2 return value = 1
Exiting fib: n = 4 return value = 3
Entering fib: n = 3
Entering fib: n = 2
Exiting fib: n = 2 return value = 1
Entering fib: n = 1
Exiting fib: n = 1 return value = 1
Exiting fib: n = 3 return value = 2
Exiting fib: n = 5 return value = 5
Entering fib: n = 4
Entering fib: n = 3
Entering fib: n = 2
Exiting fib: n = 2 return value = 1
Entering fib: n = 1
Exiting fib: n = 1 return value = 1
Exiting fib: n = 3 return value = 2
Entering fib: n = 2
Exiting fib: n = 2 return value = 1
Exiting fib: n = 4 return value = 3
Exiting fib: n = 6 return value = 8
fib(6) = 8
```

Figure 1 shows the pattern of recursive calls for computing fib(6). Now it is becoming apparent why the function takes so long. It is computing the same values over and over. For example, the computation of fib(6) calls fib(4) twice and fib(3) three times. That is very different from the computation we would do with pencil and paper. There we would just write down the values as they were computed and add up the last two to get the next one until we reached the desired entry; no sequence value would ever be computed twice.

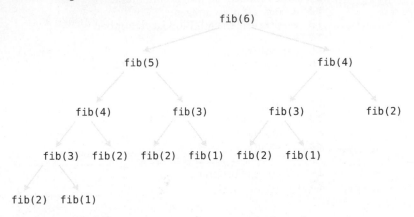

Figure 1   Call Pattern of the Recursive fib Function

If we imitate the pencil-and-paper process, then we get the following program.

sec04/loopfib.py

```
1  ##
2  #   This program computes Fibonacci numbers using an iterative function.
3  #
4
5  def main() :
6     n = int(input("Enter n: "))
7     for i in range(1, n + 1) :
8        f = fib(i)
9        print("fib(%d) = %d" % (i, f))
10
11 ## Computes a Fibonacci number.
12 #  @param n an integer
13 #  @return the nth Fibonacci number
14 #
15 def fib(n) :
16    if n <= 2 :
17       return 1
18    else :
19       olderValue = 1
20       oldValue = 1
21       newValue = 1
22       for i in range(3, n + 1) :
23          newValue = oldValue + olderValue
24          olderValue = oldValue
25          oldValue = newValue
26
27       return newValue
28
29 # Start the program.
30 main()
```

Program Run

```
Enter n: 50
fib(1) = 1
fib(2) = 1
fib(3) = 2
fib(4) = 3
fib(5) = 5
fib(6) = 8
fib(7) = 13
. . .
fib(50) = 12586269025
```

This function runs *much* faster than the recursive version.

In this example of the fib function, the recursive solution was easy to program because it exactly followed the mathematical definition, but it ran far more slowly than the iterative solution, because it computed many intermediate results multiple times.

Can you always speed up a recursive solution by changing it into a loop? Frequently, the iterative and recursive solution have essentially the same performance. For example, here is an iterative solution for the palindrome test:

```python
def isPalindrome(text) :
    start = 0
    end = len(text) - 1
    while start < end :
        first = text[start].lower()
        last = text[end].lower()
        if first.isalpha() and last.isalpha() :
            # Both are letters.
            if first == last :
                start = start + 1
                end = end - 1
            else :
                return False

        if not last.isalpha() :
            end = end - 1

        if not first.isalpha() :
            start = start + 1

    return True
```

This solution keeps two index variables: start and end. The first index starts at the beginning of the string and is advanced whenever a letter has been matched or a non-letter has been ignored. The second index starts at the end of the string and moves toward the beginning. When the two index variables meet, the iteration stops.

Both the iteration and the recursion run at about the same speed. If a palindrome has n characters, the iteration executes the loop between $n/2$ and n times, depending on how many of the characters are letters, because one or both index variables are moved in each step. Similarly, the recursive solution calls itself between $n/2$ and n times, because one or two characters are removed in each step.

In such a situation, the iterative solution tends to be a bit faster, because each recursive function call takes a certain amount of processor time. In principle, it is possible for a smart compiler to avoid recursive function calls if they follow simple patterns,

Occasionally, a recursive solution runs much slower than its iterative counterpart. However, in most cases, the recursive solution is only slightly slower.

but Python's compiler does not do that. From that point of view, an iterative solution is preferable.

EXAMPLE CODE   See sec04/looppalindromes.py in your eText or companion code for the iterative version of the palindrome program.

In many cases, a recursive solution is easier to understand and implement correctly than an iterative solution.

However, many problems have recursive solutions that are easier to understand and implement correctly than their iterative counterparts. Sometimes there is no obvious iterative solution at all—see the example in the next section. There is a certain elegance and economy of thought to recursive solutions that makes them more appealing. As the computer scientist (and creator of the GhostScript interpreter for the PostScript graphics description language) L. Peter Deutsch put it: "To iterate is human, to recurse divine."

11.5 Permutations

The permutations of a string can be obtained more naturally through recursion than with a loop.

In this section, we will study a more complex example of recursion that would be difficult to program with a simple loop. (As Exercise ●●● P11.15 shows, it is possible to avoid the recursion, but the resulting solution is quite complex, and no faster).

We will design a function that lists all permutations of a string. A permutation is simply a rearrangement of the letters in the string.

For example, the string "eat" has six permutations (including the original string itself):

```
"eat"
"eta"
"aet"
"ate"
"tea"
"tae"
```

Using recursion, you can find all arrangements of a set of objects.

© Jeanine Groenwald/iStockphoto.

Now we need a way to generate the permutations recursively. Consider the string "eat". Let's simplify the problem. First, we'll generate all permutations that start with the letter "e", then those that start with "a", and finally those that start with "t". How do we generate the permutations that start with "e"? We need to know the permutations of the substring "at". But that's the same problem—to generate all permutations—with a simpler input, namely the shorter string "at". Thus, we can use recursion. Generate the permutations of the substring "at". They are

```
"at"
"ta"
```

For each permutation of that substring, prepend the letter "e" to get the permutations of "eat" that start with "e", namely

```
"eat"
"eta"
```

Now let's turn our attention to the permutations of "eat" that start with "a". We need to produce the permutations of the remaining letters, "et". They are:

```
"et"
"te"
```

We add the letter "a" to the front of the strings and obtain

```
"aet"
"ate"
```

We generate the permutations that start with "t" in the same way.

That's the idea. The implementation is fairly straightforward. In the permutations function, we loop through all positions in the word to be permuted. For each of them, we compute the shorter word that is obtained by removing the ith letter:

```
shorter = word[ : i] + word[i + 1 : ]
```

We compute the permutations of the shorter word:

```
shorterPermutations = permutations(shorter)
```

Finally, we add the removed letter to the front of all permutations of the shorter word.

```
for s in shorterPermutations :
    result.append(word[i] + s)
```

As always, we have to provide a special case for the simplest strings. The simplest possible string is the empty string, which has a single permutation—itself.

Here is the complete program.

sec05/permutations.py

```
1   ##
2   #   This program computes permutations of a string.
3   #
4
5   def main() :
6       for string in permutations("eat") :
7           print(string)
8
9   ## Gets all permutations of a given word.
10  #   @param word the string to permute
11  #   @return a list of all permutations
12  #
13  def permutations(word) :
14      result = []
15
16      # The empty string has a single permutation: itself.
17      if len(word) == 0 :
18          result.append(word)
19          return result
20      else :
21          # Loop through all character positions.
22          for i in range(len(word)) :
23              # Form a shorter word by removing the ith character.
24              shorter = word[ : i] + word[i + 1 : ]
25
26              # Generate all permutations of the simpler word.
27              shorterPermutations = permutations(shorter)
28
29              # Add the removed character to the front of each permutation
30              # of the simpler word.
31              for string in shorterPermutations :
32                  result.append(word[i] + string)
33
34      # Return all permutations.
35      return result
36
37  # Start the program.
38  main()
```

Program Run

```
eat
eta
aet
ate
tea
tae
```

Compare the permutations.py and triangle.py programs. Both of them work on the same principle. When they work on a more complex input, they first solve the problem for

Computing & Society 11.1 The Limits of Computation

Have you ever wondered how your instructor or grader makes sure your programming homework is correct? In all likelihood, they look at your solution and perhaps run it with some test inputs. But usually they have a correct solution available. That suggests that there might be an easier way. Perhaps they could feed your program and their correct program into a "program comparator", a computer program that analyzes both programs and determines whether they both compute the same results. Of course, your solution and the program that is known to be correct need not be identical—what matters is that they produce the same output when given the same input.

How could such a program comparator work? Well, the Python interpreter knows how to read a program and make sense of the classes, functions, and statements. So it seems plausible that someone could, with some effort, write a program that reads two Python programs, analyzes what they do, and determines whether they solve the same task. Of course, such a program would be very attractive to instructors, because it could automate the grading process. Thus, even though no such program exists today, it might be tempting to try to develop one and sell it to universities around the world.

However, before you start raising venture capital for such an effort, you should know that theoretical computer scientists have proven that it is impossible to develop such a program, *no matter how hard you try.*

There are quite a few of these unsolvable problems. The first one, called the *halting problem,* was discovered by the British researcher Alan Turing in 1936. Because his research occurred before the first actual computer was constructed, Turing had to devise a theoretical device, the *Turing machine,* to explain how computers could work. The Turing machine consists of a long magnetic tape, a read/write head, and a program that has numbered instructions of the form: "If the current symbol under the head is *x*, then replace it with *y*, move the head one unit left or right, and continue with instruction *n*" (see figure below). Interestingly enough, with only these instructions, you can program just as much as with Python, even though it is incredibly tedious to do so. Theoretical computer scientists like Turing machines because they can be described using nothing more than the laws of mathematics.

Expressed in terms of Python, the halting problem states: "It is impossible to write a program with two inputs, namely the source code of an arbitrary Python program *P* and a string *I*, that decides whether the program *P*, when executed with the input *I*, will halt—that is, the program will not get into an infinite loop with the given input". Of course, for some kinds of programs and inputs, it is possible to decide whether the program halts with the given input. The halting problem asserts that it is impossible to come up with a single decision-making algorithm that works with all programs and inputs. Note that you can't simply run the program *P* on the input *I* to settle this question. If the program runs for 1,000 days, you don't know that the program is in an infinite loop. Maybe you just have to wait another day for it to stop.

Such a "halt checker", if it could be written, might also be useful for grading homework. An instructor could use it to screen student submissions to see if they get into an infinite loop with a particular input, and then stop checking them. However, as Turing demonstrated, such a program cannot be written. His argument is ingenious and quite simple.

Suppose a "halt checker" program existed. Let's call it *H*. From *H*, we will develop another program, the "killer"

Alan Turing

a simpler input. Then they combine the result for the simpler input with additional work to deliver the results for the more complex input. There really is no particular complexity behind that process as long as you think about the solution on that level only. However, behind the scenes, the simpler input creates even simpler input, which creates yet another simplification, and so on, until one input is so simple that the result can be obtained without further help. It is interesting to think about this process, but it can also be confusing. What's important is that you can focus on the one level that matters—putting a solution together from the slightly simpler problem, ignoring the fact that the simpler problem also uses recursion to get its results.

program K. K does the following computation. Its input is a string containing the source code for a program R. It then applies the halt checker on the input program R and the input string R. That is, it checks whether the program R halts if its input is its own source code. It sounds bizarre to feed a program to itself, but it isn't impossible. For example, a word counting program can count the words in its own source code.

When K gets the answer from H that R halts when applied to itself, it is programmed to enter an infinite loop. Otherwise K exits. In Python, the program might look like this:

```
r = Read program input
if check(r, r) :
    done = False
    while not done :
        done = False   # Infinite loop
else :
    return
```

Now ask yourself: What does the check function answer when asked whether K halts when given K as the input? Maybe it finds out that K gets into an infinite loop with such an input. But wait, that can't be right. That would mean that check(r, r) returns False when r is the program code of K. As you can plainly see, in that case, the killer program exits, so K didn't get into an infinite loop. That shows that K must halt when analyzing itself, so check(r, r) should return True. But then the killer program doesn't terminate—it goes into an infinite loop. That shows that it is logically impossible to implement a program that can

check whether *every* program halts on a particular input.

It is sobering to know that there are *limits* to computing. There are problems that no computer program, no matter how ingenious, can answer.

Theoretical computer scientists are working on other research involving the nature of computation. One important question that remains unsettled to this day deals with problems that in practice are very time-consuming to solve. It may be that these problems

are intrinsically hard, in which case it would be pointless to try to look for better algorithms. Such theoretical research can have important practical applications. For example, right now, nobody knows whether the most common encryption schemes used today could be broken by discovering a new algorithm. Knowing that no fast algorithms exist for breaking a particular code could make us feel more comfortable about the security of encryption.

Program

Instruction number	If tape symbol is	Replace with	Then move head	Then go to instruction
1	0	2	right	2
	1	1	left	4
2	0	0	right	2
	1	1	right	2
	2	0	left	3
3	0	0	left	3
	1	1	left	3
	2	2	right	1
4	1	1	right	5
	2	0	left	4

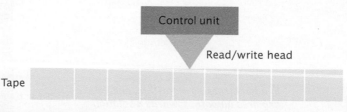

The Turing Machine

11.6 Backtracking

Backtracking examines partial solutions, abandoning unsuitable ones and returning to consider other candidates.

Backtracking is a problem solving technique that builds up partial solutions that get increasingly closer to the goal. If a partial solution cannot be completed, one abandons it and returns to examining the other candidates.

Backtracking can be used to solve crossword puzzles, escape from mazes, or find solutions to systems that are constrained by rules. In order to employ backtracking for a particular problem, we need two characteristic properties.

1. A procedure to examine a partial solution and determine whether to

   - Accept it as an actual solution.
   - Abandon it (either because it violates some rules or because it is clear that it can never lead to a valid solution).
   - Continue extending it.

2. A procedure to extend a partial solution, generating one or more solutions that come closer to the goal.

Backtracking can then be expressed with the following recursive algorithm:

> Solve(partialSolution)
>   Examine(partialSolution).
>   If accepted
>   Add partialSolution to the list of solutions.
>   Else if not abandoned
>   For each p in extend(partialSolution)
>   Solve(p).

Of course, the processes of examining and extending a partial solution depend on the nature of the problem.

As an example, we will develop a program that finds all solutions to the eight queens problem: the task of positioning eight queens on a chess board so that none of them attacks another according to the rules of chess. In other words, there are no two queens on the same row, column, or diagonal. Figure 2 shows a solution.

In this problem, it is easy to examine a partial solution. If two queens attack each other, reject it. Otherwise, if it has eight queens, accept it. Otherwise, continue.

It is also easy to extend a partial solution. Simply add another queen on an empty square.

In a backtracking algorithm, one explores all paths towards a solution. When one path is a dead end, one needs to backtrack and try another choice.

© Lanica Klein/iStockphoto.

Figure 2
A Solution to the Eight Queens Problem

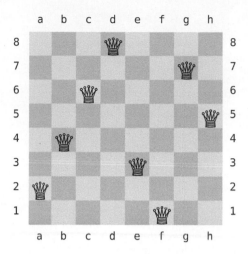

We represent a partial solution as a list of strings, where each string gives a queen position in the traditional chess notation. For example,

```
["a1", "e2", "h3", "f4"]
```

The examine function checks whether two queens in a partial solution attack each other:

```
def examine(partialSolution) :
    for i in range(0, len(partialSolution)) :
        for j in range(i + 1, len(partialSolution)) :
            if attacks(partialSolution[i], partialSolution[j]) :
                return ABANDON
    if len(partialSolution) == NQUEENS :
        return ACCEPT
    else :
        return CONTINUE
```

The extend function takes a partial solution and makes eight copies of it. Each copy gets a new queen in a different column.

```
def extend(partialSolution) :
    results = []
    row = len(partialSolution) + 1
    for column in "abcdefgh" :
        newSolution = list(partialSolution)
        newSolution.append(column + str(row))
        results.append(newSolution)
    return results
```

The only remaining challenge is to determine when two queens attack each other diagonally. Here is an easy way of checking that. Compute the slope and check whether it is ±1.

This condition can be simplified as follows:

$$(\text{row}_2 - \text{row}_1)/(\text{column}_2 - \text{column}_1) = \pm 1$$

$$\text{row}_2 - \text{row}_1 = \pm(\text{column}_2 - \text{column}_1)$$

$$|\text{row}_2 - \text{row}_1| = |\text{column}_2 - \text{column}_1|$$

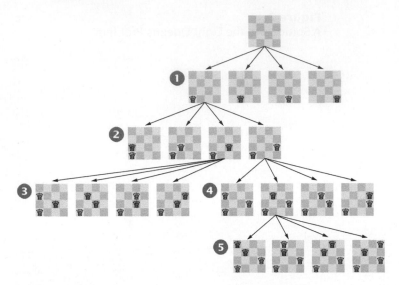

Figure 3   Backtracking in the Four Queens Problem

Have a close look at the solve function in the queens.py program below. The function is a straightforward translation of the pseudocode for backtracking. Note how there is nothing specific about the eight queens problem in this function—it works for any partial solution with an examine and extend function (see Exercise ••• P11.19).

Figure 3 shows the solve function in action for a four queens problem. Starting from a blank board, there are four partial solutions with a queen in row 1 ❶. When the queen is in column 1, there are four partial solutions with a queen in row 2 ❷. Two of them are immediately abandoned. The other two lead to partial solutions with three queens ❸ and ❹, all but one of which are abandoned. One partial solution is extended to four queens, but all of those are abandoned as well ❺. Then the algorithm backtracks, giving up on a queen in position a1, instead extending the solution with the queen in position b1 (not shown).

Our example program solves the problem with eight queens. When you run the program, it lists 92 solutions, including the one in Figure 2. Exercise ••• P11.21 asks you to remove those that are rotations or reflections of another.

sec06/queens.py

```
 1  ##
 2  #   This program solves the eight queens problem using backtracking.
 3  #
 4
 5  def main() :
 6      solve([])
 7
 8  COLUMNS = "abcdefgh"
 9  NQUEENS = len(COLUMNS)
10  ACCEPT = 1
11  CONTINUE = 2
12  ABANDON = 3
13
```

```
14  ## Prints all solutions to the problem that can be extended from
15  #   a given partial solution.
16  #   @param partialSolution the partial solution
17  #
18  def solve(partialSolution) :
19     exam = examine(partialSolution)
20     if exam == ACCEPT :
21        print(partialSolution)
22     elif exam != ABANDON :
23        for p in extend(partialSolution) :
24           solve(p)
25
26  ## Examines a partial solution.
27  #   @param partialSolution the partial solution
28  #   @return ACCEPT if it is a complete solution, ABANDON if it is invalid,
29  #   or CONTINUE otherwise
30  #
31  def examine(partialSolution) :
32     for i in range(0, len(partialSolution)) :
33        for j in range(i + 1, len(partialSolution)) :
34           if attacks(partialSolution[i], partialSolution[j]) :
35              return ABANDON
36     if len(partialSolution) == NQUEENS :
37        return ACCEPT
38     else :
39        return CONTINUE
40
41  ## Checks whether one position attacks another. Positions are given as
42  #   strings with a letter for the column and a number for the row.
43  #   @param p1 a position
44  #   @param p2 another position
45  #   @return True if the positions are in the same row, column, or diagonal
46  #
47  def attacks(p1, p2) :
48     column1 = COLUMNS.index(p1[0]) + 1
49     row1 = int(p1[1])
50     column2 = COLUMNS.index(p2[0]) + 1
51     row2 = int(p2[1])
52     return (row1 == row2 or column1 == column2 or
53        abs(row1 - row2) == abs(column1 - column2))
54
55  ## Extends a partial solution to the next column.
56  #   @param partialSolution a partial solution to the problem
57  #   @return a list of all partial solutions that have a queen added in the
58  #   next column
59  #
60  def extend(partialSolution) :
61     results = []
62     row = len(partialSolution) + 1
63     for column in COLUMNS :
64        newSolution = list(partialSolution)
65        newSolution.append(column + str(row))
66        results.append(newSolution)
67     return results
68
69  # Start the program.
70  main()
```

Program Run

```
['a1', 'e2', 'h3', 'f4', 'c5', 'g6', 'b7', 'd8']
['a1', 'f2', 'h3', 'c4', 'g5', 'd6', 'b7', 'e8']
['a1', 'g2', 'd3', 'f4', 'h5', 'b6', 'e7', 'c8']
  . . .
['f1', 'a2', 'e3', 'b4', 'h5', 'c6', 'g7', 'd8']
  . . .
['h1', 'c2', 'a3', 'f4', 'b5', 'e6', 'g7', 'd8']
['h1', 'd2', 'a3', 'c4', 'f5', 'b6', 'g7', 'e8']'
```

(92 solutions)

WORKED EXAMPLE 11.2

Towers of Hanoi

The "Towers of Hanoi" puzzle has a board with three pegs and a stack of disks of decreasing size, initially on the first peg (see Figure 4).

The goal is to move all disks to the third peg. One disk can be moved at one time, from any peg to any other peg. You can place smaller disks only on top of larger ones, not the other way around.

Legend has it that a temple (presumably in Hanoi) contains such an assembly, with sixty-four golden disks, which the priests move in the prescribed fashion. When they have arranged all disks on the third peg, the world will come to an end.

Problem Statement Help out by writing a program that prints instructions for moving the disks.

Consider the problem of moving d disks from peg p_1 to peg p_2, where p_1 and p_2 are 1, 2, or 3, and $p_1 \neq p_2$. Because $1 + 2 + 3 = 6$, we can get the index of the remaining peg as $p_3 = 6 - p_1 - p_2$.

Now we can move the disks as follows:

- Move the top $d - 1$ disks from p_1 to p_3
- Move one disk (the one on the bottom of the pile of d disks) from p_1 to p_2
- Move the $d - 1$ disks that were parked on p_3 to p_2

The first and third step need to be handled recursively, but because we move one fewer disk, the recursion will eventually terminate.

It is very straightforward to translate the algorithm into Python. For the second step, we simply print out the instruction for the priest, something like

```
Move disk from peg 1 to 3
```

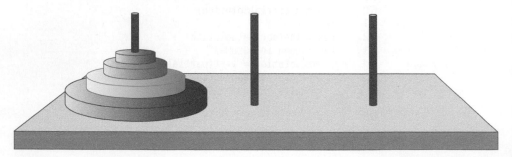

Figure 4 Towers of Hanoi

worked_example_2/towersofhanoimoves.py

```
 1  ##
 2  #   This program prints instructions for solving a Towers of Hanoi puzzle.
 3  #
 4
 5  def main() :
 6      move(5, 1, 3)
 7
 8  ## Print instructions for moving a pile of disks from one peg to another.
 9  #   @param disks  the number of disks to move
10  #   @param fromPeg  the peg from which to move the disks
11  #   @param toPeg  the peg to which to move the disks
12  #
13  def move(disks, fromPeg, toPeg) :
14      if disks > 0 :
15          other = 6 - fromPeg - toPeg
16          move(disks - 1, fromPeg, other)
17          print("Move disk from peg", fromPeg, "to", toPeg)
18          move(disks - 1, other, toPeg)
19
20  # Start the program.
21  main()
```

Program Run

```
Move disk from peg 1 to 3
Move disk from peg 1 to 2
Move disk from peg 3 to 2
Move disk from peg 1 to 3
Move disk from peg 2 to 1
Move disk from peg 2 to 3
Move disk from peg 1 to 3
Move disk from peg 1 to 2
Move disk from peg 3 to 2
Move disk from peg 3 to 1
Move disk from peg 2 to 1
Move disk from peg 3 to 2
Move disk from peg 1 to 3
Move disk from peg 1 to 2
Move disk from peg 3 to 2
Move disk from peg 1 to 3
Move disk from peg 2 to 1
Move disk from peg 2 to 3
Move disk from peg 1 to 3
Move disk from peg 2 to 1
Move disk from peg 3 to 2
Move disk from peg 3 to 1
Move disk from peg 2 to 1
Move disk from peg 2 to 3
Move disk from peg 1 to 3
Move disk from peg 1 to 2
Move disk from peg 3 to 2
Move disk from peg 1 to 3
Move disk from peg 2 to 1
Move disk from peg 2 to 3
Move disk from peg 1 to 3
```

These instructions may suffice for the priests, but unfortunately it is not easy for us to see what is going on. Let's improve the program so that it actually carries out the instructions and shows the contents of the towers after each move.

We represent each tower as a list of disks. Each disk is represented as an integer indicating its size from 1 to n, the number of disks in the puzzle. There are three towers, so a configuration of the puzzle is a list of three lists, such as this one:

```
[[5, 2], [4, 1], [3]]
```

The move function first carries out the move, then prints the contents of the towers:

```
def move(towers, disks, fromPeg, toPeg) :
    if disks > 0 :
        other = 3 - fromPeg - toPeg
        move(towers, disks - 1, fromPeg, other)
        diskToMove = towers[fromPeg].pop()
        towers[toPeg].append(diskToMove)
        print(towers)
        move(towers, disks - 1, other, toPeg)
```

Here, the index values are 0, 1, 2. Therefore, the index of the other peg is 3 - fromPeg - toPeg. Here is the main function:

```
def main() :
    NDISKS = 5
    disks = []
    for i in range(NDISKS, 0, -1) :
        disks.append(i)
    towers = [disks, [], []]
    move(towers, NDISKS, 0, 2)
```

The program output is

```
[[5, 4, 3, 2], [], [1]]
[[5, 4, 3], [2], [1]]
[[5, 4, 3], [2, 1], []]
[[5, 4], [2, 1], [3]]
[[5, 4, 1], [2], [3]]
[[5, 4, 1], [], [3, 2]]
[[5, 4], [], [3, 2, 1]]
[[5], [4], [3, 2, 1]]
[[5], [4, 1], [3, 2]]
[[5, 2], [4, 1], [3]]
[[5, 2, 1], [4], [3]]
[[5, 2, 1], [4, 3], []]
[[5, 2], [4, 3], [1]]
[[5], [4, 3, 2], [1]]
[[5], [4, 3, 2, 1], []]
[[], [4, 3, 2, 1], [5]]
[[1], [4, 3, 2], [5]]
[[1], [4, 3], [5, 2]]
[[], [4, 3], [5, 2, 1]]
[[3], [4], [5, 2, 1]]
[[3], [4, 1], [5, 2]]
[[3, 2], [4, 1], [5]]
[[3, 2, 1], [4], [5]]
[[3, 2, 1], [], [5, 4]]
[[3, 2], [], [5, 4, 1]]
[[3], [2], [5, 4, 1]]
[[3], [2, 1], [5, 4]]
[[], [2, 1], [5, 4, 3]]
[[1], [2], [5, 4, 3]]
[[1], [], [5, 4, 3, 2]]
[[], [], [5, 4, 3, 2, 1]]
```

That's better. Now you can see how the disks move. You can check that all moves are legal—the disk size always decreases.

EXAMPLE CODE See worked_example_2/towersofhanoi.py for the complete program.

You can see that it takes $31 = 2^5 - 1$ moves to solve the puzzle for 5 disks. With 64 disks, it takes $2^{64} - 1 = 18446744073709551615$ moves. If the priests can move one disk per second, it takes about 585 billion years to finish the job. Because the earth is about 4.5 billion years old at the time this book is written, we don't have to worry too much whether the world will really come to an end when they are done.

11.7 Mutual Recursion

> In a mutual recursion, cooperating functions or methods call each other repeatedly.

In the preceding examples, a function called itself to solve a simpler problem. Sometimes, a set of cooperating functions or methods calls each other in a recursive fashion. In this section, we will explore such a **mutual recursion**. This technique is significantly more advanced than the simple recursion that we discussed in the preceding sections.

We will develop a program that can compute the values of arithmetic expressions such as

```
3+4*5
(3+4)*5
1-(2-(3-(4-5)))
```

Computing such an expression is complicated by the fact that * and / bind more strongly than + and -, and that parentheses can be used to group subexpressions.

Figure 5 shows a set of **syntax diagrams** that describes the syntax of these expressions.

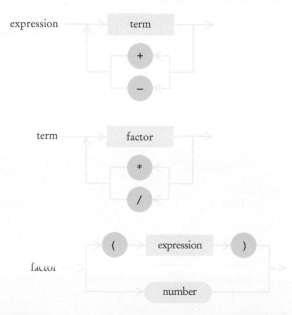

Figure 5 Syntax Diagrams for Evaluating an Expression

To see how the syntax diagrams work, consider the expression 3+4*5:

- Enter the *expression* syntax diagram. The arrow points directly to *term*, giving you no alternative.
- Enter the *term* syntax diagram. The arrow points to *factor*, again giving you no choice.
- Enter the *factor* diagram. You have two choices: to follow the top branch or the bottom branch. Because the first input token is the number 3 and not a (, follow the bottom branch.
- Accept the input token because it matches the number. The unprocessed input is now +4*5.
- Follow the arrow out of *number* to the end of *factor*. As in a function call, you now back up, returning to the end of the *factor* element of the *term* diagram.
- Now you have another choice—to loop back in the *term* diagram, or to exit. The next input token is a +, and it matches neither the * or the / that would be required to loop back. So you exit, returning to *expression*.
- Again, you have a choice, to loop back or to exit. Now the + matches one of the choices in the loop. Accept the + in the input and move back to the *term* element. The remaining input is 4*5.

In this fashion, an expression is broken down into a sequence of terms, separated by + or -, each term is broken down into a sequence of factors, each separated by * or /, and each factor is either a parenthesized expression or a number. You can draw this breakdown as a tree. Figure 6 shows how the expressions 3+4*5 and (3+4)*5 are derived from the syntax diagram.

Why do the syntax diagrams help us compute the value of the tree? If you look at the syntax trees, you will see that they accurately represent which operations should be carried out first. In the first tree, 4 and 5 should be multiplied, and then the result should be added to 3. In the second tree, 3 and 4 should be added, and the result should be multiplied by 5.

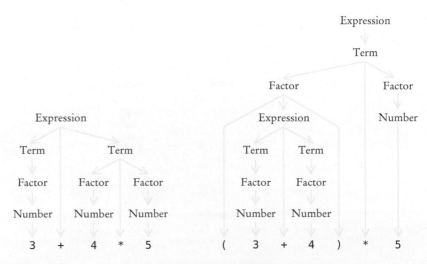

Figure 6 Syntax Trees for Two Expressions

At the end of this section, you will find a program that evaluates these expressions. The program makes use of a tokenize function that breaks up an input string into tokens—numbers, operators, and parentheses. (For simplicity, we only accept positive integers as numbers, and we don't allow spaces in the input.)

To compute the value of an expression, we implement three functions: expression, term, and factor. The expression function first calls term to get the value of the first term of the expression. Then it checks whether the next input token is one of + or -. If so, it calls term again and adds or subtracts it.

```python
def expression(tokens) :
    value = term(tokens)
    done = False
    while not done and len(tokens) > 0 :
        nextToken = tokens[0]
        if nextToken == "+" or nextToken == "-" :
            tokens.pop(0)    # Discard "+" or "-"
            value2 = term(tokens)
            if nextToken == "+" :
                value = value + value2
            else :
                value = value - value2
        else :
            done = True

    return value
```

The term function calls factor in the same way, multiplying or dividing the factor values.

Finally, the factor function checks whether the next token is a (. If not, the token must be a number, and the value is simply that number. However, if the next token is a (, the factor function makes a recursive call to expression. Thus, the three methods are mutually recursive.

```python
def factor(tokens) :
    nextToken = tokens.pop(0)
    if nextToken == "(" :
        value = expression(tokens)
        tokens.pop(0)    # Discard ")"
    else :
        value = nextToken

    return value
```

To see the mutual recursion clearly, trace through the expression (3+4)*5:

- expression calls term
  - term calls factor
    - factor consumes the (input
    - factor calls expression
      - expression returns eventually with the value of 7, having consumed 3 + 4. This is the recursive call.
    - factor consumes the) input
    - factor returns 7
  - term consumes the inputs * and 5 and returns 35
- expression returns 35

As always with a recursive solution, you need to ensure that the recursion terminates. In this situation, that is easy to see when you consider the situation in which expression calls itself. The second call works on a shorter subexpression than the original expression. At each recursive call, at least some of the tokens are consumed, so eventually the recursion must come to an end.

sec07/evaluator.py

```python
1  ##
2  #   This program evaluates arithmetic expressions.
3  #

5  def main() :
6     expr = input("Enter an expression: ")
7     tokens = tokenize(expr)
8     value = expression(tokens)
9     print(expr + "=" + str(value))

11 ## Breaks a string into tokens.
12 #   @param inputLine a string consisting of digits and symbols
13 #   @return a list of numbers (made from the digits of the input) and symbols
14 #
15 def tokenize(inputLine) :
16    result = []
17    i = 0
18    while i < len(inputLine) :
19       if inputLine[i].isdigit() :
20          j = i + 1
21          while j < len(inputLine) and inputLine[j].isdigit() :
22             j = j + 1
23          result.append(int(inputLine[i : j]))
24          i = j
25       else :
26          result.append(inputLine[i])
27          i = i + 1
28    return result

30 ## Evaluates the expression.
31 #   @param tokens  the list of tokens to process
32 #   @return  the value of the expression
33 #
34 def expression(tokens) :
35    value = term(tokens)
36    done = False
37    while not done and len(tokens) > 0 :
38       nextToken = tokens[0]
39       if nextToken == "+" or nextToken == "-" :
40          tokens.pop(0)    # Discard "+" or "-"
41          value2 = term(tokens)
42          if nextToken == "+" :
43             value = value + value2
44          else :
45             value = value - value2
46       else :
47          done = True

49    return value

51 ## Evaluates the next term found in the expression.
```

```
52  #  @param tokens the list of tokens to process
53  #  @return the value of the term
54  #
55  def term(tokens) :
56     value = factor(tokens)
57     done = False
58     while not done and len(tokens) > 0 :
59        nextToken = tokens[0]
60        if nextToken == "*" or nextToken == "/" :
61           tokens.pop(0)
62           value2 = factor(tokens)
63           if nextToken == "*" :
64              value = value * value2
65           else :
66              value = value / value2
67        else :
68           done = True
69
70     return value
71
72  ## Evaluates the next factor found in the expression.
73  #  @param tokens the list of tokens to process
74  #  @return the value of the factor
75  #
76  def factor(tokens) :
77     nextToken = tokens.pop(0)
78     if nextToken == "(" :
79        value = expression(tokens)
80        tokens.pop(0)    # Discard ")"
81     else :
82        value = nextToken
83
84     return value
85
86  # Start the program.
87  main()
```

Program Run

```
Enter an expression: 3+4*5
3+4*5=23
```

TOOLBOX 11.1
Analyzing Web Pages with Beautiful Soup

Web pages are written in HTML, the Hypertext Markup Language. HTML pages are made up of *elements*, which are comprised of content enclosed in a pair of matching tags. The tags tell the browser how to display the content. Unfortunately, not all HTML pages on the Web are properly formed—it is common to have missing or mismatched element tags. Browsers can tolerate minor errors and show the pages as best as they can. But for programmers who need to analyze web pages, tagging errors are very annoying.

In this Toolbox, you will learn the basics of the Python library named Beautiful Soup, which can be used to turn "tag soup" into properly nested structures. (Refer to Toolbox 2.1 if you have not already installed the libraries as explained there.)

Web Page Basics

HTML pages start with a *root element*. Each element can have children. The root element has two children, named head and body, and the child elements themselves have children. Here is an example of a web page:

```
<html>  # The root element
    <head>
        <title>First Presidents</title>
    </head>
    <body>
        <p>The first three presidents of the United States were</p>
        <ol>
            <li><a href="en.wikipedia.org/wiki/George_Washington">
                George Washington</a></li>
            <li><a href="en.wikipedia.org/wiki/John_Adams"> </a>
                John Adams</li>
            <li><a href="en.wikipedia.org/wiki/Thomas_Jefferson">
                Thomas Jefferson</a></li>
        </ol>
    </body>
</html>
```

In this example, the body element has two children: a paragraph and an ordered list (with tag names p and ol). The ordered list has three children that are list items (with tag name li). (For more about HTML, see Appendix F.)

When you pass a string containing HTML (such as a web page) to Beautiful Soup, you get an object representing the HTML document:

```
import bs4
doc = bs4.BeautifulSoup(html)
```

In general, when e is a tag, then e.contents is a list of its children. For example,

```
root = doc.contents[0]
```

stores the html element of the page in root. You can now examine its children. However, root.contents is a list of *five* children: the head and body elements, and the text around them, which consists entirely of blank spaces.

```
firstChildren = root.contents  # blank space, head, blank space, body, blank space
```

You will see in Exercise ••• Toolbox P11.27 how you can get rid of the blank spaces. Beautiful Soup doesn't do this by default because it is not always easy to tell when a blank space is document text, and when it separates tags.

The children of an element can be a mixture of tags and text. Here is how to distinguish between them:

```
if type(child) == bs4.element.Tag :
    child is a tag with name child.name
else :
    child is a text element with contents str(child)
```

If child is a tag, you get its name as child.name. If it is a text element, str(child) is the contents as a Python string.

For accessing the *attributes* of a tag (for example, the href attribute of a hyperlink tag a), you use the [] operator, as you do with a dictionary:

```
if child.name == "a" :
    link = child["href"]
```

By visiting children and, recursively, their children, you can traverse an HTML document to find the elements and attributes that are of interest to you—see Exercise •• Toolbox P11.28.

Because finding elements is such a common operation, the Beautiful Soup library provides a function for that purpose. The call

```
elements = doc.find_all("a")
```

yields all elements whose beginning tag name is a.

Writing a Web Crawler

You can use the Beautiful Soup library to create a web crawler, a program that browses the World Wide Web to collect information from web pages as the pages are visited. Search engines such as Google use web crawlers to collect and index web page content to facilitate fast searches. A web crawler is also used to collect web page addresses and the links between the pages in order to map a portion of the Web.

Here, we are going to write a web crawler that browses the Web to collect the addresses of all web pages that can be reached in three steps from the hyperlinks on a given page.

To accomplish this, you first need to read the entire contents of a web page and search for all hyperlinks on that page that point to other web pages. The same process must then be repeated on each of those pages until you have traveled at most three links away from the initial page. This naturally leads us to a recursive algorithm:

> *Open and parse the web page.*
> *For each link on the page*
>   *Get the URL of the link.*
>   *If the URL refers to a web page and it has not been visited*
>   *Add the URL to the list of visited pages.*
>   *Recursively search the new page.*

To keep track of the distance, or the *depth*, of the search, we can maintain a counter that is reduced for each step from the initial page. The forward search ends when the counter reaches 0.

Our function will have three inputs: the address of the web page, the number of steps to search from this page, and a list of addresses for those pages encountered during the crawl.

```
def crawl(address, depth, visited) :
```

On the first call to the recursive function, the main function creates a list into which the web page addresses will be added. After the list is filled by the crawl function, its contents are printed to show the URLs encountered during the crawl:

```
def main() :
    url = input("Start with URL: ")
    visited = []
    crawl(url, 3, visited)
    print(visited)
```

In Toolbox 7.3, you learned how to open a web page and obtain a response object:

```
response = urllib.request.urlopen(address)
```

To parse the web page and find all the hyperlinks, you can use the tools provided by the Beautiful Soup toolkit.

To use the toolkit, you create an instance of the BeautifulSoup class (defined in the bs4 module) and pass it the response object that resulted from opening the web page:

```
doc = bs4.BeautifulSoup(response)
```

The web page is automatically read and decoded. If there is any problem with connecting to the server or parsing the response (for example, if the URL points to an image), then an exception will be raised. A try/except block can be used to skip such URLs.

To find all the hyperlinks on the web page, you use the find_all method, which returns a list of links, one for each <a> tag found on the page.

```
links = doc.find_all("a")
```

These tools can be used to implement the recursive crawl function as shown in the following program.

toolbox_1/webcrawler.py

```
1  ##
2  #  This program browses the Web to collect the addresses of all web pages that can
3  #  be reached by following the hyperlinks within three steps from an initial page.
4  #
5
6  import bs4
7  import urllib.request
8
9  def main() :
10     url = input("Start with URL: ")
11     visited = []
12     crawl(url, 3, visited)
13     print(visited)
14
15  def crawl(address, depth, visited) :
16     if depth == 0 :
17        return
18     try :
19        response = urllib.request.urlopen(address)
20        doc = bs4.BeautifulSoup(response)
21        print("Visiting " + address)
22        for link in doc.find_all("a") :
23           href = link["href"]
24           if href[0:4] == "http" and href not in visited :
25              visited.append(href)
26              crawl(href, depth - 1, visited)
27     except :
28        return
29
30  main()
```

CHAPTER SUMMARY

Understand the control flow in a recursive computation.

- A recursive computation solves a problem by using the solution to the same problem with simpler inputs.
- For a recursion to terminate, there must be special cases for the simplest inputs.

Design a recursive solution to a problem.

Identify recursive helper functions for solving a problem.

- Sometimes it is easier to find a recursive solution if you make a slight change to the original problem.

Contrast the efficiency of recursive and non-recursive algorithms.

- Occasionally, a recursive solution runs much slower than its iterative counterpart. However, in most cases, the recursive solution is only slightly slower.
- In many cases, a recursive solution is easier to understand and implement correctly than an iterative solution.

Review a complex recursion example that cannot be solved with a simple loop.

- The permutations of a string can be obtained more naturally through recursion than with a loop.

Use backtracking to solve problems that require trying out multiple paths.

- Backtracking examines partial solutions, abandoning unsuitable ones and returning to consider other candidates.

Recognize the phenomenon of mutual recursion in an expression evaluator.

- In a mutual recursion, cooperating functions or methods call each other repeatedly.

REVIEW EXERCISES

- **R11.1** Define the terms
    - **a.** Recursion
    - **b.** Iteration
    - **c.** Infinite recursion
    - **d.** Recursive helper function

- **R11.2** Outline, but do not implement, a recursive solution for finding the smallest value in a list.

- **R11.3** Outline, but do not implement, a recursive solution for sorting a list of numbers. *Hint:* First find the smallest value in the list.

- **R11.4** Outline, but do not implement, a recursive solution for generating all subsets of the set $\{1, 2, \ldots, n\}$.

- **R11.5** Exercise ••• P11.15 shows an iterative way of generating all permutations of the sequence $(0, 1, \ldots, n-1)$. Explain why the algorithm produces the correct result.

- **R11.6** Write a recursive definition of x^n, where $n \geq 0$. *Hint:* How do you compute x^n from x^{n-1}? How does the recursion terminate?

- **R11.7** Improve upon Exercise • R11.6 by computing x^n as $(x^{n/2})^2$ if n is even. Why is this approach significantly faster? *Hint:* Compute x^{1023} and x^{1024} both ways.

- **R11.8** Write a recursive definition of $n! = 1 \times 2 \times \cdots \times n$. *Hint:* How do you compute $n!$ from $(n-1)!$? How does this recursion terminate?

- **R11.9** Find out how often the recursive version of the `fib` function calls itself. Keep a global variable `fibCount` and increment it once in every call to `fib`. What is the relationship between `fib(n)` and `fibCount`?

- **R11.10** Let moves(n) be the number of moves required to solve the Towers of Hanoi problem (see Worked Example 11.2). Find a formula that expresses moves(n) in terms of moves($n-1$). Then show that moves(n) = $2^n - 1$.

- **R11.11** Trace the expression evaluator program from Section 11.7 with inputs 3 – 4 + 5, 3 – (4 + 5), (3 – 4) * 5, and 3 * 4 + 5 * 6.

PROGRAMMING EXERCISES

- **P11.1** Given a class `Rectangle` with instance variables `width` and `height`, provide a recursive `getArea` method. Construct a rectangle whose width is one less than the original and call its `getArea` method.

- **P11.2** Given a class `Square` with instance variable `width`, provide a recursive `getArea` method. Construct a square whose width is one less than the original and call its `getArea` method.

- **P11.3** Write a recursive function `reverse(text)` that reverses a string. For example, `reverse("Hello!")` returns the string `"!olleH"`. Implement a recursive solution by removing the first character, reversing the remaining text, and combining the two.

▪▪ **P11.4** Redo Exercise • P11.3 with a recursive helper function that reverses a substring of the message text.

▪ **P11.5** Implement the reverse function of Exercise • P11.3 as an iteration.

▪▪ **P11.6** Use recursion to implement a function

```
def find(text, string)
```

that tests whether a given text contains a string. For example, find("Mississippi", "sip") returns True.

Hint: If the text starts with the string you want to match, then you are done. If not, consider the text that you obtain by removing the first character.

▪▪ **P11.7** Use recursion to implement a function

```
def indexOf(text, string)
```

that returns the starting position of the first substring of text that matches string. Return −1 if string is not a substring of the text. For example, s.indexOf("Mississippi", "sip") returns 6.

Hint: This is a bit trickier than Exercise •• P11.6, because you must keep track of how far the match is from the beginning of the text. Make that value a parameter variable of a helper function.

▪ **P11.8** Using recursion, find the largest element in a list.

Hint: Find the largest element in the subsequence containing all but the last element. Then compare that maximum to the value of the last element.

▪ **P11.9** Using recursion, compute the sum of all values in a list.

▪▪ **P11.10** Using recursion, compute the area of a polygon. Cut off a triangle and use the fact that a triangle with corners (x_1, y_1), (x_2, y_2), (x_3, y_3) has area

$$\frac{|x_1y_2 + x_2y_3 + x_3y_1 - y_1x_2 - y_2x_3 - y_3x_1|}{2}$$

▪▪ **P11.11** The following function was known to the ancient Greeks for computing square roots. Given a value $x > 0$ and a guess g for the square root, a better guess is $(g + x/g) / 2$. Write a recursive helper function def squareRootGuess(x, g). If g^2 is approximately equal to x, return g, otherwise, return squareRootGuess with the better guess. Then write a function def squareRoot(x) that uses the helper function.

▪▪▪ **P11.12** Implement a function substrings that returns a list of all substrings of a string. For example, the substrings of the string "rum" are the seven strings

```
"r", "ru", "rum", "u", "um", "m", ""
```

Hint: First generate all substrings that start with the first character. There are n of them if the string has length n. Then generate the substrings of the string that you obtain by removing the first character.

▪▪▪ **P11.13** Implement a function subsets that returns a list of all subsets of the characters of a string. For example, the subsets of the characters of the string "rum" are the eight strings

```
"rum", "ru", "rm", "r", "um", "u", "m", ""
```

Note that the subsets don't have to be substrings—for example, `"rm"` isn't a substring of `"rum"`.

■■■ **P11.14** In this exercise, you will change the `permutations` function of Section 11.5 (which computed all permutations at once) to a `PermutationIterator` (which computes them one at a time).

```
class PermutationIterator :
    def __init__(self, s) :
        . . .
    def nextPermutation(self) :
        . . .
    def hasMorePermutations(self) :
```

Here is how you would print out all permutations of the string `"eat"`:

```
iter = PermutationIterator("eat")
while iter.hasMorePermutations() :
    print(iter.nextPermutation()
```

Now we need a way to iterate through the permutations recursively. Consider the string `"eat"`. As before, we'll generate all permutations that start with the letter `"e"`, then those that start with `"a"`, and finally those that start with `"t"`. How do we generate the permutations that start with `"e"`? Make another `PermutationIterator` object (called `tailIterator`) that iterates through the permutations of the substring `"at"`. In the `nextPermutation` method, simply ask `tailIterator` what *its* next permutation is, and then add the `"e"` at the front.

However, there is one special case. When the tail generator runs out of permutations, all permutations that start with the current letter have been enumerated.

Then

- Increment the current position.
- Compute the tail string that contains all letters except for the current one.
- Make a new permutation iterator for the tail string.

You are done when the current position has reached the end of the string.

■■■ **P11.15** The following program generates all permutations of the numbers $0, 1, 2, \ldots, n-1$, without using recursion.

```
def main() :
    NUM_ELEMENTS = 4
    a = list(range(1, NUM_ELEMENTS + 1))
    print(a)
    while nextPermutation(a) :
        print(a)

def nextPermutation(a) :
    i = len(a) - 1
    while i > 0 :
        if a[i - 1] < a[i] :
            j = len(a) - 1
            while a[i - 1] > a[j] :
                j = j - 1
            swap(a, i - 1, j)
            reverse(a, i, len(a) - 1)
            return True
        i = i - 1
    return False
```

```
def reverse(a, i, j) :
    while i < j :
        swap(a, i, j)
        i = i + 1
        j = j - 1

def swap(a, i, j) :
    temp = a[i]
    a[i] = a[j]
    a[j] = temp

main()
```

The algorithm uses the fact that the set to be permuted consists of distinct numbers. Thus, you cannot use the same algorithm to compute the permutations of the characters in a string. You can, however, use this program to get all permutations of the character positions and then compute a string whose ith character is word[a[i]]. Use this approach to reimplement the permutations function of Section 11.5 without recursion.

■■ **P11.16** Extend the expression evaluator in Section 11.7 so that it can handle the % operator as well as a "raise to a power" operator ^. For example, 2 ^ 3 should evaluate to 8. As in mathematics, raising to a power should bind more strongly than multiplication: 5 * 2 ^ 3 is 40.

■■■ **P11.17** Implement a DiskMover class that produces the moves for the Towers of Hanoi puzzle described in Worked Example 11.2. Provide methods hasMoreMoves and nextMove. The nextMove method should yield a string describing the next move. For example, the following code prints all moves needed to move five disks from peg 1 to peg 3:

```
mover = DiskMover(5, 1, 3)
while mover.hasMoreMoves() :
    print(mover.nextMove())
```

Hint: A disk mover that moves a single disk from one peg to another simply has a nextMove method that returns a string

```
Move disk from peg source to target
```

A disk mover with more than one disk to move must work harder. It needs another DiskMover to help it move the first $d-1$ disks. The nextMove method asks that disk mover for its next move until it is done. Then nextMove issues a command to move the dth disk. Finally, it constructs another disk mover that generates the remaining moves.

It helps to keep track of the state of the disk mover:

- BEFORE_LARGEST: A helper mover moves the smaller pile to the other peg.
- LARGEST: Move the largest disk from the source to the destination.
- AFTER_LARGEST: The helper mover moves the smaller pile from the other peg to the target.
- DONE: All moves are done.

■■■ **P11.18** *Escaping a Maze*. You are currently located inside a maze. The walls of the maze are indicated by asterisks (*).

```
* *******
*     * *
* ***** *
* * *   *
* * *** *
*   *   *
*** * * *
*     * *
******* *
```

Use the following recursive approach to check whether you can escape from the maze: If you are at an exit, return `True`. Recursively check whether you can escape from one of the empty neighboring locations without visiting the current location. This function merely tests whether there is a path out of the maze. Extra credit if you can print out a path that leads to an exit.

■■■ **P11.19** The backtracking algorithm will work for any problem whose partial solutions can be examined and extended. Provide a `PartialSolution` class with methods `examine` and `extend`, a `solve` method that works with this class, and a subclass `EightQueensPartial-Solution` that provides concrete `examine` and `extend` methods.

■■■ **P11.20** Using the `PartialSolution` class and `solve` method from Exercise ■■■ P11.19, provide a class `MazePartialSolution` for solving the maze escape problem of Exercise ■■■ P11.18.

■■■ **P11.21** Refine the program for solving the eight queens problem so that rotations and reflections of previously displayed solutions are not shown. Your program should display twelve unique solutions.

■■■ **P11.22** Refine the program for solving the eight queens problem so that the solutions are written to an HTML file, using tables with black and white background colors for the board and the Unicode character `"\u2655"` for the queen.

■■ **P11.23** Generalize the program for solving the eight queens problem to the n queens problem. Your program should prompt for the value of n and display the solutions.

■■ **P11.24** Using backtracking, write a program that solves summation puzzles in which each letter should be replaced by a digit, such as

```
send + more = money
```

Your program should find the solution $9567 + 1085 = 10652$. Other examples are `base + ball = games` and `kyoto + osaka = tokyo`.

Hint: In a partial solution, some of the letters have been replaced with digits. In the third example, you would consider all partial solutions where k is replaced by 0, 1, ... 9: `0yoto + osa0a = to0yo`, `1yoto + osa1a = to1yo`, and so on. To extend a partial solution, find the first letter and replace all instances with a digit that doesn't yet occur in the partial solution. If a partial solution has no more letters, check whether the sum is correct.

■■ **P11.25** The recursive computation of Fibonacci numbers can be speeded up significantly by keeping track of the values that have already been computed. Provide an implementation of the `fib` function that uses this strategy. Whenever you return a new value, also store it in an auxiliary list. However, before embarking on a computation, consult the list to find whether the result has already been computed. Compare the running time of your improved implementation with that of the original recursive implementation and the loop implementation.

■■■ **Graphics P11.26** *The Koch Snowflake.* A snowflake-like shape is recursively defined as follows. Start with an equilateral triangle:

Next, increase the size by a factor of three and replace each straight line with four line segments:

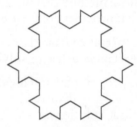

Repeat the process:

Write a program that draws the iterations of the snowflake shape. Prompt the user to press ENTER, after which the next iteration is produced.

■■■ **Toolbox P11.27** Write a function that removes ignorable white space from an HTML document that was read with Beautiful Soup (see Toolbox 11.1). Ignore white space that occurs between two elements, unless it occurs adjacent to these elements:

```
b, big, i, small, tt
abbr, acronym, cite, code, dfn, em, kbd, strong, samp, var
a, bdo, br, img, map, object, q, script, span, sub, sup
button, input, label, select, textarea
```

(These elements are called "inline elements" in HTML because they can be contained inside textual material.)

■■ **Toolbox P11.28** Reimplement the `find_all` method of Beautiful Soup by writing a function that accepts an HTML tag as a string and yields a list of all descendant tags with a given tag name. Use recursion in your solution.

CHAPTER 12

SORTING AND SEARCHING

CHAPTER GOALS

To study several sorting and
searching algorithms

To appreciate that algorithms for the same
task can differ widely in performance

© Volkan Ersoy/iStockphoto.

To understand big-Oh notation

To estimate and compare the performance of algorithms

To write code to measure the running time of a program

CHAPTER CONTENTS

One of the most common tasks in data processing is sorting. For example, a list of employees often needs to be displayed in alphabetical order or sorted by salary. In this chapter, you will learn several sorting methods as well as techniques for comparing their performance. These techniques are useful not just for sorting algorithms, but also for analyzing other algorithms.

Once a list of elements is sorted, one can rapidly locate individual elements. You will study the *binary search* algorithm that carries out this fast lookup.

12.1 Selection Sort

In this section, we show you the first of several sorting algorithms. A *sorting algorithm* rearranges the elements of a collection so that they are stored in sorted order. To keep the examples simple, we will discuss how to sort a list of integers before going on to sorting strings or more complex data. Consider the following list values:

```
     [0] [1] [2] [3] [4]
      11  9  17   5  12
```

> The selection sort algorithm sorts a list by repeatedly finding the smallest element of the unsorted tail region and moving it to the front.

An obvious first step is to find the smallest element. In this case the smallest element is 5, stored in values[3]. We should move the 5 to the beginning of the list. Of course, there is already an element stored in values[0], namely 11. Therefore we cannot simply move values[3] into values[0] without moving the 11 somewhere else. We don't yet know where the 11 should end up, but we know for certain that it should not be in values[0]. We simply get it out of the way by *swapping* it with values[3]:

```
     [0] [1] [2] [3] [4]
       5  9  17  11  12
```

Now the first element is in the correct place. The darker color in the figure indicates the portion of the list that is already sorted.

In selection sort, pick the smallest element and swap it with the first one. Pick the smallest element of the remaining ones and swap it with the next one, and so on.

© Zone Creative/iStockphoto.

Next we take the minimum of the remaining entries values[1] . . . values[4]. That minimum value, 9, is already in the correct place. We don't need to do anything in this case and can simply extend the sorted area by one to the right:

Repeat the process. The minimum value of the unsorted region is 11, which needs to be swapped with the first value of the unsorted region, 17:

Now the unsorted region is only two elements long, but we keep to the same successful strategy. The minimum value is 12, and we swap it with the first unsorted value, 17:

```
[0] [1] [2] [3] [4]
 5   9  11  12  17
```

That leaves us with an unprocessed region of length 1, but of course a region of length 1 is always sorted. We are done.

This algorithm will sort any list of integers. If speed were not an issue, or if there simply were no better sorting method available, we could stop the discussion of sorting right here. As the next section shows, however, this algorithm, while entirely correct, shows disappointing performance when run on a large data set.

Special Topic 12.2 discusses insertion sort, another simple sorting algorithm.

sec01/selectionsort.py

```python
1  ##
2  #    The selectionSort function sorts a list using the selection sort algorithm.
3  #
4
5  ## Sorts a list, using selection sort.
6  #   @param values the list to sort
7  #
8  def selectionSort(values) :
9     for i in range(len(values)) :
10       minPos = minimumPosition(values, i)
11       temp = values[minPos]    # Swap the two elements
12       values[minPos] = values[i]
13       values[i] = temp
14
15  ## Finds the smallest element in a tail range of the list.
16  #   @param values the list to sort
17  #   @param start the first position in values to compare
18  #   @return the position of the smallest element in the
19  #   range values[start] . . . values[len(values) - 1]
20  #
21  def minimumPosition(values, start) :
22     minPos = start
23     for i in range(start + 1, len(values)) :
24        if values[i] < values[minPos] :
25           minPos = i
26
27     return minPos
```

sec01/selectiondemo.py

```
1  ##
2  #  This program demonstrates the selection sort algorithm by sorting a
3  #  list that is filled with random numbers.
4
5  from random import randint
6  from selectionsort import selectionSort
7
8  n = 20
9  values = []
10 for i in range(n) :
11     values.append(randint(1, 100))
12 print(values)
13 selectionSort(values)
14 print(values)
```

Program Run

```
[65, 46, 14, 52, 38, 2, 96, 39, 14, 33, 13, 4, 24, 99, 89, 77, 73, 87, 36, 81]
[2, 4, 13, 14, 14, 24, 33, 36, 38, 39, 46, 52, 65, 73, 77, 81, 87, 89, 96, 99]
```

12.2 Profiling the Selection Sort Algorithm

To measure the performance of a program, you could simply run it and use a stopwatch to measure how long it takes. However, most of our programs run very quickly, and it is not easy to time them accurately in this way. Furthermore, when a program takes a noticeable time to run, a certain amount of that time may simply be used for loading the program from disk into memory and displaying the result (for which we should not penalize it).

In order to measure the running time of an algorithm more accurately, we will use the time() library function from the time module. It returns the seconds (as a floating-point value) that have elapsed since midnight at the start of January 1, 1970. Of course, you don't care about the absolute number of seconds since this historical moment, but the difference of two such counts gives us the number of seconds in a given time interval.

Here is how to measure the sorting algorithm's performance:

sec02/selectiontimer.py

```
1  ##
2  #  This program measures how long it takes to sort a list of a
3  #  user-specified size with the selection sort algorithm.
4  #
5
6  from random import randint
7  from selectionsort import selectionSort
8  from time import time
9
10 firstSize = int(input("Enter first list size: "))
11 numberOfLists = int(input("Enter number of lists: "))
12
```

```
13  for k in range(1, numberOfLists + 1) :
14      size = firstSize * k
15      values = []
16      # Construct random list.
17      for i in range(size) :
18          values.append(randint(1, 100))
19
20      startTime = time()
21      selectionSort(values)
22      endTime = time()
23
24      print("Size: %d Elapsed time: %.3f seconds" % (size, endTime - startTime))
```

Program Run

```
Enter first list size: 1000
Enter number of lists: 6
Size: 1000 Elapsed time: 0.042 seconds
Size: 2000 Elapsed time: 0.166 seconds
Size: 3000 Elapsed time: 0.376 seconds
Size: 4000 Elapsed time: 0.659 seconds
Size: 5000 Elapsed time: 1.035 seconds
Size: 6000 Elapsed time: 1.506 seconds
```

To measure the running time of a function, get the current time immediately before and after the function call.

By starting to measure the time just before sorting, and stopping the timer just after, you get the time required for the sorting process, without counting the time for input and output.

The table in Figure 1 shows the results of some sample runs. These measurements were obtained with an Intel dual core processor with a clock speed of 3.2 GHz, running Python 3.2 on the Linux operating system. On another computer the actual numbers will look different, but the relationship between the numbers will be the same.

The graph in Figure 1 shows a plot of the measurements. As you can see, when you double the size of the data set, it takes about four times as long to sort it.

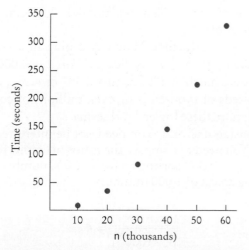

n	Seconds
10,000	9
20,000	38
30,000	85
40,000	147
50,000	228
60,000	332

Figure 1   Time Taken by Selection Sort

12.3 Analyzing the Performance of the Selection Sort Algorithm

Let us count the number of operations that the program must carry out to sort a list with the selection sort algorithm. We don't actually know how many machine operations are generated for each Python instruction, or which of those instructions are more time-consuming than others, but we can make a simplification. Simply count how often a list element is *visited*. Each visit requires about the same amount of work by other operations, such as incrementing indexes and comparing values.

Let n be the size of the list. First, you must find the smallest of n numbers. To achieve this, you must visit n elements. Then swap the elements, which takes two visits. (You may argue that there is a certain probability that you don't need to swap the values. That is true, and one can refine the computation to reflect that observation. As we will soon see, doing so would not affect the overall conclusion.) In the next step, you need to visit only $n-1$ elements to find the minimum and then visit two of them to swap them. In the following step, $n-2$ elements are visited to find the minimum. The last run visits two elements to find the minimum and requires two visits to swap the elements. Therefore, the total number of visits is

$$
\begin{aligned}
n + 2 + (n-1) + 2 + \cdots + 2 + 2 &= \left(n + (n-1) + \cdots + 2\right) + (n-1) \cdot 2 \\
&= \left(2 + \cdots + (n-1) + n\right) + (n-1) \cdot 2 \\
&= \frac{n(n+1)}{2} - 1 + (n-1) \cdot 2
\end{aligned}
$$

because

$$
1 + 2 + \cdots + (n-1) + n = \frac{n(n+1)}{2}
$$

After multiplying out and collecting terms of n, you find that the number of visits is

$$
\tfrac{1}{2}n^2 + \tfrac{5}{2}n - 3
$$

This is a quadratic equation in n. That explains why the graph of Figure 1 looks approximately like a parabola.

Now simplify the analysis further. When you plug in a large value for n (for example, 1,000 or 2,000), then $\frac{1}{2}n^2$ is 500,000 or 2,000,000. The lower term, $\frac{5}{2}n - 3$, doesn't contribute much at all; it is just 2,497 or 4,997, a drop in the bucket compared to the hundreds of thousands or even millions of comparisons specified by the $\frac{1}{2}n^2$ term. Just ignore these lower-level terms.

Next, ignore the constant factor $\frac{1}{2}$. You need not be interested in the actual count of visits for a single n. You need to compare the ratios of counts for different values of n^2. For example, you can say that sorting an list of 2,000 numbers requires four times as many visits as sorting an list of 1,000 numbers:

$$
\frac{\left(\frac{1}{2} \cdot 2000^2\right)}{\left(\frac{1}{2} \cdot 1000^2\right)} = 4
$$

The factor $\frac{1}{2}$ cancels out in comparisons of this kind. We will simply say, "The number of visits is of order n^2". That way, we can easily see that the number of comparisons increases fourfold when the size of the list doubles: $(2n)^2 = 4n^2$.

> Computer scientists use big-Oh notation to describe how fast a function grows.

To indicate that the number of visits is of order n^2, computer scientists often use **big-Oh notation**: The number of visits is $O(n^2)$. This is a convenient shorthand. (See Special Topic 12.1 for a formal definition.)

To turn a polynomial expression such as

$$\tfrac{1}{2}n^2 + \tfrac{5}{2}n - 3$$

into big-Oh notation, simply locate the fastest-growing term, n^2, and ignore its constant coefficient, $\frac{1}{2}$ in this case, *no matter how large or small it may be.*

You observed before that the actual number of machine operations, and the actual amount of time that the computer spends on them, is approximately proportional to the number of element visits. Maybe there are about 10 machine operations (increments, comparisons, memory loads, and stores) for every element visit. The number of machine operations is then approximately $10 \times \frac{1}{2}n^2$. As before, we aren't interested in the coefficient, so we can say that the number of machine operations, and hence the time spent on the sorting, is of the order of n^2 or $O(n^2)$.

> Selection sort is an $O(n^2)$ algorithm. Doubling the data set means a fourfold increase in processing time.

The sad fact remains that doubling the size of the list causes a fourfold increase in the time required for sorting it. When the size of a list increases by a factor of 100, the sorting time increases by a factor of 10,000. To sort a list of one million entries (for example, to create a telephone directory), takes 10,000 times as long as sorting 10,000 entries. If 10,000 entries can be sorted in about nine seconds (as in our example), then sorting one million entries requires more than one day. You will see in the next section how one can dramatically improve the performance of the sorting process by choosing a more sophisticated algorithm.

Special Topic 12.1

Oh, Omega, and Theta

We have used big-Oh notation somewhat casually in this chapter to describe the growth behavior of a function. Here is the formal definition of big-Oh notation: Suppose we have a function $T(n)$. Usually, it represents the processing time of an algorithm for a given input of size n. But it could be any function. Also, suppose that we have another function $f(n)$. It is usually chosen to be a simple function, such as $f(n) = n^k$ or $f(n) = \log(n)$, but it too can be any function. We write

$$T(n) = O(f(n))$$

if $T(n)$ grows at a rate that is bounded by $f(n)$. More formally, we require that for all n larger than some threshold, the ratio $T(n) / f(n) \le C$ for some constant value C.

If $T(n)$ is a polynomial of degree k in n, then one can show that $T(n) = O(n^k)$. Later in this chapter, we will encounter functions that are $O(\log(n))$ or $O(n \log(n))$. Some algorithms take much more time. For example, one way of sorting a sequence is to compute all of its permutations, until you find one that is in increasing order. Such an algorithm takes $O(n!)$ time, which is very bad indeed.

Table 1 shows common big-Oh expressions, sorted by increasing growth.

Table 1 Common Big-Oh Growth Rates	
Big-Oh Expression	Name
$O(1)$	Constant
$O(\log(n))$	Logarithmic
$O(n)$	Linear
$O(n \log(n))$	Log-linear
$O(n^2)$	Quadratic
$O(n^3)$	Cubic
$O(2^n)$	Exponential
$O(n!)$	Factorial

Strictly speaking, $T(n) = O(f(n))$ means that T grows no faster than f. But it is permissible for T to grow much more slowly. Thus, it is technically correct to state that $T(n) = n^2 + 5n - 3$ is $O(n^3)$ or even $O(n^{10})$.

Computer scientists have invented additional notation to describe the growth behavior of functions more accurately. The expression

$$T(n) = \Omega(f(n))$$

means that T grows at least as fast as f, or, formally, that for all n larger than some threshold, ratio $T(n) / f(n) \geq C$ for some constant value C. (The Ω symbol is the capital Greek letter omega.) For example, $T(n) = n^2 + 5n - 3$ is $\Omega(n^2)$ or even $\Omega(n)$.

The expression

$$T(n) = \Theta(f(n))$$

means that T and f grow at the same rate—that is, both $T(n) = O(f(n))$ and $T(n) = \Omega(f(n))$ hold. (The Θ symbol is the capital Greek letter theta.)

The Θ notation gives the most precise description of growth behavior. For example, $T(n) = n^2 + 5n - 3$ is $\Theta(n^2)$ but not $\Theta(n)$ or $\Theta(n^3)$.

The notations are very important for the precise analysis of algorithms. However, in casual conversation it is common to stick with big-Oh, while still giving an estimate that is as good as one can make.

Special Topic 12.2

Insertion Sort

Insertion sort is another simple sorting algorithm. In this algorithm, we assume that the initial sequence

```
values[0] values[1] . . . values[k]
```

of a list is already sorted. (When the algorithm starts, we set k to 0.) We enlarge the initial sequence by inserting the next list element, values[k + 1], at the proper location. When we reach the end of the list, the sorting process is complete.

For example, suppose we start with the list

| 11 | 9 | 16 | 5 | 7 |

Of course, the initial sequence of length 1 is already sorted. We now add `values[1]`, which has the value 9. The element needs to be inserted before the element 11. The result is

| 9 | 11 | 16 | 5 | 7 |

Next, we add `values[2]`, which has the value 16. This element does not have to be moved.

| 9 | 11 | 16 | 5 | 7 |

We repeat the process, inserting `values[3]` or 5 at the very beginning of the initial sequence.

| 5 | 9 | 11 | 16 | 7 |

Finally, `values[4]` or 7 is inserted in its correct position, and the sorting is completed.

The following function implements the insertion sort algorithm:

```python
## Sorts a list, using insertion sort.
#   @param values the list to sort
#
def insertionSort(values) :
    for i in range(1, len(values)) :
        nextValue = values[i]

        # Move all larger elements up.
        j = i
        while j > 0 and values[j - 1] > nextValue :
            values[j] = values[j - 1]
            j = j - 1

        # Insert the element.
        values[j] = nextValue
```

How efficient is this algorithm? Let n denote the size of the list. We carry out $n - 1$ iterations. In the kth iteration, we have a sequence of k elements that is already sorted, and we need to insert a new element into the sequence. For each insertion, we need to visit the elements of the initial sequence until we have found the location in which the new element can be inserted. Then we need to move up the remaining elements of the sequence. Thus, $k + 1$ list elements are visited. Therefore, the total number of visits is

$$2 + 3 + \cdots + n = \frac{n(n+1)}{2} - 1$$

Insertion sort is an $O(n^2)$ algorithm.

We conclude that insertion sort is an $O(n^2)$ algorithm, on the same order of efficiency as selection sort.

Insertion sort has a desirable property: Its performance is $O(n)$ if the list is already sorted—see Exercise ••• R12.17. This is a useful property in practical applications, in which data sets are often partially sorted.

Insertion sort is the method that many people use to sort playing cards. Pick up one card at a time and insert it so that the cards stay sorted.   © Kirby Hamilton/iStockphoto.

EXAMPLE CODE   See `special_topic_2/insertiondemo.py` in your eText or companion code for a program that illustrates sorting with insertion sort.

12.4 Merge Sort

In this section, you will learn about the merge sort algorithm, a much more efficient algorithm than selection sort. The basic idea behind merge sort is very simple.

Suppose we have a list of 10 integers. Let us engage in a bit of wishful thinking and hope that the first half of the list is already perfectly sorted, and the second half is too, like this:

| 5 | 9 | 10 | 12 | 17 | 1 | 8 | 11 | 20 | 32 |

Now it is simple to *merge* the two sorted lists into one sorted list, by taking a new element from either the first or the second sublist, and choosing the smaller of the elements each time:

5	9	10	12	17	1	8	11	20	32		1									
5	9	10	12	17	1	8	11	20	32		1	5								
5	9	10	12	17	1	8	11	20	32		1	5	8							
5	9	10	12	17	1	8	11	20	32		1	5	8	9						
5	9	10	12	17	1	8	11	20	32		1	5	8	9	10					
5	9	10	12	17	1	8	11	20	32		1	5	8	9	10	11				
5	9	10	12	17	1	8	11	20	32		1	5	8	9	10	11	12			
5	9	10	12	17	1	8	11	20	32		1	5	8	9	10	11	12	17		
5	9	10	12	17	1	8	11	20	32		1	5	8	9	10	11	12	17	20	
5	9	10	12	17	1	8	11	20	32		1	5	8	9	10	11	12	17	20	32

In fact, you may have performed this merging before if you and a friend had to sort a pile of papers. You and the friend split the pile in half, each of you sorted your half, and then you merged the results together.

The merge sort algorithm sorts a list by cutting the list in half, recursively sorting each half, and then merging the sorted halves.

That is all well and good, but it doesn't seem to solve the problem for the computer. It still must sort the first and second halves of the list, because it can't very well ask a few buddies to pitch in. As it turns out, though, if the computer keeps dividing the list into smaller and smaller sublists, sorting each half and merging them back together, it carries out dramatically fewer steps than the selection sort requires.

Let's write a mergesort.py module that implements this idea. When the mergeSort function sorts a list, it makes two lists, each half the size of the original, and sorts them recursively. Then it merges the two sorted lists together:

© Rich Legg/iStockphoto.

In merge sort, one sorts each half, then merges the sorted halves.

```python
def mergeSort(values) :
    if len(values) <= 1 : return
    mid = len(values) // 2
    first = values[ : mid]
    second = values[mid : ]
    mergeSort(first)
    mergeSort(second)
    mergeLists(first, second, values)
```

The mergeLists function is tedious but straightforward. You will find it in the code that follows.

sec04/mergesort.py

```python
1   ##
2   #   The mergeSort function sorts a list, using the merge sort algorithm.
3   #
4
5   ## Sorts a list, using merge sort.
6   #   @param values  the list to sort
7   #
8   def mergeSort(values) :
9      if len(values) <= 1 : return
10     mid = len(values) // 2
11     first = values[ : mid]
12     second = values[mid : ]
13     mergeSort(first)
14     mergeSort(second)
15     mergeLists(first, second, values)
16
17  ## Merges two sorted lists into a third list.
18  #   @param first  the first sorted list
19  #   @param second  the second sorted list
20  #   @param values  the list into which to merge first and second
21  #
22  def mergeLists(first, second, values) :
23     iFirst = 0      # Next element to consider in the first list.
24     iSecond = 0     # Next element to consider in the second list.
25     j = 0           # Next open position in values.
26
27     # As long as neither iFirst nor iSecond is past the end, move
28     # the smaller element into values
29     while iFirst < len(first) and iSecond < len(second) :
30        if first[iFirst] < second[iSecond] :
31           values[j] = first[iFirst]
32           iFirst = iFirst + 1
33        else :
34           values[j] = second[iSecond]
35           iSecond = iSecond + 1
36
37        j = j + 1
38
39     # Note that only one of the two loops below copies entries.
40     # Copy any remaining entries of the first list.
41     while iFirst < len(first) :
42        values[j] = first[iFirst]
43        iFirst = iFirst + 1
44        j = j + 1
45
46     # Copy any remaining entries of the second list.
47     while iSecond < len(second) :
48        values[j] = second[iSecond]
49        iSecond = iSecond + 1
50        j = j + 1
```

sec04/mergedemo.py

```python
1   ##
2   #   This program demonstrates the merge sort algorithm by
3   #   sorting a list that is filled with random numbers.
4   #
5
```

```
 6  from random import randint
 7  from mergesort import mergeSort
 8
 9  n = 20
10  values = []
11  for i in range(n) :
12      values.append(randint(1, 100))
13  print(values)
14  mergeSort(values)
15  print(values)
```

Program Run

```
[8, 81, 48, 53, 46, 70, 98, 42, 27, 76, 33, 24, 2, 76, 62, 89, 90, 5, 13, 21]
[2, 5, 8, 13, 21, 24, 27, 33, 42, 46, 48, 53, 62, 70, 76, 76, 81, 89, 90, 98]
```

12.5 Analyzing the Merge Sort Algorithm

The merge sort algorithm looks a lot more complicated than the selection sort algorithm, and it appears that it may well take much longer to carry out these repeated subdivisions. However, the timing results for merge sort look much better than those for selection sort.

Figure 2 shows a table and a graph comparing both sets of performance data. As you can see, merge sort is a tremendous improvement. To understand why, let us estimate the number of list element visits that are required to sort a list with the merge sort algorithm. First, let us tackle the merge process that happens after the first and second halves have been sorted.

Each step in the merge process adds one more element to values. That element may come from first or second, and in most cases the elements from the two halves must be compared to see which one to take. We'll count that as 3 visits (one for values and one each for first and second) per element, or $3n$ visits total, where n denotes the length of values. Moreover, at the beginning, we had to copy from values to first and second, yielding another $2n$ visits, for a total of $5n$.

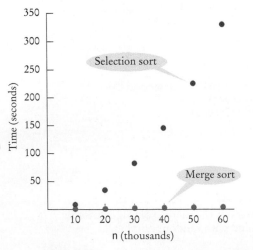

n	Merge Sort (seconds)	Selection Sort (seconds)
10,000	0.105	9
20,000	0.223	38
30,000	0.344	85
40,000	0.470	147
50,000	0.599	228
60,000	0.729	332

Figure 2 Time Taken by Merge Sort and Selection Sort

If you let $T(n)$ denote the number of visits required to sort a range of n elements through the merge sort process, then you obtain

$$T(n) = T\left(\frac{n}{2}\right) + T\left(\frac{n}{2}\right) + 5n$$

because sorting each half takes $T(n/2)$ visits. Actually, if n is not even, then you have one sublist of size $(n-1)/2$ and one of size $(n+1)/2$. Although it turns out that this detail does not affect the outcome of the computation, you can assume for now that n is a power of 2, say $n = 2^m$. This way, all sublists can be evenly divided into two parts.

Unfortunately, the formula

$$T(n) = 2T\left(\frac{n}{2}\right) + 5n$$

does not clearly tell you the relationship between n and $T(n)$. To understand the relationship, evaluate $T(n/2)$, using the same formula:

$$T\left(\frac{n}{2}\right) = 2T\left(\frac{n}{4}\right) + 5\frac{n}{2}$$

Therefore

$$T(n) = 2 \times 2T\left(\frac{n}{4}\right) + 5n + 5n$$

Do that again:

$$T\left(\frac{n}{4}\right) = 2T\left(\frac{n}{8}\right) + 5\frac{n}{4}$$

hence

$$T(n) = 2 \times 2 \times 2T\left(\frac{n}{8}\right) + 5n + 5n + 5n$$

This generalizes from 2, 4, 8, to the kth power of 2:

$$T(n) = 2^k T\left(\frac{n}{2^k}\right) + 5nk$$

Recall that we assume that $n = 2^m$; hence, for $k = m$,

$$T(n) = 2^m T\left(\frac{n}{2^m}\right) + 5nm$$

$$= nT(1) + 5nm$$

$$= n + 5n\log_2(n)$$

Because $n = 2^m$, you have $m = \log_2(n)$.

To establish the growth order, you drop the lower order term n and are left with $5n\log_2(n)$. Drop the constant factor 5. It is also customary to drop the base of the logarithm because all logarithms are related by a constant factor. For example,

$$\log_2(x) = \log_{10}(x) / \log_{10}(2) \approx \log_{10}(x) \times 3.32193$$

Hence we say that merge sort is an $O(n\log(n))$ algorithm.

Merge sort is an $O(n \log(n))$ algorithm. The $n \log(n)$ function grows much more slowly than n^2.

Is the $O(n \log(n))$ merge sort algorithm better than an $O(n^2)$ selection sort algorithm? You bet it is. Recall that it took $100^2 = 10{,}000$ times as long to sort one million records as it took to sort 10,000 records with the $O(n^2)$ algorithm. With the $O(n \log(n))$ algorithm, the ratio is

$$\frac{1{,}000{,}000 \log (1{,}000{,}000)}{10{,}000 \log (10{,}000)} = 100\left(\frac{6}{4}\right) = 150$$

Suppose for the moment that merge sort takes the same time as selection sort to sort a list of 10,000 integers, that is, about 9 seconds on the author's test machine. (Actually, it is much faster than that.) Then it would take about 9×150 seconds, or about 23 minutes, to sort a million integers. Contrast that with selection sort, which would take over a day for the same task. As you can see, even if it takes you several hours to learn about a better algorithm, that can be time well spent.

In this chapter we have barely begun to scratch the surface of this interesting topic. There are many sorting algorithms, some with even better performance than merge sort, and the analysis of these algorithms can be quite challenging. These important issues are often revisited in later computer science courses.

EXAMPLE CODE See sec05/mergetimer.py in your eText or companion code for a program that times the merge sort algorithm.

Special Topic 12.3

The Quicksort Algorithm

Quicksort is a commonly used algorithm that has the advantage over merge sort that no temporary lists are required to sort and merge the partial results.

The quicksort algorithm, like merge sort, is based on the strategy of divide and conquer. To sort a range values[start] . . . values[to] of the list values, first rearrange the elements in the range so that no element in the range values[start] . . . values[p] is larger than any element in the range values[p + 1] . . . values[to]. This step is called *partitioning* the range.

For example, suppose we start with a range

| 5 | 3 | 2 | 6 | 4 | 1 | 3 | 7 |

Here is a partitioning of the range. Note that the partitions aren't yet sorted.

| 3 | 3 | 2 | 1 | 4 | | 6 | 5 | 7 |

You'll see later how to obtain such a partition. In the next step, sort each partition, by recursively applying the same algorithm on the two partitions. That sorts the entire range, because

In quicksort, one partitions the elements into two groups, holding the smaller and larger elements. Then one sorts each group.

© Christopher Futcher/iStockphoto.

the largest element in the first partition is at most as large as the smallest element in the second partition.

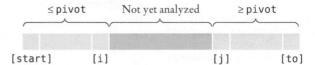

Quicksort is implemented recursively as follows:

```
def quickSort(values, start, to) :
   if start >= to : return
   p = partition(values, start, to)
   quickSort(values, start, p)
   quickSort(values, p + 1, to)
```

Let us return to the problem of partitioning a range. Pick an element from the range and call it the *pivot*. There are several variations of the quicksort algorithm. In the simplest one, we'll pick the first element of the range, values[start], as the pivot.

Now form two regions values[start] . . . values[i], consisting of values at most as large as the pivot and values[j] . . . values[to], consisting of values at least as large as the pivot. The region values[i + 1] . . . values[j - 1] consists of values that haven't been analyzed yet. At the beginning, both the left and right areas are empty; that is, i = start - 1 and j = to + 1.

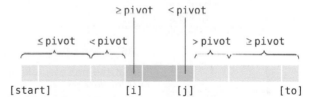

Partitioning a Range

Then keep incrementing i while values[i] < pivot and keep decrementing j while values[j] > pivot. The figure below shows i and j when that process stops.

Extending the Partitions

Now swap the values in positions i and j, increasing both areas once more. Keep going while i < j. Here is the code for the partition function:

```
def partition(values, start, to) :
   pivot = values[start]
   i = start - 1
   j = to + 1
   while i < j :
      i = i + 1
      while values[i] < pivot :
         i = i + 1
      j = j - 1
      while values[j] > pivot :
         j = j - 1
      if i < j :
         temp = values[i]    # Swap the two elements.
         values[i] = values[j]
         values[j] = temp
   return j
```

On average, the quicksort algorithm is an $O(n \log(n))$ algorithm. There is just one unfortunate aspect to the quicksort algorithm. Its *worst-case* run-time behavior is $O(n^2)$. Moreover, if the pivot element is chosen as the first element of the region, that worst-case behavior occurs when the input set is already sorted—a common situation in practice. By selecting the pivot element more cleverly, we can make it extremely unlikely for the worst-case behavior to occur. Such "tuned" quicksort algorithms are commonly used, because their performance is generally excellent.

Another improvement commonly made in practice is to switch to insertion sort when the list is short, because the total number of operations using insertion sort is lower for short lists.

EXAMPLE CODE   See special_topic_3/quickdemo.py in your eText or companion code for a program that demonstrates the quicksort algorithm.

Computing & Society 12.1   The First Programmer

Before pocket calculators and personal computers existed, navigators and engineers used mechanical adding machines, slide rules, and tables of logarithms and trigonometric functions to speed up computations. Unfortunately, the tables—for which values had to be computed by hand—were notoriously inaccurate. The mathematician Charles Babbage (1791–1871) had the insight that if a machine could be constructed that produced printed tables automatically, both calculation and typesetting errors could be avoided. Babbage set out to develop a machine for this purpose, which he called a *Difference*

Engine because it used successive differences to compute polynomials.

For example, consider the function $f(x) = x^3$. Write down the values for $f(1)$, $f(2)$, $f(3)$, and so on. Then take the *differences* between successive values:

```
1
    7
8
    19
27
    37
64
    61
125
    91
216
```

Repeat the process, taking the difference of successive values in the second column, and then repeat once again:

```
1
    7
8       12
    19      6
27      18
    37      6
64      24
    61      6
125     30
    91
216
```

Now the differences are all the same. You can retrieve the function values by a pattern of additions—you need to know the values at the fringe of the pattern and the constant difference. You can try it out yourself: Write the highlighted numbers on a sheet of paper and fill in the others by adding the numbers that are in the north and northwest positions.

This method was very attractive, because mechanical addition machines had been known for some time. They consisted of cog wheels, with 10 cogs per wheel, to represent digits, and mechanisms to handle the carry from one digit to the next. Mechanical multiplication machines, on the other hand, were fragile and unreliable. Babbage built a successful prototype of the Difference Engine and, with his own money and government grants, proceeded to build the table-printing machine. However, because of funding problems and the difficulty of building the machine to the required precision, it was never completed.

While working on the Difference Engine, Babbage conceived of a much grander vision that he called the *Analytical Engine*. The Difference Engine was designed to carry out a limited set of computations—it was no smarter than a pocket calculator is today. But Babbage realized that such a machine could be made *programmable* by storing programs as well as data. The internal storage of the Analytical Engine was to consist of 1,000 registers of 50 decimal digits each. Programs and constants were to be stored on punched cards—a technique that was, at that time, commonly used on looms for weaving patterned fabrics.

Ada Augusta, Countess of Lovelace (1815–1852), the only child of Lord Byron, was a friend and sponsor of Charles Babbage. Ada Lovelace was one of the first people to realize the potential of such a machine, not just for computing mathematical tables but for processing data that were not numbers. She is considered by many to be the world's first programmer.

Topham/The Image Works.

Replica of Babbage's Difference Engine

12.6 Searching

Searching for an element in a list is an extremely common task. As with sorting, the right choice of algorithms can make a big difference.

12.6.1 Linear Search

Suppose you need to find your friend's telephone number. You look up the friend's name in the telephone book, and naturally you can find it quickly, because the telephone book is sorted alphabetically. Now suppose you have a telephone number and you must know to what party it belongs. You could of course call that number, but suppose nobody picks up on the other end. You could look through the telephone book, a number at a time, until you find the number. That would obviously be a tremendous amount of work, and you would have to be desperate to attempt it.

This thought experiment shows the difference between a search through an unsorted data set and a search through a sorted data set. The following two sections will analyze the difference formally.

If you want to find a number in a sequence of values in arbitrary order, there is nothing you can do to speed up the search. You must simply look through all elements until you have found a match or until you reach the end. This is called a **linear** or **sequential search**. It's the algorithm used by Python's in operator when determining whether a given element is contained in a list.

How long does a linear search take? If we assume that the target element is present in the list values, then the average search visits $n/2$ elements, where n is the length of the list. If it is not present, then all n elements must be inspected to verify the absence. Either way, a linear search is an $O(n)$ algorithm.

Here is a function that performs linear searches through values, a list of integers. When searching for a target, the search function returns the first index of the match, or -1 if the target does not occur in values.

> A linear search examines all values in a list until it finds a match or reaches the end.

> A linear search locates a value in a list in $O(n)$ steps.

sec06_1/linearsearch.py

```
1  ##
2  #   This module implements a function for executing linear searches in a list.
3  #
4
5  ## Finds a value in a list, using the linear search algorithm.
6  #   @param values the list to search
7  #   @param target the value to find
8  #   @return the index at which the target occurs, or -1 if it does not
9  #   occur in the list
10 #
11 def linearSearch(values, target) :
12    for i in range(len(values)) :
13       if values[i] == target :
14          return i
15
16    return -1
```

sec06_1/lineardemo.py

```
1  ##
2  #   This program demonstrates the linear search algorithm.
```

```
3   #
4
5   from random import randint
6   from linearsearch import linearSearch
7
8   # Construct random list.
9   n = 20
10  values = []
11  for i in range(n) :
12      values.append(randint(1, 20))
13  print(values)
14
15  done = False
16  while not done :
17      target = int(input("Enter number to search for, -1 to quit: "))
18      if target == -1 :
19          done = True
20      else :
21          pos = linearSearch(values, target)
22          if pos == -1 :
23              print("Not found")
24          else :
25              print("Found in position", pos)
```

Program Run

```
[18, 5, 12, 4, 11, 12, 19, 1, 13, 14, 12, 18, 8, 10, 15, 20, 1, 6, 20, 3]
Enter number to search for, -1 to quit: 2
Not found
Enter number to search for, -1 to quit: 3
Found in position 19
Enter number to search for, -1 to quit: 5
Found in position 1
Enter number to search for, -1 to quit: 7
Not found
Enter number to search for, -1 to quit: 11
Found in position 4
Enter number to search for, -1 to quit: 13
Found in position 8
Enter number to search for, -1 to quit: 17
Not found
Enter number to search for, -1 to quit: 19
Found in position 6
Enter number to search for, -1 to quit: -1
```

12.6.2 Binary Search

Now let us search for a target in a data sequence that has been previously sorted. Of course, we could still do a linear search, but it turns out we can do much better than that. Consider the following sorted list values. The data set is:

[0] [1] [2] [3] [4] [5] [6] [7] [8] [9]

| 1 | 4 | 5 | 8 | 9 | 12 | 17 | 20 | 24 | 32 |

We would like to see whether the target 15 is in the data set. Let's narrow our search by finding whether the target is in the first or second half of the list. The last value in the first half of the data set, values[4], is 9, which is smaller than the target. Hence, we should look in the second half of the list for a match, that is, in the sequence:

```
[0] [1] [2] [3] [4] [5] [6] [7] [8] [9]
 1   4   5   8   9  12  17  20  24  32
```

The middle element of this sequence is 20; hence, the target must be located in the sequence:

```
[0] [1] [2] [3] [4] [5] [6] [7] [8] [9]
 1   4   5   8   9  12  17  20  24  32
```

The last value of the first half of this very short sequence is 12, which is smaller than the target, so we must look in the second half:

```
[0] [1] [2] [3] [4] [5] [6] [7] [8] [9]
 1   4   5   8   9  12  17  20  24  32
```

It is trivial to see that we don't have a match, because $15 \neq 17$. If we wanted to insert 15 into the sequence, we would need to insert it just before values[6].

A binary search locates a value in a sorted list by determining whether the value occurs in the first or second half, then repeating the search in one of the halves.

This search process is called a **binary search**, because we cut the size of the search in half in each step. That cutting in half works only because we know that the sequence of values is sorted.

The following function implements binary searches in a sorted list of integers. The binarySearch function returns the position of the match if the search succeeds, or –1 if the target is not found in values. Here, we show a recursive version of the binary search algorithm.

sec06_2/binarysearch.py

```
 1  ##
 2  #   This module implements a function for executing binary searches in a list.
 3  #
 4
 5  ## Finds a value in a range of a sorted list, using the binary search algorithm.
 6  #   @param values  the list in which to search
 7  #   @param low the low index of the range
 8  #   @param high the high index of the range
 9  #   @param target the value to find
10  #   @return the index at which the target occurs, or -1 if it does not
11  #   occur in the list
12  #
13  def binarySearch(values, low, high, target) :
14     if low <= high :
15        mid = (low + high) // 2
16
17        if values[mid] == target :
18           return mid
19        elif values[mid] < target :
20           return binarySearch(values, mid + 1, high, target)
21        else :
22           return binarySearch(values, low, mid - 1, target)
23
24     else :
25        return -1
```

EXAMPLE CODE   See sec06_2/binarydemo.py in your eText or companion code to run a binary search.

Now determine the number of visits to list elements required to carry out a binary search. Use the same technique as in the analysis of merge sort. Because you look at the middle element, which counts as one comparison, and then search either the left or the right sublist, you have

$$T(n) = T\left(\frac{n}{2}\right) + 1$$

Using the same equation,

$$T\left(\frac{n}{2}\right) = T\left(\frac{n}{4}\right) + 1$$

By plugging this result into the original equation, you get

$$T(n) = T\left(\frac{n}{4}\right) + 2$$

This generalizes to the kth power of 2:

$$T(n) = T\left(\frac{n}{2^k}\right) + k$$

As in the analysis of merge sort, you make the simplifying assumption that n is a power of 2, $n = 2^m$, where $m = \log_2(n)$. Then you obtain

$$T(n) = T(1) + \log_2(n)$$

Therefore, binary search is an $O(\log(n))$ algorithm.

That result makes intuitive sense. Suppose that n is 100. Then after each search, the size of the search range is cut in half, to 50, 25, 12, 6, 3, and 1. After seven comparisons we are done. This agrees with our formula, because $\log_2(100) \approx 6.64386$, and indeed the next larger power of 2 is $2^7 = 128$.

Because a binary search is so much faster than a linear search, is it worthwhile to sort a list first and then use a binary search? It depends. If you search the list only once, then it is more efficient to pay for an $O(n)$ linear search than for an $O(n \log(n))$ sort and an $O(\log(n))$ binary search. But if you will be making many searches in the same list, then sorting it is definitely worthwhile.

> A binary search locates a value in a sorted list in $O(\log(n))$ steps.

12.7 Problem Solving: Estimating the Running Time of an Algorithm

In this chapter, you have learned how to estimate the running time of sorting algorithms. As you have seen, being able to differentiate between $O(n \log(n))$ and $O(n^2)$ running times has great practical implications. Being able to estimate the running times of other algorithms is an important skill. In this section, we will practice estimating the running time of list algorithms.

12.7.1 Linear Time

Let us start with a simple example, an algorithm that counts how many elements have a particular value:

```
count = 0
for i in range(len(values)) :
   if values[i] == searchedValue :
      count = count + 1
```

What is the running time in terms of n, the length of the list?

Start with looking at the pattern of list element visits. Here, we visit each element once. It helps to visualize this pattern. Imagine the list as a sequence of light bulbs. As the ith element gets visited, imagine the ith bulb lighting up.

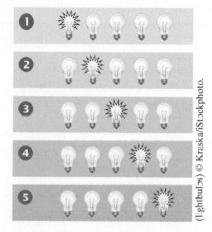

(lightbulbs) © Kraska/iStockphoto.

Now look at the work per visit. Does each visit involve a fixed number of actions, independent of n? In this case, it does. There are just a few actions—read the element, compare it, maybe increment a counter.

Therefore, the running time is n times a constant, or $O(n)$.

What if we don't always run to the end of the list? For example, suppose we want to check whether the value occurs in the list, without counting it:

A loop with n iterations has $O(n)$ running time if each step consists of a fixed number of actions.

```
found = False
i = 0
while not found and i < len(values) :
   if values[i] == searchedValue :
      found = True
   else :
      i = i + 1
```

Then the loop can stop in the middle:

Found the value

Is this still $O(n)$? It is, because in some cases the match may be at the very end of the list. Also, if there is no match, one must traverse the entire list.

12.7.2 Quadratic Time

Now let's turn to a more interesting case. What if we do a lot of work with each visit? Here is an example. We want to find the most frequent element in a list.

Suppose the list is

8	7	5	7	7	5	4

It's obvious by looking at the values that 7 is the most frequent one. But now imagine a list with a few thousand values.

8	7	5	7	7	5	4	1	2	3	3	4	9	12	3	2	5	$\cdots$	11	9	2	3	7	8

We can count how often the value 8 occurs, then move on to count how often 7 occurs, and so on. For example, in the first list, 8 occurs once, and 7 occurs three times. Where do we put the counts? Let's put them into a second list of the same length.

values: | 8 | 7 | 5 | 7 | 7 | 5 | 4 |

counts: | 1 | 3 | 2 | 3 | 3 | 2 | 1 |

Then we take the maximum of the counts. It is 3. We look up where the 3 occurs in the counts, and find the corresponding value. Thus, the most common value is 7.

Let us first estimate how long it takes to compute the counts.

```
for i in range(len(values)) :
    counts[i] = Count how often values[i] occurs in values
```

A loop with n iterations has $O(n^2)$ running time if each step takes $O(n)$ time.

We still visit each list element once, but now the work per visit is much larger. As you have seen in the previous section, each counting action is $O(n)$. When we do $O(n)$ work in each step, the total running time is $O(n^2)$.

This algorithm has three phases:

1. Compute all counts.
2. Compute the maximum.
3. Find the maximum in the counts.

We have just seen that the first phase is $O(n^2)$. Computing the maximum is $O(n)$—look at the algorithm in Section 6.3.4 and note that each step involves a fixed amount of work. Finally, we just saw that finding a value is $O(n)$.

The big-Oh running time for doing several steps in a row is the largest of the big-Oh times for each step.

How can we estimate the total running time from the estimates of each phase? Of course, the total time is the sum of the individual times, but for big-Oh estimates, we take the *maximum* of the estimates. To see why, imagine that we had actual equations for each of the times:

$$T_1(n) = an^2 + bn + c$$

$$T_2(n) = dn + e$$

$$T_3(n) = fn + g$$

Then the sum is

$$T(n) = T_1(n) + T_2(n) + T_3(n) = an^2 + (b + d + f)n + c + e + g$$

But only the largest term matters, so $T(n)$ is $O(n^2)$.

Thus, we find that our algorithm for finding the most frequent element is $O(n^2)$.

12.7.3 The Triangle Pattern

Let us see if we can speed up the algorithm from the preceding section. It seems wasteful to count elements again if we have already counted them. Can we save time by eliminating repeated counting of the same element? That is, before counting `values[i]`, should we first check that it didn't occur in `values[0] ... values[i - 1]`?

Let us estimate the cost of these additional checks. In the ith step, the amount of work is proportional to i. That's not quite the same as in the preceding section, where you saw that a loop with n iterations, each of which takes $O(n)$ time, is $O(n^2)$. Now each step just takes $O(i)$ time.

To get an intuitive feel for this situation, look at the light bulbs again. In the second iteration, we visit `values[0]` again. In the third iteration, we visit `values[0]` and `values[1]` again, and so on. The light bulb pattern is

If there are n light bulbs, about half of the square above, or $n^2/2$ of them, light up. That's unfortunately still $O(n^2)$.

Here is another idea for time saving. When we count `values[i]`, there is no need to do the counting in `values[0] ... values[i - 1]`. If `values[i]` never occurred before, we get an accurate count by just looking at `values[i] ... values[n - 1]`. And if it did, we already have an accurate count. Does that help us? Not really—it's the triangle pattern again, but this time in the other direction.

That doesn't mean that these improvements aren't worthwhile. If an $O(n^2)$ algorithm is the best one can do for a particular problem, you still want to make it as fast as possible. However, we will not pursue this plan further because it turns out that we can do much better.

A loop with n iterations has $O(n^2)$ running time if the ith step takes $O(i)$ time.

12.7.4 Logarithmic Time

Logarithmic time estimates arise from algorithms that cut work in half in each step. You have seen this in the algorithms for binary search and merge sort.

In particular, when you use sorting or binary search in a phase of an algorithm, you will encounter logarithms in the big-Oh estimates.

Consider this idea for improving our algorithm for finding the most frequent element. Suppose we first *sort* the list:

$$8 \quad 7 \quad 5 \quad 7 \quad 7 \quad 5 \quad 4 \quad \longrightarrow \quad 4 \quad 5 \quad 5 \quad 7 \quad 7 \quad 7 \quad 8$$

That cost us $O(n \log(n))$ time. If we can complete the algorithm in $O(n)$ time or even in $O(n \log(n))$ time, we will have found a better algorithm than the $O(n^2)$ algorithm of the preceding sections.

To see why this is possible, imagine traversing the sorted list. As long as you find a value that is equal to its predecessor, you increment a counter. When you find a different value, save the counter and start counting anew:

values:	4	5	5	7	7	7	8
counts:	1	1	2	1	2	3	1

Or in code,

```
count = 0
for i in range(len(values)) :
   count = count + 1
   if i == len(values) - 1 or values[i] != values[i + 1] :
      counts[i] = count
      count = 0
```

That's a constant amount of work per iteration, even though it visits two elements:

$2n$ is still $O(n)$. Thus, we can compute the counts in $O(n)$ time from a sorted list. The entire algorithm is now $O(n \log(n))$.

Note that we don't actually need to keep all counts, only the highest one that we encountered so far (see Exercise •• P12.7). That is a worthwhile improvement, but it does not change the big-Oh estimate of the running time.

An algorithm that cuts the size of work in half in each step runs in $O(\log(n))$ time.

Programming Tip 12.1
Searching and Sorting

When you write Python programs, you don't have to implement your own sorting algorithms. The list class provides a sort method that can be used to sort the elements in a list.

```
values = [ . . . ]
values.sort()
```

In earlier versions of Python, the sort method used the quicksort algorithm. In the current version, sort uses a hybrid algorithm that combines the insertion and merge sort algorithms.

You can also search a list using the in operator. Because the operator can be used on both sorted and unsorted lists, it uses the linear search algorithm to determine if an element is in the list. To perform a binary search on a sorted list, you must provide your own implementation of the algorithm and use it instead of the in operator.

Special Topic 12.4
Comparing Objects

In application programs, you often need to sort or search through collections of objects. The sort method defined for the list class can sort any type of data, including objects from user-defined classes. That method, however, cannot know how to compare arbitrary objects. Suppose, for example, that you have a list of Country objects. It is not obvious how the countries should be sorted. Should they be sorted by their names or by their areas? The sort method cannot make that decision for you. Instead, it requires that the objects be comparable using the < operator.

You can define the < operator for your own classes (see Section 9.11). For example, to sort a collection of countries, the Country class would need to implement the __lt__ method:

```
class Country :
    . . .
    def __lt__(self, otherCountry) :
        return self._area < otherCountry._area
```

This method determines if the area of the self country is less than the area of the otherCountry. As the list is being sorted, this method is called each time two objects need to be compared to determine which precedes the other. Now you can use the sort method to sort a list containing Country objects.

WORKED EXAMPLE 12.1
Enhancing the Insertion Sort Algorithm

Problem Statement   Implement an algorithm, called *Shell sort* after its inventor, Donald Shell, that improves on the insertion sort algorithm of Special Topic 12.2.

Shell sort is an enhancement that takes advantage of the fact that insertion sort is an $O(n)$ algorithm if the list is already sorted. Shell sort brings parts of the list into sorted order, and then runs an insertion sort over the entire list, so that the final sort doesn't do much work.

A key step in Shell sort is to arrange the sequence into rows and columns, and then to sort each column separately. For example, if the list is

65 46 14 52 38 2 96 39 14 33 13 4 24 99 89 77 73 87 36 81

and we arrange it into four columns, we get

$$
\begin{array}{cccc}
65 & 46 & 14 & 52 \\
38 & 2 & 96 & 39 \\
14 & 33 & 13 & 4 \\
24 & 99 & 89 & 77 \\
73 & 87 & 36 & 81
\end{array}
$$

Now we sort each column:

$$
\begin{array}{cccc}
14 & 2 & 13 & 5 \\
24 & 33 & 14 & 39 \\
38 & 46 & 36 & 52 \\
65 & 87 & 89 & 77 \\
73 & 99 & 96 & 81
\end{array}
$$

Put together as a single list, we get

14 2 13 5 24 33 14 39 38 46 36 52 65 87 89 77 73 99 96 81

Note that the list isn't completely sorted, but many of the small numbers are now in front, and many of the large numbers are in the back.

We will repeat the process until the list is sorted. Each time, we use a different number of columns. Shell had originally used powers of two for the column counts. For example, on a list with 20 elements, he proposed using 16, 8, 4, 2, and finally one column. With one column, we have a plain insertion sort, so we know the list will be sorted. What is surprising is that the preceding sorts greatly speed up the process.

However, better sequences have been discovered. We will use the sequence of column counts

$$
\begin{aligned}
c_1 &= 1 \\
c_2 &= 4 \\
c_3 &= 13 \\
c_4 &= 40 \\
&\cdots \\
c_{i+1} &= 3c_i + 1
\end{aligned}
$$

That is, for a list with 20 elements, we first do a 13-sort, then a 4-sort, and then a 1-sort. This sequence is almost as good as the best known ones, and it is easy to compute.

We will not actually rearrange the list, but compute the locations of the elements of each column. For example, if the number of columns c is 4, the four columns are located in the list as follows:

65				38				14				24				73			
	46				2				33				99				87		
		14				96				13				89				36	
			52				39				4				77				81

Note that successive column elements have distance c from another. The kth column is made up of the elements values[k], values[k + c], values[k + 2 * c], and so on.

Now let's adapt the insertion sort algorithm to sort such a column. The original algorithm, with the outer loop rewritten as a while loop, is:

```
i = 1
while i < len(values) :
    nextValue = values[i]
```

```
# Move all larger elements up.
j = i
while j > 0 and values[j - 1] > nextValue :
   values[j] = values[j - 1]
   j = j - 1

# Insert the element.
values[j] = nextValue
i = i + 1
```

The outer loop visits the elements values[1], values[2], and so on. In the kth column, the corresponding sequence is values[k + c], values[k + 2 * c], and so on. That is, the outer loop becomes

```
i = k + c
while i < len(values) :
   . . .
   i = i + c
```

In the inner loop, we originally visited values[j], values[j - 1], and so on. We need to change that to values[j], values[j - c], and so on. The inner loop becomes

```
while j >= c and values[j - c] > nextValue :
   values[j] = values[j - c]
   j = j - c
```

Putting everything together, we get the following function:

```
## Sorts a column, using insertion sort.
#  @param values the list to sort
#  @param k the index of the first element in the column
#  @param c the gap between elements in the column
#
def insertionSort(values, k, c) :
   i = k + c
   while i < len(values) :
      nextValue = values[i]
      # Move all larger elements up.
      j = i
      while j >= c and values[j - c] > nextValue :
         values[j] = values[j - c]
         j = j - c

      # Insert the element.
      values[j] = nextValue
      i = i + c
```

Now we are ready to implement the Shell sort algorithm. First, we need to find out how many elements we need from the sequence of column counts. We generate the sequence values until they exceed the size of the list to be sorted:

```
columns = []
c = 1
while c < len(values) :
   columns.append(c)
   c = 3 * c + 1
```

For each column count, we sort all columns:

```
s = len(columns) - 1
while s >= 0 :
   c = columns[s]
   for k in range(c) :
      insertionSort(values, k, c)
   s = s - 1
```

How good is the performance? Let's compare with quicksort and insertion sort:

```
firstSize = int(input("Enter first list size: "))
numberOfLists = int(input("Enter number of lists: "))

for k in range(1, numberOfLists + 1) :
   size = firstSize * k
   values = []
   # Construct random list.
   for i in range(size) :
      values.append(randint(1, 100))
   values2 = list(values)
   values3 = list(values)

   startTime = time()
   shellSort(values)
   endTime = time()
   shellTime = endTime -startTime

   startTime = time()
   quickSort(values2, 0, size - 1)
   endTime = time()
   quickTime = endTime -startTime

   for i in range(size) :
      if values[i] != values2[i] :
         raise RuntimeError("Incorrect sort result.")

   startTime = time()
   insertionSort(values3)
   endTime = time()
   insertionTime = endTime -startTime

   print("Size: %d Shell sort: %.3f Quicksort: %.3f Insertion sort: %.3f seconds"
      % (size, shellTime, quickTime, insertionTime))
```

We make sure to sort the same list with all three algorithms. Also, we check that the result of the Shell sort is correct by comparing it against the result of the quicksort algorithm.

Finally, we compare with the insertion sort algorithm.

The results show that Shell sort is a dramatic improvement over insertion sort:

```
Enter first list size: 1000
Enter number of lists: 6
Size: 1000 Shell sort: 0.004 Quicksort: 0.002 Insertion sort: 0.049 seconds
Size: 2000 Shell sort: 0.007 Quicksort: 0.004 Insertion sort: 0.198 seconds
Size: 3000 Shell sort: 0.011 Quicksort: 0.007 Insertion sort: 0.456 seconds
Size: 4000 Shell sort: 0.015 Quicksort: 0.009 Insertion sort: 1.067 seconds
Size: 5000 Shell sort: 0.021 Quicksort: 0.012 Insertion sort: 1.313 seconds
Size: 6000 Shell sort: 0.023 Quicksort: 0.015 Insertion sort: 1.873 seconds
```

However, quicksort outperforms Shell sort. For this reason, Shell sort is not used in practice, but it is still an interesting algorithm that is surprisingly effective.

You may also find it interesting to experiment with Shell's original column sizes. In the shellSort function, simply replace $c = 3 * c + 1$ with $c = 2 * c$. You will find that the algorithm is about three times slower than the improved sequence. That is still much faster than plain insertion sort.

EXAMPLE CODE   In your companion code, you will find worked_example_1/shelltimer.py that compares Shell sort to quicksort and insertion sort.

CHAPTER SUMMARY

Describe the selection sort algorithm.

- The selection sort algorithm sorts a list by repeatedly finding the smallest element of the unsorted tail region and moving it to the front.

Measure the running time of a function.

- To measure the running time of a function, get the current time immediately before and after the function call.

Use big-Oh notation to describe the running time of an algorithm.

- Computer scientists use big-Oh notation to describe the growth rate of a function.
- Selection sort is an $O(n^2)$ algorithm. Doubling the data set means a fourfold increase in processing time.
- Insertion sort is an $O(n^2)$ algorithm.

Describe the merge sort algorithm.

- The merge sort algorithm sorts a list by cutting the list in half, recursively sorting each half, and then merging the sorted halves.

Contrast the running times of the merge sort and selection sort algorithms.

- Merge sort is an $O(n \log(n))$ algorithm. The $n \log(n)$ function grows much more slowly than n^2.

Describe the running times of the linear search algorithm and the binary search algorithm.

- A linear search examines all values in a list until it finds a match or reaches the end.
- A linear search locates a value in a list in $O(n)$ steps.
- A binary search locates a value in a sorted list by determining whether the value occurs in the first or second half, then repeating the search in one of the halves.
- A binary search locates a value in a sorted list in $O(\log(n))$ steps.

Practice developing big-Oh estimates of algorithms.

- A loop with n iterations has $O(n)$ running time if each step consists of a fixed number of actions.
- A loop with n iterations has $O(n^2)$ running time if each step takes $O(n)$ time.
- The big-Oh running time for doing several steps in a row is the largest of the big-Oh times for each step.
- A loop with n iterations has $O(n^2)$ running time if the ith step takes $O(i)$ time.
- An algorithm that cuts the size of work in half in each step runs in $O(\log(n))$ time.

REVIEW EXERCISES

- **R12.1** What is the difference between searching and sorting?

- **R12.2** *Checking against off-by-one errors.* When programming the selection sort algorithm of Section 12.1, a programmer must make the usual choices of < versus <=, len(values) versus len(values) - 1, and from versus from + 1. This is fertile ground for off-by-one errors. Conduct code walkthroughs of the algorithm with lists of length 0, 1, 2, and 3 and check carefully that all index values are correct.

- **R12.3** For the following expressions, what is the order of the growth of each?
  - **a.** $n^2 + 2n + 1$
  - **b.** $n^{10} + 9n^9 + 20n^8 + 145n^7$
  - **c.** $(n + 1)^4$
  - **d.** $(n^2 + n)^2$
  - **e.** $n + 0.001n^3$
  - **f.** $n^3 - 1000n^2 + 10^9$
  - **g.** $n + \log(n)$
  - **h.** $n^2 + n \log(n)$
  - **i.** $2^n + n^2$
  - **j.** $\dfrac{n^3 + 2n}{n^2 + 0.75}$

- **R12.4** We determined that the actual number of visits in the selection sort algorithm is
  $$T(n) = \tfrac{1}{2}n^2 + \tfrac{5}{2}n - 3$$

  We then characterized this function as having $O(n^2)$ growth. Compute the actual ratios

  $$T(2{,}000)/T(1{,}000)$$
  $$T(5{,}000)/T(1{,}000)$$
  $$T(10{,}000)/T(1{,}000)$$

  and compare them with

  $$f(2{,}000)/f(1{,}000)$$
  $$f(5{,}000)/f(1{,}000)$$
  $$f(10{,}000)/f(1{,}000)$$

  where $f(n) = n^2$.

- **R12.5** Sort the following growth rates from slowest to fastest growth.

$O(n)$	$O(\log(n))$	$O(2^n)$	$O(n\sqrt{n})$
$O(n^3)$	$O(n^2 \log(n))$	$O(\sqrt{n})$	$O(n^{\log(n)})$
$O(n^n)$	$O(n \log(n))$		

■ **R12.6** Suppose algorithm *A* takes five seconds to handle a data set of 1,000 records. If the algorithm *A* is an $O(n)$ algorithm, approximately how long will it take to handle a data set of 2,000 records? Of 10,000 records?

■■ **R12.7** Suppose an algorithm takes five seconds to handle a data set of 1,000 records. Fill in the following table, which shows the approximate growth of the execution times depending on the complexity of the algorithm.

	$O(n)$	$O(n^2)$	$O(n^3)$	$O(n \log(n))$	$O(2^n)$
1,000	5	5	5	5	5
2,000					
3,000		45			
10,000					

For example, because $3000^2/1000^2 = 9$, the $O(n^2)$ algorithm would take 9 times as long, or 45 seconds, to handle a data set of 3,000 records.

■ **R12.8** What is the growth rate of the standard algorithm to find the minimum value of a list? Of finding both the minimum and the maximum?

■ **R12.9** What is the big-Oh time estimate of the following function in terms of *n*, the length of values? Use the "light bulb pattern" method of Section 12.7 to visualize your result.

```
def swap(values) :
    i = 0
    j = len(values) - 1
    while i < j :
        temp = values[i]
        values[i] = j[i]
        j[i] = temp
        i = i + 1
        j = j - 1
```

■ **R12.10** Trace a walkthrough of selection sort with these lists:

a. 4 7 11 4 9 5 11 7 3 5

b. –7 6 8 7 5 9 0 11 10 5 8

■ **R12.11** Trace a walkthrough of merge sort with these lists:

a. 5 11 7 3 5 4 7 11 4 9

b. 9 0 11 10 5 8 –7 6 8 7 5

■ **R12.12** Trace a walkthrough of:

a. Linear search for 7 in   –7 1 3 3 4 7 11 13

b. Binary search for 8 in   –7 2 2 3 4 7 8 11 13

c. Binary search for 8 in   –7 1 2 3 5 7 10 13

■■ **R12.13** Your task is to remove all duplicates from a list. For example, if the list has the values

4 7 11 4 9 5 11 7 3 5

then the list should be changed to

4 7 11 9 5 3

Here is a simple algorithm. Look at values[i]. Count how many times it occurs in values. If the count is larger than 1, remove it. What is the growth rate of the time required for this algorithm?

■■■ **R12.14** Modify the merge sort algorithm to remove duplicates in the merging step to obtain an algorithm that removes duplicates from a list. Note that the resulting list does not have the same ordering as the original one. What is the efficiency of this algorithm?

■■ **R12.15** Consider the following algorithm to remove all duplicates from a list. Sort the list. For each element in the list, look at its next neighbor to decide whether it is present more than once. If so, remove it. Is this a faster algorithm than the one in Exercise ●● R12.13?

■■■ **R12.16** Develop an $O(n \log(n))$ algorithm for removing duplicates from a list if the resulting list must have the same ordering as the original list. When a value occurs multiple times, all but its first occurrence should be removed.

■■■ **R12.17** Why does insertion sort perform significantly better than selection sort if a list is already sorted?

■■■ **R12.18** Consider the following speedup of the insertion sort algorithm of Special Topic 12.2. For each element, use the enhanced binary search algorithm described in Exercise ●● P12.15 that yields the insertion position for missing elements. Does this speedup have a significant impact on the efficiency of the algorithm?

■■ **R12.19** Consider the following algorithm known as *bubble sort*:

> While the list is not sorted
>   For each adjacent pair of elements
>   If the pair is not sorted
>   Swap its elements.

What is the big-Oh efficiency of this algorithm?

■■ **R12.20** The *radix sort* algorithm sorts a list of n integers with d digits, using ten auxiliary lists. First place each value v into the auxiliary list whose index corresponds to the last digit of v. Then move all values back into the original list, preserving their order. Repeat the process, now using the next-to-last (tens) digit, then the hundreds digit, and so on. What is the big-Oh time of this algorithm in terms of n and d? When is this algorithm preferable to merge sort?

■■ **R12.21** A *stable sort* does not change the order of elements with the same value. This is a desirable feature in many applications. Consider a sequence of e-mail messages. If you sort by date and then by sender, you'd like the second sort to preserve the relative order of the first, so that you can see all messages from the same sender in date order. Is selection sort stable? Insertion sort? Why or why not?

■■ **R12.22** Give an $O(n)$ algorithm to sort a list of n bytes (numbers between –128 and 127). *Hint:* Use a list of counters.

■■ **R12.23** You are given a sequence of lists of words, representing the pages of a book. Your task is to build an index (a sorted list of words), each element of which has a list of sorted numbers representing the pages on which the word appears. Describe an algorithm for building the index and give its big-Oh running time in terms of the total number of words.

■■ **R12.24** Given two lists of n integers each, describe an $O(n \log(n))$ algorithm for determining whether they have an element in common.

■■■ **R12.25** Given a list of n integers and a value v, describe an $O(n \log(n))$ algorithm to find whether there are two values x and y in the list with sum v.

■■ **R12.26** Given two lists of n integers each, describe an $O(n \log(n))$ algorithm for finding all elements that they have in common.

■■ **R12.27** Suppose we modify the quicksort algorithm from Special Topic 12.3, selecting the middle element instead of the first one as pivot. What is the running time on a list that is already sorted?

■■ **R12.28** Suppose we modify the quicksort algorithm from Special Topic 12.3, selecting the middle element instead of the first one as pivot. Find a sequence of values for which this algorithm has an $O(n^2)$ running time.

PROGRAMMING EXERCISES

■ **P12.1** Modify the selection sort algorithm to sort a list of integers in descending order.

■■ **P12.2** Write a program that automatically generates the table of sample run times for the selection sort algorithm. The program should ask for the smallest and largest value of n and the number of measurements and then make all sample runs.

■ **P12.3** Modify the merge sort algorithm to sort a list in descending order.

■ **P12.4** Write a telephone lookup program. Read a data set of 1,000 names and telephone numbers from a file that contains the numbers in random order. Handle lookups by name and reverse lookups by phone number. Use a binary search for both lookups.

■■ **P12.5** Implement a program that measures the performance of the insertion sort algorithm described in Special Topic 12.2.

■ **P12.6** Implement the bubble sort algorithm described in Exercise •• R12.19.

■■ **P12.7** Implement the algorithm described in Section 12.7.4, but only remember the value with the highest frequency so far:

```
mostFrequent = 0
highestFrequency = -1
n = len(values)
for i in range(n) :
    Count how often values[i] occurs in values[i + 1] ... values[n - 1]
    If it occurs more often than highestFrequency :
        highestFrequency = that count
        mostFrequent = values[i]
```

■■ **P12.8** Implement the following modification of the quicksort algorithm, due to Bentley and McIlroy. Instead of using the first element as the pivot, use an approximation of the median. (Partitioning at the actual median would yield an $O(n \log(n))$ algorithm, but we don't know how to compute it quickly enough.)

If $n \leq 7$, use the middle element. If $n \leq 40$, use the median of the first, middle, and last element. Otherwise compute the "pseudomedian" of the nine elements values[i * (n - 1) // 8], where i ranges from 0 to 8. The pseudomedian of nine values is med(med(v_0, v_1, v_2), med(v_3, v_4, v_5), med(v_6, v_7, v_8)).

Compare the running time of this modification with that of the original algorithm on sequences that are nearly sorted or reverse sorted, and on sequences with many identical elements. What do you observe?

■■■ **P12.9** Bentley and McIlroy suggest the following modification to the quicksort algorithm when dealing with data sets that contain many repeated elements.

Instead of partitioning as

(where ≤ denotes the elements that are ≤ the pivot), it is better to partition as

However, that is tedious to achieve directly. They recommend to partition as

and then swap the two = regions into the middle. Implement this modification and check whether it improves performance on data sets with many repeated elements.

■ **P12.10** Implement the radix sort algorithm described in Exercise ●● R12.20 to sort lists of numbers between 0 and 999.

■ **P12.11** Implement the radix sort algorithm described in Exercise ●● R12.20 to sort lists of numbers between 0 and 999. However, use a single auxiliary list, not ten.

■■ **P12.12** Implement the radix sort algorithm described in Exercise ●● R12.20 to sort arbitrary int values (positive or negative).

■■■ **P12.13** Write a program that sorts a list of Country objects in decreasing order so that the most populous country is at the beginning of the list.

■ **P12.14** Implement the binarySearch function from Section 12.6.2 without recursion.

■■ **P12.15** Consider the binary search algorithm from Section 12.6.2. If no match is found, the binarySearch function returns −1. Modify the function so that if target is not found, the function returns $-k - 1$, where k is the position before which the element should be inserted.

■■ **P12.16** Implement the merge sort algorithm without recursion, where the length of the list is a power of 2. First merge adjacent regions of size 1, then adjacent regions of size 2, then adjacent regions of size 4, and so on.

■■■ **P12.17** Implement the merge sort algorithm without recursion, where the length of the list is an arbitrary number. Keep merging adjacent regions whose size is a power of 2, and pay special attention to the last area whose size is less.

■■■ **P12.18** Use insertion sort and the binary search function from Exercise ●● P12.15 to sort a list as described in Exercise ●●● R12.18. Implement this algorithm and measure its performance.

■ **P12.19** Supply a class Person that implements the comparison operators. Compare persons by their names. Ask the user to input ten names and generate ten Person objects. Determine the first and last person among them and print them.

■■ **P12.20** Sort a list of strings by increasing *length*.

■■■ **P12.21** Sort a list of strings by increasing length, and so that strings of the same length are sorted lexicographically.

PYTHON OPERATOR SUMMARY

The Python operators are listed in groups of decreasing precedence in the table below. The horizontal lines in the table indicate a change in operator precedence. Operators with higher precedence bind more strongly than those with lower precedence. For example, x + y * z means x + (y * z) because the * operator has higher precedence than the + operator. Looking at the table below, you can tell that x and y or z means (x and y) or z because the or operator has lower precedence.

The *associativity* of an operator indicates whether it groups left to right, or right to left. All operators in Python have left to right associativity except exponentiation, which has right to left associativity. For example, the - operator binds left to right. Therefore, x - y - z means (x - y) - z. But the ** operator binds right to left, and x ** y ** z means x ** (y ** z).

Operator	Description	Reference Location
[]	Index	Section 2.4.4, Section 6.1.2
[:]	Slice operator	Special Topic 6.3
()	Function call or method call	Section 2.2.4
.	Method or instance variable access	Section 2.4.5, Section 9.2
**	Exponentiation	Section 2.2.2
+ *(unary)*	Positive	Section 2.2.1
– *(unary)*	Negative	Section 2.2.1
~ *(unary)*	Bitwise *not*	Appendix E
*	Multiplication	Section 2.2.1
/	Real division	Section 2.2.1
//	Floor division	Section 2.2.3
%	Integer remainder	Section 2.2.3
*	Sequence replication	Section 2.4.2
+	Addition	Section 2.2.1
+	Sequence concatenation	Section 2.4.2
-	Subtraction	Section 2.2.1

Operator	Description	Reference Location
<<	Bitwise shift left	Appendix E
>>	Bitwise shift right	Appendix E
&	Bitwise *and*	Appendix E
^	Bitwise exclusive *or*	Appendix E
|	Bitwise *or*	Appendix E
in	Membership test: in container	Section 3.8, Section 6.3.5
not in	Membership test: not in container	Section 3.8, Section 6.3.5
is	Identity test: is an alias	Section 9.10.1
is not	Identity test: is not an alias	Section 9.10.1
<	Less than	Section 3.2
<=	Less than or equal	Section 3.2
>	Greater than	Section 3.2
>=	Greater than or equal	Section 3.2
!=	Not equal	Section 3.2
==	Equal	Section 3.2
not	Boolean *not*	Section 3.7
and	Boolean "short circuit" *and*	Section 3.7
or	Boolean "short circuit" *or*	Section 3.7
if - else	Conditional expression	Special Topic 3.1
lambda	Anonymous function	Not covered

PYTHON RESERVED
WORD SUMMARY

Reserved Word	Description	Reference Location
and	Boolean *and*	Section 3.7
as	Used as part of an try or with clause to specify an alternate name for an object	Section 7.5
assert	An assertion that a condition is fulfilled	Not covered
break	Breaks out of the current loop	Special Topic 4.2
class	Defines a class	Section 9.2
continue	Skips the remainder of a loop body	Not covered
def	Defines a function or method	Section 5.2, Section 9.2
del	Removes an element from a container	Not covered
elif	An alternative conditional branch statement	Section 3.4
else	The alternative clause in an if statement	Section 3.1
except	The handler for an exception in a try block	Section 7.5
finally	A clause of a try block that is always executed	Section 7.5
for	A loop for iterating over the elements of a container	Section 4.6
False	The false Boolean value	Section 3.7
from	Used with the import statement to include items from a module	Section 2.2
global	Declares a variable to have global scope	Section 5.8
if	A conditional branch statement	Section 3.1
import	Includes within a module the individual items or the full contents of another module	Section 2.2 Special Topic 2.1
in	Container membership test	Section 3.8
is	Test whether a variable is an alias	Section 9.10
lambda	Used to create an anonymous function	Not covered

Reserved Word	Description	Reference Location
None	A special value indicating a non-existent reference	Section 9.10
not	Boolean *not*	Section 3.7
or	Boolean *or*	Section 3.7
pass	A place holder when a statement is required	Not covered
raise	Raises an exception	Section 7.5
return	Returns from a method	Section 5.4
True	The true Boolean value	Section 3.7
try	A block of code with exception handlers or a finally handler	Section 7.5
with	A block of code that is executed within a specific context	Special Topic 7.4
while	A loop statement	Section 4.1
yield	Returns the result of a generator function	Not covered

THE PYTHON STANDARD LIBRARY

This appendix provides a brief description of all functions and classes from the standard Python library and the custom graphics module that are used in this book.

Built-in Functions

- **abs**(x)

  This function computes the absolute value $|x|$.

  Parameters: x A numerical value

  Returns: The absolute value of the argument

- **bytes**()
- **bytes**(x)

  This function creates a new bytes sequence. If no argument is given, an empty bytes sequence is created. With an integer argument, it creates a bytes sequence with the given number of zero bytes. If a sequence argument is provided, a bytes sequence is created that contains the elements of that sequence.

  Parameters: x An integer or a sequence

  Returns: The new bytes sequence

- **chr**(x)

  This function creates a string containing a single character whose Unicode value is x.

  Parameters: x An integer value

  Returns: A string containing the character with Unicode value x

- **dict**()
- **dict**(*container*)

  This function creates a new dictionary. If no argument is given, it creates an empty dictionary. If *container* is a dictionary, a duplicate copy of that dictionary is created. Otherwise, if *container* is a sequence of immutable objects, the elements of the container become keys of the new dictionary.

  Parameters: *container*   A sequence or dictionary from which the new dictionary is created

  Returns: The new dictionary

- **float**(x)

  This function converts a string or an integer to a floating-point value.

  Parameters: x A string or numerical value

  Returns: A new floating-point value

- **hash**(*object*)

  This function creates a hash value for *object*. Hash values are used to compare dictionary keys.

  Parameters: *object*   An object of any type

  Returns: The integer hash value

- **input**()
- **input**(*prompt*)

  This function obtains a sequence of characters from the user via the keyboard (standard input). If an argument is supplied, the *prompt* string is displayed to the console window (standard output) before characters are input.

  Parameters: *prompt*   A string displayed as the prompt to the user

  Returns: A string containing the characters entered by the user

- **int**(x)

  This function converts a number or string to an integer.

  Parameters: x A string or numerical value

  Returns: The new integer object

- **isinstance**(*object*, *name*)
- **isinstance**(*object*, *nametuple*)

  This function determines whether an object is an instance of a class or one of its subclasses. The second argument can be a single class name or a tuple of class names. If a tuple is supplied, the function determines whether the object is an instance of any of the classes specified in the tuple.

  Parameters: *object*   An object of any type

                 name   A single class name

                 nametuple   A tuple of class names

  Returns: True if the object is an instance of any of the classes provided as arguments, False otherwise

- **issubclass**(*class*, *name*)
- **issubclass**(*class*, *nametuple*)

  This function determines whether a class is a subclass of another class. The second argument can be a single class name or a tuple of class names. If a tuple is supplied, the function determines whether the class is a subclass of any of the classes specified in the tuple.

- **len**(*container*)

  This function returns the number of elements in a container.

  Parameters: *container*   A container

  Returns: An integer indicating the number of elements

- **list**()
- **list**(*container*)

  This function creates a new list. With no argument, it creates an empty list. If *container* is a list, a duplicate copy of that list is created; if it is a dictionary, a list containing the keys of the dictionary is created. If the container is a sequence, the new list contains the sequence elements.

  Parameters: *container*   A container whose elements are used to create the new list

  Returns: The new list

- **max**(*arg₁*, *arg₂*, ...)
- **max**(*container*)

  This function returns the largest value in a collection. If one argument is supplied and it is a container, the largest element in the container is returned. The container must not be empty. If multiple arguments are supplied, the function returns the largest of those values.

  Parameters: *container*   A container

  $arg_1, arg_2, \ldots$ Values of any type that are comparable

  Returns: The largest value in a collection

- **min**(*arg₁*, *arg₂*, ...)
- **min**(*container*)

  This function returns the smallest value in a collection. If one argument is supplied and it is a container, the smallest element in the container is returned. The container must not be empty. If multiple arguments are supplied, the function returns the smallest of those values.

  Parameters: *container*   A container

  $arg_1, arg_2, \ldots$ Values of any type that are comparable

  Returns: The smallest value in a collection

- **next**(*iterator*)

  This function returns the next item from a container or iterator.

  Parameters: *iterator*   An iterator object or container that can be used with the for loop

  Returns: The next item from the iterator or container. If there are no additional items, a StopIteration exception is raised

- **open**(*filename*, *mode*)

  This function opens a text or binary file named *filename* and associates it with a file object. A file can be opened for reading, writing, or both reading and writing. When a file is opened for reading, the file must exist or an exception is raised. When a file is opened for writing and the file does not exist, a new file is created; otherwise the contents of the existing file are erased. When a file is opened in append mode and the file does not exist, a new file is created; otherwise new text is appended to the end of the existing file.

  Parameters: *filename*   A string indicating the name of the file on disk

  mode   A string indicating the mode in which the file is opened for a text file: read ("r"), write ("w"), append ("a"), and read/write ("r+"). For a binary file: read ("rb"), write ("wb"), append ("ab"), and read/write ("rb+").

  Returns: A file object that is associated with the file on disk

- **ord**(*char*)

  This function returns the Unicode value for a character.

  Parameters: *char*   A string containing one character

  Returns: The Unicode value of the character in the string

- **print**()
- **print**(*arg₁*, *arg₂*, ...)
- **print**(*arg₁*, *arg₂*, ..., end=*string*, sep=*string*, file=*fileobj*)

  This function prints its arguments (*arg₁*, *arg₂*, ...) to the console window (standard output), separated by the sep string and followed by the end string. If no argument is supplied, the function simply starts a new line. By default, the arguments are separated by a blank space and the last argument is followed by a newline character (\n), which starts a new line. To suppress the new line at the end, specify the empty string as the end string (end=""). To use a string other than a blank space to separate the arguments, specify a new sep string. To print to a text file instead of standard output, specify the file object as the file= argument.

Parameters: arg_1, arg_2, ...   The values to print

end=*string*   An argument indicating that *string* is to be printed following the last argument value

sep=*string*   An argument indicating that *string* is to be printed between the argument values

file=*fileobj*   An argument indicating the text file object *fileobj* to which the arguments arc to be printed

- range(*stop*)
- range(*start*, *stop*)
- range(*start*, *stop*, *step*)

This function creates a sequence container of integer values that can be used with a for statement. The sequence of integers ranges from the *start* value to one less than the *stop* value in increments of the *step* value. If only the *stop* value is supplied, *start* is 0 and *step* is 1. If only the *start* and *stop* values are supplied, *step* is 1.

Parameters: *start*   An integer indicating the first value in the range

stop   An integer indicating a value that is at least one larger than the last value to be included in the range

step   An integer indicating the step between each value in the sequence

Returns: An iterator object that can be used with the for statement

- round(*value*)
- round(*value*, *digits*)

This function rounds a numerical value to a given number of decimal places. If only *value* is supplied, it is rounded to the closest integer.

Parameters: *value*   The integer or floating-point value to be rounded

digits   The number of decimal places

Returns: The argument rounded to the closest integer or to the given number of decimal places

- set()
- set(*container*)

This function creates a new set. If no argument is supplied, it creates an empty set. If *container* is a set, then a duplicate copy of that set is created; if it is a dictionary, a set containing the keys of the

dictionary is created. Otherwise, if *container* is a sequence, the new set contains the unique elements of the sequence.

Parameters: *container*   A container whose elements are used to create the new set

Returns: The new set

- sorted(*container*)

This function creates a sorted list from the elements in *container*. The elements are sorted in ascending order by default.

Parameters: *container*   A container whose elements are to be sorted

Returns: The new sorted list

- str(*object*)

This function converts an object to a string.

Parameters: *object*   The object to be converted

Returns: The new string

- sum(*container*)

This function computes the sum of the elements of *container*, which must contain numbers.

Parameters: *container*   A container of numerical values to be summed

Returns: The sum of the container elements

- super()

When a method is called on the object that this function returns, the superclass method is invoked.

- tuple()
- tuple(*container*)

This function creates a new tuple. If no argument is supplied, it creates an empty tuple. If *container* is a tuple, a duplicate copy of that tuple is created; if it is a dictionary, a tuple containing the keys of the dictionary is created. Otherwise, if it is a sequence container, the new tuple contains the sequence elements.

Parameters: *container*   A container whose elements are used to create the new tuple

Returns: The new tuple

Built-in Classes

dict Class

- *d* = dict()
- *d* = dict(*c*)

This function creates a new dictionary. If *c* is a dictionary, a duplicate copy of that dictionary is created. Otherwise, if *c* is a sequence of immutable objects, the sequence elements are the keys of the new dictionary. If no argument is provided, it creates an empty dictionary.

Parameters: *c*　A dictionary or sequence from which the new dictionary is created

Returns:　The new dictionary

- *value = d[key]*

The [] operator returns the value associated with *key* in the dictionary. The key must exist or an exception is raised.

- *d[key] = value*

The [] operator adds a new *key/value* entry to the dictionary if *key* does not exist in the dictionary. If *key* does exist, *value* becomes associated with it.

- *key* **in** *d*
- *key* **not in** *d*

The **in/not in** operators determine whether *key* is in the dictionary *d*.

- **len**(*d*)

This function returns the number of entries in the dictionary.

Parameters: *d*　A dictionary

Returns:　An integer indicating the number of dictionary entries

- *d*.**clear**()

This method removes all entries from the dictionary.

- *d*.**get**(*key*, *default*)

This method returns the value associated with *key*, or *default* if *key* is not present.

Parameters: *key*　The lookup key

default　The value returned when the key is not in the dictionary

Returns:　The value associated with the key or the default value if the key is not present in the dictionary

- *d*.**items**()

This method returns a list of the dictionary entries. The list contains one tuple for each entry in the dictionary. The first element of each tuple contains a key and the second element contains the value associated with that key.

Returns:　A list of tuples containing the dictionary entries

- *d*.**keys**()

This method returns a list of the dictionary keys.

Returns:　A list containing the keys in the dictionary

- *d*.**pop**(*key*)

This method removes *key* and its associated value from the dictionary.

Parameters: *key*　The lookup key

Returns:　The value associated with the key

- *d*.**values**()

This method returns a list of the dictionary values.

Returns:　A list containing the values in the dictionary

list Class

- *l* = **list**()
- *l* = **list**(*sequence*)

This function creates a new list that is empty or contains all of the elements of *sequence*.

Parameters: *sequence*　A sequence from which the new list is created

Returns:　The new list

- *value = l[position]*

The [] operator returns the element at *position* in the list. The position must be within the legal range or an exception is raised.

- *l[position] = value*

The [] operator replaces the element at *position* in the list. The position must be within the legal range or an exception is raised.

- *element* **in** *l*
- *element* **not in** *l*

The **in/not in** operators determine whether *element* is in the list.

- **len**(*l*)

This function returns the number of elements in the list.

Parameters: *l*　A list

Returns:　An integer indicating the number of elements in the list

- *l*.**append**(*element*)

This method appends *element* to the end of the list.

Parameters: *element*　The element to append

- *l*.**index**(*element*)

This method returns the position of *element* in the list. The element must be in the list or an exception is raised.

Parameters: *element*　The element to locate

Returns:　The position in the list that contains the element

- *l*.**insert**(*position*, *element*)

  This method inserts *element* at *position* in the list. All elements at and following the given position are moved down one position.

  Parameters: *position* Position where the element is to be inserted

  element The element to insert

- *l*.**pop**()
- *l*.**pop**(*position*)

  This method removes the last element from the list or the element at *position*. All elements following the given position are moved up one position.

  Parameters: *position* Position of the element to remove

  Returns: The removed element

- *l*.**remove**(*element*)

  This method removes *element* from the list and moves all elements following it up one position. The element must be in the list or an exception is raised.

  Parameters: *element* The element to be removed

- *l*.**sort**()

  This method sorts the elements in the list from smallest to largest.

set Class

- *s* = **set**()
- *s* = **set**(*sequence*)

  This function creates a new set that is empty or a copy of *sequence*. If *sequence* contains duplicate values, only one instance of any value is added to the set.

  Parameters: *sequence* A sequence from which the new set is created

  Returns: The new set

- *element* **in** *s*
- *element* **not in** *s*

  The in/not in operators determine whether *element* is in the set.

- **len**(*s*)

  This function returns the number of elements in the set.

  Parameters: *s* A set

  Returns: An integer indicating the number of set elements

- *s*.**add**(*element*)

  This method adds *element* to the set. If the element is already in the set, no action is taken.

  Parameters: *element* The new element

- *s*.**clear**()

  This method removes all elements from the set.

- *s*.**difference**(*t*)

  This method creates a new set that contains the elements in set *s* that are not in set *t*.

  Parameters: *t* A set

  Returns: The new set that results from set difference

- *s*.**discard**(*element*)

  This method removes *element* from the set. If the element is not a member of the set, no action is taken.

  Parameters: *element* The element to be removed from the set

- *s*.**intersection**(*t*)

  This method creates and returns a new set that contains the elements that are in both set *s* and set *t*.

  Parameters: *t* A set

  Returns: The new set that results from set intersection

- *s*.**issubset**(*t*)

  This method determines whether set *s* is a subset of set *t*.

  Parameters: *t* A set

  Returns: True if *s* is a subset of *t*, False otherwise

- *s*.**remove**(*element*)

  This method removes *element* from the set. If *element* is not in the set, an exception is raised.

  Parameters: *element* The element to be removed

- *s*.**union**(*t*)

  This method creates and returns a new set that contains all elements in set *s* and set *t*.

  Parameters: *t* A set

  Returns: The new set that results from set union

str Class

- *s* = **str**()
- *s* = **str**(*object*)

  This function creates a new string that is empty or the result of converting *object* to a string.

  Parameters: *object* The object to be converted

  Returns: The new string

- *substring* **in** *s*
- *substring* **not in** *s*

  The in/not in operators determine whether *substring* is in the string *s*.

- `len(s)`

  This function returns the length of the string *s*.

  Parameters: *s*   A string

  Returns: An integer indicating the number of characters in the string

- `s.count(substring)`

  This method returns the number of non-overlapping occurrences of *substring* in the string *s*.

  Parameters: *substring*   The string to look for

  Returns: The number of occurrences of the substring in the string

- `s.endswith(substring)`

  This method determines whether string *s* ends with *substring*.

  Parameters: *substring*   The string to look for

  Returns: True if string *s* ends with *substring*, False otherwise

- `s.find(substring)`
- `s.find(substring, begin)`

  This method returns the lowest index in string *s* where *substring* begins, or −1 if *substring* is not found. If the *begin* argument is supplied, the search is performed on the contents of string *s* within the sequence of characters starting at index *begin* through the end of the string.

  Parameters: *substring*   The string to look for

  begin   The starting index within string *s* at which the search begins

  Returns: The position where *substring* begins in the string

- `s.isalnum()`

  This method tests whether the string *s* consists of only letters and digits and contains at least one character.

  Returns: True if both conditions are true, False otherwise

- `s.isalpha()`

  This method tests whether the string *s* consists of only letters and contains at least one character.

  Returns: True if both conditions are true, False otherwise

- `s.isdigit()`

  This method tests whether the string *s* consists of only digits and contains at least one character.

  Returns: True if both conditions are true, False otherwise

- `s.islower()`

  This method tests whether the string *s* consists of only lowercase letters and contains at least one character.

  Returns: True if both conditions are true, False otherwise

- `s.isspace()`

  This method tests whether the string *s* consists of only white space characters (blank, newline, tab) and contains at least one character.

  Returns: True if both conditions are true, False otherwise

- `s.isupper()`

  This method tests whether the string *s* consists of only uppercase letters and contains at least one character.

  Returns: True if both conditions are true, False otherwise

- `s.lower()`

  This method returns a new string that is the lowercase version of string *s*.

  Returns: A new lowercase version of the string

- `s.lstrip()`
- `s.lstrip(chars)`

  This method returns a new version of string *s* in which white space (blanks, tabs, and newlines) is removed from the front (left end) of *s*. If an argument is provided, characters in the string *chars* are removed instead of white space.

  Parameters: *chars*   A string specifying the characters to be removed

  Returns: A new version of the string

- `s.replace(old, new)`

  This method returns a new version of string *s* in which every occurrence of the string *old* is replaced by the string *new*.

  Parameters: *old*   The substring to be replaced

  new   The substring that replaces the old substring

  Returns: A new version of the string

- `s.rstrip()`
- `s.rstrip(chars)`

  This method returns a new version of string *s* in which white space (blanks, tabs, and newlines) is removed from the end (right end) of *s*. If an argument is provided, characters in the string *chars* are removed instead of white space.

Parameters: *chars* A string specifying the characters to be removed

Returns: A new version of the string

- s.**rsplit**(*sep*, *maxsplit*)

This method returns a list of words from string *s* that are split starting from the right end of the string using substring *sep* as the delimiter. At most *maxsplit* + 1 words are made.

Parameters: *sep* A substring specifying the separator used for the split
maxsplit The maximum number of splits

Returns: A list of words that results from splitting the string

- s.**split**()
- s.**split**(*sep*)
- s.**split**(*sep*, *maxsplit*)

This method returns a list of words from string *s*. If the substring *sep* is provided, it is used as the delimiter; otherwise, any white space character is used. If *maxsplit* is provided, then only that number of splits will be made, resulting in at most *maxsplit* + 1 words.

Parameters: *sep* A substring specifying the separator used for the split
maxsplit The maximum number of splits

Returns: A list of words that results from splitting the string

- s.**splitlines**()

This method returns a list containing the individual lines of a string split using the newline character \n as the delimiter.

Returns: A list containing the individual lines split from the string

- s.**startswith**(*substring*)

This method determines whether string *s* begins with *substring*.

Parameters: *substring* The substring to look for

Returns: True if string *s* starts with *substring*, False otherwise

- s.**strip**()
- s.**strip**(*chars*)

This method returns a new version of string *s* in which white space (blanks, tabs, and newlines) is

removed from both ends (front and back) of *s*. If an argument is provided, characters in the string *chars* are removed instead of white space.

Parameters: *chars* A string specifying the characters to remove

Returns: A new version of the string

- s.**upper**()

This method returns a new string that is the uppercase version of string *s*.

Returns: A new uppercase version of the string

File Input/Output

Common Methods and Functions

The following methods and functions are common to both text and binary files.

- **open**(*filename*, *mode*)

This function opens a text or binary file named *filename* and associates it with a file object. A file can be opened for reading, writing, or both reading and writing. When a file is opened for reading, the file must exist or an exception is raised. When a file is opened for writing and the file does not exist, a new file is created; otherwise the contents of the existing file are erased. When a file is opened in append mode and the file does not exist, a new file is created; otherwise new text is appended to the end of the existing file.

Parameters: *filename* A string indicating the name of the file on disk
mode A string indicating the mode in which the file is opened Modes for a text file are: read ("r"), write ("w"), append ("a"), and read/write ("r+"). Modes for a binary file are: read ("rb"), write ("wb"), append ("ab"), and read/write ("rb+").

Returns: A file object that is associated with the file on disk

- f.**close**()

This method closes an open file. It has no effect if the file is already closed.

- f.**seek**(*offset*, *relative*)

This method moves the file marker to the given byte *offset*. The *relative* argument indicates whether the file marker is to be moved relative to the beginning of the file (SEEK_SET), the current position of the file marker (SEEK_CUR), or the end of the file (SEEK_END).

Parameters: *offset*   An integer indicating the number of bytes to move the file marker

relative   One of the constants SEEK_SET, SEEK_CUR, or SEEK_END (defined in the os module)

Returns: The new absolute position of the file marker

- f.**tell**()

This method locates the current position of the file marker.

Returns: The absolute position of the file marker

Text File Methods

The following methods can be used with text files.

- f.**read**()
- f.**read**(*num*)

This method reads the next *num* characters from a file opened for reading and returns them as a string. If no argument is supplied, the entire file is read and its contents returned in a single string. An empty string is returned when all characters have been read from the file.

Parameters: *num*   An integer indicating the number of characters to be read

Returns: A string containing the characters read from the file

- f.**readline**()

This method reads the next line of text from a file opened for reading and returns it as a string. An empty string is returned when the end of file is reached.

Returns: A string containing the characters read from the file

- f.**readlines**()

This method reads the remaining text from a file opened for reading and returns it as a list of strings in which each element of the list contains a single line of text from the file.

Returns: A list of strings containing the lines of text read from the file

- f.**write**(*string*)

This method writes *string* to a file opened for writing.

Parameters: *string*   The string to be written

Binary File Methods

The following methods can be used with binary files.

- f.**read**()
- f.**read**(*num*)

This method reads the next *num* bytes from a binary file opened for reading and returns them as a bytes sequence. If no argument is supplied, the entire file is read and its contents returned in a single bytes sequence.

Parameters: *num*   An integer indicating the number of bytes to be read

Returns: A bytes sequence containing the bytes read from the file

- f.**write**(*data*)

This method writes a sequence of bytes to a binary file opened for writing.

Parameters: *data*   A bytes sequence

csv Module

reader Class

- r = **reader**(*filename*)

This function creates a new reader object that can be used to iterate over the contents of a CSV file. The file must exist or an exception is raised.

Parameters: *filename*   A string containing the name of the CSV file

Returns: The CSV reader object

writer Class

- w = **writer**(*filename*)

This function creates a new writer object that can be used to create a new CSV file. If the file does not exist, a new file is created; otherwise the contents of the existing file are erased.

Parameters: *filename*   A string containing the name of the CSV file

Returns: The CSV writer object

- w = **writerow**(*row*)

This method adds the next row of column data to the CSV file. The data must be provided as a sequence of strings or numbers.

Parameters: *row*   The sequence of strings or numbers comprising the next row

email.mime.multipart Module

- m = MIMEMultipart()

  This function creates and returns a MIME Message object that is used to create e-mail messages.

  Returns: A Message object

Message Class

- m.add_header(*field*, *value*)

  This method adds a new header entry to the e-mail message. A header entry consists of a field and its corresponding value.

  Parameters: *field*   A string containing the name of an e-mail message header field

  value   A string containing the value associated with the given header field

- m.attach(*content*)

  This method adds content to the body of the e-mail message. *content* must be a MIME content object.

  Parameters: *content*   A MIME content object that contains the content to be added

email.mime.text Module

- MIMEText(*data*, *type*)

  This function creates a new MIME content object that stores the text provided in *data*.

  Parameters: *data*   A string containing the text to be stored in the MIME content object

  type   A string containing the MIME encoding type of the text; common values include "plain" and "text"

  Returns: A MIME content object

email.mime.image Module

- MIMEImage(*data*)

  This function creates a new MIME content object that stores the raw data of an image. The new content object is initialized with the supplied *data*.

  Parameters: *data*   A string containing the raw image data

  Returns: A MIME content object

email.mime.application Module

- MIMEApplication(*data*)

  This function creates a new MIME content object that stores application-specific data such as PDF documents and spreadsheets. The new content object is initialized with the supplied *data*.

  Parameters: *data*   A string containing the application-specific data

  Returns: A MIME content object

json Module

- dumps(*d*)

  This function converts the entire contents of a dictionary to a JSON-formatted string.

  Parameters: *d*   A dictionary from which the JSON string is created

  Returns: A JSON-formatted string

- loads(*s*)

  This function converts a JSON-formatted string to a dictionary. Numerical values specified in the JSON string are converted to the their appropriate data type: integer or floating-point.

  Parameters: *s*   A string containing data stored in the JSON format

  Returns: A dictionary containing the data obtained from the JSON string

math Module

- e

  This constant is the value of e, the base of the natural logarithms.

- pi

  This constant is the value of π.

- acos(*x*)

  This function returns the angle with the given cosine, $\cos^{-1} x \in [0, \pi]$.

  Parameters: *x*   A floating-point value between −1 and 1

  Returns: The arc cosine of the argument, in radians

- asin(*x*)

  This function returns the angle with the given sine, $\sin^{-1} x \in [-\pi/2, \pi/2]$.

  Parameters: *x*   A floating-point value between −1 and 1

  Returns: The arc sine of the argument, in radians

- atan(*x*)

  This function returns the angle with the given tangent, $\tan^{-1} x \in (-\pi/2, \pi/2)$.

  Parameters: *x*   A floating-point value

  Returns: The arc tangent of the argument, in radians

- **atan2**(y, x)

  This function returns the angle with the given tangent, $\tan^{-1}(y/x) \in (-\pi, \pi)$. If x can equal zero, or if it is necessary to distinguish "northwest" from "southeast", use this function instead of atan(y/x).

  Parameters: y, x Two floating-point values

  Returns: The angle, in radians, between the points $(0, 0)$ and (x, y)

- **ceil**(x)

  This function returns the smallest integer $\geq x$.

  Parameters: x A floating-point value

  Returns: The smallest integer greater than or equal to the argument

- **cos**(x)

  This function returns the cosine of an angle given in radians.

  Parameters: x An angle in radians

  Returns: The cosine of the argument

- **degrees**(x)

  This function converts radians to degrees.

  Parameters: x An angle in radians

  Returns: The angle in degrees

- **exp**(x)

  This function returns the value e^x, where e is the base of the natural logarithms.

  Parameters: x A floating-point value

  Returns: e^x

- **fabs**(x)

  This function returns the absolute value $|x|$ as a floating-point value.

  Parameters: x A numerical value

  Returns: The absolute value of the argument as a floating-point value

- **factorial**(x)

  This function returns $x!$, the factorial of x.

  Parameters: x An integer ≥ 0

  Returns: The factorial of the argument

- **floor**(x)

  This function returns the largest integer $\leq x$.

  Parameters: x A floating-point value

  Returns: The largest integer less than or equal to the argument

- **hypot**(x, y)

  This function returns the Euclidean norm $\sqrt{x^2 + y^2}$.

  Parameters: x, y Two numerical values

  Returns: The length of the vector from the origin to the point (x, y)

- **log**(x)
- **log**(x, *base*)

  This function returns the natural logarithm of x (to base e) or, if the second argument is given, the logarithm of x to the given base.

  Parameters: x A number greater than 0.0

                     base   An integer

  Returns: The logarithm of the argument

- **log2**(x)
- **log10**(x)

  This function returns the logarithm of x to either base 2 or base 10.

  Parameters: x A number greater than 0.0

  Returns: The logarithm of the argument to either base 2 or base 10

- **radians**(x)

  This function converts degrees to radians.

  Parameters: x An angle in degrees

  Returns: The angle in radians

- **sin**(x)

  This function returns the sine of an angle given in radians.

  Parameters: x An angle in radians

  Returns: The sine of the argument

- **sqrt**(x)

  This function returns the square root of x, $\sqrt{x}$.

  Parameters: x A floating-point value ≥ 0.0

  Returns: The square root of the argument

- **tan**(x)

  This function returns the tangent of an angle given in radians.

  Parameters: x An angle in radians

  Returns: The tangent of the argument

- **trunc**(x)

  This function truncates a floating-point value x to an integer.

  Parameters: x A floating-point value

  Returns: The whole number part of the argument as an integer

os Module

- SEEK_CUR
- SEEK_END
- SEEK_SET

  These constants are used with the seek method to indicate the position from which the file marker is offset: SEEK_CUR indicates the offset is relative to the current position of the file marker, SEEK_END is relative to the end of the file, and SEEK_SET is relative to the beginning of the file.

- **chdir**(*path*)
  This function changes the current working directory to *path*.
  Parameters: *path*   A string containing the absolute or relative name of a directory

- **getcwd**()
  This function returns the complete path name of the current working directory.
  Returns: A string containing the name of the current working directory

- **listdir**()
- **listdir**(*path*)
  This function returns a list containing the names of the entries (files, subdirectories) in the current directory or the directory given by *path*.
  Parameters: *path*   A string containing the absolute or relative name of a directory
  Returns: A list of strings containing the names of entries in a directory

- **remove**(*filename*)
  This function deletes an existing file.
  Parameters: *filename*   A string with the absolute or relative name of an existing file

- **rename**(*source*, *dest*)
  This function renames or moves a file.
  Parameters: *source*   A string with the absolute or relative name of an existing file
  dest   A string containing the new absolute or relative name for the file

os.path Module

- **exists**(*path*)
  This function determines whether *path* refers to an existing file or directory.
  Parameters: *path*   A string containing the absolute or relative name of a directory or file
  Returns: True if the file or directory exists, and False otherwise

- **getsize**(*path*)
  This function returns the size of a file whose name is specified by *path*.
  Parameters: *path*   A string containing the absolute or relative name of a file
  Returns: The size of the file in bytes

- **isdir**(*path*)
  This function indicates whether *path* refers to a directory.
  Parameters: *path*   A string containing the absolute or relative name of a directory
  Returns: True if *path* is the name of a directory, False otherwise

- **isfile**(*path*)
  This function indicates whether *path* refers to a file.
  Parameters: *path*   A string containing an absolute or relative name of a file
  Returns: True if *path* is the name of a file, False otherwise

- **join**(*path*, *name*)
  This function appends a file or directory name to a path, including the appropriate path separator for the operating system being used.
  Parameters: *path*   A string containing an absolute or relative path name
  name   A string containing the file or directory name to be appended to the path
  Returns: A string containing the new path name

random Module

- **randint**(*first*, *last*)
  This function returns the next pseudorandom, uniformly distributed integer in the range from *first* to *last* (inclusive) drawn from the random number generator's sequence.
  Parameters: *first*, *last*   The first and last values in the integer range
  Returns: The next pseudorandom integer $\geq$ *first* and $\leq$ *last*

- **random**()
  This function returns the next pseudorandom, uniformly distributed floating-point number between 0.0 (inclusive) and 1.0 (exclusive) from the random number generator's sequence.
  Returns: The next pseudorandom floating-point number $\geq$ 0.0 and < 1.0

re Module

- **split**(*pattern*, *string*)

  This function splits the *string* at each occurrence of the given regular expression *pattern* and returns the collection of substrings in a list.

  Parameters: *pattern* a string containing a regular expression pattern used to determine where the given string is split

  string a string to be split based on the given expression pattern

  Returns: A list containing the substrings or words that result from splitting the string

shutil Module

- **copy**(*source*, *dest*)

  This function copies the entire contents of a source file to a directory or a new file.

  Parameters: *source* A string with the absolute or relative name of an existing file

  dest A string containing the absolute or relative name of an existing directory or the new file

smtplib Module

SMTP Class

- *c* = **SMTP**(*host*, *port*)

  This function creates a new SMTP (Simple Mail Transfer Protocol) object for connecting to an e-mail server in order to send an e-mail message.

  Parameters: *host* A string containing the host name of the e-mail server

  port An integer value that indicates the network port number on which the connection to the e-mail server is made

  Returns: The SMTP connection object

- *c*.**starttls**()

  This method creates the connection to the e-mail server and turns on secure communications.

- *c*.**login**(*username*, *password*)

  This method logs in to the e-mail server using the provided credentials.

  Parameters: *username* A string containing the user name of the account from which the message will be sent

  password A string containing the password of the account

- *c*.**send_message**(*msg*)

  This method transmits an e-mail message from your computer to the server, which in turn sends it to the appropriate recipients.

  Parameters: *msg* A correctly constructed Message object that contains header entries and body content for an e-mail message

- *c*.**quit**()

  This method closes the connection to the server and quits the e-mail session.

sys Module

- **argv**

  This variable references the list of string arguments passed to the program via the command line.

- **exit**()
- **exit**(*message*)

  This function terminates the program. If an argument is provided, *message* is displayed before termination.

  Parameters: *message* A string to be printed to the console window

time Module

- **sleep**(*seconds*)

  This function pauses the program for a given number of seconds.

  Parameters: *seconds* The number of seconds to pause the program

- **time**()

  This function returns the difference, measured in seconds, between the current time and midnight, Universal Time, January 1, 1970.

  Returns: The current time in seconds since January 1, 1970

urllib.parse Module

- **urlencode**(*params*)

  This function creates a string that contains a sequence of URL arguments that are formatted for use in the urllib.request.urlopen function. The arguments to be included in the string are specified as key/value pairs in the provided dictionary.

  Parameters: *params* A dictionary containing the key/value pairs of the URL arguments

  Returns: A string containing a correctly formatted URL argument sequence

urllib.request Module

- **r = urlopen(*url*)**
  This function connects to a web page and opens it for reading. An HTTPResponse object is returned, which handles the actual reading.
  Parameters: *url* A string containing the universal resource locator (URL) of the web page to be read
  Returns: An HTTPResponse object

HTTPResponse Class

- **r.read()**
  This method reads the body of the web page and returns it as a byte sequence.
  Returns: A byte sequence containing the entire contents of the web page body

- **r.close()**
  This function closes the HTTPResponse object and disconnects from the web page.

ezgraphics Module

The ezgraphics module is based on components from an open source project. Visit the http://ezgraphics.org web site for more information about the project and to browse tutorials on using its full range of features.

GraphicsWindow Class

- **w = GraphicsWindow()**
- **w = GraphicsWindow(*width*, *height*)**
  This function creates a new graphics window that contains an empty graphics canvas. The size of the canvas defaults to 400 by 400 pixels unless the width and height values are provided.
  Parameters: *width*, *height* The size in pixels of the canvas contained in the window
  Returns: The graphics window object

- **w.canvas()**
  This method returns a reference to the graphics canvas contained in the window.
  Returns: A reference to the graphics canvas

- **w.close()**
  This method closes the graphics window and permanently removes it from the desktop. It cannot be used after it has been closed.

- **w.getKey()**
  This method gets and returns the next key pressed by the user. The program pauses and waits for the user to press any key.
  Returns: A string indicating which key was pressed

- **w.getMouse()**
  This method gets and returns the location of the next mouse button click on the canvas. The program pauses and waits until the user clicks a mouse button in the canvas area.
  Returns: A two-element tuple (*x*, *y*) containing the canvas coordinates of the mouse pointer when the button was clicked

- **w.hide()**
  This method hides or iconizes the graphics window. The window remains open and usable, but it is not visible on the desktop. If the window is not valid, an exception is raised.

- **w.isValid()**
  This method determines whether the graphics window is valid (opened).
  Returns: True if the graphics window is valid (opened) or False if it is closed

- **w.setTitle(*title*)**
  This method sets the text to be displayed in the title bar of the window.
  Parameters: *title* The string to be the window title

- **w.show()**
  This method displays the graphics window on the desktop. If it is not valid, an exception is raised.

- **w.wait()**
  This method keeps the graphics window open and waits for the user to click the "close" button in the title bar or for the program to call the close method.

GraphicsCanvas Class

- **c.clear()**
  This method clears the canvas by removing all geometric shapes and text that were previously drawn on the canvas.

- **c.drawArc(*x*, *y*, *diameter*, *startAngle*, *extent*)**
  This method draws a circular arc on the canvas. The style used to draw the arc is specified using the setArcStyle method. The default style ("slice") draws pie slices.
  Parameters: *x*, *y* The coordinates of the top-left corner of the arc's bounding square

diameter   The size of the circle (given as an integer) on which the arc is drawn
startAngle   The angle (given in degrees) around the outside of the circle at which the arc begins. An angle of zero degrees is the line that passes through the center of the circle parallel to the *x*-axis
extent   The size of the arc given as an angle in degrees

Returns: An integer value that uniquely identifies the arc, chord, or pie slice on the canvas

- `c.drawImage(`*image*`)`
- `c.drawImage(`*x*, *y*, *image*`)`
  This method draws an image on the canvas. The image is drawn with its top-left corner at position (0, 0) or the given (*x*, *y*) position on the canvas. When the (*x*, *y*) coordinates are not provided, the canvas is resized to tightly fit around the image.

  Parameters: *x*, *y*   The coordinates of the top-left corner of the image
  image   A GraphicsImage object containing the image to be displayed

  Returns: An integer value that uniquely identifies the image on the canvas

- `c.drawLine(`x_1, y_1, x_2, y_2`)`
  This method draws a line between two points.

  Parameters: x_1, y_1 The coordinates of the starting point given as integers
  x_2, y_2 The coordinates of the end point given as integers

  Returns: An integer value that uniquely identifies the line on the canvas

- `c.drawOval(`*x*, *y*, *width*, *height*`)`
  This method draws an oval on the canvas.

  Parameters: *x*, *y*   The coordinates of the top-left corner of the bounding rectangle
  width, *height*   The width and height of the bounding rectangle

  Returns: An integer value that uniquely identifies the oval on the canvas

- `c.drawPoint(`*x*, *y*`)`
  This method draws a single point on the canvas.

  Parameters: *x*, *y*   The coordinates of the point given as integers

  Returns: An integer value that uniquely identifies the point on the canvas

- `c.drawPoly(`*sequence*`)`
- `c.drawPoly(`x_1, y_1, x_2, y_2, x_3, y_3, ...`)`
  This method draws a polygon on the canvas using the vertices provided as a series of *x*- and *y*-coordinates. The coordinates can be provided in a sequence container as a single argument, or as multiple arguments.

  Parameters: *sequence*   A list or tuple of integer values that specify the coordinates of the polygon vertices. It must contain at least six values
  $x_1, y_1, x_2, y_2, x_3, y_3, ...$ The integer coordinates of the polygon's vertices

  Returns: An integer value that uniquely identifies the polygon on the canvas

- `c.drawRect(`*x*, *y*, *width*, *height*`)`
  This method draws a rectangle on the canvas.

  Parameters: *x*, *y*   The coordinates of the top-left corner of the rectangle
  width, *height*   The width and height of the rectangle

  Returns: An integer value that uniquely identifies the rectangle on the canvas

- `c.drawText(`*x*, *y*, *text*`)`
  This method draws text on the canvas. The text is drawn relative to the anchor point (*x*, *y*). The default position of the anchor point is the northwest corner of the bounding box that surrounds the text. If the string contains newline characters, multiple lines of text will be drawn.

  Parameters: *x*, *y*   The anchor point coordinates
  text   The string containing the text to be drawn

  Returns: An integer value that uniquely identifies the text on the canvas

- `c.drawVector(`x_1, y_1, x_2, y_2`)`
  This method draws a line between two points with an arrowhead at the end point.

  Parameters: x_1, y_1 The coordinates of the starting point given as integers
  x_2, y_2 The coordinates of the end point given as integers

  Returns: An integer value that uniquely identifies the vector on the canvas

- `c.height()`
  This methods returns the height (vertical size) of the canvas.

  Returns: The height of the canvas

- *c*.**width**()
  This methods returns the width (horizontal size) of the canvas.
  Returns: The width of the canvas

- *c*.**setAnchor**(*position*)
  This method sets the anchor position used when drawing new text on the canvas. The position is a point on the bounding box that surrounds the text; it is specified as a geographic direction.
  Parameters: *position*   The anchor position given as a string, which must be one of "n", "s", "e", "w", "nw", "ne", "sw", "se", or "center"

- *c*.**setArcStyle**(*style*)
  This method sets the style used to draw new arcs on the canvas. An arc can be drawn three ways: as a pie slice in which lines are drawn from the perimeter to the circle's center, as an arc in which only the perimeter section is drawn, or as a chord in which the ends of the arc are connected with a straight line.
  Parameters: *style*   The arc style given as string; must be one of "slice", "arc", or "chord"

- *c*.**setBackground**(*name*)
- *c*.**setBackground**(*red, green, blue*)
  This method sets the background color of the canvas. The color can be specified by name or by the values of its red, green, and blue components.
  Parameters: *name*   The color name given as a string
  red, green, blue   Integers in the range 0 through 255

- *c*.**setColor**(*name*)
- *c*.**setColor**(*red, green, blue*)
  This method sets both the fill and outline color used to draw new shapes and text on the canvas to the same color. The color can be specified by name or by the values of its red, green, and blue components.
  Parameters: *name*   The color name given as a string
  red, green, blue   Integers in the range 0 through 255

- *c*.**setFill**()
- *c*.**setFill**(*name*)
- *c*.**setFill**(*red, green, blue*)
  This method sets the color used to fill new shapes drawn on the canvas. The color can be specified by name or by the values of its red, green, and blue components. If no argument is given, the fill color is cleared.
  Parameters: *name*   The color name given as a string
  red, green, blue   Integers in the range 0 through 255

- *c*.**setFont**(*family, style, size*)
  This method sets the font used to draw new text on the canvas. A font is specified by three characteristics: *family*, *size*, and *style*.
  Parameters: *family*   The font name given as a string, which must be one of "arial", "courier", "times", or "helvetica"
  style   The font style given as a string, which must be one of "normal", "bold", "italic", or "bold italic"
  size   The point size of the font given as a positive integer

- *c*.**setHeight**(*size*)
  This method changes the height of the canvas.
  Parameters: *size*   A positive integer indicating the new height

- *c*.**setJustify**(*style*)
  This method sets the justification used when drawing multiple lines of text on the canvas.
  Parameters: *style*   The style given as a string; must be one of "left", "right", or "center"

- *c*.**setLineWidth**(*size*)
  This method sets the width of new lines drawn on the canvas.
  Parameters: *size*   An integer value ≥ 0

- *c*.**setLineStyle**(*style*)
  This method sets the style used to draw new lines on the canvas. Lines can be solid or dashed.
  Parameters: *style*   The line style given as a string, which must be either "solid" or "dashed"

- *c*.**setOutline**()
- *c*.**setOutline**(*name*)
- *c*.**setOutline**(*red, green, blue*)
  This method sets the color used to draw new lines and text on the canvas. The color can be specified by name or by the values of its red, green, and blue components. If no argument is given, the outline color is cleared.
  Parameters: *name*   The color name given as a string
  red, green, blue   Integers in the range 0 through 255

- *c*.**setWidth**(*size*)
  This method changes the width of the canvas.
  Parameters: *size*   A positive integer indicating the new width

GraphicsImage Class

- *i* = GraphicsImage(*filename*)
- *i* = GraphicsImage(*width*, *height*)

  This function creates a new graphics image that can be used to create or manipulate an RGB color image. An empty image of a given size can be created or an image can be loaded from a file.

  Parameters: *filename*   A string containing the name of a GIF or PPM image file

  width, *height*   The size of the new empty image

  Returns: The graphics image object

- *i*.clear()

  This method clears the image and sets the pixels to be transparent. The size of the image is not changed.

- *i*.copy()

  This method creates a copy of the image.

  Returns: The duplicate graphics image object

- i.getPixel(*row*, *col*)

  This method returns the color of a specified pixel in the image. The color is returned as a three-element tuple containing the red, green, and blue component values.

  Parameters: *row*, *col*   The vertical and horizontal coordinates of the pixel

  Returns: A tuple containing the color component values

- *i*.getRed(*row*, *col*)
- *i*.getBlue(*row*, *col*)
- *i*.getGreen(*row*, *col*)

  These methods returns the corresponding color component value of a specified pixel in the image.

  Parameters: *row*, *col*   The vertical and horizontal coordinates of the pixel

  Returns: The color component value as an integer

- *i*.height()

  This method returns the height (vertical size) of the image.

  Returns: The height of the image

- *i*.save(*filename*)

  This method saves a copy of the image to a file in the GIF image format.

  Parameters: *filename*   A string containing the name of the GIF image file

- *i*.setPixel(*row*, *col*, *red*, *green*, *blue*)
- *i*.setPixel(*row*, *col*, *color*)

  This method sets the color of a specified pixel in the image. The color can be specified by individual values for its red, green, and blue components or by a three-element tuple that contains the three component values (red, green, blue).

  Parameters: *row*, *col*   The vertical and horizontal coordinates of the pixel

  color   A tuple containing three integers in the range 0 through 255

  red, *green*, *blue*   Integers in the range 0 through 255

- *i*.width()

  This method returns the width (horizontal size) of the image.

  Returns: The width of the image

turtle Module

- backward(*distance*)

  This function moves the turtle distance amount along a straight line in the opposite direction.

  Parameters: *distance*   The number of pixels to move the turtle

- clear()

  This function clears the turtle's drawing from the window, but does not move the turtle.

- forward(*distance*)

  This function moves the turtle *distance* amount along a straight line in the current direction.

  Parameters: *distance*   The number of pixels to move the turtle

- goto(*x*, *y*)

  This function moves the turtle to the absolute (*x*, *y*) position in the window.

  Parameters: *x*, *y*   The coordinates of the window position given as integers

- heading()

  This function returns the turtle's current heading in degrees.

  Returns: The current heading as a floating-point value

- hideturtle()

  This function hides the turtle. The hidden turtle cannot draw on the window.

- **home()**
  This function moves the turtle to the origin (0, 0) and sets the heading to the east.

- **left(*angle*)**
  This function turns the turtle left by *angle* degrees.
  Parameters: *angle*   The angle given as a floating-point value

- **pencolor(*colorname*)**
- **pencolor(*red, green, blue*)**
  This function sets the color of the pen the turtle uses to draw on the window. The color can be specified by name or by the values of its red, green, and blue components.
  Parameters: *colorname*   The color name given as a string
  red, green, blue   Integers in the range 0 through 255

- **pendown()**
  This function puts the pen down to draw when the turtle moves.

- **pensize(*width*)**
  This function sets the thickness of the line drawn by the turtle to width pixels.
  Parameters: *width*   The width given as an integer.

- **penup()**
  This function picks up the pen to stop the turtle from drawing when it is moved.

- **reset()**
  This function clears the turtle's drawing from the window, moves the turtle to the origin (0, 0), and sets the heading to the east.

- **right(*angle*)**
  This function turns the turtle right by *angle* degrees.
  Parameters: *angle*   The angle given as a floating-point value

- **showturtle()**
  This function shows the turtle. The turtle must be visible to draw on the window.

THE BASIC LATIN AND LATIN-1 SUBSETS OF UNICODE

This appendix lists the Unicode characters that are most commonly used for processing Western European languages. A complete listing of Unicode characters can be found at http://unicode.org.

Table 1 Selected Control Characters			
Character	Code	Decimal	Escape Sequence
Tab	'\u0009'	9	'\t'
Newline	'\u000A'	10	'\n'
Return	'\u000D'	13	'\r'
Space	'\u0020'	32	

Table 2 The Basic Latin (ASCII) Subset of Unicode

Char.	Code	Dec.	Char.	Code	Dec.	Char.	Code	Dec.
			@	'\u0040'	64	`	'\u0060'	96
!	'\u0021'	33	A	'\u0041'	65	a	'\u0061'	97
"	'\u0022'	34	B	'\u0042'	66	b	'\u0062'	98
#	'\u0023'	35	C	'\u0043'	67	c	'\u0063'	99
$	'\u0024'	36	D	'\u0044'	68	d	'\u0064'	100
%	'\u0025'	37	E	'\u0045'	69	e	'\u0065'	101
&	'\u0026'	38	F	'\u0046'	70	f	'\u0066'	102
'	'\u0027'	39	G	'\u0047'	71	g	'\u0067'	103
(	'\u0028'	40	H	'\u0048'	72	h	'\u0068'	104
)	'\u0029'	41	I	'\u0049'	73	i	'\u0069'	105
*	'\u002A'	42	J	'\u004A'	74	j	'\u006A'	106
+	'\u002B'	43	K	'\u004B'	75	k	'\u006B'	107
,	'\u002C'	44	L	'\u004C'	76	l	'\u006C'	108
-	'\u002D'	45	M	'\u004D'	77	m	'\u006D'	109
.	'\u002E'	46	N	'\u004E'	78	n	'\u006E'	110
/	'\u002F'	47	O	'\u004F'	79	o	'\u006F'	111
0	'\u0030'	48	P	'\u0050'	80	p	'\u0070'	112
1	'\u0031'	49	Q	'\u0051'	81	q	'\u0071'	113
2	'\u0032'	50	R	'\u0052'	82	r	'\u0072'	114
3	'\u0033'	51	S	'\u0053'	83	s	'\u0073'	115
4	'\u0034'	52	T	'\u0054'	84	t	'\u0074'	116
5	'\u0035'	53	U	'\u0055'	85	u	'\u0075'	117
6	'\u0036'	54	V	'\u0056'	86	v	'\u0076'	118
7	'\u0037'	55	W	'\u0057'	87	w	'\u0077'	119
8	'\u0038'	56	X	'\u0058'	88	x	'\u0078'	120
9	'\u0039'	57	Y	'\u0059'	89	y	'\u0079'	121
:	'\u003A'	58	Z	'\u005A'	90	z	'\u007A'	122
;	'\u003B'	59	[	'\u005B'	91	{	'\u007B'	123
<	'\u003C'	60	\	'\u005C'	92	|	'\u007C'	124
=	'\u003D'	61	]	'\u005D'	93	}	'\u007D'	125
>	'\u003E'	62	^	'\u005E'	94	~	'\u007E'	126
?	'\u003F'	63	_	'\u005F'	95			

Table 3 The Latin-1 Subset of Unicode

Char.	Code	Dec.	Char.	Code	Dec.	Char.	Code	Dec.
			À	'\u00C0'	192	à	'\u00E0'	224
¡	'\u00A1'	161	Á	'\u00C1'	193	á	'\u00E1'	225
¢	'\u00A2'	162	Â	'\u00C2'	194	â	'\u00E2'	226
£	'\u00A3'	163	Ã	'\u00C3'	195	ã	'\u00E3'	227
¤	'\u00A4'	164	Ä	'\u00C4'	196	ä	'\u00E4'	228
¥	'\u00A5'	165	Å	'\u00C5'	197	å	'\u00E5'	229
¦	'\u00A6'	166	Æ	'\u00C6'	198	æ	'\u00E6'	230
§	'\u00A7'	167	Ç	'\u00C7'	199	ç	'\u00E7'	231
¨	'\u00A8'	168	È	'\u00C8'	200	è	'\u00E8'	232
©	'\u00A9'	169	É	'\u00C9'	201	é	'\u00E9'	233
ª	'\u00AA'	170	Ê	'\u00CA'	202	ê	'\u00EA'	234
«	'\u00AB'	171	Ë	'\u00CB'	203	ë	'\u00EB'	235
¬	'\u00AC'	172	Ì	'\u00CC'	204	ì	'\u00EC'	236
-	'\u00AD'	173	Í	'\u00CD'	205	í	'\u00ED'	237
®	'\u00AE'	174	Î	'\u00CE'	206	î	'\u00EE'	238
¯	'\u00AF'	175	Ï	'\u00CF'	207	ï	'\u00EF'	239
°	'\u00B0'	176	Ð	'\u00D0'	208	ð	'\u00F0'	240
±	'\u00B1'	177	Ñ	'\u00D1'	209	ñ	'\u00F1'	241
²	'\u00B2'	178	Ò	'\u00D2'	210	ò	'\u00F2'	242
³	'\u00B3'	179	Ó	'\u00D3'	211	ó	'\u00F3'	243
´	'\u00B4'	180	Ô	'\u00D4'	212	ô	'\u00F4'	244
µ	'\u00B5'	181	Õ	'\u00D5'	213	õ	'\u00F5'	245
¶	'\u00B6'	182	Ö	'\u00D6'	214	ö	'\u00F6'	246
·	'\u00B7'	183	×	'\u00D7'	215	÷	'\u00F7'	247
¸	'\u00B8'	184	Ø	'\u00D8'	216	ø	'\u00F8'	248
¹	'\u00B9'	185	Ù	'\u00D9'	217	ù	'\u00F9'	249
º	'\u00BA'	186	Ú	'\u00DA'	218	ú	'\u00FA'	250
»	'\u00BB'	187	Û	'\u00DB'	219	û	'\u00FB'	251
¼	'\u00BC'	188	Ü	'\u00DC'	220	ü	'\u00FC'	252
½	'\u00BD'	189	Ý	'\u00DD'	221	ý	'\u00FD'	253
¾	'\u00BE'	190	Þ	'\u00DE'	222	þ	'\u00FE'	254
¿	'\u00BF'	191	ß	'\u00DF'	223	ÿ	'\u00FF'	255

GLOSSARY

Abstract class　A class that cannot be instantiated.

Abstract method　A method with a name, parameter variables, and return type but without an implementation.

Accessor method　A method that accesses an object but does not change it.

Actual parameter　The argument actually passed to a function or method.

Algorithm　An unambiguous, executable, and terminating specification of a way to solve a problem.

API (Application Programming Interface)　A code library for building programs.

Argument　A value supplied in a function or method call, or one of the values combined by an operator.

Assignment　Placing a new value into a variable.

Association　A relationship between classes in which one can navigate from objects of one class to objects of the other class, usually by following object references.

Asymmetric bounds　Bounds that include the starting index but not the ending index.

Big-Oh notation　The notation $g(n) = O(f(n))$, which denotes that the function g grows at a rate that is bounded by the growth rate of the function f with respect to n. For example, $10n^2 + 100n - 1000 = O(n^2)$.

Binary file　A file in which values are stored in their binary representation and cannot be read as text.

Binary operator　An operator that takes two arguments, for example $+$ in $x + y$.

Binary search　A fast algorithm for finding a value in a sorted sequence. It narrows the search down to half of the sequence in every step.

Bit　Binary digit; the smallest unit of information, having two possible values: 0 and 1. A data element consisting of n bits has 2^n possible values.

Body　All statements of a function or method or statement block.

Boolean operator　An operator that can be applied to Boolean values. Python has three Boolean operators: and, or, and not.

Boolean type　A type with two possible values: True and False.

Bounds error　Trying to access a sequence element that is outside the legal range.

Bug　A programming error.

Built-in function　A function defined by the language itself that can be used without having to import a module.

Byte　A number made up of eight bits. Essentially all currently manufactured computers use a byte as the smallest unit of storage in memory.

Byte code　Instructions for the Python virtual machine.

Call stack　The ordered set of all methods and functions that currently have been called but not yet terminated, starting with the current method or function and ending with main.

Case sensitive　Distinguishing upper- and lowercase characters.

Central processing unit (CPU)　The part of a computer that executes the machine instructions.

Character　A single letter, digit, or symbol.

Class　A programmer-defined data type.

Class variable　A variable defined in a class that has only one value for the whole class, and which can be accessed and changed by any method of that class.

Command line　The line the user types to start a program in DOS or UNIX or a command window in Windows. It consists of the program name followed by any necessary arguments.

Comment　An explanation to help the human reader understand a section of a program; ignored by the interpreter.

Compiler　A program that translates code in a high-level language (such as Python) to machine instructions (such as byte code for the Python virtual machine).

Compile-time error　An error that is detected when a program is compiled.

Compound statement　A statement construct that consists of a header and statement block. The header ends with a colon (:).

Computer program　A sequence of instructions that is executed by a computer.

Concatenation　Placing one string after another to form a new string.

Concrete class　A class that can be instantiated.

Constant　A value that cannot be changed by a program. In Python, constants customarily have names consisting of all uppercase letters.

Constructor   A sequence of statements for initializing a newly instantiated object.

Container   A data structure, such as a list, that can hold a collection of objects and provides a mechanism for managing and accessing the collection.

Data member   Another name for an instance variable.

Data records   A collection of data fields pertaining to a common entity.

Data type   See **Type**

De Morgan's Law   A law about logical operations that describes how to negate expressions formed with *and* and *or* operations.

Debugger   A program that lets a user run another program one or a few steps at a time, stop execution, and inspect the variables in order to analyze it for bugs.

Dictionary   A container that keeps associations between key and value objects.

Directory   A structure on a disk that can hold files or other directories; also called a folder.

Dot notation   The notation *object.method(arguments)* or *object.variable* used to invoke a method or access an instance variable.

Driver module   The main module among a set of modules in which execution of the program begins.

Dynamic method lookup   Selecting a method to be invoked at run time. In Python, dynamic method lookup considers the class of the actual object (implicit parameter) to select the appropriate method.

Encapsulation   The hiding of implementation details.

Escape character   A character in text that is not taken literally but has a special meaning when combined with the character or characters that follow it. The \ character is an escape character in Python strings.

Escape sequence   A sequence of characters that starts with an escape character, such as \n or \".

Exception   A class that signals a condition that prevents the program from continuing normally. When such a condition occurs, an object of the exception class is raised.

Exception handler   A sequence of statements that is given control when an exception of a particular type has been raised and caught.

Expression   A syntactical construct that is made up of constants, variables, function and method calls, and the operators combining them.

Extension   The last part of a file name, which specifies the file type. For example, the extension .py denotes a Python file.

Fibonacci numbers   The sequence of numbers 1, 1, 2, 3, 5, 8, 13, ..., in which every term is the sum of its two predecessors.

File   A sequence of bytes that is stored on disk.

File marker   The position within a random-access file of the next byte to be read or written. It can be moved so as to access any byte in the file.

Flag   See **Boolean type**

Floating-point number   A number that can have a fractional part.

Floor division   Taking the quotient of two integers and discarding the remainder. In Python the // symbol denotes floor division. For example, 11 // 4 is 2, not 2.75.

Folder   See **Directory**

Formal parameter   Parameter variable.

Format operator   The percent sign (%) used to generate a formatted string.

Function   A sequence of statements that can be invoked multiple times, with different values for its parameter variables.

Garbage collection   Automatic reclamation of memory occupied by objects that are no longer referenced.

Global variable   A variable whose scope is not restricted to a single function or method.

Hand execution   See **Walkthrough**

Hard disk   A device that stores information on rotating platters with magnetic coating.

Hardware   The physical equipment for a computer or another device.

Hash function   A function that computes an integer value from an object in such a way that different objects are likely to yield different values.

Header   A component of a compound statement that ends with a colon (:).

High-level programming language   A programming language that provides an abstract view of a computer and allows programmers to focus on their problem domain.

IDE (Integrated Development Environment)   A programming environment that includes an editor, compiler, and debugger.

Immutable object   An object whose data cannot be modified.

Importing a module   Including the contents of a separate Python module for use within the current module.

Inheritance   The relationship between a more general superclass and a more specialized subclass.

Initialize   Set a variable to a well-defined value when it is created.

Inner class   A class that is defined inside another class.

Instance of a class   An object whose type is that class.

Instance variable   A variable defined in a class for which every object of the class has its own value.

Integer   A number that cannot have a fractional part.

Lexicographic ordering   Ordering strings in the same order as in a dictionary, by skipping all matching characters and comparing the first non-matching characters of both strings. For example, "orbit" comes before "orchid" in lexicographic ordering. Note that in Python, unlike a dictionary, the ordering is case sensitive: Z comes before a.

Library   A set of modules that can be included in programs.

Linear search   Searching a container (such as a set or list) for an object by inspecting each element in turn.

List   A mutable sequence that grows or shrinks dynamically as new elements are added or removed.

Literal   A notation for a fixed value in a program, such as –2, 3.14, 6.02214115E23, "Harry", or "H".

Local variable   A variable whose scope is a function or method.

Logical operator   See **Boolean operator**.

Logic error   An error in a syntactically correct program that causes it to act differently from its specification. (A form of run-time error.)

Loop   A sequence of instructions that is executed repeatedly.

Loop and a half   A loop whose termination decision is neither at the beginning nor at the end.

Machine code   Instructions that can be executed directly by the CPU.

Magic number   A number that appears in a program without explanation.

Merge sort   A sorting algorithm that first sorts two halves of a data structure and then merges the sorted halves together.

Method   A sequence of statements that has a name, may have parameter variables, and may return a value. A method, like a function, can be invoked any number of times, with different values for its parameter variables, but a method can only be applied to an object of the type for which it was defined.

Modification read   User or file input read within an event-controlled loop that modifies the loop variable. Used in conjunction with a priming read.

Modulus   The % operator that computes the remainder of an integer division.

Mutator method   A method that changes the state of an object.

Mutual recursion   Cooperating functions or methods that call each other.

Nested loop   A loop that is contained in another loop.

Networks   An interconnected system of computers and other devices.

Newline   The "\n" character, which indicates the end of a line.

No-argument constructor   A constructor that takes no arguments.

None reference   A reference that does not refer to any object.

Number literal   A fixed value in a program this is explicitly written as a number, such as –2 or 6.02214115E23.

Object   A value of a class type.

Object-oriented programming   Designing a program by discovering objects, their properties, and their relationships.

Object reference   A value that denotes the location of an object in memory.

Off-by-one error   A common programming error in which a value is one larger or smaller than it should be.

Opening a file   Preparing a file for reading or writing.

Operator   A symbol denoting a mathematical or logical operation, such as + or &&.

Operator associativity   The rule that governs in which order operators of the same precedence are executed. For example, in Python the - operator is left-associative because a - b - c is interpreted as (a - b) - c, and ** is right-associative because a ** b ** c is interpreted as a ** (b ** c).

Operator precedence   The rule that governs which operator is evaluated first. For example, in Python the and operator has a higher precedence than the or operator. Hence a or b and c is interpreted as a or (b and c). (See Appendix A.)

Out-of-range error   Attempting to access an element whose index is not in the valid index range; bounds error.

Overloading   Giving more than one meaning to a method name.

Overriding Redefining a method in a subclass.

Parameter passing Specifying expressions to be arguments for a method or function when it is called.

Parameter variable A variable of a method or function that is initialized with a value when the method or function is called.

Permutation A rearrangement of a set of values.

Polymorphism Selecting a method among several methods that have the same name on the basis of the actual types of the implicit parameters.

Primary storage Electronic circuits that can store data as long as they have electric power.

Priming read User or file input read before the start of an event-controlled loop that initializes the loop variable. Used in conjunction with a modification read.

Primitive type A data type provided by the language itself.

Programming The act of designing and implementing computer programs.

Prompt A string that tells the user to provide input.

Pseudocode A high-level description of the actions of a program or algorithm, using a mixture of English and informal programming language syntax.

Public interface The features (methods, variables, and nested types) of a class that are accessible to all clients.

Python interpreter A program that translates Python source code into byte code and executes it in the Python virtual machine.

Python shell A user interface that can be used to interact with the Python interpreter.

Quicksort A generally fast sorting algorithm that picks an element, called the pivot, partitions the sequence into the elements smaller than the pivot and those larger than the pivot, and then recursively sorts the subsequences.

Raise an exception Indicate an abnormal condition by terminating the normal control flow of a program and transferring control to a matching except clause.

Random access The ability to access any value directly without having to read the values preceding it.

Recursion A strategy for computing a result by decomposing the inputs into simpler values and applying the same strategy to them.

Recursive function or method A function or method that can call itself with simpler values. It must handle the simplest values without calling itself.

Redirection Linking the input or output of a program to a file instead of the keyboard or display.

Reference See **Object reference**

Regular expression A string that defines a set of matching strings according to their content. Each part of a regular expression can be a specific required character; one of a set of permitted characters such as [abc], which can be a range such as [a-z]; any character not in a set of forbidden characters, such as [^0-9]; a repetition of one or more matches, such as [0-9]+, or zero or more, such as [ACGT]; one of a set of alternatives, such as and|et|und; or various other possibilities. For example, [A-Za-z][0-9]+ matches Cloud9 or 007 but not Jack.

Relational operator An operator that compares two values, yielding a Boolean result.

Reserved word A word that has a special meaning in a programming language and therefore cannot be used as a name by the programmer.

Return value The value returned by a method or function through a return statement.

Roundoff error An error introduced by the fact that the computer can store only a finite number of digits of a floating-point number.

Run-time error An error in a syntactically correct program that causes it to act differently from its specification.

Scope The part of a program in which a variable is defined.

Secondary storage Storage that persists without electricity, e.g., a hard disk.

Selection sort A sorting algorithm in which the smallest element is repeatedly found and removed until no elements remain.

Sentinel A value in input that is not to be used as an actual input value but to signal the end of input.

Sequence A container that stores a collection of values that can be accessed by an integer index.

Sequential access Accessing values one after another without skipping over any of them.

Sequential search See **Linear search**

Set A container that stores an unordered collection and provides for the efficient addition, location, and removal of elements.

Short-circuit evaluation Evaluating only a part of an expression if the remainder cannot change the result.

Sign bit The bit of a binary number that indicates whether the number is positive or negative.

Software   The intangible instructions and data that are necessary for operating a computer or another device.

Source code   Instructions in a programming language that need to be translated before execution on a computer.

Source file   A file containing instructions in a programming language such as Python.

Standard library   The collection of modules that come with the interpreter and are available for use in every Python program.

State   The current value of an object, which is determined by the cumulative action of all methods that were invoked on it.

Statement   A syntactical unit in a program. In Python a statement is either a simple statement or a compound statement.

Statement block   A group of one or more statements, all of which are indented to the same indentation level.

Stepwise refinement   Solving a problem by breaking it into smaller problems and then further decomposing those smaller problems.

String   A sequence of characters.

String literal   A string in which the characters are explicitly specified within the source code.

Stub   A function or method with no or minimal functionality.

Subclass   A class that inherits variables and methods from a superclass but may also add instance variables, add methods, or redefine methods.

Superclass   A general class from which a more specialized class (a subclass) inherits.

Symmetric bounds   Bounds that include the starting index and the ending index.

Syntax   Rules that define how to form instructions in a particular programming language.

Syntax diagram   A graphical representation of grammar rules.

Syntax error   An instruction that does not follow the programming language rules and is rejected by the compiler. (A form of compile-time error.)

Tab character   The "\t" character, which advances the next character on the line to the next one of a set of fixed positions known as tab stops.

Table   A tabular arrangement of elements in which an element is specified by a row and a column index.

Terminal window   A window for interacting with an operating system through textual commands.

Text editor   A software application used to enter the contents of a text file like the statements of a program or the contents of a data file.

Text file   A file in which values are stored in their text representation.

Token   A sequence of consecutive characters from an input source that belong together for the purpose of analyzing the input. For example, a token can be a sequence of characters other than white space.

Trace message   A message that is printed during a program run for debugging purposes.

Traceback   A printout of the call stack, listing all currently pending method calls.

Tuple   An immutable sequence similar to a list.

Type   A named set of values and the operations that can be carried out with them.

Unary operator   An operator with one argument.

Unicode   A standard code that assigns code values consisting of two bytes to characters used in scripts around the world. Python stores all characters as their Unicode values.

Unit testing   Testing a function or method by itself, isolated from the remainder of the program.

User-defined data types   A data type, not provided by the language, that is defined by the user. In Python, class definitions are used to specify user-defined data types.

Variable   A symbol in a program that identifies a storage location that can hold different values.

Virtual machine   A program that simulates a CPU that can be implemented efficiently on a variety of actual machines. A given program in Python byte code can be executed by any Python virtual machine, regardless of which CPU is used to run the virtual machine itself.

Walkthrough   A step-by-step manual simulation of a computer program.

White space   Any sequence of only space, tab, and newline characters.

Window   A desktop component that contains a frame and title bar.

Wrapper class   A class that provides a new simplified interface for an existing class.

INDEX

Note: Page numbers followed by t indicate tables; those preceded by A indicate appendices.

ILLUSTRATION CREDITS

Icons

Common Error icon (parrot): © Eric Isselée/iStockphoto.

Computing & Society icon (trebuchet): © Stephen Coburn/123RF.com.

How To icon (compass): © Steve Simzer/iStockphoto.

Paperclips: © Yvan Dube/iStockphoto.

Programming Tip icon (balloon): © Mikhail Mishchenko/123RF Limited.

Self Check icon (stopwatch): © Nicholas Homrich/iStockphoto.

Special Topic icon (trumpets): © modella/123RF.com.

Toolbox icon: (tools) mattjeacock/Getty Images, Inc.; (chalice) Paul Fleet/Getty Images, Inc.

Worked Example icon (binoculars): © Tom Horyn/iStockphoto.

Chapter 4

Page 175–178 (left to right, top to bottom):

Gogh, Vincent van *The Olive Orchard:* Chester Dale Collection 1963.10.152/National Gallery of Art.

Degas, Edgar *The Dance Lesson:* Collection of Mr. and Mrs. Paul Mellon 1995.47.6/National Gallery of Art.

Fragonard, Jean-Honoré *Young Girl Reading:* Gift of Mrs. Mellon Bruce in memory of her father, Andrew W. Mellon 1961.16.1/National Gallery of Art.

Gauguin, Paul *Self-Portrait:* Chester Dale Collection 1963.10.150/National Gallery of Art.

Gauguin, Paul *Breton Girls Dancing, Pont-Aven:* Collection of Mr. and Mrs. Paul Mellon 1983.1.19/National Gallery of Art.

Guigou, Paul *Washerwomen on the Banks of the Durance:* Chester Dale Fund 2007.73.1/National Gallery of Art.

Guillaumin, Jean-Baptiste-Armand *The Bridge of Louis Philippe:* Chester Dale Collection 1963.10.155/National Gallery of Art.

Manet, Edouard *The Railway:* Gift of Horace Havemeyer in memory of his mother, Louisine W. Havemeyer 1956.10.1/National Gallery of Art.

Manet, Edouard *Masked Ball at the Opera:* Gift of Mrs. Horace Havemeyer in memory of her mother-in-law, Louisine W. Havemeyer 1982.75.1/National Gallery of Art.

Manet, Edouard *The Old Musician:* Chester Dale Collection 1963.10.162/National Gallery of Art.

Monet, Claude *The Japanese Footbridge:* Gift of Victoria Nebeker Coberly, in memory of her son John W. Mudd, and Walter H. and Leonore Annenberg 1992.9.1/National Gallery of Art.

Monet, Claude *Woman with a Parasol—Madame Monet and Her Son:* Collection of Mr. and Mrs. Paul Mellon 1983.1.29/National Gallery of Art.

Monet, Claude *The Bridge at Argenteuil:* Collection of Mr. and Mrs. Paul Mellon 1983.1.24/National Gallery of Art.

Monet, Claude *The Artist's Garden in Argenteuil (A Corner of the Garden with Dahlias):* Gift of Janice H. Levin, in Honor of the 50th Anniversary of the National Gallery of Art 1991.27.1/National Gallery of Art.